T0351373

SIGILLUM UNIVERSITATIS SCOLARIUM STUDII PRAGENSIS

KAARLE NORDENSTRENG

THE RISE AND FALL OF THE INTERNATIONAL ORGANIZATION OF JOURNALISTS BASED IN PRAGUE 1946–2016

USEFUL RECOLLECTIONS PART III

CHARLES UNIVERSITY
KAROLINUM PRESS 2020

KAROLINUM PRESS
Karolinum Press is a publishing department of Charles University
Ovocný trh 560/5, 116 36 Prague 1, Czech Republic
www.karolinum.cz

Set and printed in the Czech Republic by Karolinum Press
Layout by Jan Šerých with regard to first edition by Aila Helin
Second, revised edition, first in Karolinum Press

A catalogue record for this book is available from the National Library
of the Czech Republic.

ISBN 978-80-246-4505-6
ISBN 978-80-246-4524-7 (pdf)

The original manuscript was reviewed by Professor Emeritus Stanislav Perkner
(Humphreys University in Stockton, California) and Professor Verica Rupar
(Auckland University of Technology, New Zealand).

CONTENTS

Part Two – Recollections of the IOJ

Appendices – Documentation on the IOJ

Ing. Václav Slavík
(22. 3. 1937 – 26. 2. 2014)
is the main source of documents used for this book. He worked in the IOJ Secretariat from 1966 until 1992 in various tasks involving studies and documentation, notably as director of the International Journalism Institute (IJI). He was originally to have been the co-author of this book but he sadly passed away before the work proceeded from the compilation of materials to the systematic writing of the chapters. However, his personal recollections are included. The book is dedicated to the memory of this invaluable Czech professional.

PREFACE

This book is a sequel to *Useful Recollections: Excursion into the History of the International Movement of Journalists,* Parts I and II, published by the International Organization of Journalists (IOJ) in Prague, 1986 and 1988 respectively.[1] The first two volumes were written by the Finnish President (Kaarle Nordenstreng) and the Czech Secretary General (Jiří Kubka) of the IOJ at the time, covering the prehistory of the IOJ from the 1890s to 1945 and the first 20 years of the IOJ until 1966.

The original intention was to continue writing a third volume to record the history of the IOJ until the late 1980s. However, history itself derailed the plan: Kubka was removed from the IOJ in 1988, while I was first kept busy by the unstable ground of the IOJ after the "Velvet Revolution" in late 1989 and then as ex-President was only looking in from outside when the IOJ began to disintegrate. However, in 1994, when a hundred years had passed since the first international congress of the "press people" in Antwerp, I began work on the third volume. The work has progressed slowly, delayed by many other projects, but now – 26 years later – it has finally materialized.

Actually the project produced two books. First, *A History of the International Movement of Journalists* (2016) pooled separate histories of all the international associations of journalists into a single volume – the IOJ being just one of five main organizations throughout the 120 years of history. That book, co-authored with me by four academic colleagues, was published in England by Palgrave Macmillan, the three volumes of *Useful Recollections* being its major source. Consequently, the present volume of the trilogy should be seen as a more detailed chronicle of the IOJ.

The story of the IOJ offers an intriguing perspective on history from the eve of the Cold War in the 1940s until the new millennium. The IOJ was founded in 1946 as a truly universal association of professional journalists, but the Cold War caused it to split, whereby it turned into one of the Soviet-dominated "democratic international organizations" – along with those of

---

1 Both parts were translated into French and published by the IOJ. All the titles are out of print but the English originals are freely available online at http://books.google.com (search "useful recollections").

women, youth, students, lawyers, scientific workers and trade unions as well as radio and television organizations – with the bulk of its membership in the socialist countries of central and eastern Europe.

However, in the 1950s and 1960s the IOJ membership spread to the developing countries of the global South and by the 1970s it had become the world's largest international non-governmental organization in the media field. Its growth continued in the 1980s, thanks to the financial means generated in Czechoslovakia through a number of commercial enterprises run by its headquarters in Prague – with the approval of the Government and the Communist Party of the country. Yet this success story was brought to a halt by the Velvet Revolution and the IOJ began to lose its political and material base in the country. The post-communist government even ordered the headquarters to be expelled, leaving only a nominal presence in the Czech Republic. Meanwhile, the once flourishing activities throughout the world disappeared.

Thus the history of the IOJ is really the story of the rise and fall of an empire. Today most of the earlier core IOJ member unions have moved to the International Federation of Journalists (IFJ), which was established in 1952 as a Western antipode to the IOJ. The IFJ used to be a bitter rival of the IOJ during the Cold War period but now it enjoys fairly universal support.

The present Part III of *Useful Recollections* is not only a new volume as a sequel to the earlier two parts, but also the complete story of the IOJ from its antecedents until the present day. The book is unique, as no complete history of the IOJ has so far been published.

The book consists of three parts. First, ten thematic chapters present the story of the IOJ written as conventional history, proceeding chronologically and illustrated by a number of photos, followed by an overview in the final chapter. An epilogue concludes Part One. Second, 18 personal recollections by selected authors from inside and outside the IOJ provide perspectives on the organization and its principal actors. Third, a number of documents as appendices complement those already published in the two earlier volumes of *Useful Recollections* and in the Palgrave Macmillan book. The photos and documents displayed as figures in this book were chosen to be mostly complementary to those included in the earlier volumes. Accordingly, the three volumes together serve as comprehensive reference material on the IOJ.

The unpublished materials used as sources for this book and the earlier volumes are stored in the National Archives of the Czech Republic. Official publications of the IOJ are mostly to be found in the collections of *Klementinum*, the National Library of the Czech Republic. Several IOJ publications are also in the collections of the library of the Faculty of Social Sciences at Charles University. Details of the sources used appear in the Bibliography at the end.

I am the main author – both as a media scholar and as a former President. One might wonder how it is possible to reconcile these different roles. My response to such doubts is, first, that writing any history is inevitably more or less subjective, and personal experience may even add valuable elements to the narrative. Second, in this case I have benefitted from a great deal of unique inside knowledge and documentation accumulated during the nearly 15 years of my presidency. I do concede a certain bias attributable to my Finnish background and to the lifelong home base of the IOJ in Czechoslovakia, which accounts for the prominence of these two countries in this book.

I consider it my moral obligation to tell the story of the IOJ honestly and openly for posterity. I do not claim to present the definitive account but rather history as I see it, with the advantage of personal involvement.

After my earlier co-author Jiří Kubka left the IOJ in 1988, and passed away in 1992, I began to work with Václav Slavík, who, when retiring from the IOJ in 1992, took with him a lot of documentation, while most of the archives were lost in the lamentable shambles of the Secretariat in the 1990s. Slavík was first envisaged as my co-author, but his failing health and finally his death in early 2014 did not allow it. Yet a substantial part of the personal recollections in Part Two of this book is written by him. Also, his invaluable documentation served as source material for much of the rest of the volume. It is with good reason that this book is dedicated to his memory.

In addition to Slavík, I wish to acknowledge the assistance of three former employees of the IOJ: Rudolf Převrátil, Chief Editor of IOJ publications 1985–90; Leena Paukku, Secretary for Europe 1987–91; Josef Komárek, Legal Advisor of the Secretary General 1994–97 and Director of Mondiapress 1997–.

Special support was provided by Markéta Ševčíková, who thoroughly studied the IOJ for her Master's thesis (2008) and for a PhDr. thesis (2015) at the Charles University. Ševčíková also prepared with me a paper on the rise and fall of the IOJ for presentation at the 6th European Communication Conference of ECREA in Prague in November 2016. On that basis we wrote in 2017 a joint article on journalist organizations in Czechoslovakia, published in the online journal *Media and Communication*.[2] The article includes an overview of the political history of Czechoslovakia from 1918 to the 1990s, providing a context to understand the story of the IOJ in this country.

These colleagues and friends deserve my sincere thanks. Special thanks are due to those colleagues, both from inside and outside the IOJ, who shared their personal recollections for this book in Part Two.

2 https://www.cogitatiopress.com/mediaandcommunication/article/view/1042.

Two more acknowledgements on my home front at the University of Tampere: Virginia Mattila, who meticulously checked the English of the texts, and Aila Helin, who skillfully processed the photos of varied quality and expertly did the model layout of the book.

Finally, I am grateful to the Faculty of Social Sciences at the Charles University for including this book in the publishing programme of the Karolinum Press. And the Karolinum team deserves a diploma for patience for having worked under the extraordinary conditions of the pandemic.

Kaarle Nordenstreng
Tampere, September 2020

PART ONE
HISTORY OF THE IOJ

CHAPTER 1
PREHISTORY 1894–1945[1]

THE STARTING POINT IN THE 1890s

The first national associations of journalists began to appear in the UK, France and other countries in the second half of the 19th century. At first they were mostly informal guild organizations. Although at that time most journalists were already wage earners, they were not always closely associated with the trade union movement, which was rapidly getting organized. Journalists as creative writers typically considered themselves as independent publishers. Thus the first organizations of the field were associated with both the journalists and the owners of the press. Yet there were also organizations which followed a clear trade union orientation, such as the syndicate established in the Netherlands in 1884 and the syndicate of French journalists founded in 1886. In the UK, the National Union of Journalists was established in 1907 and affiliated to the British Trade Union Congress in 1920. This was the pattern for most national associations of journalists established after 1900 in Scandinavia, Australia, the USA and elsewhere.

The newspaper publishers and editors were even faster to organize than journalists. In the UK, the Newspaper Society was founded as early as 1836 to safeguard the interests of British newspaper owners. In the USA, the American Newspaper Publishers' Association was founded in 1887.

By the 1890s journalists and publishers in most European countries were more or less organized – not everywhere in solid associations but at least as loose fraternities around a common profession. Newspapers were growing along with increasing advertising and the press achieved a higher profile both in politics and as a form of industrial modernization.

Obviously the time was ripe for national groups to be internationally connected for mutual benefit: to learn from each other, to create rules for transborder sales of news, and above all to strengthen the profession's prestige.

---

1 This chapter is based on *Useful Recollections, Part I*, "The Shaping of International Co-operation: From the 1880s to the 1940s" (Kubka & Nordenstreng, 1986, pp. 41–85). The quotes below are taken from this book. More on the early associations can be found in *A History of the International Movement of Journalists* (Nordenstreng & al., 2016, pp. 42–124).

The initiative for international conferences and a permanent international organization in the field was made at a small meeting of British, French and Belgian journalists arranged by the Institute of Journalism in London in 1893. This led to the convening of the **International Congress of the Press in Antwerp** (Belgium) on 7–11 **July 1894**, in connection with a World Exposition which took place in that city that year for several months.

According to Antwerp newspaper reports, the Congress was attended by over 400 participants. The conference proceedings[2] lists in the programme over 60 delegates from 17 European countries, including the three conveners and Germany, Austria, Switzerland, Italy, Spain, Portugal, The Netherlands, Denmark, Norway, Sweden as well as Russia. The only delegate from outside Europe was from New Zealand. No Americans, either North or South.

The agenda and discussions are well documented in the proceedings. Six plenary sessions during three days discussed a wide range of topics, including the definition of a journalist, the characteristics of the profession, professional education, Sunday work, and problems faced by women journalists. Special attention was paid to issues of copyright.[3]

On the agenda was naturally also the question of how to continue the congresses and to establish a permanent association. Accordingly, the Antwerp Congress launched the **International Union of Press Associations (IUPA)**. This first international organization of journalists was formally established only two years later, once its constitution was drawn up and adopted by the next two congresses in Bordeaux (1895) and Budapest (1896). IUPA was based in Paris and by 1900 its congress was attended by 69 associations from 24 countries, representing over 10,000 journalists and publishers.

IUPA's congress met altogether 15 times between 1894 and 1914, when World War I disrupted regular activities. Participants came mostly from the European countries but occasionally also from Turkey, Egypt, Argentine, Brazil, Mexico and Japan. After the war the first disagreement erupted about admitting members from the former Central Powers, and by 1927, when the congress was able to meet again, it had lost much of its momentum to a new federation (FIJ). Moreover, in 1933 the newspaper publishers also established their own federation. Nevertheless, IUPA survived until 1938.

Consequently, while IUPA had a spectacular beginning, inspiring a generation of professionals to engage in international co-operation, its idea as a com-

---

2 *1er Congrès International de la Presse* (1894). This 104-page publication surfaced in some libraries and served as the main source on how the international movement really started (for both Kubka & Nordenstreng and for Björk). The proceedings contain as appendices five lengthy presentations, including Aaron Watson's "On Copyright, or the Protection of Literary Property" and Grace Stuart's "English Women in Journalism".

3 See Björk (1996) and Nordenstreng & al. (2016).

mon platform for both publishers and working journalists did not meet the challenges of the early 20th century and was therefore doomed to disappear.

Meanwhile, Czech journalists were active in creating a sub-regional Association of Slavonic Journalists in 1898. Prague also served later in 1929 as the venue of an important FIJ Executive Committee meeting.[4]

THE FIJ BETWEEN THE WORLD WARS

In the early 20th century there was a boom of international organizations. For the news media, these included special sectors of the press – the periodic press, the sporting press, the Roman Catholic press and even revolutionary-proletarian writers – as well as regionally based organizations such as the Imperial Press Union (1909, later the Commonwealth Press Union). A particular case was the Geneva-based **International Association of Journalists accredited to the League of Nations (IAJA)**.[5]

The most important of the post-World War I organizations was to be the international association of journalists, established in 1926 with the name **Fédération Internationale des Journalistes (FIJ)**. It was based on the initiative of the French Journalists' Syndicate, which hosted a founding meeting in Paris on 12–13 June 1926, attended by unions of journalists from 21 countries. The initiative was prompted by the ILO which already in 1925 launched an international survey on the working conditions of journalists.[6] In the name of the commission which had prepared the meeting, Stéphen Valot of the French Syndicate pointed out that the profession of journalists was becoming increasingly international, making it imperative for journalists to be organized on an international level.

During the discussion in Paris, certain doubts were first voiced about the relations of the new organization to IUPA and IAJA. Yet after its special character was explained, the doubts were allayed and those present unanimously took a decision to set up a new organization. Its statutes, drawn up by the hosts, were then approved. The FIJ was defined to be an association of national organizations of journalists whose members were to be exclusively professional journalists, affiliated to the permanent editorial office of a news-

4 See Holoubek (1976).

5 The League of Nations, predecessor of the United Nations, and the International Labour Organization (ILO), played an important role in promoting press policies in the 1920s and early 1930s. See *Useful Recollections, Part I* (1986, pp. 69–73); Nordenstreng & al. (2016, pp. 80–104).

6 The results of the survey were published in *Conditions of Work and Life of Journalists* (1928). Excerpts from this report are reproduced as an annex in *Useful Recollections, Part I* (1986, pp. 91–107).

paper or a news agency and who derived their main income from journalistic work. Thus the goal of the organization was clearly to safeguard the rights and trade union benefits of professional journalists and to improve their working conditions. Among the statutory tasks were the following:

> The elaboration, preservation, and publication of statistical and other documents of a nature to assist in the work of defending professional interests;
> The study of formulas capable of bringing about the institution of standard contracts for individual or collective employment, and the general surveillance of the enforcement of these contracts wherever they have been accepted;
> The extension to journalists of all countries of the advantages and the rights won by national associations.

After the founding meeting in Paris, Valot sent out an invitation to the **1st FIJ Congress** (Figure 1.1). This Congress, which officially constituted the organization, took place in Geneva in the premises of ILO on 24–25 September 1926. It was attended by unions representing journalists from 16 European countries, including Czechoslovakia. Russian publishers and journalists, who were active in the launching of IUPA and attended its first congresses, were no longer prominently present in international professional associations after the turn of the century – certainly not after 1917. Attending as observers at the 1st FIJ Congress were the ILO and the International Institute of Intellectual Cooperation (the predecessor of UNESCO) as well as the Secretariat of the League of Nations and the IAJA.

The congress heard a report by ILO on the working conditions of journalists in different countries and pledged to help in the successful completion of its international survey. The congress also declared that it would strive for these freedoms to be guaranteed by law through its member unions.

At the time of its establishment, the FIJ united 25,000 journalists through its national member associations. By joining the Federation, each association implicitly acknowledged the principles of a syndicalist organization the main task of which was the conclusion of working contracts, the setting of minimum wages and the acknowledgement of a court of arbitration as an institution to settle disputes between journalists and the newspapers for which they worked.

The FIJ had a permanent secretariat in Paris, administrated by a Secretary General elected for four years, and an Executive Committee composed of two members for every country affiliated and meeting annually. A bureau, composed of the President and Vice-Presidents, Treasurer, Secretary General and his deputies, was to meet more frequently. The President was elected for two years and the congresses had to be convoked every two years. Stéphen Valot was an obvious choice for Secretary General, and the first President was Georges Bourdon of the French Syndicate.

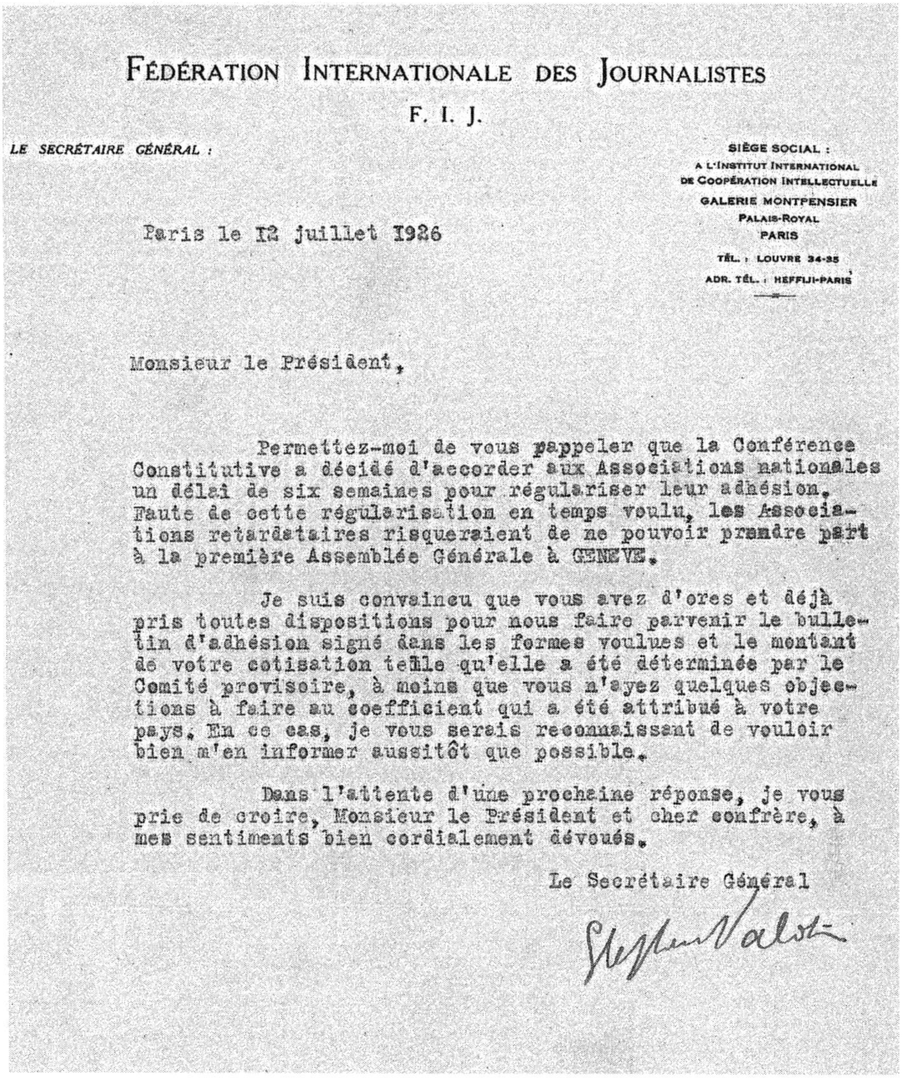

FÉDÉRATION INTERNATIONALE DES JOURNALISTES

F. I. J.

LE SECRÉTAIRE GÉNÉRAL :

SIÈGE SOCIAL :
A L'INSTITUT INTERNATIONAL
DE COOPÉRATION INTELLECTUELLE
GALERIE MONTPENSIER
PALAIS-ROYAL
PARIS

TÉL. : LOUVRE 34-35
ADR. TÉL. : HEFFIJI-PARIS

Paris le 12 juillet 1926

Monsieur le Président,

Permettez-moi de vous rappeler que la Conférence Constitutive a décidé d'accorder aux Associations nationales un délai de six semaines pour régulariser leur adhésion. Faute de cette régularisation en temps voulu, les Associations retardataires risqueraient de ne pouvoir prendre part à la première Assemblée Générale à GENEVE.

Je suis convaincu que vous avez d'ores et déjà pris toutes dispositions pour nous faire parvenir le bulletin d'adhésion signé dans les formes voulues et le montant de votre cotisation telle qu'elle a été déterminée par le Comité provisoire, à moins que vous n'ayez quelques objections à faire au coefficient qui a été attribué à votre pays. En ce cas, je vous serais reconnaissant de vouloir bien m'en informer aussitôt que possible.

Dans l'attente d'une prochaine réponse, je vous prie de croire, Monsieur le Président et cher confrère, à mes sentiments bien cordialement dévoués.

Le Secrétaire Général

Stephen Valot

Figure 1.1 The circular letter of the FIJ to national journalist organizations after its founding conference in June 1926, inviting all to the constitutive 1st Congress in Geneva. The seat and address of the FIJ was established at the International Institute of Intellectual Cooperation (predecessor of UNESCO) where the FIJ had its address until September 1939.

In the first years of its existence the FIJ flourished. In early 1927 it issued a list of collective contracts in different countries with an index of subjects included in them, and at the end of the year it published a draft model contract drawn up on the pattern of existing instruments. It also continued the ILO survey on the profession and began compiling media laws in European nations.

In those years, issues of a more general character appeared among problems of a purely professional nature, such as concessionary fares on railways and ships for journalists and the setting up of schools for journalists. The FIJ was active in these issues and attended the League of Nations conference of press experts in Geneva dealing with better and cheaper international transfer of information that could "help calm down public opinion in different countries".

The FIJ Executive Committee, which met in Vienna in May 1927, noted with satisfaction that more organizations had joined the Federation, including those of Australia, Switzerland, the Netherlands and Latvia. On the other hand, a problematic matter of principle was raised by the application for membership of an association of Russian journalists – a group of Czarist refugees based in Paris, while the FIJ practically ignored the new world of revolutionary journalism being created in the Soviet Union.

The **2nd FIJ Congress** was convened in Dijon (France) in November 1928 (Figure 1.2). It approved positions and activities on several important issues, such as concentration in the press industry, an international identity card for journalists, a new phenomenon of "radiophonic journalism" as well as a code of ethics and a tribunal of honour for the profession. Georges Bourdon voluntarily handed over the FIJ presidency to the head of the *Reichsverband der deutschen Presse*, Georg Bernhard.

Various projects were developed further in 1929 by the FIJ Executive Committee, meeting in Prague and Antwerp. The global economic depression brought a new item to the agenda – unemployment. Nevertheless, the main attention was paid to issuing the international journalist's card and to establishing the tribunal of honour. The ruling of the tribunal began as follows:

1. In defence of the honour of the profession it is necessary to draw up strict rules determining the rights and duties of journalists as regards the good reputation of private and public persons.
2. As regards conflicts between journalists from different countries, the committee declares that no theory or comments are banned, but they must not be based on consciously distorted facts or on them known to be false.
3. Every journalist is responsible for the information he has personally obtained. The sending to any newspaper of false or intentionally distorted information so as to poison the international atmosphere shall be put before the tribunal. If the informer's bad intentions are proved, he will be subject to strict sanctions.

Numéro 49 NOVEMBRE 1928

le journaliste

ORGANE DU SYNDICAT NATIONAL DES JOURNALISTES

Association de Défense et de Discipline Professionnelles

FONDÉE EN 1918

126 rue de Provence
PARIS
Bureaux ouverts de 10 heures à midi et de 2 heures à 7 heures

Paraît tous les mois
Téléphone : LOUVRE 55-37 — 55-38

Sommaire

Un journaliste digne de ce nom

prend la responsabilité de tous ses écrits, même anonymes, tient la calomnie la diffamation et les accusations sans preuves pour les plus grandes fautes professionnelles, n'accepte que des missions compatibles avec sa dignité professionnelle, s'interdit d'invoquer un titre ou une qualité imaginaire, pour obtenir une information, ne touche pas d'argent dans un service public ou une entreprise privée où sa qualité de journaliste, ses influences, ses relations seraient susceptibles d'être exploitées, ne signe pas de son nom des articles de pure réclame commerciale ou financière, ne commet aucun plagiat, ne sollicite pas la place d'un confrère ni ne provoque son renvoi en offrant de travailler à des conditions inférieures, garde le secret professionnel, n'abuse jamais de la liberté de la presse dans une intention intéressée. (*Déclaration du Syndicat*, juillet 1918).

LE CONGRÈS DE LA F.I.J.

« ... un groupement de forces comme il n'en existe pas d'autres exemples dans le monde intellectuel. Il est ailleurs des organisations plus fortes en effectifs; il n'en est pas de plus cohérentes par la rigueur de la constitution interne et de mieux préparées à l'action par la netteté du programme. »

(Extrait de l'ouvrage publié par le B. I. T. sur les Conditions de travail et de vie des journalistes.)

Les journalistes français ne sauraient donner trop d'attention aux importantes assises qui, dans quelques jours, s'ouvriront à Dijon.

Du 15 au 18 novembre, la Fédération Internationale des Journalistes y tiendra son assemblée générale statutaire, qui sera la seconde après l'assemblée générale de Genève, en 1926. La constitution de la F.I.J. veut en effet que le Congrès soit convoqué tous les deux ans pour se prononcer sur la direction générale de la Fédération, résoudre les questions étudiées par le Comité Exécutif et choisir son président. Dans l'intervalle, la conduite de la Fédération est assurée par le Comité Exécutif (qui se réunit tous les six mois dans une ville différente et qui, jusqu'à présent, a successivement délibéré à Genève, Vienne, Paris et Cologne), et par son Bureau, qui siège tous les mois à Paris.

L'honneur et le soin d'organiser le Congrès revenant cette année à la France, pays du président sortant, nous avons pensé que nos hôtes nous sauraient gré de les conduire au cœur d'une grande et illustre région française; aussitôt que nous nous sommes ouverts à lui de notre dessein, M. Gaston Gérard, député-maire de Dijon, avec la promptitude de décision qu'on lui connaît, l'a fait sien, et c'est ainsi que, par la vertu de sa bonne grâce, la F. I. J. est assurée de trouver à Dijon un accueil digne d'elle et de la cité qui la recevra, et que ses délibérations auront lieu dans le palais des ducs de Bourgogne.

LA F. I. J.

Il est temps que les journalistes français comprennent que la F. I. J. est une grande institution, l'une des plus belles et des mieux charpentées qu'ait enfantées, depuis dix ans, l'esprit international. Internationale, elle l'est, au plein sens du mot, d'intention, de construction et d'action, et ceux qui la dirigent se sont appliqués à lui conserver son caractère essentiel, qu'elle ne laisserait entamer que pour s'affaiblir. Mais nous avons en même temps la fierté de nous rappeler qu'elle est une création française, que son secrétaire général, Stephen Valot, cheville ouvrière de l'institution, est français, que son siège social est à Paris, qu'en la constituant nos confrères étrangers ont entendu placer à sa tête un président français.

Ainsi sortie du Syndicat National des Journalistes, qui, en la créant, a manifesté sa force vitale et du même coup l'ampleur de son action professionnelle, elle lui fait grandement honneur sans doute, mais nous pensons aussi qu'elle mérite d'être, pour tout le journalisme français et pour notre pays, un sujet d'orgueil. Elle ne nous aura pas médiocrement aidés à obtenir les sécurités et les garanties depuis longtemps reconnues à nos confrères étrangers. Sans elle, le projet de Contrat collectif établi par le Syndicat National ne serait pas ce qu'il est. Sans elle, il serait privé d'un des arguments les plus forts qui nous permettent de le justifier auprès des directeurs. Ainsi aura-t-elle, en ce qui nous concerne, rempli une de ses premières fonctions, qui est de mettre au service des efforts particuliers et nationaux le rayonnement d'une force collective et internationale.

La F. I. J. répondait si bien à un besoin universel, que son succès a eu quelque chose de foudroyant. D'emblée, elle a réuni les plus grandes associations professionnelles d'Europe : la National Union anglaise (4.800 membres), le Reichsverband allemand (4.300 membres), l'Organisation autrichienne (1.650 membres), etc... Elle rassemble aujourd'hui à peu près l'unanimité des nations européennes, plus l'Australie, et cela fait déjà environ 25.000 journalistes. Elle est entrée en rapport avec les Etats-Unis et l'Amérique latine : le moment ne semble pas très éloigné où elle formera le faisceau fortement noué de tous les journalistes du monde. Nous disons tous les journalistes, car la France est le seul pays où les journalistes, au mépris de tous leurs intérêts corporatifs, aient eu l'inconséquence de se disséminer en une infinité d'associations. Partout ailleurs, sauf exceptions justifiées par des circonstances particulières, ils ont eu la sagesse de se réunir en un seul organisme chargé de les défendre. C'est cet organisme unique en chaque nation qui la représente à la F.I.J., et la puissance de la Fédération est en ceci que la motion votée à Vienne en 1927 interdit aux associations affiliées d'adhérer à nulle autre organisation internationale.

En relations régulières avec la Société des Nations, le Bureau International du Travail et l'Institut International de Coopération intellectuelle, elle participe à leurs travaux et y a sa place chaque fois qu'il y est question de la condition des journalistes. Elle a un siège dans la Commission des Travailleurs intellectuels, récemment créée par le B. I. T., et si l'on veut savoir quel est son crédit auprès des grands organismes internationaux nés de la guerre et qui sont comme des laboratoires où les peuples essayent de confronter et d'entremêler leurs âmes avec leurs intérêts, que l'on prenne la peine de lire plus loin l'extrait que nous reproduisons du grand ouvrage que le B. I. T. vient de publier sur la condition des journalistes dans le monde entier.

Figure 1.2 The information bulletin of the French National Syndicate of Journalists regularly covered news and events of the FIJ. The 2nd FIJ Congress in Dijon was naturally a leading topic of the bulletin in November 1928.

The International Tribunal of Honour of Journalists[7] was formally established by the **3rd FIJ Congress** convened in Berlin in October 1930 (Figure 1.3). There H.M. Richardson, General Secretary of the UK National Union of Journalists (NUJ) was elected as the new FIJ President, while Valot was re-elected as Secretary General. Richardson was a firm supporter of an international code of honour as well as a court of honour to monitor it. This position not only highlighted high moral principles but also reflected the libertarian press freedom whereby the news media should be kept free from governmental regulation.

Richardson introduced the Tribunal of Honour at its opening ceremony in The Hague in October 1931 as the FIJ's contribution to the cause of peace. His speech ended as follows:

> I do not anticipate that this court will often be called into session, because I believe that journalists, like everyone else, are recognizing more and more readily the inadequacy of a narrow nationalism as a basis for even national well-being. More and more is being realised that the nations of the world are one, and that an injury to one nation is an injury to all.
>
> So far as the ethics of journalism are concerned, the International Federation seeks to inculcate that belief positively by endeavouring to improve the status of journalists of all countries, and negatively by bringing into public odium those journalists who are false to the ideal of their profession, which is the accurate recording of events and the reasoned comment upon authentic facts.

In hindsight, these words appear both prophetic and ironic – prophetic because the tribunal soon became paralyzed, and ironic as narrow-minded nationalism was propagated rather than discouraged by the rise of fascism in Germany and elsewhere in Europe. The proceedings of the FIJ throughout the 1930s show that the time for lofty ideas and initiatives such as the Tribunal was over and that journalists and their organizations became hostages of declining economics and of rising contradictions in politics.

Nevertheless, the **4th FIJ Congress** in London in October 1932 continued to promote collective contracts, copyright and support for unemployed journalists.[8] Moreover, the Congress discussed the role of the press in the main-

---

7 The background and launching of the Tribunal in The Hague in October 1931 are presented in *Le Tribunal d'honneur international des journalistes* (1932). Excerpts from this booklet are reproduced as an annex in *Useful Recollections, Part I*. A summary is given *Useful Recollections, Part I* (1986, pp. 63–69).

8 The time of this 4th FIJ Congress was mistakenly given to be February 1933 in *Useful Recollections, Part I* (1986, p. 74). All the FIJ congresses except the last (7th) one in 1939 were held every two years as determined in the statutes.

DEUTSCHE PRESSE

ZEITSCHRIFT FÜR DIE GESAMTEN INTERESSEN DES ZEITUNGSWESENS
ORGAN DES REICHSVERBANDES DER DEUTSCHEN PRESSE E.V.
20. JAHRGANG NR. 43 BERLIN-SCHÖNEBERG, 25. OKTOBER 1930

Herausgeber: Reichsverband der deutschen Presse, Geschäftsführend. Vorsitz. Dir. G. Richter. Schriftleitung: Otto Schabbel, Berlin W 10, Tiergartenstraße 16. Fernsprecher: Kurfürst 2694

Friedrich Ernst Hübsch Verlag, Gesellschaft mit beschränkter Haftung, Berlin W 62, Maaßenstraße 34 Fernsprecher: Amt Lützow 2212 und 2851 / Postscheck-Konto: Berlin 146997. Telegr.-Adresse: Hübschverlag

Alle Einsendungen für die Schriftleitung an den Reichsverband der deutschen Presse, Berlin W 10, Tiergartenstraße 16. Sprechstunde: 12 bis 1 Uhr. — Fernsprecher: Amt Kurfürst 2694

Erscheint Sonnabends. Jedes Postamt und der Verlag nimmt Bestellungen an. Bezugspreis monatl. Mk. 2.—, einzeln Mk. 1.—. Anzeigen laut Tarif. Anzeigenschluß: Mittwoch. Erfüllungsort: Berlin-Mitte

Zum Kongreß der Fédération Internationale des Journalistes

in Berlin vom 22. bis 25. Oktober 1930

Gruß des Herrn Reichsministers des Auswärtigen Dr. Curtius

Es ist mir eine besondere Freude, die Teilnehmer an dem 2. Kongreß der „Fédération Internationale des Journalistes" in der Hauptstadt des Deutschen Reiches als Gäste begrüßen zu können.

Die Organisation der „F.I.J." hat in den vier Jahren ihres Bestehens bewiesen, daß der Gedanke, der zu ihrer Gründung geführt hat, lebenskräftig ist. Die „F.I.J." verfolgt den Zweck, durch regelmäßige Aussprache und Regelung vom nationalen Boden aus die internationale Gemeinschaft zu befestigen, die internationale Gegensätzlichkeit aber zu beseitigen. Dementsprechend will die „F.I.J." durch ihre Einrichtungen und Verhandlungen die Kräfte der nationalen Presseverbände wahren und dadurch kräftigen, daß sie die internationale Gemeinschaft pflegt.

In diesem Sinne begrüße ich die bevorstehende Berliner Tagung der „F.I.J." und wünsche ihrem Arbeitsprogramm den besten Erfolg.

Curtius

Figure 1.3 The host of the 3rd FIJ Congress, *Reichsverband der deutschen Presse*, published on the front page of its journal in October 1930 a letter of welcome from the German Minister of Foreign Affairs.

tenance of peace, confirming the doctrine that freedom of the press had to be defended particularly at a time when it was endangered by economic and political interests. This freedom, it was pointed out, was seated in the conscience of the journalist, and this conscience could maintain its full power only if collectively expressed. Its best guarantee was the will of professional journalists to respect the rules of honour of their profession as manifested by the International Tribunal of Honour.

An emphasis on peace and responsible reporting also came from the League of Nations, which convened further meetings of press experts in Copenhagen in 1932 and Madrid in 1933 and other meetings in the context of the World Disarmament Conference. These all were actively attended by the FIJ, also drawing attention to the question of inaccurate news and how to combat false information.[9]

However, all initiatives were paralyzed by the political developments, with media and democracy under increasing pressure all over Europe, especially – but not only – in Germany, where Hitler became Chancellor in January 1933 and the Parliament dissolved itself in February. Meanwhile, the FIJ continued its activities and organizational life after the 4th Congress in London, where Herman Dons of Belgium was elected as the new President.

The biggest problem for the FIJ's promotion of freedom of journalism turned out to be an increasingly common phenomenon in Europe: the rise of fascism, which defined the media as an instrument of the state. The proceedings of the FIJ Executive Committee in Budapest in June 1933 demonstrated the FIJ's inconsistent application of membership policy. The big German union, the *Reichsverband der Deutschen Presse*, had sent no delegates. A Dutch delegate, reporting first hand from his experience in Berlin, described the Nazi faction in the *Reichsverband* as amateur journalists bent on crowding out the old elite. In its conference in April 1933, the majority of the members of the *Reichsverband* voluntarily submitted to a ban on communist and Jewish journalists from the profession, who were forced to emigrate or incarcerated in concentration camps. After that in the Budapest meeting, hosted by the Hungarian fascist state and union, the Dutch, Polish, British and Belgian representatives called for the expulsion of the *Reichsverband*. Since the majority remained hesitant as to the wisdom of expelling one of its strongest members, the final resolution did indeed condemn Nazi persecution, but only suspended the *Reichsverband's* membership.

---

9 A reminder of the widespread support for this approach was the fact that the newly founded International Federation of Newspaper Publishers Associations even proposed a convention for the immediate retracting and correction of false news. (FIADEJ, later FIEJ is the predecessor of today's WAN-IFRA.)

The **5th FIJ Congress** was held in Brussels in October 1934. Paul Bourquin of Switzerland was elected as the new President and Valot was re-elected once again as Secretary General. The Congress admitted a significant new member: the American Newspaper Guild (ANG) established one year before with some 10,000 members representing about half of journalists in the USA. A less pleasant matter in the Congress was the discussion concerning the application for admission of an association of German refugee journalists. The application was submitted by Georg Bernhard, former FIJ President and of Jewish origin. He appeared before the Congress describing the circumstances under which he and his colleagues had been forced to leave the *Reichsverband* and emigrate. Yet his application was rejected by a majority in the Congress on the grounds that the association did not have a "national character" – something that the *Reichsverband* was considered to have although connections with it had been suspended because of its adherence to a Nazi position on journalism.

Similar problems arose with Spain, Italy and other countries. It became clear that more and more countries had divided factions of journalists who could not be admitted to the FIJ as nationally representative collectives with a clear press freedom position. Disagreement mounted among the FIJ members about how to navigate in the politically stormy waters. Still, in 1935 the Executive Committee meeting in Helsinki could note with satisfaction that FIJ had member organizations in all European countries except the Soviet Union and Italy. Furthermore, it had member organizations in the USA, Brazil and Australia. Discussions were under way with Indian and Japanese journalists to join the FIJ.

The **6th FIJ Congress** met in Bern (Switzerland) in September 1936. The FIJ was ten years old, but it was in no mood for celebration. From the outset, discussion centred on the problem of press freedom. The participants were divided into two camps. One stressed its fidelity to the principle of freedom of the press as formulated in the FIJ statute. The other questioned whether it was really reasonable to uphold this formulation of the FIJ statute if freedom of the press was becoming a rarity throughout Europe. After a long and passionate discussion the Congress decided to keep the statute unchanged but to organize a poll on the problem among member unions. This was a compromise which exposed the crisis which had been fomenting inside the FIJ since 1933.

A resolution was adopted appealing to the world press to lend its support to a peace policy and thus help to avert the danger of international conflicts. Given the real situation in the world and the press at that time, the resolution was mere wishful thinking. Karl Eskelund of Denmark was elected as the new FIJ President.

After this the FIJ proceedings of the Executive Committee meetings in Vienna 1937 and Paris 1938 show how the organization, while continuing to debate press freedom and conditions for membership under increasingly difficult conditions, still managed to pursue such professional matters as limiting working hours and promoting deontological codes. Yet one topic was missing from the proceedings: a serious discussion of the concept of freedom of expression and of journalism. It was certainly looming behind the debates and controversies but it was kept under the carpet – obviously not to allow professional activities to be threatened by ideological and political clashes.

Escalating political problems in Europe led to a change of venue of the **7th FIJ Congress** from Denmark to Morocco and Strasbourg, but finally it was convened at Bordeaux in July 1939. It adopted an important document: the Professional Code of Honour for Journalists. Beyond this, there is little to be put on the historical record from this Congress – apart from the fact that it was the last FIJ Congress, with Archibald Kenyon of the UK elected as its President.

One of the first tasks of the new President was to join the Secretary General in appealing to the member unions for solidarity with those IFJ colleagues who were affected by the war (Figure 1.4). The circular letters from the secretariat discontinued in spring 1940.

In June 1940 Hitler's troops marched unopposed into Paris. The FIJ bureau was taken over by the Nazis and its archives confiscated.

DEVELOPMENTS DURING WORLD WAR II

In October 1940 a conference was held between the *Reichsverband* of the German Press and the fascist National Syndicate of French Journalists, which decided to "replace the International Federation of Journalists, a provocation centre, and a representative of Jewish-democratic intellectual thinking operating from Paris to corrupt journalists all over the world". One year later, in December 1941, the so-called **Union of National Unions of Journalists** was set up in Vienna. Its head was Wilhelm Weiss, editor-in-chief of the main National Socialist newspaper, the *Völkischer Beobachter*, and chairman of the *Reichsverband* of the German Press.

At the same time, in December 1941 when World War II had been raging for two years, a new organization was established in London called the **International Federation of Journalists of Allied or Free Countries (IFJAFC)**, which:

> regards itself as holding in trust the spirit and work of the Fédération Internationale des Journalistes. Its fundamental principle is to safeguard and support the freedom of the Press; its activities will be guided by this and by the resolve to see the FIJ re-established on a stronger, universal basis after the war.

FÉDÉRATION INTERNATIONALE
DES JOURNALISTES
F. I. J.

Leeds, ~~PARIS~~ le 1er Octobre 1939

LE SECRÉTAIRE GÉNÉRAL
STEPHEN VALOT

N°

PIÈCES JOINTES

Dear Friend and Collegue,

It is my duty and desire tó support in the strengest possible manner the elcquent and moving appeal that has been adressed to the organisations of the F.I.J. by Mr Stephen Valot.

It happens that both Mr. Valot and myself are citizens of countries engaged in the war. I am sure that no journalist will for one moment on that account attribute to us any motive of selfish concern in the appeal we make to those who are happily at peace for their help in the humanitarian and fraternal task of relieving the tragic needs arising from the war.

In our own organisation we face grave problems -- reduced membership and income, difficulties of one sort and another due to the departure of members on activeservice, new responsibilities to their wives and families, reduced opportunities of employment in consequence of smaller papers. We face these problems with inevitably diminished means and with the certain prospect of largely increased demands on all our resources.

But we make this international appeal on the ground of international solidarity, professional interest, fraternal duty and practical sympathy for all our organisations [illegible]

With fraternal greetings,
Yours most sincerely,

A. KENYON

President, Federation Internationale des Journalistes

[signature]
SECRÉTAIRE GÉNÉRAL

Figure 1.4 In autumn 1939 the FIJ was naturally preoccupied by the escalating war. The first circular letter about its impact on member unions and journalists was issued by Stéphen Valot (in French) in August and in October he and the President signed a joint appeal. There the seat is changed to a temporary address.

At the time of its second Congress in October 1942, the IFJAFC had members in Australia, Brazil, Belgium, Britain, Czechoslovakia, "Free France", Greece, The Netherlands, Norway, Poland, the USSR and Yugoslavia. Its president was Archibald Kenyon of the UK, its two Vice-Presidents Alexander Sverlov of the USSR and Tor Gjesdal of Norway, its treasurer Jiří Hronek of Czechoslovakia and its secretary L. A. Berry of the UK.

The IFJAFC was guided by "the resolve to see the FIJ re-established on a stronger, universal basis after the war". On this basis an appeal was launched by its last Congress, which met in London in March 1945, to set up a new organization with the widest possible participation of journalists from all over the world. It took another year until March 1946 when finally a letter of invitation was issued to the IFJAFC members and other potential participants to attend the World Congress of Journalists in Copenhagen in June that year.[10]

10 The letter is reproduced in *Useful Recollections, Part II* (Nordenstreng & Kubka, 1988, pp. 10–11).

CHAPTER 2
FOUNDING 1946–47[1]

COPENHAGEN 1946

The war-time Federation IFJAFC, carrying the legacy of the pre-war FIJ, convened the **World Congress of Journalists in Copenhagen** on 3–9 **June 1946** (Figure 2.1). This Congress was a manifestation of the positive post-war spirit: the Danish Parliament building in a country liberated from fascism accommodated 165 delegates from 21 countries[2], in the presence of the Crown Prince of Denmark and high-ranking representatives of the new United Nations.

The official report of the Congress[3] begins with the following summary:

> Its formation followed the voluntary dissolution, in separate meetings on June 3, of the Fédération Internationale des Journalistes (F.I.J.), which was founded in 1926, and of the International Federation of Journalists of Allied or Free Countries (I.F.J.A.F.C.), which from 1941 carried on the idea of international co-operation of democratic journalists.
>
> The I.O.J. is therefore soundly based in a respected tradition and experience of work for international co-operation in journalism. Its formation, indeed, was foreseen in the 1941 constitution of the I.F.J.A.F.C. which pledged the establishment of a journalists' international on a stronger, universal basis after the war.

---

1 This chapter is based on *Useful Recollections, Part II* (Nordenstreng & Kubka, 1988, pp. 9–28). The quotes below are taken from this book. Much of the text also appears in *A History of the International Movement of Journalists* (Nordenstreng & al., 2016, pp. 125–132). These books include chronologies of relevant events throughout the history of the IOJ, including its prehistory from 1893 on.
A summary of the founding years 1946–47 is provided by a chronicle published in the IOJ magazine *The Democratic Journalist* 6–7/1966 on the occasion of the 20th anniversary of the Organization (available online at http://books.google.com, search "democratic journalist").
Appendix 1 provides a list of all meetings of the IOJ statutory bodies from 1946 to 1996. The Presidium members throughout this period are listed in **Appendix 2**.

2 Australia, Belgium, Czechoslovakia, Denmark, Finland, France, Greece, Iceland, Netherlands, New Zealand, Norway, Peru, Poland, South Africa, Sweden, Switzerland, Turkey, United Kingdom, USA, USSR, Yugoslavia.

3 Published in July 1946 as *I.O.J. Bulletin No. I.* It is reproduced as Annex 2 in *Useful Recollections, Part II* (1988, pp. 101–120).

Kronprinsen ved Aabningsmødet.

Journalistkongressen.

Referat af de tre Dages Forhandlinger i Folketingssalen.

UNGE DAMER modtog den internationale Journalistkongres' Delegerede i Rigsdagshuset med naa Buketter, lyserøde Roser til Damerne og mørkde Nelliker til Herrene. Blomsterne, Kongressens aukke Emblem og det lille Navneskilt paa Reverset .mt Flagene udenfor Bygningen var det eneste Udyr. Præcis Kl. 9 samledes alle Delegerede og Gæster ; lidt efter kom Kongressens Protektor, Kronprins ·ederik. Formanden for Danske Journalisters Fællespræsentation, Redaktør *Niels Hansen*, bød i en kort ılkomsttale paa Engelsk og Fransk Velkommen til ınmark. Saa talte Finansminister *Thorkil Kristensen*, r repræsenterede Udenrigsminister Gustav Rasmusn. Thorkil Kristensen takkede paa den danske Beıknings Vegne Pressen i den frie Verden for den Opıntring, den havde været for Befolkningen her i Lant under Krigen. Endvidere udtalte Finansministeren:

»Nazismen og dens Metoder lærte os alle, hvad Frid er værd, ogsaa Pressefriheden. Vi fik en haard ktie i, hvor vigtigt, ja fundamentalt det er for Deıkratiets Bestaaen og Udvikling, at der er en fri Presse. Jeg har derfor med Interesse bemærket, at Pressens Frihed staar paa Konferencens Program. Vi ønsker, at Kongressen under sin Drøftelse af Metoder til at sikre Pressens Frihed i det moderne Verdenssamfund vil naa til gode Resultater, saa Hindringer af enhver Art for en fri Udøvelse af Journalistens ansvarsfulde Gerning maa ryddes af Vejen.«

Kronprinsen fik derefter Ordet og udtalte paa Engelsk: »Idet jeg byder Dem Velkommen og ønsker Dem Held med Kongresens Arbejde, erklærer jeg hermed Kongressen for aabnet.«

Deltagerne i Mødet rejste sig og klappede, og dermed var Festiviteterne overstaaet. Præsidenten for The International Federation of Journalist in Allied and Free Countries, Mr. *Kenyon* tog straks Ordet og holdt en Tale, der baade var en smuk Hilsen til Danmark og en tankevækkende Introduktion til de senere Forhandlinger paa Kongressen om de store principielle Spørgsmaal. Mr. Kenyon udtalte:

Figure 2.1 a The journal of the Danish Union of Journalists featured extensive coverage of the Copenhagen Congress in text and photos.

JOURNALISTEN 11

Den nye Ledelse: Fra venstre Morel, Murray, Kenyon, Bean, Gjesdal og Sverlov.

ncen mellem Kravet om Frihed og Ansvarsfølel-
Presse-Monopoler er Faren for Pressen, hvadenten
:r Statsmonopoler eller private Monopoler. En Na-
.lisering af Pressen fører til Diktatur og dermed
rig.
:scalakis, Grækenland, forelagde en Resolution, der
:t skarpt præciserede Forpligtelsen for de natio-
Journalistorganisationer til at arbejde for fuld
:d. Delegationen foreslog, »at alle Repræsentanter
ı nye Pressesammenslutning, der er samlet her,
afgive en højtidelig Forsikring om, at der er ab-
Pressefrihed i deres respektive Lande og at dette
ı Betingelse »sino non qua« for at deltage i den
nationale Federation.«
dvidere ønskede den græske Delegation, at man
le opfordre Regeringerne til at give alle frem-
: Journalister fuld Frihed til at undersøge Lande-
›olitiske, sociale og andre Forhold.
ıkussionen om Pressefriheden fortsattes Onsdag
'en med et Indlæg af den russiske Delegerede
Surkov, der bl. a. udtalte:
:ressens og Radioens Rolle i det moderne Samfund
ıa betydelig, at Friheden ikke udelukkende kan
vor personlige Ejendom. I den franske Resolution
der kun om Pressens Frihed, men der siges intet
ournalistens Ansvar. Nogle Journalister har, som
e ved, brugt Pressens Frihed imod Folkenes sande
Derved blev Pressefriheden blot Frihed til at for-
Forholdet mellem Nationerne. Ingen anden Stat
'æret Genstand for saa mange Løgne som Rus-
Vi har kun det ene Krav og Ønske, at man skri-
'andheden om Forholdene i vort Land. Hos os er
ens Frihed garanteret i vor Forfatning. Journali-
ɜ lever med Folket, har delt dets Lidelser under
disse Krigsaar. Det er efter vor Mening nødvendigt, at
der skabes en Æreslov for Journalister, saaledes at
Folket kan have fuld Tillid til, hvad Pressen fortæller
og vi kan naa dertil, at Folket betragter Journalisterne
som deres Venner.«

Bean, Australien, var enig med den polske Delegation i, at en etisk Kode var nødvendig.

Herefter afsluttedes den forberedende Debat om Spørgsmaalet og en Redaktionskomité gik i Gang med at samarbejde de mange Forslag.

Dernæst talte UNO's Repræsentant, Chefen for Verdensorganisationens Informations-Tjeneste, Vicegeneralsekretær *Cohen*, om Pressens Opgaver i Arbejdet for Freden. Der er et Problem, som har meget stor Betydning i denne Forbindelse, sagde Mr. Cohen — det er Friheden til at bringe Nyheder fra hele Verden. Alle Møder i Verdensorganisationen holdes aabne for Pressen. Kun i Undtagelsestilfælde, hvor det drejer sig om Spørgsmaal, der kan berøre private Personers Anliggender, holdes der lukkede Møder. 800 Pressemænd er nu permanent knyttet til Verdensorganisationen, desuden 300 fra Radiotjenesten og mange fra Filmsproduktionen. Men man har Opmærksomheden henvendt paa, at mange smaa Lande ikke er repræsenteret. Det skyldes i mange Tilfælde økonomiske Vanskeligheder og vi er meget villige til at lytte til alle gode Raad, som man maatte kunne give os om, hvorledes Kontakten kan gøres saa god som muligt. Sikkerhedsraadet er den Institution, som har haft størst Tiltrækningskraft for Pressen. Men i det økonomiske og sociale Raad udføres en lang Række vigtige konstruktive Opgaver, som fortjener mere Opmærksomhed end de nu faar. Gennem Arbejdet i disse Instanser skal vi give Folkene over hele Verden fornyet Tillid. Af denne

Figure 2.1 b The journal reproduced the same photo of the IOJ "founding fathers" as that on the cover of *Useful Recollections, Part II* (taken from *IOJ Bulletin No. I*, July 1946).

The Congress report as well as accounts in several journals of the national unions represented in Copenhagen describe the lively debate, beginning with the election of Congress officers and ending with the establishment of the new organization. After Archibald Kenyon of the UK was elected by acclamation as the congress chairman, the election of Stéphen Valot – the French Secretary General of the pre-war FIJ – to the Congress presidium was opposed by the French delegation, which represented a post-war line with less bourgeois orientation and proposed another representative of the French member union for this position. The compromise was that both French colleagues were elected.

Opinions differed regarding "liberty of the press", but finally the Congress unanimously approved a statement of principle on this topic. Another much debated issue was whether the organization should be set up "purely on a trade union basis" as proposed by the general secretary of the British NUJ or whether it should be based on a more individualistic approach by "continental intellectualism" advocated by the Swiss delegates. The Soviet contingent supported trade unionism while also advocating the creation of "a moral code" for the profession – no doubt a code intended to eliminate fascist propaganda. The moral in this context referred to the Soviet notion of peace – after, for example, the paper *Red Star* alone had lost 17 of its 42 war correspondents. However controversial the issues, they were settled in an amicable atmosphere.

After the debate the chairman proposed that the **International Organisation of Journalists (IOJ)** be established without delay. The proposal was adopted with 16 votes, each delegation having one vote. Switzerland abstained and Turkey had not yet arrived at the Congress. The provisional constitution for the new organization was drawn up by one of the Congress committees composed of delegates from Belgium, Czechoslovakia, Denmark, Finland, France, South Africa, the UK, the USA and the USSR. In addition to these nine countries, the founding members were from Australia, Greece, Ireland, the Netherlands, New Zealand, Norway, Peru, Poland, Sweden, Switzerland, Turkey and Yugoslavia. The largest member unions came from the USSR (30,000 journalists), the USA (25,000) and the UK (8,000).[4]

The provisional constitution was adopted unanimously. Its Article 1 determines the name[5] and places the provisional headquarters in London,

4 The resolution on Press and Peace calls upon "all the 130,000 members of the International Organisation of Journalists to do their utmost in support of the work of international understanding and co-operation entrusted to the United Nations". The origin of this figure is shrouded in mystery, while the sum total of membership figures given by the national affiliates represented in Copenhagen is slightly over 80,000 (*Useful Recollections, Part II,* 1988, p. 15).

5 "Organisation" was written with s instead of z – consistent with the British spelling of the time.

where the war-time Federation also had its base. Article 2 defines the "Aims and Objects" of the IOJ as:

a) Protection by all means of all liberty of the press and of journalism. The defence of the people's right to be informed honestly and accurately.
b) Promotion of international friendship and understanding through free interchange of information.
c) Promotion of trade unionism amongst journalists.

The election of the IOJ leadership went smoothly. The six officers elected were President A. Kenyon (UK), Vice-Presidents E. Morel (France), T. Gjesdal (Norway), M. Murray (USA) and A. Sverlov (USSR) as well as Secretary-Treasurer K. Bean (Australia). Of these, President Kenyon and Vice-President Sverlov held the same positions in the war-time Federation.

Accordingly, with the founding of the IOJ in Copenhagen, the USA (Murray), USSR (Sverlov) and Scandinavia (Gjesdal) assumed leading positions in the international movement of journalists, which had so far been dominated by colleagues from continental Europe and the United Kingdom.

The first IOJ Congress report also puts on record – under the title "Dissolution of F.I.J." – that representatives of the countries which had been in the FIJ met separately under the chairmanship of its president Archibald Kenyon and resolved that "this F.I.J. ceases to function as an international organisation of journalists as from the date when the new Federation has been formed and its officers elected". Similarly the war-time IFJAFC was dissolved. Accordingly, the transfer of organizational legacy and competence was made crystal clear: the successor to the FIJ was the IOJ.

PRAGUE 1947

The **2nd IOJ Congress** was convened in Prague on 3–7 **June 1947**, hosted by the Czechoslovak Union of Journalists (Figure 2.2). The spirit continued to be fairly good and the world of journalism still united, although international politics was already moving towards the Cold War. Winston Churchill had coined the term "iron curtain" in his speech in Fulton, Missouri, in March 1946, but 1947 was the year when Americans began to take institutional steps: The Marshall Plan was directed to Western economies to shield them against Soviet influence and the Central Intelligence Agency CIA was established.

The ceremonial part of the Congress followed the grand style established in Copenhagen. The sessions took place in the *Slovanský dům* in the centre of Prague, decorated with the flags of 30 countries and a special Congress emblem. The Congress was under the patronage of the President of the Czechoslo-

deník II. světového sjezdu mezinárodní organisace novinářů

орган II. всемирного съезда международной организации журналистов

PRAHA 1947

IOJ

daily of the II. world congress of the international organisation of journalists

journal du II. congrès mondial de l'organisation internationale des journalistes

Praha, 1. VI. 1947 — 1

Mezinárodní organisace novinářů

Международная организация журналистов

International Organisation Of Journalists

L'Organisation Internationale Des Journalistes

II. SVĚTOVÝ SJEZD · II. ВСЕМИРНЫЙ КОНГРЕСС

II. WORLD CONGRESS · II. CONGRES MONDIAL

PRAHA · ČESKOSLOVENSKO

3.—10. VI. 1947

Na pozvání vlády republiky Československé a Svazu československých novinářů.

By the invitation of the Government of the Czechoslovak Republic and the Czechoslovak Union of Journalists.

По приглашению правительства Чехословацкой республики и Союза чехословацких журналистов

Under the Patronage of His Excellency

Dr. Edvard Beneš, President of the Czechoslovak Republic

Honorary Chairmen:

Mr. Josef David, Chairman of the Constituent National Assembly, Mr. Klement Gottwald, Prime Minister, Mr. Petr Zenkl, Vice-Premier, Monsignore Jan Šrámek, Vice-Premier, Mr. Zdeněk Fierlinger, Vice-Premier, Mr. Ján Ursíny, Vice-Premier, Mr. Viliam Široký, Vice-Premier, Mr. Jan Masaryk, Minister of Foreign Affairs, Mr. Václav Kopecký, Minister of Information, Mr. Vladimír Clementis, State Secretary for Foreign Affairs, Mr. Václav Vacek, Lord Mayor of Prague.

President of the Union of Czechoslovak Journalists:

Mr. Otakar Wünsch

President of the International Organisation of Journalists:

Mr. Archibald Kenyon (United Kingdom)

Vice Presidents of the I.O.J.

Mr. Eugene Morel (France), Mr. Tor Gjesdal (Norway), Mr. Milton M. Murray (USA), Mr. Alexander Sverlov (USSR).

Secretary-Treasurer of the I.O.J.:

Mr. Keith F. Bean (Australia)

Organising Committee of the Prague Congress:

Mr. Jiří Hronek (Chairman)

Mr. Zdeněk Anděl, Mr. Stanislav Budín, Mr. Evžen Cíl, Mr. Karel Hetteš, Mr. Eduard Maška, Mr. František Noska, Mr. N. Pavlović, Mr. Jindřich Prokop, Mr. Karel Zieris.

The International Organisation of Journalists

Международная организация журналистов

1

Figure 2.2 a The daily Congress Journal issued by the local organizing committee in three languages (English, French and Russian) gave a comprehensive account of the proceedings.

deník II. světového sjezdu mezinárodní organisace novinářů

орган II. всемирного съезда международной организации журналистов

PRAHA 1947 IOJ

daily of the II. world congress of the international organisation of journalists

journal du II. congrès mondial de l'organisation internationale des journalistes

Praha, 4. VI. 1947 — 3

AUSPICIOUS START OF CONGRESS

Masaryk: "If You Hit On Iron Curtain - Give Me A Ring" — IOJ Granted Consultative Status in UN — Zaslavsky Pledges Fullest Soviet Participation — Palestine Accepted

Flags of 31 States and in the midst of them the emblem of the Journalist Congress were the decoration of the Slovanský Dům where the Second World Journalists Congress was opened on Tuesday at 9 o'clock in the morning. The Congress was opened by the President of the International Organisation of Journalists, Mr. A. Kenyon. Among the guests were Minister of Foreign Affairs, Mr. Jan Masaryk, Minister of Information, V. Kopecký, State Secretary of Foreign Affairs, Dr. V. Clementis, Bulgarian Minister, Simov, the Lord Mayor of Prague, Dr. V. Vacek and the Press Attachés of Prague Embassies and officials of the Press Department of the Ministry of Information.

Mr. Jan Masaryk in his welcoming address said: "In the name of the Czechoslovak Government I welcome you all, delegates of the Second International Congress of Journalists, in Prague. I also welcome the representatives of the United Nations and UNESCO. You gentlemen represent the most divergent political viewpoints, the most varied social legislations, and often quite opposite viewpoints as to the meaning of freedom of the Press. One may expect, therefore, that the discussion will not only be interesting, but pretty lively at times. We are glad. The more often supporters [illegible] discuss and argue, the better it will be for the ordinary newspaper reader who is often unaware of what happens behind the headlines".

Mr. Masaryk went on to say that mankind which in two generations has passed through the valley of darkness and death deserves to be spared a third ordeal. The cherished ideal was to write at last, what might be called the Symphony of Peace.

The Headlines Should Grow Smaller

"You, the fellow composers of this music of the future", said Mr. Masaryk, "will use different counterpoints and different methods. But if you earnestly attempt to reach agreement on basic questions, the day will come when the present ten centimeter headlines which daily tell us of international tension, will grow smaller and be replaced, I hope, by more constructive headlines telling us about the lessening of international tensions; about not the possibility, but the necessity for agreement. Then peace will be preserved and strengthened for long time to come, which might mean, perhaps, for ever."

Mr. Masaryk went on to ask delegates not to render the United Nations ridiculous, or to be cynical in their treatment of U. N. For the time being it was the only road to our goal. If they must be critical let them be constructively so.

The UN And IOJ.

Mr. Otakar Wünsch, Chairman of the Union of Czechoslovak Journalists, then welcomed the delegates. "We Czechoslovak journalists," he said, "thank our National Front Government, and Parliament, which has recently passed a law giving our organisation the right to look after the ideological aspect of the press. By giving news on international events in a concrete and objective manner, we want to play our full part in working for the collaboration of nations, now so necessary that people may recover from the disasters of war."

Mr. Archibald Kenyon in replying to messages of welcome, spoke warmly of the spirit of hospitality which he has encountered in Prague. "We know that almost every week in Prague some international conference is being held. We can really see how Czechoslovakia has opened of the world."

Warmest greetings to the Congress from the Secretary General of the United Nations, Mr. Trygve Lie, were conveyed by his special representative, Mr. Tor Gjesdal, (Norway), who emphasised that the I. O. J. had been officially granted high consultative status on the Councils of the United Nations. The danger of having the international atmosphere poisoned by insufficient or unskilled representation of facts, or by misrepresentation, should be combated. He felt that the organisation of journalists of the five continents could do much to improve the situation.

The Report of the Executive

Mr. Bean, the Secretary Treasurer of the I. O. J. in his annual report, stated that the work of building the I. O. J. has progressed steadily, and with a vigour and success which warranted the congratulations of all affiliated organisation to the executive which the Copenhagen Congress created.

He said that the constitution provisionally agreed upon at Copenhagen would stand, except that there would be a change to the effect that members of the Executive Council should have the rights of delegates at future congresses, but not to vote apart from their national organisations.

Continued on Page 2

Масарик приветствует съезд. Председательствует Кенион
Masaryk Welcomes the Congress. Kenyon At the Chair
Masaryk salue le Congrès, Kenyon préside

DEBUT FAVORABLE DU CONGRES

Masaryk: «Si vous tombez sur le rideau de fer - prévenez moi!» — L'IOJ obtient une voix consultative à l'ONU — Zaslavsky assure pleine participation des journalistes soviétiques

Les drapeaux de 31 états, au milieu desquels se trouvait l'emblème du Congrès des Journalistes, constituèrent la décoration de Slovanský Dům, où s'ouvrit, le mardi à 9 heures du matin, le deuxième Congrès Mondial des Journalistes. Le Président de l'Organisation Internationale des Journalistes, M. A. Kenyon, inaugura le Congrès. Parmi les invités se trouvaient: M. Jan Masaryk, Ministre des Affaires Etrangères, M. V. Kopecký, Ministre de l'Information, M. V. Clementis, sous-secrétaire d'Etat aux Affaires Etrangères, le Ministre bulgare, M. Simov, le maire de Prague, M. V. Vacek, les Attachés de presse des ambassades étrangères à Prague, et les personnalités du département de la presse au ministère de l'Information.

M. Jan Masaryk dans son allocution de bienvenue prononça les mots suivants: »Au nom du gouvernement tchécoslovaque, je vous souhaite la bienvenue à tous, délégués du second congrès international des journalistes à Prague, et à vous représentants de l'U. N. O. et de l'U. N. E. S. C. O. Vous représentez, Messieurs, les points de vue politiques les plus divers et les législations sociales les plus variées, et, souvent, des points de vue opposés en ce qui concerne la manière de concevoir la liberté de la presse. On peut donc s'attendre à ce que la discussion ne soit pas seulement intéressante, mais à certains moments très vivante. Nous en sommes heureux. Plus les défenseurs de thèses politiques et sociales variées se rencontreront, discuteront et argumenteront, mieux ce sera pour le lecteur de journaux ordinaire qui ignore souvent ce qui se cache derrière les entêtes.«

M. Masaryk continua en disant que l'humanité, qui en l'espace de deux générations a traversé la sombre vallée de la mort, mérite de se voir épargner une nouvelle épreuve. L'idéal désiré était d'écrire enfin ce qui pourrait être appelé la Symphonie de la Paix.

Pour des titres plus modestes

»Vous, les compositeurs de cette musique du futur«, dit M. Masaryk, »vous allez vous servir de différents contrepoints et de différentes méthodes. Mais si vous essayez sérieusement d'arriver à un accord général sur les questions de base, le jour viendra où les titres actuels, qui ont dix centimètres de haut et qui nous parlent quotidiennement de la tension internationale, se réduiront et seront remplacés, je l'espère, par des titres plus constructifs parlant de la diminution des tensions internationales, de la nécessité, et non de la possibilité, d'un accord. Alors

Suite en page 2

УСПЕШНОЕ НАЧАЛО КОНГРЕССА

Ян Масарик: «Если найдете у нас железный занавес - протелефонируйте мне» — МОЖ получила право совещательного голоса в ООН — Заславский обещает полнейшее содействие советских журналистов — Принятие новых членов

Пестрые цвета национальных флагов 29 государств и под ними эмблема журналистов являются скромным украшением большого зала Славянского дома, в котором во вторник, 3 июня, был открыт Всемирный конгресс журналистов. Представители их выскажут на этом съезде свое мнение по поводу одного из основных факторов современной цивилизации — свободы печати. Они обсудят и другие проблемы, касающиеся прессы и журналистов, но вопрос свободы печати, за которую журналисты никогда не переставали бороться, и которую так высоко ценит именно чехословацкий народ, переживший годы геббельсовского ограничения печати, этот вопрос наложит основной отпечаток на конгресс журналистов, который открыт в городе, где сто лет тому назад работал отважный защитник свободы печати Карел Гавличек Боровский.

Шум в зале внезапно прекратился, когда вскоре после 9 часов председатель А. Кенион (Великобритания) открыл второй конгресс Всемирной организации журналистов. Среди почетных гостей при торжественном открытии конгресса присутствовали: министр иностранных дел Ян Масарик, министр информации В. Копецкий, министр внешней торговли д-р Г. Рипка, статс-секретарь д-р Вл. Клементис, болгарский посол Ш. Симов (еще недавно сам журналист), городской голова гор. Праги д-р В. Вацек и его заместительница Р. Пелант, пресс-атташе пражских посольств и представители чехословацкой печати.

Министр Масарик в своей речи приветствовал от имени чехословацкого правительства делегатов второго Международного конгресса журналистов, представителей организации Объединенных Наций и ЮНЕСКО. «Вы являетесь представителями разных политических течений, сказал он, выразителями разнообразных социальных законодательств и, часто, совершенно противоположных мнений по вопросу о свободе печати. Поэтому можно ожидать, что обмен мнениями будет не только интересным, но и очень оживленным. И мы этому рады.»

Министр Масарик сказал далее, что человечество, которое в течение двух поколений слишком много испытало, заслуживает того, чтобы было, наконец, избавлено от дальнейших страданий. Если вы искренно попытаетесь достигнуть соглашения по основным вопросам, то наступит день, когда мир будет обеспечен и укреплен на долгое время, может быть, и навсегда. Министр Масарик обратился к делегатам с просьбой не заниматься беспредметной критикой, но критикой по существу.

Затем председатель Центрального Союза чехословацких журналистов О. Вюнш приветствовал своих коллег-журналистов.

После него выступил с речью председатель Международной организации журналистов Артур Кенион.

Заместитель председателя Международной организации журналистов и директор отделения по делам информации при Организации Объединенных Наций, Тор Гиесдал передал съезду самые сердечные приветствия генерального секретаря ООН Трюгве Ли, которого он замещает.

Секретариат Организации Объединенных Наций и особенно Отделение по делам информации, заявил Тор Гиесдал, уже давно убеждены, что успех Объединенных Наций, в конце концов, зависит от общественного мнения в каждой стране, от общего понимания задач, которые стоят перед Организацией Объединенных Наций и в той же мере от соответствующей информации общественности всех стран о достижениях и целях Организации Объединенных Наций.

Мы сознаем, что эта сословная организация, со своими высокими моральными целями и идеалами, направленными к международному взаимопониманию, может быть значительным фактором при поддержке продолжительного всемирного мира и прогресса.

Мы все еще находимся в периоде между войной и миром. Возможно, что эти проблемы не являются столь серьезными, как некоторые люди любят об этом думать. Слишком вольные и неответственные речи не нужно принимать всерьез. С другой стороны, существует опасность, что международная атмосфера будет отравлена недостаточной и неумелой передачей фактов или их искажением. С этой опасностью необходимо бороться.

Журналистическая организация пяти континентов света может улучшить положение, если она будет итти вперед, имея в виду лучшие традиции своего сословия, и помнить резолюции, принятые на прошлогоднем Международном Съезде в Копенгагене.

Объединенные Нации стремятся к тесному сотрудничеству с Международной Организа-

Продолжение на 2 стр.

Figure 2.2 b No other IOJ Congress has been accompanied by such reporting on the past day's events with text, photographs and even cartoons.

vakia, Dr Edvard Beneš, who hosted a reception in Prague Castle. The opening session was addressed by the Minister of Foreign Affairs, Jan Masaryk, and a message was also received from the Prime Minister, Klement Gottwald, who, besides welcoming the guests, expressed the wish that they:

> take a good look round our country which according to certain opinions is situated behind some mythical "iron curtain". We trust that in describing their impressions of Czechoslovakia they will be faithful to the first and most dignified task of journalists, namely, to tell the truth and assist towards the victory of truth.

Amplifying this point, the Chairman of the Organizing Committee, Jiří Hronek, addressed the delegates:

> We here in Czechoslovakia are convinced that it is the function of the Press to unite, and not to divide the nations. We know of course that it is not always so, and that in times of political tension the press often obscures the situation, instead of clarifying it and encouraging a state of public opinion conducive to the lessening of international tension. I believe that one of the tasks of this Conference ought to be to create in the International Organization of Journalists a powerful instrument of world peace, a powerful defence for peace, for good neighbourliness among the nations, and an instrument of truth.

The IOJ President, Archibald Kenyon, echoed these welcoming addresses:

> The inspiration of our movement is service through friendship. In that spirit we meet in Prague, in that spirit we esteem and reciprocate the great goodwill and kindness that are being shown to us by the people, the President, the Government, and the Press of Czechoslovakia.

Kenyon also pointed out the special relationship which had been developing between the IOJ and the United Nations and, referring to the UN resolution which authorized the convocation of a Conference on Freedom of Information, he asked:

> If there is not freedom of information how can we know the facts? If we do not know the facts, how can we form right conclusions? If we do not form right conclusions, how can we act wisely and justly? We may not come to the right conclusion or act wisely if we have full information, but without knowledge we are almost certain to go wrong.

Greetings to the Congress from the Secretary-General of the United Nations, Trygve Lie, were conveyed by his special representative, Tor Gjesdal – the same Norwegian who had been elected as one of the IOJ Vice-Presidents at the Copenhagen Congress. He reported that the IOJ had been officially granted high consultative status on the UN Economic and Social Council ECOSOC. He also emphasized that the danger of having the international atmosphere poisoned by insufficient or unskilled representation of facts, or by misrepresentation, should be avoided. In his view the organization of journalists of the five continents could do much to improve the situation.

The Prague Congress was attended by 208 delegates and guests from 28 countries. In addition to those 21 countries which were present in Copenhagen, there were now also representatives from Austria, Bulgaria, Egypt, Hungary, Iran, Palestine, the Philippines, Romania, Spain (the exiled group as guests) and Venezuela. On the other hand, of those attending in Copenhagen, New Zealand, Peru and Turkey were absent from Prague. The UN was represented by Gjesdal and UNESCO's observer was the head of the division of mass communication, René Maheu, who later became its Director-General.

All those organizations attending were admitted as members, with the exception of Egypt and Iran. The applications of these two were problematic because they included not only journalists but also proprietors, and therefore the matter was referred to the Executive Committee. On this occasion the exiled group of Spanish journalists was accepted as a full member – by a majority vote after a "stormy debate" with a Soviet-American controversy.

Even more heated was the debate on the future headquarters of the IOJ.[6] In Copenhagen it was decided that London would be only the provisional base of the IOJ; now Prague offered to host the headquarters. The British, supported especially by the Americans, wanted the wartime base London to continue, while most others, including Scandinavian and Central European members, voted for Prague – either as a permanent base or as the beginning of a rotation. Hence the headquarters were moved to Prague at least until the next Congress.

The debate on the headquarters followed after the unanimous adoption of the constitution, now called "Statute".[7] There it is stipulated that the IOJ headquarters "shall be situated in such place as Congress shall determine".

---

6 This time we can follow the proceedings in greater detail in the official report, which contains ten printed pages describing the discussions, published by the new headquarters in Prague in 1947. The debates mentioned here are summarized in *Useful Recollections, Part II* (1988, pp. 19–22). Selected photos and cartoons from the Congress Journal are reproduced in the same (pp. 17–21).

7 The name of the organization was spelled in the Statute with z, but later in the 1950s and 1960s the IOJ documents and publications also used the old British spelling with s. However, between 1966 and 1991 the spelling was consistently with z.

It was inevitable then that the question of headquarters would surface as soon as the Statute was adopted.

The Article on "Aims and Objects" is essentially the same as already formulated in Copenhagen, but the new wording was more outspoken from the point of view of professional journalists (changes after Copenhagen in italics):

a) Protection by all means of the liberty of the press and of journalist*s*. The defence of the people's right to be informed *freely, fully,* honestly and accurately.
b) Promotion of international friendship and understanding through free interchange of information.
c) The promotion of trade unionism amongst journalists, *the protection of their professional rights and interests, and the improvement of their economic status.*

The membership conditions remained the same as laid down in Copenhagen. Thus only one organization from each country was eligible to affiliate, but in the event of more than one organization claiming to represent the journalists of a country, the Executive Committee was given the power to decide which organization, if any, should be admitted – subject to the decision of the following Congress.

The Statute determined that each delegation at the Congress, the supreme authority of the IOJ, should have one vote only. This was after voting down an American proposal, first also supported by the Soviets, who, however, reversed their position in the debate, that each Congress delegation should have one vote for every 1,000 members to a maximum of 10 votes. The number of members in the American Newspaper Guild was now 17,000, whereas in Copenhagen it was reported to be as many as 24,500. The same downward trend was true of membership in the Soviet Union of Journalists: in Copenhagen a figure of 30,000 was reported, but now it was explained that several thousand journalists had in fact been working on military newspapers which had since been discontinued and the actual membership figure given was 14,000. Obviously it was in the interest of unions with a large membership to report the lowest possible figure for purposes of determining the membership dues. With these lower figures the total membership of the IOJ at the time of the Prague Congress was reportedly 58,600.

Later on, the drafting committee (UK, USA, USSR, France, Norway, Austria and Yugoslavia) proposed a resolution on freedom of the press identical to the wording of the Copenhagen statement, except for the final paragraph which was replaced by a new formulation:

> The peoples of the world are weary of war, ardently desirous of peace. As men and women of good will they seek to know and to understand each other so that con-

flict shall not arise among them. It is the basic right of the people everywhere to be informed, freely, honestly, accurately, and fully. It is from this right to the people that freedom of the press is born. The IOJ on behalf of its members and on behalf of the people they serve, declares:

1. There must be free access to news and information for all journalists.
2. There must be full freedom to publish news, information and opinion without restraint beyond the essential demand of decency, honesty and integrity.
3. Pending an international convention establishing universally a free flow of news and information, all nations should be urged to enter into bi-lateral or multi-lateral treaties to this end.

The Congress adopted this resolution unanimously – another proof that it was indeed a landmark statement. The last paragraph of the Copenhagen statement, calling for a mechanism to monitor press freedom in individual countries, was now incorporated in the Statute, where it appears under the paragraph "Disputes":

> Any affiliated organization shall be entitled to lay a complaint against any other organization on the ground of unconstitutional conduct. It shall be the duty of the Executive Council[8] to investigate any such complaint and to submit to all affiliated organizations a precise of the complaint, the defence together with its findings and such recommendations as it may consider necessary. The Executive Council's precise findings and recommendations shall be submitted to the next Congress which shall have the power to suspend, censure or expel the national organization against which complaint was made.

Other resolutions were likewise unanimously adopted, and the elections of officers were also unanimous. Archibald Kenyon (UK) was re-elected as President, and Milton M. Murray (USA), Pavel Yudin (USSR), Eugen Morel (France), and Gunnar Nielsen (Denmark) were elected Vice-Presidents. Jiří Hronek (Czechoslovakia) was elected to the combined office of the Secretary General and Treasurer.

After four days and one night of intensive proceedings, the Congress came to a close at 5 a.m. on 7 June. The last point, as noted in the official report:

> By acclamation an invitation of Mr. Stijns (Belgium) was accepted that the next congress should be held in Brussels.

---

8 The earlier Executive Committee was called in this Statute a Council while its function remained the same – a broadly representative governing body between the congresses. In practice it was called Executive Committee and later renamed so.

The founding of the IOJ was completed in Prague in 1947, with a solid constitution and a fairly extensive membership as well as an established status of a non-governmental organization at the UN and UNESCO. The international movement of journalists was firmly organized and united.

One should note that the IOJ was not the only international non-governmental organization (INGO) established after World War II. The World Federation of Trade Unions (WFTU) was founded in 1945 in Paris, after a similar prehistory with another international federation during the age of the League of Nations. The same year the World Federation of Democratic Youth (WFDY) was also established in London and the Women's International Democratic Federation (WIDF) in Paris. The following year, 1946, the World Federation of Scientific Workers (WFSW) was founded in London, the International Union of Students (IUS) in Prague and the International Association of Democratic Lawyers (IADL) in Paris.[9]

Many other INGOs were established in different sectors, but these seven were to have a history similar to that of the IOJ. They all represent a wave of optimistic initiatives to enhance post-war co-operation in various sectors in the spirit of the United Nations, but became embroiled in the Cold War as fellow travellers on the Soviet side of the divided world. An intellectual catalyst for these organizations was provided by the idea of peace – Soviet style mobilizing an international movement led by the World Peace Council (WPC).[10]

---

9 For more on each of these, see Wikipedia https://en.wikipedia.org/ Also Union of International Associations (UIA), International Organizations Search https://uia.org/ybio/.

10 See Roberts (2014).

CHAPTER 3
TURMOIL IN THE COLD WAR 1948–53[1]

The promising period of founding congresses in Copenhagen and Prague soon turned to a chilling period of Cold War. The developments ensuing from 1948 to 1966 were presented in *Useful Recollections, Part II* as four phases: (1) Crisis 1948–49, (2) Results of the Cold War 1950–53, (3) Striving for Unity 1954–60, (4) Emancipation of the Third World 1961–66. Here the same sub-division is followed, but under two different chapters.

CRISIS 1948–49

Soon after the Prague congress some British and American press reports accused the IOJ of "falling under Russian influence", with the headquarters "taken over by communists" and its Secretary General named as a hardline puppet of Moscow. Such press coverage should be seen within the context of the political developments at the time: the German zones of occupation were divided into West Germany and the German Democratic Republic (1949), the North Atlantic Treaty Organization NATO was established (1949), while the Soviet Union and the new socialist countries created the Council of Mutual Economic Aid CMEA (1949) – the Soviet-led defence organization, the Warsaw Pact, being established only later (1955) after West Germany joined NATO. Already in 1947 the Soviets had set up the Information Bureau of Communist and Working-Class Parties COMINFORM.

Regarding the Czechoslovak Secretary General and Treasurer Jiří Hronek, in reality he was not a communist but a progressive patriot – one of those who due to their Jewish origin had fled the fascists and gone into exile in London and then returned to participate in the national democratic reconstruction. The American Vice-President Murray, for his part, proposed right after the Prague Congress to his own union ANG that the Americans should disaffiliate from the IOJ. His proposal was turned down by the ANG membership and

1 This chapter is based on *Useful Recollections, Part II* (1988, pp. 29–55). The quotes below are taken from this book unless otherwise noted. Some of the text also appears in *A History of the International Movement of Journalists* (Nordenstreng & al., 2016, pp. 132–142).

consequently he resigned. Then Harry Martin was elected as ANG President and assumed the American place in the IOJ leadership.

Martin represented the IOJ at the ECOSOC Sub-Commission of Freedom of Information and of the Press, which met in the temporary UN premises at Lake Success, New York in early 1948. This important session prepared articles for the draft international declaration on human rights and issued a statement of principle on the rights, obligations and practices to be included in the concept of freedom of information. Even more vital was the **UN Conference on Freedom of Information in Geneva** in **March–April 1948**. Since the IOJ was granted the highest status of an NGO at the Conference, the **IOJ Executive Committee** in a meeting in **Brussels in February 1948** prepared a set of resolutions to be taken to the UN Conference and decided to send to Geneva a delegation composed of the President, the Secretary General and both the American and the Soviet Vice-Presidents.

The resolutions agreed by the Executive Committee to be brought to Geneva contained, firstly, a general proposition to the UN's ECOSOC adopted already by the Prague congress, making eight proposals to overcome economic problems faced by the media and journalists as well as to ensure that "in all countries equal facilities of access to sources of information are granted to journalists of all countries without discrimination on ground of race, nationality, creed or politics" and also "to seek the establishment of intergovernmental machinery for the protection of journalists unjustly accused of legal or political offences".[2] Secondly, the Executive agreed to pass to Geneva two resolutions with specific recommendations: to start a "Day of Friendship and Mutual Understanding in the Press... to propagate lasting peace, real democracy, mutual understanding and friendship among nations" and to "consider (1) the possibility of formulating a *code of conduct* for journalists and newspapers in reporting and presenting news and views in international interest, and (2) of establishing under United Nations authority and with the co-operation of the IOJ and newspaper owners a *Court of Honour* before which complaints and accusations of falsification and distortion could be brought and examined". It is important to note that these resolutions were adopted unanimously, endorsed by the Americans as well as the Soviets. Accordingly, the spirit of Copenhagen and Prague still prevailed in February 1948.

The UN Conference in Geneva produced two months later a mixed bag of resolutions, the most significant of these being the draft Article 19 for the Universal Declaration on Human Rights finally adopted by the UN General Assembly in December 1948. The Conference resolutions also included a UN Draft International Code of Ethics for journalists and even the idea

2 For the full text of this resolution, see *Useful Recollections, Part II* (1988, p. 27).

of the Court of Honour was embedded in the Final Act of the Conference. However, most of the Conference proposals were frozen by the Cold War – the "Day of Friendship" proposal already at the Conference table in Geneva. Yet it was obvious that the contribution of the IOJ to the UN Conference was positive.

What definitely was not positive was a public attack by Vice-President Martin against Secretary General Hronek while the two attended the UN Conference. Actually Martin did not appear in Geneva as an IOJ Vice-President but as part of the US governmental delegation representing American trade unions. From this position Martin publicized a letter he had written to President Kenyon after the Brussels Executive, suggesting that the IOJ headquarters be moved from Prague to the West and claiming that Hronek was misusing IOJ funds for communist propaganda. Thus the new ANG President, like his predecessor, turned against the IOJ Secretary General and the Czechoslovak headquarters. Hronek replied immediately in a letter which was also made public. The tide was changing at least in the American ANG approach to the IOJ right after February 1948.[3]

No doubt this clash served the interests of those pursuing the Cold War. The forces of confrontation advanced on several fronts, from international security with the founding of NATO to the trade union movement, which was divided, both nationally and internationally, into a left-wing and mostly pro-Soviet faction on the one hand, and a right-wing and pro-western faction on the other.[4] These developments were naturally reflected within the IOJ. For example in France, Vice-President Morel, who represented the right-wing *Force Ouvrière*, withdrew and his place was taken by firm leftist forces, including Jean-Maurice Hermann, who later became the IOJ President.

---

3 Parallel to these events in early 1948 Czechoslovakia was drawn into a constitutional crisis which led to a takeover of the Social Democratic Party by pro-Soviet communists – something that was seen as a "communist coup" (see Ševčíková & Nordenstreng, 2017). Later in 1948 the same occurred in Hungary, Poland and Bulgaria.
The most dramatic event in Czechoslovakia in early 1948 was the death of Foreign Minister Jan Masaryk. This son of Czechoslovakia's first President Tomáš Masaryk had a long record as a diplomat before World War II, resigning from the service in 1938 in protest against the Nazi occupation of the country. During the war he served as the Foreign Minister of Czechoslovakia's government in exile in London and after the liberation in 1945 he continued in the same position in a coalition government. When the communists seized power in February 1948, he did not resign as did other non-communist Ministers, as he wished to preserve the formal unity of the political forces. He was found dead after falling from the window of the Ministry on 10 March 1948, with an explanation that it was suicide. However, another political version claimed that he was pushed out of the window to pave the way for a complete communist takeover.

4 See *Useful Recollections, Part II* (1988, pp. 35–36).

Figure 3.1 The United Nations Conference on Freedom of Information took place in the UN premises in Geneva in March–April 1948. In May 1948 UN Assistant Secretary-General for Public Information, Benjamin Cohen, right, talks in New York with members of the Advisory Committee of Information Experts, called by the UN Secretary-General. Next to Cohen are Vernon Bartlett, M.P. of the London *News Chronicle;* Jiří Hronek, Chief of the Political Division of the Czechoslovak Broadcasts; Raul Noriega, Mexican journalist and diplomat; and Whitelaw Reid, Vice-President of the *New York Herald Tribune.* (Photos from the UN Photo Library in New York)

It was obviously the political development relating to a communist takeover rather than what happened within the IOJ itself that was the real cause of controversy. In response to the events in Czechoslovakia, protests were also expressed by the Danish, Swedish and Norwegian unions of journalists, referring to information according to which 80 journalists had been dismissed by the local action committees. In April the Confederation of Scandinavian Unions of Journalists warned that the forthcoming session of the IOJ Executive Committee might lead to an explosion as the Czechoslovak union was bound to deliver there a full explanation of what had happened.

It was natural that Hronek was brought into the spotlight following the crucial changes in the Czechoslovak political arena during the first months of 1948 – widely and aggressively covered by the western press. Nevertheless, he is seen still in May 1948 smiling with other information experts at a UN meeting at Lake Success, New York – not as the IOJ Secretary General but as a Czechoslovak state broadcasting executive (Figure 3.1).

In the course of 1948 the situation escalated both in international relations in general and in public opinion and media coverage in particular.

Against the backdrop of these developments, the **IOJ Executive Committee** met in **Budapest in November 1948**. Attended by representatives of 15 member unions, it was indeed an explosive session, but not so much around the purges in Czechoslovakia as around the issues of war and peace. The Soviet Vice-President Yudin attacked the Americans for "waging war psychosis" and the Secretary General emphasized the journalists' obligation for peace. There was no mood for reconciliation and the American Vice-President Martin simply walked out of the meeting, while the delegates of Austria, Belgium, Sweden and the UK took no further part in it. (Figures 3.2–3)

As confirmed by the personal recollections of Klánský in Part Two of this book, the Soviets pursued a hard line which left no room for compromise.[5] Obviously the American and British delegations were also following a similar Cold War script from the opposing side, although we have no inside evidence of their motives and instructions. In any case Hronek was typically seen in the West as a puppet of the Soviet Stalinists. Yet in reality he tried to maintain a common ground, although it was hopeless under those circumstances to prevent an escalation of an East-West split.

The results of the Budapest Executive were reported in *IOJ Bulletin No. 1* of January-February 1949.[6] Its editorial by Secretary General Hronek provoked President Kenyon to single out the following formulation: "...most newspapers in Great Britain...reflecting the moods, plans and intentions of the groups to which they belong, they speak of war, they call upon their readers to hate other nations, they openly incite them to bloodshed". In a letter to Hronek in March 1949, Kenyon wrote: "I must protest against Cominform propaganda of this character being circulated through the machinery and at the expense of the IOJ!"

The unpublished correspondence between Kenyon and Hronek in 1948–49 shows that while the two leading IOJ officers had several disagreements and were clearly tied to their increasingly divergent political environments, they still tried to maintain some degree of consensus. In April 1949, after learning that the majority of the British NUJ members who voted in a referendum about the international relationship were against continuing in the IOJ, Hronek wrote to Kenyon:

> Now the NUJ and probably the Americans are solving a very complicated and a very important question with a butcher-knife instead of doing it with a surgeon's scalpel. What we need is an honest co-operation and plenty of plain talking, unity of purpose, but, of course, not a meaningless unity. About your remark that the IOJ being either political or un-political: well, I think that there is no escape from it being what you term "political". If you look at our resolutions from the very beginning, you will see that the IOJ was meant and always wanted to be political, in the broad sense of this word.

---

5 See also Klánský's testimony quoted in *Useful Recollections, Part II* (1988, p. 38).

6 Reproduced as Annex 3 in *Useful Recollections, Part II* (1988, pp. 121–122).

A NEWNES-PEARSON PUBLICATION

World's Press News

The National Newspaper of the Press, Advertising, Paper and Printing

Offices: 20, Tudor St., E.C.4. Phone: CENtral 4040

Vol. 40. No. 1,028. LONDON, NOVEMBER 25, 1948 Price 9D.

Registered at the G.P.O. as a Newspaper.

Brian Chapman is New 'Daily Herald' Managing Editor

BRIAN CHAPMAN, former managing editor of the "Daily Express" has joined the "Daily Herald" in the same capacity. His duties will include taking charge of production at night.

This appointment, announces the editor, Percy Cudlipp, is part of a rearrangement of executive duties in anticipation of larger papers. A. William Farrar, associate editor, will supervise the work of the various editorial sections during the day.

When Mr. Chapman announced his resignation "for personal reasons" in March, 1947, he had been with the Beaverbrook organisation 15 years and was right-hand man to Arthur Christiansen, editor-in-chief. In 1933 he left the chief sub-editorship of the *Evening Standard* to succeed Mr. Christiansen as editor of the *Daily Express* Manchester edition, and later returned to London as assistant editor of the *Sunday Express*. He joined the *Daily Express* in 1940 as assistant managing editor and became managing editor five years later.

Mr. Farrar, who joined the *Daily Herald* in 1940 as assistant editor, was formerly an assistant editor at the *Daily Mirror*. His appointment as associate editor is a new one in the *Herald* organisation.

U.S. Delegate Walks Out

Political Attack on Western Press Splits IOJ Executive

C. J. Bundock Refuses to Take Further Part

DECLARING "I am not authorised by my organisation to agree to the use of this meeting as a platform for partisan political propaganda," C. J. Bundock, NUJ general secretary, last Thursday refused to participate further in the International Organisation of Journalists' executive meeting in Budapest.

Jiri Hronek, head of the Czech State Information Department and Secretary-General of the International Organisation of Journalists, addressing the executive meeting at Budapest last week. Next to him is P. Yudin, USSR, editor-in-chief of "Durable Peace, People's Democracy," and on the left is Archibald Kenyon, president of IOJ.

That he did not follow the example of Harry Martin, president of the American Newspaper Guild, who walked out of the meeting altogether can possibly be put down to the fact that he felt he owed it to the president of the IOJ, Archibald Kenyon, to remain.

Mr. Martin picked up his papers and left the council meeting after Pavel Yudin, one of the Russian representatives, had made a long speech attacking the "Western capitalist Press" for warmongering.

Yudin singled out the United States, Greece, Turkey and the Netherlands as having reached the climax of inciting war. He went further and labelled Lawrence (*New York Times*), Drew Pearson (*New York Daily Mirror*), Paul Schubert (*Colliers*), Bela Kolchivari (*Look*), Keebour (*Life*) and Cecil Brown, all of America, and Jakid Yalcin, of Turkey, as "befoulers of journalism" for articles "inciting to war."

Mr. Bundock was joined in his protest by the delegates from Holland, Belgium and Sweden, who all abstained from taking further part in a meeting which was being utilised for political propaganda.

New International Body

Harry Martin told New York reporters on his arrival home this week that he would recommend the withdrawal of the American Newspaper Guild from the IOJ. He stated further that he would recommend his executive when it met in February next to join the British, Scandinavian and "other free newspaper unions" in the formation of a new international body.

What steps the NUJ will take remain to be seen. Mr. Bundock will be reporting to his NEC this week, and it may be that no final action will be announced until the next Congress of the IOJ due to be held in Brussels next May or June.

The imminence of the next Congress led to deferment of consideration of the demand made early this year by Harry Martin for the removal of Jiri Hronek, Czech State information chief, from his office of secretary-general of the Organisation.

Political Attacks

Last week's three-day executive meeting became a political platform from the moment it opened. The Hungarian delegate tabled a resolution adopting the factual report of the secretary-general, but tacked on to it a violently worded addendum criticising member-unions for the participation in war-mongering journalism and in "anti-democratic" propaganda.

When Mr. Bundock demanded a straightforward resolution which merely adopted the report the executive sought a way out of the difficulty by forming a sub-committee of five—of which Mr. Bundock and Mr. Martin were members—with instructions to produce an acceptable resolution. A three-and-a-half hour meeting of the sub-committee that night produced

(Continued on page 7, col. 1)

Return to Five-page Papers at Noon, Sunday, January 2

THE Board of the Newsprint Supply Co., Ltd., with the approval of the BoT, have decided that the return to five-page papers and to freedom of sale should take effect as from noon on Sunday, January 2. The first issues to be affected will therefore be those of the morning papers dated January 3.

This first upward step, the newsprint rationing committee states, is designed to restore for all newspapers the position prevailing before the last cut was made.

"This is the principle to which the Government has agreed," the Committee emphasises, "and it is not at this stage possible to consider any amendment to the system as it existed prior to the cut."

With freedom of sales it follows that rationing by tonnage will also be abolished from noon on January 2, when rationing will once again be operated by pages. The only exception will be that the sporting papers and certain others which were on a tonnage ration prior to 1947 will continue on that basis.

As from the agreed date, morning papers selling at 1d. will run an average of five pages per issue, those selling at 1½d. six pages, and those at either 2d. or 3d. a maximum of eight pages. Penny and three-halfpenny evenings will be allowed a five-page average, and 2d. evenings eight pages. Sunday papers will be granted eight pages per issue whatever their selling price, while weekly papers will be at six pages if

(Continued on page 4, col. 1)

of newsprint shortage.

Figure 3.2 The British special paper on the print industry gave prominent coverage to the IOJ Executive Committee right after its divisive meeting in Budapest in November 1948. The photo shows Secretary General Hronek speaking, next to Soviet Vice-President Yudin and British President Kenyon.

For your advance information! [illegible] Ever [illegible]

JOURNALIST December, 1948 177

INTERNATIONAL EXECUTIVE MEETS

by C. J. BUNDOCK

I HAVE just returned from a meeting of the Executive Committee of the International Organisation of Journalists in Budapest, and it is a sad tale I have to tell.

It seems impossible in these post-war days to work in an international organisation unless you are prepared to regard it as a battleground for conflicting political systems.

Our view has always been that, as in our own Union we do not allow party politics to intrude into our professional affairs, so in the IOJ we should assist each other in the professional matters that interest us as journalists, not as political partisans.

The Eastern View

[illegible] is not the view of the Eastern gro[illegible], and we have come back feeling that we cannot continue to participate in an organisation which is made the platform for fierce attacks by the Eastern countries on the Western.

The countries represented at the meeting were Austria, Belgium, Bulgaria, Czechoslovakia, France, Hungary, Netherlands, Palestine, Poland, Rumania, Spanish Exiles, Sweden, United Kingdom, USA, USSR and Yugoslavia.

I should mention that I understand the French union has split into three sections—one remaining with the CGT, one attaching itself to *Force Ouvriere*, and one being independent.

It was a Communist of the CGT Faction who came to Budapest. He cannot be regarded as representing the journalists of France, though no doubt he represents some.

Remitted to Congress

The Danes and I think the Norwegians were prevented from coming by fog which grounded the planes in which they would have travelled. Mr. Martin, the President of the Am[illegible]an Newspaper Guild, arrived a[illegible]te for the same reason.

M[illegible] Kenyon presided with his usua[illegible] success in that capacity, being firm in his ruling when that was necessary but always genial.

As the full Congress is to be held within six or seven months at Brussels all parties agreed that the question of the secretaryship and the headquarters should be left for decision then.

For nearly three days we discussed the Secretary's report, for, this presented the opportunity for the political barrage.

Secretary's Report

The Hungarian representative moved that the Secretary's report be noted, and that

"The Executive Committee declare that the IOJ in its capacity as an international organisation has not been a fighting and progressive international organisation of journalists.

"In the complicated international situation when a hard fight is going on between the democratic camp and the anti-democratic, between the partisans of peace and warmongers, the IOJ stands aside, which is contrary to the interests of nations and to the interests of the progressive journalists of the world.

"This has happened because after two Congresses many organisations have not given the necessary assistance to the General Secretariat in its activity and have not taken any initiative to fulfil their tasks laid down by the statutes and decisions of the Congress."

By means of such resolutions the Eastern countries seek to gain the authority of the IOJ for their claim to be the democratic and peace-loving nations opposing the undemocratic forces and warmongers.

The Hungarian was followed by a spate of speeches on the warmonger theme.

Striving to Agree

I proposed that we accept the Secretary's report as a factual statement and consider the more contentious matters on a Polish motion on the same lines.

That was not agreed, and a sub-committee consisting of the Russian, Hungarian, Polish, and American representatives and myself was appointed to try to produce an agreed draft.

We sat from about 10 p.m. on the second day to 1.30 in the morning when we broke up unable to agree.

We reported this when the committee reassembled in the morning, and were asked to go out again. We made another attempt.

Mr. Martin and I said we were prepared to support a resolution declaring that it should be the aim of all journalists to promote Peace and to work to remove the cause of misunderstanding among peoples, which we regarded as being above the political conflict, but we were not prepared to subscribe to the propaganda about warmongers, and anti-democratic forces.

Ultimately we did reach a resolution on which I cannot say Mr. Martin and I were particularly keen, but which was shorn of the objectionable phrases and on which we were prepared to compromise.

Reciprocal Holidays

During the sitting of the sub-committee two items of more legitimate business were taken. The President (Mr. Kenyon) reported on the Geneva conference of the United Nations on the Freedom of the Press and of Information.

He also suggested a scheme for reciprocal hospitality for holidays among journalists. This was approved and referred to the Secretariat for communication to the unions willing to participate in the scheme.

The Polish Resolution

When the sub-committee returned to the full committee the agreed resolution was put and carried unanimously.

Then the Polish representative moved his resolution—a long one, containing such passages as the following:

"The world has been living during the last few years in an atmosphere of steadily increasing anxiety and tension caused by 'war of nerves' or 'cold war' which is led with a growing and irresponsible ruthlessness by the capitalist groups of the Western countries."

"In this war propaganda a paramount role is played by powerful news agencies and press organs wielded by capitalist press monopolies. By means of false information and calumnies and open instigations to 'atomic war' and 'preventive war' they foment war psychosis."

"The black war propaganda is going on with increasing strength in the press of the majority of Western countries."

And much more to the same effect.

I urged the Polish representative to withdraw this resolution. We had just reached an agreed resolution after much effort in the sub-committee and this raised the conflict all over again.

He would not withdraw, and the weary succession of "warmonger" speeches began once more.

After a long attack by the Russian vice-President of the IOJ on the American press and members of the American Newspaper Guild Mr. Martin remarked—

"We have listened to a shocking thing; an attack on one of our great unions in the IOJ and I do not propose further to be a party to such proceedings."

He walked out of the Committee. I said:—

"I have made the position of my Union perfectly clear. I am not authorised to consent to the use of this International Organisation of Journalists as a platform for partisan political propaganda.

"We came here to deal with the proper business of an Executive Committee. That is the administrative business of the IOJ.

We have spent three days in political partisanship with which my Union has nothing to do. Therefore in justice to my organisation, I cannot take any further part in the proceedings."

NEWS FROM THE PRESS BALLS

Mr. O. W. Fletcher, joint editor of "Press Bowl," presenting first copies to film stars Susan Shaw and Albert Lieven at Croydon's first Press Ball staged by the editorial staffs of the "Croydon Times" and "Croydon Advertiser," which was an outstanding success. The target of £100 was doubled.

Birmingham Does It!

BIRMINGHAM has done it again. Everyone said that it would be impossible for this year's Press Ball to get anywhere near last year's total of over £2,000 for the Widow and Orphan Fund and the Newspaper Press Fund.

Well, they were wrong. A midnight film show, the ball itself—at the Grand Hotel on November 11—an industrial appeal and the publication of the stunt newspaper *Brighter Times* all helped to bring this year's figure within a few pounds of the 1947 total.

Lord Iliffe was among the guests. *Brighter Times* carried one of Giles' cartoons from THE JOURNALIST, and this has given a big fillip to sales in Birmingham of the 2s. 6d. booklet.

☆ ☆ ☆

About midnight on November 5 the lights in the ballroom of Doncaster Mansion House were dimmed—and Guy Fawkes himself was wheeled into the South Yorkshire Branch's Press Ball.

He was pushed round the floor by three 6-ft. branch members, dressed up as schoolboys, who collected coppers in the approved fashion.

The W. & O. Fund is estimated to gain £100.

So successful was the effort that the branch is to inquire into the possibility of a midnight film show.

Guy Fawkes also presided over Keighley Plot Night Press Ball.

Prizes were handed out by radio commentator Stewart MacPherson: this first post-war event to be held by the branch has realised about £50.

☆ ☆ ☆

Joining the 420 dancers at Darlington Press Ball on November 11, Film Star Maxwell Reed presented the prizes, compered a novelty elimination dance and signed hundreds of autographs.

Second to be held since the war, the Ball has re-established itself as one of the chief events in the Quaker town's social calendar.

Ayrshire's first ever Press Ball was an outstanding success, and the W & O Fund will benefit by nearly £80 from this pioneering effort.

Figure 3.3 The British NUJ journal published an article on the Budapest Executive in its December 1948 issue, written by Clement Bundock who as NUJ General Secretary played an important role in mobilizing a Western opposition against the influence of Prague and Moscow in the IOJ. A copy was sent personally by Kenyon to Hronek "for your advance information".

In July 1949, after the NUJ had announced its exit from the IOJ, Kenyon wrote to Hronek:

> I share your feeling of sadness about the split of the IOJ. I am afraid we shall have to agree to differ about the reasons for it. In my view, the cause is the party political vote so strongly sounded at the Budapest meeting [...] The general body of members of the NUJ have undoubtedly been influenced in taking the decision to leave the IOJ by what they regard as party political propaganda and the reiterated suggestions in it that unless they follow the Budapest line they are to be regarded as indecent journalists who are not interested in the preservation of peace. [...]
>
> Though disagreeing with the conduct of the IOJ at and since Budapest, I have not resigned. I do not like dramatic personal demonstrations which accentuate divisions and create fresh difficulties. So, if I am permitted to do so, I will preside at the Brussels meeting in the same spirit of objectivity which I have tried to show in the past. For I still hope that some day international journalists of all political beliefs and opinions will find a common ground for mutually beneficial co-operation, as we do in the NUJ.

In August 1949, Hronek responded to Kenyon and closed his letter as follows:

> I share your hope that a common ground for mutually beneficial co-operation of international journalists of all political beliefs can be found. May I add that in my opinion this common ground must be looked for in the IOJ which already is the existing common ground of international journalism if really co-operation and not a split is sought.

After this exchange an administrative conflict arose between the President and the Secretary General on convening the **IOJ Executive Committee** to prepare for the forthcoming 3rd Congress. Kenyon did not consider a pre-Congress Executive to be necessary, while Hronek responded to the request of the Polish and French member unions and arranged it in **Prague in September 1949**. The controversy was exacerbated by the failure of its invitation to reach Kenyon on time and consequently the President not attending the meeting. Representatives of the member unions from the Benelux and Scandinavian countries as well as from the USA were also absent. Attendees included delegates from France, central and east European countries as well as new member candidates from Albania, China, "Free Greece" and the "Eastern Occupied Zone of Germany".

In September 1949, *IOJ Bulletin No. 4* displayed a grim picture of the state of affairs (Figure 3.4). Five letters of the NUJ responding to IOJ requests and appeals were displayed on the front page as a demonstration of the totally negative approach of the British Union to international cooperation. On the second page was a brief item: "The British National Union of Journalists will disaffiliate

INTERNATIONAL ORGANIZATION OF JOURNALISTS

Organisation Internationale des Journalistes • Международная Организация Журналистов

BULLETIN БЮЛЛЕТЕНЬ 4

PRAGUE, JULY-SEPTEMBER ПРАГА, ИЮЛЬ-СЕНТЯБРЬ 1949

THE EXECUTIVE COUNCIL OF IOJ CONVENED TO PRAGUE.

CONVOCATION A PRAGUE DU COMITÉ EXÉCUTIF DE L'O. I. J. • Исполнительный Комитет МОЖ совывается в Праге.

Upon a request by the Polish Union of Journalists and the French Trade-Union of Journalists the Executive Council of the International Organisation of Journalists was convened at the Prague headquarters for September 15th in order to prepare the Brussels Congress. This decision is based on § 8 of the IOJ Constitution which says that "all motions for discussion at Congress must be in the hands of the Executive Council at least four months before the opening of the Congress. The agenda and the copies of all motions for submission to Congress should be sent to the national affiliated organisation at least two months before the opening of the Congress".

Le Comité Exécutif de l'Organisation Internationale des Journalistes vient d'être convoqué sur la demande de l'Union des Journalistes Polonais et du Syndicat National des Journalistes Français pour le 15 septembre dans la ville du siège de l'Organisation, à Prague pour y préparer le Congrès de Bruxelles. Cette décision se fonde sur le paragraphe 8 de la Constitution de l'O. I. J. qui stipule que « toutes les motions en vue d'une discussion au cours du Congrès doivent être remises entre les mains du Comité Exécutif au moins quatre mois avant l'ouverture du Congrès. L'ordre du jour du Congrès ainsi que toutes les motions qui y seront présentées doivent être envoyées aux organisations nationales affiliées en questions au moins deux mois avant l'ouverture du Congrès ».

По просьбе Польского союза журналистов и Французского профсоюза журналистов, в Праге, местопребывании ее Генерального Секретариата, 15. сентября э. г. созывается Исполнительный комитет Международной организации журналистов для подготовки Брюссельского Конгресса. Это решение основывается на пар. 8 Устава МОЖ, гласящем, что «все предложения, вносимые на обсуждение Конгресса, должны быть вручены Исполнительному комитету по крайней мере за четыре месяца до начала Конгресса. Повестка дня и копии всех предложений, предназначенных для обсуждения на Конгрессе, должны быть разосланы национальным организациям-членам по крайней мере за два месяца до открытия Конгресса».

NO... NO... NO...

The leadership of the NUJ and international cooperation. • Voici les réponses qui nous sont parvenues aux cinq lettres que nous avons envoyées à l'Union nationale les journalistes britanniques. • Приводим ответы на наши пять писем Британскому национальному союзу журналистов.

Letter No 1. is a reply to our request for information on professional, economic and social conditions of journalists in various countries.

Reply No. 2 concerns our efforts to save the life of the Greek journalist Manolis Glezos.

Reply No. 3 concerns a request for records on the fulfilment of tasks which the Executive Council resolution on war mongers put before the national organisation.

No. 4 is a rejection of our request to investigate the case of the Cyprian newspaper "Democratis" which was suppressed by British colonial authorities.

No. 5 is the negative answer to our request for an increase of per capita payments in order to enable IOJ to publish a printed journal.

To the Holiday Exchange proposal published in No. 1. of this Bulletin the NUJ didn't reply at all.

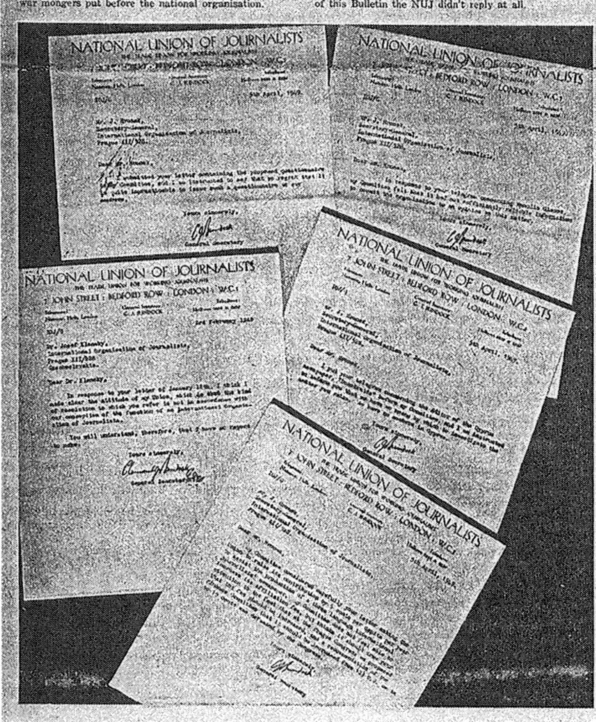

Письмо № 1 — отрицательный ответ на анкету, посланную Британскому национальному союзу журналистов. Между прочим, она была послана всем другим национальным союзам и опубликована во втором номере настоящего бюллетеня. Цель анкеты — собрать информации о профессиональном, экономическом и социальном положении журналистов в разных странах.

Письмо № 2 является отказом принять участие во всемирной кампании за спасение жизни греческого журналиста Манолис Глезоса. Французский, советский, датский, израильский, польский и многие другие национальные союзы журналистов, также как и Ассоциация корреспондентов Организации Объединенных наций в Лэйк Саксесс и другие международные и национальные организации протестовали против смертного приговора над этим героем греческого движения сопротивления против нацистов.

Письмо № 3 говорит «Нет» на наш запрос представить доклад о деятельности против военной пропаганды, согласно резолюции Исполкома, принятой 10 голосами при пяти воздержавшихся.

Письмо № 4 — отрицательный ответ на нашу просьбу помочь в расследовании случая с одной газетой на острове Кипре, запрещенной колониальными властями.

Письмо № 5 является отказом на нашу просьбу добровольно увеличить членский взнос на 5 центов в год, чтобы дать Секретариату возможность продолжать выпуск настоящего бюллетеня. Эта просьба оправдывается фактом, что бюджет МОЖ не был покрыт, вследствие отказа Гильдии американских журналистов, одной из самых крупных организаций, покрыть задолженность за два года.

На просьбу, опубликованную в февральском номере настоящего бюллетеня, о сотрудничестве национальных организаций по вопросу организации каникулярного обмена журналистов, Британский национальный союз журналистов вообще не дал никакого ответа.

La lettre n° 1 est une réponse au questionnaire envoyé aussi bien à l'Union des journalistes britanniques qu'aux autres organisations nationales et qui a été d'ailleurs inséré dans le dernier numéro de notre bulletin. Ce questionnaire devait faire état de la situation professionelle, économique et sociale des journalistes dans les différents pays du monde.

La lettre n° 2 porte le refus de prendre part à la campagne pour sauver la vie du journaliste grec Manolis Glezos.

La lettre n° 3 rejette notre demande de publier un rapport sur les mesures prises contre la propagande de guerre en accord avec la résolution de Comité exécutif adoptée par dix vois contre cinq abstentions.

La lettre n° 4 est une réponse à notre demande de procéder à une enquête au sujet d'un journal de Chypre qui avait été interdit par les autorités coloniales locales.

La lettre n° 5 rejette notre demande d'une augmentation volontaire des cotisations de membres de l'O. I. J. de 5 cents par an afin de rendre possible la publication de notre bulletin. Cette demende est justifiée par le fait que le budget de l'O. I. J. n'a pu être équilibré vu que L'American Newspaper Guild, une des plus grandes organisations membres de l'OIJ avait refusé de payer ses cotisations qu'elle devait pour deux années.

La demande publiée dans le numéro de février de ce bulletin au sujet de la coopération internationale des organisations nationales dans la question des séjours de vacances à l'étranger est restée sans réponse.

Figure 3.4 *IOJ Bulletin* September 1949. The front page of a six-page publication issued in English, French and Russian.

from the IOJ", followed by a longer piece quoting the NUJ Nottingham branch and the trade and technical branch as well as three individual NUJ members opposed to the disaffiliation. Likewise reported was the American ANG attack on the IOJ headquarters, with Secretary General Hronek's response. Another piece of news reported: "Chinese journalists want to adhere to IOJ".

Once Kenyon had received the results of the Prague Executive Committee, he wrote to Hronek on 5 October 1949:

> It is now clear from the decisions of the Executive Committee that the main purpose of the meeting was to plan the coming Congress of the IOJ as a party political demonstration. I refer particularly to Item 3 of the proposed agenda and the instruction given to you on the composition of the Congress.
>
> Item 3 of the agenda reads: "The Press and Journalists in the struggle for peace".
>
> The instruction reads: "The Executive Committee instructs the General Secretary to invite to the Congress, in addition to representatives of member organisations of the IOJ, representatives of the United Nations, representatives of the World Movement of Peace and of its progressive international organs, as well as distinguished representatives of progressive journalists, whether members or non-members of organisations affiliated to the IOJ." [...]
>
> Since the meeting of the Executive Committee in Budapest last year the IOJ headquarters in Prague has become in effect a branch office of the Cominform and the IOJ Bulletin a Cominform propaganda sheet. [...]
>
> The Executive Committee having agreed to take part in a political movement, and thus to the use of the IOJ as a party puppet, I must dissociate myself completely from this degradation of principle and purpose.
>
> I therefore resign the office of the President as from September 14th.

The resignation of Kenyon as President was followed by the withdrawal of the Belgian union's invitation to host the 3rd Congress in Brussels. In December 1949, the French member union – a branch of the communist-dominated trade union CGT – invited the Congress to Paris. However, the French state refused to grant visas to all delegates and the venue was once more changed, now to Helsinki – the capital of Finland, a country which after World War II adopted quite friendly relations with the Soviet Union, her Eastern neighbour, against which she had fought two wars between 1939 and 1944.

While the Congress arrangements were faltering in late 1949 and early 1950, the IOJ lost most of its members in Western Europe. For example, the Union of Journalists in Finland (*Suomen Sanomalehtimiesten Liitto*, SSL) – a founding member of both the IOJ and the pre-war FIJ – regretted that "the struggle between countries representing different ideological orientations within the IOJ has become more and more violent and there seems to be little hope for fruitful cooperation among journalist organizations in all countries". Therefore it discontinued its membership of the IOJ, but expressed its "wish that the political situation in the world would take such a turn that the journalist unions of the world could once more be seen in a constructive fraternal cooperation for pursuing the common interests of the press and journalists in the IOJ".

Meanwhile, Hronek with his executive secretary Klánský operated in Prague under the prevailing conditions, accepting the split and more intensive adherence to the Soviet orbit. This is confirmed by Hronek's contacts with Moscow between September 1949 and September 1950.

Documents found in the Russian State Archive of Social-Political History in Moscow[7] include, first, a letter by V. Kuznetsov, Chairman of the All-Union Council of Trade Unions, to the USSR Minister of Foreign Affairs V.M. Molotov, dated 6 September 1949 and labelled "Secret", suggesting three persons to constitute the Soviet delegation at the Executive Committee meeting in Prague on 15 September. Second, another "secret" letter from the same Council to Molotov, dated 3 March 1950, suggests a five-person delegation for the IOJ Congress in Paris scheduled for the end of March and requests the allocation of 25,000 French Francs to partly cover the expenses of the Congress. An appendix to this letter was a "Directive" for the delegation regarding the Congress agenda and how to behave and vote there. Third, a letter signed by V. Grigorian, head of the International Department of the Central Committee of the Soviet Communist Party, addressed to "Comrade Stalin", dated 21 August 1950 and classified as "Top secret", requesting permission to invite Hronek to visit Moscow for 10 days to meet with Soviet journalists in preparation for the next IOJ Congress. This clandestine visit was naturally not reported in the *IOJ Bulletin*.

No doubt the East-West division was inspired by the U.S. State Department as well as the British and French Foreign Ministries in these years.[8] Additional support came from the Marshall Plan administration in Paris, where former ANG President Martin was now working. Moreover, as was later revealed by former CIA agent Philip Agee: "In addition to propaganda against IOJ and operations to deny Western capitals for IOJ meetings, the Agency promoted the founding of an alternative international society of journalists from the free world."[9]

A candidate for such an alternative was an anti-IOJ organization called the **International Federation of Free Journalists of Central and Eastern Europe and Baltic and Balkan Countries (IFFJ).**[10] It was based on exiled

7 The author visited the Russian State Archive in November 2012 and October 2014. Key documents are reproduced as **Appendix 3** of this volume.

8 See Beyerdorf & Nordenstreng (forthcoming).

9 Agee (1977, p. 78)

10 *IFFJ* (1952) and Nekola (2017).

journalists staying in London during the war and organized mainly by a fairly large Union of Journalists of the Polish Republic and a smaller Syndicate of Czech Journalists. Both groups belonged to the war-time IFJAFC but the Polish Union was not invited to the IOJ founding Congress in Copenhagen, where Poland was represented by another national association. Accordingly, the IFFJ became a home for exiled journalists as an opposition to those unions who established the IOJ and were mainly concerned about reconstruction of post-war journalism in their respective countries.

This opposition was represented as an alternative to the IOJ at the UN Conference on Freedom of Information and it was formally established later in 1948 under the leadership of Polish exiled journalists. Political developments in Czechoslovakia and the rest of the new socialist countries gave new impetus to the IFFJ, which became a clearing house for the deprivation of freedom behind the "iron curtain". In 1952 the IFFJ was recognized by the ECOSOC Sub-Commission on the Freedom of Information and Press – at a time when the Cold War had led to a situation in which the IOJ was deprived of its relationship with the UN. However, IFFJ did not succeed in constituting itself as a true alternative to the IOJ – a role finally assumed by the IFJ.

SPLIT 1950–53

As a consequence of the development in the late 1940s, the IOJ became an organization whose core membership was made up of national journalist unions in the socialist countries of central and eastern Europe, including the recently established German Democratic Republic (GDR), and of such smaller journalists' associations in the western world which had a "progressive and democratic" orientation. In addition, the IOJ increasingly acquired members from the developing countries, including China. A special case was the socialist country of Yugoslavia: its member union was expelled from the IOJ – after Belgrade, in keeping with President Tito's policy of independence and nonalignment, turned it against Moscow.[11]

The **3rd IOJ Congress** was convened **in Helsinki** on 15–17 **September 1950**, at the invitation of a relatively small Finnish association of left-wing socialist and communist journalists (*Yleinen Lehtimiesliitto*, YLL), which replaced the nationally representative SSL as the IOJ member (Figure 3.5).

11 Again the context of the time should be recalled, including events such as the Korean War (1950–53) and the anti-communist campaigns especially in the USA (McCarthyism). In the Soviet Union and its East European allies these were years of hardline communism until Stalin died in 1953.

Figure 3.5 The 3rd IOJ Congress in Helsinki in September 1950 took place in the cultural house of the left-wing political movements. Although it was arranged at short notice and hosted by a small association, the staging was impressive, with the Government of Finland officially greeting the Congress. Prime Minister Urho Kekkonen seen here being welcomed by Secretary General Jiří Hronek. (Photos by Yrjö Lintunen, from The People's Archives in Helsinki)

The Congress was attended by 62 delegates – less than one third of those in the 2nd Congress in Prague. However, there were now more countries from which they came: 30, including the UK, the USA and Scandinavia – not from the main national unions but from smaller "progressive and democratic associations". The majority of the delegates came from eastern Europe, but Asia was also represented by unions from China, Iran, Korea, Mongolia and Vietnam, while African participants came from Algeria, West Africa and South Africa; there were no delegates from Latin America.[12]

12 No report survives from this Congress, apart from what is included in *Useful Recollections, Part II* (1988, pp. 43–49). A mimeographed report of the Secretary General exists.

The Statute of the IOJ was modified to accommodate different membership categories: (a) national unions, (b) national IOJ groups and (c) individual members. Accordingly, the IOJ abandoned its former principle of mandatory national representativeness and welcomed all likeminded groups and even individuals to join – obviously in order to welcome members from countries with no unions or from countries whose unions were hostile to the IOJ.

Otherwise the Statute was retained largely in its original form, but a major reformulation was done in the first Article on Aim and Tasks to accommodate the Cold War realities – no doubt following a Soviet line – as follows:

1. The maintenance of peace and the expansion of cooperation among nations, as well as international understanding through free, accurate and honest informing of public opinion. The struggle against the spreading of war psychosis and war propaganda, against fascist propaganda of any sort, against nationalist or racial hatred and against the creation of international tension by means of falsehoods and calumnies.
2. The protection of freedom of the press and of journalists against the influence of monopolist and financial groups. The defence of the right of every journalist to write according to his conscience and conviction. The protection of the rights of colonial peoples and national minorities to publish newspapers in their native language. Support for journalists who have been persecuted for having taken up their pens in defence of peace, justice and the liberty and independence of their countries.
3. The protection of all journalists' rights. The struggle for the bettering of the material conditions of their existence. The gathering and dissemination of all information concerning the living conditions of journalists in all countries (collective agreements, salaries, professional training). Support for the trade union movement in the struggle for journalists' demands.
4. The protection of the peoples' rights to receive free and honest information. The struggle against falsehood, calumnies and the systematic misinformation of the people by the press, as well as against every form of journalistic activity in the service of individuals or particular groups of society whose interests are contrary to those of the working masses.

The Congress elected Jean-Maurice Hermann of France as the new President with Vice-Presidents coming from the USSR, China, Poland, Finland and West Africa (see Appendix 2).

Czechoslovakia was confirmed as the site of the headquarters and Hronek was re-elected as Secretary General and Treasurer. On this basis, with a total membership of about 50,000 journalists from over 30 countries, the IOJ continued with its new profile to expand both geographically and professionally, emphasizing peace and development instead of trade unionism, although this was retained as one of the objectives in the Statute.

In the Cold War divide the IOJ stood on the eastern side with its headquarters in Prague, where the World Federation of Trade Unions (WFTU) was also based since its founding in 1945. Like the IOJ, it split after its western member unions left in 1949 and established the rival International Confederation of Free Trade Unions (ICFTU) based in Brussels. The International Union of Students (IUS) was also based in Prague and fell to the eastern side in the Cold War. The other INGOs mentioned above in Chapter 2 likewise became more or less part of the pro-Moscow alignment. Another INGO of the same kind was the International Organisation of Radio and Television (OIRT) founded in 1946, moving its headquarters from Brussels to Prague in 1950.

After the 3rd Congress in Helsinki in 1950, the IOJ consolidated its secretariat in Prague. In the beginning it was a modest desk of one executive secretary working under the guidance of Secretary General Jiři Hronek, whose main job was in the Czechoslovak international radio service (see recollections by Klánský in Part Two). It began to grow into a real secretariat located in the premises of the Czechoslovak Union of Journalists. In 1952 Hronek resigned as Secretary General[13] and was replaced by another representative of the Czechoslovak Union: Jaroslav Knobloch.

In **October 1953** the IOJ established at its **Executive Committee in Prague** the **International Fund for Solidarity with Journalists** "to support journalists, regardless of their nationality, religion or political beliefs, who for any reason are discriminated against or persecuted for giving truthful information, for their stand in favour of cooperation among nations, or in defence of national sovereignty and the democratic rights of nations". In the same year the IOJ Secretariat began to publish the **monthly review *The Democratic Journalist*** in English, French and Russian.

The Executive Committee was determined by the Statute to act as the supreme organ of the IOJ between the Congress sessions – it was a mini-Congress with representatives from all member unions. As seen in Appendix 1, the Executive Committee met almost annually: after Prague in Budapest and Sofia, and in 1957 for the first time outside Europe, in China.

Meanwhile, the **International Federation of Journalists (IFJ)** was established in **Brussels in May 1952.**[14] The founding congress was attended by 49 delegates from 14 countries (Figure 3.6). Brussels was chosen as its headquarters and Clement J. Bundock of the UK was elected as the first President.

13 According to Slavík this was a command of the Communist Party.

14 The founding congress was preceded by a preparatory conference in Paris in October 1951, attended by delegates from the UK, USA, France, Austria, Belgium and the Netherlands. Before that, in January 1951, a consultative meeting took place in Brussels – no doubt as part of the CIA-supported division of the trade union movement (*Useful Recollections, Part II*, 1988, pp. 49–50).

Figure 3.6 The participants at the IFJ founding congress in Brussels on 5–8 May 1952. (Photo from *The International Federation of Journalists*, 1977)

The constitution adopted on this occasion stipulates that membership of the IFJ "is open to national trade unions of professional journalists which are dedicated to the freedom of the press, and which conform to the definitions immediately following". The definitions specify what is meant by a trade union (in a universally valid manner) and by freedom of the press: "freedom in the collection of information, freedom of opinion and comment and freedom in the dissemination of news".

A separate paragraph – no doubt pointing at the IOJ – stated:

> Organizations of journalists which are part of international groups of journalists, whose aims are in conflict with the constitution of the International Federation of Journalists shall not be admitted as Affiliated or Associate members.

There was also a section entitled "Non-political character of the Federation":

> The International Federation of Journalists, being an organization created to deal with matters related to the practice of the profession of journalism and with the maintenance of press freedom as defined in Section II, is not concerned with questions of political philosophy and ideological conflict. It is agreed by the unions which have created the Federation that such questions are inadmissible at its deliberations.

The objects of the IFJ were laid down in the constitution as follows:

a) To do all in its power to safeguard the freedom of the press and the freedom of journalists engaged in their legitimate professional activities, and to preserve the standards of the profession.

b) To take such action as may be possible whenever a serious threat is made to the rights and liberties of the press and of journalists.
c) To promote the professional training of future journalists and the professional improvement of working journalists.
d) To promote such relations between the affiliated unions as will guarantee the goodwill and assistance of any one of the unions to members of the others who may be travelling in its territory for professional purposes.
e) To encourage the organization and growth of national trade unions of journalists.
f) To collect from the affiliated unions information concerning conditions of employment, contracts of service, benefits provided by the unions for their members, and other matters of professional interest and to supply such information to the affiliated unions.

Seen from the point of view of the IOJ, there was hardly anything in these aims and objectives that the members of the older body could not have subscribed to. As a matter of fact, most of these objectives can be found in earlier IOJ documents. Yet there is a significant difference that can be seen between this and the revised IOJ formulation regarding the freedom of the press: a critical approach to the (capitalistic) monopolization of the press is missing from the IFJ position. In addition to this, another difference can be seen between the two: the IFJ did not specify the social responsibility and ethical orientation of the journalist, whereas the IOJ made it clear ever since Copenhagen that freedom should not be misused – especially not on behalf of those who incite war.

From the perspective of the IOJ, the IFJ obviously appeared as a divisive phenomenon. It is true that the IFJ represented the majority of national unions of journalists in western Europe, North America and Australia – altogether over 40,000 from 14 countries. In the Cold War conditions it inevitably pursued a western ideological position. At the same time the IOJ, due to its composition, represented the eastern ideological position.

In terms of numbers the IOJ was bigger than the IFJ, both counting individual journalists represented through national affiliates (50,000 vs. 40,000) and counting the number of countries represented (30 vs. 14). Yet the two were typically seen as political parallels on different sides of the Cold War divide. Politically their profiles were quite different – the IFJ with its professional trade union orientation resembling the pre-war FIJ. However, organizationally it was the IOJ that continued to occupy the legal mandate of the old FIJ, while the IFJ was founded on a new territory facilitated by the western side of a Cold War rivalry.

CHAPTER 4
CONSOLIDATION 1954–66[1]

After Stalin's death in 1953, the peak of the Cold War passed and in 1954 the Foreign Ministers of the USA, the UK, France and the USSR began to prepare for a summit between "The Big Four" (Eisenhower, Eden, Faure and Bulganin). The summit took place in Geneva in July 1955 expedited by the policy of peaceful coexistence advocated by the new Soviet leader, Nikita Khruschev.

The "spirit of Geneva" also began to replace the Cold War climate in international relations among journalists, who wanted to see the same "thaw" foster their own professional movement, which had been beset by political conflicts since the late 1940s. Accordingly, a regional "World Congress of Journalists" convened in Sao Paulo (Brazil) in November 1954, called on the two international organizations of journalists – the IOJ and the IFJ – to meet for the purpose of creating a single organization which would bring together journalists of the whole world.

QUEST FOR UNITY 1954–60

The IOJ Executive Committee in Budapest in October 1954 endorsed the steps taken by the Secretariat with a view to initiating talks on collaboration with the IFJ. The latter had not responded to earlier overtures on the part of the IOJ, notably greetings sent to the 2nd IFJ congress in Bordeaux in 1954. The Executive congratulated the journalists of Latin America and the Federation of the Italian Press, who had started work to establish cooperation between the two internationals. The Executive stressed the efforts to achieve the broadest possible cooperation among journalists of all countries on the basis of their common professional interests and regardless of political differences.

Moreover, a resolution was approved expressing gratification that among journalists of various countries "a wish was expressed to hold an interna-

1 This chapter is based on *Useful Recollections, Part II* (1988, pp. 59–88). Some of the text also appears in *A History of the International Movement of Journalists* (Nordenstreng & al., 2016, pp. 142–153).

tional meeting of journalists, which would consider mutual aid to journalists so that they can better exercise their professional duties in obtaining more complete and objective information about the life of different nations, thus promoting peaceful coexistence among countries with different political systems and strengthening cultural and economic relations among countries". The Executive also expressed its support for those journalists who had formed a committee for the implementation of the idea. Hence the IOJ made a strategic move against a Cold War confrontation by supporting the idea of a "World Meeting of Journalists" – to be convened as an independent platform, yet with the organization's political and material support.

The **World Meeting of Journalists** took place **in Helsinki** on 10–15 **June 1956**, hosted in Otaniemi, the student campus of the Technical University of Helsinki. Attended by 259 journalists from 44 countries, it was the largest and most representative gathering in the history of journalism so far (Figure 4.1). At this meeting, the voices of journalists from the countries of Latin America, Asia and the Arab world were particularly strong – stronger than in the IOJ congresses held hitherto. Moreover, among the participants were representatives of journalists' unions from India, Yugoslavia, Italy, Indonesia and other countries which were not members of either of the two existing internationals.

The proceedings of the Meeting were published by the Committee for the Cooperation of Journalists in the form of a booklet.[2] The introduction to this publication states that the Meeting "exceeded all expectations":

> We are convinced that when the history of world journalism comes to be written, this International Meeting of Journalists will be recognised as a great and shining event.

The Meeting confirmed in an impressive manner the position that it is possible to achieve agreement among all journalists – as far as their professional problems are concerned – to strengthen the status of journalists in society and to improve their material conditions, educational level, etc.

On the other hand, the Meeting was not supported by the IFJ; on the contrary, its member unions were urged not to attend. Among the followers of these instructions was the Finnish Union of Journalists SSL[3]. Accordingly, it relinquished the role of local host to a smaller leftist union of journalists YLL – the same that hosted the 3rd IOJ Congress in Helsinki. The IFJ attitude did not, however, drastically limit the participation even of Western journalists, as most West European countries, the USA, Canada, Israel, Australia and

2 Extensive excerpts from this publication are reproduced as an annex in *Useful Recollections, Part II* (1988, pp. 123–161).

3 The SSL was not a founding member of the IFJ and joined it only in 1955.

Figure 4.1 The World Meeting in Helsinki was opened on 10 June 1956 by Mrs K.M. Rydberg, President of YLL. A logo of two flying pens was hanging above the podium. The President of Finland, Dr Urho Kekkonen, received key delegates in the presidential palace (see *Useful Recollections, Part II*, 1988, p. 153) and Mrs Sylvi Kekkonen received the Chinese delegation as shown here. The Minister of Foreign Affairs, Dr Johannes Virolainen hosted a reception for all delegates. (Photos by Yrjö Lintunen, from The People's Archives in Helsinki)

Japan were represented. It is also noteworthy that the delegations from the Federal Republic of Germany and from France, for example, were not only numerous but very representative; among the French participants was Jean Schwoebel, a prominent journalist of *Le Monde*.

The delegations from the developing countries were particularly impressive; the most outstanding example being the Brazilian delegation, which consisted of 38 journalists representing the entire country both geographically and politically. The same was true of the 18-man delegation from India; one of them was D.R. Mankekar who 20 years later became Chairman of the Non-Aligned News Agencies Pool. Notable names among the Latin American participants were Genaro Carnero Checa of Peru (whose efforts 20 years later led to the creation of FELAP) and Luis Suarez of Mexico (who later succeeded Checa as Secretary General of FELAP). As to the IOJ, there were participants from all its member unions – from Albania to the USSR. The President of the IOJ, Jean-Maurice Hermann, was part of the French delegation.

The IOJ President conveyed fraternal greetings from one of the existing international organizations which had supported the initiative to meet "without wishing at any time to patronise or control the development of this gathering". He regretted that the IFJ was averse to co-operating on an equal footing but said that "we should nevertheless be glad to see the beginning of friendly co-operation between our organizations". Hermann made the headlines with his comprehensive address by pointing out that journalists selling their minds are worse than prostitutes selling their bodies. Moreover, the IOJ President offered to dismantle his organization in the interests of unity.

The Brazilians proposed the setting up of a permanent body, but the Italians and especially the Yugoslavs felt that any new committee would be another "bloc organization" – a kind of third international. Consensus was achieved on the basis of an Indian thesis that what was at issue was not an organization but a movement – as Nehru had not proposed a third bloc but a movement aimed at the abolition of blocs, which was a reference to the Non-Aligned Movement launched in Bandung in 1955. Consequently, the Initiating Committee was transformed in Helsinki into the **International Committee for the Cooperation of Journalists (ICCJ)**, composed of 30 members from over 20 countries on all continents – from Australia to Chile, from the Gold Coast (Ghana) to Israel.

After four days of plenaries and commissions the meeting discussed and adopted a "Concise Protocol" and eight resolutions on various topics. In addition, a separate resolution by 30 representatives from Asian, African and Arab countries proposed "that a 'Bandung Conference' of Journalists should be held some time next year and at a convenient place in order that professional problems common to them may be discussed and decisions reached".

All in all, the World Meeting in 1956 must be regarded as a major landmark in the history of the international movement of journalists. It is true that most of the questions raised and recommendations made were not original, but had already been placed on the agenda either at the UN, UNESCO or in non-governmental professional bodies such as the IOJ (ever since Copenhagen 1946) or even the pre-war League of Nations, FIJ and IUPA (ever since Antwerp 1894). But it is nevertheless remarkable that an initiative by the profession itself brought about such a comprehensive review of various issues after several years of international tension. In today's perspective, 1956 can be seen as a very promising new beginning with a rich professional substance.

The quest for unity, on the other hand, did not fare very well after 1956. First the ICCJ joined the initiative of the Italian and Yugoslavian journalists' associations to call an international conference of all under the auspices of UNESCO, with a view to establishing a single world organization of journalists. The national unions which did not belong to either of the two internationals, including those from Brazil and India, also invited the IOJ and IFJ for preliminary talks scheduled in Brussels in early 1957. The IOJ welcomed this and was prepared to attend, while the IFJ was not. Consequently, no talks, nor a UNESCO conference. The IFJ's lack of interest was obviously due to bigger political and corporate forces from the West, as demonstrated at UNESCO's General Conference in Delhi in late 1956, when the Yugoslav delegation made the above proposal for a broad conference but failed to find consensus.[4]

While there was no progress towards the unity of the movement at large, broad international cooperation achieved on several special areas of journalism. Accordingly, travel writers and journalists established their own international federation (FIJET) in 1954 and by the end of the 1950s the IOJ had organized conferences among agricultural journalists, sports journalists, foreign affairs journalists and photojournalists. Photography became a particularly important special interest area, leading not only to a conference in 1960 but to biannual Interpress Photo exhibitions in Berlin, Budapest and Warsaw (Figure 4.2).

The intricacies of the Cold War delayed the convening of the IOJ Congress which according to the Statute was to take place every fourth year. It took twice as long after Helsinki 1950 to hold the next Congress in 1958. Before that the Executive Committee met almost every year – in 1957 for first time outside Europe, in Peking.

4 One should remember the context of contradictory political developments: the creation of the Non-Aligned Movement (NAM) to break the Cold War division after the Bandung Conference in 1955, the founding of the European Economic Community (EEC) in Western Europe after the Treaty of Rome in 1957 and the deepening of East-West conflict by building the Berlin Wall in 1961.

INTER PRESS FOTO

BERLIN

The first INTERPRESSFOTO, which was held in Berlin, was a great success and evoked lively interest. The exhibition lasted six weeks and even had to be prolonged. 256 press photographers from 32 countries took part. From the 2668 photographs received the international jury selected the 433 best for showing. The Berlin exhibition was a veritable world meeting of press photographers and a variegated review of their labours, the quality of which was of a high international level. (To the photo: View of the installation of the exhibition.)

BUDAPEST

The second INTERPRESSFOTO took place in August 1962 in Budapest. This time the exhibitors from 34 countries from all continents exhibited some 500 photographs. The importance of the exhibition lay not only in its power of communication, but also in its ability to stimulate indignation, above all concerning certain negatives aspects of life in the world today. A large number of the photographs gave direct expression to the ideas of humanity, democracy, a lasting peace and social justice. (To the photo: View of the inauguration of the exhibition.)

WARSAW

The third INTERPRESSFOTO was organized in 1964 in WARSAW. It showed 372 photographs chosen from the 1,200 pictures submitted from 21 countries. There were photographs from Algeria, Belgium, Bulgaria, Chile, Czechoslovakia, Denmark, Finland, France, the German Democratic Republic, the German Federal Republic, Poland, the U.S.S.R., and other countries. The series "The Gate of Tragedy", which received the Grand Prix, and other winning pictures spoke very clearly about the problems of our epoch. (To the photo: View of the big hall of the exhibition.)

Figure 4.2 *The Democratic Journalist* 6–7/1966 featured a supplement on Interpress Photo exhibitions 1960–64 as highlights of the first two decades of the IOJ.

Figure 4.3 IOJ President Hermann speaks with the Mexican delegate Luis Suarez during an interval at the 4th IOJ Congress in May 1958. They first met at the World Meeting in Helsinki two years earlier. (More photos of the Bucharest Congress by local agency photographers are included in *Useful Recollections, Part II*, 1988, pp. 66–67.)

The **4th IOJ Congress** took place **in Bucharest** (Romania) on 15–18 **May 1958** (Figure 4.3). With 60 delegates from 17 member unions and 21 observers, its attendance was more or less the same as in the previous Congress, except that now there were also delegates from Latin America. The proceedings confirmed the policy of the past few years, stressing "unity of journalists throughout the world" and condemning the arms race with "the policy of propagating war psychosis". Particular attention was paid to solidarity – both politically with journalists "exposed to persecution for their work in the cause of peace and mutual understanding between nations" and socio-economically by establishing rest home for journalists by the Black Sea in Varna, Bulgaria.[5]

The elections in the 4th Congress followed the pattern of the 3rd Congress. Jaroslav Knobloch, who had been appointed Secretary General in 1952, continued, but he resigned prematurely in 1959 – due to pressure from the Communist Party (as in the case of his predecessor). He was followed by Jiří Meisner (see his personal recollections in Part Two). Hermann was re-elected as President.

The **2nd World Meeting of Journalists** was held **in Baden** near Vienna (Austria) on 18–22 **October 1960**. Convened by the ICCJ it was attended by 260 journalists from 62 countries, making it another landmark in the history of journalism (Figure 4.4). Of the 260 colleagues, 118 were from Europe, 67 from Asia, 15 from Africa, 69 from the Americas and Australia, including presidents and other leading officers of 43 national associations and one international (IOJ). The Meeting was opened by the Secretary General of the Brazilian Federation of Journalists, and among the chairpersons and speakers were colleagues from all parts of the world – from Bolivia to India, from Costa Rica to Japan, from Mali to Mongolia, from South Africa to North Korea, from

5 No published report was issued of this Congress. Excerpts of the proceedings are included in *Useful Recollections, Part II* (1988, pp. 65–69).

COMITÉ INTERNATIONAL
POUR LA
COOPÉRATION DES JOURNALISTES

SECRÉTARIAT
805/p/60

Presse (I)

Vienne, I6 octobre I960

APA - AP - ANSA - TASS -
TANJUG - CTK - MTI - ADN -
DPA - UPI - HSINHUA
V i e n-n e

C O M M U N I Q U E'

" Les participants à la Deuxième Rencontre Mondiale des Journalistes, dont les travaux s'ouvriront mardi I8 octobre, à IO heures, dans le Kurhaus de Baden, ont commencé à arriver dans la capitale autrichienne. Lesavions et les trains ont débarqué les premiers délégués provenant du Japon, de Chine, du Pérou, d'Argentine, Union Soviétique, Italie, Brésil, Méxique, Liban, Allemagne, Tchécoslovaquie, Bolivie, Guyane Britannique et Angola.

L'écho soulevé par l'initiative patronée par le Comité International pour la Coopération des Journalistes, les lettres et les messages d'encouragements, les adhésions - près de 300 journalistes et 45 organisation; professionnelles de 68 pays ont annoncé leur arrivée à Baden - font de la Deuxième Rencontre Mondiale des Journalistes la plus importante assemblée de ce genre de ces dernières années

Le secrétariat général qui coordonne les préparatifs du Colloque international s'installera officiellement demain, lundi I7 octobre, dans le Kurhaus de Baden ".

Figure 4.4 The 2nd World Meeting of Journalists in Vienna in October 1960 followed the tradition established in Helsinki in 1956, with impressive conference facilities and a professional press service.

China to the UK. However, there were no representatives of the IFJ, although several of its member unions were present.

In the various plenary sessions and in three commissions those present discussed the three main items on the agenda: (1) How to facilitate the exercise of the profession; (2) Problems of the press and radio in underdeveloped countries; and (3) Ethics of the profession: rights and obligations, the role of the journalists in forming public opinion and in the evolution of international relations, obligations arising out of the UN Charter. A lot of professional substance was exposed, but in contrast to the 1956 Meeting, the proceedings in 1960 seem to have taken a direction which could easily be called "political". This was inevitable given the presence of several colleagues who were involved in a liberation struggle of their respective countries. Symptomatic in this respect was the point made by a Cuban delegate, who stated that it was only since January 1959 that there had been real journalists in his country.

The 2nd World Meeting in 1960 adopted several resolutions[6] but it was essentially a repetition – and reconfirmation – of the first one held four years earlier. It continued to highlight political issues of peace and international understanding – with more attention now to developing countries. Yet it also pursued professional and trade union matters, including an inquiry into the working conditions of journalists which was supposed to be implemented by the ICCJ and to be reported to the next World Meeting.

A notable difference from the first Meeting was that the question of achieving organizational unity was no longer at the forefront. The continuous non-response by the IFJ and the Western politics against unity at UNESCO had obviously taught a lesson to those who gathered in Baden; the optimistic visions entertained in Helsinki had proved to be largely illusions. Consequently, the IOJ remained the only structure for worldwide cooperation, along with the ICCJ, which continued to exist, albeit with a rather short-term mandate.

The role of the IFJ throughout the pursuit of unity was something that could be characterized as stubborn separatism. Accordingly, a world congress of journalists scheduled for 1956 in Montevideo did not achieve its objectives after the IFJ and its US affiliate ANG launched a campaign against this initiative on the part of Latin American journalists. Likewise, the IFJ declined an invitation to build bridges through Italy: the National Federation of the Italian Press (FNSI) proposed that its congresses in Palermo in 1954 and in Trieste in 1956 be used as neutral ground to bring the IFJ and the IOJ together through their leaders, but on both occasions the invitation was turned down by the IFJ.

Despite an inability to meet and discuss even professional matters among themselves, the two internationals were brought together at a conference

6 The resolutions are reproduced as Annex 5 in *Useful Recollections, Part II* (1988, pp. 163–168).

convened by UNESCO in Paris in December 1957 for the founding of the International Association for Mass Communication Research (IAMCR).[7] The fact that both the IOJ and IFJ Presidents were among the founding members of the IAMCR, together with media scholars and educators from East and West, shows that there was an ecumenical potential for cooperation.

EMANCIPATION OF THE THIRD WORLD 1961–66

The early 1960s was a period of accelerating decolonization in Africa and Asia. It was also a period when many national liberation movements became allies of the Soviet Union and parties to East-West conflicts, notably in Cuba (the Cuban Missile Crisis of 1962) and in Indochina (the war between North and South Vietnam since 1963). These developments politicized the context of international journalism and increasingly shifted the contradictions from Cold War-driven East-West conflicts across the "iron curtain" in Europe to North-South conflicts between the "imperialist" West and the "Third World" as the global South was called during the Cold War.

This was a stage when the effort towards unity as the leading theme in the movement was replaced by an increasing mobilization of national and regional associations of journalists in Africa, Asia and Latin America. An emphasis on the developing continents was quite obvious in the contents of *The Democratic Journalist* in 1963–65. It is also interesting to read in issue 6–7/1965 of the journal about journalism under the Yugoslav system – an article by the Secretary General of the Federation of Yugoslav Journalists, Miodrag-Žika Avramović, certainly reflects a conciliatory approach to a founding member which was expelled in 1949 at the time of the political polarization in the late 1940s.

Special attractions at this time among actual and potential members everywhere were provided by the international rest homes built by the IOJ with its member unions in Bulgaria and Hungary (Figure 4.5).

The main development in Africa was the **Pan-African Conference of Journalists in Bamako** (Mali) in May 1961, convened by the Committee for Co-operation of African Journalists. It was attended by journalists from ten countries of North and West Africa, while colleagues from several countries of East and Southern Africa wished to attend but were prevented by financial or political obstacles. The IOJ attended as an observer, but the IFJ declined the invitation. The conference adopted several resolutions, including one on the founding of the **Pan-African Union of Journalists**.[8] The 2nd Pan-African

7 See http://iamcr.org/history.

8 The first bulletin of the Union (in French) is reproduced as Annex 6 in *Useful Recollections, Part II* (1988, pp. 169–181).

Figure 4.5 The first international rest home ("recreation centre") for journalists was opened in Varna (Bulgaria) in July 1959. The hotel building had four storeys facing the Black Sea and later a 12-story tower building was added. The second international rest home for journalists was built on the shores of Lake Balaton in Hungary and opened by the IOJ President in May 1965. (Photos from *The Democratic Journalist*, 1/1965 and 6–7/1965)

Conference of Journalists took place in Accra (Ghana) in November 1963. It was opened by the President of the Republic of Ghana, Kwame Nkrumah, who on this occasion delivered an historical speech.[9]

The developments in Latin America were related to a prolonged struggle over regional federations in the Western hemisphere. Since in the 1940s there had been initiatives inspired mainly by the American newspaper publishers to create the **Inter-American Press Association (IAPA)**. It was established in 1950 under US control, leaving the professional journalists to find their own organizational solutions. One of these initiatives was the regional **World Conference in Sao Paulo** in 1954 calling for unity, but it did not survive under the shadow of IAPA and its instruments such as the **Inter-American Federation of Working Newspapermen (FIOPP)** set up in 1960 to cater for

9 Nkrumah's speech is reproduced as Annex 7 in *Useful Recollections, Part II* (1988, pp. 183–190).

the professional co-operation in accordance with the US interests in the region. However, it disintegrated when the ANG Treasurer was exposed as the channel of CIA financing to the Latin American programme.[10]

In 1962 a **Committee for Information and Co-operation of Latin American Journalists (CICPLA)** was established in Havana, leading to the founding of **the Federation of Latin American Journalists (FELAP)** with the IOJ support as late as 1976. The IOJ Executive Committee met in Havana in 1962 and *The Democratic Journalist* extended its translations to include Spanish. The IFJ for its part had as yet no notable activity in the region.

Faced by these trends throughout the developing world, the **5th IOJ Congress** was held **in Budapest** on 6–10 **August 1962** in Hungary's grand Parliament building (Figure 4.6). With 89 delegates from 28 member unions and groups as well as nearly 80 observers and guests, it manifested the growth of the IOJ especially in the Third World, from which roughly half of its members came. The newly elected Presidium reflected the same trend: of the nine Vice-Presidents, three came from Europe (Finland, Poland, USSR), while two came from Asia (China, Indonesia), one from Africa (Mali), one from the Arab world (United Arab Emirates) and two from Latin America (Cuba, Mexico). Yet the most influential Vice-President was obviously from the USSR: President of the Soviet Union of Journalists and Editor-in-Chief of *Pravda*. Hermann was re-elected as President and Meisner as Secretary General.[11]

Figure 4.6 Prime Minister of Hungary, János Kádár, meeting leading representatives of the 5th IOJ Congress in Budapest on 10 August 1962. (Photo from the Hungarian News Agency MTI. More photos in *Useful Recollections, Part II*, 1988, pp. 82–83.)

10 See *Useful Recollections, Part II* (1988, pp. 79–80).

11 This time the Congress proceedings were printed as *What is the International Organisation of Journalists* (1962).

Resolutions were adopted by the Congress on unity, on the ethics of the profession in the context of "the legitimate aspirations of the peoples for national independence, social progress, democracy, freedom and peace", on the persecution of journalists for their professional activities, as well as on social questions such as minimum wages, working hours and social benefits. Regarding holidays, the initiative was endorsed to establish a second international recreation centre at Lake Balaton in Hungary. Professional training of journalists was also emphasized, leading to the inauguration of an international school for this purpose both in Berlin (1963) and in Budapest (1964). Finally, the Congress resolved to set up an International Photography Section as the first specialized professional section in the IOJ.[12]

In general, the 5th Congress was marked by a serious orientation towards professionalism. Hungarians continued in the same professional track, highlighted among others by hosting, with the IOJ support, in 1965 the congress of the International Sporting Press Association (AIPS), a specialized association established already in 1924 with members in 33 countries – most of them strongholds of the IFJ.

A year after the IOJ Congress in Budapest, the **3rd World Meeting of Journalists** was organized in **September-October 1963**, this time as a trip aboard a **Russian ship *Litva*** cruising in the Mediterranean from Algiers to Beirut with several landfalls on the way (Figure 4.7). Attended by 260 journalists from 69 countries the Meeting held discussions and met among others President Nasser of Egypt and Archbishop Makarios of Cyprus. (For its background, see Meisner's recollection in Part Two.)

The substance of the proceedings and resolutions followed the pattern of the two earlier World Meetings, with more and more attention devoted to the developing countries of the Third World. But the Meeting also highlighted the professional inquiry initiated three years earlier in Baden, which had by now become "a unique documentation encompassing 57 countries", and it requested the ICCJ to cooperate with the ILO and UNESCO with a view to drafting model contracts of employment for journalists.[13] However, such professional and trade union initiatives were left without systematic implementation under the political circumstances of the 1960s.

Regarding **developments in Asia**, the IOJ encouraged journalists to get organized and internationally linked to "progressive forces". Its main partner in Asia was first China, which hosted the IOJ Executive Committee in Peking

12 The proposal for the setting up of a Photography Section of the IOJ was made by Vilém Kropp, photographer of the Czechoslovak daily *Práce*, on behalf of the photographic sections of several IOJ member unions.

13 The Communiqué of the Meeting is reproduced as Annex 8 in *Useful Recollections, Part II* (1988, pp. 191–193).

Figure 4.7 The 3rd World Meeting of Journalists in the Mediterranean at a ceremony of raising the Meeting's banner on the deck of *Litva* in September 1963. (Photo from *The Democratic Journalist*, 6–7/1966)

already in April 1957. Indonesia became the second stronghold, hosting the IOJ Presidium in Jakarta in February 1963 (Figure 4.8).

Two months later a regional conference of Afro-Asian journalists was organized in Jakarta. This was a sequel to an initiative originating in the 1955 Bandung conference and followed up by a special resolution signed by the Asian participants at the World Meeting in Helsinki in 1956. With further encouragement from the 2nd World Meeting in Baden in 1960, the Chinese journalists in particular were active in developing a "militant friendship" among Afro-Asian journalists, leading to the Jakarta conference, at which 48 countries were represented and which "held high the banner of the Bandung spirit", in the words of the Vice-President of the **All China Journalists' Association (ACJA)**, Chin Chung-hua, who was also IOJ Executive Committee member.[14]

14 Chung-hua wrote an article on the conference for *The Democratic Journalist*, reporting that it adopted "a programme for common struggle by Asian and African journalists – The Jakarta Declaration, and 30 resolutions on the struggle against imperialism and colonialism and other matters". The article was never published; it was found only as a manuscript among the correspondence between the IOJ and ACJA. This shows that a rapid deterioration in relations between the IOJ and its Chinese member union

Figure 4.8 President Sukarno of Indonesia greeting Olavi Laine, IOJ Vice-President from Finland, at a reception during the IOJ Presidium in Jakarta in February 1963. The IOJ was welcome to Sukarno's Indonesia – a left-leaning country interested in balancing the "imperialist influence" of the Western powers in the region. Two years later began a bloody political crisis, which ended in 1967 with a military *coup* led by General Suharto. (Photo from Olavi Laine's collection)

The Jakarta conference in April 1963 led to the establishment of the **Afro-Asian Journalists' Association (AAJA)** as a chapter in the history of Mao's "cultural revolution". This happened in the absence of the IOJ. In 1966 the AAJA issued resolutions under titles such as "China's unprecedented development of nuclear weapons demonstrates the resourcefulness of Mao Tse-tung's thought" and "AAJA condemning criminal activities of Soviet revisionists to split Afro-Asian writers' movement".

The ACJA still attended the IOJ Executive Committee in Santiago de Chile in September 1965, mounting a vehement attack on both the IOJ leadership and "the Khrushchev revisionists' general line of 'peaceful coexistence'". After this session the contacts between the IOJ and its Chinese member union practically ceased. However, the ACJA never formally discontinued its membership of the IOJ.

The first conference of Arab journalists was held in February 1965 in Kuwait and attended by 135 delegates of journalist organizations from 13 Arab countries. The IOJ attended as an observer. This quite representative meeting established the **Federation of Arab Journalists (FAJ)**.

At this time, **IOJ-affiliated schools for journalists** from developing countries were started in Berlin by the GDR Union of Journalists, in Budapest by the Association of Hungarian Journalists and in Roztěž near Prague by the Czechoslovak Union of Journalists (Figure 4.9). The Berlin school was founded under the name "College of Solidarity" for the purpose of promoting the short-term education of young journalists of countries liberated from colonialism and governed by national liberation movements. Later the Roztěž school, operated with the Czechoslovak news agency ČTK, was closed and another school opened in Prague in the 1980s. The Bulgarian Union of Journalists and the Cuban Union of Journalists also established IOJ-affiliated

began in January 1963 – no doubt as a reflection of the overall political clash between China and the Soviet Union. See also Meisner's recollections in Part Two.

Figure 4.9 The German school in Berlin-Friedrichshagen occupied a large building with classroom, dining and dormitory facilities (on the left). The Czechoslovak school was first housed in a castle in Roztěž (on the right). The Hungarian school was located in central Budapest, likewise with facilities for both teaching and accommodation. (Photos from IOJ publications)

schools. Hundreds of young journalists from Africa and Asia were trained in these institutions.

Accordingly, the years 1963–65 witnessed a breakthrough in IOJ assistance for the training of journalists – in close connection with developments in Africa. In addition to such an institutionalization of professional activities within the IOJ, overall political contact was maintained with leading figures of the Third World also after the spectacular appointments during the Mediterranean cruise. For example, in March 1964 IOJ Secretary Alexander Yefremov conducted an interview with the Prime Minister of India, Jawaharlal Nehru, who stated: "The world journalist community is very powerful and your International Organization can do a lot for the benefit of mankind. It is a noble deed to draw the attention of the mass media to the needs and requirements of the developing countries."

These activities in the Third World attracted more and more members to the IOJ so that by 1966 its membership base reached 130,000 journalists in 108 countries, as shown in **Appendix 4**.

The IFJ, for its part, persevered throughout the 1960s with its separatist policy with regard to the IOJ and the World Meetings. At the same time it endeavoured to gain ground in the Third World through its own collaborators in several African, Asian and Latin American countries. An "expansion programme" led to missions to Asia and Africa, and in 1964–1967 to several three-week seminars in Nigeria, Ivory Coast, Zaire, Liberia and Ghana. The fruits of the programme were apparent at the 7th IFJ Congress in Vichy (France) in 1964, attended by 125 delegates and observers from as many as 32 countries. At this time the IFJ membership exceeded 45,000.

Consequently, in terms of numbers the IFJ was less than half the size of the IOJ. But it was evident that both organizations were viable within their own spheres and able to grow, especially in the Third World. Obviously they needed money for all the activities – especially the IOJ for the permanent schools, publications and a large secretariat in Prague. Membership fees covered only a fraction of what was needed and both organizations counted on assistance from affluent member unions.

Regarding financing, the IOJ was assisted especially by the resourceful Soviet Union of Journalists – and by the Soviet Union itself as seen in the preparation of the 3rd Congress in 1950 (Chapter 3 above and Appendix 3) as well as of the 3rd World Meeting of Journalists (Meisner's personal recollections in Part Two). It is obvious that the IOJ was financially supported by all socialist countries which hosted the IOJ congresses and activities in the 1950s–60s: Romania, Hungary, Bulgaria, the GDR and Poland in addition to the USSR and Czechoslovakia. This was done either directly through the state agencies (with the blessing of the Communist Party in question) or indirectly through the member unions concerned as was habitual with all non-governmental associations in those countries. This was the "Moscow financing" for the IOJ at the time – part of a system which similarly supported organizations in the arts, sciences, etc.

An additional source of financing alongside membership fees and state funding of the above kind was the international lottery initiated in the mid-1960s in the name of the IOJ in the socialist countries of eastern Europe. It became an important means of fundraising for the training schools and assistance to journalists in the developing countries. At the same time, it made the IOJ known to millions of people in eastern Europe which otherwise had only limited opportunities for voluntary civic activities.

As far as the IFJ is concerned, it had a problem with its American member ANG, which at one stage was used as a channel for CIA financing.[15]

Obviously there was **rivalry between the IOJ and the IFJ** regarding the Third World and in the 1960s the IOJ was making impressive headway as the Soviet-led socialist countries were largely taken as a "natural ally" of

15 This was exposed in reports in *The Washington Post* and *The New York Times* of February 1967; quoted in *Useful Recollections, Part II* (1988, pp. 87–88).

the developing countries. On the other hand, it is also obvious that not all IFJ members warmed to the idea of an ideological race with the IOJ in the developing countries. In point of fact, the CIA revelations were a big surprise to most of the IFJ constituency, including the rank-and-file members of ANG, which naturally brought the programme to a halt.

The relations of the two world organizations at this time – 20 years after the founding of the IOJ, 17 years after the withdrawal of the Western member unions, and 14 years after the founding of the IFJ – are well reflected in the *IOJ News and Information* of June 1966 (Figure 4.10). The IOJ message to the 8th IFJ Congress in West Berlin in May 1966, signed by Jiří Meisner, was very conciliatory, although written in the customary diplomatic style. In the message the IOJ "once again declares its readiness to participate in conversations on equal terms and suggests, as a first step, a discussion between representatives of your Federation and the IOJ". The message referred to the increasing contacts between the member unions of the two internationals:

> We have in mind the numerous discussions between journalist organisations and individual journalists, on the occasion of the bi-lateral conferences, Congresses and meetings, the "Round Table" meetings that have taken place in Great Britain, Poland, France, Hungary, the Soviet Union, Rumania, and so on.
>
> What is by now an everyday reality for our member unions, should be equally possible between the representatives of our two international centres.

Finally, the message invited the IFJ "responsible leaders" to attend the 6th IOJ Congress in East Berlin in October 1966 "when we are celebrating the 20th anniversary of our organization". The message was followed by a report on the 8th IFJ Congress by a staff writer. After a brief review of the professional items on the Congress agenda, the report points out that the IOJ message was also discussed and that a reply was approved:

> It was the first time a leading organ of the IFJ had concerned itself with an IOJ letter and its proposals, and to which it had replied. Up to now, all letters, appeals and proposals put forward by the IOJ have remained unanswered on the part of the IFJ. [....]
>
> The Congress once again demonstrated how thoroughly inconsistent the attitude of the International Federation of Journalists really is, for by constantly endeavouring to prove and emphasize its "a-political" nature it in fact tries to distract journalists from fulfilling their very responsible mission in contemporary society, which is, namely to do all they can to serve the vital interests of the nations and to assist them in their efforts to secure a better and more beautiful life in a world freed of the threatening dangers of wars, in their efforts for peace and freedom, for mutual understanding and friendship among nations.

Supplement to THE DEMOCRATIC JOURNALIST No. 6-7, 1966

The I.O.J. Message to the Congress of the International Federation of Journalists

The following letter was sent by the I.O.J. General Secretariat to the Presidium and delegates of the VIIIth International Federation of Journalists' Congress, in West Berlin:

Prague, April 28, 1966

To the Presidium and Delegates
of the Congress of the
International Federation
of Journalists

BERLIN (West)

Dear Colleagues,

The International Organisation of Journalists (I.O.J.) sends fraternal greetings to all the delegates at your Congress and expreses its conviction that your Congress will deal fairly with questions concerning co-operation between all international and regional organisations of journalists, in the interests of finding solutions to all the important, general, professional and social problems of concern to journalists.

Our Organisation once again declares its readiness to participate in conversations on equal terms and suggests, as a first step, a discussion between representatives of your Federation and the I.O.J.

Applying the principles of our organisation, amongst which there is that of "the maintenance of peace and the consolidation of friendship among the peoples and of mutual understanding by the free, truthful and honest informing of public opinion", we make use of this occasion to express our desires to hold a discussion with the leaders of the I.F.J., which would constitute the initial step in common succeeding actions to the advantage of the press, journalism and journalists throughout the world, who are invested with responsibilities of a primary nature in modern society and contemporary civilisation.

In the world today, which is witness to more and more dangerous international tension, which threatens to degenerate into a world war, it is our primordial task to examine ways and means of mobilizing the conscience of humanity, of guaranteeing freedom, democracy, human dignity, and a peaceful and creative life to everyone of us. Is it not then the journalists who should be denouncing the critical danger represented by the war in Vietnam? And not only in Vietnam? The entire humanity would appreciate such an effort made by us.

We reckon that, from various points of view we should be intervening in common in order to defend the interests of the free press and active journalists. On this occasion we will list only two points in which, in our opinion, it should be possible to undertake common action:

a) the defence of the purely professional and social interests of journalists;
b) research into the field of information.

We are aware that we are expressing the opinion not only of the numerous member unions of the I.O.J., but also that of numerous member unions of your Federation, by affirming that it is essential for our two organisations to deal with these questions. The best proofs of all this are the contacts that are continually growing between the member unions of your Federation and of our Organisation. We have in mind the numerous discussions between journalist organisations and individual journalists, on the occasion of the bi-lateral conferences, Congresses and meetings, the "Round-Table" meetings that have taken place in Great Britain, Poland, France, Hungary, the Soviet Union, Rumania, and so on.

What is by now an everyday reality for our member unions, should be equally possible between the representatives of our two international centres.

We repeat, once again, that we,

Figure 4.10 *IOJ News and Information* June 1966. The front page of a four-page bulletin. These were regularly issued as supplements to *The Democratic Journalist* in the 1960s.

No doubt the relations between the two internationals resembled a dialogue of the deaf. Yet by now it was an incipient dialogue, instead of one-way messages from the IOJ to the IFJ. However, the IFJ did not accept the invitation to attend the IOJ Congress on the other side of the Berlin Wall.

CHAPTER 5
EXPANSION 1966–75[1]

This chapter reviews the development of the IOJ from the 6th Congress in Berlin (1966) to the eve of the 8th Congress in Helsinki (1976). It was followed by a period of dynamic development from 1976 to 1989 which is covered in the next three chapters. After that the IOJ began to disintegrate so that by 2000 all its activities had ceased. This is covered in Chapters 9 and 10.

The focus in the present chapter is on the overall orientation and structure of the IOJ, summarizing the congresses and activities, while most details are left to be found in original documents and publications.[2] Each of these chapters begins with a list of political events to contextualize the developments of the time, as done for the earlier periods in *Useful Recollections, Part II*.

This was a period when the Third World continued its ascent in the global arena, notably in the first UN Development Decade 1960–70. Meanwhile the war between North and South Vietnam continued with the involvement of the USA and the USSR until the Americans withdrew from Saigon in 1975.

In Mao's China the Cultural Revolution began in 1966.

In 1967 the Six-Day War was fought between Israel and neighbouring Egypt, Jordan and Syria, resulting in Israel's occupation of Sinai, the West Bank, Jerusalem and the Golan Heights. The Yom Kippur War followed in 1973.

Czechoslovakia in 1968 was a special case with "Prague Spring" and the invasion by the Warsaw Pact forces in August 1968, followed by "normalization" of political life in harmony with the Soviet line.

Détente – relaxation of tension between the USSR and the USA – began in 1969 with the SALT negotiations to limit nuclear weapons, followed by the Conference on Security and Co-operation in Europe (CSCE) 1973–75 with its Final Act signed in Helsinki on 1 August 1975.

In Chile, the democratically elected government of Salvador Allende was violently overthrown by a military coup in 1973. In Portugal the Salazarian dictatorship was peacefully overthrown in 1974 and in Spain Franco's dictatorship was replaced by democracy in 1975.

---

1 This chapter is based on *Useful Recollections, Part II*, only regarding the 6th Congress in Berlin (1988, pp. 89–92) as that volume ends with 1966.

2 These are freely available as explained in the Preface.

RECORD CONGRESSES AND EXPANDING ACTIVITIES 1966–71

The **6th IOJ Congress in Berlin** (GDR) was held on 10–15 **October 1966** in the Congress Hall on the Alexanderplatz (Figure 5.1). It was attended by 138 delegates from 48 member unions, 130 observers and invited guests plus representatives of 14 international organizations.[3] In terms of numbers the Congress was twice the size of the two earlier congresses in Budapest (1962) and Bucharest (1958). The attendance reflected the membership, which had grown substantially in different parts of the world. The Congress admitted 22 national associations and groups from Africa, Asia and Latin America as new IOJ members. The number of countries with IOJ members after the 6th Congress in 1966 was 108, and the total number of journalists covered was over 130,000.[4]

Figure 5.1 The presidium of the 6th IOJ Congress in Berlin in October 1966. From the left: delegates from Colombia and the USSR; in the centre IOJ President Hermann, GDR Union President Krausz and IOJ Secretary General Meisner; on the right delegates from North and South Vietnam. (Photo from *The Democratic Journalist* 11–12/1966. This issue includes coverage of the Congress, in both text and photos.)

3 A complete list of participants is included in the Congress proceedings *Sixth Congress* (1966). The publication of 134 pages contains detailed reports of the sessions, extensive extracts from the speeches of the President, Secretary General and the Vietnamese delegation, final resolutions as well as a number of photos.

4 For a list of countries in various regions where the IOJ had members of different categories in 1966, see **Appendix 4**.

Opulent facilities for the Congress were provided in "the capital of the German Democratic Republic", with excursions around the GDR for the participants "to see for themselves the great construction achievements of its population".

The Berlin Congress can be seen as an historical point where the IOJ consolidated itself as the leading international organization of working journalists, based on its three main constituencies: national unions in the Socialist countries and in the Third World as well as progressive groups and individuals in the so-called West. The only notable exception to the overall positive development was the case of China: the All China Journalists' Association (ACJA) withdrew from participation in the IOJ activities – although it never formally renounced its membership of the IOJ.

Compared to the IFJ, the IOJ was more than twice the size in terms of journalists covered – the IOJ counting over 130,000 individual journalists against the 55,000 represented by the IFJ member unions. However, the IOJ suffered from a legitimacy problem as in 1950–52 it had lost its status as a non-governmental organization affiliated to the UN and UNESCO. This status was not restored until 1969–70.

The IOJ was now characterized by a growing preoccupation with the developing countries. This also meant that the debates and resolutions were quite political. Accordingly, more than half of the text of the resolutions adopted in Berlin concerned matters of a general political nature, beginning with a "Resolution on the Vietnam problem". On the other hand, extensive resolutions were also passed on professional and social questions, and permanent commissions were established for these two areas.

The elections reflected both continuity and expansion. Jean-Maurice Hermann was re-elected as President, while Jiří Kubka of Czechoslovakia was elected as the new Secretary General (see Slavík's recollections in Part Two). A separate office of Treasurer was assigned to the Hungarian member union's Secretary General Norbert Siklósi (see recollections by Tamás).

Of the Vice-Presidents elected at the previous Congress in Budapest, those from Mali, Poland, Finland, Mexico, the United Arab Republic, Cuba and the USSR were retained (with some new names), while Mongolia, North Korea and South Vietnam from Asia replaced China and Indonesia. In addition, Chile was made Vice-President, in the person of the Secretary of the Commission for Information and Cooperation among Journalists of Latin America. There was likewise a new Vice-President from Guinea, in the person of the President of the Pan-African Union of Journalists. Finally, a representative of the host country, the GDR, was elected Vice-President. The Soviet Vice-President was the President of the USSR Union of Journalists – always the Editor-in-Chief of *Pravda* and member of the Communist Party's Central Committee.

The Secretariat in Prague was strengthened after the 6th Congress. The Secretariat, in addition to the Secretary General and a Soviet Secretary for Europe, also acquired a German (GDR) Secretary for Africa, Asia and the Arab world, and a Columbian Secretary for Latin America. They and local assistants occupied a part of the premises of the Czechoslovak Union of Journalists, which moved in 1967 from *Vinohradská Street* in Prague 1 – a building subsequently demolished due to the reconstruction of the city centre – to *Pařížská Street* two blocks from the *Old Town Square* (Figure 5.2).

72 THE DEMOCRATIC JOURNALIST – 5-6/1967

The old, now destroyed I.O.J. quarters . . .

. . . and the new ones.

I.O.J. GENERAL SECRETARIAT MOVED TO NEW QUARTERS

The I.O.J. General Secretariat, and our editorial office along with it, moved from the buy central part of Prague to Pařížská Street — in the oldest quarter of the city, the Old Town. In the coming years this street is expected to become a second centre of Prague; it will house the offices of plane companies, of travel bureaux, of luxurious shops, and so forth. This will add to its attractions since this quarter is the site of romantic, picturesque nooks, many inns, full of crooked, narrow streets, passageways and alleys. The street branches out from the Old Town Square — the site of one of the greatest treasures in Prague, the Old Town Hall — which oll of you undoubtedly know if you have ever been to Prague. It leads to the river embankment and from there it is only a short walk to the Charles Bridge with its magnificent view of Hradčany, the Prague Castle.

The reason for the move was simple. Prague is being reconstructed, a bridge is to be built across one of its valleys and this bridge will end very close to the site of I.O.J.'s former headquarters. In addition, Prague's first underground is under construction. With such plans for modernisation and reconstruction it goes without saying that some buildings will have to be torn down. This fate has met a whole block of houses, including ours at No. 3, the former headquarters of our organisation and of the Union of Czechoslovak Journalists. This is one of the last photos of the building before it was demolished.

The new headquarters which the International Organisation of Journalists now occupies takes up practically the whole floor of two buildings that are joined together. The General Secretariat has thereby expanded its floor space and will now have its own meeting hall, lounge, and as formerly, together with the Union of Czechoslovak Journalists, a club and a restaurant.

Finally, we can only hope that in the new, better headquarters our work will be improved and more fruitful than heretofore and that the tasks which our organisation has before it will be successfully fulfilled. dgr.

Figure 5.2 The change in the IOJ premises in Prague was reported in the May–June 1967 issue of *The Democratic Journalist*.

After the Berlin Congress the IOJ headquarters began to have an **extension in Budapest** under the umbrella of the Hungarian Association of Journalists (MUOSZ), thanks to the ingenuity of its Secretary General Norbert Siklósi – now also IOJ Treasurer. As shown by Pál Tamás in Part Two, Budapest served as a politically safe haven for both professional and commercial activities carried out jointly by MUOSZ and the IOJ. Secretary General Kubka was a willing partner to Siklósi in developing new forms of commercial activity. Since 1971 these were run by the IOJ's sister company INTERPRESS Budapest with Gyorgy Stark as its director. No doubt Hungary, with her relatively liberal atmosphere, served as a model for Kubka to emulate in Czechoslovakia.

Spring 1968 was promising for such visions, but the events of August put them on hold, while the IOJ endeavoured to survive the crisis, beginning by extricating itself from the occupation of its Secretariat by the Warsaw Pact forces as shown by Slavík in Part Two. After all, the IOJ did not undergo drastic changes after the events of 1968 in Czechoslovakia. Its political and professional profile remained by and large the same, as determined by the Berlin Congress in 1966. After Kubka had ensured political space for the IOJ under pressure from hardliners in the USSR and also at home, the organization continued its operations, but with a politically more cautious approach (Figure 5.3).

Figure 5.3 The cover of *The Democratic Journalist* 12/1968 showed the new leadership of Czechoslovakia: Ludvík Svoboda, Alexander Dubček, Oldřich Černík and Josef Smrkovský. However, this issue of the journal in no way covered the developments of the "Prague Spring", apart from a photo of Svoboda being sworn in to the office of President and Dubček addressing the people's militia; also, a photo of people signing resolutions in support of the Communist Party of Czechoslovakia in summer 1968. A three-page report on changes in the journalist organization of the country by Dr Stanislav Maleček, Secretary of the Union of Czech Journalists, was published in issue 9/1968. Otherwise the IOJ publications kept quiet about the Prague Spring and its aftermath of the occupation.

However, a certain anomaly of the organizational life is shown by the fact that no IOJ statutory body met in 1968 (see Appendix 1). Usually the Executive Committee or its Presidium met once a year, but 1968 is empty. The next Congress was to be convened in Havana in 1971, five years after Berlin. This started a tradition of holding Congresses every five years instead of four – a more convenient cycle for a large organization, although the IOJ Statute required the Congress to meet once in four years.

A documentation of the IOJ activities in this period is provided by a book-form information package *The IOJ Between Two Congresses: Berlin 1966 – Havana 1971*.[5] In addition to summarizing meetings of the IOJ bodies and visits of delegations to several countries, it highlights two political events: the gala meeting in Prague in October 1967 in honour of the 50th anniversary of the Great October Revolution, and the international gathering of journalists in Leningrad in October 1969 on the occasion of the centenary of the birth of V. I. Lenin – the latter in co-operation with the Soviet Union of Journalists.

The book also shows that the IOJ was expanding to set up regional information centres, the first of which was opened in Cairo for the Arab countries and Africa. The various parts of the book are devoted to reviews of IOJ solidarity events with fighting and persecuted journalists in Vietnam, the Arab countries, Greece, South Africa and elsewhere, to activities in the social field and in the professional sphere, and to IOJ cooperation with international organizations. About one third of the book is composed of reports by the member unions. Finally, 22 appendices reproduce various documents, beginning with the IOJ Statute, the list of member organizations and the Berlin Congress resolutions and ending with the statutes of various sectorial activities such as the Social Commission, the Solidarity Lottery as well as sections and clubs for press photographers, graphic artists and motoring journalists.

The extent and variety of IOJ activities in the late 1960s looks impressive – to such a degree that one begins to wonder how well the original aims and objectives may survive in such a supermarket. It is clear that the political framework determined above all by Soviet interests set the basic tone for activities, with an overall line towards "peace, democracy and social progress".

However, within this framework ample space remained to further the social and professional interests of journalists. Yet little or no attention was paid to trade union affairs – obviously because in the socialist countries these were handled by different unions, which at the international level were represented by the World Federation of Trade Unions (WFTU) – also headquartered in Prague. As noted in Chapter 3, the trade union movement was also divided by the Cold War, with the opposing party to the WFTU, the International Confederation of Free Trade Unions (ICFTU), established in 1949 in Brussels.

A natural platform for pursuing trade union matters was the IOJ **Social Commission** established by a resolution of the Berlin Congress with a mandate "to improve social, economic and legal conditions in order to adapt them

5 For details of this and other publications, see Bibliography.

to their duties and their part in the life of modern society". While the resolution was a fairly general call for co-operation to protect and improve the working and living conditions of journalists, it provided an extensive list of topics – including conditions of employment, salaries, working hours, retirement age, etc. – to serve as a basis for systematic study. The resolution also called for an investigation of "the influence of the present technical revolution on the working and living conditions of journalists". A separate recommendation was made for "carrying out a big international inquiry into the participation and conditions of work of women in our profession". The chair and head office of the Commission were mandated to be in Bulgaria, with members coming from different continents.[6]

The Commission was constituted in 1967 and its first meeting was held in Sofia in January 1968. However, it was not until 1970 that it had commissioned a questionnaire on the social situation of journalists around the world.[7] No special activities were carried out on the technical revolution and on women journalists. In practice, most of the Commission's attention focused on the international rest homes in Varna and Balaton as well as consideration of another one with a "medical institute" in Karlovy Vary.

Obviously the conditions were not conducive to implementing all the ideas approved in Berlin. It was not only politics after the Czechoslovak events in 1968 that caused a certain slowdown in this field but also the lack of co-operation with the IFJ, which pursued its own trade union oriented activities. In such a situation it was unrealistic to convene a truly international conference on the topic together with the ILO and UNESCO, as was suggested in the Berlin resolution. A divided movement was able to deliver less for its members than would have been the case if the IOJ and IFJ had joined forces. In the late 1960s it was inconceivable for the two rivals to work together on such a vital topic as the working and living conditions of journalists.

A reminder of the realities of the day is the conference of anti-imperialist journalists organized by the Union of Journalists of the Korean People's Democratic Republic together with the IOJ in Pjongyang in 1969 (Figure 5.4).

While the IOJ was strongly influenced by international politics, its professional side was kept alive and even strengthened. This was highlighted in the Berlin Congress by the establishment of a permanent IOJ **Professional Commission**. Its mandate was to promote the IOJ training schools, to organize international conferences and regional seminars on the qualifications of journalists, to analyse the state of the media in developing countries, to edit an

6 The resolution is reproduced in *Sixth Congress* (1966, pp. 96–100), and in *The Democratic Journalist (DJ)* 11–12/1966.

7 See Vasilev (1970).

Figure 5.4 The Conference on the Tasks of Journalists of the Whole World in Their Fight Against the Aggression of U.S. Imperialism was held in Pyongyang on 18–24 September 1969. The guest of honour and main speaker was Marshall Kim Il Sung, who is here greeted by the IOJ Secretary General Jiří Kubka, next to the IOJ Vice-President from Cuba, Ernesto Vera. The conference was attended by 114 journalists from 90 countries and representatives of 13 international organizations. (Photos from *The Democratic Journalist* 11–12/1969)

international magazine on the theory and development of journalism, and to publish handbooks "to ensure the steadily growing level of our schools".[8]

The Congress resolution moreover urged the IOJ Secretariat to pursue contacts with the International Committee for Cooperation among Journalists (ICCJ) – the body behind the World Meetings in 1956, 1960 and 1963 and the inquiry into the working conditions of journalists. No follow-up on these contacts seems to have taken place, showing that the story of the ICCJ had gradually come to a natural end.

8 *Sixth Congress* (1966, pp. 92–95).

The Professional Commission was formally established in early 1968 under the leadership of the Union of Romanian Journalists. Its first meeting was held in May 1969, attended by representatives of nine member unions (from Czechoslovakia, the GDR, Hungary, Poland, Bulgaria, Romania, France, Colombia and Venezuela). Accordingly, this Commission was even slower to get organized than the Social Commission, and its role in the IOJ was not particularly significant under the post-Prague Spring conditions, as evidenced by the absence of the Soviet Union of Journalists from its constitutive meeting.

On the other hand, the Berlin Congress resolution lists a number of concrete measures "in defence of the profession", beginning with the establishment of professional unions, the issuing of journalists' cards, the defence of freelance journalists, ensuring that it is the journalist and not the enterprise that holds copyright and ending with points in the defence of the journalist's freedom to work and "backing journalists persecuted for having carried out their profession with dignity".

The IOJ Between Two Congresses has a chapter on the IOJ activities in the professional sphere.[9] It includes under "Schools, seminars, symposia" three professional events already in 1967: a Latin-American seminar on press agencies held in Havana, an international conference of economics editors in Moscow, and an international colloquium "on new trends in training journalists in connection with the scientific-technical revolution" in Prague. The colloquium took place on 3–4 November 1967, convened by the IOJ in collaboration with the Union of Czechoslovak Journalists, the IAMCR and the Charles University (Institute of History of Mass Communication). Attended by 36 representatives from 15 countries and UNESCO, it was acclaimed as "an outstanding initiative by the IOJ in the professional field" – at a time when the IOJ had not yet reinstated its formal relationship to UNESCO.

The three schools (Berlin, Budapest, Roztěž), together with related seminars, constitute the main part of professional activities, and they are naturally well summarized in this publication. The second main part of the professional sphere is composed of the Photo Section founded in 1962 (by the 5th Congress in Budapest) and the Clubs. The Photo Section organized the 4th Interpress Photo Exhibition (after Berlin 1960, Budapest 1962 and Warsaw 1964) in Moscow in 1966 and other cities in the USSR, with over two million visitors. The 5th Interpress Photo Exhibition took place in Prague in 1970. These and special exhibitions on occasions such as the 50th anniversary of the Russian Revolution in 1967 and the Olympic Games in Mexico in 1968 made the name of the IOJ widely known outside media circles. Still, the World Press Photo – an Amsterdam-based institution es-

9 Pp. 58–68; this is longer than the chapter on the social field (pp. 51–57).

tablished in 1955 to organize annual competitions for photojournalists – became far better known around the world.[10]

Of the IOJ Clubs, the most prominent was the Interpress Auto Club, established in 1965 dealing with cars and motoring. It was based in Warsaw with its own presidium and conferences held in Poland, Hungary and Czechoslovakia. In Prague it organized in 1968 an exhibition "Man and Automobile", where car manufacturers including Daimler-Benz displayed their safety features, with an international symposium on "Safe driving and the tasks of mass communication". The exhibition actually attracted 400,000 visitors. The second exhibition was held in Prague in 1970, with more displays and equally many visitors. A symposium on "Traffic safety and journalists" was attended by journalists from the GDR, Romania, Italy, France and Czechoslovakia.

The Club organized an Interpress Auto Rally, the first in Czechoslovakia in 1966, the second in Poland (Figure 5.5) and thereafter annually in different socialist countries. The last Interpress Auto Rally was organized in 1975,

95

IInd Interpress Auto Rally in Poland's Baltic Region

About Interpress — Autoclub Idea and Work

Figure 5.5 The Interpress Auro Rally was widely covered in the socialist countries, here by *The Democratic Journalist* 7–8/1966. The *Interpress Magazin* in Czechoslovakia had by 1970 quite a popular appearance.

10 See https://www.worldpressphoto.org/ While most of the winners of the World Press Photo of the Year were from the West, the fourth in 1959 was Stanislav Tereba from Prague; see https://en.wikipedia.org/wiki/World_Press_Photo_of_the_Year.

while the Club continued until the 1980s as a special-interest section of the IOJ without notable professional impact. Obviously the IOJ could present itself as carrier of quite non-political professional activities at a time when it was seen in the West as an overtly political association. On the other hand, this Club had practically no relevance for the increasing membership in the developing countries.

Another IOJ section with a closer connection to the journalistic profession was the Interpress Graphic Club founded in 1967 among art editors and lay-out professionals in newspapers and magazines. Like the Auto Club, it was organized as an international association with national chapters and its own presidium. Its first conference was held in Budapest in May 1968, attended by representatives from the GDR, Bulgaria, Hungary, Czechoslovakia and the USSR. It organized in Prague in 1967 an international exhibition of periodicals and modern press technique, visited by 28,000 journalists and specialists on the polygraphic industry. Two years later this was followed by Interpress Prague69, also extending to radio and television technique, with 56 companies from 12 countries displaying their products. This exhibition had 240,000 visitors with three expert symposia using simultaneous interpreting to five languages. One of these was "Incomtyp 69" with leading international specialists presenting typesetting by means of computers.

In this particular area the IOJ was really at the cutting edge of developments. The Graphic Club activities also led in 1968 to publishing a specialized magazine *Interpressgraphic* for technical and graphic editors of newspapers and magazines. It appeared in 5,000 copies in English and Russian. Moreover, in 1968 the IOJ expanded to commercial publishing by issuing *Interpress Magazin* in Czech language for the Czechoslovak market. This was a general-interest magazine of popular stories from home and abroad with a lot of photos – nothing to do with journalism but just published by the IOJ. First as a quarterly and since 1970 a bimonthly, it had a circulation of 120,000 and was self-supporting (Figure 5.5).

The IOJ started in the late 1960s also to publish brochures and books for professionals. These included political pamphlets such as a "Black book" in Spanish on the CIA-supported activities among Latin American journalists in 1967, but most of the books were academic, notably these: the proceedings of the colloquium on new trends in training journalists held in Prague in 1967 (in French, 1968); a collection of press laws in Scandinavian countries (in English, 1968); handbooks on news agencies and on television journalism (in English, 1970); and a collection of texts by V.I. Lenin to mark the centenary of his birth (in English, French and German, 1970).

However, the main publishing platform of the IOJ in the late 1960s was ***The Democratic Journalist*** (*DJ*), published monthly in English, French, Russian and Spanish, and distributed in 16,000 copies not only to member unions but increasingly also to journalism schools around the world. Its content was strikingly diverse and eclectic, ranging from plain documentation of relevant meetings and events and short pieces of news on the press, radio and television around the world to sharp political stories such as "Struggling Latin American journalists in solidarity with Vietnam" and "The new face of Fascist Vorster" (*DJ* 7–8/1967). On special occasions the entire issue was devoted to a political event, especially on the 50th anniversary of the "Great Socialist October Revolution" which naturally focused on the Soviet press but also had an article on the 1917 revolution and the Czechoslovak press (*DJ* 10/1967).

On the other hand, there were articles by academics such as Professor Vladimír Klimeš of Charles University[11], Professor Francesco Fattorello of the University of Rome[12] and Professor Yassen Zassoursky of Moscow State University[13]. In early 1968 the journal published a detailed report about an inquiry among members of Union of the Czechoslovak Journalists[14].

In 1969 lengthy articles were published by several internationally known academics: Jacques Bourquin from Switzerland (President of the IAMCR), Johan Galtung from Norway, Marques de Melo from Brazil, Bogdan Osolnik from Yugoslavia and Dallas Smythe from Canada.

In addition to scientific and political content the journal included a wide range of reports on journalism and media around the world – not only in Europe but especially in the developing continents of Africa, Asia and Latin America on countries such as Brazil, India and Vietnam. Each number also had a photo supplement. Although the content was uneven and the profile of the journal somewhat confusing, it provided a unique window to the world of media and journalism of its time (Figure 5.6). Mailed free of charge, with nice stamps from Czechoslovakia, it reached a relatively wide audience in different language areas, also outside the IOJ membership, including teachers and students of journalism in Western Europe and North America.

The journal first listed as its successive Editors-in-Chief the IOJ Secretary General – Knobloch, Meisner and Kubka – without any other editorial staff. However, beginning with the September issue 9/1967 a separate Editor-in-Chief appears (Dr. Lodislav Mareda) and from January 1/1968 on also editors of the English, French, Spanish and Russian versions as well as an assistant editor and an art editor. A new Editor-in-Chief is listed in the last issue of

---

11 "A few notes about the conditions for entering the journalist profession in various countries" (*DJ* 1/1967). "The scientific and technical revolution and the prospects for journalistic activity" (*DJ* 4/1967, continuing *DJ* 5–6/1967).

12 "The education of journalists" (*DJ* 11–12/1967). "Information – a social phenomenon" (*DJ* 5/1969).

13 "The training of journalists: What it is and what we should like it to be" (*DJ* 2/1968. "A criticism of the bourgeois theory of journalism" (*DJ* 5/1969).

14 See Jisl (1968).

Figure 5.6 *The Democratic Journalist* was prompt in covering the topics consonant with progressive views and not contradicting Soviet politics. Thus protection of journalists against undemocratic regimes was featured in an article by Charles University Professor Vladimír Klimeš already in 1969, at which time both journalist and publisher organizations only began to pursue the matter. The safety of journalists on dangerous missions later became a major issue for the profession. Likewise, in 1969 questions of mass media in relation to international law, including human rights, were covered extensively in articles by the academics mentioned above. Although these topics did not yet figure high on the agenda of media professionals, the *DJ* still promoted them – balancing political stories with scholarly material.

1969 (Oldřich Bureš).[15] The Editors-in-Chief were Czech and the rest of the editorial staff also from Czechoslovakia.

The Secretariat in Prague was expanded not only with editorial staff but also by two senior officers in addition to the earlier three regional Secretaries: an Italian Secretary for International Organizations (see Zidar's recollections in Part Two) and a Romanian Secretary for Professional Matters serving as Secretary of the Professional Commission.

An overview of IOJ activities covering the years 1967–90 is provided by a chronological list of events in **Appendix 5.**[16] It shows that from 1967 to 1971 the IOJ arranged or attended on average at least one event per month. These took place in various countries, mostly in central and eastern Europe. In 1967–68 the list is dominated by the activities of the IOJ Photo Section and Clubs (Auto, Graphic), but from 1969 on – after the "Prague Spring" and "normalization" – there are more and more events of a political nature, including "Consultation of IOJ member unions from the CMEA countries". From 1974 on these annual meetings were formalized and numbered until the 14th in

15 Issues 9 and 10 of 1969 did not list any Editor-in-Chief – suggesting that the transition was not smooth. The first issue with Bureš as Editor-in-Chief (11–12/1969) was devoted entirely to two political conferences: one in Leningrad on V. I. Lenin's 100th birthday and the other in Pyongyang against imperialism (see above Figure 5.4). Materials from the Lenin conference were also published throughout 1970.

16 This long list of events complements the chronology in Annex 1 of *Useful Recollections, Part II* (1988, pp. 95–100) and the timeline in Appendix I of *A History of the International Movement of Journalists* (Nordenstreng & al., 2016, pp. 181–192).

1988.[17] No doubt the IOJ was used as an instrument for coordinating the positions of the journalist unions in the socialist camp.

Despite the dominance of politics, professional activities were also promoted, notably by establishing in 1970 the Club of Agricultural Journalists.

The political tone in the IOJ activities of the late 1960s was less against imperialism than in favour of détente: creating a platform for co-operation among journalists across the East-West divide, hosted in Italy (Lignano and Capri), in Poland (Jablonna and Gdansk) as well as in Finland (Siikaranta) and Sweden (Ystad). The IOJ was among the NGOs which began to mobilize support for European security and co-operation parallel to the diplomatic conference CSCE since 1972. In this process the leaders of the IOJ and IFJ also began to meet annually. It is obvious that a key figure in this orientation of the IOJ was Oleg Zagladin, the Soviet Secretary for Europe, whose brother Vadim was a leading advocate of détente in the International Department of the Soviet Communist Party's Central Committee.

The **7th IOJ Congress in Havana** was held in the "capital of revolutionary Cuba" on 4–11 **January 1971** (Figure 5.7). It marked the 25th anniversary of the IOJ and was the first Congress to be held in Latin America, "in a country which was the first to settle accounts with American imperialist domination".[18] The Congress report documents the attendance of

Figure 5.7 The 7th Congress in Havana in January 1971 was staged in the same grandiose way as preceding congresses in Berlin, Bucharest and Budapest. (Photo: IOJ)

17 *Journalists' Affairs* 4/1974 and 4/1975. It took place still in 1989 in Cuba as Consultative Meeting of Socialist Countries' Unions of Journalists (see Appendix 5).

18 *7th Congress* (1971, p. 7).

326 participants from 84 countries (187 delegates from 64 member unions, 71 guests and 68 observers) – a new record after Berlin in 1966. Twenty new member organizations joined the IOJ in Havana, notably national associations from Bolivia, Chile, Jordan, Palestine, Sierra Leone, Somalia and Venezuela as well as groups of progressive journalists, for example from Cyprus, Greece, Japan, Spain and the USA. Whereas the number of countries where the IOJ had member unions or groups was 47 in 1966 (see Appendix 4), it was now 58.[19]

The high profile of the Congress was apparent in the greetings of political leaders from most of the socialist countries in central and eastern Europe, beginning with the USSR (Leonid Breznev), and several developing countries, including Cambodia (Norodom Sihanuk), Egypt (Anvar Sadat), Iraq (Ahmad Bakr), Syria (Hafez Assad) and Vietnam, both North (Pham Van Dong) and South (Huynh-tan-Phat). A special meeting of several hours with the Cuban leader Fidel Castro took place on a farm outside Havana.

The Congress heard an extensive report by the Secretary General Jiří Kubka, delivered in Spanish, with separate sections devoted to political developments in Europe, Asia, Africa and Latin America, followed by brief overviews of professional, social and editorial activities. Towards the end of his 39 pages long report Kubka notes:

> The period that has elapsed since the Berlin Congress has convincingly proved that the position and prestige of the IOJ among democratic journalists of the entire world are increasing. Thanks to the activity of our member unions and groups and, above all, to the activity of the unions of journalists in the socialist countries, it has been possible to propagate even more among journalists the ideas of the struggle for peace, solidarity, democracy and progress and to unify the resistance to the forces of imperialism and aggression.[20]

After pointing out that "our epoch is a period of transition from capitalism to socialism", Kubka appealed to all journalists of the world to improve their "professional qualifications in the ever-sharpening ideological struggle".[21]

Kubka's overall approach is repeated in the 20-page long General Resolution adopted by the Congress. Separate resolutions were passed "On Support for the Struggle of the Peoples of Vietnam, Laos and Cambodia" as well as "On Tribute to Che Guevara". The Congress also approved reports from the Professional and Social Commissions covering the years 1967–1970 and passed resolutions on their tasks for the period 1971–74. These reports and resolu-

19 Ibid., 1971, pp. 183–191.
20 Ibid., p. 47.
21 Ibid., pp. 50–53.

tions continued along the lines adopted in Berlin, covering several areas from schools to rest homes and co-operation with UNESCO. However, trade union activities were still absent from the IOJ agenda, while the Social Commission was now called the "Social Welfare Commission".

Moreover, the Congress adopted some amendments to the IOJ Statute, including a paragraph on the Auditing Commission, which was elected at the preceding Congress and which now was noted to be worth maintaining "for the satisfactory functioning and verification of financial operations".[22]

The elections renewed the mandate of President Hermann[23], Secretary General Kubka, Treasurer Siklósi and most of the 11 national Vice-Presidents (with some new names), however replacing the Vice-President from Mexico with another from Peru (see Appendix 2). In addition, the Vice-President from Guinea was to be named later, likewise another one to be jointly named by three member organizations of the Portuguese colonies.

An amendment of the Statute determined that the chairmen of the Social and Professional Commissions were considered associate members of the Presidium. Hence Georgi Bokov from Bulgaria and Nestor Ignat from Romania were added to the 16-man Presidium.

DÉTENTE FACILITATING BROADER CO-OPERATION 1971–75

Soon after the Havana Congress *The Democratic Journalist* published a leading article by President Jean-Maurice Hermann.[24] It provides a historical perspective of the IOJ at the time of the 7th Congress:

> It is now twenty years since I went to Helsinki to attend the Third Congress of the I.O.J. The American imperialists, who were systematically endeavoring to sever all ties between East and West, had caused a rupture in our organization which was among the first international bodies born after anti-fascist victory in 1946.
>
> This was the worst period of the Cold War. Our Congress was successfully held in a rather small hall. Yet how great our enthusiasm would have been had we been able to predict the magnificent growth of the I.O.J. over the next twenty years.

---

22 Ibid., p. 178. This amendment was followed by another one on finances, urging payment of membership fees (0.50 US $ per member per year) and to help finance, by special contributions, large international IOJ projects. Another amendment was that chairmen of the Professional and Social Commissions were to be considered associate members of the Presidium.

23 Hermann's re-election was not automatic: there was an attempt to remove him after he and the SNJ-CGT had condemned the foreign intervention in Czechoslovakia in 1968. The incident remained out of publications until 1991.

24 "Journalists and the future of the world", *DJ* 6/1971.

> The International Organization of Journalists which our opponents wanted to reduce to an insignificant body, hemmed in within its own ghetto, is today established on all continents. It has become the most important organization which exists or has ever existed in our profession.
>
> How has this continuous, unbroken success come about? It is undoubtedly due to the development of the world and the balance of forces which rule our planet.

Hermann points out that "although imperialists are still conducting aggressive actions in all too many places they are being driven more and more on to the defensive". He also notes that, while the opponents label the IOJ a "Communist organization", it has more unions and member groups in non-socialist than in socialist countries and that its strength is based on the unity whereby "Socialists, liberals, Christians, Moslems, Buddhists and free-thinkers freely associate with Communists". The core of this strategic vision is that while imperialism was on the defensive there was more room for progressive movements and that the IOJ should be seen as part of a broader worldwide front – not as part of the socialist bloc although working in alliance with it.

The developments of the IOJ during the next five years are well documented in a book with almost 300 pages which includes reports of the Presidium and Executive Committee meetings between 1971 and 1976.[25] The first of these was an extraordinary **Presidium in Prague in September 1971**, celebrating the 25th anniversary of the founding of the IOJ and held in the Great Hall of the Charles University. It was also a manifestation of "militant solidarity" with the people of Vietnam, announcing a worldwide competition of journalistic works under the heading "Peace for Vietnam".

The next **Presidium** meeting took place in **Balatonszéplak (Hungary) in September 1972.**[26] In addition to marking the 50th anniversary of the establishment of the USSR it reviewed the political and professional developments since Havana and prepared the draft agenda for the Executive Committee to be convened a year later. As a special issue related to the European developments around the CSCE, the Presidium "paid great attention to the responsibility of journalists with regard to maintenance of peace on the continent and the world over" and adopted an appeal:

> In order to contribute to the creation of a favourable climate, the International Organization of Journalists proposes to all journalists organizations in Europe to jointly

25 *The International Organization of Journalists Between Two Congresses: Havana – Helsinki 1971–1976* (1976, pp. 19–21).

26 Ibid., pp. 25–29.

draft the principles of a convention, which could become an integral part of the professional ethical norms of journalists.[27]

The Executive Committee between the two Congresses took place in **Baghdad (Iraq)** on 26–29 **September 1973** (Figure 5.8). This was the first time that an IOJ statutory meeting was convened in the Middle East and the second time it was hosted by an Arab country – the first being Algeria in 1964. The report by the Secretariat given there provides a detailed account of the activities of the IOJ since Havana.[28] Of the different regions of the world the most extensive coverage is given to Europe: how the IOJ has participated in the CSCE process with the International Committee for Security and Co-operation in Europe (meetings in Brussels – see Appendix 5) and with its own member unions in the Baltic Sea region (meetings in Jablonna, Gdansk, Siikaranta, etc.) as well as with the Italian initiatives (meetings in Lignano, Capri).

Figure 5.8 The IOJ Executive Committee in Baghdad in September 1973. A military coup, with US support, had just taken place in Chile and the seat of the lost Chilean member of the Executive Committee was symbolically empty. (Photo from *The Democratic Journalist* 11/1973)

The report for the Baghdad meeting states that the appeal on a European convention given in the Balaton Presidium was soon brought up by the IOJ

27 Ibid., p. 28. The appeal included some concrete points for discussion on such a convention.

28 Ibid., pp. 33–85.

at a press conference in November 1972 on the eve of the diplomatic CSCE talks in Helsinki. The report claims that the ideas of the IOJ were met with approval at a meeting of journalist organizations from 18 European countries held in Brussels in May 1973.[29] This meeting welcomed not only the elaboration of a convention on the ethical norms of the journalistic profession but also the preparation of a charter on the principles of co-operation among journalist organizations in Europe. Another positive signal to the IOJ in 1973 was the opening of relations with the Finnish Radio and Television Journalists' Union (RTTL), which had a much broader political basis than the old Finnish member union (YLL) and which was ready to support the idea of a European Charter. Nevertheless, one should note that the IFJ and most of its member unions were not involved in such an active CSCE process, although the IFJ leaders had joined the Italian platform and even begun to meet their IOJ counterparts (see Murialdi's recollections in Part Two).

The first meeting of the leading IOJ and IFJ representatives took place in Zürich (Switzerland) in September 1973, just before Baghdad. President Hermann gave to the Executive Committee a detailed report of the meeting, which turned out to be little more than courteous chat. The IFJ delegation was not prepared to discuss concrete activities proposed by the IOJ, including the preparation of ethical principles and a European Charter – the excuse being that they had no mandate to do so. Yet they proposed to meet again, which happened in Karlovy Vary (Czechoslovakia) in April 1974. In Baghdad the IOJ delegation was commissioned to continue the contacts with the IFJ,

> without covering the divergences still existing between the two organizations, but to make all efforts in order to find the fields of possible action in the common interest of all the profession. In the first place it is the interest to end the cold war in the mass information media and to turn them into factors permanently endorsing understanding among the peoples.[30]

A significant aspect in the Executive Committee report is the emphasis on the journalist organizations of European socialist countries, which "bring forth an immense political, moral and material contribution in the interest of all progressive journalism throughout the world".[31] Hence the pivotal role

29 Ibid., pp. 34–36. This meeting was convened by the International Committee for Security and Co-operation in Europe, based in Brussels, after an Assembly of Social Forces in Brussels in June 1972 had proposed to set up a working group on questions of mass media. The IOJ immediately picked up this idea and worked together with the Brussels Committee to convene the meeting a year later.

30 Ibid., pp. 96–97. (This quote is obviously a translation from Russian.)

31 Ibid., pp. 39–40.

of the socialist countries in the IOJ and the IOJ serving as their instrument for co-ordination, is made perfectly clear. An important decision by the Executive Committee in support of détente in western Europe was the decision to set up an IOJ office in Paris, hosted by its French member union SNJ-CGT – at the location of the IOJ President (Figure 5.9).

Figure 5.9 President Jean-Maurice Hermann was fêted in Paris on his 80th birthday, 28 February 1975. His French colleagues presented him with a pastoral staff as a mark of the overwhelming respect he enjoyed as a veteran journalist. On the left Gérard Gatinot, Secretary General of the French Journalist Syndicate SNJ-CGT; on the right Jiří Kubka and Oleg Zagladin from the IOJ. (Photo: IOJ)

After Europe, the report covers in detail the IOJ activities in the regions of Asia, the Middle East, Africa and Latin America, with separate sections devoted to professional and social activities as well as relations with international organizations. An individual event of historical importance was the first IOJ/UNESCO Colloquy on the development of media and training of journalists held in Budapest in June 1973.[32]

The Presidium met again in **Ulan Bator (Mongolia) in September 1974** and in **Bucharest (Romania) in October 1975**. These meetings[33] provide similar reviews of different regions as that of the Baghdad Executive Committee, naturally reflecting the political developments in the world such as the military coup in Chile and the final stage of the Vietnam War. The reports reveal that the IFJ was a difficult partner, causing problems in the European co-operation facilitated by the Italian FNSI as well as in the developing continents. In Europe, political tension emerged from different interpretations of

32 See *DJ* 12/1973. The second IOJ/UNESCO Colloquy took place in Visegrad (Hungary) in December 1975 (see *DJ* 2/1976).

33 *Between Two Congresses* (1976, pp. 87–140 and 141–186). See also *DJ* 11/1974.

the "third basket" in the CSCE – the sphere of humanitarian co-operation understood by the IFJ as a window of opportunity for the dissidents in eastern Europe, while the IOJ took it as encouragement to cultivate official contacts. In Latin America, a striking example of poor co-ordination was the response to the *coup* in Chile: the IOJ proposed to send there a joint IOJ-IFJ delegation endorsed by the UN, but the IFJ hastily sent a delegation of its own, followed later by a separate delegation of the IOJ.

The professional and social matters reported in these Presidium meetings essentially follow up on the same activities already listed in the Havana Congress proceedings, with some new elements such as the Social Commission's proposal to launch an international inquiry on the state of health of journalists in co-operation with the WHO and the ILO. On the other hand, no results are reported on the projects already initiated in Berlin, including inquiries on the social situation of journalists in general and women journalists in particular.

The two Presidium reports also tell about the Solidarity lottery. In Ulan Bator in September 1974 it notes that in December the lottery would be 10 years of age and during this time it had raised 50 million Czechoslovak Crowns. This was used to buy printing machines for Vietnam and various other ways "to support the struggle of the Vietnamese people, of the Chilean patriots, of the African liberation movements".[34] With all its solidarity actions (rallies, donations, etc.) and publishing outlets (posters, booklets and journal articles) the IOJ was at the forefront of worldwide campaigns about Vietnam (since the late 1960s) and Chile (since 1973).

Between Two Congresses: Havana–Helsinki 1971–1976 gives a detailed account of the publishing activities.[35] The number of books and pamphlets, including Congress proceedings in various languages, published during that five-year period was 54.[36] In the period of 1966–71 the IOJ had issued altogether 29 titles. Accordingly, the publishing activity had redoubled and moreover a parallel publishing house INTERPRESS had started its operations in Budapest in the early 1970s, issuing both books and periodicals and even producing films. *The Democratic Journalist* continued in the 1970s as before. Its periodic supplements of organizational news and information were replaced since 1973 by a fortnightly publication *Journalists' Affairs* (in four languages). It normally had about 20 pages and a modest appearance with type-written text and no photos. The first issue of 1974 was devoted largely to Vietnam and after that it carried short reports from the Secretariat and member unions as well as "From the World of the Press, Radio and Television" (Figure 5.10).

34 Ibid., pp. 138–139.
35 Also in *DJ* 7–8/1976.
36 A timely example of these is *Developing World and Mass Media* (1975).

Figure 5.10 IOJ publications in the 1970s included thematic brochures on political topics, a fortnightly news bulletin and organizational reports for Congresses.

The Presidium in Bucharest in 1975 issued a declaration on the topical 30th anniversary of the United Nations, noting that the IOJ "always fully supported the principles in the interest of strengthening peace and international cooperation".[37] The Presidium also issued a declaration "On the Historic Victory of the Vietnamese People" as well as a declaration "Against Oppression in Chile". On the political side of the Presidium was an appointment with President Nicolae Ceauşescu. Organizationally, the most important decision of the Presidium was that the 8th IOJ Congress would take place in Helsinki (Finland) in September 1976.

The choice of Helsinki as the site of the next Congress was logical, given the CSCE, which was originally a Soviet initiative, but was later taken up and organized by Finland in the early 1970s and successfully concluded in 1975 with a historical summit signing the "Helsinki Accords". The IOJ was a vociferous supporter of this political process, manifested on all occasions.

Finland also had a good record of co-operation with the IOJ: in 1950 it had hosted the 3rd IOJ Congress – after Brussels and Paris turned out to be politically impossible – and in 1956 it provided the site for the worldwide meeting of journalists. It had an IOJ member (YLL), which did not, however, represent the whole political spectrum but mainly communists – the same as the member in France. In this respect it was essential that the IOJ was able to broaden its base in Finland right across the political spectrum and this was made through the nationally representative trade union and professional association of radio and television journalists, the RTTL.[38]

---

37 *Journalists' Affairs* 20–21/1975; *DJ* 12/1975.

38 Its earlier President was Olavi Laine, since the late 1960s at the Finnish Broadcasting Company (YLE) and before that foreign news editor in the leading communist newspaper. He also belonged to the IOJ member union YLL and in that capacity held the position of an IOJ

After signing an agreement on co-operation with the IOJ in May 1974, the RTTL representative attended the Presidium in Ulan Bator and the whole RTTL leadership visited the IOJ Secretariat in Prague in December 1974, meeting there both Secretary General Kubka, new Treasurer Kìrály and President Hermann. In this way the RTTL became an active observer at the IOJ, leading in May 1975 its delegation back to Finland – Zagladin and Bureš attending a colloquium "Journalists and Détente" at the University of Tampere[39] and meeting Finland's Prime Minister and Minister of Foreign Affairs.

These discussions (Figure 5.11) paved the way for Finland to become the site of the 8th Congress. Once the Final Act of Helsinki was signed at the CSCE Summit on 1 August 1975, the YLL, the RTTL in co-operation with the main trade union of press journalists in Finland (SSL, a member of the IFJ) formed a broadly representative local organizing committee for the Congress. The preparations were officially launched in Helsinki in November 1975 with an IOJ delegation: Jiří Kubka, Oleg Zagladin and Oldřich Bureš from the Prague Secretariat as well as Alexander Losev, the Vice-President of the Union of Journalists of the USSR from Moscow. The delegation met not only the local organizing committee but also the Prime Minister, the Mayor of Helsinki, the

Figure 5.11 Bridgebuilding in Finland: The RTTL hosted the colleagues from the IOJ Secretariat in Prague several times after 1974. Here at a table outdoors on the right: RTTL leaders Reino Paasilinna, Esko Seppänen and Arne Wessberg talking to Oldřich Bureš. On the left: Eero Toukkari talking to Oleg Zagladin. In the middle: Sirkka Närhinen and Unto Miettinen. (Photo: RTTL)

Vice-President from 1962 to 1971 (see Figure 4.8 in Chapter 4). The RTTL leadership in the 1970s represented first and foremost professional and trade union interests, with political affiliations of mainly Social Democrats and Communists. The Secretary General of the RTTL at the time was Esko Seppänen, who later became a leftist member of both the Finnish Parliament and the European Parliament.

39 See *Journalists and Détente* (1975).

Director-General of the Finnish Broadcasting Company (YLE) and the secretaries of the Central Organization of the Finnish Trade Unions (SAK).

The overall development of the IOJ from the mid-1960s to the mid-1970s was growth and consolidation. The positive development was a consequence of three main trends. Firstly, the Soviet-inspired attempts to dispel the Cold War tension in Europe, with the Finnish-led CSCE diplomacy for détente, encouraged journalists' associations to co-operate across the East-West divide and pushed the IFJ to gradually abandon its hard line of separatism and anti-communism. Secondly, the developing countries found the socialist community – despite the rift with China – as a natural ally in geopolitical platforms, while at the same time the Third World was gathering its own forces around the Non-Aligned Movement (NAM). Thirdly, the IOJ was proactive in capitalizing on these trends, with the political and material assistance of its European member unions in the socialist countries.

CHAPTER 6
KEEPING PACE WITH A NEW WORLD ORDER 1976–80

The late 1970s was a period when the fresh détente and decolonization of the previous decade encouraged structural changes on a global scale, as highlighted by the UN Declaration on the New International Economic Order. The idea of a New World Order became a powerful paradigm inspiring those who aimed at overcoming East-West contradictions and North-South inequalities.

Détente with the Final Act of Helsinki prevailed, while the Cold War continued as the geopolitical context. After the Vietnam War, a conflict had erupted in Indo-China with the new Khmer Rouge regime in Cambodia fighting against Vietnam from 1975 to 1979 with the support of China.

In China Mao Tse-tung died in 1976, heralding the start of a new era with Deng Xiaoping leading the country towards a market economy.

In 1976 the Non-Aligned Movement (NAM) generated the idea of a New International Information Order parallel to the New International Economic Order. UNESCO played a central role in global media policies.

In 1979 an Islamic Revolution overthrew the Persian monarchy in Iran, turning the USA from an ally into an enemy. A war broke out between Iran and Iraq in 1980 lasting until 1988.

The superpower conflict escalated to a new wave of the Cold War after the USA decided in 1979 to deploy medium-range missiles in Western Europe.

The Soviet Union invaded Afghanistan at the end of 1979, leading to war between the USSR and the Islamic resistance supported by the USA. The cunning American strategy was to make Afghanistan into the Vietnam of the Soviet Union.

In Poland, problems in the national economy led to unrest and in 1980 gave rise to the independent trade union movement Solidarity in opposition to the government and the Communist Party.

For the IOJ the international system was to change fundamentally in its favour for the first time since the outbreak of the Cold War in the late 1940s. The IOJ tried to keep pace with the global changes, emphatically supported by the Soviet foreign policy of the time.

The present chapter covers the IOJ in the late 1970s, as manifest in the Congress of 1976 and the following three statutory meetings in 1977–79 as well as in historical developments at UNESCO.

CELEBRATING DÉTENTE IN HELSINKI AND PARIS 1976–77

The **8th IOJ Congress in Helsinki** on 21–23 **September 1976** was more than a regular assembly of the supreme body convened five years after the previous Congress; this time it was also the 30th anniversary, and held moreover in the city and the very conference centre which only a year ago had hosted the Helsinki Summit of the CSCE (Figure 6.1). This historical landmark stood as a confirmation of the international order created after World War II, helping the political atmosphere of East-West relations to be in reasonably good shape and even inspiring a view that this was the beginning of the end of the Cold War. Under these circumstances the Congress in the Finlandia Hall in 1976 was a shining manifestation of the IOJ as an advocate of détente in accordance with the political momentum of the day.

Figure 6.1 The Finlandia Hall: the site of the 8th IOJ Congress. (Photo: IOJ)

The preparations for the Congress had started in 1975, when committees were established in both Helsinki and Prague. The IOJ Secretariat set up separate working groups to prepare the Congress documents, the financial matters and the organizational questions. The Finnish committee appointed a General Secretary to coordinate the Congress preparations.[1] In early 1976 the Finn-

1 This task was assigned to Esko Seppänen, former General Secretary of the RTTL, since 1974 working as an economics journalist at YLE. The Finnish preparatory committee of three parties included in 1976: YLL President Paavo Ruonaniemi and Secretary Markku Vainio, RTTL President Seppo Heikki Salonen and General Secretary Eero Toukkari, SSL President Antero Laine. *The Democratic Journalist* (*DJ*) devoted most of its issue 9/1976 to articles on the Finnish mass media by Laine, Salonen and Toukkari among others.

ish preparatory committee visited the IOJ Secretariat, and on this occasion the President of the main Union of Journalists in Finland (SSL), Antero Laine, announced his designation as an observer at the IOJ.[2] Accordingly, the IOJ had an IFJ member union as a working partner, although the SSL did not become a formal IOJ member as double membership was not allowed by the IFJ.

The Congress report[3] states that there were 132 delegates from 65 member unions and 111 observers, guests and members of the Secretariat (Figure 6.2). Among the guests were leading officers of regional federations from Africa, the Arab world and Latin America. In addition, 110 journalists were accredited to cover the Congress. In terms of numbers it was close to Havana and Berlin but did not surpass their record numbers. A historical step forward was that the IOJ Congress was now attended for the first time by observers from the IFJ; this was four months after an IOJ delegation had for the first time attended the IFJ Congress in Vienna. The Helsinki Congress was also attended by some IFJ Western member unions, notably from the other Nordic countries and the UK. Moreover, one of the Finnish hosts was the IFJ member SSL, whose President, Antero Laine, was actually sitting in the Congress Presidium.

Figure 6.2 Newly elected President Kaarle Nordenstreng addressing the Congress in Helsinki in September 1976, behind him Saad Qassim Hammoudi, Vice-President from Iraq, next to him Vice-Presidents Viktor Afanasiev from the USSR, Harri Czepuck from the GDR and Luis Suarez from Mexico; last on the right Secretary General Jiří Kubka. (Photo from *The Democratic Journalist* 12/1976)

The high profile of the Congress was ensured by messages received from several heads of state, beginning with Finland's President Urho Kekkonen and

2 *Journalists' Affairs* 3/1976.

3 *8th Congress* (1976). Summary of the proceedings and several photos of Congress participants were also published in *DJ* 12/1976.

the Soviet Communist Party General Secretary Leonid Brezhnev and continuing with leaders of most European socialist countries, of several Middle Eastern countries as well as of Socialist Vietnam. The opening of the Congress was addressed by Finland's Minister of Foreign Affairs Kalevi Sorsa and a message from UNESCO's Director-General A.M. M'Bow was read out by the Director of the Communication Sector Gunnar Naesselund. The World Peace Council (based in Helsinki) announced that its highest medal of honour was to be granted to the IOJ. On the last day of the Congress President Kekkonen received a delegation of the newly elected Presidium (Figure 6.3).

Figure 6.3 The President of Finland, Dr Urho Kekkonen, received a delegation of the IOJ Presidium in the presidential palace on the last day of the Congress. The President, seen from behind on the left, has just received a gift from Soviet Vice-President Afanasiev, second on the right, next to IOJ President Nordenstreng. In the middle Ernesto Vera from Cuba, Salah Hafez from Egypt and Cheick Mouctary Diarra from Mali. On the left behind the President: Tsend Namsrai from Mongolia. (Photo: Lehtikuva)

The Congress admitted 11 new member unions, mostly from Latin America but also from Congo and Kuwait.[4] Among these was the Chilean Committee of the IOJ – "journalists associated in the fight against the junta" – replacing the earlier Colegio de Periodistas de Chile, which was closed down by the military regime. The number of countries in which the IOJ had members was now 109. As most of these countries already had members, this figure is practically the same as ten years earlier (see Appendix 4).

The Congress elected a new Presidium and Executive Committee, unanimously as usual, but naturally after considerable lobbying (see Nor-

4 *8th Congress* (1977, pp. 11–12). Also in *DJ* 12/1976.

denstreng's testimony in Part Two). The Presidium was expanded from 14 to 22 members by adding Vice-Presidents from Somalia, Puerto Rico, Venezuela, Mali, Guinea, France, Iraq, Sri Lanka and Mexico (see Appendix 2). Other Vice-Presidents continued with partly changing names; only Peru was dropped from the list. Kaarle Nordenstreng was elected President, Jiři Kubka continued as Secretary General and András Király was confirmed as Treasurer. In addition, former President Jean-Maurice Hermann was elected Honorary President. With the Bulgarian and Romanian chairmen of the Social and Professional Commissions, the Presidium had 25 members.

The first among formally equal Vice-Presidents was Viktor G. Afanasiev, President of the USSR Union of Journalists – by far the largest of the IOJ members – appointed to this position only a few months earlier, when he became Editor-in-Chief of *Pravda* and also a member of the Central Committee of the Soviet Communist Party. He succeeded Michail Zimyanin, who had held these positions since 1966 and who was now promoted to the Secretariat of the Party. Afanasiev was a philosopher from the Soviet Academy of Sciences and he assumed the top position in Soviet journalism with an unusual profile and as an advocate of détente.

The Executive Committee was composed of the Presidium plus about 30 members coming from all member unions except those which already had a place in the Presidium. By and large the 50+ members of the statutory bodies were divided between (1) the socialist countries of central and eastern Europe, (2) the countries of western Europe, North America, Japan and (3) the developing countries of the Third World as follows: "East" 7, "West" 6, and "South" 40. Although this is just a simple count, it demonstrates the overwhelming majority of the voices of the Global South in the IOJ membership. At the same time that the "West" had a very thin representation – Finland 2, France 2, USA 1 and Japan 1 – while the "East" with the USSR, Poland, the GDR, Czechoslovakia, Hungary, Bulgaria and Romania provided a massive potential with large unions. The "South" was again abundant in numbers but most of them represented relatively small and poorly resourced unions.

It was obvious to all at this Congress, as it had been since the 3rd Congress in 1950, that the IOJ was dominated by the Soviet Union of Journalists and its sister unions in the "East" – seen as sources of solidarity towards the member unions in the "South". This was demonstrated by the travel arrangements: most participants from outside Europe were flown by Aeroflot to Moscow and transported further to Helsinki by a Soviet train – the tickets provided either by the Soviet Union of Journalists or the IOJ – paid for mostly in rubles and other "soft currencies". No documentation survives of these finances but it is obvious that the main sources were the Soviet Union of Journalists and the IOJ with its Lottery Fund raising money from several socialist countries. An increasingly important source of funding, especially for the hard currency (US dollars), was the IOJ commercial enterprises in Czechoslovakia and Hungary.

The accommodation of all delegates at the Hotel Inter-Continental in Helsinki (adjacent to the Finlandia Hall) and the rent of the conference premises were paid for by the IOJ and totalled 240,000 Finnmarks of the day, corresponding to 172,000 Euros in 2017.[5] The travel costs in soft currencies cannot be reliably converted into Euros of today, but they surely represent at least the same level as the local expenses in Finland.

Accordingly, it can be estimated that the Congress meant an investment of about 350,000 Euros at today's prices for the IOJ and its closest partners in the socialist countries. The earlier congresses and other statutory meetings were likewise paid for mostly by the IOJ and its socialist partners, although using less hard currency than in Helsinki. A usually expensive component of the conference costs was easy for the IOJ to cover after Havana, as one of its first commercial enterprises in Czechoslovakia was an interpreting agency with both personnel and equipment for simultaneous interpreting in all IOJ languages (Czech, English, French, Russian and Spanish).

The substance of the Congress was reflected in the reports of the Secretary General and the permanent Commissions.[6] The proceedings are summarized the Congress report:

> Fifty-six speakers took part in the general discussion. Their addresses dealt with the most important professional, ethical and social questions of mass communication of today and the tasks of journalists in efforts to extend international solidarity, to reduce international tension, in the fight against imperialism, racism, apartheid, colonialism, neo-colonialism and Zionism, for the freedom of journalists and political prisoners in Chile, Argentina, South Africa, Namibia and in other countries...[7]

The main Congress resolution[8], called the "Orientation Document", begins on an optimistic note and ends with a positive appeal:

> The Congress noted with satisfaction a change in relation of forces in favour of peace, democracy, national liberation and independence, and socialism. [...]

Let us do everything we can to make information truly serve the interests of peoples struggling on the basis of their own experience so that war, racism and colonialist oppression will never again disgrace mankind.

---

5 Personal communication with Esko Seppänen, December 2017.
6 *8th Congress* (1976, pp. 17–85).
7 Ibid., p. 12. Also in *Journalists' Affairs* 19–21/1976.
8 *8th Congress* (1976, pp. 86–95). Also in *DJ* 12/1976.

The bulk of the text has a much sharper tone:

> Progressive journalists of the world have resolutely resisted and continue to resist imperialist, colonialist, neo-colonialist policy, racism and fascism. Through their truthful and objective information they helped weaken the positions of imperialism, which has lost the initiative on the international scene; they positively influenced public opinion, which understands clearly that imperialism can no longer subordinate to its will the future of peoples. [...]
>
> Colonialism broke down. The Congress enthusiastically greets the historic victories of the Vietnamese people, as well as the victories of the peoples of Laos and Cambodia. The defeat of imperialist plans in Indochina demonstrated clearly the heroic fight of peoples, supported by the solidarity of all progressive forces of the world...

The document also refers to "the glorious fight for freedom of the Korean people against imperialist intrigues" and to the struggles of the Palestinian and Lebanese people, the Cypriot people and the African peoples in newly independent colonies of Portugal, especially Angola, as well as the struggles for liberation in South Africa, Namibia and Zimbabwe. In Latin America, the document notes that "American imperialism has suffered a defeat in its attempts to blockade Cuba", while "it is necessary to recall the persecution of democratic journalists in Chile, the majority of whom continue to suffer in the prisons of the fascist junta, and the repression against journalists in other Latin American countries", including Argentina and Brazil, and "the brutal suppression of aspirations for freedom and independence of the peoples of Panama, Puerto Rico and others".

The Orientation Document welcomes the overall positive development for détente in Europe and also the consolidation of regional federations of journalists in Africa, the Arab world and most recently in Latin America, where FELAP was founded in June 1976. Still, the general approach of the document follows more or less the same political line as the previous Congresses and cannot be distinguished as an historical turning point from confrontation to détente. The final position of the Congress is written in the customary jargon with little consistency and somewhat contradictory advice for the future.

A synthesis of the IOJ's standing in the world at the time of the 8th Congress was given by the newly elected President in his closing address.[9] He singled out two overall perspectives characterizing the contemporary international arena: firstly détente and secondly "the struggle against colonialism and other forms of unjust and unequal social order – in economic as well as cultural-informational spheres". He referred to the movement of Non-

9 *DJ* 1–2/1977. The address is presented there as an article by Nordenstreng entitled "Historical tendencies are on our side".

Aligned countries "as an ever more significant force contributing to a new and more democratic world order – democratic not only in the theory of classic liberalism but in actual practice, for the benefit of the majority of the people".

Indeed, if the CSCE was the cornerstone of détente in the first half of the 1970s, it was the **Non-Aligned Movement** (NAM) that was the driving force for the decolonization of information in the second half of the 1970s. The idea of a New International Information Order (NIIO) emerged from the NAM Symposium on Information in Tunis in April 1976 and was confirmed as a political goal by the NAM Summit in Colombo in August 1976.[10] This was a most welcome concept for the IOJ which immediately began to promote it in *The Democratic Journalist*[11] and in separate publications[12].

A parallel political process in line with the IOJ's strategic line took place at **UNESCO,** which already in 1972 had approved a Soviet initiative to prepare a draft declaration "concerning the fundamental principles governing the use of the mass information media with a view to strengthening peace and international understanding and combating war propaganda, racialism and apartheid".[13] This was supposed to be an intergovernmental instrument – but in full accordance with the IOJ proposal to all European journalist organizations in 1972 to prepare a convention on professional ethics. The draft declaration was to have been adopted by the General Conference of UNESCO in Nairobi in October 1976, but after encountering vociferous criticism from the Western political and commercial circles it was shelved for another two years. The IOJ delegation at the Conference spoke in favour of its adoption.[14]

The first IOJ statutory body meeting after Helsinki was the **Presidium in Paris** on 18–19 **November 1977** (Figure 6.4). Paris was already chosen as

---

10 See Nordenstreng (2011). This is the testimony of a scholar who was personally involved in the process. The New International Information Order (NIIO) or New International Information and Communication Order (NIICO) later became known as the New World Information and Communication Order (NWICO). The IOJ used mostly NIICO.

11 The first issue devoted to it was *DJ* 4/1977, with introductory articles by Kaarle Nordenstreng & Tapio Varis (University of Tampere) and Gunnar Naesselund (UNESCO). It also included a long article by Professor Herbert Schiller (University of California, San Diego), on the doctrine of free flow of information as an American instrument of communication domination. Furthermore, it published the New Delhi Declaration of June 1976, establishing the Non-Aligned Pool of News Agencies (NANAP), and the key statement on NIIO of the Colombo Summit of August 1976. *DJ* 5/1977 continued to cover the topic with articles by authors from Yugoslavia, Singapore and India.

12 *Towards a New...* (1976); *Current Views...* (1977).

13 See *Historical Background...* (1982). Also Nordenstreng (1984, pp. 82–86).

14 The statement by the IOJ President is reproduced in *Journalists' Affairs* 22–24/1976. Also in *Reflexions Around UNESCO* (1979, pp. 5–11).

Figure 6.4 The IOJ Presidium in Paris in November 1977. From the left: Honorary President Hermann, Secretary for Europe Zagladin, President Nordenstreng, Secretary General Kubka and hosting Vice-President Gatinot. (Photo from *The Democratic Journalist* 12/1977 which also includes a photo supplement on France today and reviews on the media and journalists in France as well as Honorary President Hermann's article on the international ethics of journalists)

the venue of this Presidium in Bucharest in 1975 as it was competing with Helsinki to host the Congress itself. The Presidium provided a platform for the leadership to take a fresh look at the developments – both in the IOJ and the world at large – one year after the Congress. The Secretary General reviewed the advances of communication technology, the historical epochs of journalism and the recent IOJ activities, while the Vice-Presidents discussed topical issues such as press concentration seen from France and colonization of information seen from Cuba.[15]

The President's presentation was an overview of "Journalists and détente", especially the role and responsibility of journalists in both maintaining and overcoming Cold War contradictions. He quoted recent appeals of journalist meetings such as the Baltic Peace Days, which had recommended including the principles of the Helsinki Accords in the codes of ethics "voluntarily adopted by journalist unions, specifying thereby what is meant in practice by responsible journalism in the spirit of the Conference of Security and Co-operation in Europe (CSCE)". He noticed that the IOJ naturally supports such initiatives, but he also pointed out that "we are well aware of the difficulties involved – and they are theoretical as well as political". Therefore, initiatives such as the UNESCO draft declaration "do have our support" since "at issue here is not a 'code' for journalists but a statement of some widely-accepted principles and

15 Key speeches are published in *DJ* 2/1978. All presentations are included in their original languages in *Presidium de l'OIJ* (1978).

value positions which, according to our understanding, should be defended in any case by all responsible journalists".[16]

President Nordenstreng noted that "it is with perfect agreement with both Western and Eastern doctrines of journalism that the public is provided with 'an ever wider knowledge' about other countries, as set forth in the Helsinki Final Act", and he went on to repeat what he had addressed to the USSR Union of Journalists Congress earlier in 1977:

> In general, objective information, as it accumulates in the consciousness of the masses, will always in the final analysis serve the interest of progressive forces and be directed against those interests which attempt to resist historical tendencies. Hence an essential prerequisite for the firm progress of the peace movement and other democratic forces is a public that is adequately informed – not only about daily events but also and above all about the so-called background; that is social, economic and political conditions and structures which only makes it possible to understand what happens on the surface and how to react properly. In this respect the task of a journalist is the same as that of a scientist: to discover objective reality and to mediate a true picture of the world to one's contemporaries.
>
> Philosophically speaking, such a search for truth is based on a materialist theory of knowledge. We know that Lenin himself made a great contribution to this theory. And he also demonstrated by his own example that a practical journalist, in order to firmly serve the interests of the working people, has to be a philosopher.[17]

Finally the President highlighted the draft Convention on the principles of relations between European journalists prepared by the IOJ and recently conveyed to the IFJ, recommending the endorsement of "those principles that are supposed to lay the foundation today for inter-organizational relations [...] to strengthen the principles of peaceful co-existence in the field of journalism". He applauded the decade-old tradition of European meetings in Italy, hosted by the FNSI, and the cordial spirit of the recent meeting on Capri, indicating that "blocs indeed have begun to melt away from the map of Europe – if not yet in the military sense of the term, then at least politically". Like President Hermann after the Havana Congress in 1971, he pointed out: "We are not a bloc organization but a broad-based framework for co-operation among various forces whose interests are not confined to

---

16 *Presidium de l'OIJ* (1978), pp. 10–22. Also in *DJ* 2/1978.

17 *Presidium de l'OIJ* (1978, p. 19). *DJ* 2/1978. Obviously this reference was inspired not only by the platform – the Kremlin Congress Palace – but also by the background of the newly elected President of the USSR Union of Journalists, Viktor Afanasiev, the philosopher. More on the address and the USSR Congress in *Journalist' Affairs* 5–7/1977.

Figure 6.5 The Secretariat in Prague was firmly settled in *Pařížská* 9, the grand building of the Czechoslovak Union of Journalists which had at street level a popular bar-restaurant for journalists *Klub Novinářů*. The host union had its offices on the first floor, while the IOJ occupied the upper floors. The Secretary General's office was in the corner with an enclosed balcony and next to it was the Protocol Department taking care of travel arrangements, etc. The secretaries had their offices in this building as did the departments for publications and finances. However, the space in Pařížská could no longer accommodate the growing number of staff following the expanding activities in the 1970s. Therefore other premises were acquired in Prague for conference and translation services and other commercial companies (see Appendix 20).

the journalists' profession as such but also to peace, democracy and overall social progress".

The Presidium announced the International Journalists' Prize for the Italian FNSI and for two journalists: Gabriel Garcia Marquez from Colombia and Helso Winnie Ndadi from Namibia. In a separate ceremony the IOJ was awarded the Order of Friendship by the Socialist Republic of Vietnam "for the help it gave to the Vietnamese people in the period of struggle against American aggression, for national regeneration and the construction of socialism". At the same time, the Honorary Order of Vietnam was presented to Honorary President Hermann and Secretary General Kubka.

The secretaries were sent by respective member unions: from the USSR for Europe, from the GDR for Africa and Asia, from Cuba for Latin America, from Poland for international organizations and from Romania for professional and social matters, including the Professional Commission. The Soviet Secretary Zagladin was replaced after Paris by Boris Sakharov (former secretary of the USSR Union of Journalists). The German Secretary Helmut Bräuer was replaced after Helsinki by Hans Treffkorn (former director of the Berlin School). The Cuban Secretary was Juan Francisco Alvarez, the Polish Secretary was Mieczyslav Kieta, replaced later by Sergiusz Klaczkow, and the Romanian Secretary was Aurelian Nestor.

Each Secretary had at least one local assistant and they had at their disposal a translation service established as an IOJ subsidiary company also selling its services to outsiders. In addition, there was the Editorial Department composed of Czechoslovak staff as well as the Documentation and Information Ser-

Figure 6.6 The Hungarian based IOJ enterprise INTERPRESS in Budapest published in 1976 *Africa Mass Media*, a professional magazine in English and French. In 1977 INTERPRESS issued *Interpress Magazin* in English, a general interest annual reader of over 140 pages with a lot on pictorial material and some advertising, while a monthly popular magazine was published in Hungarian (like the one in Czech) in 150,000 copies. *Interpressgraphic*, addressed to photographers and graphic designers had started already in 1969 and grown by 1977 to a glossy quarterly magazine of nearly 200 pages with an advertising supplement of 30 pages. It was published mainly in English with sections in Russian, French, German and Spanish.

vice (see Slavík's recollections in Part Two). The Secretariat kept in touch with the member organizations not only by normal mail and periodical publications but also by telex with topical information bulletins in French (informations d'actualité) once or twice a week – 85 bulletins in 1976 and 101 in 1977. An extension of the Secretariat was the economic branch of commercial enterprises which, apart from the translation service, mainly served outside customers thereby increasing the revenue for the IOJ.

An overview of **activities in 1976–80** is provided in Appendix 5. It shows that the number of events remained less than 20 per year until 1977, but after that it burgeoned to be two or three times as many every year. The scale of activities grew dramatically, no doubt reflecting the far-ranging interests of the growing membership and also the increasing resources for the activities.

GLOBAL OUTREACH WITH UNESCO, MEXICO AND VIETNAM 1978–80

The list in Appendix 5 demonstrates how the IOJ activities became increasingly global, covering both political and professional topics such as these: the 3rd IOJ/UNESCO Colloquy in November 1977 hosted in Baghdad by the Iraqi Union of Journalists and dedicated to "Decolonization of information and the role of mass media in the development of a new international economic order",[18] the Conference of Solidarity with African and Arab People against Imperialism convened in Ethiopia in September 1978, as well as the 2nd FELAP Congress in Venezuela[19] and the international seminar by the USSR National Commission for UNESCO in Uzbekistan[20], both in 1979.

From an organizational point of view the most significant event during this period took place in Paris just five months after the Presidium: **UNESCO consultation with international and regional organizations of journalists** on 17–19 **April 1978** (Figure 6.7). Those invited were the IOJ, the IFJ, the International Catholic Union of the Press (UCIP based in Geneva) and four regional organizations: the Union of African Journalists (UAJ based in Egypt), the Federation of Arab Journalists (FAJ based in Iraq), the Federation of Latin American Journalists (FELAP based in Mexico) and the Confederation of ASEAN Journalists (CAJ based in Indonesia). These can all be classified as professional associations, mainly representing practising journalists and, apart from the IFJ, also leading editors in the socialist and developing countries.

18 *DJ* 2/1978.
19 *Journalists' Affairs* 19–20/1979.
20 *DJ* 12/1979.

Figure 6.7 The Consultative Meeting of international and regional organizations of journalists in Paris, April 1978. From the right: UNESCO host Hifzi Topuz, IFJ General Secretary Theo Bogaerts, UCIP Administrative Secretary Marcel Furic, IOJ Secretary General Kubka, President Nordenstreng, Secretary for Africa and Asia Treffkorn, CAJ Executive Secretary D.M. Sunardi, IOJ Secretary for Latin America Juan Alvarez, FELAP Secretary Hernan Uribe and Concelor Ibar Aibar. The African and Arab representatives of the UAJ and FAJ were absent. (Photo: UNESCO)

These organizations were not associated with the Western editors and publishers with their International Press Institute (IPI), the International Federation of Newspaper Publishers (FIEJ, later WAN and IFRA) and the Inter-American Press Association (IAPA). Those had since 1974 been mounting an opposition to UNESCO's communication policies, spearheaded by the World Press Freedom Committee (WPFC based in the USA), while the professional journalists' organizations were behind UNESCO and its support for the NAM-initiated New International Information Order (NIIO).[21] Actually the composition of the Paris group was dominated by the IOJ as it had fraternal relations and co-operation agreements with three of the four regional organizations (FELAP, FAJ and UAJ).

The meeting in UNESCO proved very successful: the participants agreed not only on exchange of information but on seeking possible joint actions in publications, on solidarity in support of persecuted journalists as well as on defining ethical principles for the journalistic profession. They wrote a joint letter to the Director-General and President of the Executive Board of UNESCO, expressing their willingness "for collaboration not only among the journalists' organizations themselves but also between them and Unesco".[22] They agreed to continue meeting, counting on UNESCO's travel support (one delegate per organization, as to this meeting). What followed was a series of ten meetings until 1990, held basically once a year, with four of the annual meetings even held in two separate places – all hosted by different partners in

21 Of the professional organizations, least firmly behind UNESCO was the IFJ. It even first joined the WPFC but later left when the publishers' lobbies became increasingly aggressive towards UNESCO and more openly aligned with the US and UK governments.

22 The letter is reproduced in Nordenstreng et al. (2016, pp. 205–206).

turn.[23] UNESCO only served as a facilitator, while the partners spontaneously agreed to have a Steering Committee composed of the IOJ, the IFJ and one of the regionals in turn. In practice, the main driving force was the IOJ and its President. The first joint publication was a booklet on the organizations involved, their histories, objectives, activities and statutes, issued in French and published by the IOJ in 1980. Other joint publications were to come later as shown in Chapter 8.

Appendix 5 shows that there was already a consultation at UNESCO in late 1977 involving the IOJ and the IFJ regarding the draft declaration tabled in Nairobi 13 months earlier. Actually intensive consultation on further drafting of the declaration had been ongoing at UNESCO since June 1977, when a team of three consultants was recruited to represent various geographic-political orientations – in practice the "three worlds" of East, West and South.[24] One of these consultants was the IOJ President who, like the other two (a British veteran journalist and a Peruvian diplomat), acted in a personal capacity without formally representing governments or organizations. Several rounds of consultations, on governmental as well as non-governmental level, finally led to a compromise formulation which was forwarded as a proposal by the Director-General to the next UNESCO General Conference.[25] After considerable diplomatic efforts it was approved by acclamation in November 1978.[26]

The consensus on the Mass Media Declaration of UNESCO was a landmark of détente, showing how highly controversial political issues can be resolved through negotiation. In the IOJ it was celebrated as an historical victory for its long-term policies, demonstrating how the IOJ was now an integral part of the progressive mainstream of international politics, whereas less than a decade ago it was still deprived of an affiliation with UNESCO and the UN. For UNESCO and its Director-General Amadou Mahtar M'Bow of Senegal – the first African at the top of a UN agency – the Declaration was a major triumph, both of diplomacy and of UNESCO's communication policies promoting a global balance and responsible journalism. Moreover, the political process of the Declaration had led to two other initiatives which were part of the Nairobi compromise two years earlier and which materialized in the following two years: the International Programme for the Development of Communication (IPDC) and the

23 The meetings are summarized in Nordenstreng et al. (2016, pp. 159–162), with their reports reproduced in an extensive Appendix (pp. 204–249).

24 See Nordenstreng (1984, pp. 113–114).

25 Ibid., pp. 115–122. Also in *Historical Background* (1979).

26 The complete declaration is available at http://portal.unesco.org/en/ev.php-URL_ID=13176&URL_DO=DO_TOPIC&URL_SECTION=201.html. The IOJ address at the 20th General Conference of UNESCO is published in *Journalists' Affairs* 1–2/1979.

International Commission for the Study of Communication Problems (MacBride Commission).

These developments at UNESCO should be seen against the **historical movement towards a new world order** – both in international relations overall and communication in particular. It was enthusiastically welcomed by those, including the IOJ membership, whose interests were at odds with the western-dominated existing order, while for those who had vested interests in the old order it was "a bad idea that refuses to die".[27] The forces and ideas involved should be seen as successive stages in an "information war" affecting all actors in international communication: (1) decolonization offensive by the South in the early 1970s, (2) counterattack by Western media corporations in the mid-1970s, (3) truce in the late 1970s, (4) new Western public-private offensive in the 1980s, and (5) pacification under globalization in the 1990s.[28]

The UNESCO developments in the late 1970s were outcomes of the truce for which the way was paved by détente. It was at this stage that the NAM launched its initiative for NIIO. Furthermore, the UN General Assembly passed a consensus resolution on "International relations in the sphere of information and mass communications" in December 1978, "recalling" the Mass Media Declaration just approved at UNESCO, "reaffirming the manifest need to change the dependent status of the developing countries in the sphere of information and communication" and "taking note of the decisions and recommendations on the question of information" recently taken by the NAM summit in Colombo as well as "recalling" the earlier UN Declaration on Programme of Action on the Establishment of a New International Economic Order.[29] This outspoken statement of the most representative platform of the international community confirmed the aspirations "to establish a new, more just and better balanced world information and communication order".

It was under these global perspectives that the IOJ convened the next **Presidium in Mexico City in November 1978** (Figure 6.8). The local host was Vice-President Luis Suarez of the Union of Democratic Journalists in Mexico. The President of the Republic of Mexico, Dr. José Lopez Portillo, sent a long message to the opening session, and five days later he had a friendly discussion with the Presidium members in his office. Before that the Presidium delegates and Secretariat staff had enjoyed the govern-

27 Nordenstreng (1984, p. 5). An overview is presented in its first chapter entitled "The context: A movement towards a new international order", pp. 3–77.

28 See Nordenstreng (2010) and Nordenstreng (2016).

29 The UN resolution 33/115B is available at http://www.un.org/documents/ga/res/33/ares33r115.pdf.

Figure 6.8 The Presidium in Mexico City on 9–11 November 1978. The ceremonial opening took place in the great hall of the National Anthropological Museum, while the sessions were held in the Hotel Presidente, Zona Rosa. At the table from the left: hosting Vice-President Suarez, President Nordenstreng and Secretary General Kubka. (Photo and cuttings from *The Democratic Journalist* 2/1979)

ment's hospitality on a two-day visit to the new tourist resort of Ixtapa on the Pacific Ocean.[30]

This Presidium – like Paris a year before – was attended by most of the Presidium members elected in Helsinki, including the German, Russian and Mongolian Vice-Presidents in person, while several others sent a representative. Latin American Vice Presidents from Cuba, Puerto Rico and Venezuela were naturally present as were observers from several other Latin American member unions and their regional federation FELAP. The Presidium welcomed four new IOJ members – the National Syndicate of the Editors of the Mexican Press, the journalist unions of Jamaica, Ethiopia and Western Sahara – and the Syndicate of Journalists of Portugal as an associate member.[31]

30 A swim in the Pacific was a refreshing contrast to politically flavoured talks in Mexico City. It was a special opportunity for Viktor Afanasiev – a record swimmer and a champion Russian water skiier.

31 A summary report is provided in a special issue of *Journalists' Affairs* (December 1978), including a press communique and the agreements signed by the IOJ with FELAP and ILET (Latin American Institute of Translational Studies). See also *DJ* 2/1979, which covers an overview with the Presidium and excerpts from speeches by the Secretary General, the Vice-Presidents from Cuba and Guinea, and the General Secretary of the Vietnam Journalists Association.

The content of the Presidium followed up the line adopted in Helsinki and Paris, with support for détente – now to be extended from Europe to all continents – and to the topics of the Mass Media Declaration, while expressing concern about the continuation of the arms race with a recent decision of the US Government to further develop the neutron bomb. Attention was paid to media concentration and transnational corporations as well as to the persecution of democratic journalists notably in Latin America. The Presidium also pointed out the necessity to render assistance to developing countries in setting up their own systems of mass communication and education of journalists. Furthermore, this time there was a new element in emphasizing the need to respect the sovereignty and laws of individual states, with a remark that "we cannot accept for the sacred accord on human rights to become an object of disinformation and for it to be misused for the violation of the principles of sovereignty and non-interference into the internal affairs of states".[32]

In his conclusions the President noted that the objective conditions discussed in the proceedings imposed new demands upon progressive forces which should both increase their activities and achieve better co-ordination and unity. He urged them "to develop systematic and scientifically-based planning of IOJ positions and activities" and listed several concrete steps to be taken: (1) to establish an IOJ coordination centre for the training of journalists in developing countries, (2) to prepare a plan for an IOJ institute of research and documentation, (3) to implement the recently prepared development plan for publications, including the editorial policy of *The Democratic Journalist*, (4) to develop new ways and means of increasing IOJ participation in various regions of the world, including regional centres whenever feasible, (5) to use the UNESCO-initiated co-operation between international and regional organizations as the main institutional link with the IFJ, and (6) to develop co-operation with the Non-Aligned countries in the field of information.[33]

This was the first time that an IOJ statutory body proclaimed its decisions in a list of operative conclusions. It had been customary to issue a detailed report of the Secretary General covering all topics and regions of the world, yet without a clear set of concrete actions. Separate resolutions had normally been passed only on special occasions. In Mexico City the Secretary General's report followed the old format, while it also included the elements

32 From the press communique published in *Journalists' Affairs* special issue (December 1978, p. 14). The same point is slightly reformulated in the editorial overview in *DJ* 2/1979.

33 This list, composed as an elaborate resolution in the UN style, is not included in the reports of *Journalists' Affairs* and *DJ*. It is to be found in the documentation *Between Two Congresses: Helsinki – Moscow 1976–1981* (1981, pp. 73–74).

of the President's list, however interspersed with lengthy discussion on the state of the world, media and journalists.[34] The President's list attempted to clarify the strategy of the IOJ and to make the organization more efficient and competent, both professionally and politically – something that the President was pursuing in consultation with the Soviet Vice-President (see Nordenstreng's testimony in Part Two).

The Presidium was an important step to consolidate the IOJ at a time of its dynamic growth, supported by the international situation and the UN policies. The struggle against apartheid was an example of the topics legitimated by the UN and actively promoted by the IOJ (Figure 6.9). As seen in Appendix 5, the extensive list of activities in 1978–79 includes more consultations for co-ordination inside and outside the IOJ membership and also more meetings on topics beyond the customary political issues. For example, the IOJ schools of journalism held in February 1979 the first meeting of the "IOJ Coordinating Committee for Training of Journalists" and in March the 1st Biennial of Humour and Militant Graphic Art was started in Cuba.[35]

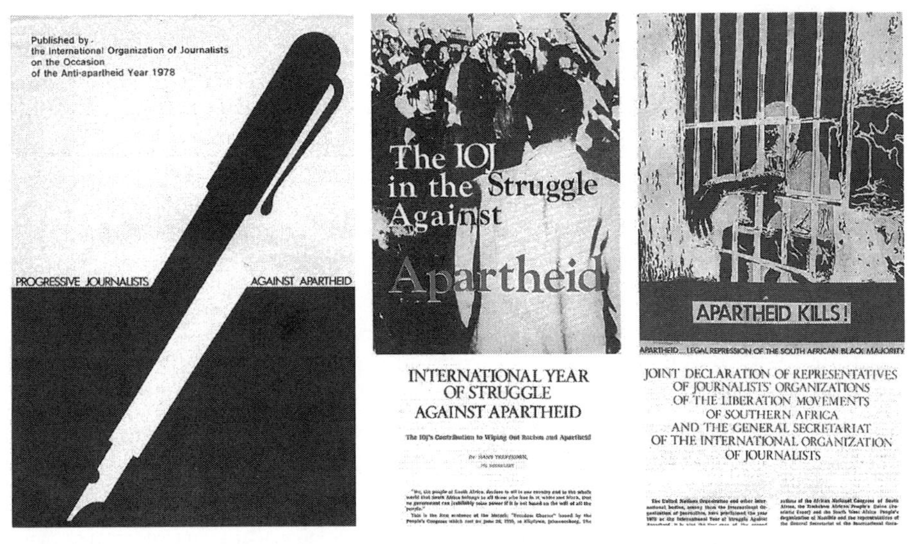

Figure 6.9 The IOJ highlighted the International Year against Apartheid in 1978 in the form of a poster, book and articles in *The Democratic Journalist*.

The IOJ publications were expanded with more books on subjects ranging from the neutron bomb to the international information order and a new series of small textbooks for the basic training of journalists was launched

34 *DJ* 2/1979.
35 *DJ* 7–8/1979.

in 1979 with its own Editorial Commission.[36] *The Democratic Journalist* continued to distribute about 20,000 copies around the world, nearly half in English and the rest in French and Spanish, with the Russian version produced in Moscow. Following the Presidium, the journal took steps to raise its profile after its 25th anniversary in 1978 (Figure 6.10). The contents, both text and photos, were as eclectic as before, combining academic articles with distinctly political materials.

Figure 6.10 *The Democratic Journalist* tried to keep up with the changing times, as shown by the first number of 1979 highlighting the International Year of the Child. A poster distributed with the journal was based on the winner of the IOJ contest "Children and the world of mass media" – a nine-year-old girl from Czechoslovakia.

In early 1979 the IOJ attended and addressed two important conferences: the first meeting of journalists of the non-aligned countries in Baghdad[37] and the UNESCO Conference of Communication Policies in Asia and Oceania in Kuala Lumpur[38]. The UNESCO conference provided a platform for the IOJ to publicize its support for the Mass Media Declaration and its promotion of professional ethics – not in the form of a strict international code but a set of principles. Meanwhile, an inventory of professional codes of ethics was presented in an IOJ book of scholarly articles.[39]

---

36 The first in the series was a 60-page pocket book *Journalism: Substance, Social Functions, Development* by the Dean of the Faculty of Journalism at Charles University in Prague, Vladimír Hudec (1979).

37 *DJ* 5/1979. The address of the IOJ President is published in *Journalists' Affairs* 5–6/1979.

38 *Journalists' Affairs* 7–8/1979.

39 *Professional Codes in Journalism*, edited by the Finnish media lawyer Lars Bruun (1979). For its introduction, see *DJ* 7–8/1979.

The calendar for 1979 abounded in visits by unions to the Prague Secretariat – beginning with Finland, Palestine and Syria, continuing with Cyprus and others as reported in *Journalists' Affairs*. Likewise, the Secretariat paid several visits to member unions – from Cuba to Mali – and signed agreements of co-operation, notably with the Union of Journalists in Finland. Various solidarity actions were now dominated by support to Vietnam against aggression from China. It was in this context that the IOJ President visited Vietnam and Kampuchea in 1979 (Figure 6.11).

Figure 6.11 While visiting Vietnam, the IOJ President was flown to Phnom Penh, the capital of Kampuchea on 6 February 1979, only four weeks after it was liberated by Vietnam from the tyrannical Khmer Rouge regime led by Pol Pot. The IOJ was the first international body to meet the new regime of the Vietnam-backed People's Republic of Kampuchea led by Heng Samrin. In front of the Presidential Palace from the time of King Norodom Sihanouk, IOJ President Nordenstreng and head of IOJ Protocol Department Ivana Čecháková next to President Samrin and the young Foreign Minister Hun Sen, who became Cambodia's Prime Minister in 1985. (Photo: IOJ)

The high profile of the Mass Media Declaration was gradually overshadowed by UNESCO's MacBride Commission, which convened meetings for governmental and non-governmental experts, attended by the IOJ, the IFJ and other major media organizations – notably on international news in Stockholm (April 1978) and on the protection of journalists in Paris (May 1979). The Commission also collected tens of background documents, one of them by the IOJ on the "Responsibility and obstacles of journalism".[40]

While UNESCO and other global perspectives dominated, the IOJ continued to keep European détente high on its agenda. The biannual Meeting of European journalists was again held in Italy in July 1979, attended by delegates from 22 unions of East and West, and followed by the 5th meeting of the leaders of the IOJ and IFJ.[41] However, at this stage the momentum for European détente was declining; for example, the draft Convention proposed two years earlier by the IOJ to the IFJ had no chance of becoming the kind

40 Background document number 53 is available at http://unesdoc.unesco.org/images/0003/000346/034643eb.pdf.

41 *Journalists' Affairs* 15–16/1979.

of charter envisioned by the IOJ since 1972. The time for the Italian initiative was soon over (see Murialdi's recollections in Part Two) and it was the broader consultative circle around UNESCO that provided the platform for the IOJ-IFJ encounters, just as foreseen in the Mexico Presidium.

The Executive Committee met in Hanoi in November 1979. This was the 19th session of the Committee since the founding of the IOJ (see Appendix 1), taking place at a time when Vietnam had been attacked by China, after Vietnam had toppled the Pol Pot regime in Kampuchea, which was supported by China. In such a tense political atmosphere the event was a manifestation of solidarity with Vietnam – both because of the actual situation and due to the historical legacy of the Vietnam War. At the same time, however, it was a platform confirming détente and the organizational reforms advocated by the Mexico Presidium. Moreover, the meeting was "a manifestation of a shared historical course" implying: "Vietnam is not alone!"

The meeting was attended by most of the nearly 70 members of the Executive Committee[42]. The sessions were held on three days, beginning with a formal opening attended by the Prime Minister of Vietnam (Figure 6.12) and ending with the adoption of a general resolution on 23 November 1979. Furthermore, the Executive Committee continued in Ho Chi Minh City, where the participants were flown on 24 November for two days. There in

Figure 6.12 The opening of the Executive Committee in Hanoi's Congress Palace on 21 November 1979. Behind the table, members of the Presidium; in the middle, President Nordenstreng between Secretary General Kubka and Prime Minister of Vietnam Pham Van Dong. Excerpts were published in *The Democratic Journalist* in 1980; before the event in 1979 articles were also published on the journalists and press in Vietnam. (Photo from *The Democratic Journalist* 1/1980, which has also an overview of the event. The proceedings were published as a book including a photo supplement.)

42 This statutory body was composed of the Presidium with 25 persons plus one representative from about 40 other member organization (unions or groups).

the Unification Palace a ceremonial session was held with an appeal to the journalists of the world.[43]

After returning to Hanoi the participants attended a reception by the Government and a group of delegates was received by the President of Vietnam (Figure 6.13). Finally, a Presidium session was held on 28 November, confirming a detailed work plan for the Secretariat General in 1980.

Figure 6.13 On the left: Prime Minister Pham Van Dong (in the middle of the front row) with delegates of the Executive Committee in front of the Government Guesthouse in Hanoi after the Government's reception on 26 November 1979. On the right: President of the Socialist Republic of Vietnam, Ton Duc Thang, with delegates on 27 November. (Photos from the proceedings *Hanoi Ho Chi Minh City* 1980)

Many political and professional issues were covered in the extensive report of the Secretary General, the reports of the Social Commission, the Auditing Commission and the Training Committee, the speeches of the Vietnamese hosts as well as 27 contributions of the Presidium delegates. For example, the Cuban delegate criticized China not only for its aggression against Vietnam and support for the Pol Pot regime in Kampuchea but also for its support to Pinochet in Chile and Somoza in Nicaragua. The Polish delegate invited the next Presidium to convene in Warsaw in 1980 and the Soviet delegate invited the next Congress to come to Moscow in 1981.

The General Resolution confirmed strong support for UNESCO's Mass Media Declaration and NAM's efforts towards a new information order. The resolution instructed the General Secretariat to prepare for the 9th Congress following the steps listed in the Mexico Presidium. The Appeal of Ho Chi Minh City summarized the positions, including condemnation of reaction-

43 The proceedings *Hanoi Ho Chi Minh City* (1980) included all key documents and speeches. See also *DJ* 2/1980. What was not included in the published reports was an intervention by Vice-President Gatinot with a communication from the French CGT deploring the Prague court's imprisonment of Václav Havel and other dissidents in Czechoslovakia. The President of the Czechoslovak Union of Journalists issued a rejoinder to this.

ary forces in various regions of the world, but ending on an optimistic note: "By carrying out these lofty tasks, we, journalists, will serve with dignity the nations and progressive mankind in its gigantic struggle for a happy future, for a life without wars and arms race."

The Executive Committee confirmed the adoption of new members since the last Congress: 11 national unions or groups, including the newly established Association of Journalists in Kampuchea, plus four associated members (from Cyprus, Portugal and Spain) and one observer (SSL from Finland). This brought the number of countries where the IOJ had large or small organizations close to 70, in addition to which there were over a hundred individual members in over 40 countries. The whole IOJ membership through its affiliates at the time was 150,000 journalists from 112 countries, as announced by the Chairman of the Vietnam Journalists Association (VJA), Hoang Tung, who represented nearly 6,000 members of the VJA.

The Executive Committee in Vietnam in 1979 stands out in the history of the IOJ as exemplary both by content and form. For background, a book was published on the IOJ's relation with Vietnam since 1950, with all the IOJ protests and appeals on Vietnam over the years and a review of the mass media in Vietnam by VJA General Secretary Luu Quy Ky.

The logistical arrangements resembled a state visit, including an hour-to-hour schedule of events printed for participants. In addition to the sessions and receptions there was a film show of the latest production of INTERPRESS Budapest on the explosion of information. On leaving Hanoi the IOJ Secretariat handed over to the hosts the simultaneous interpreting equipment used by the IOJ translation team. This donation was the latest of several solidarity gifts given by the IOJ to its Vietnamese member union since the 1960s.

An essential source of funding for solidarity was the **IOJ International Lottery** (Figure 6.14). Over 20 million tickets were sold every year in the late 1970s, with national lotteries organized in Czechoslovakia, Hungary, Bulgaria, the GDR, USSR and Mongolia as well as in Vietnam, although the latter received more than it contributed to the IOJ Solidarity Fund (Figure 6.14).

One of the long-term activities was the **Interpress Photo exhibition**, arranged biannually since 1960 in the socialist countries in turn (see Appendix 5) – most recently in Cuba immediately after the Executive Committee in Hanoi (Figure 6.14).

Like the International Lottery, the Interpress Photo exhibition reached out far beyond the IOJ membership, raising awareness of the IOJ among the wider public in the socialist countries and no doubt strengthening its political support in the ruling communist parties. Other means of engaging the public were competitions like that shown in Figure 6.10 above.

International Organization of Journalists announces two competitions

Figure 6.14 As presented in *The Democratic Journalist* 3/1980, the IOJ lottery was "the only permanent international lottery in the world". This was a major source of finance for the schools in Berlin and Budapest and furthermore produced a substantial part of the funding for various other IOJ activities. *The Democratic Journalist* gave extensive coverage to the Interpress Photo exhibition in Havana as was customary with earlier exhibitions since the 1960s (see Figure 4.2).

In general, the IOJ activities in 1980 continued the trends of previous years whereby professional and political topics were more or less in balance and all regions of the world were represented. A distinctive feature in 1980 was several UNESCO-related activities, beginning with a consultation with the IOJ and IFJ on the protection of journalists and continuing with the Intergovernmental Conference to set up the IPDC in April and in October the General Conference to adopt a compromise report of the MacBride Commission, published as a milestone book *Many Voices, One World* (1980).

The truce in the "information war" still prevailed, in spite of obvious political contradictions in topics such as NWICO, codes of ethics and protection of journalists. The IOJ gave vocal support to UNESCO against a hardening line of the western lobbies, the IOJ President welcoming the MacBride Report's compromise recommendations on professional standards and praising UNESCO for initiating the consultative meetings.[44]

Figure 6.15 In 1980 the IOJ publications distributed a flyer inviting participation in two competitions: one for international solidarity at large and another for the specific cause of the Palestinian people. Such competitions helped to mobilize the readers for closer association with the IOJ but their overall impact was rather in making a political profile for the IOJ than in recruiting new members for the Organization.

The **2nd Consultative Meeting of international and regional organizations of journalists** was held in **Mexico City on 1–3 April 1980**

44 Two addresses of the IOJ President in UNESCO's General Conference in Belgrade (1980) were published as supplements to the *IOJ newsletter* 11 and 12/1980.

(Figure 6.16). It was attended by the IOJ (4 representatives), UCIP (2) and the regional federations from Latin America FELAP (7), Asia CAJ (1) and the Arab world FAJ (4). Absent were the IFJ and the Union of African Journalists (UAJ). As for the first meeting at UNESCO in 1978, the convener was Hifzi Topuz, Director of the Section of Free Flow of Information and Communication Policies, now accompanied by Germán Carnero Roqué, UNESCO's Regional Adviser on Communication in Latin America and the Caribbean – the same Peruvian diplomat who had represented the developing countries in the 1977 consultation on the Mass Media Declaration. Major attention was attracted by President Portillo, who not only came to open the meeting but generously provided the presidential airplane to fly the participants to Cancún in the Yukatan peninsula for two days of post-conference recreation.

Figure 6.16 The President of the United States of Mexico, Dr José Lopez Portillo coming to open the Consultative Meeting in Mexico City on 1 April 1980. Greeting him IOJ President Nordenstreng next to Germán Carnero Roqué from UNESCO. On the left Marcel Furic of the International Catholic Union of the Press (UCIP) and the backview of Luis Jordá Galeana of the National Syndicate of Editors of the Mexican Press. The meeting and its results were widely covered in a supplement of the new *IOJ newsletter*.

The agenda of the meeting included several topical issues: UNESCO's Mass Media Declaration, professional ethics, the new information order, the economic and social situation of journalists, new conceptions of news and the protection of journalists. Each was discussed after being introduced either by UNESCO representatives or by experts among the participants – the new information order by ILET's Director Juan Somavia – but especially thorough was the consideration of professional ethics, leading to "a document of extraordinary importance in journalist practice called the Mexico Declaration".[45]

The year 1980 was full of events but without any statutory meeting – the first year since 1968 (see Appendix 1). The invitation presented in Hanoi by the Polish Union did not materialize, no doubt due to political turmoil in Poland related to the founding of the independent trade union Solidarity

45 The proceedings were published in *Journalists´ Affairs*, Special Issue in May 1980, and the communique with the Mexico Declaration as a supplement to the *IOJ newsletter* 1/1980. The Mexico Declaration was published also in *DJ* 6/1980.

IOJ news letter 1980 JUNE 1

THE INTERNATIONAL ORGANIZATION OF JOURNALISTS

REPRESENTANTS
OF JOURNALISTS' UNIONS MEET

On the invitation of the French journalist trade unions NSJ, CFDT and CGT, a meeting of professional journalists' trade unions and organizations of Western Europe was … with the detailed project that was discussed.

2. to organize in the coming months a new meeting which would define the modality and put into operation …

During the meeting the following information was also presented:

Paolo Murialdi, President of FNSI, informed the participants about the next meeting of European journalists …

LOTTERY

On May 12, 1980, the first draw in the IOJ's International Lottery for 1980, the only international lottery in the world, whose proceeds are used to help progressive journalist' organizations of Africa, Asia and Latin America, was held in Prague. Five lucky winners became the owners of passenger cars and dozens of others won a variety of valuable prizes. In this year's 16th IOJ Lottery, the main prizes also include a ready-built house, passenger cars, minimotorcycles, trips to the Gobi desert, trips to the seaside, etc.

Covers of IOJ publications mentioned above

Published by I.O.J. – International Organization of Journalists
Editorial office : Pařížská 9, Prague 1, Czechoslovakia
Telegram : INTORGJOUR Prague – TELEX : 012331 INJOUR C

IOJ news letter 1980 NOVEMBER 12

THE INTERNATIONAL ORGANIZATION OF JOURNALISTS

Meeting of solidarity in Kabul

IOJ Delegation Ends South-East Asia Visit

With a detailed discussion with Foreign Minister of Sri Lanka, A.C.S. … delegation was received by M.A. Bakeer Marker, parliament … Nadu, Mr. M.G. Ramachandran. The Union state Tamil Nadu has 40 …

ČSSN Seminar

The Czechoslovak Union of Journalists (ČSSN) organized a nationwide seminar from October 29 to 31 on the subject "Technical development of communication media". Leading Czechoslovak specialists from ČTK, the press, radio, television and the Czechoslovak polygraphic industry spoke about the development and consequeces of the scientific and technological revolution in the information media.

The guests included the dean …

CARNERO CHECA DIES

An outstanding Peruvian publicist and journalist, Secretary General of the Federation of Latin American Journalists and member of the IOJ Executive Committee, Genaro Carnero Checa died in Mexico on October 12, 1980.

Genaro Carnero Checa was born on April 14, 1910 in Piura, Peru. Almost 50 years of his active life have been devoted to journalism and struggle for the national and social liberation, first in Peru and, later on, in other Latin American countries. For his activities he was imprisoned several times and deported to live in exile.

In 1950, he founded the Federation of Peruvian Journalists and became its president for several terms. He wrote articles for a number …

Figure 6.17 In June 1980 the *IOJ newsletter* replaced *Journalists' Affairs* as the main vehicle of current information on the IOJ. Printed as a bulletin running to 4–8 pages on thin high-quality paper, it was issued biweekly first in English and widely distributed within and outside the IOJ members. For example, in November 1980 it reported on the IOJ delegation's visits to Afghanistan, India and Sri Lanka; the photo shows a mass rally in Soviet-backed Kabul. Among other news was a short story of a seminar on the new polygraphic industry organized by the Czechoslovak Union of Journalists and an obituary of a prominent Peruvian journalist, the founder of FELAP.

(*Solidarność*) by Lech Walesa. In this process the Polish member union – the Association of Polish Journalists (SDP) – became a platform of the power struggle between Communist and Solidarity sympathizers, leading in October 1980 to an extraordinary congress of the SDP with a sharp turn in its political direction from a traditional supporter of the government – and the IOJ – to a radical representative of the new oppositional forces.[46]

All in all, by the end of the 1970s the IOJ was the world's largest international body of mass communication professionals, bringing together 150,000 journalists and other creative media workers representing all continents and various political outlooks within a democratic and progressive orientation.

46 See Furman (2017, p. 81–82).

CHAPTER 7
PERSEVERING IN A NEW COLD WAR 1981–85

The beginning of the 1980s was a period of an unprecedented militarization in the North and debt crisis in the South. The ambitions of the 1970s for a new world order were replaced by new Cold War, while the public movements for peace, disarmament and development continued with an increasing force.

In 1981 Ronald Reagan started his first term as President of the USA with a hardline policy towards the USSR led by Leonid Brezhnev, turning the American-Soviet relations from co-operation to confrontation. Reagan's decision in 1983 to launch the Strategic Defense Initiative ("Star Wars") and the earlier Euro-missile deployment provoked mass protests involving millions of people.

The new Cold War tension fuelled local and regional conflicts, notably in Nicaragua, where the Sandinists, whose revolution had toppled Somoza's corrupt regime in 1979, were opposed by counter-revolutionaries ("Contras") organized by the USA. The US financing for Contras was based on murky arms sales in the Middle East to Iran with the intention to undermine the Hizbollah movement supporting Palestinians against Israel.

In early 1985 Mikhail Gorbachev became the leader of the Soviet Union. His main ambition was to improve the stagnant economy with radical measures of structural change (perestroika). A parallel policy of openness (glasnost) facilitated an atmosphere of political and cultural freedom. Relations with the USA improved alleviating tension and leading to negotiations for limiting nuclear weapons.

The IOJ continued its successful development in the 1980s with growing membership and increasing activities. However, it no longer enjoyed the favourable climate of détente and decolonization after 1981, when international relations turned towards a new Cold War. Weak signals of this new trend appeared in the late 1970s as dissident movements spread in the socialist countries – encouraged by the Helsinki Final Act particularly in the Soviet Union. Political tensions had been rising towards the end of the 1970s, but the truce of the information war continued until 1980. A new western offensive against UNESCO and NWICO was launched in early 1981 when Regan took office.

This chapter reviews the main IOJ developments during the first half of the 1980s.

FACING AND WAGING CAMPAIGNS 1981

At this stage the US-based media lobbies led by the World Press Freedom Committee (WPFC) began to **campaign against UNESCO and the idea of NIICO**. A landmark of this campaign was in May 1981 with the "Voices of Freedom Conference of Independent News Media" in Talloires (France) and the same message was given increasing publicity in the USA (Figure 7.1). The long-term "information war", after the truce in the late 1970s, entered the next stage of corporate offensives which continued throughout the 1980s.[1]

Commentary:
Press freedoms and economic freedoms are under attack in the UN. The defenders of each must now unite, argues historian Allen Weinstein.
Danger at the UN.

Figure 7.1 The US magazines *Time* and *Newsweek* published in February 1982 a four-page supplement paid for by the SmithKline corporation, with an alert: "Press freedoms and economic freedoms are under attack at the UN. Defenders of each must now unite." The commentary was presented as a message by a historian, but its substance was from the WPFC. The supplement was included only in the North American editions of the magazines.

Reagan himself endorsed the declaration issued in Talloires and warned that the USA might withdraw its support from UNESCO.[2] This position was based on the view that by advocating a balanced flow of international news, the protection of journalists and their codes of ethics, UNESCO was pursuing restrictions on a free market and even state control of the media – a narrative promoted by the American media corporations and supported by media owners throughout the western world. This narrative was not approved by most professional journalists and their organizations. Those convened at the Consultative Meetings took UNESCO as a safeguard of rather than threat to press freedom. Later scholars classified the corporate offensive as "a big lie".[3]

Nevertheless, the narrative about UNESCO and the UN attempting to curtail media freedom travelled well in the western publicity. The IOJ waged a counter campaign, but its influence on western public opinion was limited; due to its image it was typically viewed as a voice of Soviet-led communism

1 See Nordenstreng (2010) and Nordenstreng (2016).
2 Reagan's letter to the House of Representatives in September 1981; quoted in the above two sources.
3 Gerbner, Mowlana & Nordenstreng (1993, p. xi).

identified to be "based in Prague". The IFJ, for its part, seen safely to be "based in Brussels", was more hesitant in defending UNESCO as it shared the media owners' priority of freedom over responsibility.

A turning point in the clash of political and professional forces was the **Meeting on the Protection of Journalists** convened by UNESCO in Paris in February 1981 (Figure 7.2). The topic was raised by the MacBride Commission and left open in its Report, while continuing murders of journalists around the world made it more and more topical. Initially invited were the international and regional organizations of working journalists involved in the Consultative group[4] plus the International Commission of Lawyers and the International Association of Democratic Lawyers (IADL) – the latter belonging to the same group of INGOs as the IOJ (see Chapter 2). However, at the last minute the USA also insisted on inviting four western media proprietors' organizations: the IPI, the FIEJ, the IAPA and the WFPC (see Chapter 6). They turned the meeting, which was supposed to examine a proposal for the establishment of an international commission for the protection of journalists prepared by a French expert[5], from a consensus-seeking consultation into a platform of the four attacking UNESCO.

IOJ news letter

1981 MARCH 5

THE INTERNATIONAL ORGANIZATION OF JOURNALISTS

WEST ATTACKS UNESCO MEETING

Concerted action of USA prevented adoption of measures for personal protection of journalists on dangerous assignments

The consultative meeting, convened by the UNESCO to Paris from 16 to 18 February, 1981, which had to debate experiences, possibilities and measures for the protection of journalists on dangerous assignments, was frustrated by the U.S.A. in a prepared, directed and concerted action.

The initial invitation list comprised all international journalists' organizations (IOJ, IFJ, UCIP, FAJ, UJA, ASEAN, FELAP, FELATRAP) recognized by and since a long time cooperating with UNESCO as progress in the sphere of personal protection of journalists on dangerous assignments, the USA representatives boycotted any agreement, and went so far as to withdraw their own draft of a Final Communique in the last minute, and refused to agree with any final report.

Therefore records of UNESCO carry only the draft standpoints of both groups concerning the attainment of a consensus.

By insulting UNESCO and its General Director, Mr. M'Bow, the International Herald Tribune, The New York Times, The United Press International and The New York Times Service attempted jointly, to jeopardize all kinds of progress and to put under pressure the representatives of the developing countries.

The vice-president of the session, Cheick Mouctary Diarra, Secretary General of the Union of African Journalists, qualified this as an impudent and arrogant behaviour of Americans, behaviour which "should open the eyes" of all journalists from the developing countries.

Unesco to Consider Plan for Licensing Journalists Despite Western Objections

By Paul Lewis

PARIS — A plan to create a new international organization to license journalists and ensure that ... generally accepted rules of professional ethics" and could censure them by withdrawing identity cards.

While the plan does not attempt ... the meeting was to be closed to news coverage.

After complaints by groups representing the West, Unesco has ...

U.S. News Official Warns Unesco On Moves to Regulate Journalists

United Press International

PARIS — An American news executive said Monday that any attempt by the UN Education, Scientific and Cultural Organization to issue regulations to protect ... States — Mr. Beebe and Dana Bullen of the World Press Freedom Committee — said they were admitted only after they learned ...

THE WASHINGTON POST.

'Ethical' Censors at Unesco

There is a dangerous new burst of solicitude for the safety of journalists at the United Nations Educational, Scientific and Cultural Organization in Paris. The agency seeks opinion on a plan to license correspondents for "safe conduct" ... that feel themselves unfairly covered by the world's news media. Those that appreciate free inquiry certainly merit help in telling their stories to the world — and also in ...

Figure 7.2 The western campaign against UNESCO and those advocating the protection of journalists was in full swing in early 1981 as reported in the *IOJ newsletter*.

4 In addition to those invited to Paris in 1978 and Mexico City in 1980, a new regional organization was now invited: the Federation of Latin American Press Workers (FELATRAP). It was founded as a pro-American counterforce to FELAP – see *IOJ newsletter* 6/1980, 10 and 14/1981, 6/1982, and *The Democratic Journalist* (*DJ*) 4/1981.

5 Professor Pierre Gaborit from the University of Paris-Nord. The 10-page document is available at http://unesdoc.unesco.org/images/0004/000420/042052eb.pdf.

After the failed UNESCO consultation in February 1981 the IOJ and its Bulgarian member union convened an **International Forum for the Protection of Journalists in Varna** in October 1981, attended by delegates from 33 national unions around the world, from the regional federations UAJ, FAJ and FELAP and the IADL – but not the IFJ, nor UNESCO.[6] The proceedings of this Forum and its publication *The Black Book* (1982) focused on "the persecution of the progressive and democratic journalists", thus limiting the cause of protection in a particular sphere without seriously aiming at a broader approach also covering western mainstream journalists, not to speak of western publishers after the clash at UNESCO. The Forum appointed an International Committee for the Protection of Journalists based in Sofia. It had little international impact as it remained aloof from the UNESCO-driven consultative meetings.[7] Meanwhile, the western campaign against UNESCO went on with a massive force.[8]

It is important to remember the wider context of the US government's undermining of multilateralism at the UN and its preference for dealing with international relations bilaterally – not least in issues such as world poverty.[9] Accordingly, the US withdrawal from UNESCO in 1984, although justified in part by media policies, should mainly be seen as part of a global strategy which has been aptly described as the "Grenada of the United Nations": a warning to the international community that the USA would not tolerate being outvoted by a Third World majority in the UN – UNESCO being a small island like Grenada whose Cuban-supported Marxist government was toppled in a US invasion in 1983.

In 1981 the IOJ turned 35 and its profile was raised in publications, especially by upgrading the content and layout of *The Democratic Journalist* (*DJ*), which included more professional articles on media and journalism around the world and even reviews of scholarly periodicals, but still retaining its clearly progressive orientation (Figure 7.3). Each number of the monthly included a brief introduction "To our readers" accompanied by a list of "IOJ bodies and services" with their addresses and telex numbers: Commissions (Professional and Social), Clubs (Photo, Auto, Agri), Schools (Berlin, Budapest, Sofia), Rest Homes (Varna,

6 *IOJ newsletter* 19/1981.
7 The Committee met only once, in Nicosia (Cyprus) in late 1982; *IOJ newsletter* 24/1982.
8 For the history of mainly UN activities for the protection of journalists, see Chocarro (2017). For UNESCO documentation, see *Protection of Journalists* (1980). An example of launching the Western campaign is Righter (1978). For an overview of the campaign, see Gerbner, Mowlana & Nordenstreng (1993).
9 This was made clear in October 1981, when Reagan met leaders of 22 countries, hosted by President Portillo of Mexico in Cancún – the same resort to which the participants of the 2nd Consultative Meeting of journalists were flown in April 1980. Among the leaders addressed by Reagan were those of India (Indira Gandhi) and Tanzania (Julius Nyerere). See https://en.wikipedia.org/wiki/North-South_Summit.

The democratic 6 '81
Journalist
THE JOURNAL OF THE INTERNATIONAL ORGANIZATION OF JOURNALISTS

IOJ 35
INTERNATIONAL ORGANIZATION OF JOURNALISTS FOR PEACE AND COOPERATION

FORTY YEARS AGO NAZI GERMANY ATTACKED THE USSR

SIGNS OF A REVIVAL OF FASCISM IN THE FRG

DEFENDING THE REVOLUTION

THE DEMOCRATIC JOURNALIST INTERVIEWS IGNACIO BRIONES TORRES DEPUTY CHIEF EDITOR OF THE NICARAGUAN DAILY "BARRICADA" AND VICE-PRESIDENT OF FELAP

HOW AP AND UPI VIEW LATIN AMERICA

PHOTOGRAPHY AND REALITY

WEST EUROPEAN TELEVISION

THE SITUATION IN FRANCE AND GREAT BRITAIN AS SEEN FROM THE ITALIAN VIEWPOINT

INTERNATIONAL NEWS REPORTING AND TECHNOLOGY

JOURNALIST'S TECHNICAL MINIMUM

OPTIC FIBRE CABLE

Figure 7.3 An example of the new profile of *The Democratic Journalist*: a couple of stories on plain politics and the rest on professional issues ranging from the revolutionary struggle of Nicaraguan journalists to the "journalist's technical minimum" presenting new media technologies.

Balaton), Companies (Interpress Prague and Budapest), Publications and Lottery. The photo supplement inserted at the centre of each issue covered different topics around the world, using prominent photographers. At the end of each number was a short information section on the member unions, schools, etc. on "IOJ life", with a calendar of events for the next two months. Several issues of the monthly also featured a supplement of 4–6 pages reproducing important UN and UNESCO resolutions. All this in English, French and Spanish produced in Prague, with a different Russian edition made in Moscow.

The fortnightly *IOJ newsletter* offered more topical information on the IOJ and its positions on current affairs, in English and since 1981, also in Spanish. This and the *DJ*, together with the list of events in Appendix 5, provide an illustrative account of what was done each year. The periodicals covered a lot of news items related to journalists and their organizations, while prominent attention was given to carefully selected topics, such as the visit by an IOJ delegation to Lebanon in August 1981, after the Israeli bombing of Beirut, including a meeting with the Palestinian leader Yasser Arafat in his underground office in Beirut.[10]

10 *DJ* 10/1981. The IOJ delegation also met the political leaders of Lebanon. While visiting the front in Southern Lebanon the delegation had a remarkable guide: Leila Khaled of the PLFP – see https://en.wikipedia.org/wiki/Leila_Khaled.

The range of IOJ activities in the 1980s is shown in Appendix 5. By 1982 the number of annual events was around 40, but after that it rose to 50–60, and in 1987 to 80. So many activities required efficient machinery to maintain and organize them. To a large extent this was done with the resources of the member unions, which were fairly well co-ordinated by the IOJ, as indicated by numerous events jointly organized and also by the annual consultative meetings of member unions of the CMEA/COMECON countries. An ever growing role was played by the headquarters, thanks to the financial means accumulated by rapidly growing commercial companies of the IOJ.

The Secretariat in Prague was gradually strengthened, with normal rotation of Secretaries sent by key member unions. A new Cuban Secretary for Latin America, Miguel Arteaga, arrived in early 1981 to replace Juan Alvarez; in addition, Ruis Caro from Peru worked there for a couple of years. In late 1981 a new Romanian Secretary for Professional Matters, Viktor Stamate, came to replace the long-serving Aurelian Nestor, who among others organized the IOJ-UNESCO Colloquia, last held in Bamako in October 1980. A German Secretary for Africa and Asia, Manfred Weigand, also came to replace Hans Treffkorn, who became Director of the Berlin School, the "Werner Lamberz" International Institute of Journalism.

The schools of journalism under the IOJ umbrella included in the 1980s, in addition to the one in Berlin (founded in 1963), the IOJ International Journalist Training Centre in Budapest (founded in 1963), the George Dimitrov International Institute of Journalism in Sofia (founded in 1978), the Jose Marti International Institute of Journalism in Havana (inaugurated in 1982) and the Julius Fucik School of Solidarity in Prague (started in 1983). In addition, there was the Stefan Gheorghiu Political Academy in Bucharest and other solidarity schools opened in Baghdad in 1980, Lima in 1982 and Pyongyang in 1984, but these were only loose ly connected to the IOJ network.[11]

This chapter, like the previous one, could have been entitled Heyday, since by and large the IOJ was successful in pursuing its mission and expanding its influence in the world. On the other hand, the success was not ideal because the IOJ was constantly embroiled in the revived Cold War, with the IFJ dominating in the West, pushing the IOJ towards the East and making the Third World a contentious terrain of rivalry. But the success was still obvious under the relatively favourable conditions of international politics lasting until late 1989, when the fall of the Berlin Wall and the "Velvet Revolution" in Czechoslovakia signalled the forthcoming collapse of the socialist system in eastern Europe.

---

11 See *Budapest Berlin Sofia* (1982) and *Journalistic Training Centres* (1986).

The statutory meetings in the 1980s were held as shown in Appendix 1:

1981 October	Congress in Moscow (USSR)
1983 January	Presidium in Luanda (Angola)
1984 September	Executive Committee in New Delhi (India)
1985 January	Presidium in Quito (Ecuador)
1986 October	Congress in Sofia (Bulgaria)
1987 March	Presidium Bureau in Moscow
1987 October	Presidium in Nicosia (Cyprus)
1988 March	Presidium Bureau in Prague
1988 April	Presidium in Brasilia (Brazil)
1989 January	Presidium in Addis Abeba (Ethiopia)

These were the milestones of the decade, covered below in two parts: the first period from 1981 to 1985, including the 9th Congress in Moscow (1981), the Executive Committee in New Delhi (1984) and two Presidiums in the intervening years (1983, 1985) in the present chapter, and the second period from the 10th Congress in Sofia in 1986 through annual Presidiums to 1989 in the following chapter.

Most of these meetings resulted in a published report and they were also given wide coverage in the IOJ journal and newsletter. This and the following chapter will highlight main developments, proceeding chronologically year by year and noting, in addition to the statutory meetings, other events of significance illustrated by samples from IOJ periodicals and photos.

The **9th IOJ Congress in Moscow** was held on 19–22 **October 1981**. It took place in the House of Columns used for official functions (Figure 7.4). It was attended by 421 delegates and observers from 82 member unions, with 13 international and regional organizations and institutions as guests. Greetings were received from several state leaders[12] with personal presentations addressed by Michail Zimyanin from the Soviet authorities followed by a number of representatives from international, regional and national organizations[13]. A surprise guest was PLO Chairman Yasser Arafat, who happened to be in Moscow to meet the Soviet leadership.

IOJ President Nordenstreng opened the Congress with proud remarks:

> This moment, in this historical hall in the heart of Moscow, is a landmark in the history of world journalism. Present here are altogether 400 representatives of jour-

12 Leonid Brezhnev of the host country, Gustáv Husák of Czechoslovakia, Erich Honecker of the GDR, Fidel Castro of Cuba, Hafez Assad of Syria, Saddam Hussein of Iraq, Pham Van Dong of Vietnam and Y. Tsedenbal of Mongolia. Their messages are reproduced in the *9th Congress* (1981, pp. 17–24).

13 UNESCO (Hifzi Topuz), World Peace Council (Romesh Chandra), World Federation of Trade Unions (Ibrahim Zakariya), IFJ (Paul Parisot), FAJ (Saad Qassim Hammoudi), UAJ (Leite de Vasconcelos), FELAP (Diaz Rangel), FNSI (P.L. Vigorelli). They are summarized in the *9th Congress* (1981, pp. 9–10).

Figure 7.4 The 9th IOJ Congress in Moscow in October 1981 witnessed another record attendance. In the photo special guest Arafat speaking; on the right President Nordenstreng, on the left Vice-President Afanasjev. (From *The Democratic Journalist* 12/1981)

> nalists coming from some 100 countries of all continents. This is the most representative meeting of journalists held ever anywhere. [...]
>
> The IOJ has changed from a circle of colleagues in some 20 countries of mainly East and West to a really worldwide movement involving journalists from most of the non-aligned countries of the developing world as well. This broad-based movement of democratic journalism has become stronger and more consolidated, so that today it constitutes a leading force in the world of journalism.

He quoted both Cuba's Fidel Castro, the current President of the Non-Aligned Movement, who reminded the audience of the exploitation, starvation and militarism in the world, and Finland's President Urho Kekkonen, who suggested that the best way for ordinary people to help improve the deteriorating international situation was to take an active part in the peace movement. The IOJ President went on:

> Journalists are faced with a double challenge. First, as citizens and intellectuals we have a responsibility to participate in the peace movement which at the same time is a movement in support of the so-called Third World. Secondly, as professionals we have a responsibility to fight any justification for, or incitement to, wars of aggression and the arms race, especially in nuclear weapons, and other forms of violence, hatred or of national, racial or religious discrimination, oppression by tyrannic regimes, as well as all forms of colonialism and neo-colonialism.

He pointed out that this definition of the struggle against the violation of humanity was taken from the Mexico Declaration and continued:

> In fact, the Mexico Declaration is a promising indication of the present orientation towards peace, democracy and social progress among the working journalists in the world. Moreover, it shows that a wide front of professional forces, extending from communists to bourgeois liberals, and also involving various religious faiths from Catholic to Islamic, can be mobilized to stand for such universal values of humanism as peace and truth. On such a broad basis it is possible to arrive at a definition and codification of the universal ethics of journalism.[14]

The four-day Congress heard the customary exhaustive report of the Secretary General[15] reviewing the political situation in the world and the IOJ activities since the last Congress[16]. Reports were given by the permanent IOJ Commissions: Professional and Social Commissions as well as by the newly established Committee for Studies and Documentation and the Co-ordination Committee for the Education and Further Training of Journalists from and in Developing Countries. Likewise, the Auditing Committee gave its report. In addition to plenary sessions the Congress was divided into three working groups dealing with Peace and Security, the New International Information Order and International Solidarity. Each working group produced a report summarizing its proceedings and proposals.[17]

The main outcome of the Congress was the Orientation Document accompanied by an Appeal to the Journalists of the World.[18] The Orientation Document followed the verbose style of those of earlier Congresses, but this time it also included concrete guidelines, beginning with the mandate for future IOJ activities to be based on the Mass Media Declaration (1978) and the Mexico Declaration (1980) and ending with a number of measures for improving the methods of work of the Secretariat.

Twenty-one new member organizations were confirmed since the last Congress, most of them already admitted by other statutory bodies, from the following countries: Mexico, Ethiopia, Jamaica, Western Sahara, Bolivia, Ecuador, Honduras, Nicaragua, Canada, Brazil, Kampuchea, Afghanistan,

---

14 From the Opening Address of the IOJ President Kaarle Nordenstreng, published in *DJ* 12/1981 and in the *9th Congress* (1981, pp. 27–32).

15 Published in part in *DJ* 12/1981, and in full in *9th Congress* (1981, pp. 33–83).

16 This time no separate report *Between Two Congresses* was published as a book but just as a printout "Working documentation destined for delegates of the 9th Congress, Moscow". It contained the Secretary General's reports to the Presidiums in Paris and Mexico City, the President's report and resolution to the Presidium in Mexico, the Secretary General's report to the Executive Committee in Hanoi and several reports to the Moscow Congress.

17 *9th Congress* (1981, pp. 100–107, 117–155).

18 *DJ* 12/1981, pp. 3, 10–15, and *9th Congress* (1981, pp. 85–99, 114–116).

Nigeria, Grenada, Malta, Greece, the Arab Republic of Yemen, Poland, Zimbabwe, Guatemala and Sierra Leone. In addition, five associate members were admitted from Cyprus, Portugal, Spain, Finland and India.

The status of associate member was an innovation to accommodate the interests of certain European unions, first introduced in the Mexico Presidium (1978) and confirmed by the Hanoi Executive Committee (1979). It was not based on the Statute, which prescribed only one type of membership divided into a) national unions, b) national IOJ groups and c) individual members.

This time there were two exceptions to the customary consensus. First, the Romanian delegation abstained from voting on the new member from Kampuchea – obviously because Romania's position in international politics was to side with China.[19] Second, the new Polish member, the Trade Union of Journalists of the Polish Republic (TUJPPR), was opposed by the existing Polish member SDP, which a year earlier had been taken over by the Solidarity forces; now in Moscow it was the only delegation openly opposed to the Communist regimes. The TUJPPR had been established in May 1981 as a trade union of journalists, which, unlike the SDP, was friendly towards the IOJ and now seeking membership. This political conflict was settled by making an exception to the rule of accepting just one organization from the Socialist countries; the TUJPPR was admitted as the second member from Poland.

The total number of journalists through organizations and groups or as individuals was now 180,000 from 120 countries, as proclaimed in the Orientation Document. In this connection we have to keep in mind the absence of the Chinese member union ACJA, which remained completely aloof from any IOJ activities in the 1970s, although not officially resigning, and therefore is not included in the counts of total membership – if the ACJA had been included, the figure would have been close to 300,000. In a way the ACJA even took action against the IOJ in 1981, in inviting the IFJ leadership to visit China, as described by Bogaerts in his recollections in Part Two. This move to fraternize with the IOJ's rival was obviously due to international politics around Vietnam and Kampuchea, which made the IOJ an outspoken critic of China.

Apart from China, it is worth noting that while the IOJ membership was constantly growing, the recruitment base also had weak points, notably Yugoslavia, whose member union had been expelled during the rise of Stalinism, but since détente in the 1970s had drawn politically quite close to the

19 The Romanian delegation likewise did not approve the paragraph in the Orientation Document pledging "our firm solidarity with the peoples of Vietnam, Kampuchea, Laos and Afghanistan" and denouncing "the repeated attempts by U.S. imperialism and Chinese expansionism".

IOJ, however not joining even as an associate member. Likewise the Italian FNSI, which provided the platform for East-West dialogue in Lignano and Capri, did not join the IOJ, but finally became an IFJ member. Furthermore, some Third World unions were reluctant to join the IOJ, despite close contacts and attendance at IOJ activities, while they were courted by the IFJ. Consequently, for example the national unions in Kenya and Tunisia opted for IFJ membership, while the Indian Federation of Working Journalists was cautious about becoming a full member of the IOJ; it became just an associate member.

The elections led to further growth of the Presidium from the 25 members elected in Helsinki to 29 members including the Chairmen of the Professional and Social Commissions and the Honorary President.[20] The President, Secretary General and Treasurer were re-elected as also were Vice-Presidents from the USSR, the GDR, Mali, Guinea, France, Iraq, North Korea, Chile, Mongolia, Finland, Mexico, Vietnam and Cuba, with some new names. The Vice-Presidents from Poland and Egypt were left to be named later; in the Polish case the two member organizations were supposed to agree on a name. Earlier Vice-Presidents from Somalia, Puerto Rico, Venezuela and Sri Lanka were not re-elected and new people were elected from Nigeria, Ecuador, Syria, Nicaragua, Peru, Palestine, Japan and Mozambique. The Executive Committee members coming from the organizations which were not in the Presidium were altogether 45.[21]

In general, the 9th Congress in Moscow endorsed the positive development of the IOJ since the 8th Congress in Helsinki. The Congress closed with an optimistic perspective: the democratic and progressive movement of journalists was expanding.[22]

Right after the Congress, the Mongolian Union of Journalists hosted a **Symposium in Ulan Bator** in the spirt of the Moscow Appeal as reported in *IOJ newsletter* 20–22/1981. Attended by 50 delegates from countries in Asia and the Pacific, from India to Australia, it was an example of how the IOJ member organizations collaborated with the world body – not only to disseminate a central message but also to generate local initiatives. This Symposium endorsed the Indian plan to convene a meeting of journalists for the Indian Ocean as a Zone of Peace and suggested establishing a federation of journalists from Asia.

Moreover, during the Symposium the 10th **Interpress Photo Exhibition** was opened, making Ulan Bator another site of this biannual event, which until now had taken place only once outside Europe (Havana in 1979). The Interpress Photo had become a brand known far beyond the IOJ members,

---

20 *DJ* 12/1981 and *9th Congress* (1981, pp. 160–163).

21 *9th Congress* (1981, pp. 164–169).

22 The Closing Address of the President, in the *9th Congress* (1981, pp. 108–113).

but still limited mainly to the socialist countries. Like the Interpress Auto Club it had a predominantly professional and non-political character which helped it to gain acceptance for the IOJ, also in the West. Those exhibiting on Interpress Photo platforms also participated in the World Press Photo organization based in Amsterdam. This organization, for its part, had a representative on the Interpress Photo jury as of 1972. It was natural that the two institutions had begun to closely co-operate which was confirmed by a joint communique in Prague in 1974. The IOJ and its member unions continued to hold Interpress Photo Exhibitions in Damascus (1983), Moscow (1985), Baghdad (1987), Pyongyang (1989) and Rio de Janeiro (1991). After that the IOJ-driven Interpress Photo no longer continued as a separate institution and it was effectively replaced by the World Press Photo.[23]

A crucial development was **Martial Law in Poland** imposed by General Wojciech Jaruzelski in December 1981. This was a harsh measure by the authoritarian government placing the entire country under military control to prevent the rising opposition from gaining power. Initially there were some casualities, but the country did not descend into a civil war. Thousands of people were detained, including Solidarity leader Lech Walesa, and most non-governmental associations were suspended. This led to the closing of most editorial offices and to the dissolution of all journalist unions, including the SDP and the TUJPPR. However, the situation soon began to be normalized and in March 1982 a new journalist union was founded – the Association of Journalists of the Polish People's Republic (SDPRL) – among journalists "who tolerated military rule as the lesser of two evils", representing about half of the Polish journalists before the imposition of martial law.[24] The martial law was lifted in July 1983, but sharp divisions persisted in Polish society and its journalist community. Different journalist associations competed against each other, while the SDPRL established itself as their main representative, in due course also becoming an IOJ member and assuming the Vice-Presidency left open in Moscow.

The year 1982 was eventful – on average more than three activities per month (see Appendix 5) – and the publications show that they were far from routine events. It was a period of varied activities dominated by issues of peace and disarmament, but dogged continually by conflicts and controversies.

---

23 *DJ* 6/1990.

24 Furman (2017, p. 83). The IOJ periodicals did not cover the Polish developments after the *coup* in the SDP in October 1980 until January 1982, when the *IOJ newsletter* had a one-page report of the situation of Polish journalists. In April it reported the setting up of the SDPRL and in July a delegation of the new Association visiting the IOJ headquarters in Prague. In August the *IOJ newsletter* 15/1982 presented the SDPRL, in which "58.3 per cent of former members of the earlier association, the SDP, have entered".

PROMOTING PEACE AND CIRCUMVENTING CONFLICTS 1982–85

The 3rd Consultative Meeting of international and regional organizations of journalists, convened in **Baghdad in February 1982**, this time also including the representative of the IFJ, continued to pursue the common topics of NIICO, ethics and protection from where they were left in Mexico two years earlier, with the question of new communication technologies added to the agenda. The meeting criticized the campaigns "orchestrated by the industrial, political and military monopolies" and declared: "We are firmly devoted to the principles of the Mexico Declaration; we denounce the manoeuvres aimed at distorting the ideals underlying the new world information and communication order."[25]

The protection and safety of journalists suddenly became a major issue when four Dutch journalists were murdered in El Salvador in March 1982. El Salvador had an alarming record of journalists murdered in recent years as already reported in the Moscow Congress, but now the issue made front-page news worldwide. (Figure 7.5) The *IOJ newsletter* produced a Special Issue on this and the Secretary General of the Netherlands Union of Journalists - an IFJ member - calling for international regulations to protect journalists.

IOJ news letter

1982 APRIL

SPECIAL ISSUE

THE INTERNATIONAL ORGANIZATION OF JOURNALISTS

MORE JOURNALISTS MURDERED IN EL SALVADOR

FOUR DUTCH COLLEAGUES VICTIMS OF THE MILITARY JUNTA

Deeply shocked and with indignation the world public learned about the new crime committed by the Salvadorean military junta: Jan Kuiper, Koos Koster, Joop Willemsen and Hans ter Laag were murdered in El Salvador.

Protest of the IOJ

"The General Secretariat of the International Organization of Journalists has learned with indignation that the ruling junta in El Salvador treacherously murdered Dutch journalists Jacobus Koster, Hans Lodewijk ter Laag, Jan Cornelis Kuiper and Johannes Willemsen. Their names are added to a long list of victims of the Salvadorean government troops and fascist commandos.

"The IOJ GS most vigorously denounces this shameful deed. It expresses its deepest sympathy to the families of the murdered men and to all Dutch colleagues.

The IOJ GS also urges all journalists and the worldwide public to energetically condemn these crimes and to help in every way to put an end to the outrages of the Salvadorean junta.

The IOJ GS once again expresses its firm solidarity with the fight of the people and journalists of El Salvador."

IOJ sends special correspondent to Holland

BURIAL OF MURDERED JOURNALISTS IN HOLLAND

Public Condemnation of Salvadorean fascists

Our correspondent, who shortly after the murders in El Salvador visited Holland, has brought back first-hand material from his stay there.

IOJ news letter

SPECIAL ISSUE

1982 JUNE

THE INTERNATIONAL ORGANIZATION OF JOURNALISTS

Despite Unprecedented Confrontation Atmosphere:

COOPERATION AND UNDERSTANDING NECESSARY AMONG WORLD JOURNALISTS

The task of the day is to strengthen cooperation among journalists of good will in all parts of the world. Only in this way can we effectively contribute to the solution of the main problems facing our profession today. These include, in the first place, our responsibility for the maintenance of peace, but also our contribution to the creation of a new, more just international information order, the protection of journalists from terror and the threat of physical liquidation in countries like El Salvador, Palestine or the Lebanon, and a number of other issues. Until not long ago there was a considerable degree of agreement in the international journalist

Discussion at the Lugano congress was remarkable for the fact that professional and trade union matters, which took up a good deal of the approved congress program, were instead completely overshadowed by the artificially inflated "Polish question". Despite the resistance of a number of delegates, this "Polish" theme became the excuse for a series of crude attacks against international cooperation among journalists, and against the IOJ. The climax of this was the adoption of a provocative resolution whose essence – if we overlook the lofty sounding but demagogic rhetoric –

(continued on page 2)

The Voice of the Cold War in Lugano

IOJ Secretary General Jiří Kubka is interviewed by Newsletter.

You've just come back from Lugano, Switzerland, where the Brussels federation held its congress. Is it true that its proceedings were quite stormy?

JK: Since the time of Helsinki there has been an agreement between the Brussels federation and our international organization on the exchange of observers. I therefore had a chance to observe the IFJ congress in Lugano – and

Figure 7.5 IOJ publications exposed the political friction between the two internationals: the IOJ highlighted the loss of journalists' lives in areas of armed conflict, while the IFJ highlighted the problems in Poland, where the dissident forces had taken over the earlier IOJ member union. The IOJ accused the IFJ of having a Cold War mentality and of failing to promote the protection of journalists.

25 See the Baghdad Declaration in *IOJ newsletter* 5/1982 and *DJ* 6/1982.

Two months later another Special Issue was released with the comments of the IOJ on the **IFJ Congress held in Lugano** in May 1982. This Congress had a stormy discussion on "the Polish question", attacking the IOJ for admitting the new Polish trade union as member in Moscow and thus undermining the status of the old member SDP, which in 1990 had staged a political *coup* (Figure 7.6). However, as shown in the Special Issue, the bulk of Polish journalists were by then back in the political orientation which preceded the turn to the Solidarity line.[26] The Special Issue also exposed how the IFJ had withdrawn its support from a conference on the protection of journalists on dangerous missions scheduled to take place in the Netherlands in April. Moreover, it showed how the Congress had ignored a Finnish proposal supporting journalists' peace movement.

PRESIDENT NYERERE:

WE NEED A NEW INTERNATIONAL INFORMATION ORDER

Tanzanian President Julius Nyerere declared that international media coverage of his recent address to Tanzanians had provided him with an object lesson about the need for a New International Information Order. This was reported by the Tanzanian paper Daily News which also wrote that President Nyerere had found it difficult to recognize his own speech dealing with the national economy from the reports he had read and heard from the international media. "Let me therefore make it clear now that we in Tanzania feel that we have not been wrong in the basic thrust of our policies (socialism and self-reliance)."

President Nyerere made these remarks at a New Year's Day reception held for members of the diplomatic corps. He also repeated Tanzanian's critical attitude to the basic structure of the present-day international economic order. He pledged that Tanzania would continue to work with other Third World countries and with friends of justice everywhere to try to achieve a fundamental change—to move towards a New International Economic Order.

Figure 7.6 Julius ("Mwalimu") Nyerere, the first President of Tanzania and a prominent Third World leader, seen here in his residence in Dar es Salaam in May 1982, meeting the IOJ President. Nyerere was briefed by Nordenstreng on the international movement of journalists and Nyerere recounted Ronald Reagan's harsh message in Cancun in October 1981 (see above footnote 9). His position on NIICO was featured in *The Democratic Journalist* 4/1982. (Photo from Nordenstreng's collection)

The IOJ President was on sabbatical from his university in Finland in 1981–82 and temporarily based in Tanzania, working on books and expanding IOJ contacts to Southern Africa (Figure 7.6). For example, visiting newly independent Zimbabwe he negotiated the transfer of IOJ membership from the liberation movement ZAPU's journalist group to the new ZANU-related Zimbabwe Union of Journalists.

The expanding range of activities – both by topic and geography – was reflected in *The Democratic Journalist*.[27] The New International Information

26 *DJ* 9/1982.

27 *DJ* 7–8/1982. The Chief Editor Oldřich Bureš passed away in July 1982 and was succeeded by Jozef Belička, with Rudolf Převrátil listed as Editor. From January 1983 on, *IOJ newsletter* was also issued in French.

Order was a regular title covered by one major article in most of the issues. The topics of Journalist's Technical Minimum appear surprisingly up-to-date today – nearly 40 years later. The IOJ Secretary General himself was a driving force of new technologies as shown by his book on the explosion of information (Kubka 1977).

In June 1982 **the IOJ raised its profile at the UN** by taking the main podium in New York at the Second Special Session on Disarmament, where INGOs and peace institutes were given the floor (Figure 7.7). The IOJ was the only organization from the media field to seize this opportunity. It did so again six years later at the Third Special Session on Disarmament. In 1985–86 the IOJ President also attended the UN Committee on Information.[28]

Figure 7.7 The IOJ President addressing the UN General Assembly, Special Session on Disarmament on 24 June 1982. On the right: New York rally in support of disarmament. (Photos from Nordenstreng's collection)

In the history of the **peace movement** the early 1980s is marked as a major wave after the Vietnam War by calling for a halt to the nuclear arms race and demanding a nuclear freeze. A broad coalition of professional and grassroots organizations around the world emerged, staging mass rallies such as the one in New York during the UN conference on disarmament on 12 June 1982 with a record participation of a million people (Figure 7.7).

A significant example of how professional journalists were drawn to the peace movement is provided by Finland, where they marked October 27 as the Day of Journalists for Peace as part of the UN Week for Disarmament.[29] Various associations in the field had formed the Journalists' Peace Committee in late 1981 and declared with a broad political profile that "it is the duty of a journalist to transmit truthful information about questions of war and

28 See **Appendix 6**. The address of 1982 is also reproduced in *DJ* 10/1982. The video recording of this 10-minute presentation is available at https://sites.tuni.fi/kaarle/nordenstreng-publications/ (see 3. Conference papers and presentations).

29 *DJ* 10/1983.

peace, armament and national defence" and that the promotion of peace was seen not only as a civil virtue but an indispensable part of professional ethics – a big leap in the thinking of media professionals.[30]

The World Peace Council (WPC)[31] organized in Prague on 21–26 June 1983 the **World Assembly for Peace and Life, Against Nuclear War** (Figure 7.8). Over 3,600 participants from 132 countries were brought to the Palace of Culture in Prague, making it one of the largest peace conferences since World War II.[32] Of the participants 40 per cent came from the developing countries of the South and another 40 per cent from the West, representing various political orientations. For instance, the Finnish parliamentary delegation was headed by the Speaker coming from the Conservative Party.

The World Assembly became a huge demonstration for the "peace, freedom, independence and prosperity of all nations", as phrased in the last slogan of its Appeal, but also a strong protest against deploying new

WORLD PEACE ASSEMBLY, PRAGUE, JUNE 21–26, 1983

Appeal for Peace and Life, Against Nuclear War

Humanity stands at a crucial crossroad of history. One step in the wrong direction – and the world could be irrevocably thrown into the abyss of a nuclear war.

Never before has the arms race, [...]

[...] man and woman, resolutely standing together for peace.

The mass movement for peace is a powerful force, a determining factor in the international situation, capable of [...]

From the welcoming address by the President of the Czechoslovak Socialist Republic, Gustáv Husák

An especially acute danger is represented by plans to deploy new first-strike nuclear missiles in Western Europe. The realization of these plans will sharply increase the danger of a nuclear conflict. Such a conflict will not be limited to the continent of Europe, but will lead to a global holocaust. It is urgent to stop the deployment of missiles in Europe, to reduce all nuclear arms on the European continent and to work for the total elimination of all nuclear weapons throughout the world.

Being extremely concerned by the increasing danger of nuclear war and realizing our great responsibility to safeguard peace, we have gathered at the World Assembly for Peace and Life, against Nuclear War from 21 to 26 June in Prague, the capital of Czechoslovakia. We are citizens of 132 countries of the world, peoples of various races and nationalities, of different philosophical views, religious and political positions. We represent 1,843 national organizations, trade unions, peace, women's, youth and students' movements, political parties and churches and 108 international non-governmental organizations. Representatives of 11 intergovernmental organizations also took part in the assembly.

We declare:

Preparation for a nuclear war is the most serious crime against humanity, but war is not inevitable. It is not yet too late to prevent a nuclear holocaust, salvation is in the hands of the people themselves, of each

No to nuclear weapons in the West or in the East, around the world

Stop the arms race, nuclear and conventional

Yes to nuclear weapon-free zones

For general and complete disarmament

Peaceful political negotiations, not military confrontation

The world's resources for peace and life

Peace, freedom, independence and prosperity for all nations

JULY – AUGUST 1983

Figure 7.8 The World Peace Assembly in Prague in June 1983 was widely covered in *The Democratic Journalist* (7–8 and 9/1983). It included a dialogue of journalists with its steering committee seen here, from the right: Antero Laine from the SSL (Finland), Norma Turner from the JANE (UK), Alice Palmer from the BPA (USA), Phan Quang from the VJA (Vietnam), H. Werner from the dju (FRG) and H.L. Yilma from the EJA (Ethiopia). (Photo from Phan Quang's collection)

30 Nordenstreng (1984).

31 See https://en.wikipedia.org/wiki/World_Peace_Council The WPC was founded in 1950 and soon became a central force among pro-Moscow INGOs, including the IOJ (see Chapter 3).

32 *DJ* 7–8/1983. See also in *IOJ newsletter* Special issue in June and 14/1983.

American missiles in Europe. The voice of over 1,800 national organizations, political parties and churches as well as over 100 INGOs could not be dismissed as "Soviet propaganda", as the Western Cold War position attempted to do.[33]

The last two conference days were devoted to dialogues in 12 special interest groups, one of them convened by the IOJ and consisting of 200 journalists around the world. The introduction was given by Leena Paukku, the Secretary General of the Finnish Journalists' Peace Committee, and the rapporteur of the group was Wim Klinkenberg, Vice-President of the Netherlands Union of Journalists. He was also a member of the IFJ Bureau and operated in the 1980s as an open friend of the IOJ, opposing the Cold War mindset, which still prevailed in the IFJ as seen in the Lugano Congress.

Four months after the World Assembly the **Congress of West European Journalists for Peace** took place in Korpilampi, near Helsinki – beginning on October 27, the Day of Journalists for Peace. This was a much smaller event, attended by 40 journalists from 10 western European countries, including national unions from Germany (dju), Portugal (SJP) and Cyprus (CUJ). The invitation was from the Union of Journalists in Finland (SSL) and the Finnish Journalists' Peace Committee. Although the hosts only succeeded in persuading few western European IFJ member unions to attend, the Congress served as a reminder that "the movement keeps growing".[34]

In general, the year 1983 of the IOJ was not only dominated by activities for peace, as can be seen in Appendix 5: the list of activities also featured many other topics, including hotspots in Afghanistan, Southern Africa, Central America, Palestine, Cyprus and the most recent Grenada after the US invasion. A peculiar part of the western campaign was the "Bulgarian connection" of the attempted assassination of the Pope in November 1982.[35] A combination of the political objectives of peace and anti-imperialism was the **World Conference in Pyongyang** organized by the Korean Journalists' Union in co-operation with the IOJ, FAJ, FELAP and UAJ (Figure 7.9).[36]

Outside the sphere of journalism, 1983 had been proclaimed by the UN as **World Communication Year**, highlighting the importance of media

33 Extensive coverage of the Assembly was given in *DJ* (7–8 and 9/1983) and *IOJ newsletter* (14/1983), including short statements by participants such as Luis Echeverria, former President of Mexico, and Hortensia Allende, widow of former President Salvador Allende of Chile.

34 The title of a story on the Congress in *DJ* 12/1983. See also report and Final document in *IOJ newsletter*, Special issue November 1983.

35 See *DJ* 12/1983 and 7–8/1986.

36 *IOJ newsletter* 15/1983. The Final Declaration of the Conference was issued as a documentary supplement of *DJ* 9/1983.

IOJ news letter 1983 AUGUST 15 15

THE INTERNATIONAL ORGANIZATION OF JOURNALISTS

WORLD CONFERENCE OF JOURNALISTS AGAINST IMPERIALISM AND FOR FRIENDSHIP AND PEACE

The Main Thing Is To Safeguard Peace

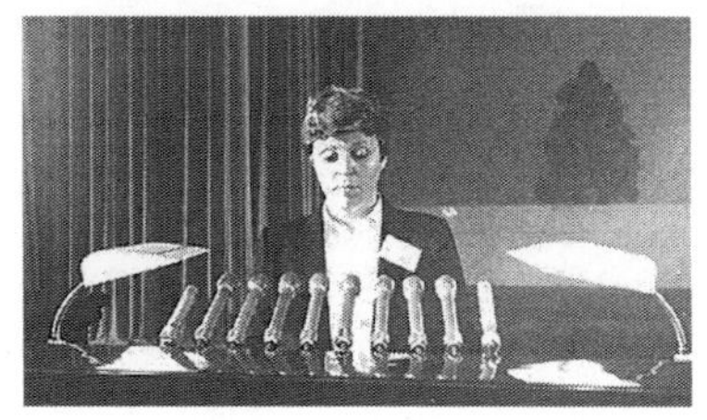

Figure 7.9 The World Conference of Journalists in Pyongyang in July 1983 was in the same grand style as that in 1969, with the opening in a stadium and a welcoming banquet with Kim Il Sung himself. Participants from 118 countries included three from Finland – Irmeli Palmu of the YLL speaking as the representative from Europe. (Photos from the Conference organizers)

and providing symbolic power to journalist organizations. For the IOJ it was also important that the idea of NIICO was now upheld by a **UN-UNESCO Round Table on NWICO**, which first met in Igls (Austria) in September 1983.[37]

The next organizational milestone of the IOJ after the Moscow Congress was the **Presidium in Luanda** on 27–29 **January 1983** – the first statutory IOJ meeting in sub-Saharan Africa. In the words of the representative of the ruling party MPLA, this meeting was considered "as an expression of militant solidarity not only with the People's Republic of Angola, but also with all the front-line states".[38] Attended by 54 participants from 30 countries, the Presidium received a report on the activities of the IOJ General Secretariat since the 9th Congress. New membership applications were approved by the journalist unions of Benin, Senegal, Mauritius, Surinam and Trinidad. After a general debate, the Presidium approved a work plan for 1983 and issued a declaration condemning racism – all documented in the report.

The following **Presidium in Paris** on 22–23 **November 1983** was called "enlarged" as its first day on 22 November was staged as a **Forum of Journalists for Peace**. Marking the 5th anniversary of the Mass Media Declaration, the Forum was addressed by the Deputy Director-General of UNESCO in charge of communication. In addition to contributions by 24 colleagues from inside and outside of the IOJ it heard a talk by Seán

37 *DJ* 12/1983.
38 *IOJ Presidium Luanda* (1983, p. 14).

Figure 7.10 The Paris Presidium in November 1983 was accompanied by a broader forum to highlight the Mass Media Declaration of UNESCO and its MacBride Commission. On the same occasion the Consultative Meeting of Journalists concluded its meeting which had begun in Prague in June.

MacBride (Figure 7.10), winner of the Nobel and Lenin peace prizes and chairman of the famous UNESCO Commission in the late 1970s. The final Statement of the Forum summarized the eventful year of peace campaigns around the world.

The Presidium received the customary report of the Secretary General and reports of the permanent IOJ Commissions (Social Commission, Training Commission and Commission for Studies and Documentation). A general debate included 16 presentations by the Presidium members and the President's closing remarks. New affiliations were admitted from the US National Alliance of Third World Journalists and the Finnish Social Democratic Association of Journalists. International Journalist Prizes for 1983 were awarded to Ernesto Vera from Cuba and Antero Laine from Finland.[39]

A major activity in 1983 was the **4th Consultative Meeting of international and regional organizations of journalists** hosted by the IOJ in two parts: **Prague on 18–19 June** and **Paris on 20 November**. The first part in Prague was attended, in addition to the IOJ, by delegations of the IFJ (President, General Secretary and representative of FELATRAP), of the Catholic UCIP (Administrative Secretary and Board member) and of the Arab FAJ (Secretary General and Assistant Secretary General) as well as representatives

39 See *IOJ Presidium Paris November 1983* (1984); *IOJ newsletter* 23/1983; *DJ* 1/1984. In his opening address President Nordenstreng among other things stressed the proposal made in his UN speech in June 1982 to set up a representative professional body for reviewing the performance of the press in matters of arms race and disarmament, and now in his concluding remarks Nordenstreng announced that Seán MacBride had agreed to lead such a commission.

of the Latin American FELAP and African UAJ. The ASEAN CAJ apologized for not being able to attend. UNESCO, which sponsored the meeting, was represented by the new Director of the Division of Free Flow of Information and Communication Policies, Hamdy Kandil; its former Director Hifzi Topuz attended as an observer. Also attending was a representative of ILO. Opening speeches were delivered by the Deputy Prime Minister of Czechoslovakia, Dr. Karol Laco, and the President of the Czechoslovak Union of Journalists, Zdeněk Hoření (Figure 7.11).

Figure 7.11 The 4th Consultative Meeting took place in the new IOJ conference hall at *Bílá Hora* in June 1983. In the opening session standing IOJ President Nordenstreng, next to him Deputy Prime Minister Laco, Journalist Union President Hoření and Secretary General Nolč. Last on the left: Kandil of UNESCO; last on the right: Furic of UCIP. (Photo from *4th Consultative Meeting* 1984)

The topics covered by the meeting were (1) protection of journalists, (2) implementation of the Mass Media Declaration of UNESCO, (3) socio-economic conditions of journalists, (4) ethics and further elaboration of the Mexico Declaration, (5) future consultative meetings. All items were thoroughly discussed, but most time was devoted to examining a revised version of the Mexico Declaration on the basis of preparation by the IOJ-UCIP-FELAP working group appointed in Mexico City. The 200-page report includes detailed proceedings with essentials transcribed from the tape-recorded discussions – a unique documentation of how the controversial topics were handled in the consultative meetings. The agreements were summarized in a final communique.

The second part of the meeting took place in Paris on 20 November 1983, towards the end of UNESCO's General Conference and before the IOJ enlarged Presidium. The meeting, held in the regional office of the IOJ, was attended by all organizations involved since 1978, except the IFJ; now FELATRAP was also listed as a regional partner. The IFJ General Secretary had confirmed his participation in advance, also sharing materials relating to the ethics document, but he was prevented from attending by illness and no one else from the IFJ attended, either. The meeting followed up the items of the Prague agenda and the published report again reproduced the proceedings in detail, including the final drafting of the document on professional ethics.

The most important outcome of the meeting was the revised version of the Mexico Declaration, **International Principles of Professional Ethics in Journalism.**[40] This was a consensus formulation after long and careful preparation – not an international code of ethics but a set of principles "as an international common ground and as a source of inspiration for national and regional codes of ethics [...] intended to be promoted autonomously by each professional organization through ways and means most adequate to its members". Issued in the name of 400,000 journalists, represented together by the organizations involved, the document, however, avoided introducing these principles as "agreed"; the Preamble only describes the process of their preparation in the consultative meetings since 1978. This was done to accommodate the hesitation of some IFJ affiliates.[41]

Even with a soft introduction it was indeed a "historical document", as the comments by the IOJ President were entitled in a brochure which was distributed later: the 10 principles "constitute the first time ever that the profession of journalism has manifested itself in a universal declaration of ethics".[42] The IOJ promoted it in publications, including the poster, and in conferences – initially at a high-level Media Conference of the Non-Aligned (NAMEDIA) in New Delhi only a couple of weeks after the document was issued (Figure 7.12).[43]

The next, **5th Consultative Meeting was held in Geneva** at the headquarters of the ILO on 5–6 **July 1984**. Attended by representatives of the IOJ, IFJ, UCIP, FELAP and UAJ, its main task was to prepare the World Conference on the Working Conditions and Security of Journalists to be convened

40 The document is available at https://research.uta.fi/ethicnet/country/international-principles-of-professional-ethics-in-journalism/.

41 Nevertheless, the IFJ later asked for the following sentence be added to the footnote about the participants of the consultative meetings: "The IFJ did not attend the conclusive meeting of this process in Paris, 20 November 1983, which issued the document."

42 *International Principles* (1985 and 1988). Also in *DJ* 2/1985 and in Nordenstreng & Topuz (1989, pp. 250–255). Admittedly, the IFJ had already adopted in 1954 the Declaration of Principles on the Conduct of Journalists ("Bordeaux Declaration"), but under the Cold War conditions it was far from universal.

43 *NAMEDIA Final Report and Documents* (New Delhi: NAMEDIA, 1984). Also in *DJ* 2/1984. In addition to the IOJ President the Conference was addressed by the Prime Minister of India, the Director-General of UNESCO and the Secretary-General of ITU among others.

Figure 7.12 During the NAMEDIA Conference in Delhi on 9 December 1983, Prime Minister Indira Gandhi received the IOJ President in her office. Mrs Gandhi was at the time Chairperson of the Non-Aligned Movement and she shared with Nordenstreng her dim view of the US-sponsored war of the "Contras" against the revolutionary government of Nicaragua. (Photo from the Indian News Agency)

in Mexico City in early 1985.[44] This joint initiative was a new beginning in the history of attempts to protect journalists – now as part of a larger package also including employment and new technologies.[45] For the IOJ it effectively replaced the Bulgarian initiative of 1981, and for the IFJ it meant that the Federation was again ready for joint activities with the IOJ and the rest of the Consultative group in protecting journalists – after its U-turn in the Lugano Congress two years earlier.

In addition, the meeting issued on 6 July 1984 a joint statement in support of UNESCO.[46] This statement, signed by the IFJ Secretary General, the IOJ President, the UCIP Administrative Secretary, the FELAP Secretary General and the UAJ Deputy Secretary, was a powerful intervention at a moment when the western campaign kept accusing UNESCO of threatening press freedom, while American opinion was divided on the wisdom of the Reagan administration's decision to withdraw from the Organization.[47] The US-led pressure against UNESCO was accumulating and the Thatcher administration in the UK was also threatening to withdraw. A version of the same statement was issued as a press release during the General Conference of UNESCO in Sofia in October 1985, by which time the western campaign was being specifically directed against Director-General M'Bow.[48]

The Executive Committee met in New Delhi in September 1984. After a preparatory meeting of the Presidium, the Executive Committee held its

44 UNESCO had already promised support for this and now FELAP announced that the Mexican Government had confirmed to host it. It was agreed that the Conference would be under the auspices of UNESCO, ILO and the International Red Cross and that it would be organized by FELAP and co-sponsored by the other parties of the Consultative group.

45 A background document by Hernan Uribe of FELAP was published in *DJ* 11/1984.

46 The statement is reproduced as **Appendix 7**. It also includes the press release of 23 October 1985, covered on the following day in The *International Herald Tribune*.

47 For overviews, see *DJ* 12/1984 and 1/1985. The question of the American withdrawal was addressed in *IOJ newsletter* 2/1985 and *DJ* 3, 4 and 12/1985.

48 See *Hope and Folly. The United States and UNESCO 1945–1985* (Preston, Herman & Schiller, 1989). M'Bow's interview was published in *DJ* 7–8/1985.

Figure 7.13 The leading officers of the IOJ documentation and publication services, Václav Slavík (on the left) and Rudolf Převrátil (in the centre) conferring with the President of Czechoslovak Union of Journalists, Zdeněk Hoření (on the right) in the early 1980s in the bar of Hotel Inter-Continental. This top hotel in Prague close to the IOJ Secretariat was a favourite venue for organizational meetings and accommodating foreign guests. (Photo: IOJ)

sessions on 20 and 23 September. These were attended by 56 members and over 50 guests and observers. Various topics were discussed and key documents were approved, including the report on the activities of the General Secretariat since the 9th Congress and reports by the permanent Commissions – after Moscow also the new Commission for Studies and Documentation and the Training Commission.[49]

The Executive Committee ended with a political declaration, pointing out "the adventurous, militaristic policies of world imperialism, led by the Reagan Administration". The declaration shared the concern about these policies with the 7th NAM Summit held in New Delhi the previous year, and also expressed its support for the Soviet proposals "aimed at reducing international tension and returning to the policies of détente".[50]

The second and third days of the meeting were devoted to the **International Seminar** on the "Role and responsibility of journalists in promoting the New International Information and Communication Order and in averting the danger of war in the Indian Ocean". Staged as a larger forum of 300 participants, the Seminar was highlighted by a message from Prime Minister Indira Gandhi and an open letter addressed to UN Secretary General Javier Perez de Cuellar in support of the UN, UNESCO, the Mass Media Declaration and the International Principles of Professional Ethics in Journalism.[51]

---

49 *IOJ Executive Committee New Delhi 1984* (1985, pp. 25–104). In addition, the membership affiliations approved in Luanda were confirmed and further applications were approved among others for associate membership from the Tanzanian Journalists Association (TAJA) and the Indian Federation of Working Journalists (IFWJ).

50 Ibid., pp. 106–107. In addition to the declaration, three resolutions were adopted: on the IOJ tasks and activities, a protest against the IFJ's plan to hold its Bureau meeting in Jerusalem and a call for a ceasefire in the Iraq-Iran war (Ibid., pp. 107–109). Also in *IOJ newsletter* 20/1984 and in *DJ* 11 and 12/1984.

51 *IOJ newsletter* 20/1984. Also in *DJ* 11/1984. The same *DJ* included a statement by the IOJ General Secretariat on the murder of Indira Gandhi, which had happened only five weeks after the Executive Committee.

The year 1985 followed the pattern of previous years, as graphically shown in the coverage of ***The Democratic Journalist***, with the struggle between peace and war as the overall framework (Figure 7.14). Most stories were overtly political but there were also strictly informative pages on media technology, journalist organizations and a "Chronicle" inside the back cover with brief news items on member unions. An exemplary case was a series of articles by the Indian P. Sainath on militarism and media in *DJ* 4–7/1985. The topics covered were many, including the protection of journalists written by experts of the International Committee of the Red Cross (ICRC).[52]

Figure 7.14 *The Democratic Journalist* provided extensive coverage of media and journalists in different parts of the world – from Nicaragua, Grenada, Ecuador and Cuba to Afghanistan, South Africa, Indonesia and Vietnam. Europe, especially Germany, was prominent in the 40th anniversary of the end of World War II. An international exhibition "The Militant Poster" in Prague in May–June 1985 was greeted by President Gustáv Husák *(DJ* 9/1985).

In addition to its own statutory bodies and the Consultative group, the IOJ continued to participate with other relevant INGOs, including the International Association for Mass Communication Research (IAMCR/AIERI).[53]

As agreed at the 5th Consultative Meeting in Geneva, the World Conference on Working Conditions and Security of Journalists was scheduled to be convened in Mexico City in March 1985. However, it did not materialize, due to the mounting pressure from Western governments and the media proprietor lobbies. Instead, the ICRC invited both the Consultative group and the

52 By Hans-Peter Gasser in *DJ* 12/1984 and 1/1985; by Alain Modoux in *DJ* 3/1985.

53 Its biennial Congress in 1984 was held in Prague, where the IOJ hosted with it a workshop on journalism education; see *IAMCR/AIERI* (1986).

media publishers to a **Round Table on the Safety of Journalists on Dangerous Professional Missions** in Mont Pelerin, near Vevey in Switzerland on 24–25 **April 1985.**[54] While the cancelling of the Mexico Conference was a setback for the Consultative group, particularly FELAP and the IOJ, the ICRC was welcomed as a neutral platform to advance the controversial project. Yet the outcome of the Round Table was meagre: all that could be agreed was the setting up of a "Hot Line" to the ICRC to help journalists in difficulties while on dangerous missions.[55]

The next **Presidium was held in Quito** from 28 June to 2 **July 1985** (Figure 7.15). It followed the customary pattern of opening addresses by the host country and the IOJ President, followed by the Secretary General introducing the Secretariat's report on the activities since the last statutory meeting. As usual, it approved this report and reports of the permanent Commissions and welcomed new membership applications[56].

IOJ news letter

1985 JULY

13–14

QUITO IOJ PRESIDIUM

THE INTERNATIONAL ORGANIZATION OF JOURNALISTS

Against Disinformation in Latin America

IOJ PRESIDIUM MEETS IN QUITO, ECUADOR

Commentary on Report of the Activity of the IOJ General Secretariat • 10th IOJ Congress in Sofia in 1986 • IOJ International Journalists Prizes for 1985 • Jiří Kubka Receives Highest Award from the UNP

Figure 7.15 Special attention in Quito was devoted to disinformation in Latin America on the basis of a report by the Deputy Secretary General of FELAP, Hernan Uribe. The same problems of information imperialism were reported by Presidium members from Africa and Asia. A delegation of the Presidium was received by the President of the Republic of Ecuador León Febres Cordero. The delegates also visited the Equator (see Quang's recollections in Part Two). The proceedings of this Presidium was published in Spanish only, while large reports were published in English and French in *DJ* 2 and 3/1986.

The Presidium ended with the release of a communique summarizing the proceedings with political remarks on various countries around the world, especially in Latin America and Africa. It recalled the recent end of military regimes in Argentine, Brazil, Bolivia and Uruguay, while "the struggle

54 *IOJ newsletter* 10/1985. The IOJ position for the Mt. Pelerin Round Table was published in *DJ* 12/1985.

55 *IOJ newsletter* 21/1985. See https://www.icrc.org/en/publication/0394-hotline-assistance-journalists-dangerous-assignments. The IOJ Documentation and Information Service (DIS), upgraded in 1983 into the IOJ Institute of Studies and Documentation (ISD), started to issue reports on Persecution of Journalists.

56 In Quito there was one application: by the Black Press Institute (BPI) from the USA. See Palmer's recollections in Part Two.

against the fascist tyranny is increasing in Chile and Paraguay"; expressed support "for the heroic people of Nicaragua in their fights against Somozist counter-revolutionaries, financed and led by the US"; and condemned "the badly named 'Radio Marti' which the Cubans dub 'Radio Reagan', a farcical propaganda aggression against the people of Cuba and an infringement of their sovereignty". The Presidium "expressed its support for Angola and Mozambique and other countries in Africa struggling to defend their sovereignty and independence in the face of the imperialist threat and condemned the US support for the racist South African regime". Solidarity was expressed with "the Palestinian people struggling for their historic right to build their own independent state". An appeal was made to the governments of Iraq and Iran "to put an end to their bloody war as it only benefits the enemies of the Arab and Iranian people and the Middle Eastern reactionary forces".[57]

The Presidium approved a resolution on UNESCO, based on the statement given by the Consultative Meeting in Geneva a year before. Furthermore, it decided to celebrate the 40th anniversary of the IOJ in Prague in June 1986 and it endorsed the proposal of the Bulgarian Union to convene the 10th Congress in Sofia in October 1986.

The Presidium was attended by most of the 29 members and nearly 20 people from the Secretariat, including 10 simultaneous interpreters. As most delegates were unable to pay their travel costs, these were mainly met by the IOJ and its East European member unions. But the investment gave an additional benefit: the return to various destinations via Cuba was arranged so that a stopover in Havana facilitated the Vice-Presidents' attendance at a conference of solidarity with journalists on dangerous missions and with the Cuban revolution as well as the beginning of the 4th Congress of FELAP. (See Quang's recollections in Part Two.)

In September 1985 the Finlandia Hall in Helsinki was again the venue of a conference, now marking the 10th anniversary of the signing of the CSCE Final Act. The **Congress on Journalists and Détente** on 6–9 September was hosted by the Union of Journalists in Finland (SSL), which had invited all the journalist unions of the 35 signatory countries, with the IFJ and the IOJ, to review the process of détente from the point of view of journalists.[58]

The Congress was attended by nearly 100 journalists from 26 CSCE countries, including the leaders of the two world organizations. The participants represented the mainstream politics of their respective countries, far from the journalists for peace gathered in Helsinki two years earlier. The IFJ after

---

57 *IOJ newsletter* 13–14/1985.

58 The Congress was financially assisted by Finland's Ministry for Foreign Affairs and private sponsors, notably Aatos Erkko, the publisher of Finland's leading newspaper *Helsingin Sanomat*. The Congress co-ordinator was Leena Paukku from SSL.

its 1982 Congress had taken a hard line against the socialist countries, in support of the dissident movements in Poland and elsewhere.

Many IFJ voices in Helsinki were cynical and pessimistic, but after frank discussions the conference ended in a positive atmosphere and a wish to continue such meetings.[59] Actually the international political climate improved towards the end of 1985, after Mikhail Gorbachev began to pursue his policy of *perestroika* and *glasnost*. The IOJ was quick to embrance this policy, covering his interview with the US *Time* magazine in August and the first Gorbachev-Reagan meeting in Geneva in November.[60]

Figure 7.16 The host of the Journalists and Détente Congress, SSL, was generous in providing the venue and platform, including its journal *Sanomalehtimies – Journalisten*. The UN had proclaimed 1986 the International Year of Peace – a welcome boost to the IOJ, which was preparing to celebrate the 40th anniversary of its foundation. The New Year greeting combined an anti-war image with a computer terminal, representing new technology which the IOJ was eagerly applying at the time.

59 The host SSL had compiled a package of background documents (*Journalists and Détente* 1985), followed by the proceedings (1986). A summary report was given in *IOJ newsletter* 18/1985. A dialogue between IFJ President and IOJ Secretary General during the Congress was published in *DJ* 2/1986.

60 *IOJ newsletter* 17 and 23/1985; *DJ* 1 and 2/1986. The report from Geneva was authored by Don Rojas, the IOJ Secretary for North America and the Caribbean.

CHAPTER 8
HEYDAY 1986-89

The grip of the Cold War was significantly released in the second part of the 1980s, but the world was still filled with conflicts. One of these was in Southern Africa, where the Apartheid regime of South Africa, supported by the USA, tried to retain its power nationally against the liberation movement ANC and internationally against the Namibian liberation movement SWAPO, with another front in Angola, where the South African and American backed UNITA was fighting the MPLA regime supported by the Cubans and the Soviets.

By the end of the 1980s the proxy wars in Africa were won by the Soviet side and the Apartheid regime in South Africa began to yield under increasing international pressure.

The first Intifada in the Gaza Strip and on the West Bank broke out in 1987, when Palestinians staged large-scale protests against Israel.

Behind political and military conflicts economies kept growing with an increasing role of new technologies in computers and telecommunications.

The year 1989 became a landmark of challenges to communist regimes. First, in mid-April Chinese students turned the Tiananmen Square in Beijing into a huge scene of protests. The government cleared it violently on 4 June and the "Democracy Movement" has never since staged similar protests.

In Europe, Poland's Solidarity Movement won general elections in June 1989. From September, on large demonstrations took place in the GDR, leading to the ousting of the communist leader Erich Honecker in mid-October and on 9 November the Berlin Wall fell. A wave of civil resistance advanced throughout the socialist countries, with the "Velvet Revolution" in Czechoslovakia from 17 November on. The founder of the Civic Forum, Václav Havel was appointed interim President at the end of December. Meanwhile, Nicolae Ceausescu of Romania was overthrown.

The Soviet Union was not shaken by these developments, although some signs of approaching political turmoil could be perceived in 1989. Gorbachev's reformist regime remained in charge, bringing hope of ending the arms race and Cold War.

The IOJ continued successful both at home in Prague and in various regions of the world. The present chapter highlights the main events of the IOJ success story during its last four years - until 1989, when the heyday was over.

TURNING 40 AND IN FULL FLOWER 1986–87

The anniversary celebrations began in Copenhagen on 7 June 1986 – exactly 40 years after the IOJ was founded and in the selfsame founding place. A small event was staged by the President and Secretary General, who happened to be conveniently there right after attending the IFJ Congress in Elsinor, eastern Denmark (Figure 8.1). The IOJ presented the Danish Parliament with a huge crystal vase from Czechoslovakia as a symbol of the dedication of journalists to the ideals of truth, freedom and peace.

Figure 8.1 Recalling the IOJ founding in Copenhagen, Christiansborg Palace, in June 1986 with the Post-War Foreign Minister of Denmark, Thorgil Kristensen, who had represented the Danish government at the constituent Congress in June 1946; pictured here second from the right with IOJ President Nordenstreng. Next to the left: Deputy Speaker of the Danish Parliament Povi Bronstedt discussing with the leaders of the Danish Union of Journalists, Board member Leif Larsen and President Tove Hygum. On the far left: IOJ Secretary General Jiří Kubka and IFJ Secretary General Hans Larsen. (Photo from *The Democratic Journalist* 9/1986)

Earlier in the year several other activities had taken place as seen in Appendix 5. First to note was the **6th Consultative Meeting of international and regional organizations of journalists in Brussels in January 1986**. Hosted by the IFJ with its President Kenneth Ashton and Secretary General Hans Larsen (who just replaced retiring Théo Bogaerts), it thoroughly discussed the safety of journalists (with Alain Modoux from ICRC), the social and economic conditions of journalists (with Christiane Privat from ILO), new technology and status of journalists (with IFJ and IOJ co-ordinating two studies supported by UNESCO) and the future of consultative meetings (to be continued in the 2nd part of the meeting later in 1986).[1]

1 Proceedings compiled by the IOJ as a dossier for participants, issued for every meeting from the 6th on, with accumulated documents until 1990.

Two significant meetings took place in April 1986, both attended by the IOJ. The USSR Union of Journalists hosted a **Conference on Mass Media and Human Rights** in Moscow – reflecting the western pressures and also the new Soviet policies under Gorbachev.[2] The 2nd **UN-UNESCO Round Table on NWICO** was held in Copenhagen.[3] In October 1986 the IOJ joined 2,500 delegates from 136 countries at one of the main events in the International Year of Peace: the **World Congress of Peace Forces** in Copenhagen.[4]

The main celebration of the 40th anniversary took place in Prague, in the same *Slovanský dům* in the centre of Prague where the 2nd IOJ Congress was held in June 1947 (Figure 8.2). A ceremonial session was held under the banner "40 Years in the Service of Peace, Truth and Progress" on 9 June 1986 in the presence of several Presidium members and many Czechoslovak journalists as well as two senior colleagues who had attended the founding Congress 40 years earlier. The meeting issued an "Appeal to the Journalists of the World", pointing out current problems of the arms race, especially "Star Wars", and mounting tension in different parts of the world.[5]

Figure 8.2 The "gala meeting" in June 1986 was addressed by Dr Matej Lúčan, Deputy Prime Minister of Czechoslovakia (speaking). At the table from the right: Ján Riško, President of the Czechoslovak Union of Journalists, Secretary General Kubka, President Nordenstreng and Mrs Gusta Fučíková, the widow of Julius Fučík, the Czechoslovak national hero journalist executed by the Nazis. The reception in the evening was attended among others by the first Secretary General Jiři Hronek. (Photos: IOJ)

2 Summary in *IOJ newsletter* 10/1986 and more in *DJ* 7–8 and 9/1986.
3 *DJ* 10/1986.
4 *DJ* 2/1987.
5 *IOJ newsletter* 12/1986 and *DJ* 9/1986. The Appeal was read out by Gordon Shaeffer – a British delegate at the founding Congress in 1946. *DJ* 5/1986 reviewed the 40 years of IOJ history. The first part of *Useful Recollections* was published for this occasion, providing background for the long prehistory of the IOJ.

INTERNATIONAL ORGANIZATION OF JOURNALISTS
ORGANISATION INTERNATIONALE DES JOURNALISTES
МЕЖДУНАРОДНАЯ ОРГАНИЗАЦИЯ ЖУРНАЛИСТОВ
ORGANIZACION INTERNACIONAL DE PERIODISTAS
المنظمة الصحفيين العالمية

Figure 8.3 The number of delegates and observers in Sofia did not quite reach the record of the previous Congress in Moscow. However, the number of member unions and other organizations present was greater than ever before, reflecting the growth of the IOJ and its prestige.

The **10th IOJ Congress in Sofia** was held in the Ludmila Zhivkova Palace of Culture on 20–23 **October 1986**, with the logo proclaiming the 40th anniversary of the IOJ and the five languages reminding of its multinational profile. The Congress was attended by 233 delegates from 96 member unions and 107 observers and guests; represented were 116 organizations from 97 countries plus 31 international and regional organizations and institutions – an all-time record.

As before, the Congress received messages from several heads of state, beginning with Todor Zhivkov of the host country and followed among others by Gustáv Husák of Czechoslovakia, Erich Honecker of the GDR, Wojciech Jaruzelski of Poland, Pham Van Dong of Vietnam, Yasser Arafat of Palestine and Daniel Ortega of Nicaragua.[6] The guests addressing the Congress included the IFJ President Mia Doornaert and the ICRC representative Michael Schroeder.[7]

---

6 An extensive report appeared within a couple of weeks in *IOJ newsletter* 21/1986 and two months later in *DJ* 1/1987. The customary printed report *10th Congress* was published in early 1987. More in *DJ* 2, 3 and 4/1987.

7 *DJ* 4/1987.

The national unions which had applied for membership since the 9th Congress – in total 23 – were unanimously admitted as new members, bringing the total number of journalists covered to 245,000. The largest new member union was the Brazilian FENAJ, whose President-elect Armando Rollemberg spoke on behalf of the new members.[8]

In addition to the opening and closing speeches by the President and the Secretary General's extensive report on developments during the past few years, the Congress received reports by the four permanent Commissions for Professional and Social affairs, Training and Studies and Documentation. The Congress followed the pattern established in Moscow, with three working groups focusing on peace, NIICO and pressing professional problems, especially protection and new technologies (Figure 8.4).

Figure 8.4 The Sofia Congress in October 1986 made full use of computers in processing data and text, demonstrated here by Secretary General Kubka, who was a pioneer in applying new technologies in international organizations. Voting in the Congress shown here by the delegation from Zimbabwe: Charles Chikerema in the middle and Christopher Muzavazi on the right. (Photos from *The Democratic Journalist* 1/1987)

The elections led to a Presidium of as many as 32 members, including the President, the Secretary General and the Treasurer. Of these, Nordenstreng and Kubka were re-elected with Károly Megyeri as the new Treasurer. The number of Vice-Presidents increased from 23 to 28, most of them continuing – some with new names – and new members coming from Brazil, Congo, Ethiopia, Portugal, Romania, the USA and Zimbabwe. The US Alice Palmer was the first female Vice-President since the 1950s. An addition to the Presidium was the Chairman of the Auditing Commission.

Sixty delegates took the floor in the plenary sessions and over 100 spoke in the three working groups. Each working group approved a summary re-

8 More on the new member unions, see *DJ* 2/1987.

port, the second one on NIICO quite detailed including a resolution with an appeal to the UN and UNESCO, to journalists and their organizations and especially to the IOJ Presidium and the Secretariat.[9] The main outcome of the Congress was issued in three resolutions: an Appeal, a Declaration of Solidarity and the Orientation Document.[10]

The Appeal to Journalists of the World reminded them of "the policies of the imperialist forces", urging "all colleagues in different countries to mobilize public opinion in defense of peace on our planet and to avert a nuclear catastrophe". Moreover, it called on journalists "to take more effective action to help solve the problem of hunger, to develop new types of foodstuffs, protect the environment, preserve the existing and discover new sources of energy".

The Declaration of Solidarity called on "all democratic journalists in the world to consistently strengthen their solidarity with all mass media workers, fighting, together with their peoples, for national liberation, self-determination, democracy and social progress". It covered in detail the struggles in various countries in Latin America, Asia, the Arab world and Africa, for example condemning "the policy of aggression carried out by racist South Africa against the Frontline States, especially Angola and Mozambique" and demanding the release of Nelson Mandela.

The Orientation Document pointed out that the IOJ had developed in 40 years "into the largest and most representative international association of professional journalists, uniting 250,000 journalists of different political, philosophical and religious convictions from 120 countries of all continents". It emphasized that the Gorbachev-Reagan meeting in Reykjavik had "opened up an historic possibility to eliminate nuclear weapons from our planet".

The Document concluded with concrete points by which the Congress firstly noted with satisfaction the trend towards closer co-operation with other international organizations, especially through the consultative meetings of international and regional organizations of working journalists under the auspices of UNESCO. Secondly, the Congress authorized the permanent IOJ Commissions in the fields of training and research to continue and asked the Presidium to set up working committees to deal with specific questions on peace and disarmament, professional ethics, social welfare, protection on dangerous missions and new technologies.[11] Thirdly, the Congress authorized the Secretary General to change the working methods of

9 *DJ* 1/1987; *10th Congress* (1987, pp. 64–84).

10 Ibid., pp. 89–107.

11 This was discussed in advance at the Tihany meeting of the CMEC member unions (see Appendix 5). As usual the meeting was attended by the IOJ Secretary General, belonging to the socialist camp, but for the first time also the IOJ President.

the governing bodies of the IOJ, among other things setting up a Bureau of the Presidium.

Thus the Congress gave a clear mandate for the continuation of the line first introduced in the 1978 Mexico City Presidium and confirmed by the 1981 Moscow Congress. It was a line referred to by the IOJ President in his concluding speech as "new thinking" – a slogan borrowed from Gorbachev. This line was introduced before the Congress as two proposals – see **Appendix 8**.

Following Sofia the **Secretariat in Prague** got new Secretaries by rotation: for Europe Vladimir Artyomov from the USSR; for Africa and Asia Bernd Rayer from the GDR; for Latin America Elson Conceptión from Cuba; for Professional Affairs Constantin Prisacaru from Romania and for International Organizations Marek Jurkowicz from Poland. A new Secretary for Europe and peace affairs was added from Finland: Leena Paukku – the first ever female Secretary at the IOJ.[12] Studies and documentation were installed in the International Journalism Institute (IJI) with Václav Slavík as its Director (see his recollections in Part Two).

Immediately after the 10th Congress the **2nd part of the 6th Consultative Meeting** was held in Sofia. It was hosted by the IOJ and attended by leading representatives of the IFJ, UAJ, FAJ, FELAP and CAJ[13], with UNESCO, ILO and the ICRC as observers – all of them also as guests at the IOJ Congress. The meeting concluded the agenda agreed in Brussels in January.[14] It was at the 6th meeting that those involved began to call the group "Consultative Club" and it was in Sofia that the FAJ submitted a proposal to turn the Club into a "World Council of Journalists". It was agreed that the Club would join the IOJ in organizing for UNESCO a Symposium on the Mass Media Declaration in Finland on the occasion of its 10th anniversary in 1988.

The Consultative Club was active and successful in 1987–89. With the political support of the IOJ, which endorsed it by the Congress, and the IFJ, which confirmed it by the President's address in Sofia, it began to publish books of which the first was a trilingual booklet listing journalists killed and missing in various Latin American countries and in the areas of Palestine, Lebanon and the Persian Gulf.

The **7th Consultative Meeting** was held in two parts in 1987: the first in Cairo (Egypt) in April and the second in Tampere (Finland) in December,

---

12 Paukku had worked in Finland as Chief Editor of the SSL journal *Sanomalehtimies – Journalisten*. In addition, she had been secretary of the Finnish Journalists' Peace Committee and main organizer of the 1st Congress of CSCE journalists in Helsinki.

13 The CAJ was represented by Vice-President Antonio Nieva, the President of the Philippine Union of Journalists, who became the IOJ Secretary General in 1995.

14 Reports of these meetings are reproduced in Appendix III of *A History of the International Movement of Journalists* (Nordenstreng & al., 2016, pp. 217–225).

making progress in joint projects supported by UNESCO and in consultation with the ICRC and ILO. By this time the group came to be called Consultative Club. The **8th Meeting** in 1988 was held again in two parts, both in Prague, and the **9th Meeting** in Mexico City in July 1989.[15] The Club continued to pursue its projects despite a setback in the Symposium of the Mass Media Declaration from which UNESCO withdrew after vehement opposition by the publisher organizations.[16]

The resulting three books[17] (Figure 8.5) and the whole record of the Consultative Club constitute a remarkable chapter in the history of the international movement of journalists. In fact, the position expressed by the 8th Consultative Meeting in 1988 was quoted as an overall conclusion of *A History of the International Movement of Journalists*: "the operation of the mass media should be determined primarily by the practice of professional journalism in the public interest without undue government or commercial influence", calling for the "professional autonomy of journalists as well as a measure of public accountability".[18]

Accordingly, the Consultative Club served as an ideal co-operation platform between those involved.[19] On the other hand, the most ambitious vision for turning it into a "World Council of Journalists" – an umbrella of practising journalists throughout the world – did not materialize: the proposal was first postponed from meeting to meeting and finally abandoned after thorough discussion in 1989. Opposition to the proposal came mainly from the IFJ, which was eager to maintain its distinct profile, but there was also reluctance among other partners – including the IOJ, where the Cold War mindset had widely nurtured a view whereby a merger with the IFJ was tantamount to surrender.

The role of UNESCO was crucial in bringing the partners together in 1978 and its financial support – an annual grant of 10,000 US dollars for travel costs – was essential to facilitate regular meetings. Yet in substance matters UNESCO remained in the background, while especially the IOJ and FELAP took initiatives and maintained progress.

UNESCO's support to the Consultative Club continued until 1990 despite the change of regime in UNESCO after the Senegalese M'Bow was replaced in

---

15 Ibid., pp. 226–247.

16 *DJ* 3, 10 and 11/1988. See also *The Global Media Debate* (1993, pp. 99–107).

17 *Journalists – murdered! Journalistes – assassines! ¡Periodistas – asesinados!* edited by R.H.L. Bakker (IFJ) and Mazen Husseini (IOJ); *Journalists and New Technology* prepared by John Lawrence (IFJ); *Journalist: Status, Rights and Responsibilities* edited by Kaarle Nordenstreng (IOJ) and Hifzi Topuz (Turkey). All these were published by the IOJ.

18 Nordenstreng & al. (2016, pp. 176–177) and *DJ* 11/1988. This formulation was prepared by IOJ President Nordenstreng together with Aidan White, who started as new IFJ Secretary General in 1987.

19 Since 1988 the Catholic UCIP no longer participated, but all other partners were very active attending meetings and contributing to the joint publications.

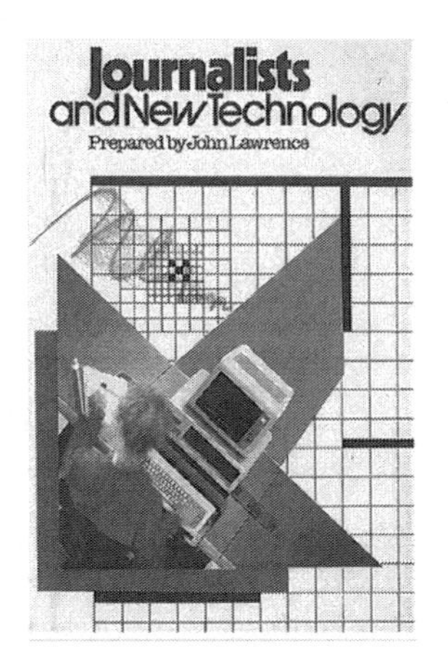

Figure 8.5 The books of the Consultative Club were prepared with good co-operation from of the organizations involved – especially the IOJ and the IFJ – while translations and publishing were generously provided by the IOJ.

1987 by the Spanish Federico Mayor as the Director-General. The change was largely due to a campaign by the western press accusing M'Bow of bad management and also of restricting press freedom in issues such as the protection of journalists. The campaign was driven by the US and UK governments, which a couple of years earlier had left UNESCO.[20] Nevertheless it succeeded in turning around especially UNESCO's media policies. For example, the ideas of the Mass Media Declaration, the MacBride Report and NWICO were effectively erased from UNESCO's programmes and replaced by a Western concept of media freedom.[21] Consequently the IOJ lost UNESCO's support for its strategic line siding with the socialist and non-aligned countries, whereas the IFJ gained support from UNESCO for its western approach.[22]

The **Presidium Bureau was held in Moscow** on 17–18 **March 1987** as a new statutory form established by the Sofia Congress. Attended by 15 of the 32 Presidium members and by 10 other representatives of member unions as well as 12 Secretaries and other members of the Secretariat (not counting the interpreters), the Bureau confirmed a new structure and composition of

20 See Preston & al. (1989) and Gerbner, Mowlana & Nordenstreng (1993).

21 UNESCO tried hard to change its image in the Western press from a government-friendly organization to an advocate of freedom and an ally of private media. For this UNESCO recruited Alain Modoux from the ICRC, first to head the Office of Public Information and later to lead the Secretariat's Division for Free Flow of Information and Communication.

22 Yet UNESCO continued to maintain normal relations with the IOJ. Director-General Mayor even sent a message of cordial greetings to the IOJ Presidium in Brasilia in April 1988; see *DJ* 6/1988.

the permanent Councils and Committees and adopted a detailed action plan for 1987 – see Minutes in **Appendix 9**.

The Minutes are self-explanatory. They were copied as material for the next full Presidium session scheduled to take place in Baghdad in October 1987. However, the venue was changed at the last minute to Nicosia in Cyprus – a decision made on practical and security grounds mainly related to the ongoing Iran–Iraq war and the deteriorating situation in the Persian Gulf. This naturally caused tension between the IOJ and its faithful member union in Iraq.[23] On the other hand, the Interpress Photo Exhibition was opened in Baghdad in late October as scheduled.

The **Presidium in Nicosia** on 21–23 **October 1987** was attended by 22 members and 10 additional representatives of member unions plus seven Secretaries (Figure 8.6).[24]

IOJ newsletter

1987 NOVEMBER

21

THE INTERNATIONAL ORGANIZATION OF JOURNALISTS

SESSION OF THE IOJ PRESIDIUM

Nicosia, October 21 to 22, 1987

Nicosia, the capital of the Republic of Cyprus, welcomed in October of this year members of the presidium of the International Organization of Journalists headed by its President Kaarle Nordenstreng and Secretary General Jiří Kubka, representatives of member organizations and secretaries of the IOJ General Secretariat.

The opening ceremony of the session was attended by the acting President of the Republic of Cyprus, Vassos Lyssarides and Dinos Michaelides, Minister of the Interior, who with sincere words welcomed members of

gress held in Sofia in 1986 – an objective and stimulating evaluation of the first results and experience gained in implementing the action plan. Discussions among journalists on setting up nuclear-free zones, participation on the mee-

In near alphabetical order the Secretary General spoke of negotiations held since the 10th Congress with member and non-member organizations of journalists and with international non-governmental organizations, e.g. on the role of the mass media in strengthening trust among nations, the mission of journalism in the developing countries and on the protection of journalists on dangerous missions. He gave details of seminars held under the auspices of the IOJ, *the inauguration of a new IOJ regional centre in Mexico, the preparation of other centres in Africa and Asia, Solidarity schools in Lagos, Portugal and Poland.* The final stage of establishing an automated information system at the IOJ is currently being undertaken, which is to serve the General Secretariat, selected organizations and IOJ member organizations.

Figure 8.6 The opening session of the Nicosia Presidium was attended by the acting President of Cyprus, Vassos Lyssarides, and the UN Special Representative in Cyprus, James Holger, who presented a certificate of "Peace Messenger" awarded by the UN Secretary General to the IOJ "in recognition of a significant contribution to the programme and objectives of the International Year of Peace". The Presidium adopted a statement "on a just solution of the Cyprus problem" and a resolution "on the situation in the Arab Gulf". Detailed reports of the proceedings were included in a customary publication.

In addition to passing political resolutions the Presidium heard the report of the Secretary General on the IOJ activities since the 10th Congress, this time focusing on professional and organizational matters, including a proposal on the establishment of IOJ regional centres. Separate reports were presented by the chairs of the Council of Studies and Documentation and the Training Council as well as of the five Committees on Peace and Disarmament, Professional Ethics, Social Issues, Protection of Journalists and New Technologies. All these

23 See exchange of telexes between Vice-President Hammoudi and President Nordenstreng, reproduced as Appendix to the Minutes of the Presidium (*The IOJ Presidium Meeting Nicosia* 1987).

24 *IOJ newsletter* 21/1987; *DJ* 1/1988; *The IOJ Presidium Meeting Nicosia* (1987).

reports were endorsed, including those on the newly established regional centre for Latin America and the Caribbean in Mexico City, the setting up of new centres in 1988 for Africa based in Addis Abeba and for the Arab world based in Algiers, with a feasibility study expected on a regional centre for Asia and another for the UN in New York/Geneva/Vienna.

The Presidium approved the Action Plan for 1987-88 and welcomed two additional member unions, from Costa Rica and Nepal. The question of membership fees was introduced by the Treasurer and it was agreed that the fee should remain the same as set in the founding Congress of 1946: 0.50 US$ per person, half to be paid in US dollars and the rest in Czechoslovak Crowns or in local currency. Member organizations would be able to apply for reductions in payments on special grounds. No details were provided on the finances but it was generally understood that there were ample means to finance the expanding activities and regional centres.

As a major issue, the President and Secretary General were invited to make a critical analysis of the IOJ Statute with a view to preparing amendments to it for the next Congress. Finally, rotating members for different regions were elected to the Presidium Bureau: Africa - Manuel Tomé, the Arab countries - Bassam Abu Shariff, Asia - Chou Chang Choun, Europe - Albino Ribeiro Cardoso, Latin America - Armando Rollemberg. Rollemberg invited the next Presidium to meet in Brasilia in April 1988.

By this time the new structure of the IOJ Councils and Committees was in place - see **Appendix 10**.

As shown in Appendix 5 the number of activities in 1987 was abundant, including among others the **2nd Congress of CSCE Journalists in Vienna** (Figure 8.7). In a common statement the hosting Austrian Union of Journalists together with the IFJ and IOJ expressed full support for the Helsinki process and called on the CSCE States to promote concrete measures and gave several recommendations to the journalist unions in these countries. It also welcomed the invitation of the Polish union to organize the third conference in 1989.[25]

Figure 8.7 The 2nd Congress of CSCE Journalists took place in the historical Hofburg palace in Vienna on 30 October – 1 November 1987. It was attended by representatives from 20 journalist unions of the CSCE countries and the two internationals, IFJ and IOJ. (Photo from the conference proceedings, 1989)

25 Proceedings of the Congress *Journalism and the Security Needs of States* (1989).

In 1988 the IOJ was close to its zenith: its membership exceeding a quarter of million – see **Appendices 11** and **12** – and the organizational structure resembling that of a large corporation – see **Appendix 13**.

APPROACHING ZENITH 1988–89

The **IOJ enterprises** attached to the Secretariat had grown from the 1970s translation and conference service "Interpress Praha" to an all-round commercial institution supplying "special services to a broad public, to scientific, research and development institutes, to social organizations, artistic unions and to communication media", as **IOJ Videopress** introduced itself. With about 1,000 people employed mainly in Prague but also in the Brno and Bratislava branches – in addition to the Hungarian Interpress Budapest – its operations included a publishing house, a conference service, an audiovisual technical documentation service, a mass media management service, a systems and programming service for computer software as well as production of technical equipment for interpreting systems and experimental purposes including space technology. The most recent ventures were small hotels and restaurants and a construction company restoring historic buildings.

Figure 8.8 The enterprise management occupied two floors in a prestigious apartment building in *Washingtonova Street*. The expanding and lucrative enterprises had come to resemble an island of capitalism in a sea of socialism. The system had been built under the guidance of Secretary General Kubka and in 1987 he recruited to it a new General Director: Miloš Jakeš Jr, the son of the Secretary General of the Czechoslovak Communist Party, who had worked for years at the headquarters of the International Union of Students (IUS) in Prague. Kubka was obviously commanded to do this by higher authorities. (Photo by Nordenstreng)

In reality the appointment of Jakeš Jr. contributed to **Kubka's resignation as the IOJ Secretary General and his replacement by Dušan Ulčák.** Ulčák was former President of the IUS and most recently the Czechoslovak Deputy Minister of Foreign Affairs in charge of developing countries. Even before the Sofia Congress Kubka had hinted that he was ready to leave, but as the Czechoslovak Union of Journalists had not found a replacement for him, he was re-elected without further discussion – like the President and the Treasurer. Now, however, a replacement was available – from outside journalism but with strong political backing, no doubt thanks to the Jakeš connection. Apart from politics there was some criticism of Kubka within the Secretariat for his authoritarian style of management and his lavish lifestyle.

The matter was formally brought up in the **Presidium Bureau in Prague on 16 March 1988**, which had been convened to prepare the forthcoming Presidium in Brasilia. According to its Minutes:

> J. Kubka informed the Bureau of his decision to resign as IOJ Secretary General, a post he has held for 22 years, as he is to act as Czechoslovakia's ambassador in Mexico. He told that he will announce this at the meeting of the IOJ Presidium in Brasilia. In this respect J. Riško announced the intention of the Czechoslovak Union of Journalists to nominate to the vacant post of IOJ Secretary General its representative Dušan Ulčák. He gave some background information about the past activities of D. Ulčák and introduced him to members of the Bureau.

The Minutes added that a number of participants expressed their great appreciation for Kubka's work and that the President believed the matter would be favourably considered by the Presidium in Brasilia. In the end Kubka did not attend the Brasilia Presidium (see Slavík's recollections in Part Two).

The Bureau in Prague was attended by 15 Presidium members and 10 representatives of member unions of the socialist countries. In addition to preparing for the next Presidium and processing the change in the Secretary General, the Bureau also discussed the IOJ publishing activities, wishing "to raise the effectiveness of the IOJ publications, to broaden their audience and to turn *The Democratic Journalist* into an influential journal of international journalism".

Actually the **IOJ publications** were flourishing towards the end of the 1980s. The flagship journal appeared monthly in English, French, Spanish and Russian with a total circulation of over 20,000 copies to 150 countries. The biweekly newsletter was issued in English, French, Spanish, German, Russian, Arabic and Portuguese in over 40,000 copies to nearly 150 countries. Non-periodical publications included books on political and professional topics, with runs of nearly 10,000 copies to 100 countries. About 10 titles were issued each year and they were promoted on the back cover of the journal (here *DJ* 10/1988).

The Democratic Journalist (*DJ*), with Rudolf Převrátil as its Chief Editor since 1985, showcased the more modern approach of the IOJ. Not only were the layout and format upgraded, with the photo supplement in full colour, but the content became more diverse: next to the customary evils of imperialism and struggle around NIICO the coverage increasingly extended to topics such as women journalists (*DJ* 11/1987), ecological journalism (*DJ* 2/1988) and journalism students (*DJ* 9/1989). The protection of journalists was featured largely with the case of French journalist Jean-Paul Kauffmann kidnapped in Lebanon (*DJ* 10/1988). The political development of *perestroika* in the Soviet Union was widely covered – as an official policy but with no insight on the challenges this posed to socialism in eastern Europe.

The **Presidium in Brasilia**, capital of Brazil, was held on 22–25 **April 1988** in the modern Itamaratu Palace, the seat of the Ministry of Foreign Affairs (Figure 8.9).[26] It was attended by 25 Presidium members (five of them substitutes) with equally many representatives of member unions and observers; in addition, six Secretaries. However, Secretary General Kubka was absent.

From the address of IOJ Secretary General Dušan Ulčák

Let me thank you for the confidence you

re will be fewer tensions and more mutual confidence. There is no doubt that journalists and the media can and must contribute substantially to this process.

Journalists and the mass media have an increasing responsibility to support the struggle for national independence and freedom now going on in the Middle East, in southern Africa and in Central America.

The role and responsibility of journalists is growing to tackle burdensome problems which the developing countries are grappling with today, such as indebtedness and information dependence. The need to defend the professional interests, rights and needs of journalists is also on the increase.

All this can and must be tackled within the framework of our organization -- the IOJ -- which during the 42 years of its exis-

Figure 8.9 The opening of the Presidium was addressed by the Governor of the Federal District of Brasilia, José Aparacido de Oliveira, and the President of the Constituent Assembly, Ulysses Guimaraes – here seen in the centre, next to IOJ President Nordenstreng, FENAJ President Rollemberg and Acting IOJ Secretary General Jurkowicz. The newly elected Secretary General Ulčák introduced himself in *The Democratic Journalist* 6/1988 as a reformist supporting a momentum towards more internal democracy and professionalism. Some thought that the reform was facilitated by the change in the Secretary General, but in reality Kubka had been as open-minded as possible under the prevailing political circumstances.

Dušan Ulčák was designated as the new Secretary General – to be confirmed by the next Executive Committee and the Congress but in practice immediately assuming full powers. The appointment was formally unanimous, although French Vice-President Gatinot raised a point of order about the procedure, noting that the Statute only allowed a substitute to replace the Secretary General between two Congresses.

The Presidium heard reports on the situation in Latin America and Brazil, leading to a resolution on the repression of journalists in Latin America

26 *IOJ newsletter* 9/1988; *DJ* 6 and 7–8/1988; *The IOJ Presidium Meeting Brasilia* (1988).

and to a declaration on the situation in Nicaragua and Panama. A resolution was also issued on the Middle East, a statement on the Iran–Iraq war, and an appeal on the situation in South Africa. Two new full members were admitted: the Lesotho Union of Journalists and the Union de Periodistas from Spain.

The customary report of the Secretary General on the IOJ activities since the last Presidium this time bypassed overviews of the political situation in the world and focused on substantive areas of IOJ activity. For example, peace and disarmament included the CSCE journalists' congress in Vienna, a round table in Vietnam on security and co-operation in Asia and the Pacific and the professional tasks of journalists, fact-finding missions to the occupied territories in Palestine and other support for peace in the Middle East as well as special working sessions in Prague to set up a system of monitoring the coverage of war and peace issues by the mass media – the President's initiative from the early 1980s (see Appendix 8). The general report was complemented by reports of the IOJ Councils, Committees, publishing activities and the regional centres.[27]

All this material was more concrete than typically in earlier statutory meetings and the Presidium admitted in its main resolution that the Secretariat "made certain steps ahead in carrying out the provisions of the IOJ Congress in Sofia". Yet the resolution emphasized "the need for greater efficiency and democracy in all levels of the IOJ structure".

In general, the Brasilia Presidium demonstrated a shift from an overtly political to a more professional approach – something that the President and western progressives had advocated all along. Now the time was ripe for a change, largely thanks to *perestroika* in the USSR.

The **Secretariat in Prague** was increased in 1988 by a new Secretary for Social Affairs, Konstantin Ivanov from Bulgaria, and a Secretary for Africa, Christopher Muzavazi from Zimbabwe – the first one from Africa. Later Sadhan Mukherjee from India was added as Secretary for Asia. Moreover, Palestinian Mazen Husseini joined as an advisor to the Secretariat; later he became Secretary for International Organizations. The Cuban Secretary for Latin America and the Caribbean was changed to Miguel Rivero. Milouš Vejvoda, Czechoslovakia's former Ambassador in Geneva, became Director of the IJI with Václav Slavík as his deputy.

The Secretariat had adopted in Kubka's last years a practice of meeting about twice a month and all matters presented with full documentation, the

27 The first regional centre had operated in Paris since 1974 headed by Vice-President Gatinot. The second centre was opened in Mexico City in 1987 headed by Cuban Vice-President Vera, who served as a full-time ambassador of the IOJ.

number of materials over 200 per year. For an example of the Secretariat agenda, see **Appendix 14.**

One should not forget the ceremonial part of the IOJ with the International Journalist Prize and the Julius Fučík Medal of Honour – see **Appendix 15**.

After the Brasilia Presidium, which naturally emphasized Latin America, attention in the IOJ was turned to Africa with the founding of the Federation of Southern African Journalists in Harare and the opening of the IOJ regional centre in Addis Abeba – both in September 1988.[28]

The last statutory meeting of the decade was the **Presidium in Addis Abeba** on 11–13 **January 1989** (Figure 8.10). Convened in the historic Africa Hall of Ethiopia's capital, it was opened by the President of the People's Democratic Republic of Ethiopia, Mengistu Haile Mariam. It was attended by 27 of the 31 Presidium members (in four cases their substitutes)[29] and 50 guests from various member unions and international organizations, including UNESCO, the Organization of African Unity and the League of Arab States.[30] The opening session was addressed by the representative of the Director-General of UNESCO. Attending were also IOJ Secretaries and 20 representatives of the Ethiopian community of journalists.[31]

Four new members – from Argentine, Barbados, the Philippines and Senegal – were admitted, bringing the total number of journalists affiliated to 256,000. The special theme of the Presidium was "Situation of the mass media in Africa, with reference to conditions of journalists", introduced by IOJ Vice-President Charles Chikerema from Zimbabwe, also Secretary General of the Union of African Journalists. The other main theme "The role of IOJ in

---

28 *IOJ newsletter* 20/1988; *DJ* 1/1989. The Federation was founded by the 3rd Conference of the journalist organizations of the Frontline States, preceded by the 2nd Conference in Arusha (Tanzania) in 1987; see *DJ* 12/1987 and 1/1988. The IOJ publications and Presidium materials used the traditional spelling Addis Ababa, whereas nowadays it is officially known as Addis Abeba.

29 The size of the Presidium had decreased to 31 in June 1988, when Honorary President Hermann passed away.

30 Among those invited to the Presidium as guests was the All China Journalists' Association – for the first time since the 1965, when ACJA discontinued its active membership. They politely regretted being unable to send a representative because the schedules of all appropriate persons were full. Another signal of opening an IOJ window to China was an article on new developments in the Chinese mass media published in *DJ* 5/1989.

31 For overviews of the Presidium, see *IOJ newsletter* 2/1989 and *DJ* 3/1989. A comprehensive report including the addresses, reports and resolutions was published as *IOJ Presidium Meeting Addis Ababa Ethiopia*, January 11–13, 1989.

IOJ newsletter

1989 JANUARY 2

THE INTERNATIONAL ORGANIZATION OF JOURNALISTS

IOJ PRESIDIUM MEETS IN ADDIS ABABA

January 11–13, 1989

The issues on the agenda included the situation of the mass media in Africa and conditions for journalists' work; the IOJ's contribution to the struggle against apartheid; membership of the IOJ and admittance of new members; a report by the General Secretary on the IOJ's activities since the Brasilia Presidium meeting; a plan of activities for 1989; and a report by the IOJ Treasurer.

SCRAPPING HARMFUL TRADITIONS

IOJ PRESIDIUM

Figure 8.10 By its size – over 100 people – the meeting resembled an Executive Committee, which actually was foreseen in the Brazil Presidium to be convened in 1989. However, for practical and financial reasons it was kept as a more limited Presidium, leaving the Executive Committee between two Congresses to be convened later. Nevertheless it was a historical meeting, both in its formal profile and substantive content. "We are increasingly leaving behind ritual in our activities, which are becoming practical and self-critical" the *IOJ newsletter* (1/1989) stated in its report on the Presidium, and *DJ* (3/1989) summarized: "The long-advocated demands for democratization and greater efficiency in the IOJ are finally beginning to take practical shape."

the struggle against apartheid" was introduced by the President of the Black Press Institute from the USA, Edward Palmer.[32]

Secretary General Ulčák presented a comprehensive report on the IOJ since the Presidium in Brasilia, focusing on democratization and efficiency and on international co-operation. Treasurer Megyeri reported on the financial aspects of the IOJ, especially the alarming failure to pay membership fees, which accounted for only six percent of the total expenditures, leaving 94 per cent to be covered from other sources including the Solidarity Fund, which in 1988 brought in over five million Czechoslovak crowns. President Nordenstreng summarized the discussions by noting with satisfaction that the IOJ was indeed proceeding along the line established in the 10th Congress and further specified in the Presidium decisions in Brasilia – the line towards democratization and rationalization.[33]

The Presidium expressed its position on the work of the IOJ Secretariat since the Presidium meeting in Brasilia in a resolution prepared by a drafting commission and unanimously approved. In addition to the general resolution, the Presidium adopted 10 documents beginning with an open letter to Nelson Mandela in Victor Vester Prison in South Africa and ending with a statement on the 40th anniversary of the Universal Declaration of Human Rights.[34]

32 *IOJ Presidium Meeting Addis Ababa* (1989, pp. 27–34).

33 Ibid., pp. 38–59.

34 Ibid., pp. 60–74.

Figure 8.11 The 3rd Congress of CSCE Journalists in Warsaw in September 1989 was addressed by the President of Poland, Wojciech Jaruzelski, here in the centre, next to the Chairman of the Association of Journalists of the Polish Republic (SDPRL), Arthur Howzan. On the left: Chairman Laine from Finland with IFJ President Doornaert; on the right: Chairwoman Prager-Zitterbart from Austria with IOJ President Nordenstreng. (Photo from the Polska Agencia INTERPRESS)

The year 1989 was full of events, including the Information Forum of the CSCE countries in London in April–May[35] and the 3rd Congress of CSCE Journalists – after Helsinki in 1975 and Vienna in 1987 – held in Warsaw in September[36] (Figure 8.11). A round table on co-operation of journalists in Europe in the fields of culture, ecology and human rights was organized by the Czechoslovak Journalists for Peace with the national Union of Journalists in Prague in March.[37] A similar thematic conference focusing on the commercialization and concentration of European media had been organized in summer 1988 by the West German Union of Media Workers in Kiel.[38]

These, like many of the events referred to above, were organized by other governmental or non-governmental organizations, with the IOJ attending as more or less active participant. There were also several activities arranged and financed by the IOJ, by the Secretariat alone or together with member unions, for example: a workshop on the World Public Opinion Campaign for Human Rights at the UN headquarters in Geneva in April, a fact-finding mission to the occupied territories in Palestine in April, the Interpress Photo competition in Pyongyang in April, a solidarity rally with Russian Lada cars from Moscow to Lagos in May–June and a training programme for peace journalists in Budapest in September.[39]

Killing and kidnapping of journalists was a continuing topic covered in most issues of *IOJ newsletter* and in June the IOJ made a proposal to convene an international conference in the forthcoming months on the protection of journalists[40].

35 *IOJ newsletter* 3 and 11/1989; *DJ* 4 and 8/1989.

36 *IOJ newsletter* 19/1989; *DJ* 12/1989. Its final Statement is reproduced in **Appendix 16**.

37 *IOJ newsletter* 6/1989; *DJ* 6/1989.

38 *DJ* 1/1979. For full list of IOJ activities in 1989, see Appendix 5.

39 These were reported in *IOJ newsletter* issues 6–19/1989 and *DJ* issues 9–10/1989.

40 *IOJ newsletter* 12/1989.

Figure 8.12 The IOJ attended as a guest the Intergovernmental Council (IGC) for the Co-ordination of Information and Communication of the Non-Aligned Countries (COMINAC), which held its 10th meeting in Harare, the capital of Zimbabwe, in August 1989. Shown here on the cover of COMINAC Newsletter with IOJ President is President of Zimbabwe, Robert Mugabe, who presided over NAM at the time, next to UJA Secretary General Charles Chikerema and Witness Mangwende, Zimbabwe's Minister of Information and Chairman of the IGC.

The IOJ was a central force of the MacBride Round Table, which was founded in Harare in October 1989 as a platform of non-governmental actors interested in maintaining NIICO at a time when UNESCO and the UN had ceased to promote it.[41]

The Secretariat held 26 formal meetings between January and December 1989, dealing with nearly 300 numbered documents. Among these were two reports on the project for monitoring media coverage of peace and war issues based on President Nordenstreng's proposal prepared in 1986 (Appendix 8). Also, there was a background paper for the trade union activities, with a set of proposals for workshops, training courses and publishing handbooks on the topic prepared by Secretaries Husseini, Ivanov and Paukku.[42] This was a significant step to making trade union matters a priority leading to such activities as a course on international labour standards for IOJ member unions held at the IOJ school in Prague in September 1990.

Accordingly, the IOJ was a hive of activity and energy throughout 1989 – indeed in its heyday. Meanwhile, the political developments in the socialist countries led to dramatic changes in the autumn.

Czechoslovakia was a special case, with a non-violent change of the political system, known as the "Velvet Revolution", occurring in a matter of days after 17 November 1989. Street demonstrations were accompanied by pockets of the Civic Forum emerging in most workplaces – including the IOJ.[43]

---

41 *IOJ newsletter* 22/1989. The Round Table held several meetings in different parts of the world until 2000; see Vincent & Nordenstreng (2016, pp. 239–292) and its home page https://indstate.edu/cas/macbrideroundtable.

42 This document is reproduced in **Appendix 17**.

43 The IOJ Civic Forum sprang up spontaneously around employees in the Secretariat and the publishing department, notably Dana Braun and Karel Hejč.

The Czechoslovak journalists, who had been prominent in the 1968 Prague Spring and who in the following "normalization" process had been pushed out of their profession, came back overnight discrediting the official Union of Journalists of the country. On 29 November they brought a letter to the IOJ Secretariat asking it to immediately announce the rehabilitation of the persecuted Czechoslovak journalists.[44] The IOJ responded to this ultimatum on 1 December with a Statement on the situation in Czechoslovakia signed by President Nordenstreng and Secretary General Ulčák, expressing the hope that all problems regarding journalists, "particularly the question of journalists who were denied in past years the right to exercise their profession, will be settled in line with the aspirations of the journalists community and of basic human rights".[45] Meanwhile, outside the IOJ a new organization was founded on 16 December: the Syndicate of Czech and Moravian Journalists.

Consequently, the decade of successful development of the IOJ ended with sinister signs of momentous change. Nevertheless, the last *IOJ newsletter* of the year reported about the new headquarters building at the corner of the Old Town Square (Figure 8.13). The outside of the 13th century building had been restored and the inside converted into a five-story modern office complex – another landmark of the IOJ heyday with a reconstruction cost of about 50 million Czechoslovak crowns and 100,000 German marks. Now it became occupied by about 50 staff of the Secretariat.

Moreover, the IOJ was a major occupant in town as it owned or rented over 70 offices or residential flats around Prague.[46] The main offices in the centre of Prague were the Secretariat in *Celetná* (A), the enterprise management in *Washingtonova* (B) and the conference service at the bottom of *Václavské náměstí* (C) (Figure 8.14). Separate buildings outside the centre were the School of Journalism on the way to the airport and in the suburb of *Bílá Hora* the conference centre, which included a restaurant and a bowling alley.

In addition to providing the Secretaries and other leading personnel with flats, the IOJ also placed at their disposal cars, registered as semi-diplomatic vehicles. The IOJ was well known in Prague for its fleet of western cars.

The magnitude of the IOJ machinery in Prague is well shown by the organizational charts in Appendix 14. A trademark of the IOJ were its distinctive conference bags and souvenirs (Figure 8.13).

On all counts the IOJ had become towards the end of the 1980s a major actor in the international arena – first and foremost as an INGO but also

---

44 The letter is reproduced in **Appendix 18**.

45 See the whole statement in *IOJ newsletter* 23/1989. A more general version of this statement was issued on 11 December as "Message of the IOJ on the eve of 1990", published in *IOJ newsletter* 1/1990 and in *DJ* 2/1990. It is reproduced in **Appendix 19**.

46 A list of these is in **Appendix 20**.

IOJ news letter

1989 DECEMBER 24

THE INTERNATIONAL ORGANIZATION OF JOURNALISTS

On December 10, 1989, the IOJ Secretariat opened its new headquarters in Prague. The simple ceremony was attended by the IOJ President Kaarle Nordenstreng and Secretary General Dušan Ulčák as well as members of the IOJ Secretariat.

The new IOJ headquarters are situated in Celetná Street near the historical Old Town Square in the restaured 13th century building. The new address of the IOJ Secretariat is Celetná 2, Prague 1, 110 00, Czechoslovakia.

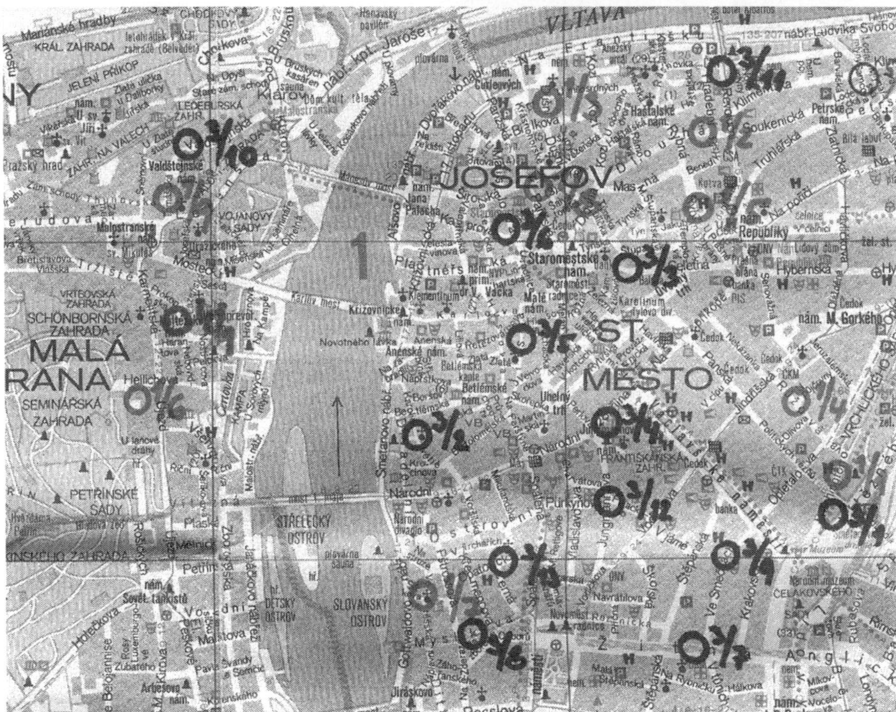

Figure 8.13 The *IOJ newsletter* reported the removal of the IOJ Secretariat to new premises. The unpublished map shows the IOJ buildings and flats in the old centre of Prague.

in relation to intergovernmental platforms. The closing assessment of the Helsinki Congress in 1976 "historical development is on our side – the initiative in the world arena is in our hands" appeared true, but only until the end of 1989.

Figure 8.13 Professionally designed conference bags were made for hosting organizations, for example in Iraq (1977) and Ecuador (1985). A sports bag served for bigger items. A large vase was a souvenir of the Executive Committee in Hanoi (1979). A drinking glass was used in the Argentinian-style restaurant *Pampa* in *Bílá Hora*.

CHAPTER 9
DISINTEGRATION 1990–97

The 1990s is known above all for the political U-turn in central-eastern Europe, where communist governments were replaced by long-oppressed opposition forces. In Czechoslovakia the Civic Forum won a landslide victory in the first general election after the communist regime in June 1990 and in July Václav Havel was confirmed as the first non-communist president since 1948. Czechoslovakia was split into the Czech and Slovak Republics in 1993.

In the Soviet Union, the Baltic republics declared independence in 1990. In August 1991 an attempted coup against Gorbachev's reformist policies led to political turmoil which ended with his resignation and Boris Yeltsin's rise to power. The USSR was dissolved by the end of 1991 and most former Soviet republics became independent.

Yugoslavia began to disintegrate in June 1991 after the republics of Croatia and Slovenia declared independence. The Yugoslav wars continued throughout the decade, ending with the war of Kosovo.

The Persian Gulf War was waged by the US-led coalition against Iraq after the latter invaded Kuwait in August 1990. The USA sought support for the war from the USSR and the rest of the UN Security Council. The successful operation encouraged the Western side to talk about a New World Order with the USA as the only superpower.

However, the Cold War was not replaced by Pax Americana. New conflicts erupted not only locally in Afghanistan, Iraq and elsewhere but also worldwide in the form of terrorism.

For the IOJ the global changes in the early 1990s were dire. The collapse of the communist regimes in central-eastern Europe and finally the end of the Soviet Union rendered void the Cold War constellation of which since the late 1940s the IOJ had been an integral part. The IOJ lost its eastern support pillar and found itself in an unwelcoming geopolitical environment.

The most serious challenge to the IOJ came from Czechoslovakia, shaking the mighty Secretariat and the commercial enterprise system behind it.

This chapter tells the story of gradual disintegration from 1990 until all IOJ activities practically ceased after 1997. The crisis year, 1990, is reviewed at some length with several appendices, whereas the rest of this period is only summarized, leaving details to be found in publications and archives.

SHAKEN BY THE FALL OF COMMUNIST REGIMES 1990

The *IOJ newsletter* began the year 1990 with a message of an optimistic worldview, next to decorative graphics wishing readers a Happy New Year.

On 8 January the leadership of the new Syndicate[1] addressed a letter to the IOJ President, announcing that **by dissolving the Czechoslovak Union of Journalists its membership of the IOJ had consequently ceased**. It continued stating that in the near future "the interests of Czechoslovak journalists with the IOJ will be considered, i.e. whether we should re-apply for membership and if so, in what form".

IOJ newsletter

1 1990/JANUARY

THE INTERNATIONAL ORGANIZATION OF JOURNALISTS

On the Year 1990

IOJ MESSAGE

As the world enters a new year and a new decade – a decade leading to the 21st century – the International Organization of Journalists (IOJ) conveys best wishes to its members and fellow journalists around the world. The IOJ hopes that the advent of a new year will lead us to a new era and that the new decade will be one of peace and progress for humanity as a whole.

This hope has been recently nurtured by the fact that developments in international relations have signalled the end of the Cold War and its ramifications. The relaxation of tension between the major powers, the progress in disarmament, the serious efforts to settle regional conflicts by peaceful means, the growing awareness of the need to overcome underdevelopment and debt in the Third World, all give rise to new prospects in East-West as well as North-South relations.

The IOJ welcomes these positive developments. At the same time it should be recalled that the IOJ was born in 1946 out of the desire of journalists all around the world to establish the broadest unity in order to assure – as its original aims and objectives stated – "the protection by all means of all liberty of the press and journalism; the defence of the people's right to be informed honestly and accurately; the promotion of international friendship and understanding through free interchange of information; and the promotion of trade unionism amongst journalists".

Unfortunately, the Cold War hampered and complicated efforts in this direction and left its mark on the world of journalism.

However, the IOJ together with other organizations of journalists has tried to overcome many of the problems

(continued on page 3)

JOURNALISM IN A COMMON EUROPEAN HOUSE

For three days, from December 11 to 13, 1989, the representatives of the Ecumenical Workshop for Information in Europe (EWIE), the International Organization of Journalists (IOJ), and the World Association for Christian Communication (WACC) came together not far from Munich to a round table meeting on the subject Transcending the Frontiers in our Common European House – Europe on the Path Leading to Mutual Rapprochement.

Religious Matters of the USSR Council of Ministers Mikhail Ivolgin, and Yuri Smirnov, another representative of the Council for Religious Matters, informed in detail about the radical changes in the situation of the Russian Orthodox Church and other

IOJ newsletter

2 1990/JANUARY

THE INTERNATIONAL ORGANIZATION OF JOURNALISTS

1990 - International Literacy Year

January 1, 1990, marked the beginning of International Literacy Year, launched by the United Nations General Assembly. UNESCO was asked to administer the events to be organized during this campaign.

At the present time there are 889 million illiterates in the world over 15 years of age, i.e. every fourth adult. Almost 98 per cent of illiterates are in the developing countries, most of them in Africa. More than 100 million children between the ages of six and eleven are unable to attend school in Asia and Africa and every third women is illiterate.

The World Conference for the Education for All, to be held in Jomtien (Thailand) from March 5 to 9, 1990, will be an important event. UNESCO, UNICEF, UN Development Program and the World Bank will be the organizers of this conference.

CZECHOSLOVAK JOURNALISTS AND NEW PERSPECTIVES

On January 6, 1990, an extraordinary congress took place in Prague of the Czechoslovak Union of Journalists (CSSN), whose almost 250 delegates unanimously decided to publicly announce the disbandment of this journalist organization. This important decision was preceded by the congresses of both national unions, the Czech and Slovak Unions of Journalists (CSN, SSN), whose decisions clearly led to this move.

The immediate impetus for such a step was the slow and unconvincing reaction of the Union to the police suppression of the student demonstration in Prague on November 17, 1989, and the events which then followed. This fact was reflected in the congress proceedings where it was said that the new social and political situation in Czechoslovakia "makes it imperative to reassess the activities and the entire existence of the CSSN". Jaroslava Marková, who since November 26, 1989, has been the Chairwoman of the newly elected administrative organ of the CSSN, stressed in her speech that what is needed is a newly conceived goal and character of the journalists' organization in Czechoslovakia which must be based on democratic principles. It must be an independent and open organization, creating good conditions for the work of journalists, providing legal protection for them, an organization which "will return the honour and authority of the journalist's card". Under J. Marková's leadership the CSSN's Presidium adopted new positions on certain earlier decisions, for instance, it invited journalists who were expelled after 1968 to return to its ranks and apologized to those who had been

(continued on page 2)

The 3rd International Conference to Support the Intifada in Occupied Palestine took place in Athens on 16th and 17th December 1989. The Conference was organized by the International Popular Committee of Artists and Intellectuals to Support the Intifada and hosted by the Panhellenic Cultural Movement.

SUPPORT THE INTIFADA

Prominent intellectuals from a number of European countries as well as leaders of organizations of solidarity with the Palestinian people took part in the meeting. The IOJ was represented by Secretary Mazen Husseini.

Intellectuals and artists from both the occupied Palestinian territories and Israel presented reports on the situation in the occupied territories and the effect of Israeli occupation and repression on the Palestinian people in the West Bank and Gaza Strip. The reports detailed the intensified brutalities and terror practised by the Israeli occupation forces against the Palestinian population, and called for stepped-up international action to put an end to Israeli occupation and to support the Palestinian Intifada.

The meeting decided to intensify its efforts to mobilise intellectuals and artists around the world in support of the Palestinian Intifada. Concrete plans of support were elaborated and a number of meetings and fora on the Intifada were held.

A view from Prague CSN congress

Figure 9.1 A report on journalism in "a common European house" was about a roundtable convened by the World Association for Christian Communication (WACC) together with the IOJ. This front page as well as that of No. 2 seems to suggest that the IOJ was on the same positive track as before. However, the report on the extraordinary congress of the Czechoslovak Union of Journalists on 6 January brought startling news: the 250 delegates unanimously decided to disband the old Union and to establish a new organization based on the new Syndicate of Czech and Moravian Journalists with a parallel Syndicate founded in Slovakia.

1 Chairperson Rudolf Zeman with vice-chairpersons Adam Černý and Vladimír Bystrov. Before the Velvet Revolution Zeman and another journalist (Jiří Ruml) had been arrested and imprisoned at which stage (on 16 November) IOJ Secretary General Ulčák sent a letter to Prime Minister Adamec requesting their release.

IOJ newsletter

3 1990/FEBRUARY

THE INTERNATIONAL ORGANIZATION OF JOURNALISTS

Lively IOJ Presidium Session

Most characteristic of the IOJ Presidium session held from January 27 to 29, 1990, in Estoril, not far from Lisbon (Portugal), was sharp – in places even vehement – discussion. The official opening was attended, among others, by the President of Portugal Mario Soares.

The main point on the agenda was the Secretariat's report on IOJ relations with other international and regional journalist organizations. In the background to all discussion and arguments, however, were developments in Eastern Europe, changes in the journalist organizations there, and their influence on the IOJ.

The Presidium approved the idea of creating a regional organization of European journalists independent of membership in the IOJ and IFJ. In order to improve IOJ activities in Europe it was decided to set up a special working group. However, proposals for practical steps leading to the gradual merger of the IOJ and IFJ, as proposed by the Finnish journalist movement, provoked sharp criticism. Several of the speakers who were against this ar-

From the IOJ Presidium Meeting

gued that the cold war has not yet ended and that such measures are premature. The general resolution, which was approved, stated, nonetheless, that the IOJ will try to unite the organized movement of journalists "without compromising our basic principles".

Another pointed discussion was around the question of how the IOJ should react to developments in Eastern Europe, especially in Czechoslovakia. The IOJ's journalist organization of the host country was disbanded and its membership in the IOJ abolished. Two new syndicates, Czech (the Syndicate of Journalists of Bohemia and Moravia) and Slovak (the Slovak Syndicate of Journalists) will decide on their attitude to the IOJ later, after a nationwide structure is created, prob-

EXTRAORDINARY CONGRESS OF GDR JOURNALISTS

On January 25 and 26, 1990, an extraordinary congress of GDR journalists was held in Berlin. It had to decide on new purposes, forms and structures of their organization.

At the beginning it made a clear break

The congress adopted new provisional

Figure 9.2 The *IOJ newsletter* No. 3 called the Presidium "lively", but in fact it was the most acrimonious statutory meeting since the outbreak of the Cold War. The other front page news on an extraordinary Congress of the GDR journalists was a reminder that the turmoil of journalist unions was not confined to Czechoslovakia. The German Congress declared: "By glorifying Stalinist policy, journalists share the guilt in the deformation of society. We are asking to be forgiven." The Germans likewise founded a new "Association of Journalists of the GDR" advocating free access to information for all citizens and striving to uphold human rights in conformity of the UN Charter. The Congress decided that the new Association remains an active member of the IOJ.

The IOJ had thus lost its member in the country of the headquarters and the enterprises supporting it. Obviously the ultimatum of the new forces after the Velvet Revolution (Appendix 18) was not taken seriously enough by the IOJ and the Syndicate was far from satisfied with the IOJ message on the eve of 1990 (Appendix 19).

The IOJ **Presidium in Lisbon-Estoril** on 27–29 **January 1990** provided a timely opportunity to assess the situation.

The Presidium was well attended: all but six of its 32 members were present in Lisbon – 5 from western Europe & the USA, 6 from central-eastern Europe and 15 from the developing countries. Also attending were other representatives of ten member unions and all the Secretaries as well as representatives of the IOJ Editorial Office and the International Journalism Institute. The report of the Presidium provides a comprehensive account of the proceedings, including summary records and the texts of key documents.

The opening addresses by the President of the Portuguese Syndicate of Journalists and the IOJ President as well as that by the President of the Republic of Portugal, Mário Soares, presented an optimistic view of the challenges facing the IOJ. President Soares reminded the Presidium that the hosting Syndicate was also a member of the IFJ and wondered "whether there is still any reason for the existence of two international organizations of journalists when there is but one world, when the news becomes known instantaneously everywhere, and when the problems of journalists are, I think, increasingly identical, regardless of the socio-political systems in which they exist".[2]

2 *IOJ Presidium Meeting Lisbon-Estoril Portugal, January 27–29, 1990* (1990, p. 29).

In his opening address President Nordenstreng recalled the 1st World Meeting of Journalists in Helsinki in 1956, where IOJ President Hermann declared that "we are ready to dissolve the IOJ if the IFJ does the same in order to unite all of us in a new world organization". At that time reunification was impossible but Nordenstreng pointed out that the Consultative Club now served as proof that "it is both natural and necessary to intensify co-operation and unity of action, leading to a reconciliation of the organized movement of journalists".[3]

The first substantive item on the agenda was "IOJ relations with other international and regional organizations of journalists", for which two background documents were prepared by the President with the Secretariat: a review of recent developments for co-operation and unity, especially in Europe[4], and a fact sheet showing in which countries of the world the IOJ, the IFJ and various regional organizations had members[5]. The ensuing discussion focused mainly on the changes in central-eastern Europe; it is extensively documented in the Presidium report.[6]

The debate was heated, exposing the controversies between members from Europe on the one hand and the rest of the world on the other, likewise between those in favour of radical change and those who defended the status quo. At the outset Bassam Abu Sharif from Palestine stressed that the majority of the IOJ member organizations came from the Third World and therefore the discussion should not be limited to eastern Europe. A contrasting view was presented by Juhani Hyttinen from Finland, emphasizing that the IOJ could not turn a blind eye to the turmoil in eastern Europe; he also regretted that the organizational crisis of the IOJ did not constitute a separate item on the agenda. Finally most of the 30 speakers did indeed discuss the acute situation in Europe starting with a brief by the Secretary General about the evolving relations with the new Czechoslovak Syndicate, while the President announced that his contacts with the new Czechoslovak organization suggested that there existed an information vacuum, even a credibility crisis, between it and the Secretariat.

Rudolf Převrátil, Chief Editor of *The Democratic Journalist*, speaking only on his own behalf, stated: "The IOJ is too committed to the former compromised regime of Czechoslovakia, failed in the fight for the freedom of the press in socialist countries and indirectly supported, at least with its silence,

---

3 Ibid., pp. 27–28.

4 Ibid., pp. 37–40. This included the quote by former President Hermann from 1956 about dissolving the IOJ in the interest of unity.

5 Ibid., pp. 43–49. This is reproduced as an appendix in Nordenstreng & al. (2016, pp. 199–203).

6 Ibid., pp. 10–18.

Figure 9.3 The IOJ journal had changed by 1990 to appear as a modern full-colour magazine. Its stories were on topical issues of media and journalism – in 1990 especially environmental journalism – and the geographical coverage extended widely from Europe to Africa, the Middle East, Asia and Latin America. Number 2/1990 was the last under Chief Editor Převrátil, who stepped down after the Lisbon Presidium and was replaced by Marek Jurkowicz, the Polish Secretary for International Organizations. The editorial policy remained unchanged.

the authoritarian systems". Secretary General Ulčák responded that Převrátil was not a member of the Presidium and expressed only his personal views, which is why there was no reason to pursue the discussion. The Secretary General also rejected the intervention of the President and disclosed that the President's original material for this agenda item was not approved by the Secretariat "because it represents the sale of IOJ interests and according to it the IOJ would become a European-centred organization". He continued: "There are at least two representatives in the leading bodies – the President and a Secretary – who work in the IOJ for somebody else and against the IOJ interests".[7]

Hyttinen followed up by expressing the opinion that the main obstacle for the IOJ in Czechoslovakia was the Secretary General. He also pointed out that "the present Minister of Foreign Affairs happened to be one of the two thousand journalists expelled from the Czechoslovak Union of Journalists after 1968".[8] Finally Hyttinen stated that "if the Secretary General does not take back his former accusation of the President and the Secretary, it would

7 All those present knew that the Secretary in question was Leena Paukku from Finland.

8 The Minister in question was Jiří Dienstbier. Until 1968 he was one of the most respected foreign correspondents in the country. After 1968 he worked as a janitor and secretly revived the suppressed newspaper *Lidové noviny*.

have serious consequences". The report adds: "The Secretary General did take back his accusations."

Viktor Afanasiev from the USSR stated that there was no cause for alarm. He supported the background document on condition that the IOJ democratic principles were not abandoned and the governing bodies of the IOJ and the IFJ were not merged. He also endorsed the founding of a European regional organization of journalists without causing detriment to the Third World journalists. Luis Suarez from Mexico agreed to seek rapprochement with the IFJ but not to disband the IOJ. Ernesto Vera from Cuba denied any prospects for an eventual merger of the IOJ and the IFJ. For him a rapprochement of the two would negatively influence the developing countries, which could become "an appendage of a European organization of journalists". Armando Rollemberg from Brazil for his part presented a long list of requirements for the IOJ to promote the right to information, pluralism, syndicalism, etc.

The representatives from Hungary and Romania announced that new unions had been founded in these countries, each continuing membership in the IOJ.

Edward Palmer from the USA inquired what would be done in the event of the Czechoslovak journalists refusing to join the IOJ and suggested a special Presidium commission to examine the IOJ's position in Czechoslovakia. This proposal was welcomed by several delegates but rejected by the Secretary General together with the Soviet and Cuban Secretaries, who wanted to allow the Czechoslovak journalists to decide for themselves on their possible membership of the IOJ and to let the Secretariat react. They thought that the very arrival of a Presidium delegation in Prague could be deemed a weakness on the part of the IOJ and that the Secretariat was well equipped to deal with the situation. The Secretary General also said that "the international character of the IOJ cannot be dependent on one country only and that the Secretary General has not been in his function owing to the fact that he is Czechoslovakian".

Chai Yong Sam from North Korea thanked the IOJ for its support for efforts to unify the two parts of the country. He suggested holding the next IOJ Congress in Pyongyang – the first time in Asia.

As the report shows, the discussion was quite animated – chaotic or refreshing, depending on the reader's perspective. Although there were moments of mutual recrimination, it ended with a formal consensus which the President summarized by three denials: no dissolution of the IOJ, no change in IOJ principles and no abandoning of the Third World.

The next items on the agenda went smoothly without major dissention. The Action Plan and Budget for 1990 included 44 events from January to December, on the average four per month. For Gérard Gatinot from France this

mladá fronta

Pátek 26. leden 1990 Ročník XLVI Číslo 22/14 072 1 Kčs

Deník čs. mládeže

poznámky

z těch, kteří na vlastní kůži pocítili jeho zvůli během jeho působení v oblasti naší zahraniční služby a kteří na[…] případech mohou […]kumentovat, že D. U[…]val nejen jako stoupenec stalinistické linie, ale i tvrdě postupoval vůči všem, kteří si dovolili mu oponovat. Zneužíval svého postavení a přátelských osobních styků s M. Jakešem, V. Bilakem, M. Štefaňákem, M. Štěpánem a dalšími.

Za svého působení v Sýrii ve[…] setrvávání ve funkci generálního tajemníka MON je ostudné nejen pro naše novináře, ale pro Česko[…]ec. […]a rádi, kdyby ti […] D. Ulčák v MON reprezentuje, řekli své slovo i k jeho novinářským kvalitám.

JUDr. R. Bobčík, ing. J. Lébl, ing. J. Opava, ing. Z. Motalík, ing. M. Musil, federální ministerstvo zahraničních věcí

MAFIE

MON: nevládní organizace pokrokových novinářů, jejímž cílem je obrana svobody tisku, dodržování pravdivosti informací, zabezpečování svobodné výměny informací, ochrana hmotných a profesionálních práv novinářů atd. (Vojtěch Honška, Jiří Kettner, Slovník mezinárodních organizací, hnutí a seskupení, Praha 1984, str. 74)

Kritizovaná MON

(lk): Na páteční tiskové konferenci v Praze, které se zúčastnili čelní představitelé Mezinárodní organizace novinářů (MON), hovořil prezident této organizace prof. K. Nordenstreng z Finska o některých aspektech minulé i budoucí práce MON. Řekl, že zástupci or-

Pokračování na str. 3

Čemu slouží?

Měl jsem na stole stručný vzkaz: Běž zítra v deset hodin na tiskovou konferenci, kterou pořádá MON, bude to zajímavé. Bylo. Poněkud jinak.

Distancujeme se od MON

(čtk): Prozatímní správní rada Syndikátu novinářů, sdružujícího českou a

MON: na jaký tón?

PRAHA (sch). Rezignaci generálního tajemníka Mezinárodní organizace novinářů (MON) ing. D. Ulčáka oznámil na […]té výjimky, ale ty se týkají především několika národních svazů, nikoli organizace jako celku.

The GUILD REPORTER, January 5, 1990 5

Revolution sweeps East European newsrooms, too

By Aidan White
Int'l Federation of Journalists

MON ztratila kredit

Má tato organizace morální právo působit v Československu?

FRÁZE, POLOPRAVDY A VÝMLUVY tvořily donedávna jádro projevů našich

Czechoslovakia: Witch-hunting and 'democracy'

Figure 9.4 On the eve of the Presidium the Czechoslovak newspaper *Mladá fronta* published a letter to the Editor by five former employees of the ČSSR Ministry of Foreign Affairs attacking Secretary General Ulčák for his activity as the ČSSR Ambassador to Syria. Thereafter negative coverage of the IOJ intensified amounting to a smear campaign. Foreign media also noted the problems of the IOJ.

was too many; he recommended fewer but better prepared activities, such as the meeting in Malaga (Spain) in April, which might lead to a European confederation of journalists.

The list of events included for the first time a budget in US dollars for each activity, ranging from 3,000 $ for a workshop on journalism and human rights in Guyana and 4,000 $ for a film show on *Intifada* in Prague to 50,000 $ for a round table on mass media and the Non-Aligned Movement in India. The total sum for these activities was 734,000 $ – on average 17,000 $ per event.

The Treasurer's Report on the financial situation in 1989 showed that the grand total expenditure of the IOJ staff, facilities and activities was nearly 50 million Czechoslovak crowns (*korunas*, Kčs) and 1.22 million US dollars (the Budget had separate categories for Kčs and US$). The report included a breakdown of these into nine, showing that almost half of the Kčs budget was spent on solidarity activities and publications/information, while nearly half of the US$ budget went to relations with journalist organizations including missions and various events. The regional centres in Budapest, Paris, Mexico and Addis took about 15 percent of the budget in both currency categories.

The total revenue in 1989 was over 54 million CZ crowns and 1.35 million US dollars. Almost half of the Kčs budget came from publishing, printing and advertising services sold to outside customers, while other enterprises (translation, data processing and other services) generated 45 percent of the local income; the solidarity lottery that year only raised about 2 million Kčs. The membership fees accounted for a mere two percent of the income.

Treasurer Megyeri once more drew attention to this abnormal situation and warned that the revenues were unstable. He pointed out that the biggest single item in the expenditure was travel, mainly flight tickets, which in 1989 consumed about 2 million Kčs and nearly half a million US$. He also warned that the IOJ financial activities would face competition and higher taxation and that all international organizations based in Czechoslovakia were now required to pay the full price of plane tickets in convertible currency.

The alerts by the Treasurer had a surprising sequel when a telex arrived from Prague on the last day of the Presidium addressed to the President and the Secretary General. Sent by the acting General Director of the IOJ enterprises, it reported about the negative publicity which the IOJ was getting in local newspapers, making the IOJ employees "gravely concerned about the future of the IOJ and its commercial activities in Czechoslovakia". It proposed that the IOJ President and "other selected members" of the IOJ leadership – conspicuously not mentioning the Secretary General – should immediately start negotiations with the appropriate officials in the country.

Before closing, the Presidium unanimously adopted several resolutions prepared by a drafting committee. A general resolution confirmed both the founding principles of the IOJ and an updated list of aims and objectives. A resolution on solidarity called for manifestations in particular against racism and neo-fascism in different parts of the world. A resolution on IOJ relations with other organizations gave strong support to the Consultative Club; it also endorsed the founding of a regional organization of journalists in Europe and recommended the appointment of an IOJ Working Group for Europe. In a resolution on developments in eastern Europe the Presidium:

- approves the activities of our Secretariat headed by the Secretary General Dušan Ulčák under the circumstances and confirms trust in his office;
- mandates the President and the Secretary General to look into the developments with a view to maintaining existing cordial relations into the national unions of the countries where these changes are taking place and to prepare an extensive report on this matter to the Executive Committee.

This resolution demonstrated how far removed its assessment was from the political reality in Czechoslovakia. A bitter reality check awaited the Secretariat staff upon their return to Prague at the end of January. First, the IOJ Civic Forum now declared that Ulčák had no mandate to represent Czechoslovak journalists and that he should therefore resign as soon as possible. At a subsequent meeting with the leaders of the Civic Forum, directors of the IOJ enterprises and their trade unions, he was told that if he did not resign, the whole organization risked facing enormous problems.

Under mounting pressure in February 1990, Ulčák announced his intention to resign. He agreed with the President to continue the technical functions of the Secretary General until March and in May his appointment was to be officially terminated at the next Presidium. During this period President Nordenstreng assumed de facto leadership of the Secretariat, and once the obstacle created by the Secretary General was removed, discussions with the Syndicate and the Government were rapidly opened.

The discussions started under conditions most unfavourable for the IOJ, as shown by the declaration issued by the Syndicate of Czech and Moravian Journalists on 20 February – see **Appendix 21**. The declaration condemned outright the historical record of the IOJ and indicated that it had no intention of joining "this discredited organization". Moreover, the Syndicate suggested that the IOJ headquarters should no longer be based in Czechoslovakia.

The first talk with the Syndicate leadership took place on 17 February 1990 and was followed by another one five days later – see the minutes of both in **Appendix 22**. These were frank talks where both sides explained their positions without reaching any conclusions. The minutes speak for themselves (see also recollections by Muzavazi in Part Two).

The next step was to meet the **Government**. The IOJ was granted an appointment on 24 February with **Deputy Prime Minister** Dr. Josef Hromádka,

IOJ NEWSLETTER 5/90

IOJ URGES SAFETY OF JOURNALISTS

(from page 1)

Husseini said, "has become in recent years one of the most dangerous." Journalists, he added, have become more and more the victims of all sorts of human rights violations. In increasing numbers

Nelson Mandela and his wife Winnie leave the prison

NELSON MANDELA Is Free!

What was regarded only a few months ago as stubborn vehemence has become a fact. On February 11, 1990, Nelson Mandela, the symbol of struggle of the

which curtail the media and strictly punish any violations.

At a meeting, in Cape Town shortly after he was released, Nelson Mandela

Figure 9.5 While having a hard time with the new political forces in Czechoslovakia the IOJ went on with business as usual as seen in the *IOJ newsletter*, reporting in March 1990 on the safety of journalists at the UN Commission on Human Rights and the great news about Nelson Mandela.

who represented a Christian Party and was also Chairman of the Ecumenical Council of Czechoslovakia. It was a polite and friendly meeting compared to the tense talks with the Syndicate – see **Appendix 23**. After the meeting Hromádka was delivered IOJ documents on professional ethics and a report on its commercial activities – see **Appendix 24**.

The developments within and around the IOJ after the Velvet Revolution were diverse and intensive, and accompanied by mounting tension. The present account gives only a summary, while a detailed chronology of relevant events until October 1990 is provided in **Appendix 25**.

An **enlarged Secretariat meeting** in Prague on 1–2 **March 1990** was held to review the developments since the Lisbon Presidium, to be briefed by the enterprise directors and to prepare for the next Presidium. In addition to the Secretaries, those attending were the President, Secretary General, Treasurer and Vice-Presidents from France, Brazil and Nigeria. After the meeting, hundreds of the staff of the IOJ enterprises gathered in a sports arena to be addressed by the President and attending Vice-Presidents.[9]

A **press conference** was held after the enlarged Secretariat to openly inform the public about the IOJ and rectify the anti-IOJ reporting. Several local and some foreign media attended, but the results were not what was expected; the press coverage mostly perpetuated the Syndicate's viewpoint. A lengthy statement by the President was practically ignored, and the IOJ was portrayed as a kind of mafia, a parasite of the sick economy of Czechoslovakia. On the other hand, the IOJ delegation had a productive meeting with the Syndicate of Slovak Journalists and the President had a constructive talk with the Director of the Czechoslovak News Agency ČTK, Petr Uhl – one of the leaders of the Velvet Revolution.

The **IOJ member unions from central-eastern Europe** met in Prague in March and reported more or less radical changes – some of them applying for IFJ membership – but none of them was intending to leave the IOJ.[10]

Despite the steps taken to resolve the situation in February–March 1990, the IOJ was faced with a mounting crisis in Czechoslovakia and the President prepared an emergency plan first to be discussed with the Soviet member union.[11] The plan included proposals for closer co-operation with the Syndicate and the IFJ, even to the point of sharing ownership of the IOJ's translation enterprise. The President also advocated an early Congress in the autumn.

9 *IOJ newsletter* 6/1990.

10 *IOJ newsletter* 7/1990.

11 The USSR Union had a new President, Ivan Laptev, the Chief Editor of *Izvestia. He* fully supported President Nordenstreng's line, also helping to stifle a conspiracy to restore Ulčák as the Secretary General if the IOJ were to be expelled from Czechoslovakia.

Although supported by the Soviets, the radical reform was brought to a standstill by a major setback in early April, when the General Assembly of the **Syndicate of Journalists decided not to join the IOJ but instead to apply for membership of the IFJ**. The Government was also lukewarm towards the IOJ with the Prime Minister turning down a request for further talks. Yet there was also positive development: the **Consultative Club held its 10th meeting** successfully hosted by the IFJ in The Hague in mid-April, approving an Action Plan for the safety of journalists.[12] As to the European meeting in Malaga at the end of April, it turned out a flop after the IFJ decided not to participate in this IOJ initiative to establish a European confederation.

Meanwhile, the **Secretariat in Prague** worked intensively with the President. On 2 April 1990 he issued a statement on temporary arrangements in the Secretariat – see **Appendix 26**. Accordingly, President Nordenstreng assumed responsibility for foreign accounts[13] and Acting Secretary General Rayer for personnel[14].

The Secretariat met almost weekly[15] and another **enlarged Secretariat meeting** was held on 6–7 **April 1990** in Špindlerův Mlýn, a mountain resort close to the Polish border. Actually it was a mini-Presidium attended by 12 Presidium members or their representatives from Brazil to the USSR[16] and over 20 persons from the Secretariat. The meeting reviewed widely the situation inside the IOJ and its relation to the host country as well as to the IFJ. The state of member unions in central-eastern Europe was discussed and it was agreed that a delegation should visit them urgently. Furthermore, the meeting received a progress report by a committee on the revision of the IOJ Statute.[17] Regarding finances, the meeting missed

12 *IOJ newsletter* 8/1990. A positive signal also came from the UK, where the NUJ's Annual Delegate Meeting stated that the Cold War divisions in the international trade union movement were an anachronism and that the IFJ and the IOJ should have better working relationships, even to the point of merging the two.

13 In April the President and the Secretary General visited the banks in Nuremberg, where the IOJ had its foreign accounts, and Ulčák was paid 40,000 US$ in compensation for the loss of income until his normal pension age (a customary practice in the West).

14 Later in April Acting Secretary General Rayer dismissed IJI Director Vejvoda immediately after his past as a high-ranking intelligence officer became public knowledge.

15 Altogether 30 regular Secretariat meetings were held in 1990. Their minutes were accompanied by 330 attachments providing full documentation on all issues.

16 The Soviet representative was an influential Secretary of their Union of Journalists, Michail Poltoranin, who later became Minister of Information and Deputy Prime Minister under President Boris Yeltsin.

17 The Statute revision was first mandated by the Presidium in Nicosia (1987). An ad hoc committee to prepare a draft for revision was appointed in the Brasilia Presidium (1988).

Figure 9.6 The Balaton Presidium was opened by the IOJ President and the General Secretary of the Hungarian Association of Journalists, Gábor Bencsik, welcoming the President of the Hungarian Republic, Arpad Göncz, who was making his first public appearance as the newly elected Head of State. President Göncz recommended the IOJ "to take the same way as we did, where sharp and serious discussions always resulted in sincere efforts to obtain a compromise". This good wish turned out to be quite far from later realities in the IOJ – as well as in Hungary itself. The photo here is from a report on the Presidium published a couple of months later in *The Democratic Journalist* 7–8/1990.

a contribution by the Auditing Commission requesting it to report to the Executive Committee.[18]

Finally the enlarged Secretariat decided to convene the Presidium in early May. President Nordenstreng and Acting Secretary General Rayer were mandated to prepare the agenda and materials in light of the discussions in the meeting. The Hungarian Association of Journalists offered to host the Presidium in a resort hotel at Lake Balaton.

The **Presidium in Balatonfüred** was held on 6–8 **May 1990** (Figure 9.6). It was attended by 29 of the 32 elected members or their representatives, 13 other delegates of member unions, 10 Secretaries and a dozen others from the Secretariat, including several enterprise directors.[19]

The first item on the agenda was the resignation of Secretary General Ulčák and the appointment of a successor, introduced with a copy of Ulčák's letter of resignation (28 February 1990) and his speech in the Presidium. It was followed by a long and heated discussion – at times quite emotional, filling nearly half of the Presidium minutes. The debate was mostly about the pressure from the new Czechoslovak Syndicate and the technical staff of the IOJ apparatus exerted upon the Secretary General and about whether the Secretariat and the President had exceeded the mandate of the Lisbon Presidium. In the debate Ulčák accused President Nordenstreng and Secretary Paukku of forcing his resignation; both rejoined that they acted

18 In addition, the President initiated after the meeting an invitation to the KPMG Europe accountant company based in Amsterdam to carry out an audit of the IOJ enterprises.

19 *IOJ Presidium Meeting Balatonfüred Hungary*, May 6–8, 1990, pp. 34–35. As in the earlier Presidium report from Lisbon, this contains detailed minutes with the main documents as enclosures.

within their respective mandates. Secretary Muzavazi likewise responded to accusations that the Secretariat had worked behind the back of the Secretary General; on behalf of his colleagues he stated that they never put themselves above the elected bodies.

Most of the over 20 speakers expressed acceptance of Ulčák's resignation, but there were two Vice-Presidents who proposed that the resignation be withdrawn and the Secretary General continue until the next Congress. French Vice-President Gatinot read out a statement by his SNJ-CGT criticizing the IOJ for having made mistakes, especially during the past six months and proposing that Gatinot be elected Secretary General. Ulčák endorsed his candidacy. The candidacy of the Acting Secretary General Rayer was proposed by Nigerian Vice-President Izobo. President Nordenstreng did not campaign for either of the two candidates but made it clear that he considered Rayer a better choice to manage the present crisis until the next Congress.

In a secret ballot Gatinot received 13 votes and Rayer 12 votes. On the following day the American delegate Edward Palmer, who had missed the ballot due to a delayed flight, announced that he would have voted for Rayer. (See Muzavazi's recollections in Part Two.)

The other items on the agenda – the situation in central and eastern Europe, the new strategy of the IOJ, the new IOJ Statutes, the IOJ's economic activities and enterprises, the membership applications and the meeting of the Executive Committee – were considered in a more dispassionate way, following up various documents from the enlarged Secretariat meeting. The Press Union of Liberia was accepted as a new member, while several applications from India and one from Thailand were returned for further preparation.

The next Executive Committee meeting was confirmed to be convened in Amman (at the invitation of the Jordanian government received in March) beginning on 13 October, to be preceded by a session of the Presidium. It was determined to hold the Congress by the end of 1990 in Europe and a Steering Committee was appointed to prepare these meetings with the following composition: President Nordenstreng, Secretary General Gatinot, Treasurer Megyeri and Vice-Presidents Suárez, Izobo, Abu Sharif, Laptev and Palmer.

The General Resolution unanimously decided on "more emphasis on professional and trade unionist aspects, social responsibility, and ethical and humanistic values". The resolution stressed that the IOJ sought to promote the worldwide unity of journalists "within the Consultative Club and other international fora".

The Presidium did not make the life of the IOJ in Prague any easier, rather the contrary. The Syndicate continued suspicious[20] and the government was

20 The first action of the new Secretary General in cancelling a meeting with the Syndicate scheduled right after the Presidium for Secretaries Rayer and Paukku was any-

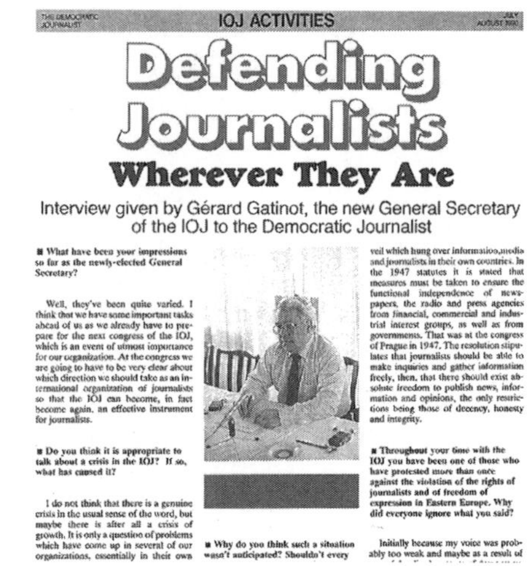

IOJ ACTIVITIES 7

Defending Journalists Wherever They Are

Interview given by Gérard Gatinot, the new General Secretary of the IOJ to the Democratic Journalist

■ What have been your impressions so far as the newly-elected General Secretary?

Well, they've been quite varied. I think that we have some important tasks ahead of us as we already have to prepare for the next congress of the IOJ, which is an event of utmost importance for our organization. At the congress we are going to have to be very clear about which direction we should take as an international organization of journalists so that the IOJ can become, in fact become again, an effective instrument for journalists.

■ Do you think it is appropriate to talk about a crisis in the IOJ? If so, what has caused it?

I do not think that there is a genuine crisis in the usual sense of the word, but maybe there is after all a crisis of growth. It is only a question of problems which have come up in several of our organizations, essentially in their own

■ Why do you think such a situation wasn't anticipated? Shouldn't every

veil which hung over information,media and journalists in their own countries. In the 1947 statutes it is stated that measures must be taken to ensure the functional independence of newspapers, the radio and press agencies from financial, commercial and industrial interest groups, as well as from governments. That was at the congress of Prague in 1947. The resolution stipulates that journalists should be able to make inquiries and gather information freely, then, that there should exist absolute freedom to publish news, information and opinions, the only restrictions being those of decency, honesty and integrity.

■ Throughout your time with the IOJ you have been one of those who have protested more than once against the violation of the rights of journalists and of freedom of expression in Eastern Europe. Why did everyone ignore what you said?

Initially because my voice was probably too weak and maybe as a result of

Figure 9.7 The new Secretary General Gatinot came out of the close-run election overflowing with confidence. In an interview published in the July-August issue of *The Democratic Journalist*, he admitted that the IOJ had gone through a period of stagnation, due to countries which were controlling information, media and journalists. Gatinot portrayed himself and his French union as critical voices against such policies over the years. He also assured that the gulf of confidence with the Czechoslovak journalists could be overcome. The interview reflected a fairly optimistic view that problems could indeed be solved. However, it soon became obvious that the problems were getting worse – with Gatinot himself a part of them.

far from friendly, especially after it began to examine the financial dealings of the former regime. **President Havel's Press Secretary** Michael Žantovský had already indicated in April 1990 that the IOJ's bad record included financial support from the Communist Party[21], but these claims were denied by the IOJ. Now, in the middle of May 1990, Žantovský repeated the allegation with a copy of a classified document from 1974 showing that the IOJ received 2.5 million Czechoslovak crowns from the state budget on instructions from the Communist Party. After this the IOJ made a thorough search of its records and did indeed discover such transfers in 1973 and 1974.

The IOJ replied to Žantovský on 1 June 1990 with a detailed account and paid back these amounts to the state. The IOJ President, Secretary General and Treasurer gave their assurances that the current leadership had been totally unaware of these dealings, although it was common knowledge in the earlier socialist countries that cultural organizations were subsidized by the state in various ways. Finally on 5 June a meeting was held in the Prague Castle between the Press Secretary and the IOJ President and Secretary General, clearing the air and laying the matter to rest.

However, the Government did nothing to alleviate the political pressure on the IOJ, especially after the federal election on 8–9 June 1990 confirmed that the Civic Forum was by far the largest party in the Parliament. After this the political atmosphere was increasingly hostile towards the IOJ and also

thing but helpful; Gatinot wanted to be present in person, but he arrived in Prague only a week later. He also cancelled the invitation to the Amsterdam-based accountant company intended to make an audit of the IOJ enterprises.

21 At this stage the IOJ President issued a statement suggesting that an extraordinary Congress be immediately convened (see Appendix 25).

towards the WFTU and the IUS, as manifested in the **Government's Resolution** (831 of 20 August 1990) **to terminate the activities of international non-governmental organizations in Czechoslovakia**.

Meanwhile the IOJ continued its activities according to the plan approved by the Presidium (see Appendix 5). For example, in July 1990 the first meeting of the IOJ European Group took place in Sofia and a presidential mission was carried out in Israel and in the occupied Palestinian territories; in August an academic seminar on models in journalism was held in Hungary; in September the 2nd MacBride Round Table was convened in Prague. These and a host of other activities were covered in the *IOJ newsletter*. Several articles critically assessing the IOJ appeared in *The Democratic Journalist*.

The Steering Committee appointed by the Presidium to prepare for the Executive Committee (EC) and the Congress held five meetings between June and October 1990; in practice it operated as a mini-Presidium during these months.[22] Initially the Committee acceded to the President's proposal to convene both the EC and the Congress already in September (in Prague), but after consulting all members of the Presidium in June, it decided to hold the EC in October in Amman as agreed in Balaton, followed by the Congress in November (in London, Paris or Geneva). Meanwhile, the EC and Congress agenda and various working materials were meticulously prepared.

In August 1990 the Gulf War had erupted, rendering Amman a problematic venue for the EC. The Steering Committee held its meeting in Amman in mid-September, recommending that the EC be convened there on the dates envisaged "if the political situation in the Gulf doesn't deteriorate seriously". If Amman were to prove impossible, an alternative was foreseen to hold the EC just before the Congress and the venue to be either Paris or Warsaw.

In early October, when several delegates and also some Secretariat staff declined to travel, the President gave a gloomy summary of the prospects for Amman as a venue and the final Steering Committee meeting in Prague took a majority decision that the EC should be relocated to Paris in November to be followed by the Congress one month later in Warsaw. The decision to cancel Amman was made after a long debate and against the position of the Palestinian Vice-President Abu Sharif and Secretary Husseini; they even called for the President's resignation because of his "partisan and biased positions".

The IOJ was approaching its statutory meetings deeply divided and surrounded by heated geopolitical tensions – with a loss of 44,000 US$ in unused flight tickets and hotel rooms.

22 The minutes of these meetings, with related documents, provide an authentic view of the complicated way towards the EC and the Congress. They, like all the Secretariat meeting minutes, are available in the National Archives of the Czech Republic.

The Executive Committee met in Paris on 17–20 **November 1990**, preceded by a one-day **Presidium.** Of the 32 Presidium members 22 were present in person (17) or through a representative (5). In addition, 52 other EC members attended, with 24 observers and 17 members of the Secretariat; altogether well over 100 people. Although the Vice-President from Iraq was absent, the overall attendance was as wide and balanced as usual in these meetings.

The published report of the meeting[23], like those of the two earlier Presidiums in 1990, included detailed minutes (Presidium 8 pages and EC 25 pages) followed by key speeches and resolutions as annexes (over 60 pages). The minutes were "taken by V. Slavík".

The Presidium received the President's review on the work of the Congress Steering Committee, especially the decision not to go to Amman, which was criticized by Vice-President Abu Sharif and Secretary Husseini.[24] The main task of the Presidium – to provide the EC with a draft agenda, time-table, standing orders and background documents – was processed by consensus.

The EC itself was opened by the IOJ President and SNJ-CGT General Secretary Michel Diard. The occasion was low key compared to previous statutory meetings – no president or minister of the host country.

New members were confirmed: 15 national organizations from all continents, most of which had already been admitted by the Presidium. In addition, the new IOJ Association of Germany, founded by members of the recently discontinued GDR union, was admitted as an associate member.

The EC received several reports on the development of the IOJ and its finances. Also included were the documents prepared by the Steering Committee on New Strategy, Unity of International Journalist Movement, Draft Statutes and Report on Right to Information and Protection of Journalists.[25]

---

23 *IOJ Executive Committee Meeting Paris, November 17–20, 1990* (1991). A detail in the lists of attendance is a reminder of how the world was changing in these months: Secretary Bernd Rayer was in May (Balatonfüred) designated as being from the "GDR", while in November (Paris) he was designated as being from the "Federal Republic of Germany". The list of Vice-Presidents included George Izobo (Nigeria), whose mandate was questioned in a letter faxed to the meeting claiming that he was no longer the leader of the Nigerian union. Consequently, Izobo was temporarily suspended from the position of IOJ Vice-President pending the results of an investigation by the Secretary General. For an overview of the EC, see *IOJ newsletter* 23/1990 and *DJ* 1/1991.

24 In late October 1990 President Nordenstreng privately suggested meeting Vice-President Abu Sharif to deliberate the contentious issues. Abu Sharif proposed meeting in a small hotel outside Zürich but Nordenstreng waited for him in vain; he never showed up. Obviously the credibility gap was too deep for off-the-record negotiation.

25 In addition, a letter by former Secretary General Kubka was informally distributed, condemning President Nordenstreng for misleading the Brasilia Presidium into removing him and engineering the election of Ulcak. He requested to be rehabilitated,

The documents were not scrutinized in detail. The debate around them was extensive and conducted in both plenary and in five regional groups, but it added little new to earlier debates in the two Presidiums.[26] Most delegates spoke about their respective national interests and no consensus emerged on how to resolve the current crisis of the IOJ. Instead, there was a division into two groups in an atmosphere of mutual distrust: one faction forming around the President, including especially the Soviet and most European unions, and the other around the Secretary General, including especially the Arab and most of the Latin American unions.

The question of the date when the Congress should be held was solved by first voting whether it be already in December. The proposal was supported by 28 votes, with 39 against and six abstentions. After considering several invitations for the venue it was unanimously agreed that the 11th Congress would be convened in Harare, Zimbabwe, in the second half of January 1991. This decision was taken while Iraq was a target of both diplomatic and military mobilization by the US-led coalition heading towards the Gulf War.

All the documents, containing numerous strategic positions and operative proposals, were unanimously approved as working material for the Congress. The General Resolution adopted at the end of the EC sharpened the overall positions taken by the earlier Presidiums that the "IOJ should undergo profound changes of character, structure and overall policy" with "total commitment to democratize the organization and to put an end once and for all to past practices and mistakes". However, the resolution did not seriously deal with the existential crisis of the IOJ in Czechoslovakia, merely stating that every effort should be made "to maintain the IOJ headquarters in Prague and to correct all past deformations that have negatively reflected on relations with the journalists of the host country".

Two days after the EC in Paris, the ČTK News Agency announced that the **Government had decided that the IOJ and the IUS "must terminate their activity in Czechoslovakia"**. Somewhat cryptically the announcement noted that the government "enjoined Foreign Minister Jiří Dienstbier to discuss the question with top officials of the two organizations which should end their activities on Czechoslovak territory on June 30, 1991 at the latest".

No such discussion took place in the few weeks preceding the Congress, which was set to take place in Harare on 24–29 January 1991. Yet the threat

---

while expressing support to Gatinot. The letter remained without notable attention and was not acted upon.

26 Some financial details attracted major attention, especially the 40,000 US$ paid to former Secretary General Ulčák, for which Secretary General Gatinot criticized the President. The 100,000 US$ paid to the Paris centre in 1989 was also raised – by the Soviet delegate criticizing the Secretary General.

of expulsion from Czechoslovakia, first announced back in August, continued to hang over the IOJ, with uncertainty spreading among the Secretariat personnel and the enterprises.

STRUGGLING FOR SURVIVAL 1991–97

Entering the year 1991 the IOJ was not only pressed by the threat of expulsion but by the mounting crisis in the Middle East. The Gulf War broke out as "Operation Desert Storm" in the middle of January, while the Secretariat was busy with the final preparations for the Congress, including tens of flight tickets to bring delegates and staff members to Harare. Airlines flying to Southern Africa were operating normally and the host union in Zimbabwe gave its assurance that the conditions for arranging the Congress were good. Nevertheless, the Gulf War created anxiety about travelling.

In this situation Secretary General Gatinot sent out on 16 January – a week before the scheduled beginning of the Congress – a message to all Presidium and EC members asking whether they considered it wise to hold the Congress in Harare starting 24 January and if they were ready to participate. President Nordenstreng was strongly opposed to this consultation, which in his opinion created confusion and invited hesitation. He sent a message to the same recipients on the following day stating that it was not justified to call off the Congress in Harare which had been duly agreed on by the Executive Committee in Paris and since then thoroughly prepared: "The Congress will be held as announced and all delegates who can make it should go to Harare."

The **11th IOJ Congress** was held **in Harare** on 24–29 **January 1991** (Figure 9.8). After all, a large number of delegates, except those from Arab countries in the war region, did indeed make it to Harare. Some 200 persons attended, of whom 138 were delegates representing 84 journalists' organizations from 82 countries and the rest observers and guests including nine international and regional organizations of journalists. The attendance was fairly high given the response to the Secretary General's question on the eve of the Congress: the Presidium members were evenly divided between those who wanted to go on as agreed and those who preferred postponement, while of the 63 members of the EC at large who responded, 38 had been in favour of postponement. Despite hesitation during the escalating Gulf War, most delegates had arrived in Harare. The attendance was clearly less than in the past two Congresses (Sofia 1986, Moscow 1981) but roughly the same as in Helsinki in 1976.

First, on 23–24 January, the **Presidium** convened, with 25 of its 32 members present (seven of these represented by their delegates). After a heated

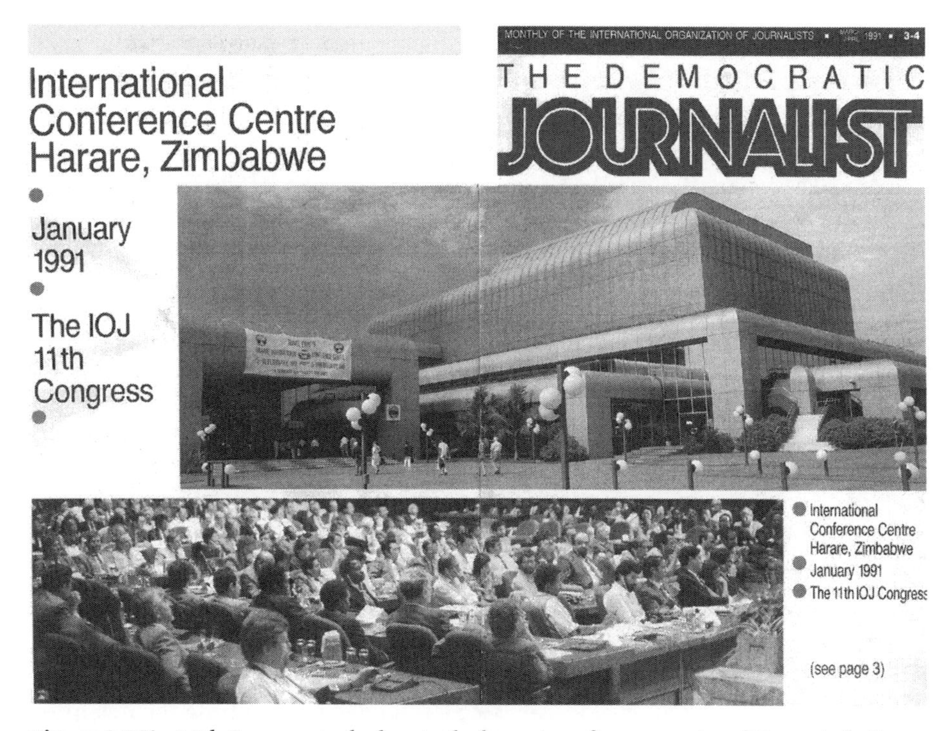

Figure 9.8 The 11th Congress took place in the largest conference centre of the capital of Zimbabwe as shown by the cover of the IOJ journal 3-4/1991.

debate on whether the Congress should be held at all given the absence of most Arab delegates, it was agreed that the necessary quorum of 51 per cent was indeed present (Cuba with the support of Palestine proposed 75 per cent and Congo 2/3). A message was sent to all member organizations in the Arab countries unable to attend eliciting their opinions on issues on the Congress agenda by any available means of communication. Also, a resolution on information aspects of the Gulf War was issued. Finally, the Presidium agreed on the draft standing orders and proposed the Congress commissions.

The Congress itself started on 24 January and lasted for five days. It was widely reported in *IOJ newsletter* 3-4/1991 and *The Democratic Journalist* 3-4/1991 but no separate Congress report was published – for the first time since the 4th Congress. The proceedings, summarized in **Appendix 27**, were made available to the Secretariat some months after Harare. The fact that it remained unpublished evidences the incipient disarray in the Secretariat.

The proceedings speak for themselves and the published reports provide additional material, including the text of the new Statutes in the *DJ* 3-4/1991. In short, the Congress documents manifested a radical shift from a fairly political to a clearly professional orientation. The specific declaration on Relations with Czechoslovakia complied with the demands presented by the Syndicates as well as the Government in the country and the declaration on IOJ Headquarters provided a constructive basis for avoiding the threat of expulsion.

The result of the elections was an outcome of heavy lobbying as shown by Muzavazi's recollections in Part Two. It was obvious that there were two main factions competing for ultimate power within the organization: one around the President advocating for radical change towards a united world organization and the other around the Secretary General clinging to the distinctive nature of the IOJ. The first had a predominantly European perspective, while the second mainly reflected the views of the global South. These became evident right after the Velvet Revolution in late 1989, were consolidated in the developments during 1990 and were finally precipitated by the Gulf War.

The election of the Secretary General became a testing ground for the two factions, seen largely as a battle between pro-West reformers and pro-South conservatives. Gerard Gatinot's candidacy for the position of Secretary General was clear well before the Congress and he had a highly efficient French campaign team, whereas the other candidate – first Bernd Rayer and then Christopher Muzavazi – was presented only during the Congress and with a less conspicuous campaign. In the vote Gatinot got 88 votes against Muzavazi's 60. Gatinot and his supporters also succeeded in obtaining the new post of Deputy Secretary General as Mazen Husseini defeated Muzavazi.

The election of the President was less intense with 91 votes for Armando Rollemberg against 52 for Luis Suarez. The Treasurer's post was won by Marian Grigore from Romania in a tight vote against Andrzej Ziemski from Poland. The list of all elected officers (see Appendix 27) was fairly balanced, but the success of Gatinot with Husseini in landing the key executive posts gave the impression that the balance of power was tilting towards the conservative old guard. This assessment was made on the spot by the Finnish, German and Soviet delegations – the USSR Union of Journalists was still the largest IOJ member – as well as those from central-eastern Europe who were sympathetic towards the Czechoslovak non-members. They were disappointed and stepped back with a wait-and-see mode, whereas the Hungarian delegation announced on the spot that this member would break off its relations with the IOJ. Harare ended with poor prospects for a reconciliation in the international movement of journalists.

The new IOJ leaders had quite a different perspective when interviewed for the IOJ publications (*IOJ newsletter* 5/1991 and *DJ* 3–4/1991): "My credo is clear: pluralism, democracy, openness" (Rollemberg); "I view the future optimistically" (Gatinot). And their views got some support in April when the Czechoslovak **Government climbed down from its earlier position of 1990** conceding that there were no legal grounds for the expulsion of the IOJ from the country. The Syndicates of Czech and Slovak Journalists immediately responded by urging the Government to abandon its new position.

The IOJ **Secretariat** was in a less optimistic state after Harare as is apparent in Muzavazi's recollections: no more regular meetings and Russian Secretary Artyomov dismissed in February. Meanwhile, **President Rollemberg** and his assistant Ramsés Ramos moved to Prague, becoming a permanent part of the headquarters. The new **Executive Committee** composed of 14 elected officers – corresponding to the earlier Presidium – **met in Prague** on 6–9 **May 1991**, welcoming the Government's decision and confirming the plan of action for the year with priority for trade union struggles, professional training and the unity of the international journalist movement. It was decided to reorganize the Secretariat on a thematic rather than a regional basis focusing on trade unions, training and publications.

On 21 August 1991 the Government took another decision whereby the **Ministry of the Interior withdrew the right of the IOJ to have its seat in Prague and engage in activities in Czechoslovakia**. This was the first legally valid decision on expulsion, while the earlier Government announcements had been more political positions. The IOJ responded with a letter to the Minister of the Interior and with a legal appeal on 10 September 1991, stressing that after the Congress the IOJ was no longer the same organization on which the earlier expulsion rulings were made in 1990.

This started a legal process with various steps through the Prosecutor General, the Supreme Court of Prague and the Constitutional Court, which in March 1997 finally dismissed all legal actions brought by the IOJ. During the process a distinction was made between the seat and the activities in the country, at one stage rejecting the legal seat but allowing activities. However, the final verdict covered both aspects.

The response to the new expulsion decision was the main issue in the **Executive Committee meeting in Rio de Janeiro in September 1991**. In the discussion 2nd Vice-President Angelov criticized the activities since Harare for being cosmetic while "conservative forces are still in command in the IOJ and radical changes are necessary". He proposed the forthcoming Council meeting to be turned into an Extraordinary Congress, but others did not agree.

The meeting also considered the Auditing Commission's report, which was not approved in the Congress, and the report of the committee set up at the Congress to investigate financial issues. Several irregularities were found and the Treasurer, his Deputy and Chairman of the Auditing Commission were charged with completing the investigation. Secretary General Gatinot was implicated in many of the irregularities and his role was heavily criticized by President Rollemberg, who asked for his suspension until the matter was solved. The meeting decided to relieve Gatinot of his office and put him on suspension until the forthcoming Council meeting. During this time Deputy Secretary General Husseini was authorized to serve as Acting Secretary General.

The Executive Committee decided to put on hold various projects and activities, to cut down drastically various expenses and to reduce the IOJ staff. Accordingly, it decided to close the school in Prague and use its building for the IJI and the Editorial Board which were to be merged. It also decided on a number of priority projects, including an IOJ computer network and databank linking the 50 largest member organizations.

The new **IOJ Council** with 82 representatives of member organizations from 72 countries met **in Sana'a** (Yemen) on 22–26 **November 1991**. It decided that Deputy Secretary General Husseini would assume the administrative and financial functions while Secretary General Gatinot was heading only the political sphere. It approved a plan to rationalize expenses by drastic cuts in personnel and a revision of the privileges enjoyed by the leading officers. It also decided to take steps to close the regional centre in Addis Abeba and to set up a regional centre for the Arab countries based in Sana'a and another centre for Asia and Oceania based in Pyongyang "with a mandate to maintain its independence from the government and political parties as well as to defend political pluralism in the region". The Council approved a long message by President Rollemberg on the strategic line of the IOJ. Finally, the Council elected seven new members to the Executive Committee, one for each of the regions. Recommendations of the Council also led to the discontinuation of *The Democratic Journalist* at the end of 1991. The *IOJ newsletter*, biweekly since 1980, began to appear only once a month or less.

In February 1992 the IFJ and the IOJ leaders signed a joint statement on co-operation in three areas of activity, reproduced in **Appendix 28**. President Rollemberg also submitted a proposal for concrete joint actions on trade unionism and media concentration, protection of journalists on dangerous missions and journalists in European economic integration. He continued with further proposals when addressing the IFJ Congress in June. However, the IFJ was reluctant to implement the joint statement – it preferred to keep a certain distance to the IOJ, taking it as a competitor which was in trouble.

The **Executive Committee met in Madrid** on 24–25 **April 1992** in order to consider the future location of the IOJ headquarters in light of the decision of the Czechoslovak Federal Ministry of the Interior. Five offers to host the IOJ were on the table: Bucharest, Madrid, Paris, Rio de Janeiro and Vienna. In a secret ballot Madrid got most votes. This was a preliminary decision to be confirmed by the Congress. The meeting also discussed other issues, especially the financial difficulties calling for reduction of expenditures and the IOJ enterprises to guarantee their profitability for the organization.

Figure 9.9 The Executive Committee in Prague in October 1992 decided to publish a new quarterly review *Le Monde des Journalistes* replacing the old monthly journal *The Democratic Journalist*, to be published by the Paris centre. The first issue of the new quarterly was published in 1993 in French and included an exclusive interview with President Aristide of Haiti by Secretary General Gatinot. Other stories covered the UN Conference on Human Rights, the situation of journalists in former Yugoslavia and several other topical issues – in a magazine style reminiscent of the discontinued *DJ*. No English version appeared and no further issues were published even in French.

Another **Executive Committee meeting in Prague** on 19–22 **October 1992** asked the leadership to prepare for transferring the headquarters to Madrid if the Czechoslovak authorities confirmed their decision to expel the IOJ. The meeting also decided to carry out several activities, including missions to former Yugoslavia and Haiti, training courses in Africa and the Arab world as well as seminars in Russia and The Philippines.[27]

Accordingly, the IOJ organized and attended various events in 1992 and 1993 but they were far fewer than before, reflecting the reduced budget and fewer staff. Since 1992 not only the Russian secretary Artyomov but also the German and Zimbabwean secretaries Rayer and Muzavazi as well as the Finnish secretary Paukku were missing. Nevertheless, while downsizing its activities the IOJ still maintained an infrastructure and level of activities which surpassed that of the IFJ. In 1993 the IOJ raised its profile by calling for a World Journalist Forum[28] and issuing a declaration at the World Conference on Human Rights in Vienna[29].

On the other hand, the IOJ lost its Finnish members, who no longer believed in its renewal: full member YLL (host of the 3rd Congress in 1950) and associate member SSL (founding member in 1946, leaving in 1949 and returning in 1981). Thus the Finns joined the Hungarians, who had left shortly after Harare. The Russians did not leave but remained passive, partly because of the transformation of their union after the end of the Soviet Union.

The next meeting of the **Executive Committee** took place **in Paris** on 26–29 **April 1993**. The meeting urged the transfer of headquarters to Madrid

27 See *IOJ newsletter* 1992 August, September and October–November.

28 See *IOJ newsletter* 1993 March.

29 Reproduced in *IOJ newsletter* 1993 July–August and as a pamphlet entitled *On the right to information* (1993).

Figure 9.10 At the end of 1993 the Secretariat had to vacate *Celetná* 2 at the corner of the Old Town Square. The owners of the building before the late 1940s demanded its restitution and the IOJ got no compensation for the major investment it had made in the reconstruction. The Secretariat moved to *Mánesova* 79 in Prague 2, an upper-middle-class residential area some distance from the centre. The office had four rooms in the basement for an annual rent of over half a million Czech crowns – with three-year advance contracted by Gatinot. (Photo by Nordenstreng)

be implemented without delay, while the IOJ enterprises were foreseen to continue in the Czech Republic (after the federal state had been split in 1992) under a professional management enabling their modernization. Deputy Secretary General Husseini having recently resigned[30], it was decided that his post remain vacant until the next Congress – with full powers of the Secretary General reverting to Gatinot. Asian Vice-President Tsegmidin Munkhjargal (Mongolia) had passed away and his functions were transferred to Antonio Nieva (The Philippines).[31]

At this stage President Rollemberg and his assistant moved to Madrid to establish the new IOJ headquarters, while the main Secretariat remained in Prague. For outsiders this highlighted the shaky state of the IOJ, in addition to the reduced activities – not least the disappearance of *The Democratic Journalist* and the closing of the International Journalism Institute IJI.

Under these circumstances, in December 1992, the IOJ received a proposal from the International Association for Mass Communication Research (IAMCR) to **re-establish the IJI** as a joint venture with this scholarly INGO, the World Association for Christian Communication (WACC), the IOJ and the Czech Syndicate of Journalists – see **Appendix 29**. President Rollemberg replied in April 1994 welcoming the idea of a joint foundation – not to be based at the IOJ school in Prague but at the IOJ premises in Paris.[32] This would have

30 Husseini resigned after the General Union of Palestinian Writers and Journalists had sent a letter to the IFJ claiming that the IOJ Deputy Secretary General had not been a proper representative of the Union.

31 See *IOJ newsletter* 1993 April–June.

32 See Rollemberg's letter in Appendix 29. His preliminary plan did not make it onto the Executive Committee's agenda. The initiative was strongly opposed by Secretary General Gatinot – not only because he disliked academic activities associated with former President Nordenstreng but also because of Rollemberg's intention to use it as a reason to occupy the IOJ premises in Paris.

meant losing a political deal with the Czech Syndicate[33], but in any case the IAMCR proposal was disregarded by the IOJ.

The **Executive Committee** met again **in Barcelona** on 6–9 **December 1993**. President Rollemberg opened the meeting with a positive statement, admitting that "we have endured three years of varied crisis" and that this meeting "has the task of ending the actual confusion, resolving divergences which may have arisen within the leadership and approving measures aimed at the urgent modernization of our organization". He submitted to the meeting 12 "Projects for resolution" extending from the IOJ's archives to the purchase of a computerized system for the headquarters in Madrid. His proposal for the plan of action in 1994 included eight events at a total expense of close to 300,000 US$ and his total budget estimate for 1994 was nearly two million US$.[34]

However, instead of processing the proposals the meeting turned into a sharp criticism of Rollemberg's working methods and administration. In this examination several members called either for his return to Brasilia or his suspension or resignation. No doubt there had been lobbying for these options by the Secretary General's camp. After this confrontation **Rollemberg tendered his resignation**, which was accepted, and 1st Vice-President Manuel Tomé became the Acting President.[35] For Rollemberg's side of the story, see his recollections in Part Two and **Appendix 30** including excerpts of his 28-page letter to his successor in January 1994.

In addition to the case of the President, the Executive Committee adopted a work plan for 1994, with priority for training actions and protection of journalists. It admitted new membership applications from associations in Peru, Panama and the Czech Republic[36]. The meeting also speeded up the preparations for the 12th Congress planned for November 1994. After the

33 The deal involved a major donation of the valuable school property in exchange for resuming relations between the IOJ and the Syndicate, informally negotiated by Nordenstreng and the Syndicate veteran Vlado Kašpar.

34 Main items of the overall budget were (in US$): Headquarters in Madrid 273,000; Leadership salaries 126,000; Regional centres and bureaus 290,000 (of which eight ranging from 10,000 to 60,000); Events and travel 450,000; Archives and computer services 150,000; Solidarity fund and emergency service 100,000; Executive Committee and Auditing Commission meetings 200,000; 12th Congress 350,000.

35 See *IOJ newsletter* November 1993 – January. *IOJ newsletter* February–April 1994 reported that the IOJ Secretariat held a working meeting in Madrid in January 1994, specifying the plan of action and budget for 1994. Also discussed was "the anti-IOJ campaign launched by the former President", in response to which a circular was sent to member organizations.

36 The application from the Czech Republic represented a small group of journalists who disagreed with the Syndicate's position.

meeting the leaders went to Madrid to attend a reception at the inauguration of the IOJ new headquarters.[37]

The **Executive Committee meeting in Prague** on 17–18 **June 1994** had three proposals for hosting the 12th Congress: in Jordan, Poland and Vietnam. Amman was chosen as it would be the first time that the IOJ Congress was held in the Arab region – and also "a way of settling a historical debt" (Figure 9.12). Three working groups were appointed to prepare the Congress materials on orientation, organization and updating the Statutes. The meeting adopted a statement on the unity of the world journalist movement, particularly joint action with the IFJ with a view to the "unification of the two organizations".[38]

Figure 9.11 Meeting with HM King Hussein in Amman in June 1994 when preparing for the 12th IOJ Congress. From the left: Suleiman Al-Qudah, President of the Jordanian Journalist Association, Interpreter Ms. G. Lama, Gérard Gatinot, IOJ Secretary General, King Hussein, Joseph Kosseifi, IOJ Executive Committee member from Lebanon and Mahboub Ali, Manager of the IOJ Arab centre in Yemen. (Photo from Al-Qudah's collection)

Another **Executive Committee meeting in Prague** on 27–28 **November 1994** set the date for the Congress to be 28–31 January 1995 and determined the details of its attendance, agenda, etc. The question of unity was discussed with different perspectives including a confederation open to all international, regional and national organizations. After the meeting the IOJ hosted a delegation of the British NUJ which was trying to bring the two world organizations together. The *IOJ newsletter* September–December 1994 covering these topics was the last issue of this publication.

By this time the headquarters in Madrid were closed, while the expulsion from Prague remained pending in the legal process. Meanwhile, the Secretary General had lost his political base in France. As shown by Diard's recollections in Part Two, the SNJ-CGT took a decision in September 1994 not to renew Gatinot's mandate in the forthcoming Congress.

---

37 See *IOJ newsletter* November 1993 – January 1994. Regarding the persecution and assassination of journalists, the meeting established an international committee for the protection of journalists and freedom of the press, chaired by Jean-Paul Kaufmann from France with Eleazar Diaz Rangel from Venezuela and Sani Zorro from Nigeria as vice-chairs.

38 *IOJ newsletter* May–August 1994.

Figure 9.12 Opening ceremony of the 12th IOJ Congress in Amman in the Cultural Centre of the Hashemite Kingdom of Jordan on 28 January 1995. At the Presidium table from the right: Al-Qudah from Jordan, Tomé from Mozambique, Gatinot from France and Suarez from Mexico. (Photos from Al-Qudah's collection)

The **12th IOJ Congress** took place **in Amman** on 28–31 **January 1995** (Figure 9.12). It was presided over by Vice Prime Minister and Minister of Information Khaled Karaki, who read an address from King Hussein, appealing to journalists to assume responsibility to society for the defence of liberty and justice and cautioning that nobody should presume to monopolize the truth.

Attending were about 100 delegates representing 69 member organizations from 65 countries. Guests included representatives of UNESCO, the Red Cross, the IFJ, the Union of African Journalists and the Federation of Arab Journalists. This time a printed report was published[39], with the Secretary General's preliminary report, the Treasurer's report and summary of the Executive Committee before the Congress. Of these, reproduced in **Appendix 31** are the Treasurer's report and the results of the elections.

The **Presidium** met for the last time **on the eve of the Congress in Amman.** The draft agenda, regulations and composition of the Congress presidium were approved and the materials for the Congress were processed. This time an explosive debate was sparked by the reports of the Secretary General and the Treasurer as Diard describes in his recollections. Obviously economy and Secretary General Gatinot's record in it was the heart of the matter.

The Congress continued to discuss the reports. Finally the Secretary General's report was not approved – in fact rejected (36 votes with 33 abstentions) while the Treasurer's report, amended by the Executive Committee, was approved (54 votes for, 2 against and 15 abstentions). New member organizations were admitted from Chile, Congo, Czech Republic, Ecuador, Ethiopia,

39 *12th Congress* (1995).

Panama, Peru and Zambia, while applications from the Dominican Republic, France and India were referred for further examination. For the French case, see Diard's recollections in Part Two.

Amendments to the Statutes were thoroughly considered and overwhelmingly approved. These remained more or less the same as the Statutes revised in Harare, including a list of 12 aims and objectives, but the organizational structure was simplified by eliminating the Council and leaving the Executive Committee as the only body under the Congress. It was composed of seven main officers – the President, two Vice-Presidents, the Secretary General with a deputy and the Treasurer with a deputy – plus seven regional Vice-Presidents and seven other members representing the regions.

Elections held by secret ballot produced the results reproduced in Appendix 31; see also recollections by Al-Qudah in Part Two. It was a new team with only a handful of those who had served in the earlier leadership (see Appendix 31).[40]

Figure 9.13 President Al-Qudah from a moderate Arab country typified the average IOJ orientation (photo by Nordenstreng in 2016). Secretary General Antonio Maria Nieva from the Philippines combined a strong track record in professional journalism and social activism on national as well as international levels. Nieva is shown here with Phan Quang, Vice-President for Asia in the Amman Congress (photo from Quang's collection).

The new Secretary General moved to Prague in April 1995, operating from the Secretariat in *Mánesova Street* with a handful of employees. No other members of the Executive Committee settled in Prague; the Deputy Secretary General from Zimbabwe, Kindness Paradza, wanted to do so but was turned down due to lack of resources. Nieva was quick to tackle the political, economic and legal problems of the IOJ, keeping the Executive Committee informed by "Internal briefings" from April 1995 on; the first two of those are reproduced partly in **Appendix 32**.

---

40 The Presidential election was won by Suleiman Al-Qudah against Andrzej Ziemski, Secretary General of the Polish member union SDPRL, with a 2/3 majority. This union played an active role in the Congress also by submitting a proposal for revising the Statutes.

Journalists INTERNATIONAL

June 1995

IOJ, IFJ Issue Landmark Plea To Stop Bloodletting in Algeria

Intervene for Peace, Qudah Asks OIC

President Qudah

'Murders in the Name of Allah'

The June IOJ-IFJ Declaration

Figure 9.14 To relaunch a periodical publication for the IOJ an informative bulletin *Journalists International* was started in June 1995, also in French translation. In size and style it resembled the earlier *IOJ newsletter*. Two issues came out in 1995 and four in 1996 and in 1997. In its year-end 1995 issue the *Journalists International* proudly announced: "IOJ leaps into cyberspace" with its own electronic mail and a homepage, shown in **Appendix 33**.

Secretary General Nieva was extremely efficient in restoring order to the IOJ despite the scarcity of resources and a host of problems in the enterprises, which were handled under a Supervisory Board and with the help of lawyers[41].

During this process of consolidation after the Congress, in March 1995, the Ministry of the Interior of the Czech Republic took a decision on the legal appeal lodged by the IOJ in 1992 against the ruling on the expulsion of the IOJ from Czechoslovakia (until the end of 1992 still a federal state), effectively confirming the expulsion of the IOJ from the country. As shown in Nieva's Internal briefing No. 2 (Appendix 32), the IOJ lodged in May 1995 another legal appeal against this latest ruling – with fairly optimistic expectations.

Under these conditions the new **Executive Committee** held its first meeting in **Prague in June 1995**. It was attended by all but two of the elected members. Those attending as observers were directors of regional centres in Sana'a, Mexico City and Pyongyang as well as representatives of the member associations in India and the Czech Republic. The report of this meeting includes the Secretary General's draft Action Plan, Conclusions and Proceedings, recording all the individual interventions, of which extracts are reproduced in **Appendix 34**.

These documents are self-explanatory as is **Nieva's report in 1996** entitled "IOJ: It lives yet to fight one more year" – see **Appendix 35**. It presented a gloomy but still hopeful assessment of the IOJ and its infrastructure for the next statutory meeting which turned out to be its last.

The **Executive Committee** met in **Hanoi** in **July 1996** (Figure 9.16). Attending were all but four of the 21 elected members and the Chairman of the

41 One of these was Josef Komárek, recruited in 1994 as advisor to Secretary General Gatinot. After the Amman Congress he became Secretary General Nieva's main legal advisor and later the director of the Mondiapress commercial company owned by the IOJ.

Figure 9.15 The IOJ Solidarity School in Prague was located at *Červený vrch* between the city centre and the airport, and was well established by the end of the 1980s as seen in this brochure. The new leadership converted it into a two-star hotel in 1994, advertised in every issue of the *Journalists International* after No. 5 (September–October 1996).

Auditing Commission as well as the director of the Pyongyang Centre and the Berlin School and two leaders of the national organization in the Philippines. Present at the inaugural session were the Malesian and Vietnamese leaders of the Confederation of ASEAN Journalists (CAJ).[42]

The Executive Committee endorsed Secretary General Nieva's report and declared unification of the journalists' movement an urgent concern in light of the new and increased dangers confronting journalists around the world. As noted by President Al-Qudah: "When reporters and editors are killed or put in prison, when newspapers are silenced, all journalists must close ranks." The meeting condemned the murder of an Irish journalist and pledged solidarity with 2,500 striking journalists and media workers in Detroit, USA. A number of resolutions were adopted concerning Palestinian, Algerian and Nigerian journalists, women journalists, etc. The National Federation of Media Workers in the Philippines (KAMMPI) was admitted as a new member.

Figure 9.16 Executive Committee in Hanoi, July 1996. Secretary General Nieva speaking. (Photo from Quang's collection)

42 See *Journalists International* edition No. 4 (July–August 1996). Detailed minutes of the meeting were prepared but not reproduced here; they are available in the IOJ collection at the National Archives of the Czech Republic.

The Executive Committee was followed by a 50th anniversary jubilee at Hanoi's Ho Chi Minh Museum, attended by Deputy Prime Minister Phan Van Khai, who presented personal felicitations from Prime Minister and National Assembly Chairman Vo Van Kiet. The IOJ presented a Scroll of Honour and Jubilee Medallion to 20 Vietnamese journalists for their outstanding contribution to the cause of international journalism. The Vietnam Journalists Association (VJA) for its part presented the Vietnam Press Medal to four IOJ leaders and two CAJ leaders. Phan Quang, President of the VJA and IOJ Vice-President for Asia-Oceania, said that holding the celebration in the museum named after Ho Chi Minh was doubly meaningful since Vietnam's founding President was himself a journalist.

The evening of "Golden Memorabilia" on 27 November 1996 was an example of Antonio Nieva's excellence in upholding the spirit despite drastic financial cuts which had reduced the Secretariat staff to less than 15 (Figure 17).

Journalists INTERNATIONAL

IOJ

IOJ, IFJ Ready Landmark Joint Action

Unchain Palestinian Newsmen, Israel asked

Golden Memorabilia

Nov. 27: An Affair To Remember

What's Inside

Journalists Close Ranks in Landmark Project

Sub-Center for C. Asia in Ulan Bator

Figure 9.17 The celebration of the 50th anniversary continued on its home ground in Prague on the premises of the former Julius Fučík School of Solidarity, as reported by the *Journalists International* (No. 6, November–December 1996). The IOJ Scroll of Honour was awarded to two former Secretary Generals, Kubka (posthumously) and Meisner, as well as 14 former IOJ employees including Václav Slavík (studies), Libuše Jelínková (publications) and Alena Kulhavá (finance).

After successfully concluding the Executive Committee meeting in Hanoi, Nieva saw his main task to be repairing the "serious damage wrought on the IOJ in the last four years".[43] Nieva believed that the IOJ could now concentrate on its professional work. In September 1996 he met with IFJ General Secretary Aidan White at UNESCO in Paris, admitting that they had nearly 30 common member unions and the pressures around the profession demanded unity. In October he reopened co-operation with the International Institute of Journalism Berlin (IIJB), beginning with photo-journalism workshops in India and The Philippines.

43 From Nieva's personal email to Nordenstreng on 19 August 1996, telling how he had been "actually fighting for survival here in Prague, fending off an attempt by a cabal of employees to crab control of the Secretariat and the IOJ properties. They tried to set off the leadership against each other [...], but they didn't succeed this time. I have had to fire some people in coming to grips with the problem, but the worst is over."

The expulsion saga continued in September 1996 with a decision of the Supreme Court of Prague against the IOJ's appeal of May 1995. In December 1996 a constitutional complaint was lodged with the Constitutional Court, which on 4 March 1997 dismissed the IOJ's appeal against the Supreme Court. However, in August 1997 the IOJ submitted a complaint to the European Court of Human Rights.

It was in such a situation that Antonio Nieva died of an aggressive liver cancer on 13 October 1997.

Figure 9.18 At the beginning of 1997 Nieva moved the Secretariat to *Londýnská* 60, closer to the Centre, with three rooms and storage space for an annual rent of less than 200,000 Czech crowns. This office has been kept until these days by the IOJ and its commercial company Mondiapress. The storage in the basement has preserved the employment and salary files of all IOJ and Mondiapress personnel from the 1970s on as required by law. Director of Mondiapress Josef Komárek pictured here in front of the office in 2015. (Photo by Nordenstreng)

CHAPTER 10
DEMISE 1998–2016

In the late 1990s the world had settled into the post-Cold War constellation whereby former socialist countries in central and eastern Europe were politically closer to the USA than to the EU with NATO as their security umbrella.

Russia followed its own course, first in rogue capitalism under President Boris Yeltsin and after 2000 in a form of increasingly state-dominated capitalism with its own socio-political order under President Vladimir Putin.

The USA, with Russia in decline and no counterweight in eastern Europe, enjoyed hegemony until terrorist attacks on its iconic centres on 11 September 2001 demonstrated its vulnerability.

Terrorism backed by Islamic extremism mobilized by Al-Qaida and ISIS became a challenge to all western countries. Civil wars continued in Iraq and Afghanistan. The conflict between Israel and the Palestinians in the occupied territories continued with several wars in Gaza since 2008.

China loomed larger in the global economy, followed by India and other countries in the global South, the BRICS grouping since 2006 highlighting the non-western challenge.

By the 2010s the world had become multipolar, both economically and culturally. The US-led unipolar worldview was giving way to a scenario with a clash of civilizations.

The media field was in turmoil, with the old mass media being challenged by new social media.

After Secretary General Nieva's death in October 1997, the IOJ was left adrift like a ship in a stormy sea with no-one at the helm, as shown by Al-Qudah in his recollections in Part Two. Guidelines came from the President in Amman and the Treasurer in Sofia, while the management of the Secretariat and the overseeing of the commercial companies were left to legal advisor Komárek, who had become Nieva's right hand man in dealing with the state authorities, local properties and personnel.

Most commercial IOJ enterprises were sold or liquidated, leaving Mondiapress owned by the IOJ as its formal base. In addition, two minor IOJ companies remained: Technical Service in Prague and Sprint-Press in Bratislava.

LAST ACTIVITIES 1998

The first event after Nieva's death was an informal **meeting of the core IOJ leadership in Berlin** in connection with the inauguration of the new IIJB premises on 15-16 **March 1998** (Figure 10.1). It was proposed by Vice-President Phan Quang to IIJB Director Rüdiger Claus and the invitation was sent to selected Executive members (see recollections by Claus and Quang in Part Two). It turned out to be the last meeting of the IOJ leadership, attended by President Al-Qudah, Treasurer Angelov from Bulgaria, Deputy Secretary General Paradza from Zimbabwe, 2nd Vice-President Nagamootoo from Guyana, Vice-President for Latin America Hernandez from Cuba and Vice-President for Asia Quang from Vietnam. In addition, Komárek from Prague and former IOJ Secretary for Africa Christopher Muzavazi from the UK attended.

Figure 10.1 IOJ leaders in Berlin, March 1998. On the left: hosting IIJB director Claus, next to IOJ President Al-Qudah. Second row far right: Phan Quang. (Photo: IIJB)

The main results of the meeting were reflected in a circular sent to all IOJ members by President Al-Qudah, dated in Amman on 5 April 1998. It reminded them that after the Amman Congress the current leadership had inherited a difficult financial situation: "the budget for all the professional and administrative work of the Organization was about 200,000 US dollars per annum, against 2.5 million dollars per annum during the years 1991–95". Still, it was assumed that the IOJ would continue to publish a newsletter or a monthly magazine on a subscription basis.

Members were requested to pay their fees regularly and to provide up-to-date membership figures – something that had never really succeeded – but this time there was a new idea to generate income: an international press identity card accredited by UNESCO and issued for 10 US$ for journalists of the member unions in the developing countries and for 30 US$ to those in Europe and North America. The member unions would get 30 per cent of the card revenue allowing them to pay their annual fees.

None of these ideas ever materialized; they apparently got lost in the continuous downsizing of the Secretariat. The number of persons employed in the Secretariat – including some managerial staff of the commercial companies – was 21 in 1997, whereas in 1993 it had been 37. From 1997 to 2002 it dwindled further to 10.

The last membership list in the records is from 1997 and includes names and contact information of 111 national associations: 14 from Europe, 4 from North America, 33 from Africa, 12 from the Arab world, 19 from Asia & Oceania, 23 from Latin America and 6 from the Caribbean. This is an impressive array of membership which, however, under the circumstances, had no longer services from the IOJ and not even contacts with the Secretariat.

An historically significant activity was the leadership's visit to China in July 1998 as reported in the recollections by Al-Qudah and Quang in Part Two. This was a breakthrough meeting with the leadership of the All-China Journalists Association (ACJA) – an IOJ member since 1950, which, after the Cultural Revolution in 1965, turned into a self-declared outsider. The IOJ had made several attempts to bring it back to active membership since the 1970s, most recently by inviting the ACJA to attend the Amman Congress, to be met with only polite excuses. Thanks to the special contacts of Vice-President Quang the IOJ now succeeded for the first time in opening real talks with them (Figure 10.2).

Before his death Secretary General Nieva had already entertained an idea that China should be attracted to activate its membership and at the same time to assist in securing the IOJ finances. President Al-Qudah's proposal to hand over the IOJ leadership to the Chinese was a bold step in materializing this idea. However, it met with no serious response from the ACJA. The Chinese obviously saw it as a desperate attempt by a crumbling empire to avoid ultimate disaster.

Figure 10.2 IOJ delegation in Beijing, July 1998. From the left: IOJ President Al-Qudah, ACJA President Zhao Hua Ze, IOJ Vice-President Quang and IOJ Treasurer Angelov. (Photo from Quang's collection)

THE LINGERING END 1999–2016

In April 1999 the European Court of Human Rights gave its verdict concerning the IOJ's complaint on the decision of the Czech Republic's Constitutional Court in 1997. The Court found in favour of the Czech Republic and against the IOJ. The decade-long legal battle about the IOJ's expulsion from the Czech Republic had come to the end.

However, even after this decision Prague continued to be the base of the IOJ in a subtle way. The Ministry of the Interior, which was empowered to decide which NGOs could have a legal seat in the Republic, had annually confirmed that the IOJ was indeed entitled to conduct activities in the country but not to have its seat there. The decision was not signed by the Minister but by a less senior functionary. Since 2000 the permission had not even included any conditions, noting that the seat of the IOJ was in *Londýnská*. A new law in 2014 transferred the power to decide about NGO seats to the City Court of Prague, but the status of the IOJ remained unchanged.

Meanwhile, at the turn of the millennium the IOJ already made it clear that it had no professional activity in the Czech Republic but only limited commercial activity through the Mondiapress and the Technical Service companies, while professional work was under the President in Jordan.

The last major property of the IOJ in Prague was the former School of Solidarity, used at the end of the 1990s as Hotel Mondial. In 2002 it was sold for 41 million Czech crowns or 1.15 Million US dollars (minus 7 percent tax and estate agent's commission). This was used to pay overdue salaries of 10 people of the Secretariat for one year and nearly half of it was held in reserve for the annual expenses of the IOJ and Mondiapress. The rest was transferred to the office of the President in Amman for operative activities.

President Al-Qudah attended meetings of the Arab Federation of Journalists and the IOJ Centre for the Arab world was operational until 2007. The IOJ President issued a statement during the Gaza War in 2008, after which there were no longer serious signs of life from the IOJ. The last meeting between President Al-Qudah, Treasurer Angelov and Mondiapress Director Komárek was in Cairo in 2007; thereafter the IOJ was practically defunct. Only Mondiapress remained in Prague with Komárek and two part-time employees.

Figure 10.3 Nordenstreng discovering the lamentable state of IOJ documents and publications in a warehouse outside Prague in 2011. The storage space in the village of *Dolany* was rented by Gatinot in 1994, when the *Washingtonova* offices were vacated. Nieva was distressed when visiting it in 1995 and at seeing photos damaged by leaking water. It was kept until 2012, when Komárek had it cleared out. (Photos from Nordenstreng's collection)

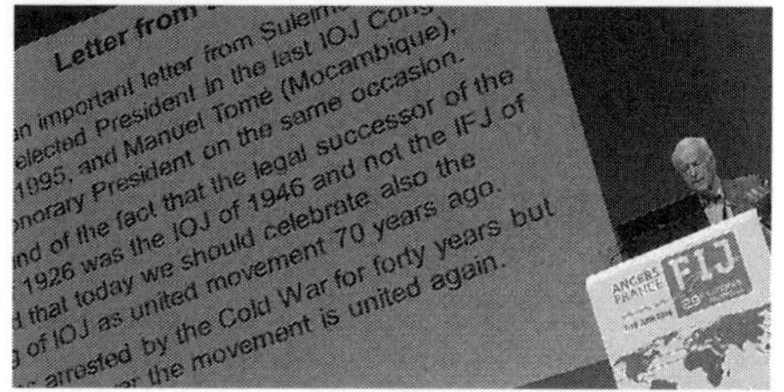

Figure 10.4 IOJ letter to IFJ Congress in Angers presented by Nordenstreng in a history panel on 7 June 2016. Other panelists from the right: V. Bogdanov (Russia), W. Mayer (Germany), A. Bellanger (IFJ General Secretary), J. Boumelha (IFJ President), F. Boissarie and M. Diard (France). (Photos by Juha Rekola)

In the 2010s, when the IOJ was in fact dead but not formally proclaimed so, many people in the profession wondered what had happened to the IOJ. When the present book began to take shape its main author started to promote a joint statement by the IOJ and the IFJ leaders declaring that the historical legacy of the IOJ would be passed on to the present IFJ. The idea of such a "decent burial" of the IOJ was welcomed by the IFJ President Jim Boumelha and also approved by IOJ President Al-Qudah; however, IOJ Treasurer Angelov objected until he passed away in 2014.

The idea finally materialized as a unilateral statement by the last two IOJ Presidents, presented to the IFJ Congress in 2016 – exactly 70 years after the founding of the IOJ. The letter is reproduced in **Appendix 36**.

CHAPTER 11
OVERVIEW 1946-2016

The 70 year-long story of the IOJ is told above in chapters based on different stages in the development of both the organization and the wider world. Figure 11.1 illustrates the history as nine main periods of organizational development with four crucial turning points in world affairs and the 12 IOJ Congresses placed on the timeline.

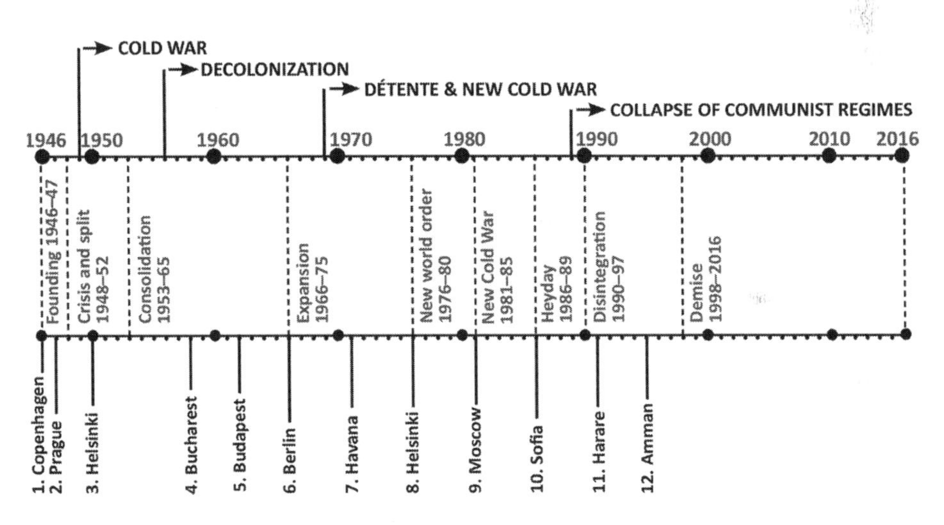

Figure 11.1 Timeline of the IOJ history in nine periods with four turning points of international politics and the twelve IOJ Congresses.

The four turning points in world affairs and the nine periods of the organizational history serve as reminders of the successive stages through which the IOJ developed. In reality the stages are not distinct but overlapping, and the world affairs are cumulative with various elements occurring in parallel.

The following visualization of the history of the IOJ condenses the nine organizational periods into six by merging the five periods between 1953 and 1990 into just two overall eras in those nearly four decades – with two distinct periods both at the beginning and at the end of the timeline.

ienik II. světového sjezdu mezinárodní organisace novinářů

daily of the II. world congress of the international organisation of journalists

journal du II. congrès mondial de l'organisation internationale des journalistes

PRAHA 1947 IOJ

Mezinárodní organisace novinářů
Международная организация журналистов
International Organisation Of Journalists
L'Organisation Internationale Des Journalistes
II. SVĚTOVÝ SJEZD · II. ВСЕМИРНЫЙ КОНГРЕСС
II. WORLD CONGRESS · II. CONGRÈS MONDIAL
PRAHA · ČESKOSLOVENSKO

1 Founding | 1946–47
The founding Congress in Copenhagen (1946) followed by the 2nd Congress in Prague (1947) elected the first IOJ leaders: President from the UK, Vice-Presidents form France, Norway, USA and USSR. The first Secretary-Treasurer was from Australia, the second one elected in Prague to run the headquarters from Czechoslovakia.

There's no place like HOME NOTES

World's Press News

The National Newspaper of the Press, Advertising, Paper and Printing

Offices: 30, Tudor St., E.C.4. Phone: CENtral 4040

LONDON, NOVEMBER 25, 1948

Brian Chapman is New 'Daily Herald' Managing Editor

U.S. Delegate Walks Out

Political Attack on Western Press Splits IOJ Executive

C. J. Bundock Refuses to Take Further Part

2 Crisis and split | 1948–52
Cold War confrontation of 1948 led to a split with western member unions leaving the IOJ. The 3rd Congress in Helsinki (1950) was limited to the Soviet-led eastern camp with unions from China and other developing countries. Two years later the western unions founded the International Federation of Journalists (IFJ) in Brussels.

3 Consolidation and growth | 1953–72
Membership grew in the Third World; their students were sent to schools in Berlin and Budapest. European members enjoyed IOJ hotels on the Black Sea and Lake Balaton. The IOJ Congresses grew in size from Bucharest (1958) to Budapest (1962), Berlin (1966) and Havana (1971). *The Democratic Journalist* became the IOJ flagship.

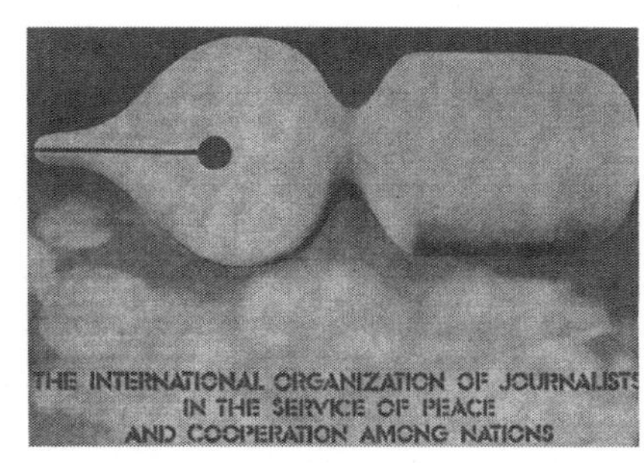

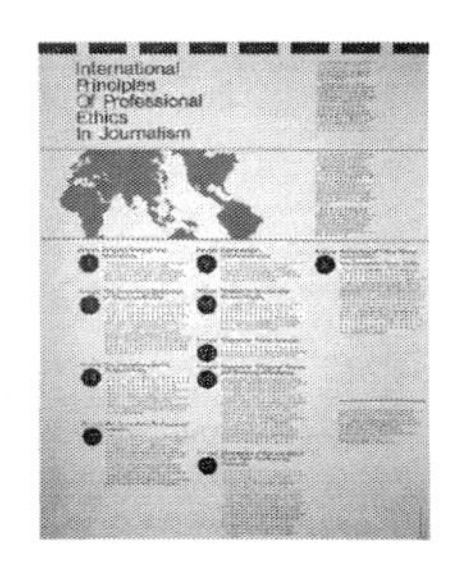

4 Détente and co-operation | 1973–89

Solidarity was manifested with Vietnam, Chile, Palestine and southern Africa. More professional activities were also provided in training, publications, studies and meetings. The 8th Congress in Helsinki (1976) was a breakthrough of détente followed by East-West and North-South co-operation with the IFJ and regional federations, fostered by UNESCO.

5 Disintegration | 1990–97

Collapse of communist regimes in central-eastern Europe in late 1989 shook the foundations of the IOJ. The Czechoslovak member union was abolished in 1990 and the new Syndicate refused to join, leading the Government to expel the IOJ. The Congress in Harare (1991) flagged reforms but the new divided leadership failed to prevent disintegration.

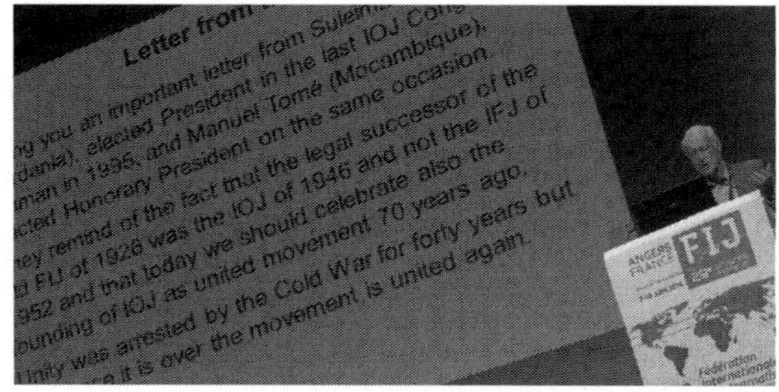

6 Demise | 1998–2016

After the last energetic Secretary General died in 1997, the IOJ had no operational Secretariat and no sustainable financial basis. The leadership offered the ailing IOJ to the Chinese association in 1998, met by silence. The end of the IOJ was a letter by the last two Presidents to the IFJ congress in 2016 – an offshoot of working on this history book.

THE IOJ HISTORY IN BRIEF[1]

The story of the IOJ began in 1946 and ended in 2016; so it reached the age of 70. However, since 1997 it had been virtually dead, and thus its active life lasted for 51 years. Its predecessors had still shorter lives: the IUPA, founded in 1894, was active for only 20 years, and the FIJ, founded in 1926, did not even last for 15 years. The IOJ should indeed be seen in the context of a history of over 120 years.[2]

The IOJ makes a particularly colourful chapter in this history. Its first two congresses in Copenhagen (1946) and Prague (1947), with journalists' associations mainly from the countries on the victorious side in World War II, took place in a post-war atmosphere of joy and optimism. However, only two years later, in 1948, the Cold War began and a wave of changes in political systems in central and eastern Europe led to the division of Europe into East and West, separated by the "iron curtain". The IOJ was part of this battleground, becoming embroiled in Cold War politics. It lost its West European and North American members, except for left-leaning sympathizers there. The western unions established a new International Federation of Journalists (IFJ) in Brussels in 1952 – as part of the "free West" countering the "communist East".

Meanwhile, the IOJ gained new members in Africa, Asia and Latin America. In 1966 its membership amounted to 130,000 journalists in 108 countries, while the IFJ had 55,000 journalists in 31 countries. The heyday of the IOJ was in the late 1980s, when its membership had grown close to 300,000 and its operations included journalism schools and publishing houses in central-eastern Europe and regional centres in the developing world. They and numerous international meetings were financially supported by a unique system of commercial enterprises in Czechoslovakia and Hungary – a veritable island of capitalism in a sea of socialism. Counted by its membership reach and activities in Prague, Budapest, Berlin and several regional centres, it was the biggest non-governmental organization in the media field overall.

Then suddenly the fall of the Berlin Wall and the Velvet Revolution in Czechoslovakia in late 1989, followed by the collapse of communist regimes in central and eastern Europe, transformed global geopolitics. The IOJ was

---

1 The preceding visualization and the following passage are based on a paper presented at the European Communication Conference of ECREA in Prague in 2016 (http://www.uta.fi/cmt/en/contact/staff/kaarlenordenstreng/publications/ECREA_paper_2016.pdf). For a short version of the IOJ history, see also Ševčíková & Nordenstreng (2017).

2 See Nordenstreng (2014) and *A History of the International Movement of Journalists* (Nordenstreng & al., 2016).

immediately shaken: its headquarters and operations, seen by the new forces in Czechoslovakia as a minion of the old repressive regime, came under sharp attack and its local member union – the legal base of its seat in Prague – was closed down and replaced by a new Syndicate of Czech and Moravian Journalists, which did not want to affiliate with the IOJ but leaned towards the IFJ. Several negotiations were held by the IOJ leadership with the Syndicate and the Czechoslovak Government in 1990, but the leadership was divided about how far it should go and the IOJ decision-making bodies gave mixed signals especially by electing the new Secretary General. The concessions from the IOJ side were always seen to be "too little, too late".

Nevertheless, in early 1991 at its 11th Congress in Harare, the IOJ was still the world's largest INGO in the media field. However, the pressures for change from central and eastern Europe, particularly Czechoslovakia, were overwhelming, and the situation was exacerbated by discord within the new leadership. Financial resources were dwindling and activities in training, publishing, etc. were gradually discontinued. Member unions one after another decided to join the IFJ, while most of them also remained members of the IOJ. By the end of the 1990s the IOJ had in fact disappeared from the scene.

In short, the IOJ was founded as a united platform for professional journalists but it lost this role during the Cold War, becoming a partisan representative of journalists from the socialist and developing countries, while at the same time supporting efforts to reunify the movement. When the Cold War ended, the IOJ not only failed to regain the united platform lost 40 years earlier but also disintegrated to the point of extinction. Its once mighty institutions had disappeared, while its western counterpart in the Cold War, the IFJ, had emerged as the new universal platform, which counted among its membership a considerable part of IOJ members. As seen in Appendix 11, most European unions had also become IFJ members by 1997, while the double members from other regions were relatively few.

At the legal level, the post-communist government of Czechoslovakia ordered the headquarters to be expelled from the country in 1991. The expulsion was processed by the courts for eight years, while the country was divided into Czech and Slovak Republics. In 1997 the IOJ appeals to the Constitutional Court finally came to the end of the legal road but, as a last resort, the IOJ still submitted a complaint to the European Court of Human Rights, which, however, in 1999 ruled against the IOJ.

Meanwhile there was a natural end to the IOJ in the Czech Republic after 1997 since by that time its financial base had practically collapsed and the once flourishing activities throughout the world faded away. The commercial enterprises, which had earned money to pay for the professional activities, were brought to an end and no savings were left to maintain even a minimal secretariat. The last statutory meeting was the Executive Committee in Hanoi in 1996. No Congress was convened since 1995 – even to dissolve the IOJ. The sudden death of the last Secretary General in 1997 sealed its fate.

The expulsion consequently became a non-issue, and the IOJ was after all allowed to retain in Prague a small legal entity – the Mondiapress company owned by the IOJ – which was not to be involved in any professional or political activity. Such activities, if any, were outsourced to a pro forma office of the last President in Amman (Jordan).

With this arrangement the IOJ was from the late 1990s on *de facto* dead, but *de jure* still alive. As the years passed by, the member unions did not take any serious initiatives to revitalize the IOJ. They seem to have taken it for granted that history had passed it by and several of them joined the only remaining worldwide organization, the IFJ. The fate of the IOJ was sealed by a letter from the last two IOJ Presidents, addressed to the 29th IFJ Congress in Angers (France) in June 2016 (Appendix 36).

RECOUNTING KEY ASPECTS

COLD WAR DIVISION AND ATTEMPTS AT UNITY

Looking at the big picture, the IOJ was indeed embroiled in Cold War politics. Founded in post-World War II conditions on a relatively neutral and pluralistic ground, it was rapidly taken over by the eastern side of the Cold War big politics. This left the field open for a corresponding western organization, leading to the founding of the IFJ.

The two adversaries continued to consolidate their respective membership spheres and increasingly to search for new members in the developing countries. Until the early 1990s the IOJ was more successful in this, but it never really surpassed its rival. The IFJ managed to retain its dominance in the western countries in Europe, North America and Australasia, and to gain a foothold in several western-oriented countries in the global South. This perpetuated the division of the movement – with the IOJ as the eastern pillar.

Accordingly, the IOJ was widely stigmatized as a “communist” or “Soviet” organization[3] – no matter how much it supported détente and

3 See Muzavazi’s recollections in Part Two. Nordenstreng met similar prejudices in the late 1980s at the UN and his Finnish background did not help to neutralize the

universal principles. In reality the IOJ had been strategically behind the attempt at a reunification of the movement ever since the World Meeting of Journalists back in 1956. However, because the IFJ and the western powers preferred to retain the division and thus to isolate the IOJ, the World Meeting cannot now be seen as such "a great and shining event" as it was foreseen to appear "when the history of world journalism comes to be written".[4]

A second attempt to reunite the movement of journalists was made in the 1980s through the UNESCO-initiated consultative meetings of international and regional organizations of journalists.[5] They developed into a unique platform for co-operation not only between the two internationals but also the regional federations in Africa, the Arab world, Asia and Latin America.[6]

The proposal for a World Council of Journalists in 1986 was an ambitious plan to achieve worldwide unity on a federative basis.[7] It was thwarted by the IFJ but the idea was kept alive by the Consultative Club until 1990. However, after that it was the IOJ that was instrumental to burying it: after being the leading partner, it completely ignored the Club, obviously due to internal turmoil and confusion. The IOJ merely reiterated its readiness for unity – with stronger and stronger statements – while the IFJ was the less interested in real unity the more the IOJ was seen to be in decline.

The Cold War mindset did not fall with the Berlin Wall and the Soviet Union; it persisted as an ideological filter into the new millennium. This legacy was a decisive factor throughout the 1990s in both the internationals with IFJ elements still suspicious of the sincerity of the IOJ and the IOJ with an influential old guard and a Third World lobby equally distrustful of the opposite side. As shown by the IOJ debates in 1990, the watershed came with the developments in central and eastern Europe: those from Europe mostly realized that at issue was a far-reaching dynamic – changing the course of history – whereas those from outside Europe mostly understood that it was rather an accidental change with no fundamental bearing on the future of the international system.

---

anti-IOJ attitude of the pro-western director of UNESCO's communication sector in the early 1990s. Likewise Al-Qudah still in the mid-1990s heard comments from the Jordanian government about the IOJ as part of the communist front.

4 See Chapter 4.

5 See Chapter 6.

6 See Chapter 7.

7 See Chapter 8.

CZECHOSLOVAKIA – FOR GOOD AND ILL

Czechoslovakia occupied a central place in the big picture because the IOJ headquarters had been in Prague since 1947. And it was not just a formal seat but an exceptionally strong base for co-ordination and support of activities. Czechoslovakia also meant that the IOJ became in 1948 an integral part of the socialist system in central-eastern Europe, led by the Soviet Union and the respective communist parties. This system had profound repercussions in journalism in Czechoslovakia both when the system was introduced in 1948 and when it was abolished after the Velvet Revolution in 1989.[8] Moreover, the Prague Spring in 1968 and its aftermath with about 1,500 journalists forced out of the profession was a time bomb which 21 years could not defuse.

Accordingly, the IOJ entered the post-socialist era in 1990 with a heavy burden of the past – both political and moral. In addition, as pointed out in Appendix 25, most of the material resources since the 1970s were generated through commercial companies established under the privileged umbrella of the Communist Party and Government of Czechoslovakia. Thus the licence to make money brought the IOJ into a symbiotic relationship with the former regime. The financial fortune became inseparable from the burden of the past and the IOJ became a virtual hostage of the communist system.

In this context, the virulence of the attack of Czech journalists against the IOJ in 1990 appears understandable but still extraordinary. Other socialist countries in central-eastern Europe experienced the same system change but in none of them except Czechoslovakia did the journalist union with a new post-socialist orientation immediately desert the IOJ and rush to the IFJ. Czechoslovakia was unique and there the conflict was undoubtedly fuelled by the reputation of the IOJ Secretariat and its commercial enterprises as a privileged empire. Meanwhile, the newborn Syndicate of Journalists did not lay much blame on the old Union of Journalists, which was a fellow traveller with the IOJ under the former communist regime. One may indeed ask whether the IOJ was made into a scapegoat: denouncing it as a totally discredited organization served to collectively exonerate the majority of journalists from wider political blame.

In hindsight, the IOJ failed in 1990 to draw clear and rapid conclusions on the drastic changes in the world. Instead, it observed only slowly and reluctantly what was happening. It was indeed appropriate to begin Chapter 9 on disintegration right after the Velvet Revolution in 1990.

8 See Chapter 3 and Ševčíková & Nordenstreng (2017).

ACTIVITIES AND FINANCES

As shown by Figure 11.1, the IOJ's active life continued for 50 years, whereas in the last 20 years it was practically dead – contrary to the hopeful poster of the 50th anniversary. Appendix 5 provides concrete evidence of the intensity and extent of the activities until 1990. From 1967 to 1977 the number of activities per year was under 20 (less than half a page in the list). From 1978 to 1982 the number was annually 30–50; after 1983 it was over 50; in 1988 and in 1989 it exceeded 90 per year.

The growth followed the increase in financial revenue, which by the end of the 1980s came mostly from the commercial enterprises owned and operated by the IOJ. The membership fees accounted for only a few per cent of the Organization's total income, while the Solidarity Lottery, which brought in substantial income in the 1970s, was no longer lucrative. The Treasurer's report for the Harare Congress disclosed that in 1989 the enterprises accounted for about 90 per cent of the IOJ's income, which was altogether about three million US dollars (including the Czechoslovak crowns converted into US$).

Roughly half of the financial resources went on the Secretariat and its extensions: Publishing House, School of Solidarity, International Journalism Institute and various services of translation, information technology, etc. In 1990 they employed some 600 persons, with a further 600 working in the other commercial enterprises. The core staff of the Secretariat numbered 20–25, including the Secretaries, whose travel costs were considerable. Since 1991 the annual expenses of the President and his assistant, including travel, amounted to some 200,000 US$ and the expenses of the Secretary General and his Deputy were of the same order.

The personnel figures turned sharply downwards after 1991: in 1993 the IOJ had a mere 50 persons on its payroll, in 1997 about 20, in 2002 ten and in 2012 only three (in Mondiapress).

The other half of the finances was used for various activities and for the statutory meetings. For example, in 1991 the Congress in Harare cost close to one million US dollars, the Council in Sana'a half a million and the Executive Committee in Rio nearly 200,000 US$.

The Auditing Commission elected in Harare wrote in September 1991 in its report to the Council in Sana'a that "we found the entire financial position of the IOJ in chaos". The situation did not essentially improve until after the Congress in Amman, when the new Secretary General managed in one year to get the situation under control despite an ailing economy.[9]

9 Secretary General Nieva submitted to the Executive Committee in Hanoi in July 1996 an 8-page assessment of the situation of the remaining 10 companies, their performance and prospects for generating revenue ("The Enterprises: making them leaner,

MEMBERSHIP

The IOJ was founded in 1946 by national unions from 21 countries with the number of journalists associated through them reaching 80,000. In 1966 the membership coverage had risen to 130,000 journalists in nearly 50 collective unions or groups plus individuals from altogether 108 countries (see Appendix 4). In 1988 the number of journalists covered had doubled: 250,000 journalists in 120 countries, of which 90 had collective members (Appendix 11).

A closer look at the 1988 figures shows that the number of member unions was divided between different regions as follows:

Europe and North America	17 of which 7 in socialist countries
Africa including Maghreb	31 of which 4 in socialist countries
Asia and Oceania	23 of which 6 in socialist countries
Latin America and the Caribbean	26 of which 1 in a socialist country
Total	97 of which 19 in socialist countries

Accordingly, no more than 20 per cent of the member unions were in socialist countries. However, counting the number of journalists represented by each union, those from the socialist countries clearly outnumbered the journalists from the non-socialist countries in the West and the global South: two thirds from the socialist countries and one third from the capitalist West and non-socialist South. In this respect the IOJ did indeed lean towards the socialist East, but it was by no means a bloc organization – unlike its western counterpart the IFJ, which only had members in non-socialist countries.

In 1991 the IOJ membership already exceeded 300,000 journalists and 100 unions (Appendix 12). Despite the problems since 1990, several new members joined until 1996 and most of the old members were still included in the last membership list in 1997; only a handful had dropped out by then, while over twenty had also joined the IFJ.

Consequently, the IOJ enjoyed a record membership while it was already disintegrating; its reputation and legacy were strong enough to sustain confidence in an organization that was failing fast. Several new members came from countries born after the USSR (Ukraine, Moldavia) and reoriented after an authoritarian rule (Ethiopia, Libya). On the other hand, vital old members from Finland and Hungary had left the IOJ in the early 1990s.

---

more efficient"). A more extensive briefing on the enterprises and their personnel problems was Nieva's confidential document of 15 pages addressed to President Al-Qudah and Treasurer Angelov on 15 January 1996. Both documents are available in the IOJ collection at the National Archives of the Czech Republic.

Of all the IOJ members, the most significant historical role was played by the Soviet and Polish unions in eastern Europe, the Finnish and French unions in western Europe and the Cuban union in Latin America. However, most decisive overall was the Czechoslovak union, which ensured the operative apparatus of the IOJ in Prague.

EPILOGUE

The preceding chapters provide an account of the rise of the IOJ from the mid-1940s to the end of the 1980s and its rapid fall after the Velvet Revolution in the 1990s. In parts the presentation may appear heavy going, but this is an inevitable consequence of remaining true to the facts and endeavouring to remain objective. On the other hand, the chronicle is by no means exhaustive; it cannot cover all details of a broad international landscape and its actors. However, all essential aspects are at least touched upon – if not in the text, at least in the appendix documentation.

The result, with the anthology of personal recollections in Part Two, is less than coherent and rather a panoply of the evidence extant on this organization. My ambition was not to construct a simple story but to provide a set of materials which will hopefully inspire further research.

And yet, three overall questions remain.

SO WHAT? WHAT IF? WHAT NEXT?

SO WHAT – DOES THIS BOOK TEACH ANY LESSONS?

Although the book delivers no sensational revelations, it contributes discoveries which enhance our knowledge of the IOJ – once the world's largest international non-governmental organization in the media field. While it does not challenge the earlier view of the IOJ, it offers new insights and details helping us to better understand journalists and their international networking. In any case the book project makes a contribution to this page of history by compiling whatever documentation has survived on the IOJ and by preserving it in the National Archives of the Czech Republic.

The lessons of this exercise are manifold. The overall lesson is the same as concluded in the byproduct of this book project – the first all-round history of the international movement of journalists:

> ...international journalist organizations are always constrained by the political environment. It is naïve and self-deceptive to believe that international journalists

and their associations could ever be completely apolitical. However, the movement is not deterministically driven by politics; it is also driven by professional interests with greater or lesser autonomy...[1]

The history of the IOJ with all its turns lends convincing support to this overall conclusion, but it also provides several specific lessons:

- While overall political structures determine the main course of history, considerable leeway remains for *subjective factors and pure chance* to influence the course of events and developments. Good examples of the subjective factors are provided by the IOJ Secretary Generals, particularly Jiří Kubka (1966–88) and Antonio Nieva (1995–97) as positive cases and Gérard Gatinot (1990–95) as a negative case. And telling examples of the role of pure chance in history are the close-run vote on Gatinot as acting Secretary General in the Balaton Presidium of May 1990 and the death of Nieva in October 1997.
- The socialist countries in central and eastern Europe constituted a political environment typically called totalitarian, but in fact this left considerable *room for manoeuvring* in maintaining international contacts, arranging events and issuing publications. An impressive example of pragmatic activities is the commercial enterprise system of the IOJ. The IOJ is also a shining example of the grey area within the "Communist bloc behind the Iron Curtain", which was more complex by far than the Cold War stereotypes.
- *Tactical attempts to influence political trends* were unsuccessful in Czechoslovakia after the Velvet Revolution. The most obvious case of this was Gérard Gatinot's attempt to win the confidence of the new Government by virtue of his defence of the repressed dissidents including Václav Havel in 1979: Gatinot simply could not persuade the new forces to change their image of him as a Stalinist. Also, new IOJ President Armando Rollemberg's offer to the Czech Syndicate to resume the IOJ Secretary General's position failed to convince the Syndicate.
- As is well known in the business world, *discord among leaders creates confusion and loss of direction* throughout any organization. A striking example of this is the conflict between President Rollemberg and Secretary General Gatinot with his Deputy in 1991–93. This conflict was preceded by a rift developing in 1990 between the radical reformers led by President Nordenstreng with the Soviets and other east Europeans on the one side, and those adhering to the *status quo* led by Secretary General Gatinot with the Arabs and Latin Americans on the other. Such internal divisions have a pernicious effect on an organization.

---

1 Nordenstreng & al. (2016, 180).

- Much value in leading international organizations is lost by *neglecting the institutional memory* while leaders are typically immersed in their present interests and not concerned with the historical legacy. Even if the IOJ did retain its original post-war peace mission constantly on the agenda, its leaders typically paid only lip service to the events and struggles of the past and did not draw serious lessons from what was discovered in the book *Useful Recollections*. In my own case, I concede negligence in not meeting and interviewing former secretaries Hronek, Klánský and Meisner during their lifetimes.

WHAT IF – COULD THE IOJ HAVE HAD A DIFFERENT FATE?

Given the role of subjective factors and pure chance in making history, there is indeed merit in the wisdom of hindsight and in posing the question "what if?". This is not mere speculation for its own sake but a serious research stream known as *counterfactual history*[2]. In some cases history could really have taken a different turn with different people at the helm and different roads taken.

For example, if, instead of Gérard Gatinot, Bernd Rayer had been elected acting Secretary General in Balaton (May 1990), the election in Harare (January 1991) could very well have resulted in the election of Christopher Muzavazi or someone else more acceptable to the Czechoslovak Syndicate and Government. Also, if Antonio Nieva had not passed away in October 1997, he might have been able to avoid the final demise and reach an agreement with the IFJ about a merger with face saved on both sides.

Apart from the election of individuals, different strategic choices could have changed history. A crucial case was the Consultative Club, which since 1990 was smothered in the demise despite its potential both to save the IOJ and to achieve unity of the movement. Another missed opportunity was the IAMCR's proposal to re-establish the IJI as a joint venture with the Czech Syndicate – a last-ditch attempt to achieve reconciliation with the Czechs. The demise was not inevitable.

WHAT NEXT – IDEAS FOR FURTHER STUDY

Not only alternative histories but also many other aspects of the IOJ are open to further study, making full use of the archive materials which have

---

2 See, for example, Cowley (1999).

been preserved, although many of these were irresponsibly lost in the 1990s. While this book is a comprehensive first history of the IOJ, it is far from being definitive. It invites closer examination of specific aspects such as these:

- The *sharp denunciation of the IOJ* in post-socialist Czechoslovakia opens an intriguing perspective to analyse the political and cultural dynamic in societies under transition. In principle the IUS and the WFTU were in the same situation, yet the IOJ suffered exceptionally harsh treatment. Was the IOJ indeed a scapegoat?
- The *information and communication technology* – computers and programming – employed by the IOJ since the mid-1980s was a resource which was advancing by leaps and bounds in 1990, while the whole Secretariat and enterprise system ran into trouble. Was the IOJ a unique enclave of new technology in Czechoslovakia at the time or was it a manifestation of a broader national trend?
- The whole *commercial enterprise system* of the IOJ awaits scholarly investigation. How did it develop and exactly what did it include? Of particular interest are its hundreds of employees, who, after 1989, became actively involved in the post-socialist business community. To what extent did the IOJ serve to prepare the ground for capitalism in the new Czechoslovakia?[3]
- The role of *intelligence agencies* in and around the IOJ remains uncharted territory which also warrants attention. No doubt the Secretariat staff in Prague included some agents working under cover; a few of them were even named in the anti-IOJ coverage by the local press in 1990. However, this was never a dominant feature of the IOJ, contrary to insinuations by western agencies.[4]
- Finally, the story of the IOJ merits comparison with what happened to the other INGOs founded after World War II, and which, during the Cold War, adopted the same pro-Soviet stance as the IOJ. The IOJ was the only one of these to go under, while the others continue in new circumstances and at new locations, although with lower profiles.

There is indeed both an intellectual challenge and a practical opportunity to continue examining the IOJ story.

---

3 This topic was proposed in Ševčíková (2015).

4 The CIA reports on the IOJ, disclosed through the U.S. Freedom of Information Act, include practically nothing beyond conventional demonizing of the INGOs with a pro-Soviet line. Similar was *Counterpoint*, "A monthly report on Soviet Active Measures" (published by Walter Spiegel in Canterbury, UK), which had in its March 1988 issue (Vol. 3, No. 10) an article on the IOJ "Leading the Soviet Attack on the Freedom of the Press".

PERSONAL REFLECTIONS

It is obvious from the preceding chapters and especially from my testimony in Part Two below that I have mixed feelings about serving as the IOJ President. Maybe I was a "useful idiot" – the phrase which Lenin was said to have used in referring to the progressive western friends of the new communist state – but I do not fundamentally regret the decision to accept the nomination. It has been an exciting journey for me, giving a lot of experience and insight into international affairs – through talks with a dozen heads of state and the UN Secretary General and observation of the dynamics behind international organizations, non-governmental as well as intergovernmental. It also gave me vital new perspectives as a scholar for the study of global communication and the role of media in society.[5]

However, all this was at a high cost of time and energy taken out of my academic and family life. After all, the IOJ Presidency was my second job next to a full-time professorship in Finland, except for a few months on leave in 1978, 1987 and in 1990. I also suffered from political stigma as a fellow traveller of the Soviets in my Finnish environment. On the other hand, I incurred no financial costs as the IOJ Secretariat provided me with all the travel expenses and a small local budget for hosting regular meetings with the Finnish IOJ members.

My overall motivation for this voluntary work was an idealistic desire to change the world for the better by influencing developments in journalism – in part the same dedication that sustained me as an academic educator and researcher. It is fair to ask to what extent I succeeded and whether it was worth all the effort. The demise of the IOJ belongs to the history after my time, but even in the heyday of the late 1980s, during my presidency, it was more the political and economic circumstances than the personal role of the leaders that determined the success. Still, some role is left for individuals in the course of history, and in this respect I do venture to claim some credit.

Nevertheless, I cannot help looking back critically at how I as the IOJ President operated throughout 1990 in the middle of the drastic political change in Czechoslovakia and rest of the world. I failed to ensure that "my side" maintained leadership of the main course of developments in the Organization and I permitted the "opposing side" to distract and gradually gain control of the machinery. A turning point was the vote on acting Secretary General in the Balatonfüred Presidium in May (see Chapter 9 and Muzavazi's recollections in Part Two). In hindsight, I regret not having prevented

5 See the conclusions and discussion in my presentation at the University of Helsinki https://sites.tuni.fi/uploads/2020/03/d020f118-ioj-history.pdf.

the vote in the absence of two important Presidium members (from Zimbabwe and USA) and not making it clear to hesitant members what really was at issue. I was naïve in allowing opponents to take advantage of formal democratic procedures and in not using my presidential powers to ensure a majority for my side.

My self-criticism about events in 1990 also extends to the strategic line I pursued on the situation of the IOJ and its political environment. My intuition in advocating a rapid change was obviously correct, but I was not forceful enough in pursuing it against the distractions coming from inside and outside the Organization. I failed to provide sufficiently decisive leadership with a clearly articulated strategy which would have persuaded those who were vacillating. I was too conciliatory, letting various interests democratically battle things out and not trying to sway opinions – contrary to what Manuel Tomé thought according to Muzavazi's recollections. Paradoxically, as a communication scholar I failed to communicate to the Presidium and Executive Committee members the alarming points of the crisis, especially the vital role of the enterprises. Moreover, as a graduate in psychology I failed to maintain trust in relations with strategic colleagues in the Secretariat and the leadership.

Of course, it is easy to be wise after the event. Moreover, given the prevailing conditions, the big picture would hardly have been fundamentally changed even by a more forceful leadership. Even if the perspectives of counterfactual history merit serious consideration, it is obvious that the IOJ and the rest of us were mere background figures in a historical drama written by the geopolitical forces ultimately driving societies and the global order.

Those forces were quite favourable towards the geopolitical constellation of the IOJ in 1976, when I started my presidency and declared: "Historical tendencies are on our side". At that time I enjoyed being an instrument of progressive development, with highlights such as the Mass Media Declaration of UNESCO (1978). A decade later, while the IOJ was still in full flower, the new Cold War manifested in such setbacks as the cancelling of the symposium on the 10th anniversary of the Mass Media Declaration (1988). I was commissioned by UNESCO to prepare it, on behalf of the IOJ and other international and regional organizations of journalists, but the project no longer enjoyed overwhelming geopolitical support; the relations of global power were changing with the relative weakening of the socialist East and the developing South.

With experiences like these I can testify that the IOJ was an object rather than a subject of history.

PART TWO
RECOLLECTIONS OF THE IOJ

From inside the IOJ

Josef Klánský: A young man in a young organization (1947–50)
Jiří Meisner: Managing the IOJ to adulthood (1958–66)
Václav Slavík: The age of achievement with Jiří Kubka (1966–92)
Ferdinando Zidar: The story of my expulsion (1972)
Pál Tamás: The IOJ empire in Kadarist Hungary (1972–74)
Alice Palmer: The IOJ and the American black press (1983–91)
Christopher Muzavazi: From heyday to chaos (1988–92)
Michel Diard: The French factor (1946–98)
Rüdiger Claus: A journalist trainer's perspective (1984–98)
Phan Quang: Mission accomplished, heritage lives on (1974–98)

Testimony of the last four IOJ Presidents

Kaarle Nordenstreng: Bridgebuilding in a volatile world (1976–90)
Armando Rollemberg: From dream to disappointment (1991–93)
Manuel Tomé: Acting in crisis (1994)
Suleiman Al-Qudah: Towards the end (1995–2016)

From outside the IOJ

Théo Bogaerts: Three decades in the IFJ (1952–85)
Hifzi Topus: A quarter of a century at UNESCO (1959–83)
Paulo Murialdi: Bringing the IOJ and the IFJ together (1974–84)
Wolfgang Mayer: Trying to overcome rivalry (1986–2000)

FROM INSIDE THE IOJ

JOSEF KLÁNSKÝ: A YOUNG MAN IN A YOUNG ORGANIZATION*

"I have a four days' job for you", a friend told me in the early summer of 1947. "Journalists from all over the world will have a congress in Prague and their host, the Union of Czechoslovak Journalists, is looking for somebody who can translate English and Russian."

I was then a young man of 26, one of the few survivors of the Holocaust, who was just completing his studies interrupted by the Nazi occupation and the war and preparing for his final exams at the Faculty of Law at Charles University in Prague. My job as a Czech-Russian-English translator with UNRRA had just reached its end, because this post-war relief and rehabilitation organization, having fulfilled its humanitarian mission, was closing down its activities. I was short of money and accepted my friend's offer.

So it happened that one day I entered a hall full of chatting people, with a banner over the still empty platform conveying that I was at the 2nd Congress of the International Organization of Journalists.

"I am not sure whether we shall need your services at all", one of the Czech organizers told me. "They did not arrive!"

"Who did not arrive?" I asked with apprehension.

"The Russians. They promised to attend, but for quite a long time we did not hear from them. Never mind. Take a seat and listen. At least you will get some idea of what we are talking about. And for today you will be paid anyway."

After the obligatory opening speeches, mutual welcoming and thanks, I learned from the reports that during World War II journalists from the Allied countries together with journalists from Nazi-occupied European countries established in London an association of free journalists and that after the war, in 1946 in Copenhagen, this war-time initiative had led to the formation of the IOJ – an umbrella organization of journalists' national trade unions. Although the Soviet Union did not have any specific journalists' union at that time (journalists instead belonged to the trade union of workers of the polygraphic industry), it joined the IOJ.

---

* The author was IOJ Executive Secretary 1947–50. Written in February 1995.

At last their delegation arrived, and the proceedings of the Congress were interrupted to welcome them. The names of the delegates from Moscow were unknown to me, but it was stressed that it was a high-ranking delegation. But why on earth didn't they arrive in time or at least inform the organizers about their delay? It was then a puzzle, but later, during the 40 years under communism, we learned to understand such phenomena: travelling abroad, contacts with foreigners, participation in events together with people from the West, were gaps in the Iron Curtain, strictly supervised by the regime. Any decision on who should be permitted to cross the borders had to be approved by the respective authorities, the lower ranks transferring decision-making, if possible, to their superiors. Anyway, this delegation had finally received its exit visa approval and I could start interpreting.

Only one item on the agenda led to discussions stormy enough to remain fixed in my memory: The controversy about the seat of the IOJ; whether its headquarters should remain in London or be transferred to Prague. And whether the post of Secretary General should remain in the hands of the incumbent holder, a London-based Australian, or taken over by the Czech candidate. The vote was in favour of Prague and Jiří Hronek, the Scandinavians and other delegations from Western Europe having supported the Easterners' choice. The capital of then still pluralistic Czechoslovakia apparently seemed to them a better place for the IOJ than the capital of a major power, still the metropolis of a colonial empire. The Czech post-war press, owned exclusively by political parties, trade unions and other "people's organizations" was considered by many a worthy experiment, granting more freedom to the press than did the Rothermeres, Beaverbrooks and other press barons of Fleet Street in London.

When the Congress came to an end, the new Secretary General Hronek made me an offer to become Executive Secretary at the IOJ's new headquarters in Prague. As my contract with UNRRA was just expiring I was free to say yes. My four days' job at the Congress grew into a long-term employment. Having a regular income, I could marry my girlfriend: the IOJ Secretary General accepted my invitation to be a witness at my wedding in October 1947. After 48 years, this marriage still lasts.

The IOJ Prague office began its activities in summer 1947 in the House of the Czechoslovak Union of Journalists near the upper end of Wenceslas Square. This house was later torn down to make room for the building of the former Federal Parliament, which today houses Radio Free Europe.

For one and a half years I was the only employee of the IOJ, compared with nearly 1,600 people working for it and its various activities four decades later, when the IOJ Secretariat General was expelled from Prague by the post-Communist regime in the early 1990s. An example of the validity of Parkinson's Law or a specific case of permanently sustainable development?

Alone in the office I had to fulfil the duties of Executive Secretary, bulletin editor, press-cards distributor, accountant, translator, typist, etc. Once or twice a week I went to see the Secretary General – at that time an unpaid honorary post – whose main work was that of editor-in-chief of Radio Prague Newscast. I brought with me the incoming mail and IOJ letters for his signature, and we discussed the tasks to be done.

Being located in the same building as the Czech journalists' union and their club, I got acquainted with many of them and started to write stories for their papers. I became a journalist *en passant*, simultaneously passing my exams to become a Doctor of Laws. I also took part in an essay contest of the United Nations, on the "Role of the Individual in the United Nations" and my essay was among the ten prize-winning entries in this worldwide contest. The award was a one-month study scholarship at the UN headquarters.

In February 1948 I took part in an IOJ leadership meeting in Brussels. I do not remember at all what we discussed there, because the Czechoslovak participants of this meeting were fully preoccupied with events at home. When our plane left Prague, our country was still a pluralistic multiparty democracy with a strong Communist party having the largest representation in parliament and government. When we returned home after the Communist take-over of 25 February 1948, Czechoslovakia was practically a one-party dictatorship on its way to becoming a Soviet satellite.

Having completed preparations and sent out invitations for the next IOJ Executive Committee meeting due to be held in Luxembourg, my request for a month's leave to visit the UN as one of its essay-contest winners was approved by Hronek. I interrupted my journey in Paris where the UN General Assembly held its 1948 session at the Palais de Chaillot. Soon after arriving there I received an urgent telegram message from Hronek to return to Prague immediately. I had to cancel my flight to New York, apologize to the UN Department of Public Information for suddenly changing the timetable of my visit, ask for an adjournment and do a lot of other inconvenient things, connected with such an unexpected change. What on earth was happening?

Back in Prague, I was told by Hronek that the Soviet Trade Union of Polygraphic Workers categorically refused to participate in the Executive meeting in Luxemburg and insisted that it be held in Budapest instead. Why did Secretary General Hronek not send them to hell? First, they were the largest member organization of the IOJ. Second, Hronek knew that we were now living in the Soviet orbit: the decision not to go to Luxembourg was not taken by polygraphic workers, but by some high authority in the background; to say "no" to Soviet orders endangered not only one's position, but was a threat to his freedom and life as well.

I had to cancel my trip to the UN in order to write to the IOJ Executive members about the change of the scene of the next Executive meeting, without any acceptable explanation why Luxembourg had to be replaced by Budapest. An awkward exchange of letters followed, illustrating the fact that the Cold War had hit the IOJ. Most invited Executive members, including British IOJ President Archibald Kenyon, nevertheless turned up in Budapest in November 1948.

A sort of secret Party caucus was called the night before the opening of the meeting by the Head of the Soviet delegation Pavel Yudin, member of the Central Committee of the Soviet Communist Party (who later served as Soviet Ambassador to China). I myself was not invited to the event but Hronek told me what instructions the delegates from the "people's democracies" were given. He seemed to be quite upset, since he was aware of the fact that these instructions meant a split in the IOJ. The Soviets wanted nothing less than a resolution condemning a number of top American journalists (e.g. the Alsop brothers) as warmongers and the expulsion of the Union of Yugoslav Journalists from the IOJ for being "Titoist renegades and agents of Anglo-American imperialism". It was quite evident that neither President Kenyon nor the delegates of the American Newspaper Guild or the British Union of Journalists would vote for such resolutions. Some delegates from Eastern European countries and, as far as I know, Hronek himself tried to convince the Soviet delegates that a more moderate and balanced wording could perhaps lead to some form of compromise. But Yudin remained stiff-necked and steadfastly insisted that their resolutions must be passed. They apparently had their orders from Moscow – who knows, maybe from Stalin himself, and back at home not fulfilling them might have been considered to be their failure, a lost battle in the raging Cold War.

The Soviet-sponsored resolutions were passed, and the majority of Western delegates left Budapest, making no secret of their intentions to quit the IOJ. Thus the IOJ became for the next four decades a Soviet-dominated front organization.

For me personally, the Budapest meeting brought about some other troubles as well. At a dinner-party the Hungarian organizer seated my wife, who accompanied me to Budapest, nearer to the President than a female editor-in-chief, who was an official member of the Czechoslovak delegation, and this *faux pas* in the protocol caused some annoyance. But still worse, somebody in the Soviet delegation, introduced as a representative of the youth press, but more probably a secret service bodyguard of Yudin, told me that his chief wanted to talk to me. I went to Yudin's room. He asked me on whose direction had I taken part in the UN essay contest, what its topic was and how it was that I alone was the winner and rewarded with a trip to the USA. I explained that I participated in the contest of my own free will, that there were ten prize-winning essays from different countries of the world and that I was not invited by the Americans but by the United Nations, of which Czechoslovakia was a member. I pointed out that on the contrary I had difficulties to get a US visa and that UN Secretary General Trygve Lie had to intervene on my behalf with the US immigration authorities. However, everything I told him was apparently not convincing enough. He warned me of the dangers facing me in imperialist America and asked about the attitude of the Czechoslovak Communist Party on this matter. I had to admit that it did not occur to me that my participation in the UN essay contest had to be considered on a political level. "Without approval by the Czechoslovak Party you cannot go to America. Ask Comrade Geminder in Prague about his opinion!"

Since I had to fly to New York the day after our anticipated return from Budapest, I had to cancel my next day's flight from Budapest to Prague and travel on the night train to be in Prague early in the morning. At the Central Committee of the Communist Party of Czechoslovakia I was told that Comrade Geminder was busy, that I should ask for a date and wait for my turn. Bedřich Geminder was head of the External Department of the Central Committee and believed at that time to be one of the most powerful men in the country.

My flight was booked for the next day, and my 30-day stay in New York had to take place before the end of 1948. It was late November and I could not wait. I told Geminder's secretary that I was sent to him by Yudin and was to see him without delay. He received me immediately and I told him my story. You should have come earlier, he said. What can we do at this stage? They invited you, paid for your ticket, so you must go! And next day I went.

This episode would not be complete without a remark about what happened three years and a few months later. In an anti-Semitic campaign against so-called "cosmopolitan elements", I was dismissed from my job at ČTK, the Czechoslovak News Agency, declared unsuitable for any intellectual employment and sent as manual labourer to a machine factory to get nearer to the working class. One of the reasons given for my dismissal from journalism was that three years ago I was sent to America by the criminal traitor Geminder! He was at that time one of the many arrested former party leaders, and in 1952, together with former Party Secretary General Rudolf Slánský and a number of mostly Jewish functionaries, including the journalist André Simone, he was sentenced to death in a show trial and hanged.

Around that time the IOJ Secretariat in Prague moved to its new premises in the building of the ČTK News Agency. A second staff member, Mrs Milena Králová, also speaking four or five languages, was hired for the IOJ administration, leaving bulletin-editing, correspondence to member organizations and preparations for the next Executive meeting and the third IOJ Congress on my agenda.

After Budapest, things changed rapidly. One after the other national member unions from the West withdrew from the IOJ or just broke off their contacts with the Prague headquarters. The IOJ was stripped of its consultative NGO status at the UN. Archibald Kenyon resigned from his post of IOJ President and publicly denounced the activities of the Prague Secretariat. In the Western press the IOJ was called – not without reason – a front organization and a tool of Soviet propaganda. Why not without reason? While taking up every case of "progressive" journalists in Western countries or their colonies who got into conflict with the law or authorities of their countries, the IOJ closed its eyes to the systematic discrimination against and persecution of anti-communist or merely nonconformist journalists in the "people's democracies" of the communist East, including Czechoslovakia.

The IOJ also faced big financial problems. The American Newspaper Guild ceased paying its per capita membership fees to the IOJ already before the Budapest Executive Committee meeting, and the other Western member unions followed suit. The only remaining member union with a large membership, that of the Soviet Union, did not pay its fees either. The final decision on what to do with the IOJ, whether to keep it alive or let it fall, had apparently not yet been taken in Moscow. The situation was so bad that for a period the IOJ did not have money to pay the salaries of its employees.

I did not feel comfortable in this atmosphere of *avant de mourir* and I started to work at the neighbouring ČTK New Agency while fulfilling part-time duties for the IOJ. I promised Hronek to assist at the preparations for the next Congress, due to take place in 1949 in Brussels. But the Belgian Union of Journalists withdrew from the IOJ and refused to organize the congress in Brussels. French journalists, affiliated with the communist-dominated CGT Trade Union, proposed to hold the congress in Paris, but later rescinded that offer claiming that some participants might not be granted visas by the French authorities. The remnants of the IOJ Executive Committee met in Czechoslovakia in 1949. Since it was decided that the next Congress should not be organized in a communist-ruled country, an invitation by a splinter association of Finnish left-wing journalists to hold the congress in Helsinki was accepted.

The third IOJ Congress in 1950 in Helsinki approved the policy adopted in Budapest and opened the IOJ doors to splinter groups and individual members. This was my last appearance as an IOJ executive officer. Newly elected IOJ President Jean-Maurice Hermann of the daily newspaper *Libération* invited me to Paris to brief him on the IOJ agenda, but the Czechoslovak Ministry of the Interior withdrew my passport and refused to issue me an exit permit. Hronek was soon also purged from his position and replaced by a more reliable – from the regime's point-of-view – Secretary General.

This is the conclusion of my eyewitness report. Never since did the IOJ render any assistance to me or other journalists in my country when being discriminated against or persecuted. I myself was banned from journalism and publishing activities for about 30 years: in 1952–1962, for being, as alleged by the then Communist authorities, a "cosmopolitan type of bourgeois origin", and in 1970–1989, for having opposed the Soviet invasion of Czechoslovakia and its occupation. During the 1950s and 1960s I could follow from outside the happenings in the IOJ under General Secretaries Knobloch, Meisner and Kubka; my former colleague Milena Králová keeping me informed. After the Soviet invasion in 1968 she was also sacked from the IOJ Secretariat and subsequently migrated with her family to Switzerland.

In the 1970s and 1980s I occasionally had dinner in an IOJ restaurant, and my children and grandchildren bought IOJ lottery tickets from street-corner vendors. Banned from journalism, I made my living as a translator-interpreter, concluding contracts with my clients often with the IOJ Translation and Interpretation Service as an intermediary. The IOJ became a large but hardly transparent multinational moneymaking enterprise, with questionable revenue and expenses, dealing in a series of activities having nothing to do with press and journalism. This mammoth of 1989, with a staff of nearly 1,600 people, had little in common with the IOJ of 1947, at whose cradle I stood.

JIŘÍ MEISNER: MANAGING THE IOJ TO ADULTHOOD*

The circumstances of Jiří Meisner's appointment to the position of IOJ Secretary General in 1958–59 were characteristic of the times that held sway in Czechoslovakia and other Eastern bloc countries. The Communist Party was making decisions on everything, including the candidature for the office of IOJ General Secretary. Before he joined the IOJ, Meisner worked for the daily *Rudé právo* published by the Central Committee of the Czechoslovak Communist Party (KSČ). At the editor-in-chief's office in September 1958, Meisner learned from the Head of the Press Department of the KSC Central Committee that he was going to become the new IOJ General Secretary. As a Party Member Meisner could only agree. When he asked whether the Union of Czechoslovak Journalists would agree with the change, he was told not to worry about it. According to Meisner, the Union was informed only after he had taken up his post at the IOJ.

It was also typical of the times that the former Secretary General Jaroslav Knobloch didn't pass on the agenda to Meisner personally. Other staff of the Secretariat were the most influential Soviet Secretary Petrov, Karl Burkhardt from the German Democratic Republic and Dante Cruicchi from Italy. Meisner thought that the reason why Knobloch was quickly removed was not the initiative of the Czechoslovak Journalists Union but a dispute between IOJ Secretary General Knobloch and the Soviet Secretary Petrov. Soon Petrov was himself removed and replaced by J. Shatskov. Somewhat later Shatskov fell from favour with Moscow and was replaced by A. Jefremov.

In connection with the change of Secretary General a delegation of Soviet journalists was going to visit Prague. Among others there was also the editor-in-chief the newspaper *Izvestia*, Alexei Adzhubei, the son-in-law of Nikita Khrushchev. At the time the Secretariat was located in four small rooms at the Czechoslovak Press Office. After Meisner had pointed out the unworthy accommodation of these 11 people working for the IOJ Secretariat to a member of the Ruling Council of the KSČ Central Committee and Minister of Information Václav Kopecký, the latter promptly decided to move the IOJ into the Union of Czechoslovak Journalists' building. The IOJ was given seven rooms there and the Soviet delegation could arrive. It was an improvisation in the Soviet manner and so it continued until the building was, after eight long years, pulled down.

When Meisner joined the IOJ he didn't know much about the institution and so he decided to act according to the international situation at the time. The Khrushchev denunciation of Stalin had brought hopes of a more liberal

* The author was IOJ Secretary General 1958–66. Written by Václav Slavík in spring 2001 based on Meisner's interview, translated from Czech by Rudolf Převrátil.

regime not only in the economy and culture of the USSR but also in those of the satellite countries. More liberal politics in the USSR had an impact on international politics. The "spirit of Geneva", which arose in 1954 at the meeting of Foreign Affairs Ministers after Stalin's death, gave rise to hopes that the politics of peace would overcome the Cold War. After the Bandung Conference in 1955 a new group of independent non-aligned nations started to form. This group formed in the spirit of Pancasila – five Rules of Peaceful Coexistence – started to influence international developments. These new voices for coexistence were reflected in journalistic circles too, and there were calls for the merging of the two international journalists' organizations. These voices came from various directions, but not from the IFJ. The IFJ obviously wasn't thinking about cooperation with the IOJ, let alone merging with it.

The calls for the unification of both international journalists' organizations had already appeared before Meisner joined the IOJ at the 1st World Meeting of Journalists held in Otaniemi, near Helsinki in 1956. The IFJ was invited but none of its members took part.

Conciliatory overtures in international relations led Meisner to develop the activities of the IOJ in keeping with these trends of peaceful coexistence and progress towards the independence of colonies and dependent territories. At the same time he was aware of the fact that the IOJ could not ignore questions such as freedom of information, the profession of journalism, journalistic ethics and the training of journalists. It seemed that the development of peaceful coexistence and of the "spirit of Bandung" could help to clarify and also resolve the basic questions of journalism.

This shifting of priorities in journalistic aims was expressed at the 2nd World Meeting of Journalists in Baden near Vienna in 1960. More than half of the 260 participants were from developing countries and many journalistic groups and important individuals from the Third World attended. Whereas in Otaniemi the emphasis was put upon the problems and ethics of journalism, in Baden there was a clear move towards political issues, questions of national liberation and peaceful coexistence. This was also helped by international developments, including the American intervention in Vietnam. Early in 1961 in Belgrade the 1st Conference of Non-Aligned Countries was held, which greatly reinforced the polities of detente.

The influence of the developing countries also started to grow in the UN. Whereas there were only 12 developing countries in the UN in 1945, in 1964 there were 64 of them and others were to follow.

Under these circumstances there was more and more interest in the IOJ. Journalists from developing countries started to come and visit the Secretariat in Prague, and they participated more in the IOJ activities. The interest in the IOJ also grew because of the training activities for journalists from developing countries organized by the IOJ and its affiliates, for example in Hungary for journalists, in Czechoslovakia for press agency workers and in East Berlin for photojournalists. The IOJ also supported journalists in Africa and the Pan-African Union of Journalists through a regional seminar for journalists in Algiers, a fund in support of Lumumba and others.

Efforts to create an independent national press and radio were obvious at the Second Pan-African Journalists' Conference in Accra (Ghana), where the IOJ also participated as an observer. The aims proclaimed by the conference were symptomatic: support for the liberation movement in Africa through press, radio and TV broadcasting, and with the aid of the mass media to help to settle disputes among African states. The Pan-African Union existed in Accra until 1966, the time when the Ghanaian President Nkrumah was overthrown in a coup.

The influence of the IOJ in Asia was rather different. The IOJ was developing cooperation with the Indian Federation of Working Journalists (IFWJ). Its delegation in Baden at the 2nd World Meeting of Journalists was preoccupied with problems about trade unions and cooperation with both international journalist organizations. Important for the IOJ penetration in Asia was the cooperation with the Indonesian Organization of Journalists which led to the meeting of the IOJ Presidium in Jakarta in February 1963. The meeting however didn't produce any noteworthy results. The Afro-Asian Conference of Journalists in April of that year, also held in Jakarta, showed why. The IOJ delegation arrived in Jakarta but was prevented from taking part in the Conference. This was as a result of pressure applied by the All China Association of Journalists (ACJA), which reflected the wide gulf between China and the Soviet Union and the consequences of the start of the Maoist "Cultural Revolution". Later on, the Chinese Union withdrew its representative from the IOJ Presidium. China was then followed by organizations of journalists from Indonesia and Ceylon (now Sri Lanka). Following the Chinese initiative the Afro-Asian Journalists' Organization was set up, which refused to cooperate with the IOJ. The attitude of Chinese journalists towards the IOJ on the other hand helped to strengthen the cooperation between the IOJ and the IFWJ.

Relations with the Vietnam Journalists Association (VJA) were different again. North Vietnam was already at war with the USA. The struggle against the USA was the main and only interest of North Vietnam, including journalists of the limited mass media (for instance Vietnamese press and radio broadcasts didn't even monitor the landing of American astronauts on the moon). In 1964 the VJA received an IOJ delegation which included IOJ Secretary General Meisner. The delegation was also received by President Ho-Chi Minh with the idea that it was possible to speak about closer cooperation following the resolution of the situation in Vietnam. The Vietnamese cooperated with countries which helped them, including China and the USSR. Later on, after the war was over, the IOJ provided material support towards the development of the Vietnamese mass media.

The IOJ had a similar relationship with Cambodia. On the way back from Hanoi in 1964, Meisner stopped in Phnom Penh. He was received by Prime Minister Prince Norodom Sihanouk, who was informed about IOJ activities but he also postponed changes in relations between the Cambodian journalists and the IOJ until such time as the conflict in Indochina was over.

In Latin America during the time of General Secretary Meisner the main focus of the IOJ was the Union of Cuban Journalists (UPEC) and the IOJ influence in Latin American countries. In 1962 the IOJ Executive Committee had a session in Havana. Fidel Castro also made a speech to the participants. The issue of extending IOJ activity in South American countries was on the agenda. The Cuban press agency Prensa Latina gave its assistance with this.

The driving force for the cooperation of Latin American Journalists was the Committee for Information and Cooperation of Latin American Journalists (CICPLA) set up in Havana in 1962. A representative of the Uruguayan journalists became General Secretary. The aim of the committee was to call a regional conference, where a permanent organization of Latin American journalists would be founded.

IOJ activity had a good reception in Chile. In 1965 the IOJ Executive Committee Meeting took place in Santiago, Chile. The IOJ delegation was also received by President Frey.

After that session in Santiago the members of the IOJ Executive Committee visited Peru, Uruguay, Brazil, Panama and Colombia. In Chile, Colombia and Peru, groups of IOJ journalists were set up. The Colombian members were especially active. They appointed their representative Marco Tulio Rodriguez as the next secretary of the IOJ Secretariat in Prague.

The IOJ tried to increase its influence in an original way: the IOJ organized the 3rd World Meeting of Journalists in September and October 1963, this time on board a ship, the *Litva*. The Soviet steamer departed from Odessa and cruised around the Mediterranean calling in at a few Mediterranean ports. The agenda of 260 journalists from 69 countries of all continents was dealt with on board. During the stops in Naples, Algiers, Tunis, Libya, Alexandria, Cyprus, Athens, Beirut and Istanbul the participants met with local journalists. In Egypt they were received by President Nasser and in Cyprus by President Makarios. The delegation of the 3rd World Conference "popped off" by plane to Accra where at the time preparations were under way for the 2nd Pan-African Conference of Journalists, which then took place in November. The delegation was received by President Nkrumah.

The growing influence of the IOJ in the developing countries, which was linked to developments in the international situation, made the IFJ also work more actively in Third World countries. The growth in activity of the IFJ had already been announced at the meeting in Bern 1960. IFJ Vice-President Bradley (USA) then visited many countries in sub-Saharan Africa. The main engine of IFJ activity in the developing countries was the American Newspaper Guild (ANG), which was the main financial supporter of the IFJ. It was also admitted on 18 February 1967 by the American newspaper *The Washington Post* that the ANG had received about one million US dollars from the CIA since 1961 for operations in the developing countries. It was a scandal which the IOJ used to its best advantage.

In the Socialist countries there was no such *Washington Post* that would write about the financing of the IOJ activities. The IOJ subsisted on contributions from member organizations. However, exceptional projects were financed with outside assistance, mainly from the USSR. For instance, Meisner went to Moscow to negotiate about the outstanding contribution for the 3rd World Meeting of Journalists. Because the man who had to make the decision – Head of the Press Department of the Soviet Union Central Committee Ilyichov – was on holiday at that time, Meisner went to see him at a Crimean sanatorium. Ilyichov reacted positively to the organization of the World Meeting on board ship and the finance was provided. The main expenses – the cruise, food, etc. – were paid by the Soviets.

While the IOJ activities increased, the financial demands also grew. The situation started to improve in 1963, when the IOJ was allowed by the Czechoslovak government to undertake business activities in the country. The setting up of the International Lottery of IOJ journalists provided a considerable source of revenue. The lottery tickets were sold publicly in the USSR, the GDR, Bulgaria and partly in Hungary. Profits were sent to the participating countries and the lottery became very popular. The first lottery was held in 1965. Secretary General Meisner thus acquired the finance that was necessary for the further development of the IOJ. But he was no longer there to see the realization of his plans. After eight years in his post he left the IOJ.

He didn't leave the IOJ of his own free will, but in the same way as he was nominated, that is, on the instructions of the KSČ Central Committee. In September 1966 just before the meeting of the IOJ Executive Committee he was informed that the Central Committee had decided on his removal. He knew the reason was his personal dispute with the Head of the Press Secretariat of the Central Committee about a matter that had nothing to do with the IOJ. There was no way that he could protect himself from such intrigues. The proposal of the Central Committee Secretariat was obviously also accepted by the Union of Czechoslovak Journalists. Their representative then proposed Meisner's removal as a motion of the Union of Czechoslovak Journalists at the 6th Conference of the IOJ in 1966 in Berlin. Meisner was then employed at the Czechoslovak Ministry of Foreign Affairs and was sent as the Czechoslovak ambassador to North Vietnam.

After some years I asked Meisner to provide me with his evaluation of the IOJ during his tenure in the 1960s. He said:

> The IOJ was in fact the extended hand of European Socialist countries under the guidance of the USSR. In the sixties the IOJ took advantage of the growing liberation movements in Third World countries and the policy of peaceful coexistence of the Eastern bloc, which tried to present the USSR and Socialist countries as the main and only proponents of peace.

This approach was successful in the sixties and attracted many followers from Third World countries. The influence of the IOJ was strengthened or weakened according to developments in the political situation in different countries and continents. The bulk the IOJ members were from the Socialist countries, obeying the USSR with the exception of Romania, which during the Ceausescu regime tried to play a less dependent role in international affairs. That was apparent, for instance, in December 1965, when there was a conference of journalists from the Balkan countries in Bucharest, with Yugoslavia present but not the USSR. Because of this reticent attitude of the Romanians, they were not present at some consultations of journalist unions from the Socialist countries.

Journalists' organizations from West European countries were usually members of the IFJ. The situation was more complicated in France, where some of journalists formed a group within the CGT trade union, which was an IOJ member. Finland had a similar situation. In other West European countries it was mainly individual journalists who cooperated with the IOJ, usually editors of Communist or radical papers.

Although no anti-Communist press was allowed in Socialist countries, in many Western and also developing countries the IOJ profited from democratic and liberal governments which tolerated opposition groups. The IOJ was obviously concerned with the issues of democracy, liberty and freedom of thought. Freedom was looked at only from the angle of Communist interest, and class and liberation on movements.

The activity of IOJ President, Jean-Maurice Hermann from France was summed up by Meisner as follows:

> Hermann always tried to manage the IOJ according to the statutes of the IOJ on the widest possible international basis, although he must have known about the flagrant breach of ethical and professional journalistic principles in the Socialist countries. He was a realist and pragmatist who was building on political reality, that is, the existence of two world camps, where it was necessary to swim between two barriers. He always tried to consider the IOJ as more than a tool of the USSR and so he was often in dispute with the USSR representatives. They did not, however, during Meisner's time at the IOJ,

ever openly oppose Hermann. They needed him as a non-Communist, Western individual and so they only tried to sway the implementation of his proposals. The Soviets were especially careful in monitoring Hermann's efforts to unify the international movement of journalists as they were afraid of too much Western influence on the IOJ. The mainstream policy of the IOJ – the drive towards peaceful coexistence – was promoted by Hermann very energetically on a long-term basis.

VÁCLAV SLAVÍK: THE AGE OF ACHIEVEMENT WITH JIŘÍ KUBKA*

In the words of the famous song by a Czech Jazz musician of the thirties Jaroslav Ježek: "Life is only luck, one day you are down, the next day up." I often thought of those words when I became an employee of the IOJ Secretariat. It was perhaps a stroke of good luck that the Secretary General of the IOJ Jiří Meisner made me one of the members of the IOJ team in 1966. He was not interested in my class origin, nor did he mind that I wasn't a member of the Czechoslovak Communist Party (KSČ). To him it was obviously more important that I was a university graduate, that I had 12 years of work experience partly in the field of international relations, and that I spoke some foreign languages.

Such an attitude was very rare at the time of the Communist regime. Although Meisner was the Secretary General of an international organization which wasn't formally under the control of any Czechoslovak institution, as a member of the KSČ he was undoubtedly accountable to its Central Committee.

Owing to the fact that I was employed by the IOJ I stopped feeling like a second-class citizen and no longer felt depressed that I didn't have a working-class background and that I had never joined the KSČ.

In the IOJ Secretariat I was instructed by Meisner to set up an International Relations Department (Diplomatic Protocol). Later on – during the tenure of Secretary General Jiří Kubka – I worked as an assistant to Italian Secretary Ferdinando Zidar. His task was to regain for the IOJ its consultative status at UNESCO and at the UN Economic and Social Council (ECOSOC). Zidar completed his task but he didn't get any appreciation: he was accused by the Czechoslovak authorities of helping the Italian journalists to maintain contacts between the Czech emigrants in Italy and the dissidents in Czechoslovakia. This led to a recommendation from the Czechoslovak authorities that he should leave the country (see his own story below).

Before Zidar's departure in 1972, Kubka asked me to build within the IOJ "a department which could give an answer to any question". And so the IOJ Documentation and Information Service was founded. It became in due course, with strong support from IOJ President Kaarle Nordenstreng, an autonomous institution, the International Journalism Institute (IJI). The activity of the IJI between 1986 and 1992 was used and appreciated not only by international, regional and national journalist organizations but also by journalism scholars, faculties of journalism, the UN, UNESCO, ILO and many

* The author was a specialist in the IOJ Secretariat 1966–86 and Director of the International Journalism Institute 1986–92. Jiří Kubka was IOJ Secretary General 1966–88. Written in spring 2001, translated from Czech by Rudolf Převrátil.

non-governmental organizations, including Amnesty International, which were involved in defending journalists.

I retired from the IOJ in 1992 after 26 years, during which I had the opportunity to meet a lot of interesting and important journalists, researchers and people from different organizations. But the most vital reflections of these years are associated with the Velvet Revolution and my long working relationship with General Secretary Jiří Kubka.

At the beginning of January 1990, the Czechoslovak Union of Journalists, which had been an IOJ member since its inception in 1946, ceased to exist. The Union was replaced by the Syndicate of Czech and Moravian Journalists as well as the Syndicate of Slovak Journalists. The new syndicate did not join the IOJ, and consequently since that moment the IOJ had its seat in a country where it had no member organization. In a statement by the Syndicate on 20 February 1990, the IOJ became the target of a very sharp attack and was accused of "persistently violating for more than 40 years all principles of protection of the freedom of expression and independence of journalists which were part of its own programme. It put itself fully in the service of totalitarian regimes in Czechoslovakia and other countries of Eastern Europe and became their loyal and obedient tool." The Syndicate further demanded that Czechoslovakia and Prague could no longer remain the seat of the IOJ and that the IOJ headquarters be moved to another country. Attacks based on half-truths and also lies appeared in the campaign mixed with earnest critical articles.

It is obvious and understandable that the IOJ was criticized by many throughout its existence. The reasons for this criticism can be traced to the IOJ Statutes and to the fact that the IOJ had its headquarters in a country which came under a totalitarian regime in 1948, as well as to the fact that persons holding the office of IOJ Secretary General were endowed with vast powers, while being simultaneously subject to very strong pressures on the part of the regime.

As far as the IOJ Statutes are concerned, they expressed a certain concept of journalism and journalists' mission in society – that peace is the ultimate goal of humanity and that mass media and journalists should develop their activities in its interests. This was natural in the atmosphere immediately after World War II when the Statutes were drawn up. This philosophy, however, was reflected in a rather simplified way in the IOJ Statutes. Their main shortcoming was the very superficial way in which the rights and obligations of individual governing bodies were worded. Practical life showed that what was extremely problematic was the clause stating that the IOJ Secretary General is the legally acknowledged governing authority ("statutory governing organ"), while stipulating at the same time that "he/she is responsible for the smooth operation of IOJ", i.e. not only its Secretariat but the organization as a whole. Another clause said that the Secretary General ensures the operation of the IOJ "under the control of the Presidium".

One might wonder why these drawbacks in the Statutes had not been remedied in the course of several decades although some additions were occasionally made. This is evidence of an utterly disparaging attitude to the basic legal document that is vital for the operations of any democratic organization. It was as late as October 1987 at the IOJ Presidium meeting in Nicosia that the IOJ President demanded a review of the IOJ Statutes – a request that was approved at the IOJ Presidium meeting held in Brazil in March 1988.

A certain rigidity in the Statutes notwithstanding, marked progress can be seen in the practical policies and positions of the IOJ during the past decades. This is true of such important areas as relations to and cooperation with international governmental and nongovernmental organizations, including the IFJ, the changing approach to such issues as freedom of expression, the social status of journalists, professional ethics, etc. The most important part in all this until 1976 was undoubtedly played by Kubka. When Prof. Nordenstreng was elected to the office of IOJ President, Kubka got a partner who took over a number of tasks which the IOJ had in the international area, professional training of journalists and other activities which were important for the IOJ. Nevertheless the huge burden of organizing and coordinating the immense field of IOJ activities and providing the necessary resources had to be shouldered by Kubka as before. Thanks to the entrepreneurship, managerial and political skills of Kubka, the IOJ enterprises Videopress in Czechoslovakia and Interpress Budapest kept expanding and provided hundreds of thousands of dollars for the IOJ. These resources made it possible to finance activities which were absolutely beyond reach of any other organization of journalists.

Kubka, however, was not only a successful entrepreneur active in a large international journalist organization. He was also a journalist of high professional level, broad education and rich fantasy. As a politician he was trying to be a hard realist but at heart he remained a romantic cherishing many unrealizable dreams. Often they remained unrealized because the reality of the Cold War did not allow them to happen.

KUBKA'S CAREER AND ACHIEVEMENTS IN THE IOJ

When Kubka was elected Secretary General at the 6th IOJ Congress in Berlin in November 1966, he was fairly well qualified for the post. Son of a well-known Czech writer and diplomat, he had an excellent education. He started his professional career as an army journalist. After the end of the Korean War he became a Czech representative in the UN International Supervisory Commission which supervised the truce between North Korea and South Korea on the 38th parallel. Young and sensitive Kubka perceived the destitution in which people were living in that developing country, and the terrible desolation caused by the Korean War. This experience became the source of his lifelong anti-war stance. After his return to Czechoslovakia in 1954 Kubka behaved, as witnessed by his contemporaries, in a pragmatic manner. He did not agree with the practices of the regime but did not revolt; he always treated his collaborators with decency. He pursued his career as a journalist in the army press.

In the sixties, Kubka was active in the Union of Czechoslovak Journalists. It was this organization, in which Kubka held the office of secretary at that time, that proposed him as a candidate for IOJ Secretary General in 1966.

Kubka took up his new job as the top IOJ executive with all his energy, making full use of his education, knowledge and experience. His arrival marks a period of rapid growth in the IOJ: year by year, many new member organizations were joining the IOJ, professional and social activities expanded, necessary financial resources were ensured. Thanks to Kubka, the IOJ reached its golden age and became a really worldwide organization of professional journalists. His merits are evident and indisputable. IOJ President Jean-Maurice Hermann was a great support for him especially during his first years in office. However, as Hermann's years advanced, his activities and influence decreased and consequently for many years, until 1976, when Nordenstreng was elected IOJ President at the 8th IOJ Congress in Helsinki, Kubka was the only engine driving the development of IOJ.

Four IOJ Congresses were held during Kubka's term in office: the 7th Congress in Havana in 1971 (326 participants, 64 member organizations represented), the 8th Congress in Helsinki in 1976 (243 participants, 65 member organizations), the 9th Congress in Moscow in 1981 (421 participants, 82 member organizations), and the 10th Congress in Sofia in 1986 (340 participants, 96 member organizations). The expenses for these congresses, which included free air tickets for many representatives of journalist organizations from developing countries, were enormous. Also very expensive – although somewhat less than the congresses – were the meetings of the IOJ Executive Committee. Kubka was the main organizer of four such meetings (Hungary, Iraq, Vietnam, India). The number of participants at these IOJ Executive Committee meetings was in many cases comparable to the number of participants at IFJ Congresses. After all, the meetings of the IOJ Executive Committee Presidium also incurred substantial costs, especially considering that seventeen Presidium meetings were held during Kubka's time in office.

A huge expansion of the IOJ membership took place during the period in which Kubka held the office of IOJ Secretary General. There were fewer than 140,000 journalists and individual members from 108 countries associated with the IOJ after its 6th Congress in 1966. The total number of member organizations, groups and committees was 49. After 22 years of Kubka's work in the IOJ, there were 105 member organizations and associated organizations, and the total IOJ membership reached a respectable level of 250,000. There were 83 member organizations from the developing countries of Africa, Asia, Latin America and the Caribbean representing 80% of IOJ membership. This fact, on the other hand, again shows that it was up to the IOJ to cover the expenses connected with participation of representatives from the developing countries in various meetings because they were unable to meet such expenses themselves.

Indeed, the above figures cannot render the whole range of various professional, social and publishing projects that the IOJ developed and implemented during the time when Kubka was its chief executive officer. Nor is it in my power to describe in detail that abundance of various activities characteristic of the IOJ in the years 1966–1988. Nevertheless I would like to present at least some facts that can tell something about that period.

In the professional and social areas, international commissions have to be mentioned which were transformed into IOJ Councils later in 1986. Specifically, these were the Commission for Social Issues (since 1967), the Professional Commission (since 1968), the Commission for Studies and Documentation and the Commission for Training of Journalists (since 1981). Training of journalists was provided in IOJ by IOJ schools in Budapest and Berlin (since 1963). On the initiative of Kubka, another six IOJ schools were established in Bucharest and Sofia (in 1977), Baghdad (1980), Prague and Havana (1983), and Pyongyang (1985). The clubs and sections have already been mentioned. Large international exhibitions of photojournalism held under the title Interpress Photo should also be noted. The first exhibition of this kind was presented in Berlin in 1960. By the end of 1987, there had been 13 such exhibitions, with the team of Kubka participating in the production of nine of them in Europe, Latin America and Asia.

The IOJ Documentation and Information Service was set up thanks to Kubka at the IOJ General Secretariat. That service was transformed into the IOJ Institute for Studies and Documentation in 1983. Its task was to gather and process information on mass media and journalism. A specialized IOJ database was developed from this information with the help of computer technology. The output was placed at the disposal of the IOJ General Secretariat and member organizations. Since the beginning of 1986, the Institute had enjoyed extensive autonomy and developed broad international activities under its new name, the International Journalism Institute (IJI).

Kubka attached great importance to the publishing activities of the IOJ. During his term in office, the IOJ published the monthly *Democratic Journalist* in four languages as its official paper, supplemented by the fortnightly *IOJ*

Newsletter appearing in six languages. The IOJ also published a professional magazine *Interpressgraphic* and a rather popular Czech-language *Interpress-Magazin* which became an interesting source of income for the IOJ. By the time of Kubka's departure from the IOJ, the number of books and booklets published by the organization had reached 186. During the initial two decades of its existence the IOJ produced altogether six publications; during the 22 years of Kubka's term in office their number reached 180. Book publishing in Czechoslovakia was subject to many limitations until 1989 (lack of printing facilities, paper shortages, etc.). If the IOJ was able to publish a number of books every year comparable to the output of many medium-sized Czechoslovak publishing houses, it was indeed a respectable performance.

The ever expanding international activities of the IOJ also meant an increasing financial burden on the IOJ budget. The financial resources of the IOJ, however, were rather limited. Member dues were actually paid by only some of the member organizations from the Socialist countries. Only the current expenses of the IOJ Secretariat could be covered from this source. After the 6th IOJ congress, the number of international representatives in the IOJ Secretariat was increased. Secretaries from the USSR, the GDR and Colombia were joined by Italian secretary Ferninando Zidar, who had worked in the General Secretariat since 1968. A secretary from Romania arrived in 1969. Polish and Bulgarian secretaries entered later on. As a result, the Secretariat consisted of Secretary General Kubka and six secretaries sent to the IOJ headquarters by member unions. Meetings of the IOJ Secretariat at that time were also attended by the IOJ Treasurer from Hungary and the director of the first IOJ regional centre in Cairo. After the 7th IOJ congress, a secretary sent by the Cuban Union of Journalists joined the Secretariat. He shared responsibility for the American region with his colleague from Colombia, and later one from Peru.

When the current operating costs of the Secretariat were covered, there were no resources left for various meetings, seminars, publishing, journalist training and other projects in the professional and social areas. At the same time, member organizations from the developing countries, which constituted an overwhelming majority of the IOJ membership, were not only unable to pay membership dues but, on the contrary, often asked for financial support from the IOJ. Kubka, being an excellent manager, was able to recruit professionals who helped him to set up special sections in the Secretariat entrusted with the task of providing financial resources for the IOJ. He expanded the IOJ International Lottery and established a specialized section for exhibitions, a translation-interpreting-conference service and a publishing house within the IOJ. With the help of those sections the IOJ was able to cover its expenses – hard currency (dollar) expenses in particular – from its own resources for the first time in 1970. These sections were transformed into a separate company IOJ Videopress in 1974. A similar company was established in Hungary already in 1971 under the name Interpress Budapest.

How did these sections work? It may be said as an example that as soon as one year after Kubka's election to the office of IOJ Secretary General, Interpress Graphic Club was set up in IOJ. This international club arranged large international exhibitions of printing technology and magazine production in Prague in 1967, 1969 and 1974. These were really big events. For example, already at the first exhibition in 1967, 56 companies presented their products on stands covering an area of 10,000 square metres, and 240,000 visitors came to see them. Another club, Interpress Auto Club, had arranged Interpress Rallies every year since the mid-1970s and set up two big international exhibitions "Man and Automobile" in Prague in 1968 and 1970. Each of the two exhibitions, supplemented by an international symposium, was visited by approximately 400,000 people.

AFTER PRAGUE SPRING

Kubka's plans for the further development of economic activities in the IOJ, so promising in the period of Prague Spring, when the IOJ host country under Alexander Dubček tended towards democratization, were dashed by the invasion of Czechoslovakia by Warsaw Pact troops on 21 August 1968.

The seat of the IOJ was no exception from the general occupation rule. When we, members of the Secretariat staff, entered the building of the Czechoslovak Union of Journalists on 22 August to get to the IOJ offices on the 3rd floor, we were welcomed by Kalashnikov rifles held by Soviet soldiers who blocked the bottom of the staircase and the lift entrance. We were allowed only to the Club of Journalists – a restaurant on the ground floor. The Czech staff of the IOJ gathered there, joined by the then IOJ Secretary Marco Tulio Rodriguez (Colombia). The secretaries from the Warsaw Pact countries Sepp Fischer (GDR) and Pavel Yerofeyev (USSR) did not show up. Nor was Kubka present. He was in the FRG at that time and because he was, according to his own words, stopped on the Czechoslovak border and not allowed to enter the country, he left for East Berlin to contact the Union of Journalists of the GDR and ask help for the IOJ. Marco Tulio Rodriguez prepared with our assistance a text which asked IOJ member organizations, on behalf of the IOJ General Secretariat, to protest against the illegal occupation of the IOJ headquarters. Until this day I recall the uneasy feelings I had when smuggling the text, hidden on my bare body under my shirt, out of the building under the gun barrels to have it sent out by telex from a nearby travel agency. It was sent to the AFP in Paris with a request to pass on the information to the UNESCO offices.

In the following days, the IOJ staff met in a Prague hotel. Information, appeals to the world public, documentation and film negatives were sent from that place to Western countries with the help of Czechoslovak Airlines pilots. Representatives of the secretariat also visited the Soviet embassy in Prague to protest against the occupation of the IOJ and the headquarters of the Czechoslovak Union of Journalists. They disproved propaganda claims to the effect that arms were found in the building. Embassy press secretary Yakovlev had by then got the blockade lifted. IOJ Secretary Pavel Yerofeyev (USSR) showed – as far as the circumstances permitted – his solidarity with protest actions taken by the Secretariat. Due to this he was recalled from the IOJ and forced to retire. Marco Tulio Rodriguez was likewise forced to leave under pressure from the Union of Journalists of the USSR. Fortunately nothing happened to me. Nevertheless I was discriminated against for long years to come by not being allowed to participate in IOJ meetings held in Western countries despite the fact that Kubka was, in general, well-disposed towards me.

The IOJ Secretariat held its first meeting in the de-blocked building on 3 September 1968 in the presence of IOJ President Hermann. That meeting, among others, approved the steps taken by IOJ representatives in the preceding days and asked the authorities to facilitate the normal operations of the Czechoslovak Union of Journalists.

After August 1968, IOJ secretaries from the Socialist countries were ordered to "normalize" the IOJ Secretariat without scruples. The Soviets placed great faith in the new secretary Igor Modnov, who replaced P. Yerofeyev. Fortunately, journalists from the FRG warned the IOJ Secretariat that Modnov was known in the FRG as a Soviet embassy officer photographed while emptying a "dead box" and that the affair was publicized by the prominent magazine *Der Spiegel*. The IOJ Secretariat insisted that Modnov be recalled and so he was replaced by a new secretary, Oleg Zagladin, a well-educated journalist and brother of Gorbachev's advisor Vadim Zagladin who in his thinking belonged rather to the post-Brezhnev era.

Nevertheless the position of Kubka as IOJ Secretary General was seriously threatened after 21 August 1968. His dismissal was urged particularly by the Union of Journalists of the USSR Executive Secretary Viacheslav Chernyshev, who was a general in Soviet counter-intelligence and a veteran of the Spanish Civil War. Chernyshev greatly resented Kubka's sympathy with Prague Spring, his more than friendly relations with the leaders of the Czechoslovak Union of Journalists in 1968 and also the fact that as early as in April 1968 he donated CZK 200,000 to journalists rehabilitated by Dubček's regime. Kubka resisted the "normalization" of the IOJ secretariat among others by establishing contacts with the National Federation of the Italian Press (FNSI).

Assisted by the President of the Czechoslovak Union of Journalists Vlado Kašpar, he asked the FNSI to send a secretary to the IOJ regardless of the fact that the FNSI was not member of the IOJ. The FNSI complied with the request and sent Ferdinando Zidar. The Italian Communist Party was very influential at that time and the USSR could not afford to totally disregard it. At the same time the PCI sharply criticized the occupation of Czechoslovakia. Consequently, the new secretary from Italy was expected to strengthen those forces in the IOJ Secretariat which opposed the occupation and to try to defend the IOJ against increasing pressures coming from the post-Dubček Czechoslovak regime which only executed orders given by the invaders.

Kubka was successful in his resistance to Chernyshev, but he had to give up many of his plans and look for ways of enabling the IOJ to survive and operate in Prague under the increasingly difficult conditions of a Communist regime that blindly obeyed all instructions coming from Moscow. Paradoxically this regime became more papal than the Pope because at the moment when Gorbachev's *perestroika* was well under way in the Soviet Union, the regime of Czechoslovak President G. Husák, and CPCZ General Secretary M. Jakeš were still governing the country in the spirit of Brezhnev.

Kubka, a born diplomat, was able to get along well with the rulers of Czechoslovakia even in those difficult times and obtained various permits for business operations allowing the IOJ to earn as many resources as needed for its ever expanding activities. Although he was put under the strict surveillance of the Communist Party, he did not become its blind servant, as they probably wished and the IOJ staff, amounting to hundreds of persons, could work in Czechoslovakia under conditions far more liberal than those in other Czech enterprises and institutions. In a country with a planned Socialist economy Kubka succeeded in building enterprises earning millions of US dollars in a way that was current in the capitalist West. This, however, eventually became fatal for Kubka. The regime of the time could not tolerate such business activities which were not under its own control.

KUBKA'S END IN THE IOJ

In 1985 the Central Committee "recommended" Kubka to appoint a new director of the IOJ Videopress enterprises in Czechoslovakia and proposed three candidates for the position. None of them suited Kubka. Finally, however, he decided in favour of one of them, Miloš Jakeš, who was the son of Party General Secretary M. Jakeš. Kubka hoped that his name alone would open the doors of the Czechoslovak authorities for the IOJ and that the prosperity of the IOJ would thereby be assured. This was indeed a good judgment. Under M. Jakeš junior, IOJ enterprises were increasingly profitable. However, M. Jakeš developed megalomaniac plans to obtain huge financial resources for the IOJ by illegal methods which he could afford as a son of the CP General

Secretary. Kubka disapproved, and this became the reason for his conflict not only with Jakeš junior but the whole totalitarian regime in Czechoslovakia. This conflict could only mean catastrophe for Kubka.

Kubka had a strong personality. For long years he had successfully resisted pressures from the largest IOJ member organization, the Union of Journalists of the USSR, as well as pressures from the Union of Czechoslovak Journalists, in which he served as a presidium member. Now he also faced pressures from the totalitarian regime exerted through the Communist Party, on the one hand, and through the son of the Party's General Secretary on the other. Kubka gave in to those pressures at the beginning of 1988 and was forced to leave the IOJ.

The methods used against Kubka must have been brutal, but anyway he was made - against his own will - to inform the IOJ bureau meeting in mid-March 1988 about "his" decision to resign from the office of IOJ Secretary General which he had held for 22 years and substitute this by his appointment to the post of Czechoslovak Ambassador to Mexico. At the end of March, before the IOJ Presidium meeting in Brazil, he wrote a letter to the IOJ President saying among others:

"As I am fully occupied by preparations for my future mission, I cannot take part in the Presidium meeting. Allow me therefore to ask you to excuse my absence with all Presidium members and inform them about my decision and my new mission. At the same time allow me to present a proposal for appointing Dušan Ulčák to the office of Presidium member, whom I warmly recommend."

In reality, the IOJ Secretary General was deprived of his passport by the Czechoslovak authorities to make his presence at the Presidium meeting in Brazil impossible. The regime did not want to risk any accident. What would happen if Kubka changed his mind and told the truth to all 28 IOJ Vice-Presidents? Also, the recommendation of Ulčák as a candidate for the Presidium and consequently as a future IOJ Secretary General was made by Kubka against his own convictions. Ulčák was not a journalist but an exponent of the regime prevailing in Czechoslovakia from the Brezhnev era. And why was he proposed to become IOJ Secretary General? Evidently at the instigation of M. Jakeš junior, his colleague of many years in the International Union of Students.

With Ulčák holding the top executive office in the IOJ, the Jakeš mafia took full hold of the IOJ management. Fortunately, its rule did not last long. The Velvet Revolution in Czechoslovakia in November 1989 marked its end. Ulčák was forced to retire from the office of IOJ Secretary General at the beginning of April 1990.

FERDINANDO ZIDAR: THE STORY OF MY EXPULSION*

Now that Czechoslovakia has become a democratic country, thanks to the Velvet Revolution, which demonstrated the strength, wisdom and unity of the Czech and Slovak peoples, it is useful to look back at the slow, heavy years that preceded it. They weighed heavily on the IOJ too, even though it is an international organization whose status and principles are largely inspired by freedom. If there is a genuine desire to go through with the radical turnabout, which is in the heart of every journalist, it is necessary to reflect on an incident that took place in Prague, with me as a central character, when I was working as an IOJ secretary.

It was an evening in late January 1972. I was on my way home from the theatre when I was surrounded by three people who furtively showed me their identity papers and introduced themselves as agents of the state security service, the StB. Straight away they asked me if I was Ferdinando Zidar, member of the Italian Communist Party (PCI) and secretary of the IOJ. When I said yes, they asked me to follow them, to "answer a few questions".

We got into a big black Tatra, which set off, preceded by one car and followed by another. After about three-quarters of an hour we came to a village I did not recognize. The agents invited me into a beautiful house set in a huge garden full of trees. Three people were waiting for me in a room. A colonel in another room was following what was going on. One of the agents told me that they wanted to talk to me about the violation of Article 16 of the Law on Public Security – the article relating to activities considered "subversive". "If everything goes well", he said, "it won't take long; you could go home tomorrow". All they wanted from me was a list of all my contacts, which meant a list of everybody I knew in Czechoslovakia.

Naturally, I refused because my past as an antifascist and partisan led my conscience to respect the principles of democracy no matter what the cost. So they persisted for a while and then, as we say in Italy, changed their tune: they let me know that I was accused of having maintained relations with people who had been purged from the Czechoslovak Communist Party and others who held "antisocialist opinions". According to them all my friends were engaged in activities hostile to the government. And I was accused of collaborating with them. They claimed I had acted as a liaison person with political émigrés. In addition I was supposed to have delivered messages and money abroad, taking advantage of my frequent trips to Paris as IOJ representative at UNESCO. And then a piece of pure theatre: they took hundreds of photographs out of a fat packet, photos of me with these alleged "subversives"

* The author was IOJ Secretary of International Organizations 1968–72. Reprinted from *The Democratic Journalist* 10–11/1990, p. 12.

in the street and in restaurants and cafés. In particular there were photos of me with Milan Hubl, with whom I enjoyed a deep friendship based on my respect for his tenacity, his highly developed intelligence and broad culture.

After so many years have passed I don't remember the names of the other "subversives". On the whole they were very serious, very intelligent people, true democrats. Some of them were communists, believers in "socialism with a human face", as we called it then; others were socialists or had different ideals.

Of course I denied every accusation, mostly to avoid causing problems for my friends, I just said that they were my best friends and they had nothing to do with Article 16 and so nothing to do with so-called "subversive activities". The discussion became more heated and the tone more polemic. Several times they suggested I worked with the state security, stressing that the StB should be considered to be a more advanced part of the false accusations made against Slánský and others which had led to their death sentences and executions, only to be subsequently rehabilitated. My questioners replied "You would do better to look at who rehabilitated them and how" (they evidently hinted at the opinion of conservatives in the Communist Party, who looked at the rehabilitation as the doing of revisionists). When I accused them of persecuting people just for their ideas and not for anything they had done, they claimed "We are political police and not bureaucratic". The interrogation lasted forty-eight hours and became increasingly fraught as we hurled insults at each other. The result was the ritual accusation of "having taken part in espionage activities".

In the end they announced my expulsion from Czechoslovakia with my departure set for the next day. I could not take anything with me. They told me they would draw up an inventory of my things and post them to me after I had left. Then I was taken back to Prague where I went straight to my office at the IOJ. Everybody had already heard the news of my expulsion. I found a small bunch of flowers on my desk, and a souvenir, left by my secretary and other staff, doubtless without the participation of my colleagues. This gesture of solidarity moved me.

The *Rudé právo* of February 25, 1972 published a list of the many people arrested during the preceding months for "criminal activities undertaken in collaboration with centres of ideological and political propaganda run by émigrés in the capitalist countries". And *Rudé právo* went on "Among these people are some journalists and other visitors to Czechoslovakia who came here as contacts with foreign and domestic enemy elements".

The leadership of the IOJ – as it did in other cases when foreign and Czechoslovak journalists were arrested or physically attacked – unquestioningly accepted the police version and in its reply to the protest note sent by the National Federation of the Italian Press (FNSI) over my expulsion, the leadership stated that "Dr. Zidar violated the rules of hospitality from which he benefited and he also compromised the statutes of the general secretariat which, as an international and extraterritorial body, cannot interfere in the internal affairs of the host country".

As for the statutes mentioned above, it must be pointed out that they call for – literally – the greatest freedom of information and action for journalists. In addition it is a fundamental duty of every journalist worthy of the name to look for information everywhere, not just from government and official sources but from opposition circles as well, in order to get a realistic picture of the situation.

To consider the ideas of the opposition as "subversive" even if they are only ideas is an attitude typical of dictatorial and oppressive governments. That is why the FNSI firmly rejected the evaluation of the IOJ leadership.

The PCI daily newspaper, *L'Unità*, also showed its solidarity with the persecuted, writing "We have never heard any objections from the leaders of the IOJ, who are now accusing Comrade Zidar, about the correct way in which he carried out his work".

So that then is the story of the past. Today it should be evaluated in the thoughts of all those who believe in democracy and the links that exist between all journalists. It is only to be hoped that the new leaders of the IOJ – when determining the radical changes with the new Congress – will be able to draw some meaningful lessons from it.

* * *

Additional remarks by Ferdinando Zidar in 1995 in response to Kaarle Nordenstreng's questions:

The IOJ seemed to me an organization which was partly professional – in the Statute clearly professional – but in fact strongly coloured by politics, in a sense Communist. However, the relation between the IOJ General Secretary and the Czechoslovak government was not obvious.

My approach to the IOJ was not in accordance with its political line and I often disagreed with it. I considered the IOJ policy for the benefit of progressive forces in the world to be very limited because of its sectarian politics.

PÁL TAMÁS: THE IOJ EMPIRE IN KADARIST HUNGARY*

As a fresh university graduate in 1972, I found employment at the Hungarian Association of Journalists (MUOSZ) in Budapest. It was a strange place in the city in those years. On the one hand the profession of a journalist in late communist Hungary was highly political: the journalist was both a servant and a partner, in some cases, even an initiator of political actions. In the eyes of the majority, maybe not the newsmen themselves but the national media elite, it was part of the political establishment. The headquarters of the Association were located in an elegant palace on the Andrassy, a neighbourhood characterized by the late 19th century villas of the former monetary aristocracy. Their club and restaurant was one of the very few places where people of letters met, but being located in the middle of the contemporary borough of embassies it was also a much loved place among diplomats. Altogether it was at that time an almost ideal place for the generation and exchange of gossip, a personal news market and meeting place of and with foreigners. During the 1960s it was the scene – together with a dozen similar projects – of the first reforms pursuing a sort of compromise of the Communist Party with the educated strata. The very existence of such a place was itself a political overture, a symbolic gesture on the part of the Party to and for the media intelligentsia.

After the uprising of 1956, in which the journalists, including former Party agitators, played an active role, the political technologists of power consolidation were really brutal in managing the press. Virtually all the staff writers in political dailies and in the cultural press were simply fired, the university-based journalist education in Budapest was not reorganized; it was liquidated. The political press was understood to be the organ of Party propaganda, and many important faces and voices of earlier years were banned from the profession by a sort of *Berufsverbot* for years. Several journalists taking a direct part in the uprising or organizing distributive networks for independent information were arrested. At the same time in the eyes of the mainstream Western press the new Kadar regime was a Russian puppet and not a legitimate representative of political power in Hungary. To a certain extent the government was isolated in the West and was simultaneously not totally "safe enough" for some Soviet hardliners. But from the early and mid-1960s Kadar did really control the country and society and already started to seek compromises both on the international scene and with local cultural and media elites.

Yet such concepts and ambitions could not be brought to fruition without the heroes or at least drivers of our story. In the Hungarian case it is my under-

* The author was research fellow at the MUOSZ 1972–74. Written in November 2014.

standing that the real protagonist of the story in and around the "new pact" of the Party with the media elite was one single individual, namely Norbert Siklósi (1924–2008). He hired me on the recommendation of Pal Gabor, his deputy and the supervisor of education in journalism. In the period 1958–73 Siklósi was Secretary General of MUOSZ. He was a very gifted organizer, a master of informal networks among journalists, politicians, Party bureaucrats, and the industrial elite of that time. As a young worker of Jewish origin in the garment industry he joined the Left, and indeed he was still very young in 1950 when joining the staff of *Szabad Nep* (main Party paper of the country at that time), where he remained until 1954. In October 1956 the writers and their association, the Writers' Union, took a crucial role in mobilizing or even preparing the political revolt. Therefore, when at the beginning of 1957 Siklósi was nominated State Commissar of the writers' and journalists' associations – while their normal operations were temporarily suspended – it meant assuming an extraordinarily sensitive role. No doubt the Party leadership knew him to be a hardliner in 1956. However, he quickly opened the doors, offered many skeptical media professionals various options to return to the press and reinstated a sort of normality in the Association. In 1957 MUOSZ elected him Secretary General – doubtless with Party approval.

Siklósi's professional skills made him a fascinating proposition. He was neither a classical Party *apparatchik*, nor a staff writer (he was practically unknown as a man of letters), but a wonderful manager with the instincts of a real businessman. He understood that step-by-step reforms alone would not suffice to establish a new pact with the journalists, but that actions were needed to improve their living conditions, and that these, together with the reforms, could create a stable and loyal majority around the new Kadar model. The model was not self-evident for the Kadarist *agit-prop* people, but he could offer them some guarantees and in this way he cleared more space for further actions. In the early 1960s he created the journalist club described above, reinstated a health insurance scheme which offered special services to journalists – much better than the national health plan – and created exchange programmes for professional trips aboard in a country where foreign travel was a truly rare privilege for practising journalists. He was even able to attract funding from state sources and industrial donations for journalist vacation homes. The largest and best of these was a special hotel in Balatonszeplak, an elegant spa by the largest lake in Hungary.

Almost from the beginning the Association offered exchange quotas for other Eastern European journalist unions and started to use the IOJ as a symbol of its foreign network. In the case of the vacation hotel this was actually a persuasive argument when applying for direct investments in it from the Hungarian state.

Siklósi and his friends understood that by using the IOJ as an umbrella they could create themselves more room to manoeuvre with the local State and Party control. At the same time, the Hungarian economic reform of the 1960s and the softening Party control of the press created for the IOJ leadership a unique window of opportunity not only to implement projects for training foreign journalists and creating international networks of specialist journalists, but also to establish commercial enterprises for generating revenue. These were probably more advanced than anything in pre-1968 Czechoslovakia and not available anywhere else in the Communist countries. Siklósi was elected as IOJ Treasurer in 1966 and he held that position until 1974.

The Hungarians and the IOJ used the emerging options for joint future actions. In this development an important role was played in the early 1970s by a Budapest-based Russian emissary, Sergej Jerofeev. He was not a Russian supervisor but an asylum seeker in a strange form. Having been first Vice-President (practically executive director) of the Soviet Union of Journalists in Moscow in the Khrushchev era, Jerofeev was dismissed after the 1964 coup against him. First he was sent to the IOJ in Prague, and later to Budapest. As an energetic man he disliked being driven into exile even in those sweet forms, but, being a democratic and gently individual he was very easygoing in his local contacts. However, in 1973 he was recalled to Moscow. His adult son and his Jewish daughter-in-law left Russia for the West, after which he was no longer eligible even for sweet exile. He died relatively young at home, and was never replaced as a Budapest-based IOJ coordinator either by a former media manager, or anybody else from Russia or Prague.

As early as in 1962 the IOJ organized a congress in Budapest – with 200 journalists from 60 countries, demonstrating its ability to support the Kadar government, which was still quite isolated internationally due to its post-1956 revanchist politics. In that congress the IOJ mandated the establishment of an International Journalist Training Center in Budapest and decided to formalize the IOJ relationship with the Balatonszeplak vacation hotel and later to extend it with a second building – the ownership still remaining with MUOSZ. The next IOJ congress in 1966 elected Siklósi Treasurer of the IOJ.

In 1966 the Hungarian Association organized in Balatonszeplak a Pan-European journalism conference, where informal contacts took place between representatives of the IOJ and the FIJ, its Western counterpart.

The years until 1973–74 were the best in Siklósi's life. He was the most appropriate East European media manager for that time – able to manipulate, open to legally permitted but unorthodox financial solutions, sensitive to others' initiatives. He and the IOJ established in Hungary international commercial publishers, film studios, journals, earning money for the IOJ – a small empire of modern media enterprises operating in that twilight zone of what was possible and permitted in a Communist country of the 1960–70s. Their *INTERPRESS Magazine* published as a monthly for the small Hungarian market had in its heyday a circulation of 240,000. Siklósi found a manager to run the Hungarian IOJ empire: Gyorgy Stark, a man able to operate between the legal and the quasi-legal, almost a "Western entrepreneur" in some eyes, or a minor gangster in the eyes of others.

In 1974 Siklósi was dismissed from his post of Secretary General of MUOSZ. He was not excluded from the actual media elite but moved from political to economic-managerial functions. In the next 15 years, until his retirement, he was the executive director of the largest Hungarian newspaper publisher (first Lapkiado, later Pallas). He was again efficient, now without formal ties, but continued to cooperate with and even control the Hungarian IOJ empire for a few more years.

In the 1970s the age of reforms was over in Hungary, Party *apparatchiks* pushed MUOSZ to elect a new Secretary General: Andras Kiraly, a former Head of the Press division in the Budapest Party apparatus. Formally the IOJ functions of Siklósi – constituting an extraordinary case at that time – were automatically transferred to Kiraly. I did not know him personally, but as far as I remember, he was in no way outstanding. I cannot say how the IOJ reacted to his nomination. But later in Prague they seemed to like him: when in 1983, reacting to the critics inside MUOSZ he was replaced in Budapest as Secretary General, he could continue to function as the IOJ Treasurer.

Meanwhile, inside Hungary Stark continued to operate the IOJ empire. The Foreign Ministry continued favourable towards its projects, so they condoned its further commercial actions and partial transfers of money to Prague.

The Balatonszeplak vacation enterprise continued as a popular international place not only in the 1970s but also in the 1980s. For that generation of media elites it established itself as one of the most desirable locations of the Kadarist regime. Leading editors, the first TV anchors, the first generation of well established Hungarian and East European movie-makers, foreign correspondents of big Hungarian national dailies – a very special mixture of those obedient to the regime and the famous and talented of that time mixed with international journalists emulating the lifestyle of their opposite numbers in the West.

Later in the 1980s a smaller resort was established in Gödöllö, a provincial town outside Budapest. This was an exclusive hideaway for the elite of the elite, with accommodation in bungalows, a dining hall with superb cuisine, a swimming pool, a sauna and a tennis court. There the IOJ and MUOSZ leadership as well as their special guests could enjoy the good life.

The International Training Center continued to function with a clientele from the Third World journalist associations. The original broader educational perspectives disappeared, but in 1974–80 a new building was granted to them from Hungarian governmental sources. The directors of the Center were usually former press attachés or other people from the Foreign Ministry, continuing to play their little games with similar Western structures and counterparts. That part of activities, in the delightful Buda hills in an elegant building, was isolated from the Hungarian media training and communication research of the time, and also from the routine life in the national Association.

By and large, in the 1970s the IOJ with its Hungarian institutions was an important window on the world – a vantage point of modernity and the *Dolce Vita* for the Hungarian media elites, contributing to a strange feeling of stability and relative comfort in the Kadarist model. For the Hungarian media elite the IOJ was not a "progressive", "leftist" or "communist" journalists' organization, but a large international body of the profession incorporating them. Most of them were not interested in the political agenda of the organization, and to a certain degree they were apolitical also in their everyday opinions. At the same time they felt a sort of deprivation of globalism in their lives. The local IOJ projects offered them a set of alternative feelings, adding to their direct experience and real environment.

ALICE PALMER: THE IOJ AND THE AMERICAN BLACK PRESS*

In 1982 Richard Durham, author, radio dramatist, and founding editor of the *Muhammad Speaks* newspaper, with the largest black readership in the US, asked Edward (Buzz) Palmer, Co-Chair of the Black Press Institute (BPI), to meet Finnish Professor Kaarle Nordenstreng, President of the IOJ, at the St. Louis airport during his stopover. BPI's Co-Chair, Dr. Alice Palmer and Professor Jan Carew (author, poet, developer of early Black Studies programs at Princeton and Rutgers universities, and Professor and Founding Chair of the African American Studies Department at Northwestern University) met with Prof. Nordenstreng and told him about the BPI's intention to expand the world views of black journalists through their publication, *The Black Press Review*. Without hesitation, Nordenstreng handed Carew and Palmer $100. Alongside Richard Durham, he became one of the first financial supporters of the BPI.

At one of Nordenstreng's later visits to the US, Buzz Palmer said to him that it would be very productive for members of the black press, led by the BPI, to receive first-hand knowledge of countries in Eastern Europe and the USSR to make their own assessments of these areas. A week later Nordenstreng sent Palmer a telegram tasking him to put together a delegation of 15 black journalists. Members of the delegation were chosen for their high journalistic standards, for geographical and gender representation, and as part of a mix of black journalists who worked for black newspapers and for mainstream media. The delegation visited Moscow, Prague, East Berlin, and smaller towns, meeting with journalists, officials and NGOs. They had interviews with *Izvestia* and *Pravda*.

The BPI and the IOJ also worked on other joint programs. With the assistance of the IOJ, the BPI organized exchanges with USSR journalists and with the Syndicate of Mexican Journalists. Soviet journalists visited the U.S. to meet with black journalists and NGOs in Atlanta, Chicago, and Washington, DC, and to speak at major universities in Chicago and the DC area. Rafael Moseev, International Secretary of the Soviet Union of Journalists, spoke at the University of Illinois at Chicago, met with the President of the University of Maryland, and met with Dr. Frank Morris, Dean of Graduate Studies at the Historically Black University Morgan State. He also met with the board of the *Chicago Defender*, a legendary black newspaper.

The Mexican Syndicate hosted a BPI-led delegation for meetings in Mexico City, including one with a former President of Mexico. The IOJ also arranged for Ohio University Political Science Professor Robert Rhodes to

* The author was IOJ Vice-President 1986–91. Written in December 2015.

have observer status at the United Nations, which gave the BPI additional entry to international affairs. A planned exchange between Black American and Russian scholars, in cooperation with the Canadian/USA Institute, never materialized as the USSR imploded in the late 1980s.

The IOJ-BPI joint programs enabled black journalists to take their own measures of issues in areas of the world too often dismissed or stereotyped by mainstream Western media and scholars. For example, during one IOJ conference in Moscow, Alice Palmer and other Western and developing country journalists visited Patrice Lumumba University, which provided free education primarily in science and engineering to students from developing countries in Africa, Asia, and the Middle East. Although the equipment and facility would not compare with advanced Western universities, the level of educational rigor was high, and students from villages and small towns who were not likely candidates for scholarships to Western universities were being educated to the benefit of their country's advancement. During this visit, Alice Palmer met Charles Chikerema, Editor of the *Daily Herald* in Zimbabwe, with whom the BPI developed bi-lateral relations.

Alice Palmer served as one of the IOJ Vice-Presidents in 1986–90 and headed the IOJ Peace Committee. She went to a women's conference outside Moscow, which brought together women from anti-apartheid and civil rights organizations that early on recognized the significant role women must play in all areas. It was attended by the wives of many of the ANC freedom fighters, who were still imprisoned at the time.

A special project with a permanent outcome was the IOJ's hosting of Jan Carew in Prague for a few months in 1984 while he wrote his book on the revolutionary history of Grenada, *Grenada: The Hour Will Strike Again*. In the Acknowledgements of his book Carew writes: "Special thanks must go to Buzz and Alice Palmer, my colleagues at the Black Press Institute. It was Buzz's idea that the history should be written at this time. The International Organization of Journalists press directors and editors were very discrete, helpful, and left the entire business of the historical content of the work to me. And special thanks are due to all those who treated me with such warmth and hospitality during my sojourn in Prague. Renewing my acquaintance with that marvelous city after thirty years was an experience that was very rewarding." Moreover, in *Episodes in My Life: The Autobiography of Jan Carew* (2015), Carew writes: "I left Prague in 1951 [where I had been a student for 2 years], not expecting to return, but found myself returning in the mid-1980s. I had wanted to write a book on Grenada following the US invasion in 1983 and was invited by the International Organization of Journalists to complete my work in Prague. Therefore, as a guest of the IOJ, I was provided comfortable lodging for several months. And two years later, the IOJ published my history *Grenada: The Hour Will Strike Again*."

Regarding the BPI's involvement in the IOJ governing bodies, Buzz Palmer represented Alice in crucial Presidium sessions in 1990 in Estoril, Portugal (January) and in Balaton, Hungary (May). In Estoril he was calling for a contingency plan in case the ongoing Velvet Revolution in Czechoslovakia would break the political and economic base of the headquarters. He was unimpressed by Vice-President Rollemberg's assessment and proposals to meet the challenge. In Hungary, Buzz's plane to Budapest arrived late, and although he took a taxi to the meeting place at Lake Balaton, he missed the crucial vote on the Secretary General, thus 'helping' Gerard Gatinot to beat Bernd Rayer.

One of the final meetings of the IOJ was in Sana'a (Yemen) in October 1991, attended again by Buzz Palmer. He was dismayed to see opportunistic members of the organization, anticipating its demise, attempting to transfer the IOJ's financial assets to their own organizations. The IOJ had significant holdings and had been an economic engine in Czechoslovakia's infrastructure. Particularly ignoble was the representative of the French syndicate Gatinot, who, as newly elected Secretary General, was claimed to have brought significant amounts of money from Harare to Paris. In Sana'a the scurrilous attacks on former President Nordenstreng, charging him with mismanagement, were the most heinous of those final days.

In hindsight, the IOJ at its height was the only journalist organization that regularly brought together journalists from around the world with different ideological and political interests, from small and large papers and media outlets, to address matters of world interest and those concerning the rights and safety of journalists. At a time when the world has acknowledged its interconnectedness, the gaping void left by the demise of the IOJ is even more deeply troubling as there is no venue now for such broad-based international gatherings. How enlightening it would be to meet regularly with journalists from the BRICS countries as that consortium evolves, and from Greece and other countries as they struggle with debilitating, destructive economic downturns. Moreover, the direct connections to organizations such as the Non-Aligned Movement when the IOJ sent representatives to work with people such as the late Professor Archie Singham at the UN have been lost.

As the world wades through the troubling morass of antipathies and sharp divisions between rich and poor, racial animosities, anger against immigrants and the buying-up of media and politicians, the IOJ will be sorely missed.

CHRISTOPHER MUZAVAZI: FROM HEYDAY TO CHAOS*

I had never heard of the IOJ until 1985, when I became secretary of the then newly formed Zimbabwe Union of Journalists (ZUJ). I was a news reporter on the national television and radio broadcast based in the country's second largest city, Bulawayo. In 1986 an invitation from the IOJ arrived for a ZUJ delegation to attend the 10th IOJ Congress in Sofia (Bulgaria). We accepted the invitation. A two-man delegation, chairman Charles Chikerema and I, attended. The conference opened with a devastating announcement for us from the Southern Africa region – the President of Mozambique, Samora Machel, had just died in a plane crash. I lost track of the opening speeches, because I was seeking out the Mozambican colleague Manuel Tomé, who was leaving the conference to return home.

I was familiar with the themes of the conference, most of which emanated from the UNESCO debate of the time – the quest for a New International Information and Communication Order aimed at correcting the bias that came with the western hegemony on the flow of news around the world. As an activist by default, I was also tied to solidarity with the people of South Africa and Namibia fighting against the hideous apartheid as well as with the states of Southern Africa subjected to acts of military destabilisation by the Pretoria regime. Moreover, I felt solidarity with the people of Palestine – this was the time of the Intifada in its infancy. And I naturally thought that journalists had a duty to promote peace among nations as opposed to war mongering.

By the end of the congress, Chikerema was elected to the IOJ Presidium. I was co-opted onto the Peace Committee, which was charged with the task of raising awareness to the perils of nuclear armament. I returned to Harare a week later, as a fringe member of the IOJ structure. About nine months later, I received an invitation to attend a meeting of my IOJ Committee in Prague. The meeting took place at the Inter-Continental Hotel, a couple of hundred metres away from the IOJ headquarters in *Pařížská Street*. The Committee was chaired by Alice Palmer from the Chicago-based Black Press Institute. For me it was educative and enlightening as regards the then current contemporary debates about armament and how to network with peace activists in both industrialised and developing countries.

Chikerema attended an IOJ Presidium meeting in Brasilia in 1988. Upon his return, he informed me that the IOJ was seeking an African at the Secretariat and that the African members of the Presidium had asked Zimbabwe to fill the post. Someone in Brasilia had mentioned that I would be suitable as

* The author was IOJ Secretary for Africa 1988–92. Written in January 2016.

I was already involved in the Peace and Disarmament Committee. The Secretary for Africa, Bernd Rayer from the GDR, visited Zimbabwe in June 1988, to formalise the posting.

As the time of my departure approached, I went around the media houses bidding farewell to colleagues and friends. When I called in at the national news agency, its Editor-in-Chief remarked that the IOJ was a Soviet Union front. I dismissed his remark by saying that's what the Western media claim.

In July 1988 I arrived back in Prague to take up my post. My first assignment took me back to Zimbabwe, to prepare a meeting for the launching of the Federation of Southern African Journalists, which was to work under the auspices of the IOJ. This brought in national journalist organisations from the Southern African region, Angola, Botswana, Lesotho, Mozambique, Tanzania, Zambia and the host country Zimbabwe, and from the liberation movements of South Africa, the African National Congress (ANC) and Pan-Africanist Congress (PAC). Also attending this conference was the then secretary general of the International Federation of Journalists (IFJ), Aidan White. He had just been in South Africa hosted by the Media Workers' Association of South Africa (MWASA). On the Harare programme he was an observer, but I soon realised he wanted the same level of participation as the IOJ. I told him that the event was run by Southern African journalists who determined the level of participation of the invitees. Just a week earlier I had attended a Nordic journalists union seminar where I came to realise that there was a battle for the mind of the Southern African media in the context of the Cold War. The Nordic unions appeared as soft peddlers of Western values, whereas others like Aidan White were Cold War warriors.

PRAGUE

I returned to Prague as summer 1988 ended. It was still sunny and warm, and tourists were still teeming in the Old Town quarters within which the IOJ was located in a building belonging to the Union of Czechoslovak Journalists. The Secretariat occupied the entire third floor. My department, the Secretariat for Africa, had three offices, one for myself, the other two for my colleague Bernd Rayer from the German Democratic Republic (GDR) and three Czech assistants. The Secretariat consisted of delegates from Finland, the GDR, Poland, Romania, Bulgaria, the Soviet Union and Cuba. The colleagues from Finland, Poland, Bulgaria, Romania and Cuba had been journalism practitioners. In addition, Secretary General Ulčák had brought with him to the IOJ a Palestinian advisor, Mazen Husseini.

The Secretariat work ranged from regular communication with member organisations to advocacy and campaigning. This involved travelling, which was most informative and revealing, especially about the reality of underdevelopment in Africa. I visited altogether no less than twenty countries in Europe, Africa and Asia, attending meetings and conferences.

I lived in *Jižní Město*, the South Town, just off the motorway to Moravia and on to Vienna. During a weekend in early September 1989, I noted an unusually high number on GDR registered Trabants fuelling and heading eastwards. I guessed they were heading for Hungary, but wondered why, because the summer holiday season had ended. Later that week there were stories in the BBC External service and British daily newspapers (which were my only news source), that groups of East German tourists to Hungary had jumped the border into Austria, seeking an onward move to West Germany. Some reportedly occupied the West German Embassy in Hungary requesting political asylum in West Germany. It dawned on me that these must be the motorists I had seen and had mistaken them for out-of-season holidaymakers. It did not occur to me then that I had witnessed part of an unfolding historic momentum and that it was coming home soon. The Honecker regime fell shortly afterwards.

On 13 November I thought I heard chanting and looked out of the office window, which was on the third floor in the *Pařížská Street*. I could see a small procession walking from the direction of the International Union of Students towards the Old Town Square. I realised later that the procession had made its way to *Václavské náměstí*. The next day, at almost the same time, the demonstrators marched on *Pařížská Street*, and it happened all week, growing bigger by the day. The final destination was the same square. On the evening of Friday November 17th, police took action against the student demonstrators – action that led to the fall of the communist government.

The following week, the revolution reached the third floor. The IOJ received a letter from our hosts, the Union of Czechoslovak Journalists. It contained criticism of the IOJ for its lack of solidarity with Czechoslovak journalists during the communist rule. This was unexpected. It signalled that the IOJ Secretariat was facing a crisis.

The IOJ President soon arrived in Prague. In the hastily convened meeting he pointed out that the biggest threat to the IOJ was the destabilization of the IOJ enterprises. The IOJ's existence depended on the enterprises which had grown to the equivalent of a major company. The Czech colleagues did not say much during this meeting. I could only assume they were confounded by the unfolding situation.

There was soon a demand that the Secretariat vacate the premises. Fortunately the IOJ had been refurbishing a building in *Celetná Street* across the Old Town Square. I was the first one among the secretaries to move into the new building. It was spectacular. While the facade was unaltered, the interior was modernised with a new elevator, chandeliers in the hallways on all floors. The offices had desktop personal computers, with the software made in the IOJ.

In January 1990 a Presidium meeting in Portugal was the earliest opportunity for the IOJ's highest body between congresses to discuss the political change around us. The meeting was well attended, with delegations from all the regions of the world. However, there was a notable absence: no delegates were from the Union of Czechoslovak Journalists. The IOJ Secretary General read a letter to the meeting from the Syndicate of Bohemian and Moravian Journalists which stated that the Czechoslovak Union of Journalists was no more. In its place were two Syndicates, one of Bohemia and Moravia, and the other of Slovakia. The letter also stated that these two syndicates were yet to decide about their international affiliation. This was an alarming development because it meant that the IOJ had no affiliate in its host country.

The Presidium witnessed a heated debate about what happened around the IOJ and what the IOJ should do (as covered in Chapter 9 above), but it ended inconclusively. We returned to Prague none the wiser, if not more confused and apprehensive about the fate of the Secretariat.

The priority in Prague was meeting the representatives of the Czech Syndicate. The Czech representatives agreed to meet the IOJ delegation on 17 February 1990 in the nearby Inter-Continental Hotel. The IOJ delegation consisted of President Nordenstreng and four members of the Secretariat: myself, Leena Paukku from Finland, Bernd Rayer from the GDR, and Miguel Rivero from Cuba, with Czech journalist Dana Braun as interpreter. The Syndicate delegation consisted of two men: V. Bystrov and A. Černý, Vice Chairs of the Syndicate. Bystrov insisted that the meeting was informal as the new Syndicate did not have a mandate to officially meet the IOJ. He said that the Syndicate did not see itself as being in conflict or crisis with the IOJ, but that it was the IOJ that was facing a crisis in its relation with organisations in the host country (see Appendix 22).

It soon became clear that the issue had evolved from reforms to an ideological paradigm shift. It was apparent that the Czech Syndicate and their Slovak counterpart were influenced by the dynamics of the political landscape. The socialist reformers were losing ground to those of the conservative right-wing with full-blown drive to market forms. In this situation the IOJ was deemed totally incompatible with the emerging new order.

Bystrov and Černý told us that the Syndicate was reviewing and evaluating developments over a 42-year period from 1948, and not from the Prague Spring only, as initially intended. Bystrov stated that 2,000 journalists had been persecuted during that period. While the IOJ was not liable for these persecutions, it had neglected these incidents during the entire period. The persecuted journalists in Czechoslovakia got no support from the IOJ. Černý acknowledged that the IOJ had done a lot for journalists in developing countries and progressive journalists in Western countries, but nothing for Czech journalists or for journalists in the Socialist countries for that matter. He added that the Czech Syndicate was interested in establishing contacts with journalists who had been persecuted by totalitarian regimes in Eastern Europe.

Earlier in February, Ulčák had announced that he was ready to resign as Secretary General, saying he was doing so to allow the IOJ to overcome its difficulties in the host country. The Secretariat arranged an enlarged meeting with some Vice-Presidents and several representatives of member unions. It was evident that the IOJ leaders from abroad were no wiser regarding the problem at hand. Some of them, notably those from Latin America, did not approve the Secretary General's resignation, saying it was for the Presidium or Congress to approve. There was a proposal by one of the African Vice-Presidents, George Izobo of Nigeria, that the IOJ send a delegation to visit Eastern Europe, to talk to unions in that region. There was also a suggestion from IOJ Brazilian Vice-President Armando Rollemberg to invite Nelson Mandela to Prague (he had been released from prison only a couple of months before). This rather bemused me as I had just returned from South Africa and was more attuned to political developments there. Rollemberg had yet another bemusing proposal, that the IOJ bring from Brazil a Lambada dancing troupe to Prague to charm the Czechoslovak citizens.

PRESIDIUM IN HUNGARY AND ABORTED EXECUTIVE COMMITTEE IN AMMAN

In May 1990 a Presidium meeting was convened by Lake Balaton (Hungary) to appoint an acting Secretary General and to set the date for an Executive Committee meeting which in turn would decide on the next venue and date for the Congress. The outcome of this meeting is something that I partly blame myself for. I had not anticipated that the choice of an acting Secretary would be taken by a vote. I had heard only recently that Vice-President Chikerema was not coming. I should have requested from him a written mandate for a vote in the proceedings of the Presidium.

The Presidium proceedings continued with what had become characteristic of the IOJ meetings of the time – arguments and recriminations. Some were calling for the President to step down with the Secretary General. When it was time for nominations for the post of acting Secretary General, Gérard Gatinot produced a letter from his Union proposing him for the office. The other nominee was Bernd Rayer. I explored the possibility of casting Chikerema's vote. One of the African Vice-Presidents, B.S. Mollet from the Republic of Congo, objected, saying I should stick to

Secretariat affairs. I was among those who believed that Gatinot was not suitable for the job. I did not think he had experience of working with a team. The delegate of the US Black Press Institute, Edward "Buzz" Palmer, with whom I shared similar positions on the current crisis, was running late for the meeting and missed the vote.

The vote came and Gatinot won by a single vote. My heart sank. I managed to catch the faces of IOJ enterprises senior managers who were attending as observers. Their countenances fell. I could tell that they, too, were disappointed. After a break Palmer arrived and apologised, stating that he would have voted for Rayer. Had he arrived in time and had I obtained a mandate from Chikerema, the outcome would certainly have been different. Rayer would have been attentive to the criticisms by the Czech Syndicate and also appreciated by them, given that there had been a profound change in his own country. The IOJ would have, arguably, not gone the way it did after that meeting.

Back in Prague, the Czech Syndicate refused to meet delegations from the IOJ even informally. This was undoubtedly their reaction to the outcome of the Presidium. They were unimpressed by Gatinot's election.

The Presidium decided to hold its next Executive Committee meeting in Amman Jordan. With the war looming in the Gulf, following Iraq's invasion of Kuwait, there was concern about that venue. The IOJ Secretariat was divided again. There was concern for both personal safety and the politics of it. The Czech staff was not keen on travelling to Amman, nor were some members of the Executive Committee. There was a rumour doing the rounds in Prague that if the IOJ went to Amman, expulsion from Prague would be immediate. Others insisted on going to Amman. There were good arguments for Amman, that the IOJ must be seen to be continuing solidarity with Arab colleagues. I was, however, thinking of the political implications regarding the base in Prague and opposed the Amman venue – to impress the Czech journalists, the Czech IOJ enterprise staff and the government that we were earnestly attempting to reform the organisation. In the end, the Amman meeting was aborted and an Executive Committee was to be convened in Paris.

EXECUTIVE COMMITTEE IN PARIS AND CONGRESS IN HARARE

The Executive Committee in Paris in November 1990 was the largest meeting the IOJ had convened since the political crisis began. It was a year after the "Velvet Revolution" in Prague. The atmosphere in Paris was as toxic as had been experienced in the preceding meetings since the onset of the crisis.

The main business of the Executive Committee was to find an agreeable venue for the Congress. The African delegates lobbied successfully for the congress to be held on their continent. They chose Harare (Zimbabwe) as a venue. I was not exactly keen on this, only because the ZUJ had a new leadership, most of whom were new to the task, and as such did not have the experience to host a conference of this magnitude. Chikerema shared my concern. I was now concerned that Harare should not turn out to be the necropolis of the IOJ.

For me, the main objective of the Congress was to decide on the future of the IOJ. It needed to demonstrate that it was turning over a new page in its history. A wrong choice for the position of President and Secretary General would have meant the end of the IOJ, at least in Prague. I could not see the IOJ surviving outside the Czech Republic. President Nordenstreng and I thought already in March 1990 that a high-profile journalist from the global South should be found as a candidate for the President and we ended up with Zwelakhe Sisulu from South Africa, at that time Editor-in-chief of the newspaper *New Nation* and son of the legendary Walter Sisulu who had been with Nelson Mandela on Robin Island. We both met Zwselakhe in Johannesburg on separate trips and suggested he consider running for the position of the IOJ President. I called him later and he said that he had agonised over the issue, but given the pressure of his anti-Apartheid work, and the demands of the IOJ work in this current crisis, he would fail in both. He would not stand. President Nordenstreng now looked at Armando Rollemberg from Brazil as a candidate for President – a trade union leader and the head of the second largest member union of the IOJ.

A colleague from the South African IOJ affiliate suggested to me that I should stand for the position of Deputy Secretary General saying I now had the necessary experience. The IOJ President was diligently trying to find a combination of leadership that would make the IOJ acceptable to the new political order in the host country and also move the organisation forward in the changed international political environment. He suggested that I stand for the post of Secretary General. The figures we had suggested that if Rollemberg and I were presented as a team, we would carry a majority of the votes. We thought we had the support of most European and Africans delegates, minus the Nigerians, Congolese and Senegalese. When the vote came, I lost to Gatinot. I was nominated again for the position of Deputy Secretary General, running against Husseini. The ZUJ delegates assured me that I had sufficient support to win the post. However, Husseini was promoted by the Palestine solidarity card and I lost again.

The following morning, one of the Czech secretarial staff introduced me to a gentleman from the Czech embassy in Harare. Shaking my hand, he said the outcome of the elections was unfortunate. I took it to mean that the election of Gatinot was a mistake.

AFTER HARARE

I arrived back in Prague on 7 February 1991. My colleague Rayer informed me that the situation there resembled a standoff. There was no communication among the secretaries. There were neither morning meetings of the Secretariat nor other customary meetings. All correspondence, incoming or outgoing, was being vetted by Husseini. Rayer confided to me that Gatinot had requested for half a million francs to be transferred to him in Paris for the purposes of purchasing a building for the IOJ. The IOJ Director of Enterprises had, rightly, said such a decision had to be made by the Executive Committee and not by him alone.

Gatinot hosted a reception to celebrate his election as Secretary General. Leena Paukku and I were the only secretaries who attended. Gatinot said he had heard that there was a perception that he was weak. He said that he was going to prove otherwise in four weeks' time.

The week February 11–15 gave us a taste of what was coming. That week the Russian secretary Vladimir Artyomov was summoned to the Secretary General's office. He was handed a letter written in French dismissing him from the Secretariat at the end of February. A few days later the Polish Secretary Marek Jurkowicz also received a dismissal letter to leave the Secretariat in ten days. Artyomov left on 1 March. No farewell. He left in silence, the secretary from what was supposed to be the most influential member union in the IOJ.

In March 1991 members of the Executive Committee came to Prague for a meeting. I picked up Vice-President Manuel Tomé at the airport. Tomé enquired about the situation at the Secretariat as we made our way to the office. I briefed him on what was going on. He did not seem to be overly surprised, let alone alarmed. He seemed content with his position as Vice-President. He was, however, critical of former IOJ President Nordenstreng for what he called manipulating opinions. As regards myself, he said I had been manipulated by Nordenstreng into running for the post of Secretary General.

Tomé probably did not know that my duties at the Secretariat had not been limited to matters of African unions only. Ulcak had informed me soon after my coming to Prague that I was not only secretary for Africa, but an IOJ secretary. In my day-to-day work I got involved in a range of Secretariat matters and I had indeed intimate knowledge of core IOJ issues. Therefore I saw no reason why I should not have competed for the post of the Secretary General.

I was surprised that some of the colleagues wanted Gatinot to stand unopposed despite his manifest ineptitude for the job. I was also disappointed that Tomé doubted my suitability for the position. Paukku and I were the only ones who had experience in real independent organising trade unions.

I had comprehensive knowledge of the western media and had worked with foreign correspondents from the UK and USA and on odd occasions from Germany.

To our surprise the secretaries were excluded from the Executive Committee meeting – contrary to earlier custom. It turned out that the meeting marked a transformation of the IOJ Secretariat into the State of Absurdistan. Rollemberg claimed his position to be a full-time staff member at the Secretariat. He had brought with him a multi-lingual assistant, Ramses Ramos, also put on the IOJ payroll, although the IOJ was not short of translator staff. The new Treasurer from Romania, Marian Grigore, also demanded that his position be full-time to manage the IOJ finances, although the IOJ had a permanent accounting staff.

Word began to filter through to the IOJ that UNESCO was organising a conference in Windhoek, Namibia on Promoting an Independent and Pluralistic African Press from 29 April to 3 May 1991. The IOJ had not received an invitation, while the IFJ was invited – showing that the IOJ was being marginalised internationally. We demanded an invitation and subsequently got one. I was delegated to attend. This was my first IOJ duty since the Harare Congress.

In Windhoek I met Aidan White and the IJF President Mia Doornaert. At a social gathering one of the evenings, White referred to Gatinot as a Stalinist. This confirmed to me that IOJ–IFJ relations, with Gatinot leading the Secretariat, were not going to be easy. Doornaert did not engage in any conversation with me and I was convinced that she might not like to have anything to do with the IOJ.

Returning to Prague, there was yet another meeting of the IOJ Executive Committee. Again we were excluded. It was said that Gatinot did not want Rollemberg full time at the Secretariat. The EC abolished the tradition of regional representation at the Secretariat, which effectively made me redundant. Rayer and I had a meeting with US Vice-President Kevin Lynch, who briefed us about the deliberations. He informed us that the new Secretariat would have three departments: publications, training and trade unionism. Between Rayer and myself, we were the only ones with skills in training and trade unionism. Lynch promised to push us to run those departments. My contract now had two months to go. I realised that there was little possibility of my remaining in Prague. There were two other secretaries preferable to Gatinot and Husseini: Ivanov from Bulgaria and Rivero from Cuba. They did not have experience in any of the three departments, but they were loyal to Gatinot.

Tension persisted at the Secretariat. There was an Auditing Commission set up to verify some of the IOJ expenditures of the previous year, which seemed out of order. James Namakajo of Uganda, who was leading one of the auditing teams, informed me that he had received a letter from Husseini's lawyers threatening him with unspecified action if their client did not receive an apology from him. Namakajo saw this as intimidation, but stated that he was going to present the report to the EC as he saw the matter from the available evidence.

My contract at the Secretariat expired in June 1991 but it was extended for six months to allow me an orderly departure. At the end of August, Tomé arrived to lead the Secretariat, standing in for Rollemberg, who had extended his stay in Rio de Janeiro. It exposed to him the reality of the IOJ situation in Prague. After three weeks at the office, Tome summoned the remaining secretaries for a meeting, our very first as a collective in eight months since Harare. Rayer, Rivero, Ivanov and I attended. The four of us shared the same frustration at the lack of implementation of IOJ programmes and Tomé expressed his personal frustration as well over some of the programmes which were not implemented, notably the decentralisation of activities such as the lottery scheme aimed at raising funds at regional level. He said that while he accepted that this had been a transitional period, Rollemberg could not do everything on his own. There was a need for collective work. He left at the beginning of October.

A week after Tomé's departure, we were called to an enlarged Secretariat meeting. Attending were the four of us plus Husseini, Rollemberg and Alexander Angelov, Vice-President from Bulgaria. This was the first meeting we ever had with Rollemberg in the chair. There was nothing innovative in his presentation. He repeated what Tomé had already stated that there was a need to work collectively in the current crisis. At the end of the meeting, I was not convinced there was going to be any change in the working methods of Rollemberg and Gatinot.

A couple of days later we had another Secretariat meeting where Husseini produced a draft of the IOJ 1992 Action Plan. It was a very scaled down plan in comparison to the previous years. It was conceded that the IOJ could not afford to spend as it could in the past. During the nine months of 1991, it had spent a whopping 700,000 US$ through the executive meetings, auditing and investigation teams. Practically no actual programmes had been funded. A few days previously Chikerema had phoned me and was furious that the IOJ had not honoured its commitment to the Union of African Journalists (UAJ) of which he was Secretary General. The IOJ reserve was down to 6 million US$ from 11 million US$ in January that year. Various suggestions were made about how to save money. It was argued that there was no need to spend more than a million dollars between the Secretariat and projects.

There was again another appeal to work together. I reiterated in these meetings that the IOJ should not be an objective by itself but that its value came from what it did for the membership, a position that my colleague Rayer was going to repeat at another meeting. I do not think Rollemberg, Gatinot and Husseini paid attention to our sentiments. This was seen in the fact we were excluded from the Executive Council they organised in Sana'a (Yemen) about six weeks later. On his return from Sana'a, Rollemberg was his babbling self, saying nothing specific. We only learnt something when Husseini returned to the office on 16 December after a five weeks' absence. Both Rayer and I were dismissed from the Secretariat with immediate effect.

POSTSCRIPT

After 1992 I followed developments taking place at the IOJ through the International Institute of Journalism Berlin-Brandenburg.

By 1995 the IOJ only had 800,000 US$ left, having blown $9 million in four years. In the end, it was not the Czech Government or the Czech Syndicate that killed the IOJ five years after the Harare Congress. It was its own leadership after Harare that wilfully suffocated the IOJ to death. There was a toxic mixture of opportunists, self-seekers and the inept. They did little work, if any, to pursue the objectives of the IOJ. Instead, they behaved like a bunch of kids in a sweet shop.

The IOJ had no shareholders; it only had stakeholders, who had no ability to call the leadership to order. The Theatre of the Absurd, casting Rollemberg, Gatinot, Grigore and Husseini brought the mighty IOJ house down, with high drama and low humour and despair.

I was privileged in having worked at the IOJ Secretariat when it was at its best but despaired at witnessing its self-inflicted demise.

MICHEL DIARD: THE FRENCH FACTOR*

In the 20th century, journalists were facing a process of industrialization in the printed media as well as in TV and radio, where the trend was even more obvious, leading them to get organized and to initiate contacts with their colleagues from all over the world. The profession transformed itself into a wage-earning class aware of the necessity of defending their work conditions as intellectual workers under managerial pressures.

Our union, the Syndicat National des Journalistes – Confédération Générale du Travail (SNJ-CGT) was founded in 1937, when France was undergoing a total political transformation. Well-known journalists decided at the beginning of this new political period to join the workers' union movement – a powerful global union (CGT) in order to stand closer to other workers in France as well as abroad. Consequently, the SNJ-CGT was devoted to international solidarity, which represents a major part of its activities.

In 1946, when the IOJ was founded, there was in France only one union of journalists, the SNJ, which was a member of the global CGT. It was then the SNJ (CGT), but later the majority of the SNJ members decided to leave the global CGT and create an autonomous union. Those SNJ members who did not want to leave the CGT (progressive journalists with Socialist or Communist orientation) formed the SNJ-CGT, which remained as the French member union in the IOJ.

The SNJ-CGT contributed a lot to the IOJ. First, Jean-Maurice Hermann, General Secretary of the SNJ-CGT, was President of the IOJ from 1950 to 1976, and then came Gérard Gatinot, who was the head of the SNJ-CGT before becoming IOJ Vice-President from 1976 to 1990, and thereafter the IOJ Secretary General from 1990 to 1995. Finally, Jean-François Téaldi became an IOJ Vice-President for Europe in 1992 (replacing the Portuguese Vice-President after his union left the IOJ) and was elected again to this position in the last IOJ Congress in Amman in 1995.

For 45 years the SNJ-CGT leaders were loyal to the IOJ. This choice was deliberate as all of them worked for a reunification of the international movement of journalists. When the reunification finally came about at the end of the 1990s, it was due to the collapse of the IOJ after its 12th Congress in Amman in 1995.

The Amman Congress took place in a troubled atmosphere and was particularly embarrassing for our union. The Congress was opened on 28 January 1995, almost 24 hours behind schedule due to a sharp disagreement between

* The author was French delegate in the IOJ Congress in Amman (1995). Deputy General Secretary of the SNJ-CGT 1990–91, General Secretary 1991–2007. Written in June 2016, translated from French by Patrick Kamenka.

the Secretary General (Gérard Gatinot) and the Treasurer (Marian Grigore) concerning a financial issue in the IOJ budget. The outgoing Treasurer Grigore, said: "The document published in the so-called 'Treasurer's Report' was not the report I prepared. I refuse to read this document and put my name to a text which is not of my making." His report was based on the Auditing Commission for the years 1991–1994, which stated: "The IOJ is sick and therefore needs remedies. In January 1991 the IOJ had 10.3 million US dollars in bank reserves and four years later, here in Amman, we find ourselves with only $ 800,000."

The Secretary-General had prepared an alternative report, which tried to minimize the financial problems of the OIJ, but, above all, ignored the misappropriation of the outgoing management, including the lavish expenses of the leaders of Prague and the highly risky strategies of many organization-related businesses unrelated to journalism while providing the bulk of its resources. History will remember that the outgoing Secretary General Gatinot's report was unanimously rejected by the Congress.

All this exposed the symptoms of the deliquescence of the organization. The IOJ's activities were severely curtailed by internal disputes and many resignations of affiliates. After the "Velvet Revolution" in Czechoslovakia, the new government decided to expel the IOJ from the country. The government blamed the IOJ for its relationship with the former socialist regime and moreover denounced the role of tens of commercial enterprises owned by the IOJ and supposed to finance its headquarters and activities. Gérard Gatinot's nomination as the IOJ's Secretary General in 1990 was taken as provocation, while the Prague officials did not consider him to be a representative of a changing line declared by the IOJ – after he had been an IOJ leader for the past 14 years.

Under these circumstances, the SNJ-CGT began to question its role inside the international movement of journalists: should it continue as an affiliate of the IOJ and try to renew it, or should it join the IFJ along with other French unions, the SNJ and the CFDT? The attitude of Gérard Gatinot in Prague was criticized from inside our union, and during a meeting of its national committee in September 1994, the SNJ-CGT took the decision not to renew Gatinot's mandate as a member of the IOJ leadership to be elected in the Amman Congress and instead to put forward Jean-François Téaldi as its candidate. This decision was quite delicate concerning not only an activist, but also a former top leader of the union. In any case, the majority of our union members took the decision, which seemed to be most appropriate given the situation in the IOJ at the time.

Gatinot tried to overturn the decision made by the union. He initiated a so-called "Union of professionals for information and communication" composed of some of his close friends (among them even the head of a school of journalism) and he proposed that the delegates attending the Congress should become members of this association in order to have the opportunity to promote his candidacy. The delegates from the SNJ-CGT were forced to denounce this manœuvre from the rostrum as an attempt to save its former Secretary General. The vote was no surprise: affiliation of this association was refused and Gatinot lacked an organization competent to present his candidacy.

Jean-François Téaldi was elected as Vice-President for Europe. But a few months later, it was inevitable that the IOJ no longer had the capacity to work as it had exhausted the financial means to maintain any activities. Therefore the SNJ-CGT decided in June 1998 to become an affiliate of the IFJ and its membership became effective in 2000. However, our union never disaffiliated from the IOJ.

The affiliation to the IFJ was concluded after a painful process – on the one hand there was the conflict with Gatinot, who was still supported by some of our members, and also there was Hermann, who was respected by all for his support to unity between unions in France and the rest of the world. Yet joining the IFJ characterized the will of our union to contribute to the development of the international movement of journalists at a time when freedom of information was in danger, when the conditions of work were deteriorating, and when solidarity had to be not only symbolic but real.

RÜDIGER CLAUS: A JOURNALIST TRAINER'S PERSPECTIVE*

First of all I have to confess that I have never held an official position in a national, nor in an international association of journalists. I am a journalist who, after completing my journalism studies at the University of Leipzig in the early 1970s, joined the GDR (the former East German) television service. My office was in (East) Berlin and international contacts were not my field. The three letters I.O.J. were of no significance to me nor indeed to most journalists in the former GDR. The IOJ was a virtually unknown organization. The logo was to be seen in the annual solidarity bazaars and on the tickets of the International Solidarity Lottery, but it was merely a visual image.

This changed when I started to work as a lecturer at the International Institute of Journalism Berlin (IIJB) in 1984. I became a rank-and-file member of the Journalists' Association of the GDR, I found numerous publications on journalistic topics edited by the IOJ and intended for the training of journalists from Africa, Asia and Latin America. The then director of the Institute, Dr. Hans Treffkorn, had been an IOJ secretary in Prague until 1980. I learned that the IIJB cooperated closely with the IOJ and its network of journalistic training institutes on four continents. The IIJB was affiliated with the IOJ but never married to the organization as were the partner schools in Budapest and Prague, but this meant no financial dependence. I found in the diplomas presented to the IIJB students after the training courses that the Institute felt committed to the professional and ethical standards of journalists laid down in the IOJ documents.

I also learned that one of the IOJ's strengths was support for member organizations in the Third World in the form of opportunities to upgrade journalists' professional skills in workshops, seminars and courses in schools and institutes in Europe, Asia, Africa and Latin America.

In the 1980s the activities of the training units, either as part of the IOJ network of schools or affiliated to the organization, were monitored by the Coordinating Committee for the Training of Journalistic Personnel in and from the Developing Countries, founded at an IOJ Meeting in 1978 in Mexico City. The Committee was to be led by the Chairman of the Journalists' Association of the GDR and its secretary was the IIJB director. The Council's main task was to determine the major content of training, including the challenges of incipient digitalization and to harmonize the curricula of the schools.

The name was further changed to "IOJ Training Commission" and later to the "Council for Journalistic Training". What did not change was the leadership, which was in the hands of the IIJB and its director.

---

* The author was lecturer at the International Institute of Journalism in Berlin (IIJB) from 1984 and its director since 1994. Written in March 2017.

From 1984 to 1988 I was included in the work of the Commission and consequently I became more familiar with the IOJ, its work and its aims. When preparing and attending the Council meetings in Budapest (1984), Aden (1985), Berlin (1986) and Pyongyang (1987), I met representatives of the IOJ and of the partner schools in Prague, Budapest, Sofia, Aden, Havana, Accra and Luanda. Thus I myself became a member of the family. The last official meeting of the Council took place in Havana in 1988. Planned meetings in Luanda and Addis Ababa had to be cancelled due to the changes in 1989/1990.

The closest IIJB partner schools in Budapest and Prague were closed down in 1990, while the IIJB staff was busy adapting the Institute to the changing political, economic and legal environment arriving with the unification of Germany at the end of 1990. There was no welcoming party for the Institute in the all-German family of journalists and safeguarding its further existence was the most crucial issue. Apart from our training for Third World journalists which was never interrupted, international activities had no priority.

In the years between the IOJ congresses in Harare 1991 and Amman 1995 there were no substantial contacts between the IIJB and the IOJ officials. Occasional requests to Prague went unanswered. It was in autumn 1995 that I received a booklet about the Amman Congress and the results plus a personal letter from the new Secretary General, Antonio Nieva.

This was the beginning of a short but wonderful friendship. Tony had taken over the office in Prague charged with stabilizing the organization, but on a much smaller scale than before. What he found in Prague was a rather large staff and nearly empty bank accounts. He also found a lot of hostility and a spirit of obstruction. The situation in Prague was not easy for the Czech staff because the legal status of the IOJ was called into question. The newcomer with the firm intention of reorganizing the IOJ was not welcome. On his first visit to Berlin in late 1995, Tony wanted to meet the former IOJ secretary, Hans Treffkorn and spent hours with him in order to learn about the setup of the IOJ office and where to find various documents – there was no support from the Prague staff.

I will never forget how Tony told me about his sadness when he was forced to sack staff and how angry he was when he had to hire a security service for the headquarters to prevent the office equipment from "leaving" the house.

The IOJ was no longer the powerful and prosperous organization it had been five years earlier. Nevertheless, Tony tried to keep it alive and active. Several times he came to Berlin simply to have a rest and to talk with friends of whom he obviously had none in Prague. In May 1997 I was invited to travel with Tony and Treasurer Alexander Angelov to Amman to meet President Suleiman Al-Qudah and representatives of the Jordan media. One result of this visit was a Memorandum of Understanding between the IIJB and the

Jordanian Journalists' Association about support for Jordanian journalists through training facilities. Under this agreement, later in 1997, a one-week workshop on business reporting in Amman was organized and paid for by IIJB – probably the last training activity ever initiated by the IOJ.

The year 1997 found Tony desperately trying to maintain or renew the international links of the IOJ and to pave the way for co-existence with the IFJ. The last time I met him was in September 1997 in Sofia, Bulgaria, where we took part in UNESCO's European Seminar on Promoting Independent and Pluralistic Media. In October came the shock – IOJ lost its relentlessly working and fighting Secretary General and no successor was nominated. This was in fact the deathblow for the IOJ.

It was early in 1998 that I received a message from Phan Quang, Vietnam Journalists' Association, who was worried about the fate of the IOJ. He proposed holding a meeting of the IOJ executives soon in Germany. Given our long partnership with the IOJ I agreed to invite key members of the Executive Committee to have their meeting and to take part in the inauguration of a new IIJB building in March 1998. The preparatory formalities were done in cooperation with Josef Komárek, head of the IOJ enterprises in the Czech Republic.

This was the last meeting of the IOJ leaders. Later in Asia I was frequently asked about the situation of the IOJ. To find out the facts I travelled in 1999 to Prague and met Komárek in a small office in *Londýnská Street*. He described the problems with the enterprises and other property of the IOJ, how hard it was to sell the IOJ School in Prague. I learned that there was a division between the professional work and the business wing. Komárek had competence for business decisions only, while the IOJ staff remained under the competence of the elected President far away. The staff had no salaries, waiting for money from the sale of the School.

As of 2000 the IOJ disappeared from my radar, apart from contacts with former President Nordenstreng. For me its book was closed – the story of a great organization with noble aims and dedication to journalists of the poorer part of this world. Thank you, IOJ.

PHAN QUANG: MISSION ACCOMPLISHED, HERITAGE LIVES ON*

The IOJ was a familiar name among Vietnamese people, particularly those born during the war from the 1950s until the 1970s and growing up during one of the most difficult times, when Vietnam faced the consequences of war, economic recession, and isolation due to Western embargoes.

For more than 24,000 members of the Vietnam Journalists Association (VJA), the IOJ represents the International Principles of Professional Ethics in Journalism (1983), which serves as the basis for Vietnam's current Code of Ethics in Journalism. The IOJ also symbolizes the principle of protecting journalists in action. During the wars against the French, Americans, Chinese, and the Khmer Rouge, more than 400 Vietnamese journalists laid down their lives and were honored as martyrs by the Vietnamese State. At that time, the Vietnamese population was estimated at 25 million.

HISTORY OF VIETNAMESE JOURNALISTS AND THE IOJ

The Vietnam Journalists' Association (VJA) was established in April 1950, in the Viet Bac region, which housed the central organs of the resistance against the French, with Xuan Thuy, Editor-in-Chief of the daily *Cuu Quoc* (National Salvation) as its President. A VJA delegation, including Radio, the Voice of Vietnam Director Tran Lam and Thep Moi, editor of the weekly *Su That* (Truth) was sent to Finland to attend the third IOJ Congress in Helsinki (September 1950), where the VJA was officially admitted as an IOJ member. *Su That* was the predecessor of the current daily *Nhan Dan*.

As the border areas were under French control in the early 1950s, it was a difficult and dangerous journey for Tran Lam and Thep Moi to get out of Vietnam and reach Helsinki. Luckily, their return trip was much easier as the borders were cleared following the Vietnam People's Army's victory over the French Expeditionary Corps in the Far East led by Colonel Lepage and Colonel Charlton. In the daily *Cuu Quoc*, Thep Moi reported on the IOJ's strong support for Vietnam's war of resistance to achieve national independence. This was the first time the Vietnamese people had ever heard of the IOJ.

At the Potsdam conference in 1945, allied leaders decided to temporarily partition Vietnam along the 16th parallel. It was agreed that British forces would take the surrender of the Japanese forces in the South while Japanese troops in the North would surrender to China. With a green light from Brit-

* The author attended several IOJ meetings since 1974 and was IOJ Vice-President for Asia as of 1995. President of VJA 1989–2000. Written in January 2017, translated from Vietnamese by Nhat Quynh, Hong Hanh and Trinh Truong.

ain, the French army, by order of General De Gaulle, returned to the Far East in an attempt to once again impose their rule on Vietnam, Laos, and Cambodia, which they called "French Indochina". Due to a lack of accurate information, people, including the French, were unaware of the invasion. Some left-wing French parliamentarians even voted for the return of the French army to Indochina.

Leo Figueres, Editor-in-Chief of the paper *L'Avant Garde,* was among the first to reshape public opinion on the war in Vietnam. Figueres, a member of France's National Syndicate of Journalists (SNJ-CGT, IOJ member), visited Vietnam at the invitation of the VJA. In Viet Bac, he met and interviewed Ho Chi Minh and visited several organizations including the Viet Minh Front and military units. He also visited some liberated regions and met local people.

"What you have done is beyond my imagination. During the war against the Nazis, only small-sized newspapers were available in France and not on a regular basis. But you are able to issue large-sized newspapers daily, even weekly", Figueres could not contain his surprise during a tour of the premises of the newspaper *Cuu Quoc*. "I will tell the French people about France's filthy war in Vietnam. I will tell them that I've met Ho Chi Minh. He is still healthy and backed by a national unity bloc, which provides a solid foundation for him and the resistance", he added.

At a conference of journalists in France in July 1950, Figueres called on the participants to support Vietnam's war of resistance. On August 17, 1950, AFP reported that the French government had arrested Figueres, who was also a former parliamentarian from the Eastern Pyrenees and recently returned from the Viet Minh-controlled region in Indochina. He was charged with carrying his interview with Ho Chi Minh in the newspaper *L'Avant Garde*. The article sparked a heated debate in the French parliament.

After Figueres, some French press agencies and journalists went further to expose the crimes perpetrated by the French expeditionary force in Vietnam, creating a turning point in how the French public viewed the war.

For half a century, from 1945 until the late 1990s, Vietnam had constantly received generous support from IOJ leaders and member journalists, as well as non-IOJ journalists, who provided accurate and unbiased coverage of what was happening in Vietnam. Since its IOJ membership, Vietnam had participated in most of the organization's activities. Vietnamese journalists held a seat on the IOJ Presidium since 1966.

DEVELOPMENTS AFTER 1966

At the 6th Congress in Berlin in 1966, the Association of Patriotic and Democratic Journalists of South Vietnam also became an IOJ member and the journalist Nguyen Van Hieu from the liberated South Vietnam region was elected a member of the IOJ Presidium.

The IOJ gained the Vietnamese people's respect and appreciation due to the many distinguished foreign journalists, who were in South Vietnam before 1975 to inform the international community of Vietnam's just war, triggering global condemnation of the French colonialists and American imperialists. Some of those correspondents were killed on Vietnam's battlefields.

For the VJA, the visit to Vietnam by IOJ leaders like President Jean-Maurice Hermann, President Kaarle Nordenstreng and Secretary General Jiři Kubka during or after the war left lasting memories. The IOJ issued in February 1979 the "Statement of Ho Chi Minh City", condemning China's armed aggression against Vietnam in retaliation for Vietnamese volunteer soldiers' support for Cambodia's fight against the Khmer Rouge. One week later, the IOJ organized an international solidarity conference with Vietnam in Helsinki (Finland).

Following the 1975 victory, which culminated in national reunification, the VJA (whose operations covered the region from the 17th parallel to the North), and the Association of Patriotic and Democratic Journalists of South Vietnam, merged into one VJA. A conference to merge the two organizations was held in Hanoi on July 7, 1976. VJA became Vietnam's sole member of the IOJ. Adhering to Vietnam's external policy of independence, self-reliance, diversification, and multilateralization, the VJA has joined the Confederation of ASEAN Journalists (CAJ).

The IOJ influenced Vietnam and its journalists in the past half a century in three major aspects:

- The IOJ had consistently supported Vietnam's struggles for national independence, reunification, freedom, and happiness during the wars, post-war reconstruction, renewal, development, and international integration since 1946, when the organization was founded.
- The IOJ helped the VJA in training journalists. Before 1986, when Vietnam began its renewal policy, there was only one tertiary institution involved in educating would-be journalists. A few students were sent to foreign universities under scholarship programs funded by the Ministry of Education and foreign institutions. Professional IOJ schools including the Berlin Journalism Institute and the IOJ Journalism Schools in Budapest and Prague provided short courses for Vietnamese journalists. In April 1988, Phan Quang was in Havana for the 11th session of the IOJ Council for the Training of Journalists and invited to become a member of the Council headed by the President of GDR Union of Journalists E. Heinrich. The VJA planned to establish an IOJ journalism school in Hanoi with the help of the IOJ leadership and modest funding from UNESCO through the International Program for the Development of Communication (IPDC). Unfortunately, the plan went nowhere as the IOJ encountered difficulties due to changes in the world in

the 1990s, while journalism faculties were established at the National University in Hanoi and Ho Chi Minh City University. Yet the foundation laid by the IOJ enabled the VJA to build the Vietnam Journalists Training Center headquartered in the VJA building in Duong Dinh Nghe Street, Cau Giay District, Hanoi.

- The VJA attended all IOJ Congresses from Helsinki in 1950 to the last Congress in Amman in 1995, and all sessions of the IOJ Executive Committee and Presidium, including those taking place in Havana (Cuba) and Quito (Ecuador).

In all these years Vietnamese journalists tried to contribute to international media movements through the IOJ. This also gave us opportunities to learn from friends in other countries.

Personally I first joined the IOJ activities as a professional journalist in summer 1974, during the fierce war between Vietnam and the USA, when the Bulgarian government held an international exhibition of agricultural achievements in the ancient city of Plovdiv. I flew there from Vietnam via Tashkent, Moscow and Sofia. In that exhibition the IOJ Club of Agricultural Journalists held an international workshop on journalism for the development of agriculture, with the participation of journalists from different parts of the world. At the same time the GDR also introduced its agricultural achievements through an exhibition in the East German city of Leipzig and hosted an international conference on agricultural industrialization. Needless to say, these occasions were rewarding for us in a country with an underdeveloped economy mainly based on agriculture.

From 1982 on I served as a delegate of the VJA in several meetings of the IOJ leading bodies, sometimes representing VJA Chairman and IOJ Vice-President Ky Luu Quy, who continued until 1989, when I became VJA Chairman. I can say that along with my other activities in the international arena, the IOJ was a central factor taking me literally around the world to visit many countries in five continents.

In 1983 a seminar "Journalism for Peace" was held in Prague in a very broad framework. Over three thousand delegates from all continents, convened by the World Peace Council, gathered in the capital of Czechoslovakia to attend the World Assembly for Peace and Life Against Nuclear War. The activities at the Assembly were quite diverse: youth summer camp, women's meetings, dialogues between unions, between religions, and workshops among artists and journalists. The writer Nguyen Dinh Thi (1921–2003), Chairman of the Vietnam Writers' Workshop moderated literature seminars, and I myself as Chairman of the VJA, with the IOJ assistance, took care of the Press Conference.

All sessions of the IOJ also left their own marks. The meeting of the Presidium IOJ in Quito, Ecuador, in 1985, under the presidency of Kaarle Nordenstreng, remains in my mind as a special occasion. The programme issues and discussions were successfully conducted in a spirit of consensus. After the meeting, the hosts invited the Presidium to visit the Equator at latitude 0.00, longitude 78,27'9" at a height of 2,483 meters above sea level. Here is the Memorial to the French physicist La Condomine, who in 1736 led international scientists to measure the length of the Equator, thus establishing a metric measurement system used throughout the world today.

In order to attend the Presidium in Quito, I for my part had to undergo a longer journey halfway around the world. From Hanoi, I flew to Moscow and stayed there a few days to allow sufficient time to apply to the Embassy of Ecuador for an entry visa to Ecuador. From Moscow, I and the delegates from Asia, Eastern Europe and elsewhere used the Soviet airline Aeroflot to the capital city of Peru, Lima. The whole group stayed one day in Lima, waiting for a connecting flight in the equatorial direction. On the way home from Quito, we visited Havana and met with Cuban leader Fidel Castro, before returning to Moscow again using Aeroflot. From here, I had to wait to change flights to reach Hanoi.

In 1992, the Finnish Broadcasting Company organized an international seminar on mass communication and democracy, attended by directors of radio and television services from developing countries in Africa and Asia, where the public service media play a pivotal role in distributing information. I was invited as the Chief Editor of National Radio, the Voice of Vietnam, and also as Chairman of the VJA. Although the IOJ was not directly involved, the seminar took the same approach as several IOJ events during the past decade. These experiences gave us in Hanoi further inspiration and confidence to host in 1999 a conference of "ASEAN Press in 21st Century – Opportunities and Challenges". It issued the Hanoi Declaration "For a Free and Responsible Press", whereby the media, regardless of their governmental regimes, must serve first and foremost the freedom of speech of their respective peoples, while the press of all political orientations has the responsibility to provide truthful information for the benefit of its nation and to promote cooperation among countries for peace, mutual understanding and development.

LAST CONGRESS IN AMMAN

The VJA three-member delegation to the Amman Congress in 1995 was led by me as the VJA Chairman, and the other two delegates were from Hanoi and Ho Chi Minh City.

We felt uneasy about the opening session, which debated financial issues involving the previous leadership. The voting procedures to elect the new IOJ leadership were cumbersome. The election of leading Jordanian journalist Suleiman Al-Qudah to the post of IOJ President went smoothly thanks to a consensus. For the Asia-Oceania region, delegates from both India and Japan wanted to run for the Vice-Presidency, but eventually nominated a Vietnamese delegate, who was later elected. The voting continued throughout the whole afternoon and evening of January 31. The later at night it grew, the fewer participants remained, as a result of tiredness. The host country announced that the Congress should end before daybreak because the next day would be the first day of the Muslim fasting month of Ramadan. Departing from Amman, I felt this was the last Congress of the IOJ.

The new IOJ Secretary General, the well-known Filipino journalist Antonio N. Nieva, was energetic, responsible, and dedicated. He left his job, wife, and child in Manila to move to work in Prague, facing financial difficulties and an unfavorable political environment. Nevertheless, he worked hard to prepare for the next statutory meetings.

LAST EXECUTIVE COMMITTEE IN HANOI

The VJA offered to host the IOJ Executive Committee in Hanoi in July 1996, marking the 50th anniversary of the founding of the Organization. This was not foreseen in the Amman Congress, but we thought that this was the last chance for the Vietnamese to show their gratitude to the IOJ and foreign journalists who had supported and helped us through the most difficult times of our country.

The meeting was attended by representatives from 25 member countries, including IOJ Vice-Presidents Tubal Paez Hernandez from Cuba, Kevin P. Lynch from the USA, Jean-François Téaldi from France, and IOJ Honorary President Manuel Tomé from Mozambique. The Honorary President of the Confederation of ASEAN Journalists (CAJ), Bandhit Rajavatanadhanin, a Thai national, was invited to the opening ceremony.

The meeting was opened in Ba Dinh Hall, the site of Vietnam's National Assembly, with the attendance of Prime Minister Phan Van Khai and other senior leaders. Many foreign delegates showed their keen interest in two of the most prominent Vietnamese figures: General Vo Nguyen Giap, who was Deputy Prime Minister at that time, and Nguyen Thi Binh, Vice-President, former Foreign Minister, and chief negotiator of the Provisional Revolutionary Government of the Republic of South Vietnam at the Paris conference (1968–1973) on re-establishing peace in Vietnam.

After the opening speech by IOJ President Suleiman Al-Qudah and a report by Secretary General Antonio Nieva, a VJA representative presented the medal "For services to the cause of Vietnam's journalism" to key IOJ leaders including the IOJ President and the Honorary President of CAJ. IOJ leaders brought from Prague to Hanoi 20 a "Scroll of Honour" to acknowledge the

Vietnamese journalists who had contributed the most to IOJ activities over the past half century. Participants were briefed by Deputy Foreign Minister Vu Khoan about Vietnam's foreign policy, and visited places of interest in Hanoi.

At the closing ceremony, we thanked and bade goodbye to our foreign guests without saying "See you at the next session". We understood that this would be the last statutory meeting of the IOJ.

TOWARDS THE END

Next year 1997 Nieva was afflicted by an aggressive cancer and in October he died. President Al-Qudah sent me a message, asking me to travel to Manila to bid a final farewell to Nieva and convey sympathies to his family.

In fact, with the passing of Secretary General Nieva, and the absence of President Al-Qudah and Treasurer Angelov, who could not leave their home country for Prague to lead the Organization in person, the IOJ only existed in name.

In early 1998 I was in contact with Rüdiger Claus, Director of the International Institute of Journalism in Berlin, and we agreed that he would convene a meeting of selected IOJ leaders to discuss the situation of the Organization and the training programmes for poor countries in Africa and Asia to raise the level of journalistic skills through short-term training courses. This seminar in March 1998 turned out to be the last event organized by the IOJ. After that, I invited Rüdiger to Vietnam and we met many times at the meetings of the ASEAN countries.

After the Amman Congress and the Hanoi Executive Committee, the IOJ's key leaders intended to shift the organization's focus to Asia, home to the fastest growing and most densely populated countries, like China, India, and Indonesia. The IOJ President wanted me to contact Chinese colleagues, and join him and Treasurer Alexander Angelov in July 1998 on a business trip to China to propose that the All China Journalists' Association (ACJA) rejoin the IOJ. If the proposal was accepted, Al-Qudah would be ready to relinquish his presidency to an ACJA representative.

The then Chinese Ambassador to Vietnam, Li Guo Zhong, was a graduate of a university in Hanoi and fluent in Vietnamese. After learning of our plan, he enthusiastically offered his help to coordinate the relevant people. Several days later I received an official invitation from the ACJA. Al-Qudah from Amman and Angelov from Sofia flew to Hanoi, from where the three of us headed to Beijing. We were welcomed by ACJA President Zhao Hua Ze and the Association's Secretariat. We stayed in China for 10 days and visited agencies in Beijing, Shanghai, Hangzhou, and Guangzhou. Wherever we went and whoever we met, we got the same answer that Zhao gave: "Welcome to China! We appreciate your proposal. We will take it into consideration and reply later." I personally interpreted this as a refusal, in the same the way that the ACJA had declined to participate in IOJ activities since the mid-1960s, however without an official announcement of its exit from the IOJ.

After the Beijing visit, I was in Amman, meeting Al-Qudah in his newspaper and had a working lunch at his residence. Al-Qudah said he assigned Josef Komárek, a Czechoslovakian lawyer and former advisor to the IOJ Secretary General, to run at the IOJ's Secretariat in Prague for Deputy Secretary General. But I had never received any information from Prague.

I fully agreed with and applauded the IOJ letter signed by President Al-Qudah and Honorary President Manuel Tomé, presented to the IFJ Congress in Angers (France) in June 2016 by Professor Kaarle Nordenstreng. For the Vietnamese journalists and people, the message represents an official announcement of the termination of the IOJ. But what the Organization had accomplished in the half a century after World War II to promote solidarity between nations, for a free, responsible, and ethical press, for the safety of journalists, and particularly for our country Vietnam, will live on forever.

TESTIMONY OF THE LAST FOUR IOJ PRESIDENTS

In the course of its existence the IOJ had six Presidents (see Appendix 2):

Archibald Kenyon	1946–49 (3 years)
Jean-Maurice Hermann	1950–76 (26 years)
Kaarle Nordenstreng	1976–90 (14 years)
Armando Rollemberg	1991–93 (3 years)
Manuel Tomé	1994 (1 year)
Suleiman Al-Qudah	1995–2016 (21 years)

The latest of these presided over an active organization for only two years: after 1997 the IOJ was practically dormant until 2016, when it was declared defunct.

The last three Presidents were asked to look back at their respective presidencies for this book by responding to the same questions. The author of this book added his responses at the final stage. The four testimonies are presented in chronological order covering over half of the whole IOJ history.

KAARLE NORDENSTRENG: BRIDGEBUILDING IN A VOLATILE WORLD*

WHEN AND HOW DID YOU FIRST HEAR ABOUT THE IOJ AND WHAT WERE YOUR CONTACTS WITH THE IOJ BEFORE YOUR PRESIDENCY?

I knew nothing about the IOJ when I was working in the Finnish radio in the late 1950s and early 1960s. At that time radio journalists, including free-lancers, only had a loose professional association without any international contacts. The RTTL was founded in 1961 as the trade union of full-time radio and TV journalists, and I became a member in the late 1960s, when it did not yet have notable international contacts. If I had been one of the relatively

* The author was IOJ President 1976–90. Written in March 2018.

few YLL members with a far left political orientation, I would certainly have known about the IOJ, but I was a bourgeois "non-political" young fellow safely shielded from progressive movements.

My first knowledge of the IOJ was through *The Democratic Journalist* (*DJ*), which was one of the few international journals coming to the University of Tampere, my academic base since the mid-1960s. However, the journal was only of marginal interest to me, while my focus was on journalism education and research on international communication. On the other hand, since late 1960 I had been part of the so-called New Left, which was rapidly rising in Finland, too, and I was particularly encouraged in this direction during an academic exchange year 1966–67 in the USA. I consequently became more interested in the progressive content of the *DJ* and was pleased to see my articles published there and also in IOJ booklets – texts picked up from scientific conferences in Moscow (1973) and Leipzig (1974). The first IOJ officer whom I got to know while attending these conferences was Editor-in-Chief Oldřich Bureš. I found him a very friendly and open-minded person – far from a dogmatic spokesman of the socialist system but not an outspoken dissident, either.

Let me add that the only time I visited Prague before my Presidency was in September 1968 – a couple of weeks after the occupation by Warsaw Pact forces which ended the Prague Spring (see https://sites.tuni.fi/uploads/2020/05/a04e2084-prague.pdf). At that time I paid no attention to the IOJ and was totally unaware of *Pařížska* 9.

HOW DID THE PROCESS OF BEING ELECTED PRESIDENT GO AND WHAT WERE YOUR MAIN ACHIEVEMENTS AND DISAPPOINTMENTS?

In spring 1976 it came to my ears through colleagues that my name had been mentioned as a possible candidate for the IOJ Presidency in discussions between the IOJ officers and the Finnish journalist union representatives, who were preparing the IOJ Congress for September. None of those insiders contacted me. I did not take those rumours seriously and was busy pursuing my scholarly activities, which at that time focused on theories of information society and international communication policies, particularly the New International Information Order. I was privileged to witness the birth of this concept at the Symposium of Information of the Non-Aligned Movement in Tunis in April 1976 (see http://urn.fi/urn:nbn:uta-3-832).

Much later I was told that the President of the GDR Union of Journalists and its General Secretary had visited Helsinki; this Union had bilateral relations with the YLL, RTTL and SSL. In a meeting with the Finnish hosts of the forthcoming IOJ Congress the Germans had told them that I was to be proposed as the next President. The Finnish colleagues found this quite an improper way of approaching the matter; they felt that they were being dictated to in such a delicate matter, whereas normally it would have been for the member unions to propose candidates for leading positions of international organizations. The discussion ended without the Finnish unions' consent to my nomination. Later I was told that the issue was not me but the process.

Then in mid-July 1976 I received a telegramme from my colleague in Leipzig, Professor Emil Dusiska, Secretary-General of the International Association for Mass Communication Research (IAMCR), inviting me to Berlin for negotiations about the forthcoming IAMCR conference in the UK (I was one of the IAMCR Vice-Presidents). Hence I flew to Berlin on 16 August, finding there also Alexander Losev, Vice-President of the Soviet Union of Journalists, the de facto director of the Union (former head of Soviet radio). The IAMCR question was quickly covered; it turned out to be merely an excuse for extending the invitation.

Obviously the Soviets had checked my background and international activities at the IAMCR, UNESCO, etc., and found that I would be a suitable successor to Hermann (who had just turned 80) as the IOJ President – as a progressive representative of the young generation (I had just turned 35), not a member of any political party and furthermore coming from Finland, the driver of détente. Losev persuaded me to accept the challenge, but I hesitated as this would change my professional prospects from a purely academic to an international political actor, although formally I would retain my professorship in Finland and be only a part-time President. Moreover, it would change my political profile from a broad progressive to a Soviet collaborator. After two nights in Berlin I flew with Losev to Moscow, where we were joined by my friends Reino Paasilinna, Press Attaché of the Embassy of Finland, and Professor Yassen Zassoursky, Dean of the Faculty of Journalism at Moscow State University. The question was collectively deliberated on at the lunch table of a resort close to Moscow airport. Before returning to Helsinki at the end of the day I gave Losev my consent – provided that no objections would be raised at home in Finland.

In Finland I found the leaders of the journalist unions YLL, RTTL and SSL irritated at being passed over. The only Finnish full member of the IOJ, the YLL, was especially embarrassed after being pushed around by the Soviets and its President, Paavo Ruonaniemi, was far from pleased at my candidacy. Meanwhile, I had an opportunity to meet the President of Finland, Dr. Urho Kekkonen, the host of the CSCE in Helsinki a year before. I had interacted with him in various connections over the years and now informed him about the prospect of my becoming the IOJ President, to which he was positively disposed. I telexed to Losev that the matter was OK in principle, but that the Finnish unions were displeased with the way the candidacy had been processed. Losev then went to Prague, where the IOJ Secretary General had invited the President of the Finnish member union YLL. Ruonaniemi refused to go, sending the YLL Secretary Markku Vainio instead. After quite harsh pressuring by Losev the YLL finally acquiesced to proposing me as their candidate in the Helsinki Congress.

The wounds sustained during the procedure were still smarting on the eve of the Congress, but the head of the Soviet delegation, Viktor Afanasiev, succeeded in curing them in a frank meeting with the Finnish union leaders. Part of the settlement was that Ruonaniemi was elected Vice-President, while no other country had two members in the Presidium (see Appendix 2).

And now to the rest of this question about my experiences:

My main achievement in general was to strengthen the strategy for East-West détente and North-South co-operation beyond the customary boundaries determined by the Cold War contradictions. This bridge-building strategy was not my invention; it was already on its way when I became President, but with my Finnish and also my academic background I could help to modernize the IOJ machinery. Contrary to my expectations, I did not meet resistance to this strategic line from the communist power groups in any of the socialist countries – notably not from Czechoslovakia, the host of the headquarters. And the Secretariat, especially Secretary General Jiří Kubka, was quite helpful all along. I had full confidence in Kubka and his ability to manage the staff and the finances.

In pursuing my objectives I enjoyed good co-operation with the most important political actor among the IOJ influentials, President Afanasiev of the Soviet Union of Journalists. Accordingly, far from being pushed around by the Soviets, I was rather using them to endorse my initiatives. Afanasiev also supported my plan to spend the first part of 1977 as visiting professor at the University of California, San Diego (a plan already made before the talks about my Presidency) in order to work in peace on a book about normative theories of the media.

While the bridgebuilding strategy was well received in the socialist countries, I was surprised to find many obstacles placed in its way in the western countries, apparently imbued with a Cold War mindset. It did not help that as a member of the RTTL and SSL I was also associated with the IFJ at the grassroots level. By and large, however, the activities in line with détente made sufficient progress to justify their inclusion as my main overall achievement.

More specifically about my achievements, what first comes to mind is the development of the IOJ publications and the upgrading of studies and documentation, leading to the establishment of the International Journalism

Institute (IJI). A less concrete but equally significant achievement in the long run was my promotion of journalistic ethics through the Mexico Declaration (1980) and the International Principles of Professional Ethics in Journalism (1983). I can also take credit for the IOJ becoming an early and vocal advocate of the idea of the New International Information Order. Strategically speaking, my most important organizational achievement was the Consultative Club of international and regional organizations of journalists – a step towards reunification.

While acknowledging these achievements one must concede that there were many other burning issues which were not properly promoted. For example, freedom of speech and of the press was not given thorough deliberation; it was typically only evinced as an argument in the defence of journalists suffering from fascist oppression or corporate pressure. The protection of journalists was likewise focused on those under right-wing repression or those on dangerous missions, discretely avoiding the question of defending the rights of journalists in the socialist countries. The potential of a broad-based coalition of NGOs for protecting journalists was missed. Some progress in this direction was made in the work on professional ethics, but the overall approach of the IOJ was quite selective, operating with double standards, and this naturally helped to maintain the image of the IOJ as an eastern "communist" organization.

Another topic which remained too low on the agenda was the trade union matters. Although trade unionism was one of the Aims and Tasks of the original Statute of Copenhagen and Prague 1946–47, and still central in the revised Statute of Helsinki after the split in 1950, it was practically lost in the ideological struggle of the Cold War. The Secretariat had minimal contacts with the World Federation of Trade Unions (WFTU), also based in Prague, as it had with the Prague-based International Organization of Radio and Television (OIRT). In hindsight, I could have initiated an IOJ strategy on trade unionism in the 1980s at a time when media concentration and commercialization became a problem worldwide. Admittedly, the appointment of a Finnish Secretary, Leena Paukku from the SSL, in 1987 was supposed to help in this respect, and some steps were indeed taken to introduce trade union matters to the member unions. However, this topic remained secondary to the pressing issues which were threatening peace and co-operation in Europe.

Nevertheless, the IOJ activities were growing and the membership was expanding. One could even say that we were growing too much, with the favourable balance of global power depending on the Soviet-led East and NAM-led South. By and large, many developments, including the reunification of the international journalists' movement, were at a promising stage in 1989, when the collapse of the socialist system paralyzed the political and economic base of the IOJ in Czechoslovakia. Moreover, the leadership elected in the Harare Congress in January 1991 to carry on after my term was drawn into an internal fight, further reducing the possibilities to sustain the achievements.

It was a huge disappointment to witness the disintegration of the IOJ in the 1990s, beginning with the loss of the unique tradition of the Consultative Club and ending with the discontinuation of the flagship *The Democratic Journalist* and the *IOJ newsletter*. I stepped aside from the IOJ right after Harare, spending a couple of months on an academic exchange at the University of Maryland (USA), and three years later I enjoyed an academic retreat at the University of Texas at Austin – on both occasions seizing the opportunity to keep in touch with the North American IOJ members, particularly Vice-President Kevin Lynch. My contacts to the Secretariat in Prague were practically lost apart from a couple of exchanges with President Rollemberg. My last attempt to salvage at least the remnants of the IOJ legacy in Czechoslovakia (Appendix 29) failed to materialize.

The new IOJ leadership was overwhelmed in a struggle for survival and beset by infighting. My advice was not needed and it seems that in the psychological drama of downfall I was assigned the role of a character representing the burden of the past. I did not take it personally, but I was chagrined to see how the IOJ empire was rapidly crumbling. After Antonio Nieva began as the new Secretary General in 1995 my contacts to Prague were resumed, but at this stage there was nothing that I could do beyond offering him my sympathy.

In a general picture the downfall can be seen as an inevitable consequence of the geopolitical change following the collapse of the socialist system in eastern Europe in 1989–91 and the simultaneous rise of neoliberalist economies in the global South. So one could say that just as the rise of the IOJ empire was dependent on the relative strength of the East and South in a world dominated by the Cold War, the fall of the empire was an inevitable sequel to the new post-Cold War geopolitical development. However, I do not exonerate the IOJ leaders from moral responsibility for the demise of the IOJ. Although history cannot be turned back, it is still useful to ask what could have been done differently and what errors were perpetrated.

WHAT IS YOUR CURRENT ASSESSMENT OF THE IOJ, WITH THE WISDOM OF HINDSIGHT?

The bottom line is that the IOJ has been a significant project in the history of journalism and media – no doubt one of the most important INGOs in the media field. For the first two years, 1946–47, it had an ecumenical character, representing the journalists of all the allied countries from the USA to the USSR. The only journalist unions excluded were those of a markedly fascist or right-wing character, while, for example, the Finnish union was included after remaining politically neutral throughout World War II despite Finland's alliance with Nazi Germany. For Czechoslovakia and other countries under Nazi military occupation the IOJ provided a welcome platform for patriotic and democratic forces to return to national and international arenas.

However, since 1948 the IOJ was embroiled in the Cold War and hence inextricably linked to the Soviet-led part of the new geopolitical world order. In this world it was simply not possible to remain neutral. This is also shown by the story of the IFJ, which became respectively partisan on the American-led western side. The international movement of journalists was as divided as the world at large – except that the Third World did not have its own journalist organization but was largely integrated with the IOJ.

A serious attempt was made in the second half of the 1950s to return to a more representative international movement of journalists, now on the initiative of unions from the developing countries, notably India and Brazil, but this attempt did not succeed, mainly because the IFJ, backed by the Western powers, refused to co-operate. It was only in the 1970s during détente that some space was made for a truly ecumenical approach, strongly advocated by the Finnish, Italian and Polish unions. The IOJ attempted to pursue this approach and, despite reluctance on the part of the IFJ, with the support of regional federations in Africa, the Arab world and Latin America, steps were taken in the 1980s towards a reunification of the divided movement. Yet the IOJ was not ready for rapid and full reconciliation, either; several of its members were not prepared to embrace unions of the "imperialist" side.

This development came to an end in the 1990s with the collapse of the Soviet-led East, leading to the rapid demise of the IOJ. Many long-time IOJ member unions joined the IFJ, which relaxed its previously sectarian approach and made it more ecumenical. However, numerous IOJ member unions remained unaffiliated without any international umbrella, while most regional federations also lost their momentum or disappeared. In the new millennium the world of journalism was no longer conducive to strong professional associations and trade unions of journalists, either nationally or internationally. Developments in both politics and media made it increasingly difficult for journalists to organize. Although the IOJ's last will in Angers in 2016 passed on the long legacy of the movement to the single remaining international organization, the IFJ, it is obvious that today's IFJ is not as strong and representative as the IOJ and the IFJ of the 1980s put together.

In short, my current appraisal of the IOJ is that it was bound to be inseparable from the geopolitics of the time – just as has been the case with the IFJ and the regional federations. Journalists and their associations, nationally and internationally, are by no means totally free and autonomous actors but closely tied to the political, economic and cultural structures in their respective societies. Their operating space is always more or less limited and they are far more dependent on outside (geo)political forces than organizational activists like to think.

ARMANDO ROLLEMBERG: FROM DREAM TO DISAPPOINTMENT*

WHEN AND HOW DID YOU FIRST HEAR ABOUT THE IOJ AND WHAT WERE YOUR CONTACTS WITH THE IOJ BEFORE YOUR PRESIDENCY?

The Brazilian National Federation of Journalists (FENAJ) affiliated to the IOJ while its President was Audálio Dantas, a sympathizer of the then Brazilian Communist Party – my adversary. It was on his initiative that we joined the IOJ. However, when FENAJ sent its first delegation to the IOJ Congress in Sofia in 1986, it was up to me, as President-Elect of FENAJ, to lead the Brazilian delegation. Then, in Sofia, I was elected Vice-President of the IOJ. Up to that moment, I knew very little about the organization, its history, its entrepreneurial power and its role in the Cold War conflict.

I was really surprised when I noticed that even inside the old Czechoslovakia the IOJ suffered severe political and ethical restrictions not only by the government of the time, but also by journalists themselves.

It took me some months to realize the causes for so many aversions, but I ended up discovering that the distaste for the IOJ was mainly because of its engagement – I'd even say automatic alignment – with the politics developed under the leadership of the extinct Soviet Union in the context of the Cold War. I noticed soon that the grounds for the generalized antipathy that we faced in the home country was the fact that the IOJ had withdrawn, shamefully, when the forces of the Pact of Warsaw invaded Czechoslovakia to fight the "Prague Spring".

Under the silence of the IOJ, hundreds and hundreds of Czech and Slovak journalists were fired and harshly prosecuted. Prevented from exercising journalism, they were forced to change professions. After this, there was a great resentment, an open wound, that was never healed. In addition, when I started to participate in the Executive Committee and its Presidium, I found out that the IOJ in fact reflected the Leninist model of organization with all power to the Secretary General, leaving the President with a role like that of "Queen of England".

I was even more surprised when I noticed the entrepreneurial power of our organization, owner or partner in dozens of companies in the most diverse areas not only in the home country, but also in Hungary and even in Germany and Austria. Two curious and revealing details: the Director General of the IOJ companies Milos Jakes Junior was the son of the Secretary General of the

* The author was IOJ Vice-President 1986–90 and President 1991–93. Written in April 2016, translated from Portuguese by Leonardo Custodio.

Czechoslovak Communist Party, and the IOJ Secretary General Dušan Ulčák (preceding Gerard Gatinot) was not a professional journalist but a diplomat of the Ministry of Foreign Affairs, a member of the governing body of the local Communist Party. These connections sounded very strange to me.

To be honest, the only positive fact in the midst of all that was the President, a highly recognized Finnish academic. Of course, there was also an air of renovation and hope after the fall of the Berlin Wall summarized in two fashionable words of that time: *glasnost* and *perestroika*.

When I took over the presidency of FENAJ in 1986, I had as adversaries those same people who followed the textbook of the Communist Party. But I never registered to the conservative wing. Let's say I was part of the so-called new Brazilian left, later consolidated in the Workers' Party. I was also part of the board of direction of the two first CONCLATs (Working Class National Congress) as well as a founding and active member of CUT (Unified Workers' Central).

I make these remarks to situate myself in the political spectrum in Brazil: I've always been close to the left, but never belonged to the "Stalinist" left that dominated and were responsible for the political line of the Brazilian Communist Party. Therefore, I was against the theory that the syndicalist organizations served as a "transmission belt" of the party guidelines. I defended, as did many other comrades in struggle, the syndicalist autonomy, the political pluralism and the broad freedom of expression.

As adversaries and victims of the fascist military dictatorship that for over 30 years ruled Brazil, we knew that we could only build socialism in an environment of freedom with political pluralism, syndicalist autonomy and the broad possibility of organization and expression, be it by the left, centre or right. One citizen, one vote. And that the will of the majority, assessed in a process of clean and balanced democratic dispute, prevailed. No impositions, no authoritarian guidelines from the party headquarters that considered itself "the enlightened guide of the people".

In these circumstances I started my political participation at IOJ. I used to say loud and clear: "Well, if we are an international organization of journalists, it is up to us to primarily defend the professional interests, the work conditions of journalists without any kind of discrimination, be they from *Pravda*, *New York Times* or *Jornal do Brasil*. We don't have to make political-ideological proselytism serving the preachers of side "a" or side "b" in the Cold War. If we want to recover the respect and gain the recognition of the category and of the international organizations (UN, UNESCO, Red Cross, Reporters without Borders, Article 19, etc.) we have to free ourselves from this nasty dilemma. And there is no way of exerting journalism as a profession if there is no freedom of opinion. And for freedom of opinion to exist it is fundamental that there is a regime that guarantees, widely, political pluralism.

HOW DID THE PROCESS OF BEING ELECTED PRESIDENT GO AND WHAT WERE YOUR MAIN ACHIEVEMENTS AND DISAPPOINTMENTS?

It was on this path that my improbable candidacy to the IOJ leadership gained body, density and became victorious in the Congress of Harare. In fact, this empathy, in my opinion – reflected so many years later – happened naturally: the delegations present in the Congress, especially those from countries that belonged to the Communist bloc, identified immediately with my thinking. Deep, deep inside, they heard from the mouth of a Brazilian leftist journalist everything they had wanted to hear for a long time.

I was elected President, but Gérard Gatinot, tied to the French CGT, representative of the old Stalinist sector, was confirmed as Secretary General. That is, the new directive board of the IOJ was hopelessly divided from the outset. In the Congress of Harare itself there was the first battle. Led by Gatinot, they wanted to maintain the old structure, with all its power in the hands of the Secretary General, leaving the President only with the ceremonial mission of presiding over the sparse meetings of the Executive Committee.

The serious crisis in which the organization was nonetheless favored some changes in the organizational model of the IOJ. The IOJ bank accounts, the operations higher than a certain limit, had to be done with double signatures: the Secretary General and the President. Even though they had offered me vast infrastructure to remain living in Brazil (office space, employees, cars and financial support), I insisted on moving to Prague. Gatinot grudgingly swallowed my decision. And there I went, accompanied by the brilliant assistant Ramsés Ramos, to live in Prague and working in an excellent cabinet on the second floor of the unforgettable headquarters located in the famous Old Square.

It wasn't easy. Soon I started facing the maneuvers and diatribes of the Secretary General. There were many, diverse and continuous. Gatinot tried to sabotage my initiatives. I was, at some point, even fearful for my life.

On the eve of the Congress of Harare, concerned about regaining the prestige and the respect of Czech and Slovak journalists, and already considering the possibility of being a candidate for the IOJ presidency, I requested an audience with the direction board of the Syndicate of Czech Journalists. With all that patrimony built on Czech territory, it seemed absurd to me that we elected a new board without representatives of local journalists and professional organizations. Therefore I presented a proposal to them: I'd be a candidate for the Presidency and would propose in my team a Czech or Slovak candidate to occupy the Secretary General, so long as the name was chosen democratically in assembly, representing the free will of the country's professionals.

The board of the Syndicate was speechless, surprised because of my unexpected proposal. They asked me for time, left for a couple of minutes and returned with the response: they had been hesitant to welcome me, they had researched my professional life and my political trajectory, they knew that I was a respected person in my country, they were pleased and truly surprised with my proposal, but they decided to refuse it. Their delegation chief summarized their position like this: "There were no conditions to rebuild an entity that had its grounds rotten." I argued that the IOJ, over time, had spread around the world. That if in Czechoslovakia its grounds were rotten, as they assessed, in many countries, like Brazil, these foundations were, on the contrary, very solid, supported by structures and organizations like FENAJ, that were very representative, legitimate and respected by journalists.

As soon as I returned to Prague as President, I decided to make a series of visits to the Czech political leadership of both the regime and the opposition. I still kept the idea that it was possible to reverse the order to expel the IOJ headquarters from Czechoslovakia. Soon I noticed that this was an impossible mission. I think they saw me as a Brazilian "Quixote", a young and wellmeaning journalist, a dreamer, but doomed to fail in that mission. No matter how much I assured them that I was there to change the path of the organization, that I had as a cornerstone of my thought and my political practice the strict defense of the democratic regime, of the pluralism of ideas and the freedom of expression, nobody believed in me. It was as if they were in front of a strange body, an alien, a being that did not fit the history of the IOJ. And, in fact, the developments of this particular plot, to my disappointment, proved they were right.

The first big confrontation in light of the inevitable change of headquarters happened to concern our destination. Where would we finally go? Gatinot, obviously, rushed to offer Paris as a first option. But I considered at the time, despite loving Paris, that it would reinforce the Stalinism that persisted in the organization. We would inevitably be subjected to the French CGT. With that in mind, with the support of a number of colleagues (Tomé, Angelov, Grigore and others) who then supported me in the Executive Committee, I decided to organize another alternative.

First, I sought to obtain a statement from the Brazilian government (at the time represented by the President Fernando Collor de Mello) in which they expressed interest in receiving the IOJ headquarters in Brasilia, the country's capital. When that alternative was secured in a formal letter to me signed by the Minister of Foreign Affairs, I looked for another possibility, a more realistic one, on European soil. That's how the hypothesis of establishing the organization in Madrid at the headquarters of the Journalists' Union UP emerged.

Madrid was favoured by the IOJ board despite the pressure of Gatinot for Paris. But this victory soon proved to be a serious mistake. The problem is that the Spanish UP lacked, in fact, representation among Spanish journalists. It was actually a ghost apparatus that for many years did not carry out needed renewals in its board. When I uncovered the farce, it was too late. We had already changed the headquarters to the Spanish capital. With Gatinot's pressure – who even started to corrupt members of the executive board of the IOJ to position themselves against my positions – the situation got out of control once and for all.

At the Executive Committee in Barcelona, meeting in December 1993, it became evident that the representatives of the Dominican Republic and the Arab countries had turned to support Gatinot and I had lost the majority. In this situation, I opted out: I returned to my country leaving a IOJ to its fate. The upsurge of the Stalinist line in my opinion represented the death sentence, which effectively happened some years later after my exit, with the robbery of the IOJ assets and a complete demoralization of the organization.

Unfortunately, I cannot present a list of achievements as my presidency turned out to be a big disappointment as shown above. I dreamed and developed a lot of ideas, but I have to admit that I executed very little of what I had wished due to the lack of objective conditions: because of the complex internal disputes and the intense sabotage I suffered. However, I take the opportunity to recall some highlights of my presidency.

Visit to Cuba: at some point, I started receiving complaints that many foreign journalists, at different times but in similar circumstances, had suffered severe violence in Havana. The aggression followed the same ritual: surrounded by "the people", the professionals were intimidated, assaulted, had their equipment stolen or damaged. Despite the complaints, nothing was done to investigate and stop those acts apparently orchestrated by the authorities, who did not even investigate the episodes.

As the IOJ President I requested explanations from Julio Garcia, the President of the Cuban Union of Journalists UPEC and Vice-President of the IOJ. I requested explanations once, twice, three times and every time I had silence as a response. That's when I decided to release a very tough public statement condemning the assaults on journalists independently of where they happened. But I decided to do more: I appointed myself president of the Biennale of Humor, an event fully financed by the IOJ. That's the way I found to travel to Havana and to stop the Cuban government from preventing my trip by denying me an entry visa to the country.

I arrived early to meet, behind closed doors with a recorder, with the board of UPEC. That's how I reported, in detail, each of the cases, instructing the colleagues to explain the inexplicable and embarrassing omission. I recorded all our difficult discussions. Having done that, I requested that they arrange a series of visits to the main Cuban media outlets (*Granma*, juventude rebelled, the radio station, the women's newspaper), but I insisted on talking directly with the journalists for 15 minutes inside the newsrooms. That's how it happened: in each newsroom, for fifteen minutes, I raised my voice supporting the thesis that socialism would only be fully victorious if it respected the pluralism of opinions, that the Single Party was detrimental to the cause and quoted Rosa Luxemburg, who observed from prison that freedom of expression was important not for the hegemonic parties, no matter how representative and respected they were, but principally for the political and ethnic minorities. On all the visits, at the end of my speech, one or two angry colleagues stood up to accuse me of working for the CIA, etc. My answer was always the same: examine my life, my career, my trajectory to know who I in fact was. I assured them that in the future, willing or not, they would realize I was right. After these meetings, always in a furtive manner, three or four colleagues came to discreetly greet me.

When I returned to Prague I received a warm visit from the Cuban secretary Miguel Rivero at the headquarters. He was very impressed with the boldness of my attitude. He said, emphatically, that I was guaranteed a special place in Cuban history when the country finally took the democratic path. To close this topic, I ordered a transcription of the recording of the meeting with UPEC, I produced a document and I decided to distribute it, in person, at the World Conference for Human Rights in Vienna.

Mission to Somalia: When I learned that several foreign journalists had been beaten to death by an angry crowd reacting to an attack by the UN peacekeeping forces in Mogadishu, I decided to organize an official mission to Somalia. I went with Colleen Roach, a media scholar from New York, accompanied by Ramsés Ramos. We went there to discuss, together with the UN officials, about ways and means to guarantee more security for journalists on dangerous missions during the coverage of war and conflicts. It was up to Colleen Roach to develop the report of the mission, which we published.

Kidnapping of Gorbachev: I was arriving home after a day at work when I heard about the kidnapping of Gorbachev in an attempted coup by the hard line of the Party, which was interested in sabotaging the ongoing process to open politics. I immediately returned to the headquarters with Ramsés Ramos. We wrote a statement asking "Where's Gorbachev?" and demanding the Soviet journalists provide a prompt response. It said that the whole world expected them to fulfill their professional duty in light of that emergency. On the following day, I ordered a translation into the other five IOJ languages and requested my secretary to buy tickets to Moscow for me and Ramsés.

I arrived in Moscow two days after the disappearance of Gorbachev. I hired a translator and made surprise visits to the main newspapers and local broadcasters starting from *Pravda*, *Izveztija* and Radio Moscow. As I had done in Cuba, I asked for direct access to the newsroom and, with the aid of a translator, before astonished colleagues impressed by such courage, I raised my voice repeating the question: "Where's Gorbachev?" I demanded a prompt response from them. At the end of the visits, the translator started crying with emotion because of my attitude. Two months later, with Gorbachev again in power, the journalists from Saint Petersburg, in recognition of my action, awarded me with a wrist watch. I was the first international organization leader to protest against the disappearance of Gorbachev. And I did it in person in an entirely unexpected way.

WHAT IS YOUR CURRENT ASSESSMENT OF THE IOJ, WITH THE WISDOM OF HINDSIGHT?

I sincerely believe that the IOJ got caught in a time warp. If we had taken advantage of the moment of change in the communist world after the events that led to the fall of the Berlin Wall to engage in severe self-criticism about the rigid ideological parameters that oriented our political action, we may have been able to recover. If we had gone through the self-criticism and promoted this kind of political-ideological recycling, we would probably have recovered the respect of international organizations (UNESCO, Red Cross, Article 19, Reporters without Borders, etc.).

With our widespread presence in over 120 countries, having the effective economic support from our enterprises, we would have been able to act in the global world carrying very important flags for the struggle for democracy, like the freedom of expression for minorities, the strengthening of public communication, the end of monopolies, and the social control of media, not to mention the rights and guarantees for journalists in general. However, unfortunately, history unfolded differently.

MANUEL TOMÉ: ACTING IN CRISIS*

WHEN AND HOW DID YOU FIRST HEAR ABOUT THE IOJ AND WHAT WERE YOUR CONTACTS WITH IT BEFORE YOUR PRESIDENCY?

My first contact with the IOJ was after its meeting at Alma Ata, at which a delegation from my National Organisation of Journalists (ONJ), which later transformed itself into a trade union, took part. In fact, contact was indirect, at a meeting where the then Vice-President of the IOJ, and member of the ONJ executive secretariat, the late Leite de Vasconcelos, gave information about the results of the gathering at Alma Ata.

In 1984, when I took on the duties of interim Secretary General of the ONJ (two years later I was elected Secretary General), I was also appointed to replace in the IOJ the prestigious journalist Leite de Vasconcelos who, regrettably, had been unable to engage in any regular professional activity for reasons of health. It was at the meeting of the IOJ Executive Committee held in New Delhi in September 1984 that I took on the duties of the IOJ Vice-President.

As of that moment, until the Congress of the IOJ in Amman in January 1995, I took part in all the meetings of the IOJ statutory bodies – Presidium, Executive Committee/Council and Congress.

In January 1991, at the 11th Congress in Harare, I was elected 1st Vice-President. It was a Congress which, judging by the openness and frankness of the debates which took place, augured a great intensification of internal democracy for the IOJ and, as a result, new developments of the organization faced with the great political and social changes on a world scale which had as their significant moments the fall of the Berlin Wall and the end of the USSR. These events had a tremendous impact on the entire world and particularly on the former Czechoslovakia, which was where the IOJ was headquartered.

Until my election, the leading bodies of the IOJ had no specific activity. I followed some activities of the IOJ through the local committee of the ONJ at the newspaper *Notícias*, where I was working, through the information which was occasionally circulated by the ONJ executive office, coming from meetings of the IOJ or from its information bulletins, for example the *IOJ newsletter*.

* The author was IOJ Vice-President 1986–93, President 1994 and Honorary President 1995–2016. Written in May 2016, translated from Portuguese by Paul Fauvet.

HOW DID THE PROCESS OF BEING ELECTED PRESIDENT GO AND WHAT WERE YOUR MAIN ACHIEVEMENTS AND DISAPPOINTMENTS?

I took on the duties of President of the IOJ, on an interim basis, in December 1993, in the middle of a crisis in the organization's leadership, which had its immediate origin in the resignation of the then President, Armando Rollemberg, during a meeting of the Executive Committee which took place in Barcelona.

Despite the success of the Harare Congress, it was still a fact that the Congress left scars on some member unions, particularly in Africa, where many hoped to see one of its Vice-Presidents, the late Zimbabwean journalist, Charles Chikerema, become the President. Strangely enough, his candidacy was not supported by his own Zimbabwe Union of Journalists, which preferred to put up another Zimbabwean as candidate for the Secretary General. But the IOJ was able to rise above these questions and advance until the moment when various obstacles and constraints began to arise, particularly as of the second half of 1992.

I took on the duties of President for slightly more than 13 months, that is from 6 December 1993 to 31 January 1995, at the Congress of Amman. I was not resident in Prague, and this did not make my activity any easier given the serious difficulties through which the IOJ was passing: lack of control over finance, drastic reduction in income, a feeling of discontent among the workers, attacks from the press of the then Czechoslovakia, and a bewildering environment of intrigue in the headquarters.

Czechoslovakia went through major changes. First, the Czech and Slovak Federal Republic was formed, and later, out of this situation two countries were born – the Czech Republic and the Republic of Slovakia. I recall that in August 1991 the IOJ received from the Minister of the Interior of the then Czech and Slovak Federal Republic an ultimatum to leave the country. The series of appeals made by the IOJ to the rulers of the country, including the then President Václav Havel, had no effect. The consequent temporary change of the headquarters to Madrid involved enormous financial costs and caused great unrest among the staff, who were essentially living in Prague. This situation exacerbated the financial difficulties through which the IOJ was passing, with the loss of one of its main sources of income, namely a travel agency, which had enjoyed a monopoly position. With the changes in the host country, including the liberalization of the economy, within a few months dozens of travel agencies had emerged.

As I said at the Amman Congress, in 13 months what was done was what the time allowed. I held a series of meetings with the staff of the Secretariat and with the workers of the companies belonging to the IOJ, to get to know their problems, to calm their spirits, and head off threats of strikes. That was achieved. It was necessary to re-establish a climate of trust and also the credibility of the organization. Some steps were taken.

We had to regularize the ownership of IOJ assets, since in some cases it was not clear, from the legal point of view, who owned the buildings and companies.

We went to London, where I met with Aidan White, the IFJ General Secretary, to discuss ways of how the two organisations could arrive at a merger, based on firmer and more regular cooperation. Although the meeting was not conclusive, the door was opened or re-opened for discussions on the matter to continue.

In Amman, I informed the Congress that I was unavailable to continue in the IOJ, because it would be incompatible with the political responsibilities I had just accepted in Mozambique (as Secretary General of FRELIMO, the ruling party). To my great surprise, the Congress delegates elected me Honorary President.

WHAT IS YOUR CURRENT ASSESSMENT OF THE IOJ, WITH THE WISDOM OF HINDSIGHT?

The assessment that can be made of the IOJ is that until the mid-1990s it played an important role in the struggle to set up a new world communication order with greater global balance. It so happened that the IOJ arose in the context of the Cold War. With the end of the Cold War, and the rise of a unipolar world, the IOJ lost its supports. In this unipolar world the IFJ survived because the countries which supported it did not fall or lose their relevance. So much so that most of the present members of the IFJ were once members of the IOJ.

And how could I not mention that the IOJ was in the vanguard of the struggle for equality, the struggle against racism and apartheid? It would be unjust not to express appreciations for the work done by the IOJ to support organizations of journalists across the world, particularly in Africa, in Latin America and in Asia. With IOJ support, some regional organizations appeared, such as the Federation of Southern African Journalists, which mounted a major campaign for the release of Nelson Mandela. But without the IOJ, these organizations were unable to sustain themselves. Hence, when the IOJ was paralyzed, they died, one might say, a natural death. Also worthy of mention is the struggle against the murder and imprisonment of journalists carried out by the IOJ across the world.

I was part of the IOJ and, as a result, I am also responsible for part of its history. And, as in any history, there were records of many achievements and many successes, despite the weaknesses, one of which was the great financial and ideological dependence on the then socialist countries. But it is an illusion to imagine "non-ideological" organizations. There is always a vision, a series of ideas and objectives which guide an organization.

We must admit that, in light of events such as the fall of the Berlin Wall and the dissolution of the USSR, we were unable to make the necessary analyses so as to take wiser decisions, to bring the IOJ into line with the new international context. Today there remains nothing for us but to consider the most dignified manner of saying farewell to its role in history.

SULEIMAN AL-QUDAH: TOWARDS THE END*

WHEN AND HOW DID YOU FIRST HEAR ABOUT THE IOJ AND WHAT WERE YOUR CONTACTS WITH IT BEFORE YOUR PRESIDENCY?

As a journalist working in this field since 1971, I used to follow the international journalism organizations, especially the IOJ and the IFJ, through the Jordanian Journalist Association (JPA), which was a member of the IOJ. After I was elected President of the JPA since 1992 for two terms until 1996, I used to follow with my colleagues the activities of the IOJ, although these activities were not that relevant to us at that time.

My first direct connection with the IOJ was through the regional IOJ office in Sana'a and the Federation of Arab Journalist in Baghdad, when the preparation of the 1995 congress started.

The regional office in Sana'a asked the JPA to host the IOJ congress in Amman. The JPA board reviewed this suggestion, but the lack of funding was an obstacle at that time. The IOJ had offered to support the JPA with 20,000 US dollars, assuming that it would locally cover the cost of accommodation, meals and other expenses except for travel expenses to and from Jordan and the fees of the translation as well as administration.

The JPA was short of funding and therefore did not approve the IOJ offer before making sure of the necessary funding. The JPA board started to look for funding from the Jordanian Government. I met with the Prime Minister and we explained all the details and the importance of holding such a congress in Amman with the attendance form 120 journalist associations from around the world. The Prime Ministry decided to allocate 80,000 Jordanian dinars to the JPA to cover the cost of the congress.

We got a cheap offer from one of the hotels for the guests' accommodation. I contacted the media organizations in Jordan and they agreed to pay for the meals during the congress. And we approached governmental and private organizations to cover the expenses of transportation and other requirements.

We contacted the IOJ and agreed to host the congress in Amman at the proposed time. A delegation from the IOJ led by Secretary General Gatinot and the Arab members of the Executive Committee Joseph Kosseifi and Mahboub Ali visited Jordan in late 1994. The delegation met with the Prime Minister, who expressed his willingness to support the congress. He complained about continuous attacks by the media on the Jordanian Government.

---

* The author was IOJ President 1995–2016. Written in May 2016, translated from Arabic by Majd Al-Qudah.

After that the delegation met with the late His Majesty King Hussein Bin Talal. I explained to him all our preparations, including the Prime Minister's willingness to support the congress. I told him that usually the IOJ complains about the government's actions against the journalists, but in our case the Prime Minister is the one who complained about the media and the journalists. His Majesty said that this means we are doing good. He asked the translator attending the meeting to tell the delegation: in the name of the JPA President we will provide all the needed support to make the congress a success. While the interpreter was speaking, she started to cough very badly, she couldn't continue her translation. His Majesty stood up and asked her if he should turn off the air condition system: "Did it bother you?" The interpreter said: "No sir, it is not the air condition."

After that the delegation didn't say anything about the Congress but asked political questions and took photos with His Majesty. When we departed I asked the translator what happened. She said that his words and humility when he talked in the name of JPA President affected her.

After that I had several meetings with the IOJ management in Prague to finalize the preparation of the congress.

HOW DID THE PROCESS OF BEING ELECTED PRESIDENT GO AND WHAT WERE YOUR MAIN ACHIEVEMENTS AND DISAPPOINTMENTS?

When the Congress started, a decision was made to appoint me as its chair.

During the Congress, the disagreements and accusations started to surface between the Secretary General, the Treasurer and the members of the Executive Committee. I started to feel that the Congress would be ruined by these disagreements. I tried to calm the situation and resolve the conflicts, obviously pleasing the delegates.

The Arab delegation started to work towards electing me President. It was a rare thing that the Arabs agreed on one thing in such situations. The proposal was welcomed by the African delegations and to some extent others. Therefore, I won the election against my Polish opponent. What paved my way were the good impressions from the Congress members while leading and organizing the proceedings.

The central IOJ leaders – President, Secretary General and Treasurer – agreed to focus on coordinated team work. Our top priorities were the following:

First, to change the bad impressions attached to the IOJ and its leadership after the Congress and Executive Committee meetings – especially the accusations regarding the financial situation in the past four years. It was unfortunate that the accusations were covered by the local and international media. In addition to that, the IOJ was seen by many as a communist organization. Some of the local media attacked the JPA's decision to host the Congress, and I was personally accused of being behind bringing communist journalists in Amman.

Therefore I contacted local and international organizations to clarify the situation confirming that the new IOJ management has a professional intention to upscale the standards of the IOJ, to provide the needed protection to the journalists and assist the member organizations to carry out their mission in the best possible way. I sent many letters to relevant parties and to the Czech Government through its embassy in Amman to explain the new direction of the new management and its focus on professionalism. Also, an IOJ delegation consisting of the President and the Secretary General met with the Assistant Director General of UNESCO in Paris. The meeting was attended by media officials at UNESCO and it was agreed on to support IOJ efforts to achieve its new mission.

Second, to complete a review of the financial situation of the Organization. According to the estimate of previous leaders, the IOJ could only survive financially six months after the Congress, while paying all its debts in Prague. The new management team mainly focused on amending the financial situation of the commercial companies. We kept receiving bad news about the state of these institutions as we learnt that they were in very bad shape and financially losing. In addition to that, the new management examined the administration in Prague aiming at minimizing the number of its staff. We were shocked to see the administrative flabbiness and nepotism.

Third, to make sure to attend all regional and international media events and continuing the cooperation with the related organizations. In this regard, the management decided to talk with the IFJ about alliance. Our Secretary General and the IFJ General Secretary met many times, but the IOJ didn't feel good about it.

Fourth, to try to save the financial situation of the IOJ, I made phone calls with number of Arab officials through colleagues in the Arab associations, especially the ones that were supported in previous years by the IOJ. I didn't receive any feedback as our reputation was not good.

Antonio Nieva's passing away was sad and shocking news in October 1997. We lost a central force to keep the IOJ together.

At that time the IOJ finances were in very bad shape. The resources barely covered the salaries of what was left of the administrative staff and its basic utilities, while the member organizations did not pay their fees in spite of constant reminders to do so. Also, no more financial resources were forthcoming from the commercial companies in spite of our efforts to amend their situation.

I and Treasurer Alexander Angelov asked the Deputy Secretary General Kindness Paradza from Zimbabwe to replace Nieva, but he said that he had a new job not allowing him to come to Prague full-time. Earlier, right after the Amman Congress, Paradza had offered to work as Deputy Secretary General in Prague, but at that time it was not justified to spend the diminishing resources for a second full-time manager.

It was also impossible for me and Angelov to move full-time to Prague because of work in our own countries. There were no other realistic alternatives to replace Nieva. While the staff was cut to a minimum and the only remaining notable property was the former school building in Prague, which was used as a temporary hotel, the secretariat soon stopped carrying out any professional tasks and it was only technically directed by a former lawyer and advisor of the Secretary General, Josef Komárek.

After Nieva's death I contacted the Chinese government to start a dialogue with the All China Journalists' Association ACJA (member since 1950 but withdrawn from active participation in 1965). The Chinese government approved receiving the IOJ delegation of the President, Treasurer and Vice-President for Asia. During the visit in July 1998 we met with a number of officials of the ACJA and we explained the situation of the IOJ and its new direction. We agreed to continue the dialogue until the ACJA would rejoin the IOJ. But it seems that the historical background and the unresolved issues between us were an obstacle in achieving this objective.

Given the lack of financial resources it was impossible for the Executive Committee to meet at any level, not to speak of another Congress. We understood that year after year the legitimacy of the IOJ was declining, but I, Angelov and Komárek still kept the nucleus of the IOJ alive. After Angelov died of cancer in 2012, Komárek and I were left alone.

WHAT IS YOUR CURRENT ASSESSMENT OF THE IOJ, WITH THE WISDOM OF HINDSIGHT?

It is clear that since my election in 1995 I have fought for the survival of the IOJ. In my opinion, it would have been possible, despite the collapse of the communist system, to avoid the IOJ's demise. If a new strategy had been in place to organize the work professionally, financially, and administratively, it would have been possible to maintain the organization in support of its members. By reforming the earlier situation with its positives and negatives, new solutions could have been found.

Unfortunately, this didn't happen as my colleagues and I faced a very difficult situation. We all made great effort to remedy matters, but without success. We came to a dead end, especially after the death of the Secretary General, and none of us was able to work full time in Prague.

As stated in the letter by Manuel Tomé and myself to the IFJ Congress in France in 2016, the fall of the Berlin Wall and the collapse of the Soviet

Union sparked in the IOJ a deterioration of what used to be the world's largest international organization of journalists and the IOJ withered into a nominal entity. Meanwhile, the IFJ grew in size and importance as many IOJ members joined it while retaining their formal membership of the IOJ. By the end of the millennium the movement had reverted to the pre-Cold World War situation, when journalists from all continents and geopolitical areas had effectively one platform for cooperation. Today it is obvious that the IFJ is the sole representative of professional journalists all around the world. However, this does not mean that the IFJ is the direct successor of the pre-war FIJ. Its legal heritage was passed on to the IOJ in 1946, and the IFJ cannot unilaterally claim the legacy of the FIJ and say that it was founded in 1926. Only the IOJ can pass on this legacy, and the IFJ must admit that its history is inseparable from that of the IOJ – the common organization founded in Copenhagen 70 years ago with high hopes, until it was split by the unfortunate Cold War.

The end of our letter in fact makes history: "As the President of the IOJ and its Honorary President elected in the last IOJ Congress in Amman in 1995, we note that the historical development has led to a natural demise of the IOJ as an operational organization. While closing this page in history, we are pleased to pass on to the IFJ the heritage of the pre-war FIJ. We wish you every success in taking good care of this valuable heritage."

FROM OUTSIDE THE IOJ

THÉO BOGAERTS: THREE DECADES IN THE IFJ*

In 1994, one hundred years after the "ler Congrès International de la Presse" which was held in Antwerp, I settled down in that lively, attractive city coming from the surroundings of Brussels, the seat of the IFJ. There I was pleased to meet a distinguished visitor, Kaarle Nordenstreng. It was a meeting between the past President of the IOJ, a man still very active – besides his academic career in Finland – in various sectors of the information on a global level, and the former Secretary General of the IFJ, now 76, who retired in 1985. Kaarle referred to a remarkable, I would add indispensable, initiative, the publication of a book on a century of activities and co-operation in the field of international journalism. And then he asked me for a contribution of personal recollections.

As I was reluctant to plunge into the huge piles of documents stored at the Brussels IFJ Headquarters, I shall try to accomplish to the best of my abilities the home-work expected of me on the basis of personal reminiscences and some papers at my immediate disposal.

Although I had a long career in the Federation, I did not attend its founding Congress in May 1952. At that time I was the Brussels correspondent of a Dutch daily based in Amsterdam.

During the summer of 1952, I was contacted by Marcel Stijns, the chief editor of a Brussels paper, and a founding member of the International Press Institute, who, during World War II, was an information officer in London of the Belgian government in exile. He proposed that I be the Secretary Treasurer of the newly created International Federation, initially on a part-time basis, as the IFJ finances did not permit it otherwise. Fortunately some years later I became the full-time Secretary General, a British colleague having been appointed Honorary Treasurer.

I attended my first IFJ meeting in the autumn of 1952. It was a session of the Bureau, then a rather intimate one as it consisted of only three members and was held in an old-fashioned London hotel in Bloomsbury Square. I very

* The author was IFJ Secretary General 1952–85. Written in May 1996.

much appreciated the typical cockney humour of our first president Clement Bundock, a former Secretary General of the National Union of Journalists. Subsequently, I made the acquaintance of the IFJ affiliates in June 1953 at an Executive session held in Vienna, at that time still under the control of the four Allied Powers.

Thereafter I was actively involved in the implementation of all IFJ decisions under the authority of the Bureau, the Executive Committee and the Congress and, more particularly, of the successive Presidents Clement J. Bundock (UK), Marcel Stijns (Belgium), Max Nef (Switzerland), Helmut Crous (Federal Republic of Germany), Henry J. Bradley (UK), Karl G. Michanek (Sweden), Paul Parisot (France) and Kenneth B. Ashton (UK).

IFJ activities, often based on the results of professional inquiries conducted among our affiliates, covered a wide range of subjects such as the social and economic conditions of journalists, the repercussions of new technologies, professional training, editorial freedom, professional secrecy and protection of copyright.

Being the Federation's Secretary General, I paid due attention to all these aspects but, perhaps due to an inner inclination, I sometimes felt more closely concerned with the safeguarding of the basic human right of freedom of information which, in the IFJ Constitution, was defined as "freedom in the collection of information, freedom of opinion and comment and freedom in the dissemination of news".

DEFENDING PRESS FREEDOM

The IFJ made a most impressive number of representations in countries all over the world where people's free access to diversified information was endangered or frankly violated, drawing the attention of those in power to Article 19 of the Universal Declaration on Human Rights. In its actions, the IFJ always maintained the greatest objectivity. Our interventions were made regardless of the political regime of the state where such infringements occurred. Countries with a totalitarian, one-party system, frequently opposed the IFJ's interventions the principle of "non-interference in internal affairs". Such arguments did not impress us when basic human rights were at stake.

IFJ affiliates themselves could always depend upon the full support of their international association when press freedom or their working conditions were in peril in their own country. While meeting in Washington in 1973, our Executive condemned the interference of the Nixon administration in the American press. Member unions regularly sought the Federation's support when they opposed economic, financial interests and monopolies, which considered press organs as mere commercial, profit-making bodies. Thus, the concept of "internal press freedom", the independence of journalists and the collective independence of the editorial staff towards the proprietors of press enterprises became of ever-growing importance in the Federation's deliberations and activities.

Paying tribute to the courageous stand of its Turkish affiliate against the military regime, which had overridden press freedom, the IFJ Congress assembled in Istanbul in 1972. It rejected all government hospitality but agreed to hear the Minister of State who, in return, had to listen to vigorous and critical speeches delivered by our president Karl Michanek and Turkish journalists. I was a member of a small IFJ delegation, which, thanks to the insistence of our national affiliate, was allowed to visit four Turkish journalists detained in Sagmolcilar Prison in Istanbul, condemned for articles they had written several years before the military coup. The publicity given to this visit certainly contributed to an earlier liberation of our combative Turkish colleagues.

Once, in 1974, returning from Kinshasa, Zaire, to Brussels I heard a personal announcement asking me to disembark in Athens, very early in the morning. The Greek colleagues had convened a special press meeting at the airport to express their gratitude towards the IFJ for its manifold representations (including fact-finding missions by journalists from Austria, the UK and the USA) during the regime of the colonels, who had so ruthlessly suppressed press freedom. Subsequently, the leaders of the Athens Union brought me to a small, picturesque Orthodox church outside the capital where I was requested to light a candle – an impressive, moving event I shall never forget.

ACTIVITIES IN AFRICA

Although, initially, the IFJ mainly consisted of European and North American journalists' unions, it endeavoured to gradually extend its relations in other continents. Contacting organizations in the so-called Third World, we always stressed the fact that the assistance we could offer was not linked to any conditions whatsoever.

Our African Journalism Institute organized several three-week seminars. I participated in those held during the 1970s in Yamoussoukro (Ivory Coast), Lomé (Togo), Nairobi (Kenya) and Maseru (Lesotho) with the generous financial support of our affiliates, mainly in Scandinavia. African participants were selected carefully, most of them having been designated by the information media of their respective countries and not by their governments. Programmes were always developed in close co-operation with the journalists of the countries concerned.

Participants appreciated being able to report frankly on their working conditions and to refer to specific difficulties they experienced in that process. Local journalists, for instance, often felt they were being discriminated against by their leaders, who frequently preferred to grant interviews to special envoys of Western media with a large dissemination. During a stopover in Johannesburg on our way to Lesotho in 1978, my Swedish colleague Hernlund and I entertained non-white South African journalists in a big hotel where they had never set foot before.

During the Maseru seminar, participants approved a strongly worded resolution on the repercussions of apartheid on their work. Subsequently Hernlund and I proceeded to Pretoria, where we delivered the text to the South African Minister of Information, Justice and Police. It provoked his wrath and indignation, but some days later punitive measures against several non-white journalists were lifted.

RELATIONS WITH THE IOJ

For several years after the founding of the IFJ there were no official contacts whatsoever between the two international organizations. It even happened at a Bureau meeting in the 1950s that one member criticized me because – just as a matter of courtesy – I replied to New Year's wishes I had received from the IOJ. Meanwhile, however, personal contacts developed at East-West meetings during the gradual decline of the Cold War.

The pending Helsinki Conference on Security and Co-operation in Europe was in the minds of the IFJ Executive Committee meeting in Washington 1973, when it held a full debate on future East-West relations. Our Bureau was instructed to "establish contacts with journalists' organizations all over the world, including the IOJ and what was called journalists' circles of the People's Republic of China, hereby clearly underlining the different conceptions concerning press freedom".

Following this decision, delegations of the IFJ and the IOJ directed by their respective presidents Karl Michanek and Jean-Maurice Hermann met in Kusnacht-Lüzern in September 1973.

A second meeting was convened in Prague and the spa of Karlovy Vary. I highly appreciated my first visit to the superb city of Prague, guided by IOJ colleagues who also invited us to a performance at the opera. However, it was obvious that there were still differences on basic principles. It was clear, for instance, that, when referring to the forthcoming Helsinki conference, the IOJ was particularly interested in the general political objectives, whereas the IFJ restricted its claims to the free flow of information and the exercise of the profession under the most appropriate conditions. Nevertheless, it felt during our meeting as if some specific initiatives could be taken jointly in the purely professional field.

This meeting took place in a pleasant, relaxed atmosphere notwithstanding a brief, minor incident. Having asked the president of the host union to authorize the IFJ delegation to pay a brief visit to a Czechoslovakian journalist who was being detained, the reply came immediately: "Mr. Bogaerts, you are most impertinent. Why ask such a question while you are here enjoying our hospitality?" When I answered that in 1972, in Istanbul, we had obtained permission to see some Turkish journalists in prison, my colleague simply replied: "We are not in Turkey here." Of course I did not pursue the matter.

Delegations of both internationals met once more in June 1975 under the bright sun of Capri, immediately after one of the International Encounters of European Journalists so perfectly organized by our friends in the National Federation of the Italian Press. The Italian colleagues, who, at that time, were affiliated with neither international, brilliantly played their role of "bridge builders", and they could hardly have chosen a more attractive location to extend their hospitality. On Capri, the two internationals approved a substantial declaration on prospects for co-operation, which was welcomed by the IFJ World Congress in Vienna (May 1976) as a "useful basis for the future development of relations between the IFJ and the IOJ".

Thereafter there were ever more numerous occasions for meetings and discussions: UNESCO's General Conferences, specific meetings convened by UNESCO on various subjects, discussions on the protection of journalists on dangerous missions organized by the International Press Institute, the activities of the "Club des journalistes européens" created by Jean Schwoebel of *Le Monde*, bilateral agreements concluded between national unions in Eastern and Western Europe, etc. Personally, I have excellent reminiscences of an East-West journalists' meeting organized in Warsaw by our Polish colleagues.

The extension of these contacts was entirely consonant with the letter and the spirit of the Final Act of the Conference on Security and Co-operation in Europe, signed in Helsinki on August 1, 1975. Obviously, the IFJ was particularly interested in the concrete proposals related to information in the so-called 3rd basket of the Final Act: "Co-operation in the humanitarian and other fields". In May 1976, the IFJ Bureau confirmed its full support for the intentions expressed in this text, more specifically regarding the exchange of information, its dissemination, the access to the sources and the improvement of the journalists' working conditions.

In June 1977 a conference was held in Belgrade with a view to examining the follow-up of the Helsinki Act. For this meeting I drafted a report on both the positive and the negative aspects of the implementation of the provisions regarding the press in the "3rd basket". It covered a wide range of subjects such as the sale of Western newspapers in Eastern Europe, difficulties experienced by foreign correspondents in obtaining a visa or a permanent working permit (either in the West or in the East), access to official or non-official sources of information, travelling restrictions, seizure of documents, etc. Let me just quote two examples from this report. In 1977, the president of the Association of Hungarian Journalists, Joseph Palfy – incidentally, a charming colleague whom I learned to appreciate – was refused an entry visa to the UK, where he intended to cover a visit by President Carter as well as a NATO summit (which he had frequently done before). No reason whatsoever was given for this measure. The BBC having transmitted an interview with Alexander Solzhenitsyn, the Soviet authorities refused a visa to its Director General for a visit to Moscow.

Such facts and many others may currently seem ridiculous and puerile to us, especially to young journalists who did not experience the political antagonisms and bickering during the Cold War.

A TRIP TO CHINA

When I started my career in the IFJ, with the political constellation in the world being then what it was, I could hardly imagine that one day I would stroll on the Great Wall as a guest of the All China Journalists' Organization.

After their break with Moscow the leaders of the People's Republic started expanding contacts with the Western World and the Chinese Journalists joined in this trend. First they invited a delegation of the Swiss Association of Journalists to their country and this organization proposed that the IFJ establish contacts with the colleagues in China. It resulted in a formal invitation to the IFJ to send representatives to the People's Republic. Thus, in July 1981, President Parisot, First Vice-President Lehni and I set off for China.

A Chinese lady fluent in French was a friendly and excellent guide during our visits to Peking, Xian, Shanghai and Hanshow. Everywhere we enjoyed a cordial welcome and delicious food. It really was a most interesting experience. Meanwhile, however, we were aware of the fact that, by inviting us, the Chinese colleagues also took the opportunity to emphasize the distance they had taken from the IOJ, which they had left for political reasons. We were told, for instance, that they immediately discarded any document sent to them by the Prague organization. Meanwhile it was clearly felt on both sides there was no specific reason whatsoever to assume that the Chinese journalists would apply for IFJ membership. There were no discussions on press freedom. Once, however, we took the opportunity of mentioning the situation of a Chinese imprisoned for having expressed opinions not corresponding to the official doctrine of the Communist Party. The deputy mayor of Shanghai replied that the man concerned had violated the laws of his country and, addressing our French colleague Parisot, he asked: "A French journalist criticizing President Mitterand wouldn't he be put in jail immediately?" Did he really mean what he said? We never knew.

At the end of an interesting and agreeable sojourn in the People's Republic we three IFJ delegates took leave of our gentle guide at Peking airport. "Alas, I said, this is the end of our gang of four!" All of a sudden, her face turned taut. She clearly had not appreciated the political references of my joke. Nevertheless, during the following years, she always sent me nice, artistic cards with kind New Year greetings.

HIFZI TOPUS: A QUARTER OF A CENTURY AT UNESCO*

I started working at UNESCO in January 1959 at the Department of Information. The Department comprised three parts: the Division of Development of Mass Communication, the Division of Free Flow of Information, and the Office of Public Information (OPI).

The first Division's main tasks were professional training of journalists, professional ethics, development of the press, and use of mass media in education. This division did research and published reports on a wide range of topics as shown in the series *Reports and papers on mass communication*.

UNESCO cooperated with most international and regional media and journalism organizations. UNESCO participated in the meetings organized by these organizations, and invited them as observers to its own meetings.

TRAINING OF JOURNALISTS

UNESCO started dealing with the training of journalists already in 1949 but a crucial effort in this area was made in 1957 when 25 governmental and professional representatives initiated the founding of regional training centres. The reasons for UNESCO to work on training issues were the role of the media in keeping peace, promoting economic development, education and culture. There were also huge technological developments in those years. The newly independent countries especially expected to utilize these developments.

France took responsibility for founding an international centre for training journalists at Strasbourg University. UNESCO supported the project and the first regional centre started by discussing international journalism training methods. Various European, African, Arab countries, and the Soviet Union and Socialist countries participated. The IOJ President at that time, Jean-Maurice Hermann, played an important role. After its opening in 1957, the Strasbourg Centre directed by Jacques Leauté organized such meetings every year.

The second regional centre of CIESPAL was founded in 1959 with the support of UNESCO in Quito, Ecuador. They too organized similar regional meetings every year. FELAP had an active role in its foundation and its activities. The third regional centre CESTI, again with UNESCO's support, was founded within Dakar University. It held regional meetings every year and organized training programmes at university level.

---

* The author was specialist on communication at UNESCO 1959–83. Written in May 2014.

In addition, UNESCO organized regional journalist training meetings in Cairo, Manila, Kampala, Nakpur, Beirut and Tunis. Professional organizations including the IOJ were invited to all these meeting. UNESCO also sent experts to member countries to enhance training for journalists and to found schools of journalism. For example, the School of Journalism in Ankara University in Turkey started in 1965 with UNESCO's support.

RESEARCH ON INFORMATION AND COMMUNICATION

UNESCO included this issue in its programme in 1957 and organized an international meeting in Paris. But prior to this, UNESCO published a bibliography on the situation of the communication research institutes in the world. Representatives from the USA, France, England, Germany, Belgium, the Netherlands, Sweden, Italy, Japan, Turkey and the Soviet Union participated in the 1957 meeting.

It was decided at this meeting to establish an organization called the International Association for Mass Communication Research (IAMCR) to enhance the international cooperation in this area. The IOJ President, Jean-Maurice Hermann, attended the founding meeting and the IAMCR. I, too, attended as a young Turkish journalist. Later, in the 1970s and the 1980s, Kaarle Nordenstreng as both President of the IOJ and Vice-President of IAMCR, contributed to the IAMCR, often in projects supported by UNESCO.

In 1978–80 Professors Kaarle Nordenstreng and Yassen Zassoursky, representing both the IAMCR and the IOJ, played effective roles to deliver research for the MacBride Commission.

MASS MEDIA CODES OF ETHICS

UNESCO analysed the situation of the professional ethics in journalism in a book called Mass Media Codes of Ethics and Councils. UNESCO's General Conference, in a resolution adopted in 1974, called for the preparation of national codes of ethics in the mass media which would be designed to promote the sense of responsibility. The IOJ organized a professional ethics conference in Budapest 18–22 July 1973. This meeting was the first of its kind in the area of ethics. Later in 1975, the IOJ again worked on the issue of ethics in developing countries, with 50 representatives participating. The resolutions of this meeting became a source for future developments.

Later the IOJ continued its work in this area by publishing a book *Professional Codes in Journalism* and compiling an inventory of journalistic codes of ethics.

PROTECTION OF JOURNALISTS

The first proposals to do something in this question came from the International Federation of Newspaper Editors after the lives of journalists following the Korean and Vietnam wars became imperilled. Later on several professional organizations made recommendations to protect journalists working on dangerous missions. The United Nations took this issue onto its agenda and UNESCO followed up in the middle of the 1970s.

An important meeting on the topic was convened by the MacBride Commission in 1978 in Stockholm. The MacBride Report of 1980 highlights this topic, although the proposals are less binding than its Chairman Seán MacBride suggested. Both the market-oriented Americans and the state-oriented Soviets were suspicious of concrete measures to protect journalists, who were seen as a potential threat to the interests of private media proprietors as well as governments.

In the 1980s UNESCO followed up the examination of measures to protect journalists. In a consultative meeting in Paris it had good cooperation with the IOJ, the IFJ and other professional journalists' organizations, but the publisher organizations disagreed – in fact they made this topic a part of their campaign against UNESCO at large, with accusations of limiting freedom of information.

CONSULTATIVE MEETINGS OF INTERNATIONAL AND REGIONAL ORGANIZATIONS OF JOURNALISTS

I was acting chief of UNESCO's Division for Free Flow of Information and Communication Policies in February 1978 when I signed a letter of invitation addressed to international and regional associations of journalists to attend a consultative meeting at the UNESCO headquarters on 17–19 April 1978. Those invited included the IOJ, IFJ, FELAP (Federation of Latin American Journalists), FELATRAP (Federation of Latin American Press Workers), FAJ (Federation of Arab Journalists), CAJ (Confederation of ASEAN Journalists), UAJ (Union of African Journalists), and UCIP (Catholic Union of the Press).

The consultation agenda was wide, extending from the protection of journalists to professional ethics, legal rights and responsibilities as well as working conditions and new technologies. The meeting went very smoothly, far from the East-West and North-South conflicts which were characteristic of many media gatherings at that time. The mood was constructive and the participating organizations were ready to continue to pursue the common issues with a view to concrete results. Consequently, further consultative meetings were convened every second year, every time more and more on the initiative of the participating organizations themselves, whereby UNESCO gradually became an observer of an autonomous "Consultative Club" of international and regional organizations of journalists. UNESCO welcomed this development in which a crucial role was played by the IOJ and its President.

Among the concrete outcomes of the consultative meetings was a landmark document *International Principles of Professional Ethics in Journalism* issued in 1983 and a book *Journalist: Status, Rights and Responsibilities* edited by Kaarle Nordenstreng and myself and published by the IOJ in 1989. Later in the 1980s the work on the protection of journalists, in cooperation with the International Committee of the Red Cross, led to a Hot Line for the safety of journalists on dangerous missions.

EVALUATION OF MY WORK AT UNESCO

I spent 25 years at UNESCO – 15 years in the Division of Development of Mass Communication (1959–1974) and eight years in the Division of Free Flow of Information and Communication policies (1975–1983). I had excellent relations with my colleagues and my directors. I will never forget the assistance of the Assistant Director-General, Tor Gjesdal, a founding member of the IOJ. He had also been the Minister of Information of the exiled government of Norway. Lloyd Sommerlad, an Australian journalist, and I had very effective cooperation. Pierre Navaux, who was the Division Director of Development of Mass Media, and I worked together in harmony for many years.

My relations with the representatives of the professional organizations were excellent, particularly with the former president, Jean-Maurice Hermann. I had read his articles in *Cahiers Internationaux* magazine for ten years prior to joining UNESCO. He was also a progressive and an independent like me.

We worked as friends with Kaarle Nordenstreng – who followed Hermann as IOJ President – throughout my career. Our friendship started at the consultative meetings, including one at his University in Tampere.

I always worked in harmony with IFJ's General Secretary, Theo Bogaerts, FELAP's revolutionist President Carnero Checa, and among the executives of IOJ Nestor Ignat, Aurelian Nestor and Gérard Gatinot.

BAD AND GOOD MEMORIES

I experienced the greatest disappointment in October 1975 in Warsaw at the General Conference of OIRT. The speech I had given as the UNESCO observer at the conference of the International Radio and Television Organization

OIRT was met with an aggressive response from the Soviet representative Sergei Lapin, and I had to leave the meeting. UNESCO did not attend the OIRT meetings in the following 4–5 years.

IPI General Secretary Peter Galliner's continuous destructive campaign against UNESCO was also among my bad memories.

At the meeting that I organized during my years at UNESCO, the IOJ and the IFJ never had any friction between them. Both organizations always agreed on issues such as the working conditions of journalists, the protection of journalists and mass media ethics. We offered grounds for these agreements.

Throughout the 25 years I spent at UNESCO, I participated in important themes such as freedom of the press, the training of journalists, the protection of journalists, and the contribution of the media to world peace. Those were the happiest years of my life.

PAOLO MURIALDI: BRINGING THE IOJ AND THE IFJ TOGETHER*

When the Cold War caused divisions in many international organizations, the organization of Italian journalists, the National Federation of the Italian Press (FNSI), decided to stay autonomous. It joined neither the IOJ, with headquarters in Prague, nor the IFJ, whose headquarters were in Brussels.

The principal motive for the Italian trade union choice was a concern to protect the unity of the class during a period of many strong ideological contradictions inside the country. In fact the FNSI included among its members media journalists and those of the organs of all political parties. The unifying characteristic of the trade union was a valid pledge to establish professional and compensatory conditions after the disastrous Fascist war.

However, for the colleagues who were leading the trade union at that time, autonomy in relation to the two international organisms did not mean isolation. When the process of détente between the two blocs started to bear its first fruits at the beginning of the 1960s, the leaders of the FNSI took the first steps to establish the relations between the IOJ and the IFJ, at least on a European level.

The Vietnam War was raging; in the Middle East there was another armed conflict brewing; but in Europe the hopes raised by Pope John XXIII, the Soviet leader Khruschev and the US President Kennedy were not gone. On the contrary, they were renewed concretely through the plans of the Conference on Security and Co-operation in Europe (CSCE).

So the FNSI, led by Adriano Falvo from 1967 until 1973, succeeded in promoting the first meeting of the European journalists in 1967 overcoming many political and ideological obstacles. In the West the Communist regime of the Eastern countries was distrusted, while on the other side the Western bloc led by the United States was mistrusted and considered "imperialists". However, under these circumstances it was deemed necessary to facilitate reciprocal relations between the trade unionists and also the journalists' associations.

The meeting was held in Lignano, a resort on the upper Adriatic, between 12 and 16 May 1967 and it was attended by trade unionists from 16 European countries and a representative of the IOJ. The leaders of the IFJ were not present. The countries represented were Austria, Bulgaria, Czechoslovakia, France, both Germanys, Ireland, Yugoslavia, Poland, Romania, Sweden, Switzerland, Turkey, Hungary, the Soviet Union and, naturally, Italy.

---

* The author was FNSI President 1974–84. Written in December 1995, translated from Italian in the Language Centre of the University of Tampere.

The results were encouraging. The final motion, carried unanimously, reaffirmed the will to defend peace and democratic freedom and directed the constitution of working groups with their headquarters in Rome to prepare the second meeting in a more concrete way.

The task of the first group was to compare the norms regulating the work of journalists in every European nation. The second group had to compare the norms that protected journalists in the area of social security and assistance.

With the prospects of common work the ice was broken and in April 1968 the meeting of the two groups started in Rome.

Another European meeting was scheduled for May 1969 in Budapest but did not take place. The Warsaw Pact troops' invasion of Czechoslovakia on 21 August 1968 shattered any hopes of détente for the union of journalists. To revive these new conciliatory steps had to be taken between the Great Powers. The signal came in 1972, when US President Nixon visited first Beijing and then Moscow.

Once more the FSNI started the work to promote a second European meeting, which was eventually held on Capri on 12–17 June 1973. This time union members from 19 countries were present. Furthermore, the president of the IFJ was present with a delegation led by a German colleague, Helmut Crous. The IOJ delegation was led by the French Jean-Maurice Hermann, who was universally respected for his sustained commitment to oppose Fascism and Nazism.

The presence of both international union organizations, even if they were not yet ready for an immediate meeting, and the frankness and the spirit of collaboration that characterized the exchange of experiences that were very different from each other, ensured the success of the meeting. It became customary to talk about the "spirit of Capri" as a hallmark of reciprocal good will.

The concluding document, approved by all the delegates, specified the objectives to be achieved: not just the primary one, contributing to consolidating peace mainly through the work of the CSCE initiated in Helsinki but also those activities directly connected to the professional practice of journalists and media, defending their autonomy and fighting against concentration as well as promoting solidarity with the colleagues persecuted for their pursuit of political motives.

The next meeting, again on Capri 23–28 June 1975, with the participation of the unions from 21 countries (in practice, no-one was missing), confirmed the success of the earlier meeting. Underlying the debate there were notably important events, both positive and negative: the war in the Middle East, the return of freedom in Greece and Portugal, the rise of a Fascist state in Chile and finally the horrible war in Vietnam.

An emotional moment of the meeting that I as President of the FNSI remember vividly was the entrance of the Portuguese colleagues, who had gained their freedom in 1974, after more than 40 years of dictatorship. An even more important event on Capri in 1975 was the direct contact between the leaders of the IOJ and the IFJ, which took place at the end of the meeting. Naturally, many opposing positions and different points of view remained, but by this time the ice was broken.

In the debate of the meeting there were two primary questions. The first concerned the journalists' participation in and their responsibility for the business aspects of the press vis-à-vis economic power and technological development. The second issue was how to improve relations between the journalists' unions of Europe, where countries had different social and political systems, in order to facilitate the work of correspondents.

The final statement, approved by all delegates, stressed the importance of engagement against the political aspects of ownership and concentration, the necessity to see technical development directed towards the growth of information and pluralism. Finally the motion recommended not just intensifying the bilateral relations between union members in different countries but also to paying attention to the cultural accords which were maturing in the CSCE.

The Italian trade union organized two more European meetings: on Capri in September 1977 and then at Saint Vincent in the Valle d'Aosta in July 1979. These two meetings were again attended by 21 delegations.

During the meeting of 1977, other improvements between the union members of countries with different social and political systems were achieved. At the same time permanent relations were established with the representatives of UNESCO. The continuing discussions on the practice of journalism during the meeting of 1979 revealed that the different conceptions of press freedom in the West and in the East limited or excluded the possibility of practical agreements.

However, the direct relations between the two internationals ensured by now were a definite merit.

We said goodbye to each other with a promise to reconvene the "committee of Capri" for a new European meeting in 1981. In spite of the commitment of many trade unionists, the Dutch and particularly the Hungarians caused international events to be postponed. The workers' rebellion in Gdansk and the rise of the Solidarity movement in Poland had received significant support in the West, starting with the Pope (John Paul II was elected in October 1978) and then in 1981 the proclamation of martial law in Warsaw wiped out conditions for promoting a new meeting.

The initiative of the Italians lasted for more than ten years. As a colleague and president of the FNSI from 1974 until 1984 I can confirm that this initiative was useful. In spite of the tensions that frequently obscured the opportunity for co-operation, concrete relations in the delicate and important area of information were established. We did indeed get to know each other and we met frequently. We ascertained that those on opposite sides of different political and social ideas could reach agreement or at least exchange experiences.

We also managed to get the two international organizations to meet each other more often than just occasionally. Those familiar with the political circumstances of the world during the 1960s and the 1970s know that our achievement was not minor.

WOLFGANG MAYER: TRYING TO OVERCOME RIVALRY*

The Berlin Wall, which divided Germany during the Cold War, was also the borderline between the IOJ and the IFJ hemispheres in Europe. Competition between these international organizations was not only for recruiting affiliates but also for recognition by other organizations like UNESCO. One of the differences was that the IFJ depended on affiliation fees, while the IOJ could profit from its various business activities. This financial aspect had an impact on this story.

On the Western side of the Wall in Germany, traditionally there were (and still are) two journalists' organizations affiliated to the IFJ: dju (Deutsche Journalistinnen und Journalisten Union – then a part of IG Medien, now under the umbrella of ver.di) and DJV (Deutscher Journalisten Verband).

In the Eastern German Democratic Republic (GDR) only the VDJ (Verband der Journalisten der DDR), which reported membership of some 9,000 journalists in 1988, was a member of the IOJ. East Germany played a very important role for the IOJ because since the 1960s its "International Institute of Journalism Berlin" (IIJB) trained journalists from all over the world. An annual "solidarity bazaar" was an activity of the VDJ which attracted much public attention. Items which journalists had received and collected while travelling abroad were sold on these occasions.

CHASING NEW MEMBERS

It was only in December 1989 that leading representatives of the two German unions met officially for the first time at a workshop in the West German town of Tutzing. In January 1990 the VDJ held an extraordinary congress and an ordinary congress followed in June. At this congress, delegates decided on the dissolution of the VDJ. This came into effect on September 30 that year.

After the unification of Germany, it was in the interests of workers and employees in the Eastern part of the country to join Western trade unions. In the media branch there was a very special situation with the two competing journalists' unions for members. Many leading officers of the dju and DJV saw a good opportunity to recruit new members in the Eastern part of Germany and to strengthen their position vis-à-vis the other union. Similar to "buyers' markets" in other branches, they considered the federal states in the East as a "membership market". When many newspapers and magazines in the former GDR were taken over by Western media houses, members of

* The author was board member of the German dju and the IFJ 1986–2016. Written in March 2014.

their workers' councils travelled to their new colleagues in the new Eastern branches to give advice. They also perceived themselves to be ambassadors of the dju or the DJV. Many of these colleagues engaged in quite aggressive propaganda for their organization. Personally, I belonged to that minority which had the simple message: "Whatever union you choose, it is just necessary to organize".

In 1990, an "IOJ Association for Germany" was created. It had three main aims: first, to continue the traditional international solidarity work of the VDJ, second, to further supply traditional IOJ International Press Cards to members of the former VDJ, and third, to promote a unification of the IFJ and the IOJ. Support for the still existing IIJB was a concrete objective of the association. However, the international press card was the main concern: some 2,500 journalists in the Eastern part of Germany had an IOJ press card. They could only get one from the IFJ if they were members of the dju or DJV. Many journalists hesitated to join the dju or DJV because the membership and card fees were higher than they had been in the VDJ, and the press card of the IFJ was also more expensive than that of the IOJ. To solve this problem, the IOJ Association lobbied hard for a combined and uniform IFJ/IOJ international press card.

The dju and IG Medien leadership supported the "IOJ Association for Germany". Their leading officers were convinced that the IOJ heritage of their colleagues in the Eastern part of Germany should be respected. During that time Holger Wenk, the President of the Association, joined IG Medien delegations to international congresses on several occasions. In return, I was personally invited as IG Medien representative, like colleagues from other IFJ unions, to participate in the IOJ Congress in Harare in 1991. I was even able to address the Congress. Holger Wenk and I were seen like a tandem in international affairs.

Time passed and the sudden death of the IOJ Secretary General, Antonio Nieva in 1997 changed many things. Nearly half a year after Nieva's death two meetings were held in Berlin between the leading representatives of the IOJ Association for Germany and representatives of the IOJ Executive Committee, including the IOJ President Suleiman Al-Qudah. For the meeting of 7 March 1998, the Association drafted a letter which should be sent to double members and other IFJ affiliates as well as a draft for a joint IFJ/IOJ international press card. The IOJ representatives rejected this initiative – they said that they would prefer to talk about all this personally at the next IFJ Congress.

More time passed, and the leadership of the Association no longer perceived a future for their organization. At the end of March 2000 Holger Wenk proposed the dissolution of the Association to a meeting of its members. Due to one of the possible scenarios, in August 2000 an agreement between the IOJ

Association for Germany and the IG Medien section in the district of Berlin-Brandenburg came into effect. Through this, the IOJ Association became the AGI/IOJ: a "working group for international activities" under the umbrella of IG Medien and in close connection with the dju. The aim of this AGI/IOJ was now to support IG Medien in its international work. It was still responsible for distributing the old IOJ International Press Card and did so for some time to come. This working group was independent in the administration of its membership and frequently had office hours in the IG Medien building for renewals of International Press Cards.

CONFLICTING AMBITIONS

At that time in 2000 it was clear that the third aim of the IOJ Association for Germany, to promote a fair unification of the IFJ and the IOJ, had become an illusion. The dju was from the outset one of the IFJ affiliates which promoted a merger of the two international organizations of journalists. But this could not succeed as the rivalry was deeply ingrained in the minds of the majority of the IFJ leaders.

First informal, then formal contacts between both international unions on the level of the general secretaries only started when the Wall fell. Soon it became declared official IFJ policy to build a single world organization of journalists. But how could this be done? Conflicting opinions and ambitions emerged in the search for an answer. Many IFJ leaders were keen to impose their own philosophy on a single world organization. In detail the IFJ strategy was inconsistent.

An IOJ Executive Committee meeting in June 1994 in Prague renewed the mandate of the IOJ leadership to pursue a programmatic unity with the IFJ "on all issues which affect journalists". The advice was "that the IOJ take a step-by-step approach towards an action programme between itself and the IFJ, and to welcome any independent measures that could realize the unification of the two organizations". At the IFJ Congress in May 1995 in Spanish Santander, a resolution was carried proposing steps to work for unity of all "genuine" journalists' unions and to look towards an open and inclusive international unity. But what was "genuine"? This word alone might show that the IFJ leaders wanted to impose their own standards.

In 1996 the different positions became increasingly obvious. Several IFJ affiliates saw a strategy for unification in double membership – that is to be members of both organizations. At least 25, possibly 30, national unions, especially in the so-called Third World, had already acquired dual membership. The board of the dju also discussed and intended to apply for IOJ membership. Others strongly opposed that idea. The French SNJ and the Dutch NVJ in May

1996 tabled a motion at the IFJ Executive Meeting in Montreal to change the statutes "in order to make it impossible to be a member of both international journalists' organizations". If a union wished to be a member of both internationals, it would then become only an associate member without voting rights. The motion referred to the increasing membership figures of the IFJ which "can from now on claim to be the organization capable of rallying the international journalists' trade union movement". This was quite distinct from a merger on an equal footing. This "capability" was certainly strengthened by the increasing fees income.

AN INITIATIVE OF IG MEDIEN

The German dju in IG Medien took another initiative in 1996. As a member of the dju federal board and the dju representative at IFJ, together with Holger Wenk and Bernd Rayer, I visited IOJ General Secretary Antonio Nieva in Prague. After our return, in a letter dated 4 September 1996, which I signed on behalf of my union, IG Medien requested the IFJ Executive Committee "to reopen the debate on contacts with IOJ and to reconsider its Montreal decisions". The letter was addressed to IFJ General Secretary Aidan White, IFJ President Jens Linde and IFJ Vice-President Gustl Glattfelder (a DJV member). IG Medien also offered its services "to moderate a meeting for an exchange of ideas between IFJ and IOJ leaders, on neutral ground in Nuremberg/Germany, half way between Brussels and Prague".

The letter closed, referring to our trip to Prague: "Nieva has several concrete ideas on specific practical projects of cooperation. They concern UNESCO as well as a joint international network to monitor media curtailment (repressive legislation and others) and violence against journalists. My union feels that the IFJ should not ignore them". The next IFJ Executive Committee met in Ljubljana in November 1996. It noted "the wish expressed by a number of IFJ unions" and indeed emphasized the need for closer cooperation between the IFJ and the IOJ. Besides the dju, especially the NUJ of Great Britain and Ireland and the unions in the Portuguese speaking world were behind this idea.

As a result of the Ljubljana meeting the Executive Committee requested the IFJ Administrative Committee to investigate, together with the IOJ, the actual state of affairs between the IFJ and the IOJ in the following four areas:

- Membership matters: to review existing membership and existing conditions for affiliation and possible criteria for admission policy in future.
- Financial affairs: to investigate the current financial crisis of the IOJ and actions taken to recover lost assets.

- Policy and constitution: to carry out a survey of the texts, policies and statutes of the IFJ and the IOJ and to examine their compatibility.
- Activities programme: to prepare a report on the activities of the two organizations covering both international and regional work.

IFJ General Secretary Aidan White informed IOJ General Secretary Antonio Nieva of this in a letter dated mid-December 1996 and asked him for a response.

At an informal meeting with White on 24 May 1997, Nieva agreed on four working groups examining the above areas and on an exchange of documentation. On 12 September White and Nieva had another formal meeting in Sofia. White complained that the IFJ had not yet received the promised documents, and Nieva confirmed that the IOJ would send them. In addition, he suggested that a fifth joint commission be established consisting of unions which are members of both the IFJ and the IOJ. In a message to the IFJ Administrative Committee White reported: "We said that this would not be appropriate". The message ended "I felt that the contacts with the IOJ should be kept as low-key as possible and should focus on getting the process we have agreed working".

At the beginning of October 1997 the IOJ finally submitted some documents to the IFJ. The sudden death of Nieva on 13 October also marked the end of the dialogue. Informing Aidan White of Nieva's death in a letter dated 21 October, IOJ president Al-Qudah wrote: "In this situation we are very sorry to inform you that the arrangement made in Sofia cannot be fulfilled in this period".

A RUDE AWAKENING

More and more IOJ affiliates applied for IFJ membership in the late 1990s. This was considered by many leading representatives of Western unions to be a victory over the old adversary. And it increased the IFJ's income from fees. Some of the new IFJ members had a rude awakening: they were in danger of being kicked out of the IFJ. Having paid one US dollar per year per member to the IOJ before (and those payments were often neglected), the financial burden of the higher membership fees of the IFJ was heavy and they could not pay these fees. The explanation was that, in contrast to the IOJ, the IFJ never had income from business activities.

For many it was a drama: journalists' unions throughout Central and Eastern Europe, having lost the backing of the IOJ, were not prepared to defend the interests of their members when Western media companies started an expansion of their business towards the East. They were driven by the greed to gain profits for their shareholders. One of the most aggressive media houses was the WAZ (Westdeutsche Allgemeine Zeitung). The IFJ policy was not really helpful. General Secretary Aidan White signed a "framework agreement" with WAZ intended to guarantee employees in Eastern countries some rights, but this agreement proved to be mere appeasement: journalists were sacked *en masse* in WAZ media and WAZ bosses in Central and Eastern Europe remained hostile to the unions. Finally, the IFJ, under pressure from the German unions, had to cancel the agreement.

WHAT WOULD HAVE BEEN IF...

Originally, the idea had been to create an "open and inclusive international unity" for journalists all over the world. By 2000 the IFJ was the sole international federation of national unions safeguarding the interests of its 170 affiliates, which the IFJ now claims to represent 600,000 journalists worldwide, but it had to work in a hostile environment. The pressure of governments and media owners on journalists' unions on the national level was harder than ever before. The struggle for press freedom and for professional rights was a greater challenge than ever before. In a changing media landscape everywhere, individual journalists needed backing to fight for sufficient conditions like income opportunities. National unions needed support to help more and more of these individual journalists. The projects which the IFJ was organizing and for which it was responsible were the instruments to meet the demands. More than 100 journalists have died on the job every year, and safety training has become one of the most important activities of the IFJ.

There may be a temptation to ask: What would have happened if it had been possible to merge the IFJ and the IOJ and to create a really open and inclusive international unity? Having once studied history at university, I consider this question purely rhetorical and not serious. History is as it happens, and this question does not solve any of the problems we are facing today.

APPENDICES
DOCUMENTATION ON THE IOJ

LIST OF APPENDICES

APPENDIX 1. MEETINGS OF THE IOJ STATUTORY BODIES 1946–96

	Congress	Executive Committee	Presidium
1946	Copenhagen, June 3–9		
		London, September 13–14	
1947		London, March 10	
	Prague, June 3–7		
1948		Brussels, February 23–24	
		Budapest, November 16–18	
1949		Prague, September 15–17	
1950	Helsinki, Sept. 15–17		
1951			Berlin, March 13–16
		Budapest, May 10–12	
1952			Vienna, December
1953		Prague, October 7–9	
1954		Budapest, October 15–17	
1955		Sofia, October 17–19	
1956			Warsaw, March 18–19
1957		Peking, April 3–4	
1958	Bucharest, May 15–18		
1959		Varna, July 23–24	
1960		Leningrad, July 7–9	
1961			Prague, January 24–27
1962		Havana, January 13–15	
			Prague, April 6–7
	Budapest, August 6–10		
1963			Jakarta, February 22–24
1964		Alger, April 27–29	
1965		Santiago, September 23–25	
1966		Třeboň, September 22–23	
	Berlin, October 10–15		
1967			Roztěž, November 29–30
1969		Balaton, May 15–18	
1970			Potsdam, June 8–9
1971	Havana, January 4–11		
			Prague, September 28–29
1972			Balaton, September 26–29
1973		Baghdad, Sept. 26–29	
1974			Ulan Bator, September 11–14

	Congress	Executive Committee	Presidium
1975			Bucharest, October 21–23
1976	Helsinki, Sept. 21–23		
1977			Paris, November 18–19
1978			Mexico City, November 9–11
1979		Hanoi, November 21–23	Hanoi, November 24, 28
1981	Moscow, October 19–22		Moscow, October 18, 23
1983			Luanda, January 27–29
			Paris, November 22–23
1984		New Delhi, September 20–23	New Delhi, September 19
1985			Quito, June 28 – July 2
1986	Sofia, October 20–23		Sofia, October 19, 23
1987			Moscow, March 17–18
			Nicosia, October 21–23
1988			Prague, March 16
			Brasilia, April 22–24
1989			Addis Ababa, January 11–13
1990			Estoril, January 27–29
			Balaton, May 6–8
		Paris, November 17–20	Paris, November 16
1991	Harare, January 24–29		Harare, January 23–24
			Prague, May 6–9*
			Rio, September 12–16
		Sana'a, November 22–26*	
1992			Madrid, April 23–25
			Prague, October 19–22
1993			Paris, April 26–29
			Barcelona, December 6–9
1994			Prague, June 17–18
			Prague, November 27–28
1995	Amman, January 28–31		Amman, January 27
		Prague, June 21–23**	
1996		Hanoi, July 11–12	

* The new Statutes adopted in Harare in January 1991 renamed the earlier Executive Committee as Council, mandated to lead the IOJ between Congresses. The earlier Presidium was now called Executive Committee, mandated to implement the Congress and Council decisions.

** The revised Statutes adopted in Amman in January 1995 renamed the Council back as Executive Committee, which from this on was the only statutory body under the Congress.

APPENDIX 2. MEMBERS OF THE IOJ LEADERSHIP 1946–96

Period	President	Vice-Presidents	Secretary General (SG) - Treasurer (T)
1946–1947	Archibald Kenyon (UK)	Tor Gjesdal (Norway) Eugene Morel (France) Milton Murray (USA) Alexander Sverlov (USSR)	SG-T Keith F. Bean (Australia)
1947–1950	Archibald Kenyon (-1949)	Eugene Morel (France) Milton Murray (USA) Gunnard Nielsen (Denmark) Pavel Yudin (USSR)	SG-T Jiří Hronek (ČSSR)
1950–1958	Jean-Maurice Hermann (France)	Doudou Guyae (West Africa) Jozef Kowalczyk (Poland) Kaisu-Mirjami Rydberg (Finland) Konstantin Simonov (USSR) Hu Tsuo No (China)	SG-T Jiří Hronek, replaced in 1952 by Jaroslav Knobloch (ČSSR)
1958–1962	Jean-Maurice Hermann	Michal Hoffman (Poland) Daniel Kraminov (USSR) Renato Leduc (Mexico) Mauri Ryömä (Finland) Deng To (China)	SG-T Jaroslav Knobloch, replaced in 1959 by Jiří Meisner (ČSSR)
1962–1966	Jean-Maurice Hermann	Hussein Fahmy (Egypt) Ching Chung Hua (China) Honorio Muñoz García (Cuba) Mamadou Gologo (Mali) Michal Hoffman (Poland) Joesoef (Indonesia) Olavi Laine (Finland) Renato Leduc (Mexico) Pavel Satyukov (USSR)	SG-T Jiří Meisner
1966–1971	Jean-Maurice Hermann	Jean-Babtiste Deen (Guinea) Mamadou Gologo (Mali) Michal Hoffman (Poland) Georg Krausz (GDR) Olavi Laine (Finland) Renato Leduc (Mexico) Hafiz Mahmoud (Egypt) Tsend Namsrai (Mongolia) Nguyen Van Hieu (South Vietnam) Kan Sang Wi (North Korea) Hernán Uribe Ortega (Chile) Ernesto Vera Méndez (Cuba) Michail Zimyanin (USSR)	SG Jiří Kubka (ČSSR) T Norbert Siklósi (Hungary)

Period	President	Vice-Presidents*	Secretary General (SG) - Treasurer (T)
1971–1976	Jean-Maurice Hermann	Ahmed Baha El-Dine (Egypt) Harri Czepuck (GDR) Djeung Djoun Ki (North Korea) J. E. Figueroa Váscones (Peru) Stanislaw Mojkowski (Poland) Tsend Namsrai (Mongolia) Alfredo Olivares Román (Chile) Paavo Ruonaniemi (Finland) Tân Dúc (South Vietnam) Ernesto Vera Méndez (Cuba) Michail Zimyanin (USSR)	SG Jiří Kubka T Norbert Siklósi, replaced in 1974 by András Király (Hungary)
1976–1981	Kaarle Nordenstreng (Finland)	Viktor G. Afanasiev (USSR) Jama Salah Ahmed (Somalia) R. A. Martínez (Puerto Rico) Ahmed Baha El-Dine (Egypt) Freddy Balzán (Venezuela) Harri Czepuck (GDR) Cheick Mouctary Diarra (Mali) Jérôme Dramou (Guinea) Gérard Gatinot (France) Saad Qassim Hammoudi (Iraq) D. Kariyakarawana (Sri Lanka) Kim Kwi Nam (North Korea) Enrique Martini (Chile) Jan Mietkowski/Józef Barecki (Poland) Tsend Namsrai (Mongolia) Paavo Ruonaniemi (Finland) Luis Suárez (Mexico) Tân Dúc (South Vietnam) Ernesto Vera Méndez (Cuba)	SG Jiří Kubka T András Király
1981–1986	Kaarle Nordenstreng	Viktor G. Afanasiev (USSR) Alhaji Bola Adedoja (Nigeria) Efraín Ruiz Caro (Peru) Jorge M. C. Rosales (Ecuador) Baba Dagamaissa (Mali) Jérôme Dramou (Guinea) Saber Falhout (Syria) Gérard Gatinot (France) Saad Qassim Hammoudi (Iraq) Eberhard Heinrich (GDR) Kim Kwi Nam (North Korea) J. M. Palacios (Nicaragua) Tsend Namsrai (Mongolia) Luu Quy Ky (Vietnam) Paavo Ruonaniemi (Finland) Bassam Abu Sharif (Palestine) Luis Suárez (Mexico) Shiro Suzuki (Japan) J. M. Varas (Chile) Leite de Vasconcelos (Mozambique) Ernesto Vera Méndez (Cuba)	SG Jiří Kubka T András Király

Period	President	Vice-Presidents**	Secretary General (SG) - Treasurer (T)
1986–1990	Kaarle Nordenstreng (Finland)	Viktor Afanasjev (USSR) Li Song Bok (North Korea) Charles Chikerema (Zimbabwe) Cheick Mouctary Diarra (Mali) Fernando Diogo (Portugal) Saber Falhout (Syria) Gérard Gatinot (France) Saad Qassim Hammoudi (Iraq) Eberhard Heinrich (GDR) Adrian Ionescu (Romania) George Izobo (Nigeria) Marian Kruczkowski (Poland) Tsukamoto Mitsuo (Japan) J. Molina Palacios (Nicaragua) Ibrahim Nafee (Egypt) Alice Palmer (USA) Armando Rollemberg (Brazil) Bassam Abu Sharif (Palestine) Bayi Sinibaguyfu Mollet (Congo) Luis Suárez (Mexico) Manuel Tomé (Mozambique) Asdrúbal de la Torre (Ecuador) Guillermo Torres (Chile) Boian Traikov (Bulgaria) Lodongiin Tudev (Mongolia) Dao Tung (Vietnam) Ernesto Vera Méndez (Cuba) Imiru Worku (Ethiopia)	SG Jiří Kubka, replaced in April 1988 by Dušan Ulčák (ČSSR), replaced in March 1990 by Bernd Rayer (GDR), replaced in May 1990 by Gérard Gatinot (France) T Károly Megyeri (Hungary)
1991–1994	Armando Rollemberg (Brazil), replaced in 1994 by Manuel Tomé (Mozambique)	Manuel Tomé (Mozambique) Alexander Angelov (Bulgaria) Bayi Sinibaguy Mollet (Congo) Tsegmid Munkhjargal (Mongolia) Fernando Diogo (Portugal) Luis Julio Garcia (Cuba) Kevin P. Lynch (USA) Yacine Mohamed Al Massoudi (Yemen) Moses Nagamootoo (Guyana)	SG Gérard Gatinot Deputy SG Mazen Husseini (Palestine) T Marian Grigore (Romania)
1995–	Suleiman Al-Qudah (Jordan)	Juan Carlos Camano (Argentina) Moses Nagamootoo (Guyana) Jean-François Téaldi (France) Ladi Lawal (Nigeria) Tubal Paez Hernandez (Cuba) Earl Bousquet (St. Lucia) Phan Quang (Vietnam) Naim Tobasi (Palestine) Kevin P. Lynch (USA)	SG Antonio Nieva (Philippines) Deputy SG Kindness Paradza (Zimbabwe) T Alexander Angelov (Bulgaria) Deputy T Shahal Careem (Sri Lanka)

* From the 7th Congress (1971) on, the chairmen of the Social Commission (Bulgaria) and the Professional Commission (Romania) were ex officio members of the Presidium.

** At the 10th Congress (1986) all Commission and Committee chairmen were elected as Vice-Presidents.

APPENDIX 3. DOCUMENTS FROM THE RUSSIAN STATE ARCHIVE 1949–50

ВСЕСОЮЗНЫЙ ЦЕНТРАЛЬНЫЙ СОВЕТ ПРОФЕССИОНАЛЬНЫХ СОЮЗОВ 13

ПРЕЗИДИУМ

6 сентября 1949 г.

№ 2437с

Москва, Калужское шоссе, 66
Дворец труда

Секретно
экз. № 1

Заместителю Председателя Совета
Министров Союза ССР

товарищу МОЛОТОВУ В.М.

I5 сентября с.г. в Праге состоится заседание Международной Организации Журналистов /МОЖ/, на котором будет обсуждаться вопрос о созыве очередного конгресса этой организации.

ВЦСПС просит разрешения направить на заседание Исполкома Международной Организации Журналистов делегацию в составе:

I. Юдина П.Ф. – редактора газеты "За прочный мир, за народную демократию", вице-председателя МОЖ / руководитель делегации/.

2. Заславского Д.И. – члена редколлегии газеты "Правда"

3. Суркова А.А. – редактора журнала "Огонек".

ПРИЛОЖЕНИЕ: копии телеграмм Генерального секретаря МОЖ Гронека.

Председатель ВЦСПС В. Кузнецов /В.Кузнецов/

В архив
Вопрос внесен в ЦК.
В.Захаров
6.IX.49.

М-4486с/6.9.49г.

Вх. 29614

т. Григорьяну –
для внесения в ЦК.
4.III.50г. В. Молотов.

ВСЕСОЮЗНЫЙ ЦЕНТРАЛЬНЫЙ СОВЕТ ПРОФЕССИОНАЛЬНЫХ СОЮЗОВ

ПРЕЗИДИУМ

3 марта 1950 г.

№ 688с

Москва, Калужское шоссе, 66
Дворец труда

Секретно

Заместителю Председателя
Совета Министров Союза ССР

товарищу МОЛОТОВУ В.М.

27 марта 1950г. в Париже состоится третий Конгресс Международной организации журналистов /МОЖ/.

ВЦСПС просит Вашего разрешения послать во Францию на Конгресс МОЖ советскую делегацию в составе:

I. Юдин П.Ф. – Главный редактор газеты " За прочный мир, за народную демократию "/руководитель делегации/

2. Заславский Д.И. – член редколлегии газеты "Правда"

3. Сурков А.А. – главный редактор журнала "Огонек"

4. Полевой Б.Н. – корреспондент газеты "Правда"

5. Жуков Г.А. – корреспондент газеты "Правда"

сроком на I5 дней.

Одновременно ВЦСПС просит Вашего разрешения ассигновать 25000 инвалютных рублей для частичного покрытия расходов по проведению конгресса.

Секретарь ВЦСПС /Л. Соловьев/

Послано
т. Маленкову Г.М.

С-т В. М. Молотова
„4" III 1950г.
Вх. № М-1084с

Проект

ДИРЕКТИВА

делегации советских журналистов на III Конгресс Международной Организации Журналистов /МОЖ/ 26-27 марта 1950г. в Париже.

I. Согласиться с повесткой дня Конгресса, предложенной Секретариатом МОЖ:

Отчет о деятельности МОЖ.
/докладчик Гронек - Ген.секретарь/
Материальное и моральное положение журналистов.
/докладчик Эрман - Франция/
Журналисты и защита мира.
/докладчики: Стилл- США
т.Заславский - СССР/
Отношение МОЖ с ООН.

2. В случае неполучения виз представителями ряда стран для участия на Конгрессе в Париже, поддержать предложение о том, чтобы заключительная часть Конграсса состоялась в Варшаве с участием 50 делегатов из парижской группы.

3. Одобрить деятельность МОЖ за период с II Конгресса. Осудить раскольников из руководства американской гильдии журналистов, союза журналистов Англии и др.стран, вышедших из МОЖ. Подчеркнуть необходимость активизации пропагандистской деятельности МОЖ и укрепления ее деятельности по сплочению прогрессивных журналистов во всех странах, независимо от того, входят их организации в МОЖ или нет, и привлечению их к участию в изданиях МОЖ.

4. По второму вопросу повестки дня выступить с сообщением о материальном положении советских журналистов, показать заботу профсоюза об улучшении экономического и социального положения работников печати, о воспитании высоких моральных качеств журналиста - честности и правдивости.

5. В докладе "Журналисты и защита мира" показать роль и задачи печати в разоблачении поджигателей войны и пропаганде дела мира. Подчеркнуть необходимость широкого и активного участия прогрессивных журналистов всех стран во всемирном движении сторонников мира. Внести предложение о принятии Конгрессом манифеста в защиту мира, демократических свобод и укрепление единства прогрессивных журналистов всех стран.

6. По вопросу о взаимоотношениях МОЖ с ООН поддержать предложение о том, чтобы МОЖ активно отстаивала в ООН вопрос о свободе печати, о честности и ответственности журналистов за свои сообщения в печати.

45
20

Копия
Сов.секретно

Товарищу СТАЛИНУ

Генеральный секретарь Международной организации журналистов Гронек Ирдж в связи с предстоящим в сентябре с.г. очередным конгрессом журналистов обратился в ВЦСПС с просьбой о представлении ему возможности приехать в СССР.

ВЦСПС (тов.Кузнецов) просит разрешения пригласить в СССР в сентябре с.г. Гронек Ирдж для переговоров с советскими журналистами по вопросам, связанным с проведением Международного конгресса журналистов.

Считаю возможным принять предложение ВЦСПС.

Проект постановления ЦК ВКП(б) прилагается.

Прошу рассмотреть.

Председатель Внешнеполитической
Комиссии ЦК ВКП(б) В. Григорьян (В.Григорьян)

21 августа 1950 года

Копии разосланы
товарищам: Маленкову
Молотову
Берия
Микояну
Кагановичу
Булганину
Хрущеву

№ 25-С-1470

11-зм

С-т В. М. Молотова
22/VIII 1950г.
Вх. № М 3240 сс

В дело
11.IX. го полит.

APPENDIX 4. IOJ MEMBER ORGANIZATIONS IN 1966

I.O.J. Member Organisations

ALBANIA: Union of Albanian Journalists.
ALGERIA: Union of Algerian Journalists.
ARGENTINA: Argentinian Federation of Press Workers.
BISSAO (Portuguese Guinea): Journalists' Group of the African Party of Independence of Portuguese Guinea and Capverd Islands.
BOLIVIA: National Grouping of Journalists.
BULGARIA: Union of Bulgarian Journalists.
CAMEROUN: National Union of Cameroun Journalists.
CEYLON: Ceylon Journalists' Association
Press Association of Ceylon.
CHILE: Chilean Committee for the International Relations of Journalists.
COLOMBIA: National Colegio of Journalists.
CUBA: Union of Journalists of Cuba.
CZECHOSLOVAKIA: Union of Czechoslovak Journalists.
DEMOCRATIC PEOPLE'S REPUBLIC OF KOREA: Korean Journalists' Union.
DEMOCRATIC REPUBLIC OF VIETNAM: Association of Vietnamese Journalists.
DOMINICAN REPUBLIC: Dominican Committee of the I.O.J.
ECUADOR: Democratic Journalists' Association of Ecuador.
FINLAND: General Union of Journalists.
FRANCE: National Syndicate of Journalists (C.G.T.).
GAMBIA: Association of Gambian Journalists.
GERMAN DEMOCRATIC REPUBLIC: Union of German Journalists.
GUINEA: National Press Syndicate of Guinea.
GUYANA: I.O.J. Members' Group in Guyana.
HUNGARY: Association of Hungarian Journalists.
INDIA: Indian Committee for Co-operation with the I.O.J.
INDONESIA: Indonesian National Group of the I.O.J.
IRAQ: Iraqi Journalists' Association.
JAPAN: Association of Korean Journalists in Japan.
MADAGASCAR: National Union of Malagasy Journalists.
MALI: National Union of Journalists of Mali.
MEXICO: Mexican Association of Journalists.
MONGOLIA: Union of Mongolian Journalists.
MOZAMBIQUE: Journalists' Group of FRELIMO (Liberation Front of Mozambique).
NICARAGUA: Journalists' Union of Nicaragua.
PANAMA: Panamian Committee of the I.O.J.
PEOPLE'S REPUBLIC OF CHINA: All-China Journalists' Association.
PERU: Peruvian Committee of the I.O.J.
POLAND: Association of Polish Journalists.
RUMANIA: Journalists' Union of the S.R.R.
SOUTH-AFRICAN REPUBLIC: South African Journalists' Circle.
SOUTH VIETNAM: South Vietnam Patriotic and Democratic Journalists' Association.
SOUTH-WEST AFRICA: Journalists' Group of the South-West African National Union (SWANU).
Journalists Branch of the South West African People's Organisation (SWAPO).
SOVIET UNION: Journalists' Union of the U.S.S.R.
SYRIAN ARAB REPUBLIC: Association of Syrian Journalists.
UGANDA: Association of Uganda Journalists.
UNITED ARAB REPUBLIC: Press Syndicate of the U.A.R.
URUGUAY: Association of the Uruguayan Press.
VENEZUELA: Venezuelan Committee of I.O.J. Members.

The Executive Committee of the I.O.J. and its Presidium

President:

Jean-Maurice HERMANN, Secretary General of the National Trade Union of Journalists (C.G.T.) — France.

Vice-Presidents:

Jean-Baptiste DEEN, Head of the Press Bureau of the President of the Republic of Guinea, Secretary General of the Federation of Workers in Information, the Press, Publishing and Books, President of the Pan-African Union of Journalists;

Mamadou El Béchir GOLOGO, Minister of Information and Tourism of the Republic of Mali, President of the National Union oj Journalists of Mali, Vice-President of the Pan-African Union of Journalists;

Michal HOFMAN, Editor in Chief of the Polish Press Agency (PAP);

Georg KRAUSZ, President of the Union of German Journalists (G.D.R.);

Olavi LAINE, President of the General Union of Journalists (Yleinen Lehtimiesliito), Finland;

Renato LEDUC, journalist, I.O.J. International Journalists', Prize, Mexico;

Hafiz MAHMOUD, President of the Press Trade Union of the United Arab Republic;

NAMSRAI, President of the Union of Mongolian Journalists;

NGUYEN van Hieu, Vice-President of the Association of Patriotic and Democratic Journalists of South Vietnam;

KANG Sang-wi, Vice-President of the Union of Journalists of Korea;

Hernán URIBE ORTEGA, Secretary General of the Chilean Committee for International Relations Among Journalists, Secretary of the Commisison for Information and Co-operation Among Journalists of Latin America;

Ernesto VERA, President of the Union of Journalists of Cuba;

Mikhail ZIMIANIN, President of the Union of Journalists of the U.S.S.R.

Secretary General:

Jiří KUBKA — Czechoslovakia.

Treasurer:

Norbert SIKLÓSI, Secretary General of the Association of Hungarian Journalists.

MEMBERS:

ALGERIA: Abdelaziz BELAZOUG, Secretary General of the Union of Algerian Journalists;

ARGENTINA: Eduardo Yazbeck JOZAMI, Secretary General of the Press Trade Union of Buenos Aires;

BOLIVIA: Fernando SIÑANI BALDIVIESO, President of the National Group of Journalists;

BULGARIA: Georgi BOKOV, President of the Union of Bulgarian Journalists;

CAMEROUN: Jules-Théodore MISSAM-HAN, Secretary General of the National Union of Camerounian Journalists;

COLOMBIA: Leopoldo VARGAS, President of the National Association of Journalists of Colombia;

CZECHOSLOVAKIA: Adolf HRADECKÝ, Secretary General of the Union of Czechoslovak Journalists;

MEMBERS OF THE I.O.J. IN 108 COUNTRIES OF THE WORLD

AMERICA	AFRICA	EUROPE	ASIA & AUSTRALIA
A — Countries in which the national organisation of journalists is affiliated to the I.O.J.:			
1. Argentina	24. Algeria	58. Albania	81. Iraq
2. Colombia	25. Cameroon	59. Bulgaria	82. Mongolia
3. Cuba	26. Gambia	60. Hungary	83. Vietnamese Democratic Republic
4. Mexico	27. Guinea	61. Poland	84. Chinese People's Republic
5. Nicaragua	28. Mali	62. G.D.R.	85. Korean People's Democratic Republic
6. Uruguay	29. Uganda	63. Romania	86. Syria
	30. U.A.R.	64. Czechoslovakia	
		65. U.S.S.R.	
B — Countries in which there is more than one organisation or more than one organisation affiliated to the I.O.J.:			
7. Bolivia	31. Madagascar	66. Finland	87. Ceylon
8. Ecuador		67. France	88. South Vietnam
C — Countries in which there are groups of members or committees of the I.O.J.:			
9. Chile	32. Bissao*		89. India
10. Guyana	33. Mozambique		90. Indonesia
11. Panama	34. South African Republic		91. Japan**
12. Peru	35. South-West Africa		
13. Dominican Republic	* so-called Portuguese Guinea		** Association of Korean Journalists in Japan
14. Venezuela			
D — Countries in which there are individual members of the I.O.J.:			
15. Brazil	36. Angola	68. Austria	92. Afghanistan
16. Canada	37. Congo/Braz.	69. Belgium	93. Burma
17. Costa Rica	38. Congo/Kinsh.	70. Great Britain	94. Cambodia
18. Salvador	39. Ivory Coast	71. Denmark	95. Cyprus
19. United States	40. Dahomey	72. Spain	96. Hong-Kong
20. Honduras	41. Ethiopia	73. Greece	97. Iran
21. Paraguay	42. Ghana	74. Italy	98. Israel
22. Puerto Rico	43. Mauritius	75. Luxembourg	99. Jordan
23. Trinidad	44. Kenya	76. Netherlands	100. Kuwait
	45. Libya	77. G.F.R.	101. Laos
	46. Malawi	78. Norway	102. Lebanon
	47. Morocco	79. Sweden	103. Malaysia
	48. Mauretania	80. Switzerland	104. Nepal
	49. Nigeria		105. Pakistan
	50. Rhodesia		106. Turkey
	51. Senegal		107. Australia
	52. Sierra-Leone		108. New Zealand
	53. Somalia		
	54. Sudan		
	55. Tanzania		
	56. Togo		
	57. Tunisia		

APPENDIX 5. CHRONOLOGY OF IOJ ACTIVITIES 1967–90*

1967	
Mar 10–11	Meeting of Presidium of Interpress Auto Club (Warsaw)
Apr 5–6	Meeting of Presidium of IOJ Photo Section (Berlin, GDR)
May 3–4	Meeting of IOJ Lottery Commission (Prague)
May 11	Meeting of Interpress Auto Club (Dolny Kazimierz, Poland)
May 12–16	1st Conference of European Journalists (Lignano, Italy)
Jun 13–15	International Conference of Modern Typography (Prague)
Jun 17–18	2nd Interpress Rally (Danzig, Poland)
Jun 20–27	Gathering of editors dealing with economic questions (Moscow)
Jun	Seminar for News Agency Editors of Latin American Countries (Havana)
Jun	Establishment of Interpress Graphic Club (Rostěž, Czechoslovakia)
Jul 20–27	Week of Solidarity with Journalists and People of Vietnam
Oct 16–17	Marking the 50th Anniversary of the Great October Socialist Revolution (Prague)
Oct 24–25	Meeting of Presidium of IOJ Photo Section (Prague)
Nov 3–4	Colloquium on New Trends in Journalistic Training in computer era (Prague)
Nov 16–17	Meeting of Presidium of Interpress Auto Club (Zakopane, Poland)
Nov 25–Dec 12	1st Interpress Exhibition Prague67
Dec	Meeting of IOJ Lottery Commission (Prague)
1968	
Jan 24–25	1st Meeting of IOJ Social Commission (Sofia)
Jan	1st number of IOJ magazine *Interpressgrafik and Interpress Magazin* (in Czech language)
Feb	Establishment of IOJ Professional Commission
Apr 23–25	International conference on publishing an IOJ Journalist Handbook (Prague)
May 3–12	1st International Exhibition "Man and Automobile" (Prague)

* Edited from dossier "IOJ Data and Documents, Special issue for internal use only" by International Journalism Institute IJI, Prague 1988 (325 pages) and later updates. This list does not include meetings of IOJ supreme bodies (see Appendix 1), nor Secretariat meetings (regular and extended). Omitted are also protests, appeals and solidarity actions concerning individual cases as well as regular courses organized by the IOJ schools in Berlin, Budapest, Roztěž-Prague, Sofia and Havana. Various meetings listed were either organized by the IOJ or attended by IOJ representatives.

May 4–10	1st Conference of Interpress Graphic Club (Budapest)
May 10–15	3rd Interpress Rally (Balatonszeplak, Hungary)
May 18	Meeting of Presidium of Interpress Auto Club (Balatonszeplak, Hungary)
Jun 24	Meeting of Presidium of IOJ Photo Section (Warsaw)
Oct 24–25	Meeting of Presidium of IOJ Photo Section (Tbilisi, USSR)
Oct	International Exhibition of Sports Photographs during Olympic Games (Mexico City)
Oct	Meeting of IOJ Lottery Commission (Prague)
1969	
Jan 17–20	1st meeting of IOJ Social Commission for international houses of journalists (Sofia)
Jan 26–27	Consultation of IOJ member unions from the CMEA countries (Roztěž, Czechoslovakia)
Mar 14	Establishment of IOJ Information Centre for Africa (Cairo, Egypt)
Mar 26–27	Meeting of Presidium of IOJ Photo Section (Sofia)
May 11	Meeting of Interpress Auto Club and 4th Interpress Rally (Dolny Kazimierz, Poland)
May 12	1st Meeting of IOJ Professional Commission (Bucharest)
May	IOJ was granted again Consultative Status at UNESCO (category B)
May	Meeting of IOJ Lottery Commission (Moscow)
Jun 9–12	Meeting of journalists from the Baltic Sea countries (Siikaranta, Finland)
Jun 11–18	2nd Interpress Exhibition Prague69 (Prague)
Sep 4–6	Gathering of European Journalists (Jablonna, Poland)
Sep 18–24	International Conference on the Fight against American Imperialism (Pyongyang)
Oct 1–5	International Gathering of Journalists on Centenary of the Birth of V.I. Lenin (Leningrad)
Nov 14	Meeting of Presidium of Interpress Auto Club (Prague)
Nov	Meeting of Presidium of IOJ Photo Section (Leningrad)
Dec	Meeting of IOJ Lottery Commission (Prague)
1970	
Apr	Meeting of IOJ Social Commission for international houses of journalists (Budapest)
May 4–5	Meeting of Presidium of Interpress Auto Club (Warsaw)
May 26	IOJ was granted again Consultative Status at UN/ECOSOC (category II)
Jun 7	International Symposium on 25th Anniversary of Potsdam Agreement (Potsdam, GDR)

Jun 21–23	Meeting of Presidium of IOJ Interpress Graphic Club (Warsaw)
Jun 26–Jul 5	2nd International Exhibition "Man and Automobile" (Prague)
Jun 27–29	Meeting of Presidium of IOJ Photo Section (Prague)
Jun 28–30	International Symposium on "Traffic Safety and Journalists" (Prague)
Jul 2–3	Meeting of Presidium of Baltic Club of Journalists (Warsaw)
Jul 22–23	Gathering of representatives of Socialist countries on training of journalists (Prague)
Sep 9–10	Preparatory meeting of IOJ Club of Agricultural Journalists (Nitra Pieany, Czechoslovakia)
Oct 8–9	2nd Conference of Club of Baltic Journalists (Ystad, Sweden)
Oct 9–11	5th Interpress Rally (Tokaj, Miszkolz, Hungary)
Nov 6–16	5th Interpress Photo Exhibition (Prague)
Dec	Meeting of IOJ Lottery Commission (Prague)
1971	
Mar 27–28	Executive Committee Meeting of Interpress Auto Club (Karl-Marx-Stadt, GDR)
Apr 21–22	Meeting of Presidium of Club of Baltic Journalists (Gdansk, Poland)
May 18	Meeting of Presidium of Interpress Auto Club (Prague)
May 26–29	Meeting of Presidium of IOJ Photo Section (Budapest)
Jun 1–10	3rd Conference of Club of Baltic Journalists (Helsinki)
Jun 3–6	6th Interpress Rally (Low Tatras, CSSR)
Jun 7–8	General Assembly of Interpress Auto Club (Pezinok, Czechoslovakia)
Jun 14	Special gathering to mark the 25th anniversary of the IOJ (Prague)
Jun 24–26	Meeting of IOJ Club of Agricultural Journalists (Prague)
Jun 29	Consultation of IOJ member unions from the CMEA countries (Prague)
Jul 5–8	Meeting of Presidium of Interpress Auto Club (Warsaw)
Sep 28–29	Meeting to mark the 25th anniversary of the IOJ (Prague)
1972	
Feb 22–23	Meeting of foreign policy journalists from the European Socialist countries (Pezinok)
Feb 29	Meeting of Presidium of Interpress Auto Club (Prague)
Mar 7–10	Meeting of IOJ Social Commission (Warsaw)
Apr 17–19	Meeting of Presidium of IOJ Photo Section (Sofia)
May 10	Meeting of graduates CTK school in Roztěž and IOJ schools in Budapest & Berlin (Prague)

May 16	Consultation of IOJ member unions from the CMEA countries (Prague)
May 18	Gathering to Mark International Day of Solidarity with the People of Vietnam (Prague)
May 31–Jun 7	Gathering of European Public Opinion on European Security and Cooperation (Brussels)
Jun 23–27	7th Interpress Rally (Uzhgorod–Lvov, USSR)
Sep 11–13	2nd Gathering of European Journalists (Jablonna)
Nov 9–24	6th Interpress Photo Exhibition (Sofia)
Dec 10–13	International jury announces prize winners of IOJ Contest "Peace to Vietnam" (Prague)
1973	
Jan 23–24	International Symposium marking Julius Fucík's 70th birthday (Prague)
Apr 3–5	Meeting of IOJ Social Commission (Sofia)
Apr 18–21	Meeting of IOJ Club of Agricultural Journalists (Roztěž, Czechoslovakia)
Apr 21–24	2nd meeting of foreign policy commentators from European Socialist countries (Prague)
May 7–14	Meeting of European Journalists on Security and Cooperation (Brussels)
Jun 18–22	1st IOJ/UNESCO Colloquy on development of media and training of journalists (Budapest)
Jun 19–21	2nd Meeting of European Journalists (Naples–Capri)
Jul 9–10	Meeting of Presidium of Interpress Auto Club (Warsaw)
Jul 21–31	10th Festival of Youth and Students (Berlin)
Jul	Contest on 25th anniversary of the foundation of the Korean People's Democratic Republic
Sep 14–15	1st meeting of IOJ and IFJ representatives (Zurich–Küssnacht)
Oct 12–14	8th Interpress Rally (Tokay, Hungary)
Oct 25–31	World Congress of Peace Forces (Moscow)
Nov 10–17	Meeting of Presidium of IOJ Club of Agricultural Journalists (Warsaw)
Nov 22–25	Meeting of Presidium of Interpress Auto Club (Zwickau, GDR)
1974	
Feb 15–17	Consultation of IOJ member unions from the CMEA countries (Prague)
Mar 21–25	International Commission to Investigate the Crimes of the Military Junta in Chile (Helsinki)
Mar 24–31	International Gathering of Journalists on Science and Technology (Moscow–Leningrad)

Apr 8–9	Celebration of 10th Anniversary of the IOJ International Centre in Budapest (Prague)
Apr 18–19	2nd meeting of IOJ and IFJ representatives (Karlovy Vary, Czechoslovakia)
May 24	Celebration of the 25th Anniversary of the World Peace Movement (Prague)
Jun 1–7	International Gathering of Journalists Dealing with Agricultural Questions (Sofia)
Jun 8–13	Meeting of IOJ Lottery Commission (Varna, Bulgaria)
Jun 21–29	3rd Interpress Exhibition Prague74 (Prague)
Jul 28	Celebration of 15th Anniversary of Establishment of the House of Journalists (Varna)
Jul 30–Aug 2	4th Congress of Federation of Arab Journalists (Damascus, Syria)
Sep 17–22	Meeting of Capri Committee for Cooperation among European Journalists (Naples)
Sep	9th Interpress Rally and Meeting of Presidium of Interpress Auto Club (Gera, GDR)
Oct 1–7	Seminar of Journalists on Agricultural Questions of CMEA Countries (Moscow)
Oct 15–16	1st Consultative Meeting of IOJ member unions from the CMEA countries (Roztěž)
Dec 11	Special meeting to mark the 10th anniversary of the IOJ International Lottery (Prague)
Dec 17–21	Constituent Congress of Union of African Journalists (Kinshasa, Zaire)
1975	
Jan 21	The IOJ Secretariat approves the statute of the Julius Fucik Medal of Honour
Jan 28	1st issue of *Interpress Magazine* in Hungarian language
Jan	Opening of IOJ Centre for Europe (Paris)
Feb 11–12	2nd Consultative Meeting of IOJ member unions from the CMEA countries (Sofia)
Mar 1	Preparatory meeting for the Third Gathering of European Journalists (Paris)
May 5–12	International Colloquium on European Security and Cooperation (Helsinki)
May 9	Meeting of Solidarity with the People of Vietnam (Berlin, GDR)
Apr 29–May 22	7th Interpress Photo Exhibition (Berlin)
Jun 2–6	Meeting of IOJ Lottery Commission (Berlin)
Jun 24–28	3rd Meeting of European Journalists (Naples–Capri)

Jun 28	3rd meeting of IOJ and IFJ representatives (Capri)
Sep 15	Inauguration of IOJ Centre for the Study of the African Press (Budapest)
Oct 5–7	Consultation on educating journalists in developing countries (UNESCO–Paris)
Oct 26–27	10th Interpress Rally (Sedlcany, Czechoslovakia)
Oct 26–30	3rd Gathering of European Journalists (Jablonna)
Dec 2–5	2nd IOJ/UNESCO Colloquy on training of journalists in developing countries (Visegrad)
1976	
Feb 3–5	Special conference in support of the Angolan people (Luanda)
Feb 20	International Consultation on *Interpressgrafik* magazine (Budapest)
Mar 1–3	Meeting of Presidium of IOJ Photo Section (Prague)
Apr 6–8	3rd Consultative Meeting of IOJ member unions from CMEA countries (Zaborow, Poland)
May 9–17	13th Congress of IFJ (Vienna)
May 30–Jun 12	FELAP Constituent Congress (Mexico City)
Jun 2–12	Meeting of IOJ Lottery Commission (Budapest)
Jun 29–30	Consultation of CMEA journalists' union secretaries for foreign relations (Roztěž)
Aug 23–Sep 3	Seminar on training of regional correspondents by IOJ & UNAJOM (Bamako, Mali)
Sep 23–26	Conference on Stopping the Arms Race, Disarmament and Release of Tension (Helsinki)
Nov 1–3	Meeting of Presidium of IOJ Photo Section (Prague)
Nov	UNESCO General Conference (Nairobi, Kenya)
Dec 14–17	5th Congress of Federation of Arab Journalists (Alger)
Dec 15–22	UNESCO Seminar in Tunis
1977	
Jan 14–16	World Forum of Peace Forces (Moscow)
Feb 22–24	Meeting of Presidium of IOJ Photo Section (Prague)
Mar 1–3	4th Congress of USSR Union of Journalists (Moscow)
Mar 7–11	UNESCO Permanent Committee of Non-Governmental Organizations (Paris)
Mar 30–31	4th Consultative Meeting of IOJ member unions from CMEA countries (Tihany, Hungary)
May 13	Round table of students of International Journalists Training Centre in Budapest
Jun 1–3	UNESCO Meeting on contribution to an ethic of communication (Paris)

Jun 20–25	Meeting of IOJ Lottery Commission (Leningrad)
Sep 27–30	4th Meeting of European Journalists (Capri)
Sep 30	4th meeting of IOJ and IFJ representatives (Capri)
Oct 14	Meeting of Club of Agricultural Journalists (Varna)
Oct 20–Dec 20	8th Interpress Photo Exhibition (Moscow)
Oct	Release of IOJ draft Convention on relations among all European Journalists
Nov 3–6	3rd IOJ/UNESCO Colloquy on decolonization of information (Baghdad)
Dec 6	Gathering of representatives of Socialist countries on training of journalists (Prague)
Dec 14–15	Meeting IOJ Social Commission on International Rest Homes for Journalists (Varna)
Dec 16	Consultative meeting of IOJ and IFJ on UNESCO draft declaration on mass media (Paris)
1978	
Jan 10–11	Consultative meeting of representatives of international democratic organizations (Helsinki)
Jan 20–22	Conference of European Youth and Students on Disarmament (Budapest)
Jan 27–29	5th meeting of International Commission for investigating crimes in Chile (Alger)
Feb 8	Meeting on the occasion of the International Year of Fight against Apartheid (Sofia)
Feb 9–12	Conference on Peace, Security and Cooperation in the Mediterranean (Athens)
Feb 26–Mar 3	International Conference of Non-Governmental Organizations on Disarmament (Geneva)
Feb	Foundation of the Georgi Dimitrov International Institute of Journalism (Sofia)
Mar 15–20	Meeting of the Women's press representatives from the Socialist countries (Warsaw)
Mar 30–Apr 1	Meeting of Andean journalists (Caracas) and Congress of Bolivian journalists (Bogota)
Apr 3–7	5th Consultative Meeting of IOJ member unions from CMEA countries (Klink–Muritz, GDR)
Apr 10–14	Visit of journalists organizations of liberation movements in Southern Africa
Apr 11–13	Meeting of Editorial Commission for IOJ textbooks (Leipzig, GDR)
Apr 16–19	Meeting of Ministers of Information of Non-Aligned Movement (Havana)

Apr 17–19	Consultative Meeting of international & regional organizations of journalists (Unesco, Paris)
Apr 24–27	UNESCO colloquy on gathering and circulating information in the world (Stockholm)
May 8–12	UNESCO expert meeting on the right to communicate (Stockholm)
May 26–27	Meeting of West European unions of journalists with French NSJ (Paris)
May 31–Jun 1	Meeting of IOJ publishing department on 25th anniversary of *The Dem. Journalist* (Balaton)
Jun 5	Round Table of students of the International Institute for Training of Journalists in Budapest
Jun 12–17	Meeting of IOJ Lottery Commission (Varna)
Jun 13	Meeting of IOJ professional clubs leading bodies (Prague)
Jun 27–28	Meeting of Council of IOJ Journalists' schools (Prague)
Jul 11–14	World Peace Council Presidium Meeting (Moscow)
Jul 28–Aug 5	11th World Festival of Youth and Students in Cuba (Havana)
Aug 28–31	ECOSOC Conference of NGOs on Actions against Apartheid (Geneva)
Sep 4–9	AIERI/IAMCR General Assembly and scientific conference (Warsaw)
Sep 13–14	Consultation on development of *The Democratic Journalist* (Prague)
Sep 15–17	Conference of Solidarity with African and Arab People against Imperialism (Addis Ababa)
Sep 18–22	14th Congress of IFJ (Nice, France)
Sep 24–29	Symposium on the occasion of the 15th anniversary of the Solidarity School in Berlin
Sep 27	Opening of new building of the International Institute for Training of Journalists in Budapest
Sep	Meeting of IOJ Social Commission (Warsaw)
Oct 2–6	UNESCO Permanent Committee of the NGOs (Paris)
Oct 2–6	Meeting of Experts for Communication Research in Latin America (Caracas, Venezuela)
Oct 5–10	Meeting of IOJ Club of Agricultural Journalists (Baghdad)
Oct 17–18	4th Gathering of European Journalists (Jablonna)
Oct 22–27	Meeting of Club of Baltic Journalists (Lubeck, FRG)
Oct 23–28	Meeting of IOJ Social Commission for International Houses of Journalists (Varna)
Nov 4	Consultation of IOJ and IFJ representatives (Paris)
Nov 4	Agreement on Friendship and Cooperation between the IOJ and the FELAP signed

Nov 11–14	Interpress Auto Club Meeting (Zakopane)
Nov 14–29	UNESCO 20th General Conference adopting the Mass Media Declaration (Paris)
Nov 29–30	Meeting of Editorial Council of the magazine *Interpress-grafik* (Budapest)
Dec 4–5	Meeting of Permanent Committee of European journalists, Capri Committee (Rome)
Dec 12–14	Meeting of IOJ Lottery Commission (Prague)
Dec 14	Meeting of UNESCO experts on initiative of the Union of Hungarian Journalists (Budapest)
Dec 15–16	Meeting of Editorial Commission for IOJ textbooks (Budapest)
Dec 18–21	UNESCO experts meeting on free and balanced flow of information (Paris)
1979	
Jan 11	Handing over journalistic equipment for the House of Journalists in Hanoi
Jan 19–21	International Committee for European Security and Cooperation Meeting (Brussels)
Jan 21–24	1st meeting of journalists of Non-Aligned countries (Baghdad)
Jan 26–28	European Forum for Disarmament by committee for European Security (Hague)
Feb 5–12	UNESCO Intergovernmental Conference on Communication Policy (Kuala Lumpur)
Feb 13	1st meeting of IOJ Coordinating Committee for Training of Journalists (Berlin)
Feb 27	Consultation of UNESCO's MacBride Commission (Paris)
Feb 27–28	International meeting on armed aggression of China against Vietnam (Ho Chi Minh)
Mar 6–8	International Solidarity Conference with Vietnam (Helsinki)
Mar 19–30	Exhibition of children's drawings by the International Journalists Solidarity Fund (Prague)
Mar 23–25	Colloquy on popularization of science and technology by French UNESCO Clubs (Nantes)
Mar	1st International Biennial of Humour (San Antonio de Los Banos, Cuba)
Apr 1–3	6th Congress of the Federation of Arab Journalists (Baghdad)
Apr 10–12	Meeting of the Permanent Secretariat of European Journalists Meetings (Budapest)
Apr 24–28	Session of the World Peace Council Presidium (Prague)

May 17–18	UNESCO seminar on protection of journalists by the MacBride Commission (Paris)
May 22–23	International Symposium on influence of media on children and youth (Prague)
May 28–31	Meeting of IOJ Lottery Commission (Bratislava)
May 30–Jun 1	Colloquy on problems of the New International Information Order (Dijon, France)
Jun 18–20	Seminar "Child and Apartheid" by UN Special Committee against Apartheid (Paris)
Jun 18–22	UNESCO Conference of NGOs (Paris)
Jun 18–23	IPI 28th General Assembly (Athens)
Jun 18–24	Meeting of IOJ Club of Agricultural Journalists (Leipzig, GDR)
Jul 2–5	5th Meeting of European Journalists (Saint Vincent, Italy)
Jul 7	5th meeting of IOJ and IFJ representatives (Saint Vincent)
Jul 17–18	6th Consultative Meeting of IOJ member unions from the CMEA Countries (Moscow)
Jul 21–24	FELAP 2nd Congress (Caracas)
Jul	ECOSOC NGOs meeting (Geneva)
Aug 25	Agreement on long-term cooperation between the IOJ and the FAJ signed in Prague
Sep 3–6	6th Summit Conference of Non-Aligned countries (Havana)
Sep 3–9	International seminar by the USSR National Commission for UNESCO (Tashkent)
Sep 8	20th anniversary of the foundation of the International House of Journalists in Varna
Oct 7–11	International seminar in support of Palestine by IOJ Social Commission (Sofia)
Dec 18–Jan 20	9th Interpress Photo Exhibition (Havana)
1980	
Jan 8	Meeting of IOJ Coordinating Committee for Training of journalists (Prague)
Jan 8	Meeting of Commission for IOJ textbooks and teaching aids (Prague)
Jan 21–22	UNESCO consultation with IOJ and IFJ on protection of journalists (Paris)
Jan 26–29	Euro-Arab Journalist Dialogue organized by FAJ (Baghdad)
Feb 2	Opening of the IOJ Solidarity School in Baghdad
Feb 17–Mar 1	Seminar for journalists from the trade union press of Africa (Paris)
Mar 3–11	Information journey of 14 West European journalists to Vietnam and Cambodia

Mar 5–8	Colloquy on tasks of press in development by the Arab Centre for Research (Amman)
Mar 9	Symposium on role of mass media in fight for peace and disarmament (Istanbul)
Mar 9–16	International conference on 110th anniversary of birth of V.I. Lenin (Ulianovsk, USSR)
Mar 18	International symposium on the 95th anniversary of birth of Egon Ervin Kisch (Roztěž)
Mar 20–21	Meeting of the Committee for European Security and Cooperation (Brussels)
Mar 26–30	Conference of Solidarity with the Palestinian People (Baghdad)
Mar 31–Apr 2	Opening of the World Press Photo exhibition (Amsterdam)
Apr 1–3	2nd Consultative Meeting of international & regional organizations of journalists (Mexico)
Apr 2–4	International meeting of journalists on 35th anniversary of victory over fascism (Kiev, USSR)
Apr 14–21	UNESCO Intergovernmental Conference on the Development of Communication (Paris)
Apr 21–25	Meeting of IOJ Lottery Commission (GDR)
Apr 22–26	Seminar in "Week of Information on the Press" (Madrid)
Apr 24–25	Preparatory meeting of IOJ Committee for Studies & Documentation (Prague)
Apr 26–27	Meeting of democratic organizations by AAPSO (Nicosia)
May 2	Meeting of journalist unions of Western Europe (Paris)
May 8–10	Meeting of the World Peace Council preparation for World Parliament of Peace (Budapest)
May 9–20	5th Latin American Seminar of Journalists, organized by UPEC, FELAP and IOJ (Havana)
May 12–16	15th Congress of IFJ (Athens)
May 15–23	18th Meeting of Journalists and Writers on Tourism, FIJET (Tuchepi, Yugoslavia)
Jun 5–7	Seminar on journalism and democracy in Latin America (Santo Domingo)
Jun 9–13	UNESCO Conference on the Mass Media Influence on the Family (Panama)
Jun 9–13	UNESCO Conference on Education for Peace (Paris)
Jun 16–19	Seminar of Interpress Auto Club (Poznan, Poland)
Jul 20–28	Journey of West European journalists to Lebanon – Syria with Palestine and Syrian unions
Aug 1	World Conference against Nuclear and Hydrogen Bombs (Japan)

Aug 19–20	Conference on decolonization & democratization of information (Potsdam–Babelsberg, GDR)
Aug 20–23	Conference of Solidarity with Egyptian Journalists organized by FAJ (Paris)
Aug 25–29	IAMCR/AIERI General Assembly and scientific conference (Caracas)
Sep 11–13	Conference of Solidarity with the fight of the Namibian people (Paris)
Sep 23–25	Preparatory meeting of International Committee on Protection of Journalists (Sofia)
Sep 23–27	World Parliament of Nations for Peace (Sofia)
Sep 29–Oct 3	4th IOJ/UNESCO Colloquy on "Role of Journalists in Developing Countries" (Bamako, Mali)
Oct 7–8	Round Table of Club of European Journalists (Madrid)
Oct 11–17	UNESCO 21st General Conference dealing with communication issues (Belgrade)
Nov 2–3	Consultative meeting of international organizations by World Peace Council (Helsinki)
Nov 10–15	Meeting of Club of Baltic Journalists (Rostock, GDR)
Nov 20–23	Seminar on New Technologies in the Mass Media (Caracas)
Dec 1–5	Meeting of IOJ Lottery Commission (Prague)
Dec 8–11	UNESCO Colloquy on Human Rights in town surroundings (Paris)

1981

Jan 19–22	Inauguration of enlarged building of Werner Lamberz Institute of Journalism in Berlin
Feb 4–5	Meeting of secretariat for international meeting of European journalists (Rome)
Feb 5	Course by Georgi Dimitrov Institute of Sofia for 75 Ethiopian journalists (Addis Abeba)
Feb 16–18	UNESCO consultation on protection of journalists on dangerous missions (Paris)
Feb 17–21	UNESCO consultation within the framework of its medium-term programme (Paris)
Feb 25–28	Signing of agreement with the Union of Journalists in Finland (SSL) as associate member
Mar 26–28	Participation in the World Congress on re-unification of Korea (Alger)
Mar 31	IOJ statement "For Peace on our Planet"
Mar	2nd International Biennial of Humour (San Antonio de los Banos, Cuba)
Apr 13–15	International seminar on TV coverage (Amsterdam)

Apr 14–16	Consultative meeting of directors of IOJ journalist schools (Bucharest)
Apr 19–21	Meeting of World Peace Council Presidium (Havana)
Apr 24–May 2	World Assembly of Journalists for solidarity with Nations of Latin America (Managua)
May 2–5	Meeting of Afro-Arab journalists (Tunis)
May 2–8	Journey of IOJ delegation to Mexico
May 3–17	Journey of IOJ delegation to Korea and Japan
May 6–9	Meeting of IOJ Lottery Commission (Budapest)
May 11–15	5th International Consultative Conference of trade unions in graphic industry (Budapest)
May 14	Meeting of IOJ Photo Section (Prague)
May 15–16	Constituent conference of National Alliance of Third World Journalists (Philadelphia, USA)
May 20–27	International Conference on Sanctions against SAR (UNESCO, Paris)
May 25	Meeting of IOJ Social Commission (Sofia)
Jun 1–7	International Conference on "Mass Media in Fight against Bourgeois Ideology" (Leningrad)
Jun 15–19	UNESCO Conference of NGOs (Paris)
Jun 23	Consultation of West European journalist unions (Paris)
Aug 17–22	Meeting of the working group on South Africa (Balatonszeplak)
Aug 28–31	International Conference of Solidarity with the Libyan Jamahiria (Tripoli)
Sep 1–2	Meeting of IOJ Coordinating Committee for Training of Journalists (Berlin)
Sep 8–9	2nd meeting of IOJ Committee for Studies and Documentation (Prague)
Sep 12–13	Meeting of leading representatives of international democratic organizations (Prague)
Sep 15	Meeting of the IOJ Auditing Commission (Budapest)
Oct 5–7	Meeting of Euro-Arab coordination committee on solidarity with Palestinian people (Rome)
Oct 14–17	International Forum on Protection of Journalists (Varna)
Oct 26–29	Symposium on journalists fighting for peace and social progress (Ulan Bator, Mongolia)
Oct 27–Nov 30	10th Interpress Photo Exhibition (Ulan Bator)
Dec 1–6	Meeting of IOJ Lottery Commission (Prague)
1982	
Jan 29–Feb 1	Conference on Disarmament and Cooperation (Vienna)
Feb 22–24	3rd Consultative Meeting of international & regional organizations of journalists (Baghdad)

Feb 23–25	Meeting of Journalists on Problems of Disarmament, Security and Peace (Bucharest)
Mar 2–4	5th Congress of USSR Union of Journalists (Moscow)
Mar 5	7th Consultative Meeting of IOJ member unions from the CMEA countries (Moscow)
Mar 11	Consultative meeting of democratic NGOs organized by the WFTU (Prague)
Mar 19–21	International Committee for European Security and Cooperation session (Brussels)
Mar 31–Apr 2	Conference on world public opinion and Special meeting on disarmament (Geneva)
Apr 17–19	Conference of journalists of the Caribbean (Saint George's, Grenada)
May 3	IOJ letter to IFJ proposing conference on protection of journalists on dangerous missions
May 9–15	Symposium on the occasion of the 100th anniversary of the birth of G. Dimitrov (Sofia)
May 11	Meeting of Presidium of IOJ Photo Section (Prague)
May 17–21	16th Congress of IFJ (Lugano, Italy)
May 31	IOJ statement concerning the unleashing of a war psychosis in the world
May 31–Jun 4	Consultation of chief editors of IOJ member union magazines (Sofia)
Jun 5–9	Visit of Carnero Roque, UNESCO regional adviser for Latin America
Jun 15–18	Conference of international centre against imperialism, zionism and reaction (Tripoli)
Jun 17–20	Symposium in support of UNESCO Mass Media Declaration (Mexico City)
Jun 21–29	2nd Special session of the UN General Assembly on Disarmament (New York)
Jun 28–29	1st session of IOJ Commission for Studies and Documentation (Moscow)
Jul 20–25	UNESCO conference on Human Rights (Strasbourg)
Jul 24–27	3rd Congress of FELAP (Panama)
Jul 25–Aug 5	Fact-finding mission to Syria and Lebanon on consequences of the Israeli aggression
Jul 26–Aug 5	UNESCO World Conference on Cultural Policies (Acapulco)
Aug 6	Press conference of fact-finding mission to Syria and Lebanon (Sofia)
Aug 6	Opening of IOJ Solidarity School in Lima

Sep 6–12	AIERI/IAMCR General Assembly and scientific conference (Paris)
Sep 7	Exhibition of drawings by Jean Eiffel (Rychnov nad Kreznou, Czechoslovakia)
Sep 13–17	Scientific conference on the occasion of the 90th anniversary of the daily *Rabotnik* (Sofia)
Sep 20	Discussion with representatives of the UN Special Committee on Decolonization (Prague)
Sep 21–26	Conference of Journalists on the 60th anniversary of the USSR (Frunze, USSR)
Sep 23–26	Conference by World Peace Council on support of the Lebanese people (Vienna)
Oct 16–19	2nd Congress of the Union of African Journalists UAJ (Cairo)
Oct 20–22	Visit of Federation of Arab Journalists delegation
Oct 27	Day of Action of European journalists for Peace initiated by the Finnish Union of Journalists
Oct 27–28	2nd session of IOJ Commission for Studies and Documentation (Moscow)
Oct 30–Nov 1	Session of Council of Chilean Journalists (Prague)
Nov 16	Session of IOJ Professional Commission (Prague)
Nov 25–Dec 4	UNESCO Special session of General Conference (Paris)
Dec 1–4	Meeting of International Committee on Protection of Journalists (Nicosia, Cyprus)
1983	
Jan 1	IOJ Institute for Studies and Documentation started to operate
Feb 12–13	Meeting of closely cooperating international organizations (Budapest)
Feb 12–15	2nd Meeting of Journalists of Non-Aligned Countries (Cairo)
Mar 18–20	2nd National Convention on Mass Communication Media (New Delhi)
Mar 22–Apr 5	Information journey of West European journalists to Afghanistan organized by IOJ
Mar 23–24	Meeting of experts on questions of an international deontological code (Budapest)
Mar 25–27	International Conference on Solidarity with Frontline States in Southern Africa (Lisbon)
Mar 26–27	3rd session of IOJ Commission for Studies and Documentation (Prague)
Apr 1–23	Conference for Peace and Independence of Nations of Central America (Managua)

Apr 15–18	International Conference in Support of Palestinian and Lebanese Peoples (Athens)
Apr 25–29	Regional Conference for Peace and Security in Asia and the Pacific (Ulan Bator)
Apr	3rd Biennial of Humour (San Antonio, Cuba)
May 3–5	Symposium on science, culture and mass media in fight for disarmament (Leipzig, GDR)
May 4–5	8th Consultative Meeting of IOJ member unions from the CMEA countries (Prague)
May 4–6	4th colloquy on Information and Documentation (Berlin)
May 11–13	24th FIPP Congress (Brussels)
May 12–18	European Encounter of Journalists (Paris)
May 13	Opening of new headquarter of IOJ Office for Europe (Paris)
May 16–25	International meeting of journalists on environmental protection and mass media (Sofia)
May 18–19	Seminar on automated information systems in running mass media (Prague)
May 22–31	IOJ delegation trip to Korean Peoples Democratic Republic
May 30–Jun 1	Session of IOJ Training Commission and directors of IOJ solidarity schools (Baghdad)
Jun 15–17	Meeting of working group to prepare an international deontological code (Prague)
Jun 18–19	4th Consultative Meeting of international & regional organizations of journalists (Prague)
Jun 21–26	World Assembly for Peace, against Nuclear War and on journalists dialogue (Prague)
Jun 28–Jul 1	Conference of African journalists (Paris)
Jul 1–2	International Committee on Protection of Journalists (Nicosia, Cyprus)
Jul 2–6	World Conference of Journalists against Imperialism and for Peace (Pyongyang)
Jul 3–9	Meeting of agricultural journalists on “Agriculture and Politics” (Warsaw)
Jul 18–21	Congress of Socialist and Progressive Union of Journalists of the Mediterranean (Malta)
Sep 5	Session of international organizations on protection of journalists by IPI (Geneva)
Sep 6	International Conference on Palestine (Geneva)
Sep 7–8	4th session of IOJ Commission for Studies and Documentation (Tashkent)
Sep 5–12	4th session of the Intergovernmental Council of UNESCO/IPDC (Tashkent)

Sep 14–19	UN-UNESCO Round Table on NWICO (Igls, Austria)
Sep 21	5th session of IOJ Training Commission (Berlin, GDR)
Sep 25–27	Session of AIERI/IAMCR International Council (Balaton-szeplak)
Sep 28	Opening of 1st course of the IOJ International School of J. Fucik in Prague
Sep 30–Oct 2	International Committee for European Security and Cooperation (Brussels)
Oct 8–9	Consultative meeting of closely cooperating international organizations (Prague)
Oct 10–13	Session IOJ Social Commission for International Rest Homes of Journalists (Budapest)
Oct 17	Opening of 1st course of the Jose Marti International Institute of Journalism in Havana
Oct 20–Dec 4	11th Interpress Photo Exhibition (Damascus)
Oct 21–23	International conference on application of UN resolutions on Cyprus (Lisbon)
Oct 22–23	8th Congress of UCIP (Dublin)
Oct 22–24	4th international exhibition "Satire in Fight for Peace" (Moscow)
Oct 25–Nov 26	UNESCO 22nd General Conference (Paris)
Oct 26–27	1st Congress of West European Journalists for Peace (Korpilampi-Helsinki)
Nov 1	Open letter of the IOJ to the progressive journalists of the world on situation in Grenada
Nov 2–5	International conference on "Journalism from Computer" (Laxemburg, Austria)
Nov 8	Conference of Solidarity with Grenada, organized by WFDY (Vienna)
Nov 14–17	2nd Vienna Dialogue on Disarmament and Detente (Vienna)
Nov 20	4th Consultative Meeting of international & regional organizations of journ. (2nd part, Paris)
Nov 21	Press conference on the 5th anniversary of UNESCO's Mass Media Declaration (Paris)
Nov 22	Forum of Journalists for Peace (Paris)
Dec 5–11	Jury of exhibition "Youth of the Eighties" organized in cooperation with UNESCO (Paris)
Dec 7–13	Conference on mass media of Non-Aligned countries organized by NAMEDIA (New Delhi)
Dec 8–12	Seminar on mass media in preserving peace and international understanding (Warsaw)

Dec 15–19	International Committee on European Security and Cooperation (Brussels)
1984	
Jan 11–12	9th Consultative meeting of IOJ member unions from the CMEA countries (Berlin)
Jan 19–26	Special session of the World Peace Council (West Berlin)
Feb 2	Celebration of the 100th anniversary of the Dutch Union of Journalists (Amsterdam)
Feb 19–25	UN session against apartheid (Vienna)
Feb 24–27	Prepararory Committee of conference on Nicaragua and Central America (Lisbon)
Feb 25–26	Meeting of closely cooperating democratic non-governmental organizations (Prague)
Feb 27–Mar 11	Journey of IOJ delegation to India
Mar 14	Session of International Committee of Solidarity with Cyprus (Helsinki)
Mar 18–21	Session of the IOJ Professional Commission (Warsaw)
Apr 12–15	Session of International Committee on European Security and Cooperation (Brussels)
Apr 16–18	Consultation of UNESCO national commissions on IPDC (Prague)
May 3–7	International Conference on Nicaragua and for Peace in Central America (Lisbon)
May 7–16	Information journey of West European journalists to Vietnam organized by IOJ
May 15	20th anniversary of IOJ Institute for Training of Journalists in Budapest (Balatonszeplak)
May 16	6th session of IOJ Training Commission with directors of IOJ schools (Balatonszeplak)
May 17–18	5th session of IOJ Commission for Studies and Documentation (Balatonszeplak)
May 19–20	International seminar on new technology and mass media by IOJ (Balatonszeplak)
May 21–26	Meeting of IOJ Lottery Commission on its 20th anniversary (Karlovy Vary, Czechoslovakia)
May 23–27	Visit of UNESCO/IPDC director Ondobo
May 28–31	Congress of the National Federation of Italian Press FNSI (Sorrento, Italy)
Jun 3–14	19th Conference of UNESCO non-governmental organizations (Paris)
Jun 4–8	17th Congress of IFJ (Edinburgh)

Jun 5–15	School of Peace by Women's Democratic International Federation (Primorsko, Bulgaria)
Jun 11–15	European Conference within framework of world disarmament campaign (Leningrad)
Jun 19–24	21st Annual Conference of Indian Federation of Working Journalists (IFWJ)
Jun 20–22	Meeting of journalists from Baltic countries within framework of "Week of Kiel" (Kiel, FRG)
Jun 25–28	Conference of journalists of Central America and the Caribbean (Managua)
Jul 5–7	5th Consultative Meeting of international & regional organizations of journalists (Geneva)
Jul 16–25	Congress of World Federation of UNESCO associations and clubs (Tokyo)
Jul 26	Celebration of 20th anniversary of founding *Interpress-magazin* (Budapest)
Aug 4–7	Round Table on role of student press by the International Union of Students (Nicosia)
Aug 27–Sep 1	Congress of AIERI/IAMCR (Prague)
Aug 28	Consultative meeting of IOJ Commission for Studies and Documentation (Prague)
Sep 21–22	Seminar on NWICO and Indian Ocean with Indian Federation of Working Journalists (Delhi)
Sep 25	Symposium "Dangerous Journalism at Home and Abroad" (Hilversum, the Netherlands)
Sep 26–27	Celebration of 25th anniversary of the foundation of Journalists' House in Varna
Sep 26–Oct 6	Seminar "Women and Mass Media" (Warsaw)
Oct 18–19	Consultative meeting of closely cooperating non-governmental organizations (Prague)
Oct 20–25	Consultation of non-governmental organizations (Vienna)
Nov 16–18	Meeting of the International Committee for European Security and Cooperation (Brussels)
Nov 17–27	Journey to India to discuss with Indian Federation of Working Journalists (IFWJ)
Nov 26–28	5th Gathering of European journalists (Jablonna, Poland)
Nov 29	Conference on New International Information and Communication Order by AAPSO (Kabul)
Dec 3–8	Meeting of IOJ Lottery Commission and drawing on its 20th anniversary (Prague)
Dec 4	Meeting of Presidium of IOJ Photo Section (Prague)

Dec 5–12	Meeting of experts on small printing machines organized by UNESCO (Mainz, FRG)
1985	
Jan 8–9	6th session of IOJ Commission for Studies and Documentation (Berlin)
Jan 11–12	10th Consultative meeting of IOJ member unions from the CMEA countries (Prague)
Jan 15–18	7th session of IOJ Training Commission (Prague)
Jan 16–28	SNJ-CGT Congress and seminar on audiovisual techniques (Paris)
Jan 24	Opening of the exhibition "Youth of the Eighties" in UNESCO (Paris)
Jan 24–29	3rd Vienna Dialogue on Disarmament (Vienna)
Jan 29–Feb 6	Visit of the Union of Tunisian Journalists delegation
Feb 22–Mar 2	Meeting of Union of African Journalists and of journalists of Non-Aligned Countries (Cairo)
Feb 26	Meeting of IOJ Professional Commission (Prague)
Mar 10–13	Visit of the Indonesian Union of Journalists delegation
Mar 11–22	Journey of journalists to USSR on the 40th anniversary of the victory over fascism
Apr 1–16	Third World Foundation 11th Meeting (Chicago)
Apr 4	Opening of the World Press Photo exhibition (Amsterdam)
Apr 9–12	Consultative meeting of closely cooperating non-governmental organizations (Helsinki)
Apr 22–29	Participation in the international meeting of journalists (Torgau, GDR)
Apr 23–25	Round Table on protection of journalists in dangerous missions (Mont Pelerin, Switzerland)
Apr 26	Opening of 1st course of IPDC journalists of Institute for Training of Journalists in Budapest
Apr	4th Biennial of Humor (San Antonio de los Banos, Cuba)
May 4–6	2nd Congress of West European journalists for peace (West Berlin)
May 7	IOJ exhibition "The Militant Posters" on 40th anniversary of end of World War II (Prague)
May 10–11	Colloquy on rights of citizens towards the press by the Press Council of Portugal (Lisbon)
May 24–25	Meeting of the AAPSO Presidium Information Committee (Prague)
May 27–29	Meeting of IOJ Lottery Commission (Berlin, GDR)
May 28–30	7th session of IOJ Commission for Studies Documentation (Balatonszeplak)

May 29–30	Seminar on new technology by IOJ Institute for Studies & Documentation (Balatonszeplak)
Jun 15–Jul 3	Session of UN Committee on Information (New York)
Jun 19	Informative meeting on the International Year of Peace organized by the UN (Vienna)
Jun 21–22	Meeting of International Committee for European Security and Cooperation (Brussels)
Jun 27–29	International colloquy "Nuclear War, Nuclear Proliferation and its Consequences" (Geneva)
Jun 30–Jul 1	Preparatory meeting of the World Congress for Peace (Copenhagen)
Jul 5	Conference on Journalists' Protection and Solidarity with the Cuban Revolution (Havana)
Jul 6–8	4th Congress of FELAP (Havana)
Jul 20–Aug 20	12th Interpress Photo Exhibition (Moscow)
Jul 26–Aug 3	12th World Festival of Youth and Students (Moscow)
Aug 22–Sep 9	Visit of American black journalists to Czechoslovakia, GDR and USSR
Aug 25–Sep 4	Meeting of journalists of Frontline States (Maputo)
Sep 6–10	Congress of journalists on 10th anniversary of signing the CSCE Final Act (Helsinki)
Sep 11–15	Interpress Auto Club Presidium Meeting (Balatonszeplak)
Sep 15–22	Conference on 10th anniversary of ASEAN Confederation of Journalists (Kuala Lumpur)
Sep 18–19	Consultation of information centres of non-governmental organizations (Prague)
Sep 21–Oct 7	National Congress of Brazilian Federation of Journalists FENAJ (Rio de Janeiro)
Sep 24–25	Consultative meeting of selected foreign columnists (Prague)
Oct 3–5	Journey of the IOJ delegation to Iraq
Oct 8–Nov 9	UNESCO 23rd General Conference (Sofia)
Oct 11–13	International Conference of Solidarity with the Fight of South African People (Addis Ababa)
Oct 12–21	Consultative meeting of closely cooperating non-governmental organizations (Havana)
Oct 29–Nov 3	International symposium on topic "Press and Democracy" (Tessaloniki, Greece)
Nov 2–6	11th Consultative meeting of IOJ member unions from the CMEA countries (Warsaw)
Nov 13–16	Seminar of the International Committee for European Security and Cooperation (Brussels)

Dec 1–7	Meeting of IOJ Lottery Commission (Prague)
Dec 7–10	8th session of IOJ Training Commission (Aden)
Dec 14–16	International Preparatory Committee for World Peace Congress (Copenhagen)
1986	
Jan 8	Visit of General Union of Palestinian Writers and Journalists (GUPWJ) delegation
Jan 9	Visit of members of Danish Organizational Committee of the World Congress for Peace
Jan 18–21	Visit of members of Union of Journalists in Finland (SSL)
Jan 18	Meeting with representatives of West European unions of journalists (Prague)
Jan 20–21	6th Consultative Meeting of international & regional organizations of journalists (Brussels)
Jan 20–24	Conference of NGOs "Together for Peace" (Geneva)
Jan 23	Statement of IOJ Secretariat on Soviet peace projects "Way to Save the Mankind"
Jan 24–26	Visit of delegation of the Union of Dutch Journalists
Jan 26–30	Celebration of 40th anniversary of the Union of Journalists of GDR (Berlin)
Jan 28–31	UNESCO Consultation on research in the communications technologies (Gothenburg)
Jan 30–31	Visit of the delegation of the Press Syndicate of Morocco
Feb 19–26	Meeting of IOJ Professional Commission (Baghdad)
Feb 24	Visit of delegation of the Korean Union of Journalists
Feb 26–Mar 1	Consultations of NGOs with ECOSOC on mutual future cooperation (Vienna)
Mar 4–28	Journey of IOJ delegation to Latin America
Mar 5	Visit of delegation of the Union of Journalists of the Democratic Republic of Afghanistan
Mar 6	Visit of delegation of the Korean Union of Journalists
Mar 11–18	Session of National Council of the Indian Federation of Working Journalists (Cuttack, India)
Apr 2–7	2nd UN-UNESCO Round Table on NWICO (Copenhagen)
Apr 9–14	AAPSO Conference on the New International Information Order (Kabul)
Apr 13–17	Conference of non-governmental organizations on termination of Iran–Iraq war (Geneva)
Apr 18–28	1st Latin American Seminar on new technologies and journalists with FELAP (Mexico City)
Apr 21–22	Conference on mass media and human rights with USSR Union of Journalists (Moscow)

Apr 21–25	Congress of the National Federation of Italian Press (FNSI) (Catania, Italy)
Apr 24–27	World Peace Council Presidium session (Sofia)
Apr 28–30	International symposium on the 25th anniversary of Radio Habana (Havana)
Apr 29	Exhibition of IOJ publications and posters to the 40th anniversary of the IOJ (Havana)
May 8–13	Meeting of IOJ Lottery Commission (Prague)
May 14–15	Seminar on International Communications and Confidence-Building in Europe (Leipzig)
May 26	Visit of the delegation of Union of Vietnamese Journalists
May 27–30	8th session of IOJ Commission for Studies and Documentation (Balatonszeplak)
May 29–30	3rd International Seminar on new technologies on the work of journalists (Balatonszeplak)
May 29–31	Session of International Committee for European Security and Cooperation (Brussels)
Jun 2–6	18th Congress of IFJ (Elsinor, Denmark)
Jun 7	40th anniversary of IOJ founding conference in Copenhagen
Jun 7–10	Visit of the delegation of the Union of Editors of Finland (TL)
Jun 9	Solemn session on the occasion of the 40th anniversary of the IOJ foundation (Prague)
Jul 2	Visit of the delegation of Nigerian Union of Journalists
Jul 17–22	Session of Solidarity Committee with Cyprus (Nicosia)
Jul 31–Aug 13	International Conference against using A and H bombs (Tokyo, Hiroshima, Nagasaki)
Aug 11	Visit of the delegation of Iraqi Journalists Union
Aug 26	IOJ General Secretariat Statement "In the interest of humanism and life on the Earth"
Sep 4–6	Conference of the Women's International Democratic Federation (Berlin)
Sep 5	Statement of IOJ General Secretariat to International Day of Journalists' Solidarity
Sep 5–9	Conference on reunification of the Korean peninsula (Pyongyang)
Sep 10–12	International scientific conference Confidence and Security (Vienna)
Sep 11–12	IOJ Auditing Commission session (Prague)
Sep 11–13	Session of IOJ Club of Agricultural Journalists (Budapest)
Sep 21–22	WFTU 11th Congress (Berlin)
Sep 24–25	Meeting of Presidium of IOJ Photo Section (Prague)

Oct 14–15	UN seminar for NGOs on how to inform about the United Nations (New York)
Oct 15–19	World Congress of Peace Forces (Copenhagen)
Oct 24–25	6th Consultative Meeting of international & regional organizations of journalists (2nd part, Sofia)
Oct 24–26	5th Congress of the Cuban Union of Journalists (UPEC) (Havana)
Oct 27–28	International Committee for European Security and Cooperation session (Vienna)
Oct 27–Nov 5	25th International Conference of the Red Cross (Geneva)
Oct 29	Visit of the delegation of Angolan Union of Journalists
Nov 10–14	12th Consultative meeting of IOJ member unions from CMEA countries (Tihany, Hungary)
Nov 12–14	Conference of Non-governmental Organizations (Geneva)
Nov 12–15	2nd congress of Portuguese journalists (Lisbon)
Nov 17–21	Meeting of IOJ Lottery Commission (Prague)
Nov 29–Dec 1	6th Gathering of European journalists (Jablonna)
Dec 18–19	7th Congress of the Union of Bulgarian Journalists (Sofia)
1987	
Jan 23–Feb 9	Visit of IOJ representative to Panama and the Dominican Republic
Feb 8–10	Congress of the General Union of Palestinian Writers and Journalists (Algeria)
Feb 12–13	Colloquy of Chilean journalists of mass media in the struggle for democracy (Paris)
Feb 26–28	Seminar "Problems of ideological struggle in propaganda" (Warsaw)
Mar 14–16	Congress of Union of Journalists of the USSR (Moscow)
Mar 15	Congress of Journalists' Union of Democratic Republic of Afghanistan (Kabul)
Mar 20–22	Seminar "Journalism and Democracy in the Southern Cone" (Santiago de Chile)
Mar 21	Statement on the International Day of Fight against Racial Discrimination
Mar 30–Apr 16	IOJ Institute for the Training of Journalists in Budapest three-week course in Ghana
Apr 4–9	5th International Biennial of Humour (San Antonio de los Banos, Cuba)
Apr 12–14	2nd Forum of the European Students of Journalism – FEJS (Porto, Portugal)
Apr 13–15	7th Consultative Meeting of international & regional organizations of journalists (Cairo)

Apr 21–23	Conference by the International Committee of Solidarity with Cyprus (Sofia)
Apr 21–27	Meeting of IOJ Training Council (Pyongyang)
May 8–16	Negotiation with Austrian Union of Journalists and participants of CSCE (Vienna)
May 10–19	International meeting on the economic development of Bulgaria (Sofia)
May 15	Message to IFJ proposing a joint stand on Information Forum of the Helsinki Final Act
May 15–17	Negotiation with Union of Journalists of Finland and Union of Dutch Journalists (Prague)
May 18–25	Celebrations of anniversaries of Finnish members, 40th of YLL and 80th of SSSL (Helsinki)
May 21	Meeting of steering committee for the revival of the European Club of Journalists (Paris)
May 22–27	13th Interpress Photo Exhibition jury meeting (Baghdad)
May 25–Jun 2	Visit of an IOJ representative to Tanzania and Ethiopia
May 26–28	5th Conference of European Reporters (Naples)
May 29–30	Meeting of International Committee for European Security and Cooperation (Brussels)
May 30–31	1st meeting of IOJ Council for Studies and Documentation and IJI Assembly (Karlovy Vary)
Jun 1	Consultative meeting for the preparation of the World Congress of Women (Geneva)
Jun 1–20	Visit of IOJ delegation to Latin America (Panama, Dominican Republic, Mexico)
Jun 3–7	Seminar on 70th anniversary of the Great October Socialist Revolution (Yerevan, USSR)
Jun 8–12	Conference of Information Ministers of the Non-Aligned Countries (COMINAC) (Harare)
Jun 13	Inauguration of the IOJ Regional Centre in Mexico
Jun 15–16	Meeting of IOJ Lottery Commission (Balatónszeplak)
Jun 15–17	Seminar "Journalism and Peace in Central America" (Mexico)
Jun 20–21	Meeting of IOJ Committee for Peace and Disarmament (Prague)
Jun 23–25	Meeting of Non-Aligned Countries' journalists on trust and understanding (Kabul)
Jun 23–27	World Congress of Women (Moscow)
Jun 27–28	9th Congress of the Czechoslovak Union of Journalists (Prague)
Jul 9–29	Discussion on freedom & responsibility in IOJ International Institute for Training (Budapest)

Jul 18–28	13th Seminar of journalists from Latin America and the Caribbean with UPEC (Havana)
Jul 22–27	2nd Congress of the World Federation of UNESCO Associations and Clubs (Madrid)
Jul 24	Letter of IOJ to Vienna meeting of CSCE with Press Conference (Vienna, Prague)
Aug 25–Sep 10	UN Special Meeting on Disarmament and Development (New York)
Sep 6	Preparation for round table on "Nuclear-free zone in the Iberian peninsula" (Karlovy Vary)
Sep 7–9	4th meeting of NGOs on "Inalienable Rights of the Palestinian People" (Geneva)
Sep 9–12	Conference of Journalists of Frontline States in Southern Africa (Arusha, Tanzania)
Sep 14–15	Consultative meeting of closely cooperating non-governmental organizations (Prague)
Sep 15	UN awards "Peace Messenger" title to IOJ for its contribution to International Year of Peace
Sep 15–16	Seminar of on new technology and international law by Karl Marx University in Leipzig
Sep 18–25	Session of the IOJ Club of Agrarian Journalists (Berlin)
Sep 19–20	Regional meeting of journalists on nuclear-free zone in Northern Europe (Åland, Finland)
Sep 24–26	Conference for peace and anti-imperialist solidarity in Asia and the Pacific (Pyongyang)
Sep 28–Oct 2	Consultations of the IJI with representatives of Yugoslav Journalism Institute (Beograd)
Oct 1	Opening of the IJI Branch in Warsaw
Oct 1–2	Symposium on transnational corporations and the mass media by NGOs (Geneva)
Oct 1–3	2nd Congress of the Association of Journalists of Poland (Warsaw)
Oct 24–Nov 24	13th Interpress Photo Exhibition (Baghdad)
Oct 26–27	Special IOJ session on media coverage of peace and war issues (Prague-Průhonice)
Oct 27	Appeal of the IOJ Committee for Peace and Disarmament on Journalists' Day for Peace
Oct 28	Presentation of IOJ Journalism Prize for J.P. Kauffmann at UNESCO (Paris)
Oct 29	Preparation for the 1st session of the IOJ Committee for New Technologies (Paris)

Oct 30–31	Colloquy on new technologies by the national syndicates in France (Paris)
Oct 30–Nov 1	2nd Congress of journalists from CSCE countries (Vienna)
Nov 2–6	24th UNESCO General Conference (Paris)
Nov 11–12	5th Congress of the Union of Mongolian Journalists (Ulan Bator)
Nov 13–14	13th Consultative Meeting of IOJ member organizations from CMEA countries (Ulan Bator)
Nov 14–26	Postgraduate course on literary genres at Jose Marti Institute of Journalism (Havana)
Nov 17–19	Meeting of Lottery Commission (Prague)
Nov 17–20	Consultation of deans of journalism faculties & schools from Socialist countries (Budapest)
Nov 28–29	Preparatory meeting of journalists of religious media on conference "Peace, Security, Ethics and Humanitarian Problems of Journalism" (Prague)
Nov 28–Dec 2	6th congress of the Syndicate of Yemeni Journalists (Sanaa, Arab Republic of Yemen)
Nov 28–Dec 6	18th session of International Council of Amnesty International (Aguas de Lindoia, Brazil)
Dec 1–4	Symposium on World Decade for Cultural Development by UNESCO (Paris)
Dec 8	Opening of the International Journalism Institute branch in Rio de Janeiro
Dec 8–11	Preparatory meeting for international peace conference in 1988 in Oslo (Sormark, Norway)
Dec 9–10	5th colloquy "Journalistic Information from Computers", by GDR Union of Journalists (Berlin)
Dec 11–13	7th Consultative Meeting of international & regional organizations of journalists (2nd part, Tampere)
Dec 12–17	1st session of IOJ Committee for Professional Ethics (Bucharest)
Dec 14–17	3rd congress of Union of African Journalists (Cairo)

1988

Jan 18–Feb 10	Visit of IOJ delegation to Brazil and Costa Rica
Jan 19–21	Round table on journalists on security and cooperation in Asia & Pacific (Ho Chi Minh City)
Jan 22–25	Information journey for a group of journalists to Kampuchea
Jan 25–27	Forum "Journalism for Peace and Sovereignty of Latin America" with FELAP (Mexico City)

Jan 28	Follow-up meeting on the media coverage of peace and war issues (Pruhonice, Prague)
Feb 2–8	8th meeting of Intergovernmental Council of UNESCO/ IPDC (Paris)
Feb 4–5	Meeting of IOJ Social Commission (Sofia)
Feb 8–11	Conference on information flow between Western and Eastern Europe (Schmitten, FRG)
Feb 9–10	Meeting of the Chairmen of IOJ Clubs (Prague)
Feb 12–23	Seminar on contemporary journalism for English-speaking Caribbean (Havana)
Feb 13–14	Round Table by IOJ Committee for New Technologies (Lisbon)
Feb 22–29	Information journey for a group of Western journalists to Angola
Mar 1	7th Congress of the Union of Journalists of Nicaragua (Managua)
Mar 3–4	12th Congress of the Union of Journalists of the GDR (Berlin)
Mar 3–5	Interpress Photo '87 Exhibition (Warsaw)
Mar 11–13	Seminar Social Security of Journalists by College of Dominican Journalists (Santo Domingo)
Mar 19–20	14th Congress of Union of Tunisian Journalists
Mar 19–22	Session of World Peace Council Presidium (Prague)
Mar 20–22	32nd session of UN Committee for Women's Rights (Vienna)
Mar 28–30	3rd meeting of Forum of European Journalism Students FEJS (Vienna)
Mar 29–31	International conference "The role of public opinion in resolving regional conflicts" (Kabul)
Apr 5–8	International forum for common future by NGO Committee for Disarmament (Geneva)
Apr 7	Agreement with IOJ and General Union of Palestinian Writers and Journalists (Prague)
Apr 8–9	Meeting of IOJ and IFJ representatives (Prague)
Apr 11–12	8th Consultative Meeting of international & regional organizations of journalists (Prague)
Apr 12	IJI Branch Office in Baghdad was founded
Apr 11–14	Colloquy on relations between UNESCO and non-governmental organizations (Paris)
Apr 12–13	AAPSO Presidium session (Budapest)
Apr 15	Presentation of IOJ film on press freedom as it is understood by Israel (Prague)

Apr 19–24	International conference “For Peace, Disarmament and Life” (Merida, Venezuela)
Apr 21–24	Conference of National Alliance of Third World Journalists (Atlanta, USA)
Apr 26–29	11th session of the IOJ Council for Training of Journalists (Havana)
Apr 26–29	International conference “Indian Ocean Zone of Peace” (Antananarivo, Madagascar)
May 16–18	5th Soviet-Finnish journalists’ seminar ”Towards a Nuclear--Weapon-Free World” (Tampere)
May 18–22	Seminar on the 500th anniversary of the discovery of America (Guadalajara, Spain)
May 21–22	Seminar of editors from peace movement publications (Stockholm)
May 25–27	International conference to put an end to the war between Iraq and Iran (Baghdad)
May 27–29	Meeting on creation of European youth magazine (Strasbourg)
May 27–29	19th IFJ Congress (Maastricht)
Jun 2–3	International symposium on “Freedom of the Press” (Tel Aviv)
Jun 2–6	Physicians for Prevention of Nuclear War (Montreal)
Jun 6–12	International seminar of agricultural journalists and IOJ Club of Agricultural Journalists (Prague)
Jun 8–9	Third UN Special Session on Disarmament (New York)
Jun 13–14	Emergency Conference in Solidarity with the Palestinian Popular Uprising (Benghazi)
Jun 13–17	21st conference of non-governmental organizations at UNESCO (Paris)
Jun 14–15	Colloquium “Europe 2000: What Kind of Television” (Munich)
Jun 14–16	Meeting of the directors of IOJ schools (Prague)
Jun 17	Meeting of closely cooperating NGOs on creation of automatized information system (Prague)
Jun 20–22	Conference “Nuclear Free Zone in Central Europe” (Berlin)
Jun 28–30	International meeting of solidarity with the Palestinian uprising (Nicosia)
Jul 15	IOJ press conference with former hostage in Lebanon, Jean-Paul Kauffmann (Prague)
Jul 18	IOJ Secretariat congratulations to Nelson Mandela on occasion of his 70th birthday

Jul 24–29	16th Conference and General Assembly of IAMCR/AIERI (Barcelona)
Aug 1–9	19th World Conference against A and H Bombs (Hiroshima-Nagasaki)
Aug 6–8	International Conference for National Reconciliation in Kampuchea (Phnom Penh)
Aug 29	Preparatory Committee for the Conference of CSCE Journalists (Vienna)
Aug 29–Sep 2	5th International NGO Meeting on the Question of Palestine (Geneva)
Sep 5–7	International meeting of journalists “For freedom of expression in Chile” (Santiago de Chile)
Sep 6–9	Session of the Interpress Auto Club – IPAC (Warsaw)
Sep 7–12	Celebration of the 40th anniversary of the foundation of DPRK (Pyongyang)
Sep 20–23	3rd Meeting of journalists organizations of Frontline States (Harare)
Sep 26	Agreement on Friendship and Cooperation between IOJ and UAJ (Addis Abeba)
Sep 27–28	Symposium on Legal Ban on Use of Force and Humanitarian Cooperation (Leipzig, GDR)
Sep 30–Oct 3	Meeting of journalists from Portuguese-speaking countries (Lisbon)
Oct 3–4	Consultative meeting of closely cooperating non-governmental organizations (Cairo)
Oct 4–10	IOJ delegation visit to Chile to closely follow the plebiscite in Chile
Oct 5–9	1st International Youth Press Festival (Tbilisi, USSR)
Oct 5–10	IOJ book exhibition at the International Book Fair (Frankfurt, FRG)
Oct 8–9	Meeting of Artists and Intellectuals for Support of Palestinian People (Athens)
Oct 10–14	25th anniversary of the foundation of International Institute of Journalism in Berlin (IIJB)
Oct 11–14	International Conference for Action to Combat Racism and Racial Discrimination (Geneva)
Oct 13	12th meeting of the IOJ Council for Training of Journalists (Berlin, GDR)
Oct 17–19	5th FELAP Congress (Acapulco, Mexico)
Oct 20–21	International symposium on new media landscape in Europe (Hamburg, FRG)

Oct 25–26	International conference on Healthier life of our society (Budapest)
Oct 25–29	Seminar of Peace Committee of Finnish Journalists (Helsinki)
Oct 29–Nov 3	Round-table on "Journalists in Europe" by USSR UJ (IOJ) and NUJ (IFJ) (Moscow)
Nov 3–8	Foreign policy commentators from socialist countries (Ulan Bator, Mongolia)
Nov 4–5	Conference of the Foreign Press Association (London)
Nov 5–6	Seminar "Cultural Imperialism in the Caribbean" (Georgetown, Guyana)
Nov 5–6	International symposium "50th Anniversary of the Reich Pogrom Night and 40th Anniversary of Universal Declaration of Human Rights" (Bonn)
Nov 7–9	Seminar "Journalism and Democratic Stability in Latin America" (Quito, Ecuador)
Nov 14–17	14th Consultative meeting of IOJ member unions from CMEA countries (Sofia)
Nov 14–18	IOJ International Lottery Commission (Prague, Czechoslovakia)
Nov 15–16	Round Table of trade union press on "Workers and Democracy in Economy and Society" (Prague)
Nov 19–29	Seminar of Latin American journalists by IOJ and UPEC (Havana)
Nov 22–29	7th Afro-Asian People's Solidarity Organization Congress (New Delhi)
Nov 25–27	2nd part of 8th Consultative Cliub Meeting (Prague)
Nov 26	2nd IOJ meeting on establishing common automatized information system (Prague)
Dec 1–2	Meeting "Trade Unions of the World for Practical Disarmament" (Limassol, Cyprus)
Dec 2–4	Consultative Meeting of Journalists from CSCE Countries (Vienna, Austria)
Dec 3–4	1st steering committee for association of European Young Journalists (Prague)
Dec 5	IOJ statement on the 40th anniversary of UN Universal Declaration of Human Rights
Dec 7–8	IOJ Photo Section Presidium meeting (Prague)
Dec 9–11	Round-table "Common Values of Journalists in Europe" by IOJ and Ecumenical Workshop for Information in Europe (Prague)

1989

Jan 6–8	Consultations of closely cooperating NGOs in UN System (Prague)
Jan 15–23	IOJ Fact-finding mission to Afghanistan (Afghanistan)
Jan 23–25	Southern Asia Media Assembly "Perception across the borders" (New Delhi)
Jan 30–Mar 10	45th Session of the UN Commission on Human Rights (Geneva)
Feb 7–11	2nd International Seminar for African Journalists "Humanity and the Media" (UAJ/ICRC) (Tunis)
Feb 13	Public hearing on "Journalists and Relief Workers in Crisis Situation" (Brussels)
Feb 14	Meeting of Advisory Board of International Institute of Journalism "Werner Lamberz" (Berlin)
Feb 16–19	9th Ordinary Congress of FTP (Sucre, Bolivia)
Feb 17–19	Regional meeting of Foreign Press Associations in Europe (Rome)
Feb 19–25	Discussion with Association of Contemporary Journalists of Turkey (Ankara)
Feb 27–Mar 4	Celebrations of 30th anniversary of Ghana Institute for Journalism (Accra)
Mar 7–13	10th session of IPDC at UNESCO (Paris)
Mar 19	International Meeting in support of SWAPO and people of Namibia for genuine independence (Lisbon)
Apr 1–9	1st part of journalist mission to Occupied Palestinian Territories and Israel (Palestine, Israel)
Apr 2–12	Interpressphoto '89 Jury session (Pyongyang)
Apr 3	50th anniversary of the Finnish Association of Magazine Editors (Helsinki)
Apr 3–7	4th Meeting of Forum for European Journalism Students (FEJS) (Tampere)
Apr 4–6	1st Meeting of European Journalism Educators with IAMCR (Tampere)
Apr 5–15	6th International Biennial of Humour (IOJ-UPEC) (S. Antonio/Baños, Cuba)
Apr 7	Round Table on Media Law in Europe (IAMCR) (Tampere)
Apr 9–11	Seminar on Role of Press in Independence Process and Integration of Latin America with FELAP (Toluca, Mexico)
Apr 12	FELAP Executive Committee meeting (Toluca, Mexico)
Apr 14–18	Discussions with All China Journalists' Association (Beijing)

Apr 19	Reporting Reality: What the Helsinki Final Act Means for Foreign Correspondents (London Mini Forum with NUJ-UK/IFJ/IOJ) (London)
Apr 25–27	First International Journalism teachers' Conference (IITJ – Budapest) (Budapest)
Apr 27	Award Ceremony of World Press Photo Contest 1989; Official Opening of the World Press Photo Exhibition 1989 (Amsterdam)
Apr 27–May 4	2nd part of journalist mission to Occupied Palestinian Territories and Israel (Palestine, Israel)
May 6–8	Meeting of closely cooperating NGOs responsible for solidarity work (WFDY) (Budapest)
May 14–16	International Seminar on Mass Media for Development (AAPSO) (Conakry, Guinea)
May 19–21	Seminar for journalists from Bolivarian countries "Journalism in the XXI Century" (Bogota, Colombia)
May 20–21	International press conference "European Community, Turkey and Freedom of Press" with Contemporary Journalists' Association Turkey (Ankara, Turkey)
May 21–23	International meeting for the inauguration of the Federation of East African Journalists Association (Kampala, Uganda)
May 21–23	International Conference "Euromedia – Challenge of the Information Age" (Vienna)
May 23–24	Presentation of IOJ sponsored film "We are journalists. Don't shoot!" (Prague, Bratislava)
May 25–27	National Workshop on New Technologies (Maracaibo, Venezuela)
May 25–Jun 26	Auto-rally Moscow–Lagos
Jun 28–30	Pan-African Conference "Peace, Disarmament and Development in Africa" (Lagos, Nigeria)
Jun 2–6	IOJ Photo-Section Presidium meeting (Berlin)
Jun 3–10	3rd part of journalist mission to Occupied Palestinian Territories and Israel (Palestine, Israel)
Jun 8–15	International meeting of agricultural journalists and Session of IOJ Club Presidium (Ulan Bator, Mongolia)
Jun 12–15	Latin American Seminar of Journalists on Integration and Communication (Havana, Cuba)
Jun 19–21	27th Congress of the International Federation of the Periodical Press (London)
Jun 22–23	Seminar on Social and Political Issues in Post-Colonial Caribbean (Bridgetown, Barbados)

Jun 26–Jul 1	UNESCO Conference on Peace in the Minds of Men (Yamoussoukro, Ivory Coast)
Jun 28–30	Pan-African Conference on Peace, Disarmament and Development (Lagos, Nigeria)
Jun 28–Jul 21	14th Interpressphoto (Pyongyang)
Jul 1–7	Symposium for Journalists from Asian and Pacific Countries (Ulan Bator, Mongolia)
Jul 1–8	13th World Festival of Youth and Students (Pyongyang)
Jul 4–11	4th part of journalist mission to Occupied Palestinian Territories and Israel (Palestine, Israel)
Jul 11–13	9th Consultative Meeting of International and Regional Organizations of Journalists (Mexico, Mexico)
Jul 19–28	IOJ fact-finding mission to Namibia (Windhoek, Namibia)
Jul 31–Aug 2	10th meeting of COMINAC (Harare, Zimbabwe)
Aug 3–9	World Conference against Atomic and Hydrogen Bombs (Organizing Committee) (Hiroshima, Japan)
Aug 11–13	Consultative meeting "Průhonice III" on monitoring media in issues of peace and war (Gödölö, Hungary)
Sep 2–10	Peace Journalists School (IOJ/WPC) (Balatonszabadi, Hungary)
Sep 6–10	Seminar "Journalist – a Mediator in Latin American Integration" (Florianopolis, Brazil)
Sep 8–16	5th part of journalist mission to Occupied Palestinian Territories and Israel (Palestine, Israel)
Sep 15–16	International Seminar "The Role of Mass Media in the Solution of Regional Conflicts" (AAPSO) (Kabul, Afghanistan)
Sep 15–17	Mass Media in a Time of Crisis – International Conference on Media and Our Common Future (Vasterås, Sweden)
Sep 16–17	3rd Congress of Journalists from CSCE Countries "From confrontation to cooperation – the challenge to journalistic work" (Warsaw)
Sep 22-23	Symposium on International Humanitarian Law with Ethiopian Red Cross (Addis Ababa)
Sep 28-Oct 1	Journalists seminar on disinformation and elections (Managua, Nicaragua)
Oct 17-26	6th part of journalist mission to Occupied Palestinian Territories and Israel (Palestine, Israel)
Oct 17–Nov 16	25th General Conference of UNESCO (Paris)
Oct 22–27	27th International Festival of Films on Scientific-Technical Programmes (Pardubice, Czechoslovakia)

Oct 2–5	International Symposium on Scientific Cooperation for Disarmament, Development and the Environment (WFSW) (Brasilia, Brazil)
Oct 9–14	32nd Assembly of World Federation of United Nations Associations (Moscow)
Oct 10–12	Consultative Meeting of Socialist Countries' Unions of Journalists (Havana)
Oct 15–21	1st World Congress "Communication for Community" (WACC) (Manila, Philippines)
Oct 27–29	MacBride Round Table on Communication (Harare, Zimbabwe)
Nov 2–3	Round Table "Survival of Civilisation and Disarmament (Moscow)
Nov 18–20	Conference on Press Councils and Press Regulatory Bodies (Kuala Lumpur, Malaysia)
Nov 18–25	14th Workshop of the Latin American Journalists (Havana)
Nov 21–26	Meeting of IOJ Committee for Professional Ethics (Bucharest, Romania)
Nov 27–30	Seminar on Population and Environment (Brasilia, Brazil)
Nov 28–Dec 1	Confederation of ASEAN Journalists 8th General Assembly and the 1st Asia Pacific Press Convention (Singapore)
Nov 30–Dec 2	Seminar "Europe, one Common Destiny" (Barcelona, Spain)
Dec 4–6	Meeting of IOJ Clubs Chairmen (Sofia)
Dec 7–9	Conference of Journalists (PAJ-Jamaica/NABJ-USA/IOJ) (Kingston, Jamaica)
Dec 11–13	2nd International Round Table of European Journalists (IOJ-EWIE) (Tutzing, FRG)
Dec 14–18	Seminar "Situation of the Press in West African Subregion, State Press, Private Press and Political Press (Dakar, Senegal)
Dec 16–17	3rd Conference to Support the Intifada in Occupied Palestine (Athens)
Dec 17–18	Conference of women journalists in print and electronic media (New Delhi)

1990

Jan 19–21	Conference for Peace, Security and Cooperation in the Red Sea, the Gulf and the Indian Ocean (Aden, PDR of Yemen)
Jan 29–Mar 9	UN Commission on Human Rights (Geneva)
Feb 14–18	International Colloquium "The Right for Information" (Yaounde, Cameroon)
Mar 1–2	Conference on mass media in Europe (Karlsruhe, FRG)
Mar 19–24	11th session of IPDC at UNESCO (Paris)

Mar 20–22	Seminar on training of journalists and preparation of text-books with IIJB (Berlin)
Mar 24–25	Workshop: Journalism and Human Rights (Georgetown, Guyana)
Mar 24–Apr 7	Fact-finding mission to Southern Africa (South Africa, Namibia, Angola, Zambia)
Mar 30–31	3rd Meeting of "Colegios" of Latin American Journalists (Santo Domingo, Dominican Republic)
Apr 2–5	Forum for European Journalism Students (Nantes, France)
Apr 9–12	Meeting of the Consultative Club of the International and Regional Organizations of Journalists (The Hague, Netherlands)
Apr 17–28	Fact-finding Mission to Eastern European Countries (Eastern Europe)
Apr 24–25	Meeting of Journalists of the Balkan Countries on Conditions of employment in mass media in the Balkans (Sofia)
Apr 28–May 1	European Meeting of Journalists (Malaga, Spain)
May 14–18	20th IFJ Congress (Baia Chia, Italy)
May 21–29	Information Seminar on Latin American and Caribbean Peace Issues (WPC) (Havana)
Jun 2–9	Meeting of Journalists from Central America (Havana)
Jun 4–10	Emergency visit to Palestinian Occupied Territories (Palestine)
Jun 19–20	International Conference "For Disarmament, Cooperation and Development in the Asia-Pacific Region" (AAPSO) (Pyongyang)
Jun 21	Round Table of CSCE Follow-up Meeting of Human Dimension (Copenhagen)
Jun 27	UN Sub-Committee on Racism, Racial Discrimination, Apartheid and Decolonization (Geneva)
Jun 27–29	Seminar on regional and local Radio and TV – Perspectives for the 90s (Prague)
Jul 4–5	Regional Meeting of the European journalist unions (Sofia)
Jul 17–18	Seminar on Media Laws in Central European Countries (Prague)
Jul 23–30	Presidential Mission to Palestinian Occupied Territories and to Israel (Palestine, Israel)
Aug 1–5	Annual Convention of the National Association of Black Journalists (NABJ) (Los Angeles)
Aug 1–9	World Conference against the Atomic and Hydrogen Bombs (Hiroshima-Nagasaki)

Aug 7–10	Seminar on Conditions of Work of Latin American Journalists (Rio de Janeiro, Brazil)
Aug 7–11	2nd Seminar on Press, Democracy, Human Rights and Development in Africa (WAJA) (Cotonou, Benin)
Aug 16	Consultation of experts on elaboration of IOJ training conception (Prague)
Aug 21–22	Meeting of Southern African Federation of Journalists (FSAJ) (Maputo, Mozambique)
Aug 22–23	Seminar on Models of Journalism with IAMCR/AIERI (Gödölö, Hungary)
Aug 26–31	IAMCR/AIERI Conference (Bled, Yugoslavia)
Sep 2–4	9th Board of Directors' Meeting of the CAJ (Batam Island, Indonesia)
Sep 4–16	2nd Peace Journalists' School (Budapest)
Sep 10–14	IOJ Course on International Labour Standards (IOJ/ILO) (Prague)
Sep 14–16	National Congress of the Association of Democratic Journalists (Johannesburg, South Africa)
Sep 19–22	Conference on "Picture, Presence and Participation of Women Journalists in Journalism of Latin America" (CNP-Venezuela/FELAP/IOJ) (Caracas, Venezuela)
Sep 20–24	Trade Union Training Course (IOJ/AHJ/IITJ) (Budapest)
Sep 21–22	Second MacBride Round Table on Communication (Prague)
Sep 24–29	3rd Conference of Ministers of Information of Non-Aligned Countries (Havana)
Oct 1–4	2nd International Journalism Teachers' Conference (Gardony, Hungary)
Oct 3–4	Seminar on Professional Ethics in Journalism (Sofia)
Oct 4–6	Conference "Caribbean Journalism and the Development Process (CAMWORK/IOJ) (Port of Spain, Trinidad and Tobago)
Oct 17–20	Seminar on Working Conditions of Journalists in Asia (IOJ/CAJ) (Bangkok, Thailand)
Oct 18–20	1st gathering of Europe's leading editors (Cardiff, United Kingdom)
Oct 22–27	7th Biennial ACCE Conference "Science and Technology – Implications for Communication Development in Africa" (Ouagadougou, Burkina Faso)
Oct 28–30	Conference of journalist organizations "Journalists of Africa: The Union Challenge" (IFJ/ UAJ) (Harare, Zimbabwe)
Nov 8–10	Round Table on Working Conditions in Maghreb Countries (AJI/Tunisia) (Tunis)

Nov 12–13	IOJ Workshop on the Question of Copyright (IOJ/WIPO) (Geneva)
Nov 14–15	International Journalist Consultation with UN Centre on Human Rights (Geneva)
Nov 28–30	Conference on Problems of New International Information and Communication Order and Cooperation among Journalists of NAM and Developing Countries (New Delhi)

APPENDIX 6. IOJ PRESENTATIONS AT THE UN 1982–88

United Nations General Assembly, Second Special Session on Disarmament, 24 June 1982

Statement of Professor Kaarle Nordenstreng, President of the International Organization of Journalists

Mr. Chairman, distinguished delegates, colleagues and friends

lt is a great honour for me to address this assembly of the international community in the name of 200,000 journalists from 120 countries. These are newspapermen and women, radio and television reporters, writers, cameramen – in short, professional workers in the mass media specialized in the task of informing the public opinion.

The aim of my organization has been ever since its foundation in Copenhagen in 1946, and I quote the first article of our statutes: "The maintenance of peace and the consolidation of friendship among peoples as well as international understanding through free, accurate and honest informing of public opinion."

It has not always been easy to pursue this aim, especially in those countries where the mass media are under a strong influence of commercial and military interests. We all know that the performance of the mass media has been far from ideal from the point of view of peace and disarmament. Often it has been a vital link in the socio-economic process which feeds arms race, by maintaining ignorance, prejudice and fear among the population, rather than by satisfying the people's right to acquire an objective picture of reality by means of accurate and comprehensive information.

Let us recall what was said 35 years ago by an authoritative commission which carried out an independent study of the press in the United States. I quote:

> With the means of self-destruction that are now at their disposal, men must live, if they are to live at all, by self restraint, moderation, and mutual understanding. They get their picture of one another through the press. The press can be inflammatory, sensational, and irresponsible. If it is, it and its freedom will go down in the universal catastrophe. On the other hand, the press can do its duty by the new world that is struggling to be born. It can help create a world community by giving men everywhere knowledge of the world and of one another, by promoting comprehension and appreciation of the goals of free society that shall embrace all men.

These words were written at the time of Hiroshima and Nagasaki. Since that time we have accumulated over a million time greater capacity for instant destruction. Therefore also the point made by the Commission on Free and Responsible Press is today a million times more serious. Especially so, since parallel to the arms race we have got hundreds of millions of poor people deprived from the most elementary human rights.

There is indeed a collective duty towards "the new world that is struggling to be born". This is how we see the contemporary movement towards new international relations in general and a new international information order in particular. This new order, understood as an integral part of the New International Economic Order, is aimed at the decolonization and democratization of the field of information and communication on the basis of peaceful coexistence between peoples.

The majority of journalists in the world support this call by the Movement of Non-Aligned Countries and its manifestations such as the Mass Media Declaration of UNESCO. A new order is in dispensable, because the status quo in the world does not promote peace, democracy and social progress. Those who are waging an ideological war against the new order – with a false image of freedom as their weapon – are in fact defending those socioeconomic structures which produce arms race and poverty.

The professional journalists today – no matter whether they are working under the sophisticated conditions of the industrialized countries, or with all the hard ships of underdevelopment, or even in the middle of a liberation struggle in Palestine, Southern Africa, Western Sahara, El Salvador, and so on – all the same, they increasingly realize that we are faced with a struggle towards a new order and that the struggle is one, however great is its variety.

But the journalists have gone further than analytically observing the situation. A significant development has taken place in the ethics of the profession, as demonstrated by a declaration given two years ago in Mexico in the name of the international and regional non-governmental organizations which unite as many as 300,000 professional journalists from all continents and various political orientations. This is what they declared, among others, and I quote:

> A true journalist stands for the universal value of humanism, above all peace, democracy, human rights, social progress and national liberation, while respecting the distinctive character, value and dignity of each culture as well as the right of each people freely to choose and develop its political, social, economic and cultural systems.
>
> Consequently, a true journalist assumes a responsibility to fight against any justification for or incitement to wars of aggression and the arms race, especially in nuclear weapons, and other forms of violence, hatred or of national, racial or religious discrimination, oppression by tyrannic regimes, as well as all forms of colonialism and neo--colonialism. This fight contributes to a climate of opinion conductive to international détente, disarmament and national development.

This socially committed journalistic ethics has recently manifested itself in the popular peace movement which is sweeping across the world, in particular the Western hemisphere. Journalists have joined other professional groups in mobilizing against nuclear extermination and in defense of peace. Typical of this contemporary movement is what was declared four months ago by the Helsinki chapter of the Union of Journalists in Finland. I quote again:

> The journalist's instrument is the word. This instrument can be used only under conditions of peace; therefore promotion of peace is the most effective way of defending freedom of speech.

What can be done in practical terms? Unfortunately professional journalists do not usually command the ultimate control of the mass media, and thus they only have a shared responsibility for how the channels of communication are being used. However, journalists for their part want to do their utmost in promoting social consciousness along the lines of the Mexico Declaration.

Among other things we are engaged in the preparation of an international code of journalistic ethics, based on the universal values held in the international community as well as on the common professional principles respected throughout the world, to be endorsed by non-governmental organizations of professional journalists at the national, regional as well as international level.

We also offer our cooperation to the United Nations in an effort to raise the standards of journalism in matters of arms race and disarmament by setting up of a presentative professional body in reviewing the performance of the press and suggesting practical means of improving the coverage.

Finally, we want to remind those engaged in the arms race that even a modest reduction of military expenditures would release financial resources for an extensive development of national and international systems of communication. Given our ethical orientation, we feel we have the moral right to demand that the governments, to begin with the permanent members of the Security Council, should curb the arms race and invest the resources thus saved to purposes of truthful and honest information.

Thank you.

Report by the IOJ President on the United Nations Committee on Information meetings in New York in 1985 and 1986

Background

The UN Committee on Information was established by a General Assembly Resolution in December 1978, right after the Mass Media Declaration of UNESCO was adopted in Paris. The Committee got two- part mandate: to oversee the establishment of the new information order (which was mainly supposed to be handled at UNESCO) and to monitor the activities of the Department of Public Information (D P!) at the UN Secretariat. Since 1979 the Committee has held an annual meeting (usually in June) the report of which has constituted the basis for a discussion and resolution on "Questions Relating to Information "at the Special Political Committee of the General Assembly (usually in October–November) leading to a final resolution by the General Assembly adopted towards the end of its session in December. The proceedings of the Committee and related General Assembly resolutions were unanimous (by consensus) until 1981. Since 1982 the USA has departed from consensus, first only with Israel but later with increasing number of western countries (in 1985 nearly 20 countries voted against the resolution in the General Assembly).

The IOJ attended the meeting of the Committee for the first time as an observer in June 1982 after the IOJ 9th Congress had demanded closer relations with the UN. This time the President was at the UN in New York mainly for the Second Special Session on Disarmament (see earlier report of that mission). On that occasion the IOJ did not seek to address the Committee but only asked the Mexico Declaration of 1980 to be distributed as background material for the members of the Committee; this was not, however, fulfilled due to either technical or political obstacles. The presence of the IOJ as an observer was also not put on record to the report of that meeting.

Committee session in 1985

The first full and official attendance of the IOJ at the Committee took place in 1985 when the President sent an advance notice to the Secretariat. Thanks to good co-operation of the Committee Chairman (comrade Willi Schlegel from GDR) the IOJ was invited to speak at the end of the general debate on the new information order (see below).

The delegation of the United States made a point of order of this to the Chairman saying that giving floor to a non-governmental organization should have been made clear to the Committee in advance. The US delegate said that an American journalist (Dana Bullen from the World Press Freedom Committee, representing the Inter-American Press Association IAPA which has the same status II with ECOSOC as the IOJ)

> had attended the Committee until yesterday. He would have been pleased to address this body had we been aware that for the first time, at least in our memory, non-governmental organizations would be invited to address the Committee on Information. That brings me to the final point: the IOJ is a well known communist organization headquartered in Prague. We will not object its being present here. We do, however, want to see another NGOs that represent points of view which are divergent from those of the IOJ to be expressed as well in this session. We regret that our distinguished Chairman...

Also the rapporteur of the Committee (a right-winger from Spain) expressed his surprise and discontent with the decision by the Chairman not shared by the rest of the Committee Presidium.

The IOJ intervention as well as the American point of order was put on record in the Press Release issued daily by the Department of Public Information. The final Report of this session of the Committee, adopted at the end of the session, mentions (under paragraph 18) that the IAPA and the IOJ participated as observers and (under paragraph 75):

> With the permission of the Committee, statements were heard by representatives of the International Telecommunications Satellite Organization (INTELSAT), and the International Organization of Journalists. One delegation expressed concern that the Committee had not previously heard statements from non-governmental organizations.

The session and the IOJ intervention got exceptional attention in the US establishment as shown by a report in the Chronicle of International Communication (see below).

The full report of the 1985 session (in English French and Spanish), together with the daily Press Release (in English only), is stored in the secretariat for international organizations as well as in the IJI.

The lack of consensus at the 1985 session led to a deep political division at the General Assembly in autumn 1985. Most western countries voted against the resolution on "Questions relating to Information" submitted by the developing countries (Group 77) with the support of the socialist countries. The main cause of disagreement was the new information order and such "political" issues as treatment of Palestine and Namibia in the UN public information activities. In general, western countries insisted that the Committee should endorse and adhere to the consensus reached at UNESCO where by the new order is defined as "continuous and evolving process". The developing countries and socialist countries refused to make explicit reference to this phrase because in the political debate it became to mean a watering down of the new order concept. Obviously the western countries intended to weaken the new order movement by diluting the concept and then gradually aiming at its total elimination from the political agenda.

Committee session in 1986

This fundamental controversy was somewhat softened in 1986 as reflected in the relatively good spirit in which the UN/UNESCO Round Table on the new order took place in Copenhagen in early April (this meeting was attended by both IOJ and IJI as reported separately to the SG).The developing countries and socialist countries showed willingness to accept now the UNESCO phrase "continuous and evolving process" at the higher political sphere of the UN and also the western countries seemed to be prepared for businesslike debate. On the other hand, the financial crisis, which was troubling the UN mainly because of the United States unilaterally cut down its contribution to the UN, added pressure at the UN Committee on Information as well. Thus the western demands to limit the UN public information activities due to financial constraints (but obviously motivated by political reasons) got new weight. Moreover, the need to achieve savings in administrative costs of the secretariat led to limit the length of the Committee session to two weeks in 1986 instead of three weeks as was the case always before.

At the beginning of the session on 23 June 1986 it became clear that the western position had not softened; on the contrary it was even more hardline than last year because now the western 'group in a joint proposal for the Committee's recommendations demanded even to change the mandate of the Committee by practically cutting out the general consideration of new information order questions. The USA, QK and some other NATO countries threatened to withdraw from the Committee unless their demands were met. Indeed, it seems that at least the USA aims that destroying the Committee – and as a first step it wants to limit it to technical questions of information only. The developing countries and socialist countries, on the other hand, are prepared to com promise as reflected in their proposals for the Committee's recommendations which were somewhat closer to the western position than the majority resolution of 1985.

The proposals of the three groups (in English, French and Spanish) are stored in the IJI, together with various working documents prepared by the UN Secretariat for this session. Also the Press Releases (in English and French) describing the debate of the first week of the Committee's session this year are filed in the IJI. Excerpts from key interventions (by Algeria, Spain, Mexico, USA and Cuba) will be published in the Democratic Journalist as a package similar to that made of last year's session (DJ 11/1985).

This time the IOJ did not address the Committee. First of all there was practically no time left for others than proper members of the Committee and in the present situation the emphasis was not in public speeches but rather in political negotiations between the three groups which took place in a working group behind closed doors. Moreover, if the IOJ had asked for the floor, then also the – IAPA would have done the same; this time they were prepared to stay throughout the meeting with several representatives (including Dana Bullen) and a written address. The IOJ President agreed with the Committee Chairman (comrade Schlegel) that we shall speak only in case the other side does it. In a friendly discussion with Dana Bullen it appeared that they wanted to speak only in case we did so, and thus it was agreed that no one will address the Committee this time. However, the presence of IAPA and IOJ at this session was put on record and will be noted in the Committee's Report.

The IOJ President was pre pared to be in New York only for one week and thus this report does not cover the final proceedings of the Committee's session. News about that has to be secured through our permanent representatives at the UN and through fraternal delegations (mainly GDR).

Prague, 29 June 1986
Kaarle Nordenstreng

Intervention by Professor Kaarle Nordenstreng at the Committee on Information, 20 June 1985

Mr. Chairman,

I represent a non-governmental, organization which brings together some 200,000 working journalists from 120 countries, most of them belonging to the Non-Aligned Movement. Like the United Nations, the International Organization of Journalists was founded in the aftermath of the Second World War as a universal forum for peaceful cooperation, in this case for the field of journalism and mass communication.

Today the IOJ is the oldest and the largest of non-governmental organizations in this field, but along with it there exist others with less universal character – either geographically or ideologically. We collaborate with these other international and regional organizations of professional journalists, thus making up a kind of "global club" which represents altogether 400,000 working journalists in the world. These organizations have held regular consultative meetings under the auspices of UNESCO since 1978; the latest one took place in Geneva in July 1984. On that occasion we issued a joint statement expressing our appreciation to UNESCO, which has facilitated these meetings between us, and I quote:

> without any interference from the side of the governments, letting professionals deal with vital issues such as codes of ethics and protection of journalists. We have all reason to support the Secretariat and the Director-General of UNESCO for their efforts in carrying out the UNESCO programmes in accordance with the Constitution for the benefit of peace, democracy, freedom of information and socio-economic progress in the world.

The statement was signed by leading representatives of my organization (IOJ), the International Federation of Journalists (IFJ), the International Catholic Union of the Press (UCIP), the Latin American Federation of Journalists (FELAP) and the Union of African Journalists (UJA).

Mr. Chairman,
I want to draw the attention of this Committee to another document issued by the "global club" of professional journalists which includes, in addition to the just-mentioned organizations, also the Federation of Arab Journalists (FAJ), the Confederation of ASEAN Journalists (CAJ) and the Federation of Latin-American Press Workers (FELATRAP). This document is called "International Principles of Professional Ethics in Journalism". Let me point out that this is indeed a historical document highly relevant to the mandate of this Committee. It is the first time that journalists have prepared for themselves a universal set of professional principles. Something like this was attempted at the U.N. in the early 1950s as a follow-up of the 1948 Conference on Freedom of Information, but without much success.

The International Principles of professional Ethics in Journalism is an independent contribution by the journalists to the establishment of a new international information and communication order. The ten principles contained in this document were prepared as an international common ground and as a source of inspiration for national and regional codes of ethics. The set of principles is intended to be promoted autonomously by each professional organization through ways and means most adequate to its members. Thus it is not an international code of conduct but a set of universal principles to be applied by the profession at the national and international level.

What is perhaps most significant in this exercise of ours is the mere fact that professionals around the world could reach consensus on principles in this delicate field. This can be taken as a promising precedent with a view of the efforts of this Committee as well.

Without going into details .of this document, let me just point out that the first of its ten principles is entitled "People's right to true information" and that this traditional basic value of journalism is accompanied among others by the following, and I quote from another principle entitled "Respect for universal values and diversity of cultures":

> A true journalist stands for the universal values of humanism ... and ... participates actively in the social transformation towards democratic betterment of society and contributes through dialogue to a climate of confidence in international relations conducive to peace and justice everywhere, to détente, disarmament and national development.

We are not afraid of combining freedom with such a responsibility that is dedicated to what might be called "United Nations ideology". As a matter of fact, speaking about freedom, we have noticed, in studying the history of French Revolution and reading again the classics of libertarian thought that the original, genuine doctrine of freedom of speech and freedom of the press was far from an abstract value void of socio-political substance. On the contrary, liberty was an ideological instrument in the hands of the raising bourgeoise in its struggle against the old feudal order. The new information order outlined at that time for example by John Stuart Mill in his famous essay "On Liberty" determined freedom of expression to be a crucial value, not because of freedom as such, but because of its potential benefit for the common good of mankind.

Mr. Chairman,

It is in this spirit that we professionals have done our homework, and we continue to do so. I hope that the same spirit finds its way to this Committee.

Thank you, Mr. Chairman.

JULY-AUGUST 1985 CHRONICLE OF INTERNATIONAL COMMUNICATION

NEW WORLD INFORMATION ORDER

NWIO Debate Dominates UNCI Meetings

In the first-ever, showdown vote taken August 30, the United Nations Committee on Information (UNCI) split 42-12 over references to the "new world information order" (NWIO) in a draft resolution drawn up during the committee's annual deliberations, June 17-July 5. The UNCI broke up in disagreement over that and lesser issues at the end of its summer session, but scheduield a two-day resumption the end of August to provide an opportunity for Third World (G-77) and Western members to consult informally on compromise language.

The vote came at the insistence of a 12-member Western group, including Japan, to demonstrate growing unity of view and a new determination to have NWIO treated throughout the United Nations system as an "evolving and continuous process." The group earlier included Greece and Turkey, both of which decided to abstain from the final balloting.

The NWIO definition over which the committee split was adopted by the United Nations Educational, Scientific and Cultural Organization (UNESCO) during its general conference in 1983. It was a major issue dividing the UNCI last year also, but a vote never came to pass because of actions by the committee chairman that deflected the disagreement upward to the Special Political Committee. The SPC can be expected to renew its own inconclusive debate sometime after the 40th General Assembly convenes this fall.

In actions leading up to the August 30 vote, the Western group did not respond to gestures indicating the G-77 was prepared to cooperate on compromise language to produce a resolution simply referencing the UNESCO document in which the NWIO definition appears. The Western group was motivated in its hardline purposes, it appears, by the desire to put the G-77 on notice that the West expects no tampering with the NWIO definiton when the 23rd UNESCO General Conference meets in Sofia this fall.

Among episodes to which the U.S. took strong exception during the main UNCI session were attacks on Raido Marti broadcasts to Cuba and the surprise, formal appearance of an official of the International Organization of Journalists (IOJ). The IOJ spokesman reported on recent international journalists meetings that voiced criticism of the American withdrawal from UNESCO and produced a new, 10-point "International Principles of Professional Ethics in Journalism" for application on national, regional and worldwide basis.

The U.S. rejected the attacks on Radio Marti in a lengthy statement and in response to the IOJ intervention said that if participation by "a well known Communist organization" is to be permitted during UNCI deliberations, the U.S. in the future would want non-governmental organizations reflecting Western views to be heard also. This would take the UNCI another step toward replacing UNESCO as the main forum for NWIO debates involving cacophonous private groups as well as governments.

INTERNATIONAL BROADCASTING

Legacy of Surrogate Radio's Strongman

Open Congressional criticism and internal, below-the-surface antagonisms within the Administration have produced a reshuffling of Reagan first-term appointees in charge of surrogate broadcasting to Eastern Europe and the Soviet Union over Radio Free Europe and Radio Liberty (RFE/RL).

The chairman of the Board for International Broadcasting (BIB), Frank Shakespeare, has been made U.S. ambassador to Portugal. His replacement is expected to be James Buckley, the former U.S. Senator from New York who since October 1982 has been the president of RFE/RL, Inc., the so-called private corporation that operates the two stations located in Munich, West Germany. Other changes that are in progress or in prospect will give RFE/RL virtually an entirely new management team and an opportunity to recoup lost prestige and professionalism about which earlier warnings were sounded (*Chronicle*, Vol. III No. 8, Vol. V No. 2).

Cables arriving in July from U.S. embassies in Eastern Europe provide the latest evidence that RFE/RL broadcasts frequently exhibit the provocative, propagandistic qualities disallowed by U.S. laws setting up the stations. American diplomats there express concern that the credibility of RFE/RL broadcasts is seriously endangered and stress that degrees of stridency eroding listener confidence and interest simply play into the hands of communist governments.

Anger over particular RFE Polish broadcasts is assumed in Washington to have played an important part in the Jaruzelski regime's adamant rejection of the Administration's ambassador-designate to Warsaw. In January of this year, after the Polish government formally protested an RFE broadcast making satirical comparisons of General Jaruzelski and Adolf Hitler, the State Department took the unprecedented step of issuing an apology disassociating itself from the broadcast. These and other embarrassments strengthened critics of Shakespeare's independent sense of foreign policy priorities and his personal manipulation of RFE/RL.

Indications of rising Congressional disapproval appear in the 1986-87 foreign relations authorization bill (H.R. 2068). It restates the importance of long-term credibility to RFE/RL "operating in accordance

United Nations General Assembly, Third Special Session on Disarmament, June 1988

Statement of Professor Kaarle Nordenstreng, President of the International Organization of Journalists

I have the pleasure of bringing to this forum the greetings of 250,000 mass-media professionals affiliated with the oldest, largest and broadest international organization of journalists in the world.

We share the gratification over the INF Treaty, and we realize that the media played a significant role in bringing about the positive turn in international relations by employing the means of mass communication between peoples "for the purposes of mutual understanding a truer and more perfect knowledge of each other 's lives," to use the words of the constitution of the United Nations Educational, Scientific and Cultural Organization (UNESCO), or, to put it in terms of the Final Act of Helsinki, by promoting "an ever-wider knowledge and understanding of the various aspects of life" in other countries.

By the same token, however, we recognize that it is the people – the general public at large – that have created the ultimate pressure for peace and disarmament, the media playing a catalytic and facilitating role. Moreover, there are among the dominant media in the world those with a tendency to foster militarism rather than disarmament, disinformation rather than fair and accurate information; and thus they continue the cold war even if Governments seem to have closed that chapter in history. This tendency, to be sure, is perpetuated by the owners and managers of the mass media – not, on the whole, by working journalists.

As far as professional journalists are concerned, their position is clear, especially in the light of the Magna Carta of contemporary journalism, the "International Principles of Professional Ethics in Journalism", issued in 1983 in the name of all major international and regional organizations of journalists, representing altogether 400,000 working journalists in all parts of the world. This is how the document characterizes the role of media workers in relation to global issues:

> A true journalist stands for the universal values of humanism, above all peace, democracy, human rights, social progress and national liberation. Thus the journalist participates actively in the social transformation towards democratic betterment of society and contributes through dialogue to a climate of confidence in international relations conducive to peace and justice everywhere, to detente, disarmament, and national development.

Accordingly, disarmament is recognized as an integral part of what might be called the universal ethic of media professionals – an ethic which begins with the pursuit of truth and ends with support for the same fundamental values as those on which the United Nations was founded. This ethic, it should be noted, is held and elaborated by the profession itself, without any interference from Governments. We stand for a free and responsible press and call for both professional autonomy of journalists and public accountability of the media.

These worthy principles must now be transferred into practical action. We need journalists talking directly to the people, as was done so effectively in the telebridges. We need constructive media criticism, based on scientific evidence, as the late Seán MacBride proposed when he called for a system of monitoring the media coverage of disarmament. My organization offers its world-wide network of journalists to build a bridge that crosses over the military-industrial complex and brings disarmament diplomacy closer to the world's people.

APPENDIX 7. STATEMENT IN GENEVA 1984 AND PRESS RELEASE IN SOFIA 1985

We representatives of international and regional organisations of journalists, uniting 400,000 working journalists in all parts of the world, express our appreciation to Unesco which has facilitated since 1978 regular consultative meetings between us, without any interference from the side of the governments, letting professionals deal with vital issues such as codes of ethics and protection of journalists. We have all reason to support the Secretariat and the Director-General of Unesco for their efforts in carrying out the Unesco programmes in accordance with the Constitution for the benefit of peace, democracy, freedom of information and socio-economic progress in the world. We especially support the initiative taken by the Director-General to establish a working group on questions relating to public information and hope that journalists be given the best possible conditions to report on Unesco's activities. At the same time, while recognising the right of free comment, we stress the importance of reporting honestly and truthfully on Unesco and the United Nations at large, in line with highest standards of journalistic ethics defined by the profession in documents such as those adopted by our organisations. Believing in the universal nature of Unesco, we hope that the professional organisations in the United States continue their call for a reconsideration of the U.S. Government's announcement to withdraw from the Organisation.

Geneva, 6 July 1984.

International Federation of Journalists (IFJ)
Secretary General

International Organization of Journalists (IOJ)
President

International Catholic Union of the Press (UCIP)
Administrative Secretary

Latin American Federation of Journalists (FELAP)
Secretary General

Union of African Journalists (UAJ)
Deputy Secretary General

23.10.85

Sofia 1985

TELEX PRESSE

SIX INTERNATIONAL AND REGIONAL ORGANIZATIONS OF JOURNALISTS DRAWN FROM ALL PARTS OF THE WORLD HAVE EXPRESSED THEIR SUPPORT FOR UNESCO'S ACTIVITIES IN THE INFORMATION AND COMMUNICATION FIELDS.

THEY INCLUDE THE PRAGUE-BASED INTERNATIONAL ORGANIZATION OF JOURNALISTS, THE BRUSSELS-BASED INTERNATIONAL FEDERATION OF JOURNALISTS, THE LATIN AMERICAN FEDERATION OF JOURNALISTS, THE AFRICAN UNION OF JOURNALISTS, THE ARAB FEDERATION OF JOURNALISTS AND THE CONFEDERATION OF ASEAN JOURNALISTS.

A STATEMENT ISSUED HERE TODAY BY THE IOJ AND SUPPORTED BY THE OTHERS SAID THAT THE ORGANIZATIONS, WHICH BRING TOGETHER 400,000 WORKING JOURNALISTS THROUGHOUT THE WORLD, EXPRESSED APPRECIATION TO UNESCO FOR FACILITATING SINCE 1978 REGULAR CONSULTATIVE MEETINGS BETWEEN THEM "WITHOUT ANY INTERFERENCE FROM THE SIDE OF GOVERNMENTS, LETTING PROFESSIONALS TO DEAL WITH VITAL ISSUES SUCH AS CODES OF ETHICS AND PROTECTION OF JOURNALISTS".

"WE WANT TO MAKE IT KNOWN THAT IN OUR EXPERIENCE UNESCO HAS NEVER SUGGESTED MEASURES DETRIMENTAL TO FREEDOM OF INFORMATION; ON THE CONTRARY, UNESCO HAS CONTRIBUTED TO A HISTORICAL MOVEMENT TOWARDS A HIGHER LEVEL OF FREEDOM THROUGH ITS SUPPORT FOR A NEW WORLD INFORMATION AND COMMUNICATION ORDER" THE STATEMENT ADDED.

IT EXPLAINED THAT SUCH AN ORDER AIMED AT THE "DECOLONIZATION AND DEMOCRATIZATION" OF INFORMATION AND COMMUNICATION AT BOTH THE NATIONAL AND INTERNATIONAL LEVELS.
"WE HAVE ALL REASON TO SUPPORT THE SECRETARIAT AND THE DIRECTOR-GENERAL OF UNESCO FOR THEIR EFFORTS IN CARRYING OUT THEIR TASKS IN ACCORDANCE WITH THE CONSTITUTION OF UNESCO FOR THE BENEFIT OF PEACE, JUSTICE, FREEDOM AND SOCIO-ECONOMIC PROGRESS IN THE WORLD" THE STATEMENT CONCLUDED.

THE STATEMENT ISSUED TODAY WAS BASED ON A SIMILAR RESOLUTION ADOPTED AT THE FIFTH CONSULTATIVE MEETING BETWEEN INTERNATIONAL AND REGIONAL ORGANIZATIONS OF JOURNALISTS HELD IN GENEVA LAST JULY.

UNESCOPRESS

APPENDIX 8. PROPOSAL FOR MAIN AREAS OF IOJ ACTIVITY AFTER THE 10TH CONGRESS 1986

Material for the extended meeting of the IOJ Secretariat, Prague, June 10–11, 1986
Material No. 1a referring to the item No. 1 of the agenda
Submitted by: K. Nordenstreng, president of the IOJ
Title: Proposals for main areas where IOJ should perform more serious and long-term activity after the 10th congress

1. **Peace and disarmament**
- analysis of media coverage and support to the system of monitoring the media [see annex below]
- analysis of ideological argumentation, language, etc.
- support to worldwide movement of journalists for peace
2. **Disinformation**
- monitoring of media coverage and in-depth exposure of cases such as Antonov, KAL 007, Nicaragua, etc.
- analysis of ideological argumentation, language, etc.
3. **Professional ethics**
- further elaboration of Principles of Professional Ethics in Journalism and assistance to national unions for their application
- support to establishment of an International Court of Honour for Journalists
4. **New International Information and Communication Order**
- monitoring of developments at UNESCO, UN, Non-Aligned Movement, etc.
- further elaboration of its principles and assistance to national unions for their application
5. **Protection of journalists in dangerous professional missions**
- collection of information on cases
- coordination of joint international action with the "consultative club" and the Red Cross
6. **New technology**
- monitoring of development in industry and media
- coordination of joint action with other journalists' organizations and the ILO
- assistance in consultation to member unions

These areas could be taken care of by special working groups to be appointed by the Congress (or Presidium).

In addition to the areas enumerated above, it is taken for granted that the following areas continue to occupy high priority and be organized along the present lines:

Publications (Democratic Journalist, Newsletter, books, etc.)
Training (schools, courses, textbooks, etc.)
Studies and documentation (Institute, dossiers, etc.)

Annex: Proposal for a System of Monitoring Media in Issues of Peace and War

The idea: to organize a permanent system of surveying and reviewing, or monitoring, the role of the mass media in peace and disarmament related issues on the basis of worldwide documentation and scientific analysis of the ways in which arms race and disarmament issues are being portrayed by the journalistic and cultural media. Although the prime target is media content or coverage, such a monitoring would naturally lead to consider also other related aspects such as media ownership and public opinion.
The system would have in a way two levels of operation. First, the primary data would be delivered by competent national and international bodies, both academic (institutes and associations of communication and peace research) and professional (organizations of working journalists). The gathering of data would be co-ordinated, and a preliminary processing of the data performed, by a central unit which could be set up by such NGOs (with consultative status at UN/UNESCO) as the IOJ, International Peace Research Association (IPRA) and the International Association for Mass Communication Research (IAMCR/AIERI).
At the second level, the final review and analysis would be done, and eventual recommendations made, by an independent international commission in line with the Brandt and Palme Commissions, not appointed by or subordinated to any intergovernmental organization. However, it would collaborate with the UN, in particular with the World Disarmament Campaign from which it might get the necessary political and financial support (some 50 000 US dollars per year). The commission would meet once a year and it would have a permanent secretariat working ideally within the above-mentioned NGO unit. The main concrete outcome of the commission would be an annual report for a wide distribution among political and professional circles – ultimately among the general public.
The idea has been entertained by myself and my colleague Tapio Varis since about 1981, and it has been shared with Seán MacBride, Luis Echeverria and Johan Galtung, among others. It has been included as an overall proposal in documents such as report of the UN disarmament seminar in Leningrad in June 1984 and the Leipzig seminar on the role of science, culture and communication in disarmament in May 1984. I have also discussed the idea with the UN Under-Secretary General on Disarmament, Mr. Marten-

son and his colleagues. MacBride has told about the idea to the UN Secretary General.
In early 1984 I thought that MacBride would assume a central role in the implementation of the idea. However, he has been too preoccupied with other things and his initial enthusiasm was somewhat reduced as the crisis around UNESCO developed towards the withdrawal of USA and UK. In spring 1985 Johan Galtung offered to host in Paris a scientific workshop on the idea, but this initiative did not materialize because of practical obstacles.
In this International Year of Peace, in connection with the 10h IOJ Congressand also in relation to the rediscovery of the International Tribunal of Honour (1931 –), it seems to me imperative that the idea be finally pushed forward. The content analysis carried out by the IOJ Commission for Studies and Documentation constitutes an important cornerstone for the new building.

Prague, 27 May 1986
Kaarle Nordenstreng

APPENDIX 9. MINUTES OF THE IOJ PRESIDIUM BUREAU IN MOSCOW 1987

MEETING OF THE IOJ PRESIDIUM - BAGHDAD, OCTOBER 20-22, 1987

اجتماع هيئة رئاسة منظمة الصحفيين العالمية بغداد ٢٠-٢٢ تشرين الاول ١٩٨٧

M I N U T E S

from the IOJ Presidium Bureau Meeting
(Moscow, March 17-18, 1987)

A. ATTENDED BY:

Bureau members:

K. Nordenstreng, J. Kubka, K. Megyeri, V.G. Afanasiev, F. Diogo, G. Gatinot, S. Q. Hammoudi, E. Heinrich, N. Dragos (by deputy of A. Ionescu), G. Izobo, A. Palmer, L. Suárez, B. Traikov, Dao Tung, E. Vera.

Member unions' representatives:

Bulgaria - S. Krstev,
Czechoslovakia - J. Valenta,
Cuba - G. García,
GDR - K. Vogel,
Hungary - P. Vajda,
Korea - Kim Kvan Su,
Mongolia - L. Tudev,
Poland - K. Krzyzagórski, M. Kruczkowski, A. Ziemski,
USSR - I. A. Zubkov, R. N. Moseev.

IOJ GS:

V. L. Artemov, E. Concepción, M. Jurkowicz, L. Paukku, C. Prisacaru, B. Sakharov, M. Weigand, D. Benová, Z. Harantová, L. Jelínková, V. Slavík, M. Chytrý.

Meeting was chaired by:

K. Nordenstreng

B. AGENDA

1. Regulations and composition of the Bureau
2. Tasks, composition and working regulations of councils and committees
3. Improvement of the General Secretariat's structure (for information)
4. Action plan for 1987
5. Presidium session in Baghdad
6. World Council of Journalists
7. International Journalists' Card (for information)
8. Miscellaneous

C. RECORD OF THE PROCEEDINGS

After the opening of the Bureau meeting, the IOJ President K. Nordenstreng checked the Bureau members' attendance by names. After this, the draft agenda was approved by all the attending participants.

To the respective points of the agenda:

To the point B1) Regulations and composition of the Bureau

On the basis of the discussion and the proposals of Bureau members a principle was adopted to hold the Bureau meeting at least twice a year. Under normal circumstances, the first meeting will be held at the beginning of the year, the second one before the opening of the Presidium session.

To the point B2) Tasks, composition and working regulations of councils and committees:

The discussion on the material focused on these issues:

- Denomination of working institutions:

  It was explained that the councils had a permanent background (schools, institute), supporting their activities, while the committees had none. This explanation allayed the doubt whether two denominations (councils, committees) were necessary.

  It was agreed to carry out further working activity within 2 councils and 5 committees.

- Mandates of councils and committees:
  During the discussions, participants emphasized the importance of individual councils and committees resulting from their responsibility for the activity in all IOJ's spheres of work. The fact that the councils and the committees are headed by the vice-presidents also demonstrates their supporting character. In order to develop the work of the councils and committees, they should be also helped by regional centres, which are supposed to influence their activity within their region. As result of the discussion, the text of certain mandates was adjusted and some chairpersons submitted new formulations.

- Financial coverage of separate actions:
  In connection with the realization of a number of actions under preparation, the discussion also highlighted the problems of their financial settlement. The SecretaryGeneral underlined that the General Secretariat covered an absolute majority of IOJ's activities and therefore it could not guarantee the financial coverage of all good and inspiring ideas which would come out from member organizations. It was concluded that the financial costs of the undertakings would be covered, within the possibilities, by the host organization and the member organizations participating in them. The General Secretariat will try to help this activity and will participate in covering these costs according to its means. The text was formulated and included into the discussed material.

- Composition of the councils and the committees:
  The councils' and the committees' respective chairpersons informed of the composition of their working institutions. As a result of the discussion, some councils and committees were complemented with other members. This is their final composition:

Composition of the Councils and the Committees.

Council for Studies and Documentation
Chairman : V. G. Afanasiev (USSR)
Members : Bulgaria, Cuba, Czechoslovakia, GDR, Hungary, Poland, Romania, USSR, IJI

Training Council
Chairman : E. Heinrich (GDR)
Members : Schools and training institutions: Bulgaria, Czechoslovakia, GDR, Ghana, India, Iraq, People's Democratic Republic of Yemen, Democratic People's Republic of Korea, Cuba, Mozambique, Tanzania, USSR, Hungary, Vietnam, Nigeria

Committee for Peace and Disarmament
Chairwoman : A. Palmer (USA)
Members : Finland, West Berlin, FRG, USSR, Hungary, Czechoslovakia, Poland, Democratic People's Republic of Korea, Zimbabwe

Committee for Professional Ethics
Chairman : A. Ionescu (Romania)
Members : Iraq, Portugal, Poland, Cuba, Finland, Morocco

Committee for Social Issues
Chairman : B. Traikov (Bulgaria)
Members : USSR, GDR, Poland, Hungary, Czechoslovakia, Syria, Ethiopia, Cuba, Democratic People's Republic of Korea

Committee for Protection of Journalists
Chairman : L. Suárez (Mexico)
Members : France, USSR, South Africa, Argentina, Chile, Nicaragua, Lebanon, Palestine, one Caribbean country

Committee for New Technologies
Chairman : G. Gatinot (France)
Members : Great Britain, GDR, Finland, Hungary, Portugal.

To the point B3)
Improvement of the General Secretariat's structure

The President and the Secretary-General gave an explanation of the material which the Bureau members was submitted for information. They emphasized that economic possibilities as well as maximum functionality of seperate links had been respected when the structure was created.

The Bureau members positively accepted the submitted structure pointing out that its rightness would be verified in the period to come, in particular when performing challenging tasks which resulted from the conclusions of the 10th Congress.

The discussion paid a profound attention to the activity of regional centres and to the countries where these centres were located. The questions concerned raison d'être of the establishment of a regional centre for the Asian continent in New Delhi. A proposal was also submitted for a regional centre in the USA, which the Secretary-General welcomed, pointing out that in case that U.S. journalists took the necessary steps, the General Secretariat would be able to quickly materialize the project. In the discussion, the location of a regional centre in Algeria was positively accepted, participants being convinced that the cooperation between Alger and Baghdad (FAJ) would be successful in all respects. The intention to establish a regional centre in Addis Ababa was supported as well. In general, there was a prevailing call for meticulous choice of journalistic personages for the leadership of the regional centres. They should be General-Secretariat's full-time employees and would be provided with all material and technical conditions for their efficient activity.

As a result of further discussion, equal workload of secretaries and vice-presidents was required. Therefore a shift of certain responsibilities was made within the framework of the General Secretariat. It was also decided to pass the responsibility for the direction of the editorial activity on the Bureau. The results of a fruitful discussion on the improved General Secretariat's structure were formulated into the revised material.

In conclusion, the President appreciated the results of the discussion as an important step in the history of the IOJ aiming at achieving the efficiency of all its links. At the same time it was emphasized that, since the 10th Congress, the structure had been coming into existence through a number of discussions which were not simple. The adopted structure should therefore keep being in force for a certain period, in order to verify its functionality. For this reason further proposals and attempts to change it should be avoided.

To the point B4) Action plan for 1987

The IOJ President explained the form of elaboration as well as the purpose of the submitted system of planning in the main spheres of the IOJ's activity. It is a document of extraordinary importance, which is, in its way, open to further elaboration, initiatives and amendments by national unions of journalists. He briefly substantiated most of the planned tasks.

The Bureau members agreed that the action plan as a whole costituted a supporting programme of the IOJ's activity for 1987, fully corresponding to the conclusions of the 10th Congress. The Bureau members therefore expressed their support to all the actions included in this plan.

During the discussion, some more actions were added into the plan:

Round table of journalists on the "Nuclear-weapon-free zone in the Iberian Peninsula"	1987 Alicante	proposed by F. Diogo
Round table of journalists on the "Nuclear-weapon-free zone in Asia and in the Pacific"	1987 Ho Chi Minh City	proposed by Dao Tung
Conference on the occasion of the Great October Socialist Revolution 70th anniversary	1987 Moscow	proposed by R. N. Moseev
Seminar oriented on the situation in the occupied Near and Middle East	1987	proposed by S. Q. Hammoudi
To organize working trips of journalists to "hot" regions before the autumn U.N. General Assembly session	1987 before August	proposed by Dao Tung
Seminar on the subject "Peace and Development", organized in cooperation with the Union of Journalists of the USSR	1988 Harare	proposed by G. Izobo

Round table on professional training of journalists and on new technologies	1987 Lisbon	proposed by F. Diogo
To discuss real possibilities of publishing "The Democratic Journalist" in Arabic	1987 Baghdad	proposed by S.Q. Hammoudi
Seminar organized by FELAP on "Democracy in Journalism, American Press, New Technologies"	1987 Central America	proposed by L. Suárez
To prepare a dossier for UNESCO General Direction in order to obtain "A" statute for the IOJ	1987	proposed by G. Gatinot
Bureau meeting in order to discuss the agenda of the Presidium and the publishing activities plan	1987 Baghdad	

During the meeting, G. Gatinot made an intervention calling for actions to be organized for the liberation of the journalists kidnapped in Lebanon. The Bureau adopted a resolution on this issue which was immediately sent out to the world mass media.

In conclusion of the discussions on the action plan, the Secretary-General informed of IOJ's financial sources. (Incomes from membership fees, Solidarity Fund, Videopress' activity). He asked to make it a rule, when putting actions forward, not only to explain the aims and the organizational ensurance, but also to always mention a financial consideration indicating who would participate in the settlement of the action.

Then the President declared that the action plan had been adopted and that it would be submitted to the Presidium at its session in Baghdad.

To the point B5) Presidium session in Baghdad

At the beginning, the President draw the attention to the changes occured in the course of the Bureau meeting. It concerned in particular the decision that this year's second Bureau meeting would take place in Baghdad prior to the Presidium session.

The conception of the preparations for the Presidium session was positively appreciated and adopted with satisfaction. The Secretary-General emphasized that the action plan would be the main item of the Presidium's agenda, pointing out that, besides the General Secretariat, all the Presidium members as well as member organizations should also participate in the fulfilment of this plan. So as to enable a thorough preparation of these discussions, the action plan will be sent out in advance.

S. Q. Hammoudi welcomed the fact that the Presidium session would be held in Baghdad assuring that the host organization would do its utmost to contribute to successful results of the dealings.

During the discussion, some of the items of the Presidium's draft agenda were amended.

To the point B6 World Council of Journalists

The President explained the history of how the idea of the World Council of Journalists had come into being and how the efforts to materialize this idea developed. He informed of its complete rejection at the IFJ Bureau session in Hong Kong.

The Bureau entrusted the President and the Secretary-General to submit the issue of the World Council of Journalists for discussion at the forthcoming consultative meeting of internatio-nal organizations of journalists in Cairo and to ensure the other partners' standpoint.

To the point B7 International Journalists' Card

After a detailed explanation by the Secretary-General, the Bureau took cognizance of the material submitted for information.

To the point B8 Miscellaneous

- L. Suárez reminded of the protection of journalists, the issue of both professional and social aspects which should also be supported by the Solidarity Fund. He invited other countries, too, to join the shared initiative of France and the USSR and thus to demonstrate international interest in this serious problem.

- G. Gatinot called for more decisive steps to be taken against the misinformation in the press. He read a declaration of the International Federation of Newspaper Publishers (Fédération internationale des éditeurs de journaux - FIEJ) on topical problems of the press requesting to discuss, on the occasion of the symposium in Tampere, the issue of the infringement on press freedom.

APPENDIX 10. MANDATES OF THE IOJ COMMISSIONS AND COMMITTEES 1987

TASKS, COMPOSITION AND WORKING REGULATIONS OF IOJ COUNCILS AND COMMITTEES

1) The IOJ councils and working committees are created on the basis of the General Resolution of the 10th IOJ Congress.

The councils and committees are responsible for their activities to the elected bodies of the IOJ (Congress, Executive Committee, Presidium, Bureau).

2) The Councils are organs of the IOJ Presidium dealing with regular activities based on permanent institutions under the IOJ (training and research institutes, schools, etc.)

The Editorial Board for Publications and Information acts in accordance with the general rules of procedure of the IOJ Councils.

3) The Committees are organs of the IOJ Presidium dealing with specific problems in the field of journalism and mass communications.

4) Councils and committees are run by chairpersons elected by the IOJ Presidium.

5) Members of the councils and committees are nominated by the respective chairpersons and confirmed by the Presidium or its Bureau. The quantity of members of councils and committees ought to garantee the effectivity of respective bodies. The chairperson may appoint a secretary, temporary bodies, etc.

6) All member organizations of the IOJ have the right to participate in the activities of councils and committees. Chairpersons of these bodies have the right to invite other organizations and institutions nonaffiliated with the IOJ to take part in the activities as consultants or observers. Specialists may be appointed by the chairperson in order to facilitate the permanent work of the councils and committees.

7) Annual plans of councils and committees are to be elaborated by the respective chairpersons and adopted by these bodies in consultation with the IOJ Secretary General and should be confirmed by the Presidium or its Bureau. A report of activities of the year passed has to be delivered on the same occasion.

8) As a general rule the expenses should be covered as far as possible by the host organization and the member organizations which are participating in the usual activities. The General Secretariat will participate in covering the expenses according to its possibilities.

MANDATES OF THE COUNCILS

Council for Studies and Documentation

a) To facilitate exchange of information between relevant research centres and to ensure that their work is properly coordinated and maximally used for the benefit of the IOJ.

b) To carry out ad hoc research projects with the aid of International Journalism Institute (IJI) and expert teams.

c) To organize international seminars, colloquies and meetings of experts.

d) To prepare proposals and supply materials for IOJ and IJI publications.

e) To help developing the IJI and to assist in establishing its membership base and in its systematical gathering, sorting out, storing and disseminating data on the mass media, journalists and their organizations, as well as in producing studies and analyses which are of interest to the IOJ and its member organizations.

Training Council

a) To collect and to transmit among IOJ member organizations information on the activities in the sphere of training and further education of journalists and to work out analyses and requirements in this sphere.

b) To encourage exchange of scientific publications, lectures, seminars, films, tapes, training materials, as well as lecturers (experts) among organizations and institutions participating in the activities of the council.

c) To coordinate the activities of IOJ Solidarity schools.

d) To prepare proposals for publishing textbooks for training of journalists within the publishing activities of the IOJ General Secretariat.

MANDATES OF THE COMMITTEES

Committee for Peace and Disarmament

a) To promote international initiatives and activities on peace and disarmament, including those submitted in the UNO.

b) To coordinate the activities of the IOJ with those of international and regional peace organizations, and to propose new ideas and new forms for their activities.

c) To organize meetings of journalists, as well as of people of other professions, on topical issues of war and peace.

d) To analyze the problems of education for peace, media coverage of peace and war issues, the phenomena of war propaganda, aggression and hatred, including racial hatred.

e) To plan IOJ publications on the subjects of war and peace.

Committee for New Technologies

1. To decide about the launching of an international inquiry on the impact of new technologies in the sphere of communication, considering four aspects:

a) trade unions:
- distribution of tasks among printers or electronic mass media technicians and journalists
- a salary rise for this new skill?
- a reduction of working hours?
- efforts against a diminuation of manpower (Murdoch example)
- to implement them so that they may be profited rather for improvement of working conditions and elimination of occupational hazards of these professions

b) medical:
- physiological consequencies and new forms of "occupational diseases"
- growing role of industrial medicine

c) deontological:
- the journalist's control of the utilization of his production

d) political:
- aggravation of the imbalance of information exchange between the developing and the industrially developed countries
- increased diffusion of the dominant ideology and its influence on culture, customs and national feelings of the peoples who are subject to this propaganda
- to require, on the contrary, that they should serve to:
  - better mutual acquaintance among peoples
  - better quality of information

2. To associate to this inquiry: UNESCO, ILO, IFJ and regional organizations of journalists, International Graphic Federation, WFTU Permanent Committee.

Committee for Social Issues

a) To carry out studies on the social situation of journalists throughout the world and to prepare proposals for the improvement of the social situation of journalists.

b) To cooperate with the international organizations dealing with social issues of mass media emploees.

c) To extend moral and material aid to journalists throughout the world facing a difficult situation (strikes, persecution, unemployment, closing down of publications, etc.).

d) To follow up the activities of IOJ International Rest Houses of Journalists. The committee can establish for that purpose a special body (subcommittee).

Committee for Professional Ethics

a) To prepare IOJ contributions to the development of professional deontology and ethics.

b) To organize the professional meetings, colloquiums and seminars on specific topics concerning the deontology and dissemination of the rules of international ethics.

c) To coordinate the activity of existing IOJ clubs and to help when necessary set up new clubs for specialized interests.

d) To organize together with the IOJ Photoreporters' Club the Interpressphoto exhibition and other international photo events.

Committee for protection of journalists and solidarity

a) To respond to various cases of journalists' exposure to personal danger in accomplishing their professional, official duties.

b) To cooperate with the Red Cross International Committee, with international, regional and national organizations of journalists in order to organize a help for the journalists who are physically endangered in accomplishing their official duties.

c) To analyse the causes of journalists' exposure to danger in accomplishing their official duties.

d) To organize various forms of help to the families of the journalists who are exposed to danger.

e) To distribute, in journalistic surroundings, the norms of international law which are a basis for international operations aiming at the protection of journalists.

APPENDIX 11. IOJ MEMBER ORGANIZATIONS IN 1988

(Secretariat document, situation by May 1988)

+ Associate member
* Listed among IOJ member organizations still in 1997.
Those which were members of the IFJ in 1997 are marked in this list in *italic*.

EUROPE		
Bulgaria	*Union of Bulgarian Journalists* *	4,500
Cyprus	*Cyprus Union of Journalists* +	120
Czechoslovakia	Czechoslovak Union of Journalists 1	7,281
Finland	General Union of Journalists (YLL)	306
	Finnish Social Democratic Association of Journalists (SSSL) +	450
	Journalists Association (TL) +	250
	Union of Journalists in Finland (SSL) +	7,579
France	*National Syndicate of Journalists* (CGT) *	1,020
Germany	Union of Journalists of the GDR 2	9,022
Greece	Group of Journalists of the IOJ in Greece *	195
Hungary	*Association of Hungarian Journalists*	5,600
Malta	Association of Progressive Journalists *	54
Poland	Association of Journalists of the PRP (SDPRL) *	6,674
Portugal	*Syndicate of Journalists* *	1,370
Romania	*Council of Romanian Journalists* *	3,000
Spain	*Federation of Paper, Graphic Arts and Soc. Comm. Workers* +	3,000
	Union of Journalists *	3,500
USSR	*Union of Journalists of the USSR* *	85,182

After its discontinuation in 1990, a new (small) Czech association is listed in 1997.

After its discontinuation in 1991, a new association of the IOJ in Germany is listed in 1997.

AFRICA		
Algeria	*Union of Algerian Journalists, Writers and Interpreters* *	600
Angola	Union of Angolan Journalists *	700
Benin	Benin Journalists' Association *	200
Botswana	Botswana Journalists' Association	60
Cameroon	National Union of Cameroonian Journalists *	47
Congo	National Union of Congolese Journalists *	700
Egypt	Egyptian Press Syndicate *	2,500
Ethiopia	Ethiopian Journalists' Association *	600
Gambia	*Gambia Press Union* *	53
Ghana	*Ghana Journalists' Association* *	620
Guinea	Association of Journalists of Guinea *	60
Guinea-Bissau	Association of Journalists of Guinea-Bissau *	56
Lesotho	*Lesotho Union of Journalists* *	15
	Writer's Association of Lesotho *	23
Madagascar	Press Syndicate of Madagascar *	30
Mali	National Union of Journalists of Mali *	80
Mauritania	Association of Mauritanian Journalists *	112
Mauritius	*Mauritius Union of Journalists* *	25
	Organization of Mauritius Progressive Journalists *	22
Morocco	*National Syndicate of Moroccan Press* *	506
Mozambique	*National Organization of Journalists* *	400
Namibia	SWAPO Branch of Journalists *	150
Nigeria	*Nigeria Union of Journalists* *	5,700
Saharawi Arab Dem. R.	Union of Journalists of Saquia el Hamra y Rio de Oro (UPESARIO) *	15
Senegal	Association of Democratic Journalists of Senegal *	52
Sierra Leone	Sierra Leone Association of Journalists *	200
Somalia	Somali Journalists' Association *	403
South Africa	South African Journalists Circle (ANC) *	550
Sudan	Sudanese Journalists' Association *	350
Tanzania	Tanzania Journalists' Association *	200
Uganda	*Uganda Journalists' Association* *	540
Zambia	Press Association of Zambia *	250
Zimbabwe	*Zimbabwe Union of Journalists* *	220

ASIA AND OCEANIA		
Afghanistan	Union of Journalists of DR of Afghanistan	1,520
Australia	IOJ Branch of Australia	15
Bangladesh	IOJ Bangladesh Group *	126
China	All China Journalists' Association 1	
DPR of Korea	Korean Journalists' Union *	10,000
India	Indian Federation of Working Journalists +	13,000
Iraq	Iraqi Journalists' Union *	3,000
Japan	Japan Journalists' Association *	600
	Association of Korean Journalists and Publishers in Japan *	400
	Japan Congress of Journalists *	1,000
Jordan	Jordanian Press Association *	250
Kampuchea	Association of Kampuchean Journalists	500
Kuwait	Kuwait Journalists' Association *	300
Lao	Association of Laotian Journalists *	400
Lebanon	Union of Journalists of Lebanon *	700
Mongolia	Union of Mongolian Journalists *	550
Nepal	National Press Club, Nepal *	300
Palestine	*General Union of Palestinian Writers and Journalists* *	3,000
DPR of Yemen	Organization of Democratic Journalists of Yemen	400
Sri Lanka	Sri Lanka Press Association *	1,123
	Union of Journalists of Sri Lanka *	458
Syria	Syrian Journalists' Union *	1,500
Vietnam	Association of Vietnamese Journalists *	6,000
Yemen Arab Republic	Yemen Journalists' Syndicate *	372

1 Did not participate in any IOJ activities after 1965.

LATIN AMERICA AND CARIBBEAN		
Argentina	IOJ Committee in Argentina *	1,017
Bolivia	Federation of Press Workers of Bolivia *	1,000
Brazil	*National Federation of Professional Journalists* (FENAJ) *	25,000
Chile	IOJ Committee in Chile	20
Colombia	National College of Journalists of Colombia *	850
Costa Rica	*National Syndicate of Journalists* *	110
Cuba	Union of Journalists of Cuba *	3,000
Dominican Republic	College of Dominican Journalists *	1,030
	National Syndicate of Press Workers *	800
Ecuador	National Union of Journalists of Ecuador *	1,500
El Salvador	National Union of Journalists of El Salvador*	82
Grenada	Media Workers Association of Grenada	82
Guatemala	Association of Democratic Journalists of Guatemala *	280
Guyana	Union of Guyanese Journalists *	127
Honduras	*Union of Journalists of Honduras* *	60
Jamaica	Press Association of Jamaica *	180
Mexico	National Syndicate of Press Editors *	3,412
	Union of Democratic Journalists *	1,200
Nicaragua	Union of Journalists of Nicaragua *	486
Panama	Syndicate of Journalists of Panama *	350
Peru	College of Journalists of Peru *	4,200
Puerto Rico	IOJ Committee in Puerto Rico	25
Saint Lucia	St. Lucia Media Workers Association *	35
Surinam	Progressive Media Workers Association of Surinam *	60
Trinidad	National Joint Action Committee *	50
Uruguay	Association of Uruguayan Press *	2,030
Venezuela	*National Syndicate of Press Workers of Venezuela* *	2,500

NORTH AMERICA		
Canada	IOJ Chapter in Canada *	30
USA	USA Chapter of the IOJ *	200
	Black Press Institute *	40
	National Alliance of Third World Journalists *	300

APPENDIX 12. SURVEY OF IOJ MEMBERSHIP IN 1988 AND 1991

(From *A History of the International Movement of Journalists*, pp. 197–198.)

Survey of the IOJ's member organizations, associated organizations and individual members
(Situation by 1 May 1988)

Region	Member organizations			Associated Organizations			Individual Members		Total	
	Number of countries	Number of organizations	Number of journalists	Number of countries	Number of organizations	Number of journalists	Number of countries	Number of journalists	Number of countries	Number of journalists
Europe	13	13	127,704	3	5	11,399	9	57	23++	139,160
Africa	31	33	16,039				13	40	44	16,079
Asia and Oceania	20	23	32,514+	1	1	13,000	4	29	25	45,543
Latin America and Caribean	24	26	49,384				2	19	26	49,403
North America	2	4	570						2	570
Total	90	99	226,211	4	6	24,399	28	145	120++	250,755

+ Does not include members of All China Journalists Association.
++ Finland Spain – represented in the IOJ, as well member organization as associated organizations.

Survey of the member organizations, associated organizations and individual members of the IOJ
(Situation by January 1991)

Region	Member organizations			Associated organizations			Individual members		Total
	Number of countries	Number of organizations	Number of journalists	Number of countries	Number of organizations	Number of journalists	Number of countries	Number of journalists	Number of journalists
Europe, North America	13	15	118,698	4	6	12,795	23	153	131,646
Africa	33	36	27,242				15	43	27,285
Asia, Oceania and Australia	21	28	89,175*				18	386	89,561
Latin America and Caribbean	22	24	52,951				20	47	52,998
Total	89	103	288,066	4	6	12,795	76	629	301,490

* Does not include of All China Journalists Association.

APPENDIX 13. IOJ ORGANIZATIONAL STRUCTURE IN 1988 AND 1990

(Secretariat document by Kubka, January 1988)

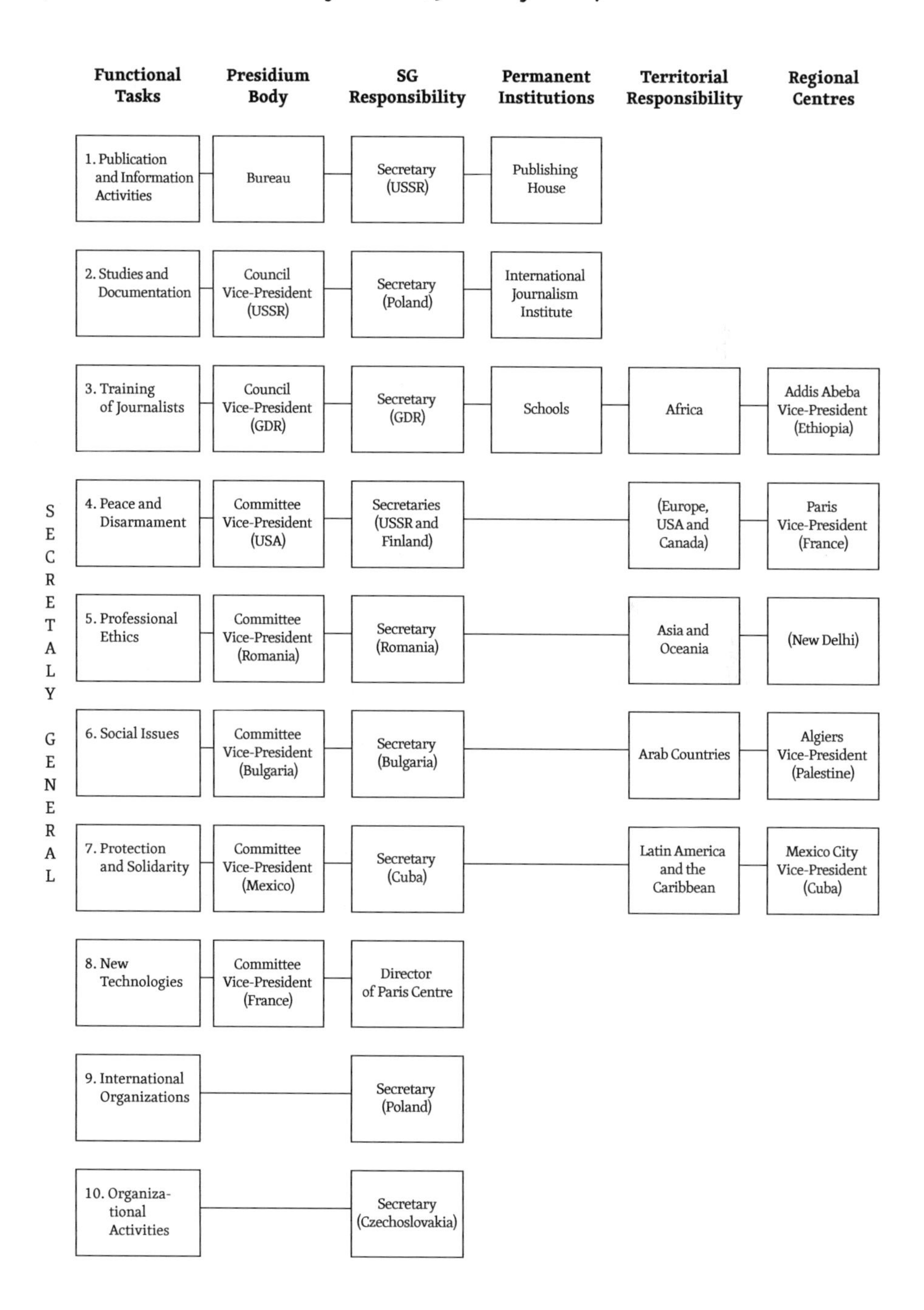

Secretariat document by Ulčák, January 1990

FOR SECRETARIAT INFORMATION
GIVEN BY: Dušan Ulčák

NO.
Date: 23-01-1990

Information on the reorganization of the administrative and economic structure of the IOJ

IOJ Secretary-General — IOJ Secretariat

IOJ Apparatus	IOJ Institutions	IOJ Enterprises
Secretariat of the IOJ SG A. Roškotová	Board of Directors Secretary: J. Kortus	Board of Directors Secretary: J. Krupica
IOJ Secretariat Office Zd. Černík	International Journalism Institute M. Vejvoda	Conference Service L. Hajda
IOJ SG Inspection Department R. Švácha	IOJ School of Solidarity M. Chytrý /temporarily/	Production and Technical Service P. Polák
Legislative and Legal Department A. Konečný	International Solidarity Lottery ---	Systems and Programming Service J. Doubravský
Centre for Information Technology Development M. Širl	Editorial Office and Publishing House, Printing Houses J. Janeček	Service for Technical Assistance Š. Rež
Personnel Department L. Rysová	Czechoslovak Editorial Office J. Blecha	International Travel Agency Š. Kačinetz
IOJ Property Administration Department V. Mírek	Interpress Magazine J. Pikous	IOJ Service in Bratislava P. Krátký
IOJ Secretariat Financial Department A. Kulhavá	Gastronomy Services F. Kozel	IOJ Service in Brno D. Prokopová
	Interpreters' Agency H. Matějčsk /temporarily/	Service for Organization and Management /L. Ficek/

APPENDIX 14. AGENDA OF THE IOJ SECRETARIAT MEETING IN MARCH 1988

Meeting of IOJ GS No. 4 - March 2, 1988

Mat. No.	Title
38/4	Visit of the delegation of Iraqi Democratic Writers, Journalists and Artists League at IOJ General Secretariat.
39/4	International conference "The Role of World Public in Solving Regional Conflicts", Kabul March 29 - 31, 1988.
40/4	Minutes of the meeting of the general secretariat No 3 - February 2, 1988.
41/4	Measures taken for establishing the "IOJ Solidarity School" in Abuja, Nigeria.
42/4	Contacts with progressive Izraeli organization and "Derech Hanitzotz/Tariq Al Sharara" weekly.
43/4	Conference on international flow of information between Western and Eastern Europe /Schmitten, FRG, February 8 - 11, 1988/.
44/4	Report on business trip to Portugal, February 11 - 19, 1988.
45/4	Materials for the IOJ Presidium meeting.
46/4	Minutes of the meeting of the general secretariat No. 3 - material No. 40; supplement of material No. 12.
47/4	Proposal of Czechoslovak Union of Journalists to award comrade Kubka the International Journalism Prize.
48/4	Invitation to Non-governmental forum for common and safe future, Geneve, April 5 - 8, 1988.
49/4	32th session of UN commission for status of women.
50/4	Solidarity plan for 1988 - 1989.

APPENDIX 15. IOJ AWARDS UNTIL 1988

IOJ INTERNATIONAL JOURNALISM PRIZE
(established by decision of the 4th IOJ Congress
Bucharest, 15-18.5.1958)

LIST OF WINNERS

1958 - Manolis Glezos (Greece)
Jacques Kayser (France)
Renato Leduc (Mexico)

1959 - Henri Alleg (Algeria)
Arpád Szakasits (Hungary)
Xuan Thuy (Vietnam)

1960 - Brian Percy Bunting (Republic of South Africa)
Editorial team of "Revolución" (Cuba)

1961 - Cho Yong Soo (South Korea - in memoriam)
Georg Krausz (GDR)
Juan Honorato (Chile)

1962 - Editorial team of "Pravda" (USSR)
Héctor Mújica (Venezuela)

1963 - Alvarez del Vayo (Spain)
Youssoufi (Morocco)

1964 - Joao Antonio Mesplé (Brazil)
Geo Bogza (Rumania)
Teaching staff of the IOJ Seminar in Algeria

1965 - Madeleine Riffaud (France)
Wilfred Burchett (Australia)
Pio Gama Pinto (Kenya - in memoriam)
Editors, reporters and technicians of the "Radio Santo Domingo"

1966 - Association of Patriotic and Democratic Journalists of South Vietnam
Gerhart Eisler (GDR)
Fabricio Ojeda (Venezuela - in memoriam)
Cedric Belfrage (USA)

1967 - Association of Journalists of the VDR
Kostas Filinis (Greece)
Kofi Batsa (Ghana)
Union of Journalists of the USSR

1968 - James Aldridge (Great Britain)

1969 - Genaro Carnero Checa (Peru)
Kim Yong Tai (Korean Peoples' Democratic Republic)
Jorge Ricardo Masetti (Argentina - in memoriam)
Journalists' team of the ORTF (France)
Monica Warnenska (Poland)

1970 - The daily "Unen" (Mongolia)

1971 - Yuri Zhukov (USSR)
Govan Mbeki (Republic of South Africa)
Juan García Ellorio (Argentina)
Elmo Gatalán Avilés (Chile)

1972 - Vu Tung (South Vietnam - in memoriam)
Luis Nelson Martírena Fabregat (Uruguay)
Unto Miettinen (Finland)

1973 - Augusto Olivares Becerra (Chile)
Ghassan Kanafani (Palestine - in memoriam)

1974 - Illegal press of Chile

1975 and
1976 - Ibrahim Amer (Egypt - in memoriam)
Luis Corvolan (Chile)
Jean Maurice Hermann (France)
Ryszard Kapuscińki (Poland)
José Manuel Ortiz García (Cuba)
Slavcho Vasev (Bulgaria)
Mikhail Zimyanin (USSR)
Association of Korean Journalists and Publishers in Japan

1977 - National Federation of Italian Press - FNSI (Italy)
Gabriel García Márquez (Columbia)
Helo Vinnia Ndadi (Namibia)
Jean Effel (France)

1978 - Augusto Carmona (Chile - in memoriam)
Union of Journalists of Nicaragua
Rudolf Singer (GDR)
Council of Journalists of Romania
Luis Suárez (Mexico)

1979 - Isao Takano (Japan - in memoriam)
Tadeusz Pasierbinski (Poland)
Hoang Tung (Vietnam)
Jorge Timossi (Argentina)

1980 and
1981 - Simon Gerson (USA)
Radio Venceremos (El Salvador)
Mamadouba Toure (Guinea)
Genzaburo Yoshino (Japan)

1982 - Aníbal de Melo (Angola)
General Union of Palestine Writers and Journalists (Palestine)
Jacobus Andreas Koster (the Netherlands - in memoriam)
Jan Cornelius Kuiper (the Netherlands - in memoriam)
Jan Johannes Willemsen (the Netherlands - in memoriam)
Hans Lodewijk Ter Laag (the Netherlands - in memoriam)
Ruth First (Republic of South Africa - in memoriam)

1983 - Ernesto Vera (Cuba)
Antero Laine (Finland)

1984 - M.Chalapathi Rau (India)
V.G.Afanasiev (USSR)

1985 - Korean daily "Rodong Sinmun"
National Union of Journalists of Ecuador

1986 - José Carrasco Tapia (Chile - in memoriam)
Hanna Muqbel (Palestine - in memoriam)

1987 - Jean-Paul Kauffmann (France)
Klemens Krzyzagórski (Poland)
Aquino Braganca and Daniel Maquinasse (Mozambique-in memoriam)

1988 - Gregorio Selser (Argentina)
Faisal Al-Husseini (Palestine)

IOJ JULIUS FUČIK MEDALS OF HONOUR
(established by decision of the IOJ Presidium session Ulan Bator, 11.-14.9.1974; statute approved at session of IOJ General Secretariat on January 21, 1975)

LIST OF WINNERS

1976

AFRICA AND ASIA

Egypt - Kamel Zoheiry
Iraq - Saad Qassim Hammoudi
- Dhia Hassan
- Fakhri Kerim
- Salah El-Din Hafez
Mali - Cheick Mouctary Diarra
Madagascar - Press Syndicate of Madagascar
Mongolia - G.Deleg
- S.Pourevjav
- O.Pountsag
- Tsend Namsrai
Palestine - General Union of Palestinian Writers and Journalists
South Africa (ANC) - M.P.Naicker
- Brian Percy Bunting
Syria - Saber Falhout
- Fuad Ballat
- Ahmad Iskander
Vietnam - Ly-Van-Sau
- Nguyen-Tan-Si (in memoriam)
- Duong-Tu-Giang
- Do-Van-Ba

AMERICA

Chile - Rolando Carasco Moya
Columbia - Alberto Zalamea
Cuba - Ernesto Vera Mendez
- Jorge Enrique Mendoza
- Comite Cubana de solidaridad con Vietnam
USA - Joe Walker
- Joseph North
Venezuela - Aristides Bastidas

EUROPE

Austria - Rudi Wengraf
Bulgaria - Dimitr Naidenov
- Mira Todorova
- Dimitr Georgiev
Czechoslovakia - Miloš Marko
- Gusta Fučíková
- Josef Valenta
- Jiří Kubka
Finland - Paavo Ruonaniemi
- Finnish Preparatory Committee for the 8th IOJ Congress

France - Jean-Maurice Hermann
- Gérard Gatinot

FRG - Werner Stertzenbach
- Wolfgang Breuer

GDR - Franz Faber
- Hermann Burkhardt
- Sepp Fischer
- Hermann Budzislawski

Hungary - Irene Komjat
- Janos Olah

Poland - Mieczyslaw Kieta
- Stanislaw Mojkowski
- Michal Hofman
- Ryszard Wojna

Romania - Nestor Ignat
- Ioan Stanculescu
- Aurelian Nestor

USSR - Daniil Kraminov
- V.Matveev
- A.K.Laurinchukas
- Oleg Zagladin

1977

EUROPE

GDR - Harri Czepuk
Italy - Dante Cruicchi
International Union of Students

1978

AFRICA

Namibia - SWAPO Branch of Journalists
Zimbabwe - Association of Journalists of Zimbabwe

AMERICA

Cuba - Revue Bohemia
Mexico - Renato Leduc
- Francisco Martínez de la Vega
Fernando Benítez

FELAP

EUROPE

GDR - Werner Lamberz International Institute of Journalism
Editorial team World Marxist Revue

1979

AFRICA AND ASIA

Mongolia - Gombo-Ochiriin Chimed
- Dambinsurengiin Tserendagva
Palestine - Bassam Abou Sharif
South Africa (ANC) - South African Journalists' Circle
Vietnam - Luu Quy Ky
- Tran Lam
- Hong Chuong
- Thep Moi
- Dao Tung
- Bui Tin

AMERICA

Cuba - Luis Gomez Wangüemert
- José Zacarias Tallet
Nicaragua - Bayar Do Arce Castaño
- Alvaro Montoya Lara - in memoriam
- Aura Ortiz - in memoriam
Porto Rico - The paper Claridad

EUROPE

Bulgaria - Stoine Krstev
- Nikola Aleksiev
- Renata Natan
Czechoslovakia - Zdeněk Hoření
GDR - Albert Norden
Poland - Vitold Lipski
- Janusz Rozskowski
- Marian Podkowinski
Romania - The daily Scinteia
- Romanian press agency Agerpress
USSR - Yassen N.Zassourski
- Spartak Ivanovich Beglov
- Sergei Nikolaevich Vishnevskij
- Iakov Alekseevich Lomko
- Vladimir Iakovlevich Serobaba
- Alexander Alexandrovich Kaverznev
World Peace Council-Romesh Chandra

1980

ASIA

Lebanon - Riad Taha - in memoriam
Mongolia - S.Chimeddamba
- D.Urzinbadam
Syria - Ahmad Iskander

AMERICA

Argentina - Roman Javier Mentaberry
Peru - Genaro Carnero Checa

EUROPE

Bulgaria - Veselin Yosifov
GDR - Helmut Brauer
- Rudi Singer
- Kurt Vogel
- Ernst Otto Schwabe
- Günter Kertzscher
- Manfred Straubing
Hungary - Hungarian press agency MTI
USSR - Genadi Iakovlevich Kovalenko
- Arkadii Afanasevich Tolstik
- Evgenii Evgenevich Grigorev
- Stanislav Nikolaevich Kondrašov
- Ivan Alekseevich Zubkov

1981

AFRICA AND ASIA

Afghanistan - Haidar Massoud
Guinea - Jerome Drâmou
Japan - Shiro Suzuki
Korea/Japan - The daily Choson Sinbo
Madagascar - Célestin Andriamanantena
Mozambique - T.Leite de Vasconcelos
Palestine - Yassir Arafat
- Majid Abou Sharar - in memoriam
PDR of Korea - Kim Gi Nam
- Chong Ha Chon
South Africa (ANC) - Govan Mbeki

AMERICA

Cuba - Nicolas Guillén
- Baldomero Alvarez Ríos
USA - Carl Winter
- John Pittman
Venezuela - Freddy Balzán

EUROPE

GDR - Hans Treffkorn
USSR - Shalva Parsadanovich Sanakoiev
- Vitali I. Sevastianov
- Ivan M.Schedrov
- Aleksander Evgenevich Bovin
- Ion Petrovich Britans
- Andrei Konstantinovich Varsobin

1982

EUROPE

USSR - Igor A.Kazanskii

1983

ASIA

Palestine	- Hani Habib - Suheil Natour - Nasri Abdul Rahman - Samer Abdallah - Rashad Abu Shawar - Ahmad Abdul Rahman - Mahmoud Labadi - Mahmoud Dawirji

AMERICA

Cuba	- Leonel Nodal Alvarez
Mexico	- Ignacio Rodriguez Terrazas

EUROPE

Cyprus	- Andreas Kannaouros
GDR	- Kurt Albrecht
Spain	- Gilles Multigner - Celso Collazos

1984

FAJ	- Hanna Muqbel - in memoriam

AMERICA

Mexico	- Manuel Buendía T.G.- in memoriam
Nicaragua	- William Ramirez

EUROPE

GDR	- Hans Frotscher - Sonja Brie
USSR	- L.N.Tolkunov - Editorial team of Komsomolskaya pravda - Vitali Korotitch - Anatoli Krasikov - Valentina Fedotova

IOJ International Journalism Institute, Budapest
IOJ editorial team of Interpressmagazin

1985

EUROPE

Bulgaria	- Dimitr Dimitrov - Serafim Severniak - Petr Kožuharov
GDR	- Editorial team of Weltbühne - Horst Sindenmann

Hungary	- Ervin Reti
	- István Kulcsar
	- Károly Matolcsy
Poland	- Zygmunt Sómkowski
	- Roman Samsel
	- Henryk Kollat
	- Julian Bartost
USSR	- M.L.Frolov
	- I.V.Vinogradov
	- A.A.Tolstik
	- N.I.Makeev
	- N.I.Peresunko
	- P.I.Troianovskii
	- V.N.Golubev
	- A.S.Prokofiev
	- F.I.Carev
	- M.A.Syrcov
	- J.I.Makarenko
	- M.D.Davitashvili
	- V.L.Skryžalin
	- J.V.Gluchov
	- A.M.Sarikov

1986

AFRICA AND ASIA

Kuwait	- Sami al-Munais
Iraq	- Sajjad al-Ghazi
	- Yaha Yassin al-Basri
	- Sabah Yassin Ali
	- Ibtisam Abdullah
Republic of South Africa (ANC)	- Nelson Mandela

AMERICA

Dominican Republic	- Orlando Martinez - in memoriam
Venezuela	- Aristid Bastidas

EUROPE

Bulgaria	- Iordan Iotov
	- Boian Traikov
	- Lalio Dimitrov
	- Kolio Gerginski - in memoriam
	- Ruben Avramov
Czechoslovakia	- Jiří Hronek
	- Jiří Meisner
	- the capitol of Prague on the 40th anniversary of of the IOJ
	- Czechoslovak Union of Journalists
GDR	- Eberhard Heinrich
	- Union of journalists of GDR

Greece	- Georgios Karantzas
	- Thanassis Georgiou
	- Vassos Georgiou
	- Costas Vidalis - in memoriam
Great Britain	- Gordon Sch"affer
USSR	- P.V.Pronin
	- E.A.Jefremov
	- I.S.Medevedev
	- M.A.Fjodorov
	- B.L.Sacharov

1987

EUROPE

Czechoslovakia	- Milan Codr
	- Vladimír Hudec
	- Vladimír Diviš
	- Karel Douděra
	- Božena Dvořáčková
	- Oldřich Enge
	- Květoslav Faix
	- Viera Gajdošová
	- Marcel Nolč
	- Leopold Podstupka
	- Jiří Stano
	- Elena Suchovská
GDR	- Manfred Weigand
	- Joachim Umann
	- Julius Waldschmidt
Hungary	- Károly Megyeri
USSR	- Jevgenii Kobelev
	- Andrei Krušinskii
	- Nikolai Solncev

ASIA

Mongolia	- Donowyn Niamsuren

1988

AFRICA AND ASIA

South Africa	- Zwelakhe Sisulu
Palestine	- Akram Haniyeh

AMERICA

Brazil	- José Gómez Talarico
Uruguay	- Rubén Acasuso

EUROPE

Cyprus	- Sevgül Udulag
GDR	- Karl-Eduard von Schnitzler

APPENDIX 16. STATEMENT OF THE 3RD CONGRESS OF CSCE JOURNALISTS 1989

Warsaw, September 17, 1989

Journalists of 20 CSCE countries met in Warsaw to further the CSCE process by improving the working conditions of journalists in the CSCE countries and the cooperation between journalists and their organizations.

The meeting took place on September 16 and 17 on the theme: "From confrontation to cooperation - the challenge to journalists at work".

It was attended by 44 representatives of 25 journalists' unions and of the International Federation of Journalists (IFJ) and the International Organization of Journalists (OIJ), and by observers of the International Journalism Institute (Prague) and the Observatoire de l'Information (Montpellier).

The participants discussed two main items:

1. Improvement of working conditions of journalists.
2. Cooperation between journalists and among national and international organizations of journalists.

The discussion was based on the CSCE final documents (Helsinki, Madrid, Vienna), the Statement of the CSCE journalists' meeting in Vienna (1987) and the proposals at the CSCE London Information Forum (April-May 1989).

On the first item, the meeting decided to seek from the CSCE governments concrete ways of putting into effect existing commitments as well as new proposals to facilitate the work of journalists.

These fall into three categories:

1. **How to get there**:

We urge all CSCE countries to issue visas to journalists within two working days of application and to establish express procedures when visas are required to cover specific events. We urge that temporary accreditation be issued within the same time limits where that accreditation is necessary.

We believe that visas should be of unlimited duration or multiple entry. In cases where a visa is refused, a full explanation for this decision should be given. A copy of this decision should be supplied to the journalists' union of the state concerned.

In countries where official accreditation is required for journalists, the accreditation should be granted as soon as possible. The procedure for investigating and/or granting the application should never exceed a one-month period.

Full accreditation should be given regardless of any political conflict between the country of origin of the journalist or media organization involved and the country that requires the accreditation.

2. How to work there

We call upon all CSCE states to remove all obstacles which hinder the work of journalists in collecting information. We believe that journalists should have unrestricted access to all sources of information, including access to the citizens of CSCE states without these citizens being required to report to the authorities and harassed or threatened as a result.

Journalists will not be required to obtain further authorization for travel within a country except for military restricted areas properly designated in advance.

3. How to report back

We believe that journalists must have the right to transmit their information by all technical means available, and that they must have the right to transport without restriction all technical equipment necessary for that purpose.

In this connection, the meeting declares that all laws and regulations in the CSCE countries which are relevant to the work of journalists must be clearly defined, publicly available and consistent with the provisions and spirit of all CSCE undertakings.

To ensure the follow up of this meeting the journalists unions in the CSCE countries will bring these demands to the attention of their governments, and present a report on the response to the IFJ or the IOJ by May 1, 1990.

On the second item, the meeting decided:

1. To draw up a list of national professional journalists' organizations in the CSCE countries. This list will be distributed to all journalists' unions concerned, for the practical use of their members.

2. To improve cooperation between journalists and their unions by means of international seminars on specific subjects, such as:

a) Rights and responsibilities: principles, laws and practices (to be organized by IFJ and IOJ)

b) Legal aspects of international broadcasting
(to be organized by the Czechoslovak union)

c) Comparative studies of media content
(to be organized by the Polish union SD PRL)

d) Media concentration in Europe
(to be organized by the Dutch union)

e) Copyright aspects
(to be organized by the IFJ in France)

f) Professional ethics of journalism
(to be organized by the International Journalism Institute, Prague)

These and other seminars will be open to interested unions of all CSCE countries.

The results of such events will be made available to all unions of CSCE countries.

3. The participants agree that there should be another meeting of the journalists of the CSCE countries in the forefield of the CSCE follow up conference in 1992. This 4th international meeting is suggested to be held on invitation of the French unions in Strasbourg in 1991.

This conference should aim at a summary of all effort to implement the given CSCE conclusions concerning the field of the free flow of information and the working conditions of journalists.

A preparatory committee of IFJ and IOJ will assist the French hosts with the organization.

The meeting welcomes the possibility offered by the Finnish delegation in the London Information Forum to organize in Helsinki, in the framework of the CSCE process, an experts' meeting on information issues during the year 1990.

The participants express their gratitude to the Journalists' Association of the People's Republic of Poland (SD PRL) for their hospitality and the excellent organization of the 3rd CSCE Journalists Meeting in Warsaw which has been an important contribution to cooperation among journalists in Europe.

APPENDIX 17. BACKGROUND PAPER FOR THE IOJ TRADE UNION ACTIVITIES 1989

FOR SECRETARIAT DISCUSSION **No.**

Given by: Mazen Husseini
Constantin Ivanov
Leena Paukku

Date: 8.11.1989

The 1st Background Paper for the IOJ Trade Union Activities

WHAT THE TRADE UNION STANDS FOR?

I * The defence and promotion of the professional and financial interests and the welfare of its members.

* The defence and promotion of the principles and practice of journalism with particular reference to the Professional Ethics in Journalism.

* The defence and promotion of the trade union principles and organization.

* The defence and promotion of copyright of its members.

* The determination of all questions affecting the professional conduct of its members.

II * The influencing over the communication policy of the country.

* The defence and promotion of freedom of the Press, broadcasting, speech and information.

* The defence and promotion of peace, equality, social justice and civil liberty.

EMPLOYMENT PROTECTION

The main function of any trade union is the protection of the jobs of its members and the betterment of their wages and conditions of work. The union will represent members whose jobs are threatened by redundancy or dismissal in the face of the employer.

Wages and working conditions are generally regulated by collective agreements between the union and the employers. Apart from wages, many other matters are covered in collective agreements, including:

* **Hours of work**
* **Paid holidays**
* **Training**
* **Paid sick and maternity leaves**
* **Grievance procedures**
* **Pension rights**

BENEFITS

Apart from general trade union services, the subscription of the members buys certain financial benefits and similar services:

* **Unemployment benefit**
  Is paid regardless of any State or other kind of benefit that members may be entitled to claim.
* **Strike benefit**
* **Grants to members in financial distress**
* **Grants to a member's dependants upon his/her death**

PROPOSALS FOR THE IOJ TRADE UNION ACTIVITIES

I Workshops

The IOJ should organize together with regional and local journalists' organizations workshops on the trade union aims such as

1. Condition of the employment in the media

* Collective agreement
* Working conditions
* Minimum salaries etc.
* New technology

2. Issues of Press Law

* The role of journalists' organizations in the relation with Press Law
* Journalists' rights and duties according to the Press Law

3. Equality of woman journalists

* The obstacles in the development of woman journalists' career
* The equality of the salary
* The representation of woman journalists in the journalists' organizations

4. Media concentration

* The role of media imperialists (Maxwell, Murdoch, Springer etc) in various continent and countries
* The influences on the communication policy and on the contents of the media
* The influences on the employment market
* Copyright; how to protect journalists' copyright

5. Copyright

* The respect of the copyright; what does it mean
* Which ways journalists have to protect their copyright; the role of the journalists' organizations

6. Freelance journalists

* Working conditions
* Fees
* Copyright problems
* Social security and pensions

The idea is to start by organizing workshops on some of those topics

2 in Africa (priority topic 1.)
1 in India
2 in Latin America
1 in Balkan peninsula
1 in Europe for EC countries (priority topic 4.)

II Trade Union Training

1. To cooperate with the representatives of the ILO in organizing trade union courses to IOJ members.

2. To begin to prepare the IOJ own course program on trade union questions, first of all for the officers and leaders of the organizations. Such a course should be immediately introduced in all IOJ schools, and help of UNESCO, ILO, etc should be sought.

III Background material

To start to prepare material for training by collecting ready materials from other national organizations on the topic of trade union. Some ideas for the contents of these booklets:

1. ABC book for trade unionist
   * Main tasks of the trade union
   * Collective agreement and collective bargaining
   * The rights and duties of members
   * The role of trade union in the protection of members' rights
   * How members act in the organization
   * etc.

2. Organizational handbook
   * The structure of the organization
   * The tasks of various bodies
   * Organization democracy
   * etc.

APPENDIX 18. LETTER TO THE IOJ FROM THE 1968 CENTER OF JOURNALISTS OF THE ČSSR 1989

CONFIDENTIAL

IOJ Secretariat
Pařížská 9
Praha 1

Prague, November 29,1989

We, representatives of the Centre of Journalists of ČSSR and representatives of Czechoslovakia in the IOJ indeed democratically elected in 1968, are addressing you with the following urgent demand:

1. To take immediate explicit position towards immediate professional rehabilitation of more than 1.000 Czech journalists as well as of hundreds of Slovak journalists which were persecuted for their activities during reviving process of 1968.

2. To inform immediately on your official position, i.e. still before tomorow's session of the Central Committee of ČSSN, the Union of Czechoslovak Journalists and present this position to the large public through mass media.

One of the IOJ goals is to fight for right of journalists to exercise freely their profession. All democratic journalists accept with pleasure the fact that you do so - but only in the regions besides the socialist countries. Czechoslovak public and Czechoslovak journalists do not know any case in which you publicly defended and supported any persecuted Czechoslovak journalist. Even your late intervention in case of release of two Czechoslovak journalists, prisoners of conscience, J.Ruml and R.Zeman, editors of "Lidové noviny",has not been done from your own iniciative but on the base of our request. Nevertheless, we know that even colleagues which officially represent their journalists union in the IOJ, requested you to intervene in this case some time ago.

In front of eyes of your Secretariat located in Prague, the struggle of our people and young journalist generation of Czechoslovakia is going on. This is the young journalist generation, which assumes today goals and aims of Prague spring '68 journalists which were struggling for democracy and for genuine freedom of expression and for free exercising of their profession. Which position up till now has been taken by the IOJ Secretariat as far as the efforts of our young colleagues are concerned? In which way and by what means has it supported them?

It seems, that the new Gorbatchev thinking and "glasnost" have not yet reached the IOJ Secretariat. It is high time to democratise deeply also the IOJ bodies if they do not want to loose their face and prestige at least in front of our Soviet, Hungarian, Polish, GDR, and of course, Czechoslovak colleagues.

But in the interest of truth it is necessary to say that the IOJ Secretariat advocated Czechoslovak journalists only in case of invasion into Czechoslovakia by armies of five States of Warsaw Treatement in August 1968. At that time not only rooms and facilities of our journalists organization were occupied but also rooms and facilities of the Secretariat of the IOJ.

This letter is being personally handed over to the IOJ Secretariat today.

Dr. František Kaucký,
Secretary General of the
Centre of Journalists of ČSSR
in 1968

Vlado Kašpar
President of the Centre of
Journalists of ČSSR in 1968

APPENDIX 19. MESSAGE FROM THE IOJ ON THE EVE OF 1990

INTERNATIONAL ORGANIZATION OF JOURNALISTS

As the world is entering a new year and a new decade - a decade leading to the 21st century - the International Organisation of Journalists (IOJ) conveys best wishes to its members and fellow journalists around the world. The IOJ hopes that the advent of a new year will lead us to a new era and that the new decade will be one of peace and progress for humanity as a whole.

This hope has been recently nurtured by the fact that developments in international relations have signalled the end of the Cold War and its ramifications. The relaxation of tension between the major powers, the progress in disarmament, the serious efforts to settle regional conflicts by peaceful means, the growing awareness of the need to overcome underdevelopment and debt in the Third World, all give rise to new prospects in East-West as well as North-South relations.

The IOJ welcomes these positive developments. At the same time it should be recalled that the IOJ was born in 1946 out of the desire of journalists all around the world to establish the broadest unity in order to assure - as its original aims and objectives stated - "the protection by all means of all liberty of the press and journalism; the defence of the people's right to be informed honestly and accurately; the promotion of international friendship and understanding through free interchange of information; and the promotion of trade-unionism amongst journalists".

Unfortunately, the Cold War hampered and complicated efforts in this direction and left its mark on the world of journalism.

However, the IOJ together with other organisations of journalists has tried to overcome many of the problems stemming out of the Cold War. Use was made of the new possibilities created by the developments in international relations, namely the Helsinki process, the growth of the Movement of Non-Aligned Countries, and the increasing role of the United Nations. Concrete results can be seen in the International Principles of Professional Ethics in Journalism (Paris, 1983), in the joint statement of the journalist organisations in the CSCE countries (Vienna, 1987) as well as in the position presented to UNESCO by the Consultative Club of International and Regional Organisations of Journalists (Prague, 1988), where it was pointed out that "the operation of the mass media should be determined primarily by the practice of professional journalism in the public interest without undue government or

---

THE INTERNATIONAL ORGANIZATION OF JOURNALISTS (IOJ) IS A NON-GOVERNMENTAL ORGANIZATION HAVING A CONSULTATIVE STATUS WITH THE UNITED NATIONS ECONOMIC AND SOCIAL COUNCIL (ECOSOC – CATEGORY II) AND UNESCO (CATEGORY B)

SECRETARIAT: Pařížská 9, 110 01 PRAGUE, CZECHOSLOVAKIA – TELEGRAMS: INTORGJOUR PRAGUE – TELEPHONE Nos.: 232 80 15, 232 83 71, 232 59 89 – TELEX No.: 122 631 JOUR C – FAX No.: 232 04 26

commercial influence. This means professionalism supported by the idea of a free and responsible press".

The IOJ welcomes the democratization process and the increased openess and commitment to the people's right to true information that is taking place in East European and other countries.

The IOJ underlines its determination to strengthen its professional approach and to step up its activities in support of the trade-union demands of journalists on the national and international levels. In line with this, it will support efforts to promote the moral and material welfare of working journalists and the defence of their status, rights and responsibilities. Its prime task is the protection of the social and economic interests of journalists, their working conditions and the right to practise their profession without discrimination of any kind. One of its major duties is to assure the respect of human rights for all, especially the safety and protection of journalists in the exercise of their profession. It will pay special attention to the question of new communication technologies, as well as to the increased concentration of the mass media, its effects on the free flow of information, and on the rights and working conditions of journalists.

On this occasion, the IOJ expresses its desire and determination to cooperate with all national, regional and international organisations of journalists in the interest of working journalists the world over and to assure the unity of action of the international community of journalists.

Kaarle Nordenstreng
IOJ President

Dušan Ulčák
IOJ Secretary General

December 11, 1989

APPENDIX 20. IOJ BUILDINGS AND PREMISES IN PRAGUE 1990

1. THE REND OF THE SERVICE OF THE DIPLOMATIC STAFF
Pronájem od Správy služeb diplomatického sboru

	THE WAY OF THE USE Způsob užití	ADDRESS Adresa
1/1	OFFICE	Washingtonova 17 F 8
1/2	OFFICE ERKOS	Dlouhá 39 a 39a E 8
1/3	RECONNSTRUCTION	Dušní 10 E 7
1/4	OFFICE IJI	Růžová 7 F 8
1/5	FLAT OF THE SECRETARY	Rybná 25 E 8
1/6	CONFERENCE SERVICE	Újezd 29 F 6
1/7	OFFICE	Vojtěšská 11 G 7
1/8	OFFICE EDITPRESS	Široká 12 E 7
1/9	OFFICE	Tomášská 8 E 6
1/10	RECONNSTRUCTION	Engelsovo nábř.76 G,H 7
1/11	OFFICE CONFER:SERVICE	Italská 16 F,G 8,9
1/12	OFFICE CONBUILD	Přemyslovská 12 G 10
1/13	OFFICE CONBUILD	Sudoměřská 1 F,G 10
1/14	FLAT OF THE SECRETARY	Donovalská 1658 K 13,14
1/15	FLAT OF THE SECRETARY	Horáčkova 1217 J 9
1/16	FLAT OF THE SECRETARY	Ketnerova 2049 J 1
1/17	FLAT OF THE SECRETARY	Bubeníčkova 1811 E,F 2
1/18	OFFICE EDITPRESS	Roosewelova 18 C,D 6
1/19	ACCOMMODATION	Mičurinova 3 D,E 7
1/20	INTERNATIONAL LOTTERY OF SOLIDARITY	U Smaltovny 17 D 8,9

2. BULDINGS OF THE IOJ
Objekty ve vlastnictví MON

2/1	TRANSPORT	Karlovarská 61 G 1
2/2	SCHOOL OF SOLIDARITY	K Červenému vrchu D 2,3
2/3	TECHNICAL SUPPORT	Karafiátova 48, I 13

3. THE REND OF THE LODGING COMPANY
Pronájem od bytového podniku

	THE WAY OF THE USE Způsob užití	ADDRESS Adresa
3/1	OFFICE, STORE	Washingtonova 17 F 8
3/2	OFFICE	K.Světlé 12 F 7
3/3	GENERAL SECRETARY	Celetná 2 F 8
3/4	CONFERENCE SERVICE	Jungmannovo nám.20 F 8
3/5	GASTRO	Jílská 7 F 7
3/6	AEROBIC	Maislova 7 E 7
3/7	RECONSTRUCTION	Žitná 27 G 8
3/8	RECONSTRUCTION	Myslíkova 31 G 7
3/9	RECONSTRUCTION	Ve Smečkách 16 F 6,8
3/10	OFFICE	Valdštejnské nám.6 E 6
3/11	OFFICE	Revoluční 8 E 8
3/12	RECONSTRUCTION	Jungmannova 30 F 8
3/13	OFFICE	Opatovická 11 F,G 7
3/14	CONFER:SERVICE, STORE	Bořivojova 122 F,G 9,10
3/15	ILS, STORE	Volavkova 15 F 2
3/16	STORE	Dostálova 273 F 16
3/17	CONBUILD	Pplk.Sochora 40 D 8
3/18	ILS, STORE	Leningradská 26 H 10
3/19	STORE	Na spojce 2 H 10
3/20	CONBUILD, OFFICE	Hradešínská 39 G 10
3/21	STORE	Kodaňská 37 G,H 10,11
3/22	CONBUILD, STORE	Kounická 40 F,G 13,14
3/23	ARANGEMENT C.S.	Na Míčánkách 1 G 10

4. THE PRIVATE REND
Pronájem od soukromníků

4/1	SYSTEMS AND PROGRAMMERS SERVICE - SPS	Maltézské nám.1 F 6
4/2	STORE C.S.	Butovická 28 J 3,4
4/3	FLAT OF THE SECRETARY	Ke Klimentce 2703 G,H 4
4/4	GARAGE	Matějská 56 B,C 5
4/5	OFFICE, INSPECTION	Moravanů 87 F,G 1
4/6	OFFICE, EDITPRESS	Na okraji 9 E,F 2,3
4/7	EDITPRESS, OFFICE	Cukrovarnická 75 E 4,5
4/8	OFFICE TECHN.SUPPORT	Na vinobraní 19 I 11,12
4/9	FLAT OF THE SECRETARY	Nám.Sv.Čecha 1 H 10
4/10	OFFICE, T.S.	U vinné révy 12 I 12
4/11	OFFICE, T.S.	U vinné révy 11 I 12
4/12	OFFICE, T.S.	V ochozu 20 I 12
4/13	OFFICE, T.S.	K rybníčkům 26 G,H 13
4/14	OFFICE, T.S.	Chrpová 21 I 13
4/15	OFFICE, T.S.	Chrpová 23 I 13
4/16	OFFICE, T.S.	Jesenická 36 I 12
4/17	OFFICE, T.S.	Jesenická 38 I 12
4/18	OFFICE, T.S.	Pošlova 10 I 12
4/19	WORK SHOP, T.S.	Azalkova 13 I 14
4/20	CONBUILD	Kladenská 61 D,E 2,4

5. ANOTHER REND
Pronájem od jiných organizací

5/1	OFFICE	Samcova 4 E 8
5/2	OFFICE	Londýnská 60 G,H 8,9
5/3	CONBUILD	Karlovo nám.7-8 G 7
5/4	CONBUILD	Šénova 1 L 12
5/5	STORE	Fabiánova 1134 H 4
5/6	GASTRO, OFICCE	Karlovarská 1/4 G 1
5/7	OFFICE EDITPRESS	Velvarská 31 D 4,5
5/8	CONBUILD, ARCHIV	Ruská 82 G 10,11
5/9	CONBUILD, Office	U Hranic 5 H 12
5/10	CONBUILD, STORE	Dřevčická F 14
5/11	OFFICE, T.S.	Ellnerové 3103-4 I 13

APPENDIX 21. DECLARATION OF THE SYNDICATE OF CZECH AND MORAVIAN JOURNALISTS 1990

Prague, 20 February (čtk)

The Contemporary Administration Council of the Syndicate of Czech and Moravian Journalists has adopted today in Prague this declaration:

The IOJ, working in Prague since 1947, has been breaking constantly during the period of 40 years all the principles of the protection of freedom of the word and independence of journalists, which were included in its programme.
This organization served fully to the totalitarian regime in Czechoslovakia and in the other Eastern European countries and it has become their loyal and obedient ideological instrument. They covered hypocritically under the veil of large activity of help to developing countries loyal assent to flagrant persecution and pursuit of journalists in the host and neighbouring countries.
The IOJ began this way in 1948 when they refused the requests of many member organizations of Western countries for the activity of protection of Czechoslovak journalists who were after the February coup d'état expelled from editorial boards by the so-called action-group committees. Then it continues by entirely passive attitude to brutal persecutions of journalists in the period of Stalinist trials in the 50's.
After 1968 it culminates by the open support of discrimination of journalists in the period of so-called process of consolidation and even by recalling of those representatives from the international Secretariat in Prague who did not agree with political development in Czechoslovakia and with persecution of journalists. The IOJ observed this line also in September 1989 when they refused unscrupulously to take into account the appeal of Czechoslovak and world journalists' public for standing for defence of imprisoned editors of "Lidové noviny".
The activity of the IOJ in Prague is the history of 40 years of betrayal of interests of journalists of host country and continuous gross violation of essential ethic principles of journalists mission.
To the fossil dogmatic character of the IOJ witnesses the fact that they still, three months after the Czechoslovak revolution of 17 November 1989, have not found a single word of apology for the betrayal committed during last decades on journalists of host and neighbouring countries. On the contrary in the meeting of its Executive Committee in the end of January 1990 in Portugal the Executive Committee has confirmed again at its Head representatives of already long ago politically and morally compromised former Czechoslovak party nomenclature.
After the end of the Czechoslovak Union of Journalists the Czechoslovak journalists' public is not a member of the IOJ. Regarding all stated facts we do not think that it is pissible for Czech and Moravian journalists to be interested in the membership in this discredited organization.
At the same time we believe that Czechoslovakia and Prague shall not be further the place of Headquarters of this organization as well as its business establishment parasiting during last decades on suffering home-side economy.

APPENDIX 22. MINUTES OF THE IOJ TALKS WITH THE SYNDICATE 1990

Minutes
on the unofficial talk of the IOJ President and an accompanying delegation of the IOJ Secretariat with representatives of the Czech Journalists Syndicate on 17 February 1990

IOJ participants:	Mr. K. NORDENSTRENG, President Mr. Chr. MUZAVAZI, Secretary Ms. L. PAUKKU, Secretary Mr. B. RAYER, Secretary Mr. M. RIVERO, Secretary
Syndicate:	Mr. V. BYSTROV, Vice-Chairperson Mr. A. ČERNÝ, Vice-Chairperson

The talk took place between 17.05 and 19.30 hrs in the suite of the IOJ President in the Hotel INTERCONTINENTAL PRAHA. MRS. D. BRAUNOVÁ (deputy editor-in-chief of "The Democratic Journalist", speaker of the IOJ Civic Forum) acted as an interpreter.

The IOJ delegation, President NORDENSTRENG in particular, confirmed the readiness of the IOJ to overcome the temporary crisis in the relations and to establish normal relations and close cooperation in the way which is desirable and necessary between the IOJ and the journalists organizations of the hosting country. The position represented by the IOJ delegation corresponded to that adopted by the IOJ Secretariat. There were no concrete promises/agreements given from the part of the IOJ delegation.

The main observations of the representatives of the Syndicate are reflected below:

After the IOJ President's summary of his discussions with the Secretariat and the staff (IOJ Board of Directors, Trade Unions Committee, Civic Forum), colleague BYSTROV, first of all, expressed his satisfaction to meet the President after the first constructive talk with him about five weeks ago. This discussion has been continued by several other official and unofficial contacts, mostly through Ms. PAUKKU.

He asked the IOJ representatives to understand the situation that the meeting still has a feature of an unofficial talk. The representatives of the Syndicate will meet representatives from friendly countries who continue to be welcomed by them. But they still don't have a mandate for discussion with the IOJ.

Colleague BYSTROV thanked for the interesting information the IOJ President had brought in his introduction. It should be acknowledged that from the part of the IOJ there were certain efforts made during the last weeks. At the same time there are also developments which have had additional negative reflections: 1/ the IOJ Presidium in Lisbon (without any detailed specification) and 2/ further development of a political climate in the country. While at the time of the last discussion five weeks ago above all the historical period since 1968 had been newly evaluated by the Syndicate, it is now the entire period of 42 years which should be analysed and newly evaluated. The IOJ could have had the possibility to work under democratic conditions in the ČSR only for half a year of 1947. This seems to be a rather short time in order to make positive estimation of an organization. Since 1948 there have been about 2000 journalists persecuted in the Bohemian parts of the country. Their fates are being grasped step by step by the Syndicate now. The Syndicate does not want and cannot ignore their interests. But the IOJ is not blamed for these persecutions said Mr. BYSTROV. Nevertheless, it is to state that this situation has remained neglected by the IOJ for all the time. The journalists persecuted in the ČSR have had never found a support at the IOJ. This question must be clarified now before the leadership of the Syndicate can submit any proposition to decide about the definition of its relationship towards the IOJ to the delegate meeting.

In Slovakia the problems seem to be similar, partly even more complicated and that thanks to some unclear economic activities of the IOJ in this part of the country. So the IOJ seems to have received a certain direct financial support from the Slovak government which is in contradiction with the IOJ Statute.

Altogether, it is to state that relatively little has been done by the IOJ during the last weeks in order to clarify this situation.

In this connection colleague ČERNÝ added that the Syndicate did not deal only with its internal affairs but it must be said that the journalists are relatively well informed about what is the role of the IOJ in the CSSR.

Colleague BYSTROV underlined that the IOJ is identified fully with the old regime which has been now overthrown. He does not know now the way out from this situation. Maybe, nobody knows the way out. Anyway, from the point of view of the Syndicate there is no time for political compromises. Of course, there is naturaly not the point reached that the government would cast the IOJ from the country. It won't go so far. But nobody can ignore the last 40 years.

Colleague ČERNÝ made a remark on this place that this is not a special problem of the IOJ only. This concerns all the international NGOs based in Prague. Colleague BYSTROV completed this with a remark that since 1947 a number of such NGOs have found their place in the ČSSR. It is now to acknowledge that the IOJ has done a lot in favour of the Third World and in favour of progressive journalists in the Western countries. But what has it done for Czechoslovak journalists? Or for journalists in any of the socialist countries? He had to use a very strong word now in order to express what the journalists had really to avoid: These persecuted journalists have been left in the lurch by the IOJ all the time. And now the IOJ comes and says let's change all this, and that in time when the old regime has been overthrown. It is very easy to take up such a position now. But why should we (Czech and Slovak journalists) now vote for anybody who did not help us before.

Colleague BYSTROV emphasized that from the point of the Syndicate there is not any conflict or a crisis in the relationship with the IOJ. It is more the IOJ which is facing crisis in relationship with organizations of the hosting country. They, the local journalists do not fee to be a part of this problem. He put the question "what can the IOJ offer to the journalists? What is the argumentation of the IOJ if we take into consideration the burden of the past." He underlined that the Slovak Syndicate shares this opinion. They have agreed upon this position in a joint coordination committee. (The coordination committee is a loose structure composed of five representatives from each Syndicate which decide irregularly about certain questions.)

On this place colleague BYSTROV made a remark that the Syndicate is interested above all in establishing contacts with persecuted journalists in other Eastern European countries in order to clear off jointly the history.

Colleague BYSTROV made also comments on economic situation of the IOJ and about the perspectives of the IOJ enterprises. He stated that the IOJ has run its enterprises practically under the protection of a monopoly position being supported or at least tolerated by the state. But this will be now over very quickly. He has his doubts if the IOJ will be able to continue its economic activities in the hitherto existing volume. The IOJ enterprises have now to face a sharp and open competition within which they have only very little chance.

The IOJ President mentioned the interest of the former Secretary General KUBKA expressed towards him to come back to the IOJ. Colleague BYSTROV confirmed that there have been similar approches taken towards the Syndicate and towards the Ministry for Foreign Affairs of the CSSR. The letters from KUBKA have been filed ad acta in the Syndicate as well as in the Ministry after taking notice. The Syndicate will not support this matter.

During the discussion the IOJ representatives pointed out several times principle and practical possibilities of cooperation, with several concrete examples, which would not be bound with the formal membership of the Syndicate in the IOJ. It was stressed that the IOJ from its part eagerly strives to create conditions for better relationship.

Colleague BYSTROV said that we do not reject the IOJ or any other organization and that IOJ has nko more special status than for example IFJ. He added that now it is up to IOJ to clear the situation. Meanwhile, Ms. PAUKKU is welcome as an ad hoc mediator, and similar role could be played by colleague RAYER as well. Our governing body has given no mandate to meet at a higher level.

Colleague ČERNÝ added that there is no conflict or trauma between us. He said that we rely on the status quo, with the IOJ headquarters in Prague and the new Syndicate defining its line. If our coordination committee would meet with your Presidium, you would just hear a negative position from our side. So let's continue like two persons living in the same house without marital relationship.

The talk has been considered to be useful by both sides.

For correctness:

Bernd Rayer
IOJ Secretary

Minutes
on the official talk of the IOJ President and acoompanying delegation of the IOJ Secretariat with the representatives of the Syndicate of Czech and Moravian Journalists on 22 February 1990

IOJ particiants: Mr. K. NORDENSTRENG, President
Mr. Bernd RAYER, Secretary

Syndicate participants: Mr. Rudolf ZEMAN, Chairperson
Mr. Vladimír BYSTROV, Vice-Chairperson
Mr. Adam ČERNÝ, Vice-Chairperson

The meeting took place at the request of the IOJ President in the office of the Syndicate.

The IOJ President explained, first of all, the immediate reason of his request to meet the leadership of the Syndicate - the declaration of Syndicate published on 20 February in the local press. The evident difference in tone between the preceding talk with colleagues BYSTROV and ČERNÝ on 17 February 1990 and the mentioned declaration resulted in the question what had happenned in the meantime that has led to this declaration.

Colleague ZEMAN welcomed the IOJ President at the "first official talk on the high level". He emphasized then that the Syndicate has been working on the new designation of its relationship to the IOJ as well as to the IFJ since last December. It will be based on the evaluation of the 40-year historical experience in the country and with the IOJ. He added then the question if the evaluation in the Syndicate's declaration did not present "a more objective estimation of this history"?

The IOJ President akcnowledged in his reply that there were unsatisfactory aspects in the history of the IOJ. He understood the declaration of the Syndicate from the specific national point of the view of the Syndicate, he said. But from the point of view of the IOJ as an universal organization there have been more clear points in the history of the IOJ than dark ones. He underlined that the IOJ is ready to make a self-critical evaluation of its past. Like all other international NGOs so the IOJ is "hostage" of its national member organizations. Within the IOJ there are observations of other member organizations which were a.o. expressed at the IOJ Presidium meeting in Lisbon as well, which take critical note of the one-sided dependence of the IOJ on the influence of the Czechoslovak Union of Journalists (ČSSN) in the past. Therefore it is necessary to clarify even the question how it had been possible that the ČSSN had not been able to represent different interests of all Czechoslovak journalists. The IOJ President put also the question if the door is definitely closed for the IOJ by this declaration. Because he had understood before that only the planned congress of the Syndicate should decide about the further shaping of the relations.

Colleague BYSTROV replied to the last remark that the Syndicate had never promised that the congress should have to decide about this question. It is fully open up to now if the question will be put on the agenda of the congress or not. The Syndicate wanted only to say that up to the date of the congress in the end of March or the beginning of April, it would be able to start discusssion on this problems.

The IOJ was very naive, he said. It is now quite evident that the journalists' unions of the socialist countries in Eastern Europe were not true journalists' organizations but instruments of the regimes.

The IOJ President made a remark that he had got an impression after the talk on 17 February 1990 that the IOJ would have been given more time in order to undertake evaluation of its face.

Colleague ZEMAN replied that the Syndicate is not member of the IOJ and therefore it does not feel to be bound by its internal procedures.

Colleague BYSTROV completed that the Syndicate had been patient for 3 months. During this time the IOJ had not found any word of excuse, it had not made any step to improve the relations. Only the first inofficial meeting with the IOJ President on 17 February 1990 gave the first signal.

Colleague ČERNÝ explaining the timing and the sharp tone of the Statement said that the IOJ Presidium in Lisbon failed with its resolution on Eastern Europe by giving the mandate to the IOJ Secretary General that means to a man who does not belong to any of the member organizations. This is absolutely unacceptable. Maybe that the representatives of the Syndicate made a mistake on 17 February 1990 in not having said the name of the Secretary General expressis verbis.

Colleague ZEMAN emphasized furthermore, that the Syndicate would concentrate in the international sphere above all on bilateral contacts with the neighbouring countries especially with the aim to clear off their common picture.

Colleague BYSTROV stated that the IOJ, apart from some few exceptions, seems not to have understood the historical situation yet. The IOJ has betrayed interests of journalists in the ČSSR for 40 years. And now the IOJ is saying: come along with us. How shall we now believe that it will be better?

Colleague ČERNÝ said that the Syndicate does not want to estimate the whole history of the IOJ but only the history of relationship between the Czechoslovak journalists and the IOJ. And in this connection there are no clear points in the history but only dark ones. And this concerns also the development of economic structures of the IOJ.

Colleague ZEMAN emphasized in the end that the leadership of the Syndicate would not refuse information exchange even with the IOJ. During the weeks to come it will concentrate fully on the forthcoming congress. Unofficial meetings continue to be useful and constructive if they will not exclude the themes of the past. He mentioned that the Czechoslovak journalists have "moral right for the IOJ property".

For correctness:

Bernd Rayer
IOJ Secretary

APPENDIX 23. MINUTES OF THE IOJ TALK WITH THE DEPUTY PRIME MINISTER 1990

Minutes
on the talk of the IOJ President Kaarle NORDENSTRENG with the Deputy Prime Minister of the CSSR Dr. Josef HROMÁDKA on 16 February 1990

The IOJ President was accompanied by the Secretaries MUZAVAZI and RAYER.

The talk was led in English without interpreter.

The IOJ President informed about the plans and activities of the IOJ in connection with the results of the IOJ Presidium meeting in Lisbon as well as on the developments in the IOJ member organizations in Eastern Europe. He underlined that despite of all changes in these countries the IOJ member organizations confirmed their active membership in the IOJ at their last congresses. They stand up for to introduce the necessary changes into the IOJ in accordance with the social developments. In this connection, he regretted the contemporary problematic situation in the relationship to the Czech and Slovak Syndicates of Journalists. The IOJ understands certain reservations and feaars of the Syndicates but is endeavouring to create conditions which would enable improvement of mutual relations. The President mentioned in this connection, also the actual dependence of the IOJ on the positions of its national member organizations and remembered critical notes about the previous dependence of the organization on the dominant influence of the ČSSN. Such a situation mustn't occur again. The IOJ is an universal organization which despite of all difficulties continues to grow and has good "ecumenical" contacts a.o. with the World Council of Churches and with the WACC.

In connection with the known attacks on the address of the IOJ the IOJ President mentioned the IOJ efforts to continue economic activities of the organization in full accordance with the legislation of the host country and in favour of both sides. He pointed out some examples of IOJ investments in the host country and declared that this activity stands open to full public control.

The IOJ President informed at the same time about a letter of the Secretary General of the IOJ which includes his intention to resign his function. The IOJ plans to hold a meeting of its Presidium possibly in Prague till the end of May at the latest which should settle this problem as well till the Congress would make the final decision. He invited the Government of the CSSR to open the meeting if the occasion arises and to inform the Presidium about the standpoint of the Government. (He reffered to the practice in Lisbon.) In case of such a decision by the enlarged meeting of the IOJ Secretaria t on 1 and 2 March 1990 the Government will be sent then an official invitation. The President offerred the Deputy Prime Minister to supply a report about the economic activities of the IOJ to him and in his person to the CSSR Government.

The Deputy Prime Minister Dr. Josef HROMÁDKA did not make any summarizing declaration during the talk. Mostly in replying to the IOJ President's declaration he outlined the following standpoints.

1. The Czechoslovak Government support the dialogue betwen all forces and at all levels. He let to know that in this sense also the continuation of contacts/dialogue between the IOJ and the Syndicates will be supported.

2. In all branches of the society an inventory is made now. Only afterwards it will be possible to make decisions. The Deputy Prime Minister said: "Give us time".

3. The Deputy Prime Minister did not let know that there would be general efforts by the Government to cease the economic activities of the IOJ now. He took notice of the examples of the useful investments by the IOJ in favour of the CSSR. He insisted on the fact that these activities must be fully "pure" and in accordance with the legislation of the country. Violation would be revenged by the Government.

4. He expressed the readeness to continue the contacts with the IOJ. In this connection he made a remark that he would welcome the economic report of the IOJ after his arrival from abroad (12 March 1990).

5. He confirmed he would expect an invitation of the Government to a possible meeting of the IOJ Presidium in Prague.

For correctness:

Bernd Rayer
IOJ Secretary

APPENDIX 24. REPORT ON THE IOJ COMMERCIAL ACTIVITIES IN CZECHOSLOVAKIA 1990

INTRODUCTION

Since the seventies, the International Organization of Journalists has been gradually setting up business enterprise so as to provide itself with resources for its widely spreading professional.

The IOJ's economic activities have been set up and have expanded gradually, without any substantial claims to investments. The necessary investments, as well as the operating costs, have been financed out of its own resources, which means that the business enterprises have been working on a principle of an entire self-financing, i.e. even without any bridging or current account credits to be given by financial institution. Its activities have mostly been oriented on Czechoslovak customers; the sphere of its export activities has always been regulated by the Czechoslovak state and therefore limited. In relation to the Czechoslovak state, where there do not exist – as a matter of principle – any exceptions not applicable to Czechoslovak enterprises as well, both the income tax and the salary taxes, artists' and writers' income taxes, etc. are paid.

The business enterprises have never been liable to the former rigid and inefficient Czechoslovak system of planning; they have been managed within the IOJ. We can say therefore that the IOJ has enterprised on its own account and at its own risk, without being supported by state credits, appropriations or loans. As a result, in the management of its economic activities the IOJ has applied highly demanding criteria, partly comparable with those applied in the management of Western companies.

Price and commercial policy have correlated with the conditions of the Czechoslovak market. We have not met with any complaints of Czechoslovak customers as regards over-pricing. Having in mind the need for good economic results and profit, the IOJ has applied professional qualification and professionalism as essential criteria in engaging its employees. The number of Communist Party members has not exceeded 20 % of full-time employees and, even in the past periods, this number did not include a series of business enterprises directors.

In our opinion, the business enterprises of the IOJ dispose of first-rate specialists, well-established and experienced in enterprising. These enterprises are useful thanks to their services, performance and products, tax returns, etc.

[...]

Tax payments

The economic effectiveness of economic departments can be characterized by the fact that their share in the origination of the Czechoslovak national revenue totals about 0.09 %. The gross income materialized, e.g., during the year 1989, totals 190.4 mil. Kčs and 11.3 mil. DEM. In the sphere of foreign business activities, the permitted financial limit has not been exceeded.

[...]

The rate of income tax levied on all the produced means has been checked regularly every year by state authorities represented by the District Financial Administration in Prague 1, where the income tax returns are filed. E.g., in the year 1989 the income tax amounting to 100.5 mil. Kčs was paid.

Taxes levied on gross wages and royalties are paid in accordance with Act No. 76/52 of the Collection of Laws. The District Financial Administration in Prague 1 checks their correctness regularly.

Health insurance payments are made in harmony with Act No. 54/56 of the Collection of Laws. The Prague Health Insurance Administration checks their correctness regularly.

SURVEY OF THE IOJ ENTERPRISES

The economic activities of the IOJ in Czechoslovakia have been materialized in its enterprises and establishments. They are the following:

Conference Service
Publishing House
Czechoslovak Editorial Office
Interpreting Agency – Artlingua
IOJ International Lottery of Solidarity
ITA Travel Agency
Production-technical Service
System and Programming Service
Service of Technical Assistance
IOJ Service Bratislava
IOJ Service Brno
Service for Organization and Control
Gastronomical Service

The individual enterprises and establishments of the IOJ represent a contribution for the national economy, wherever the state enterprises and organizations either did not manage to cover the market requirements, or the state enterprises and organizations were not interested in the mentioned activities owing to their variety or a low effectiveness and capacity. 916 full-time workers, Czechoslovak nationals, have participated in this activity.

Interpreting and translating activities that form the basis of the Conference Service have been ensuring important congresses, symposia, seminars, exhibitions etc., both in Czechoslovakia and abroad, e.g. extensive and highly professional undertakings, such as CHISA, ICALS, AAPSO (India) and medical congresses in Prague. Apart from the interpreting and translating activities, the Conference Service also provides for the services in the field of reprography for Czechoslovak organizations, institutions and the public. Furthermore, the Conference Service – Artlingua helps to bridge over the persisting shortcomings in the language preparation of employees of Czechoslovak organizations.

The Czechoslovak Editorial Office ranks among the other activities – recently 80 titles of computer literature have been published there in the section of publishing services. As far as the computer literature is concerned, in 1989 the IOJ became the supplier of the biggest number of titles on the Czechoslovak market. In cooperation with the Ministry of Education of the Czech Republic it delivered three hundred titles of university manuals, textbooks and monographs. In the sphere of culture, printed material was edited within the framework of the Prague Spring music festival. The Publishing and Printing Houses also organize emergency undertakings (symposia, biennial anniversaries, congresses) that cannot be ensured by the customer in Czechoslovakia within the required time (e.g., the 5th World Biennial of Architecture INTERARCH 89 in Sofia).

The fortnightly of the Czech Ministry of Culture "Scéna", the IOJ bimonthly "Interpress Magazin" and the encyclopedic seried "Přemožitelé času" inform regularly a wide reading public on the area of culture, theatre, film and video. The other authors', editorial and press services are afforded for the International Institute of Theatre, the Prensa Latina agency and the Czech Ministry of Education, the Interpress Magazin editorial office will edit the foreign-language quarterly GOLEM with information on the cultural life of Prague, as one of the main centres of European culture.

Today the ITA travel agency, enterprising in the area of active tourism, has been preparing an extension of its activities to the area of passive tourism. Sleeping capacities are obtained on the basis of concluded business contracts with the owners of hotel complexes. Similarly the prevailing majority of Czechoslovak travel agencies (Autoturist, Sportturist, etc.) have partly used sleeping capacities owned by other organizations. The technical conditions of the resources we use are not usually convenient, as neither the owner nor the tenants of these capacities invested in these real estates. Considering this situation, we offered the owners of these complexes a project capacity, engineering and organization of the building part of repairs, reconstructions and modernizations of these hotels. The concrete example is the materialization of the complete reconstruction and modernization of the complete reconstruction and modernization of the Atlantic hotel into the hotel of the *** category in 22 months, at the cost of approx. 0.5 mil. Kčs per bed and at the financial reimpursement of 98 % in crown and 2 % in foreign exchange. Nowadays projects for modernization and reconstruction of the Savoy hotel and partial reconstructions of Opera, Merkur, Axa and Tatran hotels are prepared.

The Production-technical Service of the IOJ implements production programmes in the area of electrotechnical manufacture, which represents significant support to the development of the Czechoslovak scientific-technical basis, as well as pronounced anti-import measures. The Production-technical Service asserts its position by manufacturing laboratory and measuring systems for the basis and applied research. Its customers are the LET Kunovice, Moravan Otrokovice and others, where the equipment was applied after a static evaluation of the L 160 plane construction. This manufacture is conditioned by the application of very modern electronic elements provided for foreign currency form the IOJ's own production. The Production-technical Service ensures the development and manufacture of medical electronics in a close cooperation with peak centres of carciology and neurology (IKEM and UVN). Another programme is the materialization of a network of automatic meteorological stations for the needs of the Czech Hydrometeorological Institute. Within a long-time concept of the Production-technical Service works on the programme of a long-distance research of the Earth, the enterprise manufactures the necessary telemetric equipment for the INTER-KOSMOS satellite programme. Another important group of products is represented by the equipment for the operation of mass media. Equipment for the titling of video signals, check of video and audio signal quality and others operate in the Czechoslovak television.

Deliveries of the IOJ Production-technical Service for the reconstruction of the National Theatre in Prague were awarded an Honourable Mention by the Czechoslovak Government. There are also the system of electronic-programmable lighting plant and other technical equipment manufactured by the Production-technical Service which operate in other Prague theatres.

The Service of Technical Assistance performs repairs and maintenance of the housing fund for the housing enterprise. In case of repairs and maintenance of real property it cooperates with the Prague National Committee, the Area National Health Authority, the Ministry of Culture and other authorities and organizations. It also contributes to the maintenance and reconstruction of clerical, historical and registered historical monuments. The Service of Technical Assistance has recently carried out a repair of the facade of the St. George's Church in Prague 3, St. Anthony's Church, participated in the repair of the State Castle of Koloděje and in other undertakings.

Within the framework of technical assistance, it provides accompanying documentation for the products of Czechoslovak enterprises exported abroad and cooperates in the project preparation of reconstructions of significant cultural-historical buildings.

As for further investments, the complete reconstruction and modernization of the Sixt's house complex in the *Celetná Street* was carried out. This complex had been taken over in a completely disconsolate condition, the undertaking was accomplished in three years at a cost of investment of approx. 50 mil. Kčs and approx. 100 thousand DEM.

The IOJ Service Bratislava renders services for enterprises and organizations in Slovakia. It functions in the sphere of interpreting and translating services, design works, editing and publishing activities, reproduction and printing works as well as in the foreign trade activities. Lately it has participated substantially in the undertakings related to the construction of paper mills of SSC Ružomberok and SMC Paskov.

The IOJ Service Brno has worked for the Czechoslovak industrial plants in the solving of problems of power savings and utilization of waste heat in economic processes with respect to ecological problems. In the field of scientific-technical calculations is has participated in the solutions of earthwork in the mining and power-generating industry as well as applications of more complex scientific-technical calculations in agriculture. It has also been developing the works for elaboration of design documentation and design tasks for agricultural enterprises.

The Service for Organization and Control participated in the elaboration of documentations and studies on introduction of the contemporary products of technical development to the area of mass information and advertising. It has contributed to the processing of control systems of the enterprises – ZTS Brno, ZTS Martin, ZVL Považská Bystrica and ZVL Skalica. In the sphere of advertising, it was the cooperation during organizing the International Exhibition of Polytechnical Facilities, Repro 89 and a number of other publicity undertakings that were among the most important.

The above stated facts are in a deep contrast with the statements published in the Czechoslovak press, where parasitizing of the IOJ economic institutions on sick Czechoslovak economy was criticized.

[...]

CONCLUSION

This report gives basic information on the economic activities performed in the IOJ enterprises and establishments. Its intention is to inform the authorities of the host country about the basic character of these activities, as well as about the conditions under which they are implemented in relation to the Czechoslovak economic system.

In the next stage of development, the economic activities of the International Organization of Journalists will be affected substantially by the change of economic climate in the Czechoslovak Socialist Republic. These influences will require necessary structural and organizing changes in both the orientation and mode of pursuing these activities. The first measures have already been accepted in this area.

All the staff of the International Organization of Journalists believe that only a positive approach of the host country towards the performance of the IOJ economic activities in Czechoslovakia will help to preserve social and legal securities of the Czechoslovak citizens employed in the IOJ, to build up the financial sources necessary for the IOJ and to pursue the activities beneficial in their consequences for the Czechoslovak economy.

APPENDIX 25. THE PRESIDENT'S REPORT ON IOJ DEVELOPMENTS IN 1989–90

Exerpts from report to the Executive Committee in Paris in November 1990

[...]

Chronology of IOJ developments from December 1989 to October 1990

The developments during the past 12 months have been too manifold and too rich in detail to allow for a comprehensive report in this connection. Therefore this is just a chronology of events which the President considers most essential for the Executive Committee to get a proper picture, with selected original documents enclosed for reference [not reproduced here].

However, first of all it must be noted that at the time of the "Velvet Revolution" the IOJ had a very poor record in defending the rights of persecuted journalists in Czechoslovakia. In this connection there was an information gap between the President and the Secretary General: I left things in the hands of the Secretariat, which this time (unlike before) assured me that effective action was to be taken, but later

I learned that the Secretary General had not done what he promised to me. Therefore I cannot accept the testimony given by Dušan Ulčák in his speech in Balatonfured as a true account of history; to say that he did enough or his utmost to defend the rights of journalists especially in Czechoslovakia appears to me as a simple lie. It is true that we all – including the President – share this burden of the past, but no-one else to my knowledge has stated without regret that all possible was done. It has already been doubtful to keep silent about our compromised record, but it would be too crude to whitewash ourselves.

My first visit to the Secretariat in the new situation was three weeks after the beginning of the new revolution in Prague. I came in early December on my own initiative with three proposals: to dismiss the Economic Director (Miloš Jakeš), to issue a clear statement in support of the changes in these countries, and to install the Finnish Secretary (Leena Paukku) as a new Deputy Secretary General. The first two were implemented, since Ulčák had already himself decided to dismiss Jakes, and there was no difficulty in formulating a joint New Year's message.

The third proposal – to appoint a neutral person next to the Secretary General who was doomed to be compromised in the political upheaval – did not get through. Obviously Ulčák took it as a first step to oust him, although this was not the intention of the Finnish side. We simply wanted to pave the way towards a normal relationship with the new Czechoslovak colleagues, and in this respect Ulčak could have taken a Finnish Deputy rather as a life jacket for himself. But he refused, showing that he was suspiciously on the defensive. In this spirit he also turned down the proposal to address the founding congress of the new Syndicate, as explained below under Comments. My mistake was to yield and to go along with this line of the Secretary General.

January

- Meeting with the Syndicate representatives and their letter to the IOJ, leaving the relationship open for positive development.
- Presidium in Estorial, where the President had no intention to suggest an immediate departure of the Secretary General – only to expose the situation in eastern Europe and in particular Czechoslovakia.
- Letter by the new Director of IOJ commercial enterprises voicing concern about negative publicity on the IOJ in the Czechoslovak media (one criticizing Ulčak during his time in the Foreign Ministry was published on the eve of the Presidium), and statement by IOJ employees' meeting convened by the Civic Forum suggesting Ulčak to leave soonest – both sent by fax to Estorial but not passed to the President.

February

- Letter by representatives of the IOJ Board of Directors, the Trade Union and the Civic Forum, handed over to the President at a meeting with them (the first time the President visited Prague since early January).
- Meetings with the Syndicate (Vice-Presidents Bystrov and Černý) and the Government (Deputy Prime Minister Hromádka), with an understanding that despite negative appreciation of the Presidium results there is room for clarifying problems and at least continuing to "live in the same house although not married".
- Declaration of the Syndicate, followed by a new meeting with its leadership (including President Zeman).
- Letter of resignation by Secretary General Ulčak.

March

- Enlarged Secretariat with press conference, issuing statement by the President (sent by mail to all member unions) which regretted the IOJ failure in the past to defend journalists particularly in Czechoslovakia and announced the convening of another Presidium to change the Secretary General and to adopt new strategy.
- Meeting with Deputy Speaker of the Federal Parliament.
- Report on IOJ economic enterprises and other materials to Deputy Prime Minister Hromádka.
- Another meeting with the Syndicate in Prague and first meeting with the Slovak Syndicate in Bratislava.

- Agreement between the President and all Secretaries present in the headquarters that Ulčak be paid a pension to cover the period from his leaving the IOJ until the normal state pension, amounting to 40,000 US dollars.
- Ulčak's appointment of Secretary Rayer as acting Secretary General during his absence (in trips and on sick leave).

April

- Agreement with the Secretary General on arrangements during a transitory period until the next Presidium, recorded as the President's letter to the Secretaries.
- In accordance with this agreement, Ulčak stopped participating the Secretariat's work and he was paid the above-mentioned pension (in one installment in Nürnberg while changing the signatures for the bank accounts).
- Enlarged Secretariat in Špindlerův Mlýn, with agreement to convene the Presidium in Hungary before the middle of May.
- Meeting with the Director of ČTK (Petr Uhl) and Minister of Information Příkazský.
- Letter by the President to the Syndicate President before its congress and after no invitation was extended to the IOJ to attend, a joint statement by the President and the Secretaries addressed to the congress.
- Invitation to an international chartered accountant company in Amsterdam to make an offer to examine the accounts of the IOJ enterprises.

May

- Official meeting with the Syndicate in Prague, with their proposal to jointly study the IOJ history and economy.
- Presidium in Balatonfured.
- New Secretary General's cancellation of earlier appointment with the Syndicate and the invitation to the Amsterdam company.
- Letter by President Havel's Press Secretary Žantovský about earlier Communist Party subsidies to the IOJ.
- Statement by the President:
  "The revelation by the Office of the President of the Republic that the IOJ has been financially supported by the Communist Party of Czechoslovakia took me by surprise which I am sure is shared by most of the leading bodies of our Organization. In this situation it is not enough to carry out a thoroughful auditing of the IOJ accounts and to proceed to a normal Congress at the end of this year as was decided at the recent Presidium session in Hungary. I consider it necessary to immediately convene an extraordinary Congress in order to completely clarify the past and present economic situation of the IOJ as well as to allow the member organizations to elect new representatives to all leading bodies including the President."

June
- Letter of response to Žantovský.
- Meeting with Žantovský (President Nordenstreng and Secretary General Gatinot).
- Steering Committee for preparing the Congress held its first meeting, suggesting to advance the Congress date to September.

July
- Meeting of the European Group in Sofia.
- Steering Committee's second meeting, concluding that majority of Presidium members do not support September as time for the Congress.
- Presidential delegation to the occupied Territories in Israel.

August
- Steering Committee's third meeting preparing for the Executive Committee documents and discussing the new situation concerning Amman after the Gulf crisis.

September
- Steering Committee's third meeting continued, with agreement to hold next meeting in Amman to examine on the spot the situation with regard to the Executive Committee.
- Steering Committee's fourth meeting in Amman.

October
- Steering Committee's consultation by telecommunication and meeting between the President, the Secretary General and the Secretaries, with conclusion to reschedule Amman.
- Steering Committee's fifth meeting fixing the Executive Committee in Paris on 17–30 November and the Congress in Warsaw on 13–18 December.

Comments

In a nutshell, the historical record of the IOJ is both positive and negative. There are achievements especially in supporting journalists in the Third World (through training, etc.) and in promoting rapprochement between colleagues in East and West (through meetings, etc.). Moreover, the IOJ has done a lot to achieve a worldwide unity of journalists. On the other hand, the IOJ has neglected to defend the rights of those journalists who did not go along with the regimes of the socialist countries as well as many developing countries. In general, the IOJ failed to pay proper attention to professional and trade union matters, while it had a heavy political and ideological orientation. The key to these so- called burdens of the past is what was perceived as the symbiotic relationship - lack of independence - which the IOJ used to have with the regimes of the socialist countries of eastern Europe. The burden was aggravated by the fact that the most flagrant neglect of defending journalists' rights is recorded in Czechoslovakia – the country where the IOJ headquarters are located and where the IOJ has established an economic base to maintain its worldwide activities.

Given the historical record of the IOJ, the changes in eastern Europe over the past year brought the IOJ into a political and economic crisis, the central aspect of which was to instill confidence in the IOJ among the newly emerged journalists organizations in those countries. An essential step to overcome the crisis was the departure of the former Secretary General. Many other moves were needed – and rapidly needed – but unfortunately the pace of change was very slow, especially after the Presidium session in Balatonfüred in May. The most important step to cope with the crisis is the Congress, because only the Congress has the organizational authority of setting the record of the past and determining the orientation for the future. The dispute within the IOJ leadership since the Presidium session in Estoril in January was largely about time: one side insisted on a rapid process with even an extraordinary Congress in the middle of the year, while the other side responded by referring to a normal statutory process and warning against a panic.

My position since December last year was consistently been in favour of a rapid change. I have been dissatisfied with the slow progress – first with the departure of former Secretary General and then with the preparation of the Executive Committee and the Congress. Especially in relation to our problems in Czechoslovakia, it can be said that our case is a typical example of the well-known syndrome "too little too late".

[...]

Host country of the IOJ: Burden and fortune of the past

The dramatic political changes in the former East Germany and Czechoslovakia in October and November 1989 made it clear that the earlier changes which had been taking place in Poland and Hungary were part and parcel of an objective and irreversible process incompassing the whole Middle and Eastern Europe with far-reaching consequences to the whole system of international governmental and non-governmental relations.

Especially the "Velvet Revolution" in the then ČSSR, which removed the old regime and started to abolish its political structures and to replace them by fully new ones, brought along a fully new situation for the IOJ in Prague. Already in November 1989 it became evident that the host organization – the Czechoslovak Union of Journalists, member or the IOJ – could not continue its existence as one of the most discredited organizations in the eyes of the new democratic forces. The Union tried first to drastically change itself, by electing a new leadership and rewriting its statutes, but his was not enough for the new forces – many of those were expelled from journalism and from the Union after the events in 1968 – and new syndicates were established to replace it in Czech and Slovak Republik.

First, in early December 1989, there was unity among the IOJ leadership about how to react to the developments, and the outcome of this was a prompt issuing of the New Year's message. But differences surfaced already in the middle of December between the President and the Secretary General about whether or not to send a message to the constitutive congress of the new Syndicate in Prague. I wanted to do it, while Dušan Ulčák was definitely against – referring to the still existing old member Union (and also hinting to me that in case I would unilaterally do it, Vice-President Gatinot would propose a vote of no-confidence in me). In the end I refrained from sending any message to this congress, but I met with the representatives of the new Syndicate on the first day after the dissolution of our old member Union in early January – without consulting the Secretary General. After this meeting the Syndicate sent us officially a letter – the only one which the IOJ has so far received from them.

As demonstrated by the record of the past 12 months, the history of the IOJ and its present crisis is inseparable from Czechoslovakia and its journalist organizations. First of all, there is the political and moral burden of the past which was pointed out above. Secondly, most of the material resources with which the IOJ has operated since the early 1970s were generated through commercial activities in Czechoslovakia, established under the privileged umbrella of the Communist Party Government of the time.

Today the IOJ is widely perceived by the new forces in the country as not only politically discredited but also economically more or less criminal. As was put to me in a discussion with the Minister of Information in April, the political past of the IOJ makes them to see red, but with the lucrative economic side of the IOJ they see double red.

We have already admitted that the IOJ failed to defend the journalists' rights in the host country. In terms of the past and present IOJ economy, we have opened our case for an objective examination, but until today we have not come across with such evidence that would justify condemning the IOJ finances to be a matter of a "monumental mafia" as is accused in the local press. A criminal process is underway against the former Economic Director (Miloš Jakeš, son of the former Communist Party Secretary General), and some minor irregularities have been spotted in the economic affairs, but by and large it seems that the IOJ money is not more dirty than any other money made by commercial enterprises under similar conditions.

However, even if we may not admit a burden of the past in terms of the economy, it remains a fact that we have accumulated a fortune mainly in Czechoslovakia at a time when we were in fact collaborators to a totalitarian regime while hundreds of colleagues in this country were underground without any support from our side. This, it seems to me, places us a moral question: Do we not owe our fortune to these colleagues, at least in part? When we are flying around the world, and extending assistance to Third World unions, we should recall that most of this money was made in Czechoslovakia, under the former regime! Since our licence to make this money came from the symbiotic relationship with the Party and Government, our financial fortune is inseparable from our burden of the past – not juridically but morally, if we want to live up with the standards of a professional organization.

I pointed out already at the Presidium session in January that since it is in Czechoslovakia where our money is being made and since the licence to print that money is given by our member union in that country, we cannot afford disregarding this country and its journalists under the new circumstances. This reasoning was a selfish one from the point of view of the IOJ, and as such it seems to me still valid. But today we have to complement this reasoning with the moral argument given above. Taken together they seem to me to put a very strong case for doing our utmost to find a solution to our problem in Czechoslovakia – instead of arrogantly disregarding the problem as an intolerable dominance by one single country in the IOJ (as suggested by past Secretary General with a considerable echo in the Presidium).

We simply cannot escape Czechoslovakia – we are their hostages because of the double effect of the political burden we have accumulated there and the financial fortune we made there (and are continuing to make). Obviously this hostage crisis is not easy to solve – now that we have lost so much time and for half a year even missed a dialogue with the most essential party in the country, the Syndicates of journalists. But still we must keep trying, at least by immediately taking the step which all parties (including the Syndicates) expect us to take: to hold the Congress and to set the record straight.

Present dispute within the IOJ: The time factor

It is natural that such a crisis in which the IOJ finds itself gets manifested in differences and even divisions among its members and within the leadership. This would happen in any social organization. As a matter of fact one may wonder how has it been possible keep the IOJ together under such circumstances – especially since in addition to the crisis around the headquarters the IOJ got involved in the Gulf crisis!

Obviously there are differences of opinion concerning strategy and tactics. However, such differences about substance have not proved to be insurmountable during the past few months – after the departure of former Secretary General. For example, there has been no major disagreement between myself and Secretary General Gatinot concerning the economic enterprises.

The main dispute has been on time, especially on the Congress date. In this connection it became clear that there are two groups or parties among us: those around the President who want an urgent solution to the problems at hand, and those around the Secretary General who want to proceed more slowly.

My own record is clear. In January I suggested the Executive Committee to meet in the middle of this year and the Congress in early autumn. In May, after the letter from the Czechoslovak President's office, I called for an extraordinary Congress at once. In June I persuaded the Steering Committee preparing the Congress to suggest to the Presidium that the Congress be convened in September, but this proposal did not get majority support (after campaigning against it by some Vice-Presidents). Finally, I (with a majority of the Steering Committee) fixed the Congress date in November – which now after rescheduling of the Executive Committee, is set to December.

APPENDIX 26. TEMPORARY ARRANGEMENTS IN THE SECRETARIAT IN APRIL 1990

FOR THE INFORMATION **No 86**
Given by: Kaarle Nordenstreng **Date: April 2, 1990**

To: Secretariat
From: President

In order to help solving the problems facing the IOJ and to ensure an effective work of the Secretariat and the economic enterprises, I agreed with the Secretary General the following:

1. Dušan Ulčák will be on leave from the office of the Secretary General beginning April 3 until the Presidium session in May which will deal with his letter of resignation.

2. Bernd Rayer will be acting Secretary General during this period, in close cooperation with Leena Paukku, while all secretaries should work as a collective team.

3. Signature rights for the IOJ foreign accounts in FRG will be transferred from Dušan Ulčák to Kaarle Nordenstreng and Vladislav Mírek on April 3.

4. Signature rights for the IOJ accounts in Czechoslovakia (Kčs and foreign currencies) will be given to Bernd Rayer together with Vladislav Mírek by April 9. Rayer will be responsible for all economic activities of the Secretariat until the time of the Presidium, while Ulčák (with Mírek) retains his signature rights in matters of the economic enterprises until a reorganization plan has been prepared by the directors by April 20.

Prague, April 2, 1990

Kaarle Nordenstreng
President of IOJ

APPENDIX 27. REPORT ON THE 11TH IOJ CONGRESS IN HARARE 1991

Summary report compiled in May 1991 by Václav Slavík in collaboration with former President Kaarle Nordenstreng and new President Armando Rollemberg

The nearly 20 documents attached to the report as appendices are not reproduced here, with two exceptions. The documents are included in the Congress materials held in the National Archives of the Czech Republic.

The Congress was held in Zimbabwe's capital Harare from 24 to 29 January 1991, with the participation of 138 delegates and over 60 observers and guests.

Opening

The opening ceremony in the Harare International Conference Centre was attended by leading representatives of the Republic of Zimbabwe: President Mugabe, Information Minister Chitepo and Foreign Affairs Minister Shamuyrarira. The President of the Zimbabwe Union of Journalists, William Bango, delivered a welcoming address on behalf of the host organization. Then the IOJ President, Kaarle Nordenstreng, delivered his opening address. President Robert Mugabe also delivered a major address. A vote of thanks was proposed by Charles Chikerema, Secretary General of the Union of African Journalists.

The opening of the working session of the Congress was greeted on behalf of the International Federation of Journalists (IFJ) by its Trade Union Development Officer, Neal Swancott, and on behalf of the trade union organization of the FRG IG Medien by Wolfgang Mayer. Participants were then acquainted with a draft resolution on the Gulf War, which was subsequently finalized and approved in the afternoon of the second day of deliberations.

Membership

The first major item on the agenda was membership and new affiliations based on two documents. Unanimously accepted as IOJ members were 20 journalist organizations from Africa, Asia, Europe and Latin America and the Caribbean (most of these had been preliminarily accepted by other statutory bodies since the 10th Congress). With the accession of these organizations the number of IOJ members exceeded 300,000 journalists belonging to 109 member and associated organizations and groups in 90 countries worldwide.

Following the adoption of the Standing Orders, the Agenda and Timetable, the Congress elected the Steering Committee (chaired by President Nordenstreng), the Nominations and Drafting Commissions (chaired respectively by Sinibaguy-Mollet of Congo and Ameyibor of Ghana) as well as a Commission for Statutes (chaired by Namakajo of Uganda). W. Bonga (Zimbabwe) was elected spokesman of the Congress.

Main Reports

The next item on the agenda was an overall review of the IOJ since the 10th Congress, based on written reports by the President, the Secretary General, the Training Council and the Council for Studies and Documentation.

A lively discussion followed the written reports and oral commentaries. The number of delegates desiring to speak in the debate was so great that it was necessary to hold an evening session on the third day of the Congress lasting until the morning of the fourth day. Fifty delegates participated, many of them addressing the Congress several times.

Most of those taking part in the debate concentrated on the issue of the future of the IOJ and primarily that of its headquarters. Even though quite controversial opinions were voiced at times, it was finally agreed that the new IOJ leadership should do its utmost to maintain IOJ headquarters in Prague. Should this not be possible, the IOJ Secretariat could be transferred – according to proposals forwarded – to one of the following locations: Berlin, Paris, Brasilia, Bucharest, Geneva, Warsaw and Madrid. The majority of delegates called for radical changes in the organization's leadership, for decentralization and democratization of its structures, for de-ideologization of the IOJ and for a reinforcement of its professional and trade union character. Demands for such changes and the election of new leading representatives should prevent a recurrence of the situation when the organization was practically governed by a few influential member organizations.

In the discussion, which was unusually frank and critical, the reasons which had led the IOJ to its present crisis were frequently pinpointed and the President and the Secretary General were spared no criticism in this respect. The two leaders answered a number of queries and defended their activities. At the suggestion of the Filipino delegate the Congress then approved their written reports as well as the reports of the Training Council and of the Council for Studies and Documentation, including their explanatory commentaries.

Finances

The next item on the agenda concerning financial and economic matters was introduced by written reports delivered by the Treasurer and the Auditing Commission as well as an oral report on IOJ enterprises. In addition, the representative of the Financial Commission, established at the meeting of the Executive Committee in Paris, explained that he had been unable to compile a report as he had not been invited to IOJ headquarters and had not received the necessary background documents.

Delegates paid considerable attention to the Treasurer's commentary. Over 20 speakers participated

in the discussion. It was stressed that this was the first time in the history of the IOJ that the issue of economic activities had been so openly and exhaustively debated at a Congress. Delegates were aware that with the changing situation in Czechoslovakia, where the absolute majority of financial resources was generated, considerably lower revenue from IOJ enterprises must be reckoned with in future. Ways of rationalizing all activities were sought, and of adopting efficiency measures and means of cutting costs. This could be achieved by introducing strategic planning for economic activities, increasing and making more effective the control of such activities by the elected bodies and drawing up alternative plans for resources other than those from Czechoslovakia.

From the discussions it became evident that the reports submitted had failed to provide answers to all contentious issues and that the President and the Secretary General did not agree on a number of issues concerning IOJ economic management. Therefore, as called for by the delegate from Egypt, the financial and economic reports were not approved and a six-member ad hoc committee was set up, composed of representatives of member unions from Egypt, Jamaica, Finland, Uruguay, Uganda and the USSR. The mandate of this committee was to thoroughly investigate the financial and economic matters pertaining to the administration and management of the IOJ and its enterprises between January 1986 and December 1990. This task was to be accomplished in three months.

Working Parties

Discussion on vital professional issues took place in the three working groups into which participants on the fourth day divided. In the first group the discussion centred on Right to Information and Protection of Journalists, in the second on Social and Trade Union Matters and in the third on issues of Unity of International Journalists' Movements.

New Strategy and Resolutions

Regarding the issue of a new strategy for the IOJ, a document was submitted drawn up by the President in consultation with Vice-Presidents Suarez and Izobo as well as some Secretaries and earlier discussed in the Presidium and the Executive Committee. A number of delegates who entered the debate on the issue supported the document, some of them proposing minor amendments. Finally the document "New Strategy and its Organizational and Financial Implications" was approved [reproduced below].

The Drafting Commission also processed a number of declarations and resolutions which were approved by the Congress [reproduced below].

Statutes

Meanwhile, the Commission for Statutes had elaborated the draft statutes with a number of paragraphs drawn up in alternative versions. These were debated in the plenary session and voted on paragraph by paragraph by all delegates. The Statutes were not merely an amended version of the earlier ones but constituted a completely new document democratically conceived in the spirit of the changes taking place in the world.

Elections

In the subsequent deliberations the following leading IOJ representatives were elected in a secret ballot:

President:	Armando Sobral ROLLEMBERG
(Brazil)	
First Vice-President:	Manuel Jorgé TOMÉ (Mozambique)
Second Vice-President:	Alexander ANGELOV (Bulgaria)
Vice-Presidents:	
for Africa	Bayi Sinibaguy MOLLET (Congo)
for Asia and Oceania	Tsegmid MUNKHJARGAL (Mongolia)
for Europe	Fernando DIOGO (Portugal)
for Latin America	Luis Julio GARCIA (Cuba)
for North America	Kevin P. LYNCH (USA)
for the Arab World	Yacine Mohamed AL MASSOUDI
(Yemen)	
for the Caribbean	Moses NAGAMOOTOO (Guyana)
Secretary General:	Gérard GATINOT (France)
Deputy Secretary General:	Mazen HUSSEINI (Palestine)
Treasurer:	Marian GRIGORE (Romania)
Deputy Treasurer:	Andrián ROJAS JAEN (Costa Rica)
Auditing Commission:	Hong JONG JIN (DPR of Korea)
	Jorge ESPINOZA (Ecuador)
	Abdellah NAANAA (Morocco)
	Victor NOVIKOV (USSR)
	Kindness PARADZA (Zimbabwe)

The Congress then decided unanimously to award the title of IOJ Honorary President to LUIS SUAREZ LOPEZ of Mexico for his lifelong activities as a journalist, for his contribution to the development of Latin American journalism and for helping to build the IOJ.

Continuing in its long-standing tradition, the Congress awarded International Journalists' Prizes for 1989 to 1991 to the following journalists: FERNANDO PESSAS (Portugal), MARIAN PODKOWINSKI (Poland), MESQUITA LOEMOS (Angola), GEORG MARKO (Bulgaria), STEFAN NACIU (Romania), and to the ASSOCIATION OF ARAB JOURNALISTS (in the occupied Palestinian territories).

Closing

In conclusion, outgoing President Nordenstreng delivered his closing speech and incoming President Rollemberg responded.

XI CONGRESS OF IOJ, Harare, Zimbabwe, January 24 - 29, 1991
XIe CONGRES DE L'OIJ, Harare, Zimbabwe, les 24 - 29 janvier 1991
XI CONGRESO DE LA OIP, Harare, Zimbabwe, enero 24 - 29, 1991
XI КОНГРЕСС МОЖ, Хараре, Зимбабве, 24 - 29 января 1991 г.
XIº CONGRESSO DA OIJ, Harare, Zimbabwe, 24 - 29 de Janeiro de 1991
المؤتمر الحادي عشر لمنظمة الصحفيين العالمية هراري ـ زيمبابوي ٢٤ ـ ٢٩ يناير / كانون الثاني ١٩٩١

Draft

Document 12

NEW STRATEGY AND ITS ORGANIZATIONAL AND FINANCIAL IMPLICATIONS

This document is based on a working paper, prepared by President Nordenstreng in consultation with Vice-Presidents Suárez and Izobo as well as some Secretaries, presented to the Balatonfüred Presidium and as well as the Executive Committee in Paris. The first conceptual part of the paper outlines the orientation of the new strategy, whereas the second organizational part outlines an alternative structure for the Secretariat and the rest of the permanent "apparatus" as compared to the present one.

a) CONCEPT AND PRINCIPLES

1. Based on the General Resolution of the Lisbon Presidium, the <u>character</u> of the IOJ rests on three cornerstones:
   - Politically, it is committed to the people's right to freedom of expression and information; to promotion of the truthfulness, openness, democratization and decolonization of the mass media; consolidation of solidarity of journalists.
   - Professionally, it is committed to the moral and material rights of working journalists, calling for trade-unionism and various ways of promoting professional ethics and protecting the professionals.
   - Organizationally, it is committed to worldwide cooperation and unity of action of all professional associations and trade-unions of journalists with the aim of achieving a unification of their organized movement.

2. This orientation is in accordance with the original founding <u>principles</u> of the IOJ, but it has not been consistently followed during the past four decades under conditions of the Cold War. Therefore it has to be stated today that the new strategy of the IOJ will
   - increase an emphasis on professional and trade-union aspects,
   - pursue the social responsibility of journalists based on human rights and other universal values,
   - adhere to pluralism in relation to various professional traditions and practices around the world,
   - evaluate the conditions of journalists and the mass media in different countries on the basis of universal principles and refrain from applying double standards.

3. The following <u>priority areas</u> are called upon by the new strategy:
   - trade union and social conditions of journalists (employment, social security, labour relations, etc.),
   - safety and protection of journalists,
   - professional ethics and standards,

- media policies (national and international aspects of ownership, control, concentration, NIICO, etc.).

Due attention should be given to issues of human rights, especially when violated by apartheid and foreign occupation, and global problems such as peace, development and environment.

4. The main forms of activity in materializing these priorities and other IOJ objectives are:
   - to gather and exchange information (fact-finding missions, studies, documentation, etc.)
   - to organize meetings, workshops, seminars, etc.
   - to organize solidarity actions, strike funds, etc.
   - to establish ad hoc committees,
   - to organize training,
   - to issue publications,
   - to monitor the performance of the mass media,
   - to represent the profession at the United Nations and its specialized agencies.

5. Where appropriate, joint action with the IFJ and the regional organizations of journalists should be pursued, as has been increasingly done through the Consultative Club. At the present stage there is potential for unity of action, with common plans and implementation mechanism, in the following matters:
   - peace and security (CSCE meetings in 1985, 1987, 1989)
   - safety and protection (brochures in 1987, 1989; joint action plan adopted in the Hague in April 1990),
   - new technologies (book in 1988),
   - status, rights and responsibilities (book in 1989)
   - ethics (collection of codes 1988),
   - employment and working conditions (ILO tripartite meeting in 1990).

   It is also possible to extend unity to the areas of:
   - surveying and evaluating the situation of journalists and the media around the world (annual report),
   - training,
   - publications,
   - representation at the UN, UNESCO, ILO, etc.

6. Beyond unity of action within the Consultative Club, there is need for the IOJ to continue joint ventures within the framework of the Non-Aligned Movement, notably through the MacBride Round Table on Communication. Similarly, joint activities should be continued and further developed with non-governmental organizations like AIERI and WACC, as well as human rights organizations such as Amnesty International and Article 19.

7. Consequently, the new strategy means, on the one hand, to lay greater emphasis on the <u>global level</u> by seeking for the broadest possible cooperation with other relevant organizations and institutions. On the other hand, the new strategy means to shift operative activities to the <u>regional level</u> and thus help strengthening the regional organizations of journalists.

* * *

b) STRUCTURE OF THE SECRETARIAT AND THE REGIONAL CENTRES

The new strategy of the IOJ, in accordance with the Orientation Document of the 10th Congress (Sofia 1986), calls for a drastic change in the organization and methods of work of the Secretariat, in particular its democratization and internationalization. What is needed in the current situation is to increase the efficiency of the apparatus which will lead to limit its size (currently there are nearly 100 full-time persons employed in Prague). Secondly, while scaling down the size of the apparatus, it should be decentralized by placing some functions at the regions and at the most important other internaional agencies. Thirdly, the Secretariat should be turned from a body where generalists hold geopolitical mandates into a body where specialists take care of professional tasks.

The following is an outline for an alternative structure to achieve this.

1. <u>Decentralization of the Secretariat</u> first of all by establishing regional centres, in addition to the present ones in Latin America and Africa, also in Asia and the Arab World and furthermore by moving the regional secretaries from the headquaters to the IOJ centres in their respective regions, working in close collaboration with the corresponding regional organizations. Thus the headquarters will no longer have "secretariats" for Africa, Latin America, etc; moreover it is better to abandon the title of an "IOJ Secretary". The centres in the regions will be essentially strengthened to include at least one regional officer (who may or may not be the director of the centre) plus 1-2 technical assistants. In order to ensure necessary cohesion, the regional officers will visit the headquarters at least once a year (common 1-2 week meeting), and they will also attend all meetings of the statutory bodies (normally one meeting per year).

   In addition to the regional centres there will be liaison offices at international organizations - according to possibilities in Geneva (UN, ILO, WIPO, ICRO, ITU), New York (UN), Paris (UNESCO) and Brussels-Strassbourg (EC, Council of Europe). Each liaison office can be composed of one part-time representative equipped with necessary facilities (fax, etc.).

   Such a decentralization will not be essentially more expensive than the present system of having regional secretaries placed in the headquarters - parallel to regional centres - especially with a view to the rising costs of living and services in Eastern Europe; economic integration will soon make the costs more or less the same throughout Europe, while costs remain lower in non-European regions. The travel costs will in both cases remain at the same level.

   A rough estimate for the annual expenses of such a network of regional centres and liaison offices (without costs of seminars etc. activities) is altogether 500.000 US$.

2. The headquarters itself includes necessary mechanism for the central management and coordination. This requires the following minimum personnel:

   * Secretary General
   * Deputy Secretary General
   * Two senior officers for specialized tasks
   * Cashier for running economic affairs (salaries, etc.)
   * 2-3 secretaries for technical assistance

   The following main fields of competence and responsibility will be divided between the four professional persons:

   - general coordination
   - economic affairs
   - member organizations and regional centres
   - international organizations and Consultative Club
   - trade union and social affairs
   - training
   - publications

   The Secretary General, Deputy Secretary General and the senior officers are recruited by consulting member organizations. No more than one of them should be from the host country. Technical assistants can be mostly from the host country.

   The cost of such a headquarters depends on the local conditions. However, the total level will be roughly 500,000 US$ annually, including costs for the premises, telecommunication and minimum travel. In addition meetings of elected bodies require on the average 100,000 US$ per year for travel and accommodation.

3. The above enumeration does not include publications (newsletter, monthly, books) which at the present level of production requires staff of about 20 persons plus running costs, altogether at the level of 700,000 US$. This can reduced to about one third, to the level of 200,000 US$, without loosing the main organ - a multilingual monthly magazine.

4. Also missing from the above outline are the schools of solidarity (presently in Budapest and Prague - the Berlin school never belonged to the IOJ but to the German Union). An estimate for their present annual expenses, transformed from local currencies to US dollars, gets up to the region of 300,000 - 500,000. In future Europe two schools will cost about US$ 800,000 per year, each with 4-7 courses of some 15 participants (including expenses for personnel, premises and air tickets to students). As to the new school about to be opened in Africa (Abuja, Nigeria), its annual running costs are estimated to be about half of the European schools (roughly US$ 200,000).

5. Likewise not included in the above listing are the persons/costs caused by studies and documentation (on protection, laws, ethics, etc.) provided by the International Journalism Institute (IJI). A separate document presents proposal for the future of the IJI.

6. By and large, the structure outlined above would mean a much smaller and cheaper permanent apparatus than the IOJ holds today but its geographic representation would be essentially broader than in the old centralized system. It would mean a real decentralization of the IOJ and at the same time strengthening of support to the regional organizations as well as the coordinating role of a universally representative common platform.

XI CONGRESS OF IOJ, Harare, Zimbabwe, January 24 - 29, 1991
XIe CONGRES DE L'OIJ, Harare, Zimbabwe, les 24 - 29 janvier 1991
XI CONGRESO DE LA OIP, Harare, Zimbabwe, enero 24 - 29, 1991
XI КОНГРЕСС МОЖ, Хараре, Зимбабве, 24 - 29 января 1991 г.
XIº CONGRESSO DA OIJ, Harare, Zimbabwe, 24 - 29 de Janeiro de 1991
المؤتمر الحادي عشر لمنظمة الصحفيين العالمية ، هراري – زيمبابوي ٢٤ – ٢٩ يناير / كانون الثاني ١٩٩١

GENERAL DECLARATIONS

- A -

1. <u>Commitment to the IOJ</u>

WHEREAS the IOJ is perceived to be in a critical state, even in a struggle to survive,

BE IT RESOLVED that members who share the original vision renew their commitment to the preservation of the organization and to the renewing of the organization in the face of the new and profound challenges of the changing times.

2. <u>General Character</u>

WHEREAS the work of journalists is rendered more effective with the support of a global organization,

BE IT RESOLVED that the IOJ declares itself to be universal in scope, independent of governments and dedicated to the unity and solidarity of journalists and their syndicates, unions and professional bodies as well as to the promotion of their rights, best interests and highest aspirations.

3. <u>Renewal Structure</u>

WHEREAS the existing organizational structure of the IOJ is perceivedd to have been significantly contributory to the operational and administrative ineffectiveness of the IOJ,

BE IT RESOLVED that a new structure be created, with statutory rules to guide and with checks and balances to ensure proper use of power and authority.

4. <u>Renewal Priorities</u>

WHEREAS the new structures mandated for the IOJ will require clear conception of the task,

BE IT RESOLVED that priority objectives be established in the statutory provisions of this 11th Congress.

SPECIFIC DECLARATIONS

- B -

1. Relations with Czechoslovakia

WHEREAS the historical background to the strained relations between the IOJ and the Czechoslovak colleagues is largely because of IOJ exercising double standards,

BE IT RESOLVED that this 11th Congress expresses profound regret that the IOJ failed to defend the Czech and Slovak journalists expelled from the profession and from their union in 1968 and subsequently, and,

BE IT FURTHER RESOLVED that among measures of resotration and reconciliation which might be taken, this Congress authorizes the Secretariat to create a special fund for the pension of those journalists and their spouses, to be initiated after proper consultation with the Czech and Slovak Syndicates of Journalists and with the Rehabilitation Committee of Journalists in Prague.

2. IOJ Headquarters in Czechoslovakia

WHEREAS the current crisis regarding the location of the IOJ Headquarters is a direct consequence of the poor relationship between the IOJ and Czechoslovak journalists,

BE IT RESOLVED that the 11th Congress mandates the setting up of a Committee including the President and Secretary General to investigate throughly and fully the history and current status of the problem,

BE IT RESOLVED that the Special Committee makes presentations to the Czechoslovak authorities expressing the unanimous wish of the delegates to the 11th Congress that the IOJ Headquarters continues to be in Prague and that the new orientation and strategy of the IOJ be presented to the Czechoslovak colleagues and to the general public and authorities in Czechoslovakia.

THEREFORE, this Congress mandates the Executive Committee to settle the problem of the IOJ Headquartes, if the need arises, on the basis of consultation with member organizations,

BE IT FURTHER RESOLVED that this Congress declares as a fundamental principle that the IOJ must never enter into relations or become involved in situations that renders it so dependent that its sovereignty or integrity is in any way threatened or undermined.

3. Protection of Journalists

WHEREAS violence against journalists in the active pursuit of their legitimate duties accounted last year for at least one hundred deaths in countries worldwide, not to mention physical and psychological injuries; in fact, even as this 11th Congres convened, the deaths of colleagues were reported in Liberia and Colombia, and, journalists are even now experiencing persecution and hostility in El Salvador, Sri Lanka, the Philippines and other countries,

BE IT RESOLVED THEREFORE that this 11th Congress issues a call to journalists everywhere to be vigilant and fearless despite adversity and hostility, and not to be intimidated by forces governmental or otherwise, acting covertly or overtly, militarily or criminally, and,

BE IT FURTHER RESOLVED that journalists everywhere take positive action in reporting acts of violence and threats of such acts against them, and,

BE IT FURTHER RESOLVED that this 11th Congress researches and reports on the situations in Africa, Latin America, Europe, Asia and the Middle East regarding the persecution of journalists who are subjected to court hearings, detention, imprisonment, beatings, etc.

4. Rights of Journalists

WHEREAS the number of murders, kidnappings and injuries to journalists are increasing at an alarming rate, especially during 1990,

THEREFORE, this Congress authorizes the Executive Committee to establish a Legal Commission to assist journalists in all parts of the world, and also, to gather information about attacks against journalists and publish such information annually in the media everywhere and furthermore, that this Congress mandates the Executive Committee to organize as soon as possible a Conference on the Protection of Journalists.

5. IOJ Training Project

WHEREAS the training of journalists has been identified as a priority of the IOJ, particularly journalists in the Third World countries,

BE IT FURTHER RESOLVED that the National Level Workshop and Asian Regional Seminar in Kathmandu, Nepal, sponsored by the IOJ and schedulred for February or March 1991, be given full publicity and support in whatever ways possible by this 11th Congress,

BE IT YET FURTHER RESOLVED that the issue of the IOJ School in Abuja, Nigeria, be referred to the Executive Committee for resolution once and for all.

6. Fund for Small Journalist Enterprises

WHEREAS the growing monopoly power of publishing ventures creates a threat for the free flow of news, dissemination of information, and for the employment and sustenance of journalists who wish to be independent of such conglomerates and so must seek alternative means for survival,

BE IT RESOLVED that this 11th Congress urges the IOJ to establish a small Journalist Enterprises Fund for unions, especially those in Africa, Asia, Latin America and the Caribbean.

7. <u>Korean Developments</u>

WHEREAS the unity of journalists within national boundaries and internationally is a fundamental objective of the IOJ,

BE IT RESOLVED that this Congress supports the efforts of the Korean people and journalists in particular for the reunification of Korea, independently and peacefully, on the basis of the Korean people, North and South, recognizing one State and one nation, with two systems of government.

8. <u>Indian Affiliation</u>

WHEREAS affiliation of journalist unions is a vital issue,

BE IT RESOLVED that this 11th Congress orders expediting of the recommendations made at the Presidium meeting here in Harare about pending applications for affiliations to the IOJ, authorizes the Executive Committee to process pending applications and make clear decisions on them as soon as possible.

9. <u>Motion of Thanks</u>

WHEREAS this 11th Congress of the IOJ was convened in Harare, Zimbabwe, from 24 to 29 January 1991, in response to the invitation of the Zimbabwe Union of Journalists,

BE IT RESOLVED that this Congress expresses its profound thanks to the people of Zimbabwe, to the President of Zimbabwe, His Excellency Robert Mugabe, who graciously declared open the Congress and delivered the main address; to the Zimbabwe Union of Journalists (ZUJ), and to the hotel management and staff for their fine hospitality.

APPENDIX 28. STATEMENT BY THE IFJ AND IOJ ON CO-OPERATION 1992

INTERNATIONAL FEDERATION OF JOURNALISTS
INTERNATIONAL ORGANISATION OF JOURNALISTS

Following an invitation extended by the IFJ a meeting of senior officers of the two organisations was held in Brussels on February 11th and 12th 1992. At the conclusion of the meeting, the IFJ and IOJ delegations issued the following statement:

Statement

"The IFJ and IOJ delegations believe that progress towards increased joint activity between the IFJ and the IOJ can only be achieved if co-operation is based upon principles of independent journalism and independent trade unionism, without regard to political or religious orientation.

The IFJ and IOJ delegations, believing that unity among journalists of the world is best achieved through practical programmes of work based upon objectives which are shared, agree to recommend to their respective governing bodies the following proposals for co-operation:

1. Safety of Journalists

Both organisations agree to give urgent priority to joint implementation of the action plan on safety of journalists previously agreed by the International and Regional Organisations of Journalists.

Both organisations, therefore, should pool resources in order to establish an effective information exchange and the widest possible network of contacts to assist all journalists working in dangerous conditions, including those working under daily conditions of censorship, intimidation or repression;

2. Copyright

Both organisations agree that immediate co-operation is needed in defence of journalists' copyright worldwide, particularly in relations with the World Intellectual Property Organisation, and that a joint meeting of the IFJ Copyright Working Party and the IOJ Copyright Committee should be organised to consider proposals for practical co-operation;

3. Trade Union Development

Both organisations note the proposal for co-operation between the IFJ and the International Journalism Institute in Berlin. Both organisations agree that this planned seminar, for journalists organisations from developing countries, which will consider strategies for trade union development should examine case studies and issues of practical and immediate concern to working journalists.

Both organisations further agree to publish jointly the results of this seminar and to use this report as a resource document to assist journalists organisations worldwide in defining issues and activities for trade union development.

These proposals, which do not interfere with the autonomy and integrity of either organisation, should provide the basis for continued dialogue between the IFJ and the IOJ."

Brussels,
February 12th 1992

ooOOOoo

Participants

IFJ	IOJ
Mia Doornaert, President	Armando Rollemberg, President
Aidan White, General Secretary	Gerard Gatinot, General Secretary
Rob Bakker	Mazen Husseini
Neal Swancott	Tom Morris
Assisted By	Assisted By
Marie Anne Paquet	Ramses Ramos

APPENDIX 29. PROPOSAL BY THE IAMCR TO RE-ESTABLISH THE IJI 1992–94

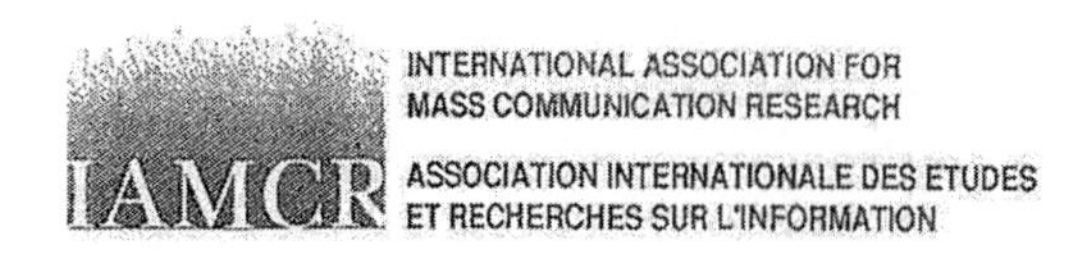

Prof. Dr. Cees J. Hamelink
President

Baden Powellweg 109-111
1069 LD Amsterdam, The Netherlands
Tel. (31) 20 - 610.15.81
Fax (31) 20 - 610.48.21
E - mail Hamelink @ IAMCR.NL

Mr. Armando Rollemberg
President I.O.J.
Celetnú 2
110 01 Prague
Czechoslovakia

Amsterdam December 12, 1992

Dear Mr. Rollemberg,

It is my pleasure to present the following letter to you on behalf of the International Association for Mass Communication Research and the World Association for Christian Communication.

We have learned that one of the consequences of the new realities in Prague is the de facto closing of the International Journalism Institute (IJI, an institutional member of the IAMCR).
We note this with regret since the IJI has become over the past few years an important resource base for documentation and contacts among media scholars. Its prime area of expertise was Central and Eastern Europe, but is has also been a unique platform for certain global aspects of journalism and mass media. For example, it has done an invaluable service by collecting and translating from various languages into a common language (English) a large number of journalistic codes of ethics -one of the best collections in the world.

We feel that it would be a great loss for the international community of media academics and professionals to be deprived of the documentation and expertise which the IJI has accumulated over the years and which it could continue to do under the new circumstances. On the other hand we understand that economc realities do not allow the IJI to continue as before sponsored exclusively by the IOJ.

Therefore we wish to approach you in order to find out whether a solution could be found to re-establishj the IJI as a joint venture between a collective of non-governmental organizations.

This could be done for example by turning the IOJ's school in Prague into an international foundation, into which also the Czech Syndicate of Journalists could be incorporated. Given the fact that this property was acquired with the means accumulated primarily in Czechoslovakia, we take it for granted that the IOJ feels itself morally obliged to invest its material assets so that they not only benefit its current members but also those professionals that constituted the base of its existence in Czechoslovakia since 1947 -including the IOJ enterprises since the 1970s.
A detailed plan can easily be prepared, once there is a basic understanding of the project. At this stage we are just sounding out whether you are interested in further developing the idea.

We do this in good faith -and recalling the fact that there exists an organic link between the IOJ and the IAMCR: the former is one of the founding memers of the latter.

We are looking forward to your kind response at your earliest convenience.

Sincerely Yours,

Prof. Dr. Cees J. Hamelink, President IAMCR
also on behalf of Rev. Carlos Valle, Secretary General WACC

INTERNATIONAL ORGANIZATION OF JOURNALISTS
IOJ PRESIDENCY

From: Armando Rollemberg
IOJ President
To: Jan Hamelinck
IAMCR President

Prague, April 9, 1993.

Dear colleague,

I am very sorry to answer to your kind letter only now. There are so many things to do and a so short time available! I apologize for it.

Your statement on the International Journalism Institute is quite true. It was a very important source of information on the situation of journalists around the world and particularly the third world countries.

Your proposal of transforming it into an international joint organization or foundation is quite interesting. We are going to have an Executive Committee meeting in April 25 to 30 in Paris, where we intend to discuss this issue. I may inform you that I have proposed last year to move IJI's main office to Paris, where IOJ has one building and to keep a filial in Prague to deal more precisely with Eastern Europe. Our building in Paris used to host the French Syndicate of Journalists-CGT and an IOJ bureau for Europe. The French Syndicate will quit the offices so we will have plenty of space. As we are moving our headquarters from Prague to Madrid soon we do not want to keep main or important offices here.

Perhaps we could discuss your idea again after the E.C.meeting. Should you kindly wait, I would write you again in May.

With my best regards,

Yours truly,

Armando Rollemberg
IOJ President

THE INTERNATIONAL ORGANIZATION OF JOURNALISTS (IOJ) IS A NON-GOVERNMENTAL ORGANIZATION HAVING A CONSULTATIVE STATUS WITH THE UNITED NATIONS ECONOMIC AND SOCIAL COUNCIL (ECOSOC – CATEGORY II) AND UNESCO (CATEGORY B)

SECRETARIAT: Celetná 2, 110 01 PRAGUE, CZECHOSLOVAKIA – TELEGRAMS: INTORGJOUR PRAGUE – TELEPHONE Nos.: 236 59 16 – TELEX No.: 122 631 JOUR C – FAX No.: 236 88 04

Professor Hamid Mowlana
President

November 21, 1994

TO: Manuel Tome, Acting President of IOJ
Alexander Angelov, Vice President of IOJ
Gerard Gatinot, Secretary General of IOJ

Dear Colleagues:

Nearly two years ago, my predecessor wrote to former IOJ President with a proposal to re-establish the International Journalism Institute (IJI) as a joint venture between the IOJ, IAMCR, and other relevant non-governmental organizations (see copy enclosed). This was a serious initiative from our side, but regretfully we received no response.

Meanwhile, the IAMCR has entered into negotiations with UNESCO (where we have consultative status A), among others, to consider how a worldwide databank of communication training institutions may be established. The institute, as proposed by us, could be made a central part of such a databank. Likewise, the IAMCR is cooperating with the Council of Europe and the European Union in the area of professional ethics of journalism, and here we also see potential for broader cooperation through the proposed institutional arrangement, given especially the good record of IJI in this field.

I, therefore, respectfully ask you to give urgent attention to our original proposal at your forthcoming Executive Committee meeting. Should you accept our proposal, in principle, we would be glad to meet with you and discuss it in greater detail in Prague during the Council of Europe conference on media policies, 7-8 December.

I would appreciate hearing from you by 3 December, after which I shall be in Budapest attending the University Forum at the CSCE conference.

Cordially,

Hamid Mowlana

Hamid Mowlana

encl.

Office of the President: School of International Service, The American University, Washington, DC 20016-8071 USA
Tel.: 1-202 885 1628 Fax: 1-202 885 2494 Email: mowlana@auvm.american.edu

DEPARTMENT OF RADIO-TELEVISION-FILM
THE UNIVERSITY OF TEXAS AT AUSTIN

CMA 6.118 · Austin, Texas 78712-1091 · FAX 512-471-4077
Undergraduate and Chair's Office · 471-4071 · Graduate Office · 471-3532

26 January 1995

To: Manuel Tome
From: Kaarle Nordenstreng
Via: Kevin Lynch
CC: Alexander Angelov

Dear friend,

I wish I could have talked with you in person but it was not possible since I have been out of Europe since early January. I am currently visiting professor at the above institution (Jose Marques de Mello from Sao Paulo is also here this spring).

As Sasha can tell you, I was in Prague in December at the European media policy conference and discussed with him a bit on the IOJ. Besides, I got through my own channels the documents of the past two IOJ Executive Committee meetings, including those on the financial situation.

Did you ever receive the enclosed letter faxed to the IOJ Prague office on the eve of the November Executive Committee? I gave to Sasha a copy of it in December; by that time he had not seen it... Until now the IAMCR has not received any response to it, and at this stage it naturally belongs to those matters to be channeled through the Congress.

I don't know whether Gerard has put it to the agenda; he might rather want to bury it (maybe that is why it never reached you in November). However, you with Sasha do have the power to take it up and push it through, even at this late moment.

I hope you realize the strategic importance of this initiative:

1) Make peace with the Czech Syndicate (under whose mandate all the IOJ money was made, beginning with Kubka's time).

2) Create a truly universal ('ecumenical') basis where the IOJ stands in alliance with IAMCR (status A with Unesco) and other NGOs of media scholars (WACC, ACCE, etc.), eventually also with IFJ and regional journalists' organizations.

3) Ensure that something permanent and honourable remains of IOJ (instead just a shameful record of loosing 10 million dollars in 5 years without notable professional performance).

It would mean a major investment or sacrifice from the IOJ's side: a good deal of its remaining property would be passed over to such an international foundation. But on return the IOJ would get a big amount of political legitimity - something that it is badly missing in its present trend towards marginalization.

As a matter of fact, this kind of new beginning to the IJI can mean also a new beginning to the Consultative Club of International and Regional Organizations of Journalists. Have you realized that this vital body (formalized in Mexico in 1989) has not met since 1990? It was perhaps the most promising forum for global collaboration among journalists, initiated by Unesco in 1978 and thereafter promoted above all by the IOJ in close collaboration with the regional federations (UJA, FAJ, FELAP, etc.). I always gave high priority to it, with achievements such as the ethical principles and the "Topuz book". The fact is that after my departure the Consultative Club has remained dormant.

And here you cannot blame Unesco or IFJ. Neither of these was really pushing it in the 1980s; it was always the IOJ that was primus inter pares. Today Unesco certainly does nothing to promote the Club, as it is under the control of World Press Freedom Committee (or as we used to say, "imperialist interests"). And the IFJ/Aidan White is, as before, only lukewarm towards the Club, as it reduces its/his hegemonistic ambitions. But the IOJ, with the regional federations, could press the Club into new life - unless it is already too late (I don't know). This would be precisely the kind of future structure which I saw Luis Suarez advocating in the Ex.Comm. session (some years after I tried to make the same point).

The new IJI initiative by the IAMCR would be a perfect and concrete way of materializing the Club idea. But it needs determination and vision. I hope that at least you and Sasha still have got those qualities left, although I do understand that you have been pressed by many domestic problems and that nowadays it is extremely difficult to bypass the iron grip of those who really control the IOJ. (Reading the documents I could not help wondering how Gerard has managed to bring back the old totalitarian style of painting black as white as vice versa...)

Good luck.

Kaarle

PS: The IAMCR was not invited to Amman but please feel free to pass publicly best regards from its President, Professor Hamid Mowlana (Iran-USA) and its Professional Education Section President, Professor Kaarle Nordenstreng (Finland)!

Encl. 3 pages

APPENDIX 30. THE PRESIDENT'S POST-RESIGNATION LETTER 1994 (EXCERPTS)

Madrid, January 12, 1994
To Manoel Tomé, 1st Vice-President of the IOJ

Dear Friend,

I have to pass on the dossier about the chairmanship of the IOJ directly to your hands. I do this by means of this open letter which I address, through your intermediary, to the Executive Committee, the affiliated organizations and the Congress of the IOJ. In this letter, I review the most important pending matters lying on my desk at the moment of my resignation, inform you about the obligations assumed in Madrid and formally pass on to you the accountancy of the IOJ and the custody of its property at the headquarters and whose list, previously checked, I present enclosed (enclosure 1).

The questions concerning my mandate are numerous and different and, therefore, I wish to specify them, without avoiding informing you sincerely about some preoccupations of mine, both old and new. For your appreciation, I am also leaving different projects elaborated before my resignation, with the intention of solving some of the most serious problems of the IOJ.

I shall begin with themes more urgent and general and then pass to those more specific. In a separate file, I am presenting you all the matters referring to the transfer of the headquarters and its installation (enclosure 2).

1. The destiny of the IOJ archives

The archives of the IOJ, including those of the International Institute of Journalism, IIJ, are piled up on the damp floor of a shed in a little town near Prague. I was shocked when I came into this shed about three months ago. Everything is left there at the mercy of the humidity of weather: papers and books are intermingled, voluminous portfolios contain documents... It is an unspeakable disaster.

I drew the attention of the Secretary General to the fact, asking him to transfer the material to a spacious and dry room, where it could be arranged and catalogued carefully. As far as I know, no specific measure has been adopted so far.

[...]

3. The financial situation and the management of the economic activities of the IOJ

Since Sanaa or, in other words, for more than two years, I have been drawing attention to the critical financial situation of the IOJ. With the enterprises disorientated and without producing any profit, some of them even making a loss, it was obvious that the IOJ had to use its reserves to continue functioning, to face the extraordinary expenses needed to indemnify the staff made redundant and to transfer its headquarters. I remember that some people called this document of mine alarmist. I repeated the alert in Madrid (enclosure 4).

Therefore, the picture painted in Barcelona and concerning the reduction of the reserves did not surprise me. It is true, but incomplete. I imagine that, as part of the plot engineered to empty the Madrid headquarters, it was deliberately omitted to say that the IOJ enterprises own more than 40 million Czech crowns (about US$ 1,300 000) in claims. And that an important part of the money that had been in banks in Germany has been changed into the capital stock of the eight enterprises restructured to become private limited liability companies.

These facts, which I am adding, obviously do not change the picture of the difficulties. A long time ago, we had a diagnosis of the crisis on our desk. As you remember, we spent many hours at meetings, talking about an adequate remedy. After two years (!), proceeding haphazardly, the Executive Committee reached two crucial decisions: to register the enterprises in the Czech Republic and in Slovakia instead of winding them up. And to look for joint ventures that would bring new capital and help us to modernize and manage them.

How many times did we conclude that we should pass on the management of the enterprises to professionals in this field? From how many members of the Executive Committee did we hear the moaning statements that we were journalists, that we did not understand anything about business and that we were not elected to manage enterprises? Even though this is not recorded in the minutes, I think that all those who attended the meeting at Courcelle still remember its decision to set up a "holding", whose Advisory Council would consist of members of the Executive Committee and which would include the economic activities of the IOJ. And that its management should be made professional.

Nothing of this has been done. Quite on the contrary, the Secretary General and the Treasurer took a fancy to the role of businessmen and installed themselves on the boards of directors of the enterprises. This was absolute nonsense, terrible amateurishness! Eight enterprises operating in an isolated way, without strategy or investment plans, in a setting made extremely difficult by the transition from the old system to market economy. Not to mention the outright hostility persisting in the Czech Republic towards the IOJ and manifested by both the authorities and important sectors of the local public opinion.

I left Barcelona with some questions stuck in my throat. When will the Executive Committee understand that the structural cause of the continuous deterioration of the finances of the IOJ lies precisely there? Is it possible that nobody remembers the 1.2 million German marks any more, lost on the purchase, and subsequent winding-up, of Japan Electronic Import? And the bankruptcy of Interpress Budapest, which led to a loss of four million dollars?

How can similar losses bee ignored? Until when will a deaf ear be turned to the remonstrances of the enterprises' managers themselves, distressed about, and puzzled by, such indecision and much great confusion?

They accused me of exceeding the President's statutory authority when insisting on making the management of the enterprises professional. But where is it said that the President should look passively at the ruin of the organization of which he is the head?

Far from this being a personal question, it is a problem essentially professional.

I am insisting on this matter for the last time and in capital letters: NOT THE SECRETARY GENERAL, STILL LESS SO THE TREASURER (AND, TO MAKE THINGS STILL WORSE, BOTH THESE MEN TOGETHER), HAS THE ABILITY TO MANAGE THE ENTERPRISES. NOT ONLY BECAUSE THEY UNDERSTAND ABSOLUTELY NOTHING ABOUT BUSINESS, BUT ALSO BECAUSE THEY ARE NOT APPOINTED TO DO THIS. Moreover, they do not breed even the minimum trust in the managers and executives. This is plain truth even if it may hurt any person whatsoever.

Frankly speaking, if we analyzed the case thoroughly, we would reach the conclusion that, in this matter (and others too), the Executive Committee was moving in circles and did not arrive anywhere. Two years were lost before the IOJ decided between winding-up or registering the enterprises. Made by Esteban Valenti, who was appointed adviser in the process of cooperation established with the IPS, the judicious diagnostic did not serve at all (enclosure 5).

The Secretary General, who had been removed from dealing with administrative matters because of his laziness, surfaced again, gradually concentrating all the powers in his hands after the resignation of the Assistant Secretary General.

[...]

10. "The World of Journalists", "The Courrier of the IOJ" and the publication policy of the Organization

Here begins another chapter of the history of my disputes with the Secretary General, which started at the very beginning of our terms of office, during a marathon of visits I made to political parties, trade-unions and the different representative bodies of the Czech and Slovak societies, trying to show that the IOJ had changed since its Harare Congress. During a visit to the European Club of Culture, I came to know the project of the publication of a book containing the material from an exhibition organized after the Velvet Revolution and concerning censorship at the time of the communist regime. The management of the Club sought financial aid to complete the publication of the material that would be distributed free of charge in the primary schools of the country.

I was accompanied by Treasurer Marian Grigore when making this visit. We considered this project to be a good opportunity for the IOJ to reappear in a positive form before the Czech and Slovak journalists and public opinion, because we would collaborate specifically in searching for the truth so many times falsified, omitted or manipulated by the totalitarian regime. We discussed the subject with the Secretary General, who expressed his agreement. Therefore, I continued with the Treasurer to negotiate the conditions of this joint venture.

On behalf of the IOJ, I wrote a letter to the management of the Club, announcing our readiness to collaborate in the publication of the book, which would cost about 40,000 dollars. The proofs of the book remained more than a month on the Secretary General's desk. When I came to him to get what he had promised, he decided to change his opinion, alleging that the IOJ should not make a book dealing exclusively with the censorship applied by the communist regime in Czechoslovakia. Either we shall make a book describing censorship in all formerly communist countries or we shall make no book at all. And, with this excuse, he categorically refused to authorize sponsorship. I felt indignant at this behavior of his. Making no bones about it, I denounced sabotage when dealing with the interested party and warned the Secretary General in writing that I would not tolerate another such offence to the authority of the President of the IOJ.

This was our first conflict. But other conflicts appeared soon afterwards, some of which merit being mentioned here.

We had not yet completed one year of administration when we decided to stop the publication "The Democratic Journalist" and to launch "The World of Journalists". Submitted by Gatinot, the proposal was approved by the Executive Committee in Rio de Janeiro unrestricted. As soon as we arrived to Prague, the Secretary General began to speak about the inefficiency of the Czech staff in the editor's office, lack of local graphic artists' creativity and the inflexibility of the IOJ printing office, arguing that the new review should be made in Paris. Despite Mazen Husseini's resistance, it was agreed that the paste-up and artwork should be made in Paris. The printing, however, was dependent on the previous presentation of its budget. At the beginning, the review should be published in English, Spanish and French.

From this moment, the Secretary General got hold of the review. Four months later, he appeared with a paste-up and several alternatives of the artwork. From time to time, always in an inappropriate way, he made some short comment on this subject. I well remember his enthusiasm when he informed us that he had obtained the permission of the Council of Europe to publish excerpts from an analysis of journalism in the region. The said document already had been widely distributed more than six months earlier. I remarked that, if the matter was not topical any more at the present moment, it would be quite out of date (?) when the review would be edited, printed and distributed in the end. By the way, on another occasion, he said that, in the first issue, he would include some excerpts from the speech I had delivered at the IFJ Congress in Montreal in June 1992.

The review first saw the light of day a few months ago, published only in French. The budget has never been discussed. Not a single line was published of the declaration we had issued in four languages at the Vienna Conference on Human Rights. On the other hand, the Secretary General's role of a protagonist becomes quite obvious after leafing through the review for the first time. In it, without consulting anyone, he appointed himself as the "director of the publication" and named an "international editorial board", consisting of myself, you and Alexander Angelov. We have never met to discuss the concept and never written a single line. This may seem to be a passing shot, but it is not. The fact is that Gérard Gatinot has made the review alone: he spent a year and some 25,000 dollars on it according to the invoices subsequently presented to the bookkeping department. And it is said nowhere in the statutes of the IOJ that the competence of the Secretary General include making a review.

We also differed over the publication of the report drawn up by the mission we had sent to Yugoslavia. Two months after the return of the delegation, we had a courageous report in English, written on a computer by Adam Novak and Jean-Philippe DeLalandre. Despite this, Gatinot insisted on carrying the material to Paris and printing a new, bilingual (French and English) version of it there. I tried in vain to convince him that the version already made would be the best alternative as soon as photocopied. First, because it was ready. Second, because this kind of work was intended for a limited public. But the Secretary General insisted on making a "cahier" in Paris. It took him more than six months, he spent several thousand dollars and used the opportunity to publish, as an illustration to the preface, his photograph when putting the mission on the plane at the Prague airport. There is a curious detail: the caption of the photograph may induce an unwary reader to think that Gatinot was present at the war front...

More recently, after my transfer to Madrid, the Secretary General also began to decide himself on what should be published or not in "The Courrier of the IOJ". In the last issue, he ordered the mission in Somalia to be removed from the front page...

In addition to my nonconformism, I use this opportunity, given by the final report, to have recorded the proposals I have been defending for years to make the publishing policy of the IOJ more dynamic. Besides, they all can be found in the set of draft resolutions I presented in Barcelona.

[...]

17. Intrigues, snares and manoeuvres

As you surely remember, at the first meeting we held after Harare, in Prague, I wondered that the correspondence addressed to me was coming opened to my office. The Assistant Secretary General explained however that this was an old practice. The whole post passed first through a department charged with getting acquainted with the content of the letters and subsequently distributing them according to the matters dealt with in them and to their addressees. I said that this was a typically Stalinist practice that would be considered a punishable crime in any moderately democratic country. And I threatened, if this practice were to continue a single day, to all a collective interview with the press and to denounce the existence of censorship in the IOJ.

This was my first "round" to make the IOJ transparent. In that case, the matter was so blatant that it was possible to denounce it and struggle against it efficiently. Thereafter, I discovered that it was much more difficult for me to put an end to the atmosphere consisting of intrigues and manipulations by the *apparat*. I could write another thousand lines here about this "culture medium" in which the IOJ continued to be immersed. During these three years, several dozens of events happened that would be suitable for illustrating this chapter of my report. The shortage of time does not allow me to do it though. However, in the files of the President's office, you will be able to check up on the truth of what I say. You will be able to find an eloquent example of snares in my correspondence with the Secretary General about the transfer and installation of the headquarters in Madrid.

However, for general knowledge, I have to expose the last of the manoeuvres, which was undertaken with the obvious aim of setting the Executive Committee against me in Barcelona. I refer to the report presented by Mr. Naanaa Abdellah on behalf of the Commission for the Audit of the Accounts of the IOJ.

[...]

That is what I call gross manipulation: a commission consisting of five members, of whom only three meet and whose report is presented at the last minute, with a false date, without being discussed by the two other representatives present at the meeting, while at least one of them openly has his protest recorded against the obvious factious character of the testimonies of the Treasurer and the Secretary General, very interested in ruining the President. In the middle of the tumultuous meeting in Barcelona, I nevertheless had the opportunity to observe that hypocrisy, lies and manipulations, i.e. the raw materials used by the leaders controlling the *apparat* to make their will prevail, are the core of the process of ruin of the IOJ.

The Berlin Wall fell in 1989, but the fact is that "glasnost" has not reached the IOJ. In fact, this is the cancer which is destroying the Organization little by little, more than do even the financial difficulties or the lack of credibility from the omissions of the past.

[...]

Conclusions

I came to Barcelona with the illusion that we were starting a new historical period of the IOJ. With the headquarters installed in magnificent premises, I took the initiative in publishing advertisements in two Spanish newspapers, asking the interested persons for curricula in view of choosing a small team: a trilingual secretary, a secretary/switchboard operator, a specialist in computer printing, an archivist and a chauffeur/messenger.

I was prompted mainly by the wish to win back so much time lost. The year 1994 would be the year of the democratization, modernization and recovery of the credibility of the IOJ. The year that would culminate in restructuring the IOJ. Everything was ready for launching this operation. We would set up a "network", re-organize the archive and recentralize the publishing activities, thus significantly enlarging the range of influence of the Organization.

In parallel, I intended to arrange a census of the affiliated organizations and to draw up a pilot study of the new statutes that would more clearly establish the strategic principles of the Organization, eliminate internal contradictions within the future leadership and guarantee a professional structure for the development of the economic activities to the IOJ.

When I became aware that the Executive Committee was getting entangled in the snare prepared by the Secretary General in collusion with the Treasurer, I lost patience and was exasperated. It became evident that the whole work done to transfer the headquarters to Madrid had been in vain. Sabotage triumphed. I realized there that al my plans, hatched so long and with such energy, would remain on paper again. I confess that, at that moment, I was dominated by a mixed feeling of disgust, frustration and impotence.

I preferred to resign my post and not to remain a prisoner of the *apparat* controlled from Prague by Gérard Gatinot and Marian Grigore, without having the minimum infrastructure to exercise the office of President, efficiently, observing, from a theatrical box (with a high salary obtained at the end of each month), the completion of the ruin of the Organization.

[...]

Yours truly,
/signed:/ Armando Sobral Rollemberg

APPENDIX 31. DOCUMENTS FROM THE 12TH IOJ CONGRESS IN AMMAN 1995

Two key documents; more in the proceedings *12th Congress* (1995)

XII CONGRESS OF IOJ, Amman, Jordan , January 28 - 31, 1995
XIIème CONGRES DE L'OIJ, Amman, Jordanie, les 28 - 31 janvier 1995
XII CONGRESO DE LA OIP, Ammán, Jordania, enero 28 - 31, 1995
المؤتمر الثاني عشر – عمان – الأردن ٢٨-٣١ كانون الثاني ١٩٩٥

IOJ TREASURER'S REPORT

On the eve of the Harare Congress, on January 1, 1991, the financial means of the IOJ were estimated at US $10,325,599, deposited in different currencies in several banks. We have to count 2,5 million dollars (il.e. 75 million Czech Korunas) of credit, respective of obligations to third parties from the past towards IOJ enterprises. After settling the bill of this Congress, and after the closure of the balance sheet for the financial year 1994 to March 1995, we will be left with a maximum total of US $800,000. It is quite justified to ask what hapened to the 11million dollars and why we haven't managed--if not to increase, at least to keep--this heritage.
The answer can be found in the details presented ion the annex, though some of these have to be accompanied by a few explanations and comments.

Because of the rumours and accusations spread all over the world concerning the origin of the IOJ financial resources, it has to be said that all the investigations made after the Harare Congress by the leadership of the IOJ and by the inspection of the Czech Ministry of Finance, have not lead to the discovery of any trace of financial support from governments, political parties or even secret organizations.

The only exception consists in a 5 million Czech Koruna financial aid received from the the Czech Communist Party. After this discovery, the leadership of the IOJ transferred this amount to the Czech Federal Government. All the rest of the financial reserves represent the profit obtained through economic activities carried out by the IOJ. It is evident that as enterprises belonging to an international organization accepted politically by the communist authorities, these have benefited from exceptional conditions: no competition, priority in obtaining raw materials (even if deficient), or reservations in hotels for clients of tourism agencies belonging to the IOJ, etc. A mere phone call from M. Ulcak or M. Jakes Jr. was enough to solve any problem.

After the fall of the communist regime and the transition to a market economy, all these advantages came to an end abruptly. The new commercial code, published in 1991, imposed the registration of enterprises in oder to be able to resume their activities. Moreover, the decision of the Federal Ministry of Interior Affairs to expel the IOJ from Czech territory had the immediate effect of the loss of trust from our best traditional clients and the attrition of our best specialists, who were attracted by more substantial salaries insured by private enterprises with foreign capital. Usually under these conditions, profits of the past have been replaced by losses in the enterprises' balance sheet. The shock did not go down well. Fears existed over the danger of confiscation of all our possessions and bank accounts, and various attempts at crisis management have been suggested, including a transfer of our assets to a foreign holding company.

Simultaneously, the debate on the opportunity fo registration along the lines of the new law went on. In search of an agreement, the Executive Committee of the IOJ designated a commission and brought in an expert from Uruguay for 3 months, which was both costly and almost froze our economic activities. The procedure of legal registration only started on January 1, 1993.

Commitments and obligations of the past

Among the 11 million dollars spent after the Harare Congress, nearly 2,25 million are not the responsibility of the new leadership. They are in fact commitments made before the congress.

1) It is firstly the expenses of the Harare congress (US $993,700), the session of the Paris presidium (US $149,058), the missed presidium in Amman (US $80,041). So, this is a first total of US $1,22 million.

2) We also have 22 million Czech Korunas, representing customs obligations and penalties for illegally imported products in the past. 4,7 million Czech Korunas have to be added for taxes for the year 1990. The total represents US $1 million. We were therefore left with approximately US $8,75 million to account for.

Mistakes and subjective factors

In its management of financial affairs, the IOJ has unfortunately made a number of mistakes:

a) The decision of President A. Rollemberg to establish himself at the headquarters of teh IOJ, which entailed considerable costs in salaries and expenses for teh administrative apparatus at the service of the president.

b) The purchase of the "Japan Electronic Enterprise" (JEE) company of Munich Germany: During the first part of 1990, the former secretary of the ION took the decision to accept the purchase proposal of a German commercial company registered with a capital of 50,000 DM for the price of 250,000 DM (the initial proposed price being 500,000 DM), with an advanced sum of 200,000 DM, but unfortunately the company went bankrupt.

The leadership could thus have seen that the company was already going bankrupt, having debts of more than 200,000 DM at the time of the transaction.

c) The retention of a Prague lawyer, M. Moravec, to sign and take decisions in his place in his quality as secretary general (quality in which a lawyer should prepare, for example, the transfer of the IOJ headquarters in Bratislava, months later the executive committee chose Madrid), in his quality as manager of MONDIAPRES LTD.

A few considerations on the use of the IOJ's financial means

At the end of this explanation on the volume of the IOJ's spending, we also have to note the way in which the sending were divided between the different areas of activity.

We will note that for the political and professional activities of the IOJ that is to say the ones that represent the very reason of the existence of our organization only 890 of the resources managed by the secretary general were used.

Another 12,56%was used to ensure the functioning of the IOJ's centers and regional offices (only for administrative costs, as for possible activities organized the IOJ paid these extra amounts that can be found in the 8% already mentioned).

The IOJ at the end of the second millenium

It was 4 years ago in Harare after my election that I promised total transparency regarding the IOJ's financial matters. I have kept my word even though most of the distinguished delegates here present do not know this. All the documents of all the executive committees (unfortunately never handed out) show so. Now, with only US $800,000 after the congress it is difficult to find a solution to elaborate a budget, even for one year, but it is 4 years to the next congress.

Even if we add US $100,000 of companies' profits (bearing in mind the volume of the social capital, it will be an ideal maximum never achieved). And if the suggestions I made in Sa'naa are accepted, suggestions that were received violently and rejected, we will still have to pay the fees of administration and communication of the headquarters. In this situation all that can be done as a conclusion is to suggest to the congress a few indispensable measures in order to ensure the survival of the IOJ.

1) Reducing all the IOJ apparatus to a small office (6 people maximum) in Prague.

2) Closing of all the regional centers and offices (including Paris, the most expensive one; the premises 58, rue Pailleron could be rented).

3) Putting an end to covering the costs for airline tickets and accommodation for participants to diverse activities. Including statutory, these obligations can be assumed by member-organizations.

4) An end to subventions of political and professional actions for 1995. (The IOJ ensuring only the logistic coordination and support of the activities organized by the member-unions or regional journalistic organizations) and the following years subventions from the UNESCO and other international and regional organizations.

5) Suspension of member organizations who do not pay their dues to the IOJ (unless, if for exceptional reasons the executive committee grants a postponement or a reduction of the payment).

6) The closing of all non-profit making companies and the sale of all non-productive material and inventory (including buildings).

XII CONGRESS OF IOJ, Amman, Jordan , January 28 - 31, 1995
XIIème CONGRES DE L'OIJ, Amman, Jordanie, les 28 - 31 janvier 1995
XII CONGRESO DE LA OIP, Ammán, Jordania, enero 28 - 31, 1995
المؤتمر الثاني عشر – عمان – الاردن ٢٨-٣١ كانون الثاني ١٩٩٥

The XII Congress of the International Organization of Journalists was held in Amman, Jordan, from January 28 through January 31, 1995.

Ninety-four delegates representing 69 member organizations from 65 countries were present at the Congress.

A new executive was elected at a duly constituted meeting of the Congress on Jan. 31.

The following officers were elected as the leadership of the IOJ:

President: Suleiman Al-Qudah, Jordan
First Vice-President: Juan Carlos Camano, Argentina
Second Vice-President: Moses Nagamootoo, Guyana
Secretary General: Antonio Ma. Nieva, Philippines
Deputy Secretary General: Kindness Paradza, Zimbabwe
Treasurer: Alexander Angelov, Bulgaria
Deputy Treasurer: Shahul Hameed Abdul Careem, Sri Lanka
Vice-President, Europe: Jean-Francois Téaldi, France
Vice-President, Africa: Ladi Lawal, Nigeria
Vice-President Latin America: Tubal Paez Hernandez, Cuba
Vice-President, Caribbean: Earl Bousquet, St. Lucia
Vice-President, Asia: Phan Quang, Vietnam
Vice-President, Arab Region: Naim Tobasi, Palestine
Vice-President, North America: Kevin Lynch, USA

Members of the Executive Committee:
Hilário Manuel Matusse, Mozambique
Luiz Carlos De Assis Bernardes, Brazil
Stanley Palmoen Sidoel, Suriname
Abdel Allateef Aouad, Morocco
José Armando Martins Morim, Portugal
Ram K. Karmacharya, Nepal

Auditing Commission:
President: Luis Castro Espinosa, Ecuador
Members: Eleanor Pratt, Ghana
Rohana Wetthasinghe, Sri Lanka
Abdellah Naanaa, Morocco
Adrian Rojas Jaen, Costa Rica

As Chairperson of the Electoral Commission, I certify that the above results are accurate.

Gail Lem, Canada
Chairperson, Electoral Commission

February 1, 1995

ORGANISATION INTERNATIONALE DES JOURNALISTES
OIJ

APPENDIX 32. INTERNAL BRIEFINGS FROM THE SECRETARY GENERAL 1995

INTERNATIONAL ORGANIZATION OF JOURNALISTS

INTERNAL BRIEFING NO. 1

FOR : MEMBERS OF THE EXECUTIVE COMMITTEE

FROM : THE SECRETARY-GENERAL

DATE : 14 APRIL 1995

1. TURNOVER OF FUNCTIONS

ON the third week of February, the incoming President, Treasurer and Secretary-General met in Prague to accomplish the necessary documentation and other paperwork related to the changeover in the directorate of the International Organization of Journalists.

This included the time-consuming but ntcessary process of notarization and registration of the election results in Amman, as attested by the Electoral Commission, in the Czech Republic, and personal appearances in the IOJ's depository banks required for the changes in check signatories.

From Feb. 13 to 20, President Suleiman Al-Qudah, Treasurer Alexander Anguelov, and Secretary-General Antonio Maria Nieva reviewed the IOJ's financial and political situation, met with the managers of the IOJ's limited companies to apprise themselves of the enterprises' problems, and laid down initial plans.

Secretary-General Nieva was briefed by outgoing Secretary-General Gerard Gatinot on pending matters requiring followup action, and met with the IOJ Secretariat staff to inform them of the leadership's new policy to cut down on all costs in order to alleviate the severe financial crisis now confronting the IOJ.

2. COLLECTIVE LEADERSHIP

Mssrs. Al-Qudah, Nieva, and Anguelov agreed, as a matter of principle, that steering the IOJ through the current crisis, the most serious in the organization's history, shall be the collective responsibility of all.

In furtherance of this commitment, all three signed a special power of attorney in favor of each other, to ensure that no vacuum ever occurs in the highest leadership in the event of the absence of one official or the other and to prevent a repetition of the top-level personality clashes that nearly tore the IOJ apart these last four years.

2. CRISIS BUDGET

The new administration enters upon its tenure confronted by the most serious financial crisis yet in the history of the organization, a grim reality that has set the IOJ's detractors to describing the 12th Congress in Amman, Jordan, as the IOJ's last congress.

The burden is on everyone in the organization -- the presidency, the Secretariat, the Executive Committee, the affiliate unions -- to prove it wrong on this, the 49th year of the IOJ.

As of the Amman Congress in January 1995, the IOJ had only U.S.$804,190.39 left in its books of accounts, down $9,521,408.61 from what the IOJ had in its coffers in 1991 when the 11th Congress convened in Harare, Zimbabwe.

2.a **DRASTIC MEASURES**

Considering that the IOJ has less than $1 million left between itself and bankruptcy, the President, Treasurer and Secretary-General agreed on drastic cost-cutting measures that will limit expenditures to about $500,000 during the year, leaving the organization with savings of $300,000 that will hopefully be replenished by proceeds from the IOJ's enterprises before the end of 1995.

Accordingly, it was agreed that the IOJ will have to go through a ''dead''* period for at least six months, beginning from January, to enable the organization to recuperate financially.

(*It means that all activities would be pared down to only those that are most necessary to minimize on expenses.)

The following cost-cutting measures were agreed to be adopted:

o All unecessary expenses would be stopped, and all existing contracts would be reviewed individually. Non-productive enterprises shall be liquidated and sold.

o For the time being, all publications -- the IOJ newsletter, the one-edition World of Journalists magazine, whose production cost the IOJ a total of $82,183 in 1994 -- would be discontinued.*

(Temporarily, printing of the IOJ Newsletter would be undertaken by mimeograph or copier.)

o For the IOJ centers, expense would be limited to salaries and office expenses. All other costs are to be slashed.

o Furthermore, operations of the Paris Center would be suspended pending consultations with the Vice President for Europe on what to do with it, while the Madrid office on Calle

Mayor, which costs the IOJ at least $5,000 a month to maintain, would be moved to a less expensive location.*

(The two actions have been carried out, with the contract for Calle Mayor discontinued, cowhile the IOJ's delegate in Madrid, Mr.Giless Multigner, is now negotiating with the Union of Journalists of Spain for office space for IOJ in its headquarters for continued representation while the problem of the IOJ's headquarters remains unresolved.)

o The support fund for political activities for 1995 shall be limited to $40,000.

o The budget for at least one Executive Committee meeting shall be limited to $50,000. The meeting shall be held in mid-June in Prague.

o The amount of $1,000 is allocated for the annual Grand Prix commitment.

o Finally, Secretary-General Nieva voluntarily accepted a 10 per cent cut in his salary for the year, in keeping with cost-saving policy, while Treasurer Anguelov agreed to waive his salary and to perform his task instead in Sofia, Bulgaria, commuting to the Czech Republic only when it is necessary. President Al-Qudah shall also not take up residence in Prague. This will save on the cost of maintaining their stay in the Czech capital.

o In lieu of salaries, as agreed, the President shall receive a monthly representation of $1,500 and the Treasurer, $1,000, in the discharge of their functions. The First and Second Vice President shall be entitled to $3,000 per annum, the Regional Vice Presidents, $1,200 per annum; and the Deputy Secretary-general and Deputy Treasurer, $1,200 also annually.

(*The total comes up to about $79,000, which will mean savings of $47,927 over last year's actual expense of $127,427 for the same line item.)

o Salaries and wages for the IOJ staff shall be kept within the $100,000 limit and those at Mondiapress, including administrative and other expanses, shall be pegged at between $200,000-$300,000 to fit into a $500,000 budget for 1995.

[...]

ANTONIO Ma. NIEVA
Secretary-General

INTERNATIONAL ORGANIZATION OF JOURNALISTS

INTERNAL BRIEFING NO. 2

F O R : The EXECUTIVE COMMITTEE

F R O M : The SECRETARY-GENERAL

R E : 26 MAY 1995

==

1. IOJ QUESTIONS ITS EXPULSION IN COURT

ON May 19, 1995, the International Organization of Journalists formally appealed before the Supreme Court its expulsion from the Czech Republic by the Ministry of the Interior.

The IOJ had 60 days from receipt of the March 8, 1995 decision handed down by Interior Minister Jan Rmel, to elevate the issue to the administration court, the deadline falling on a Saturday, May 20.

Having exhausted all administrative remedies in trying to get the Interior Ministry to reconsider its decision, judicial redress was now the only recourse left for the IOJ.

The IOJ's petition for relief, prepared by the Advocate Irena Helmova of the law office of Aure, sought basically two things:

o Restrain the Ministry of the Interior from executing the order under question while the appeal is being heard; and

(*This prayer for temporary restraining order is necessary because the appeal in itself, under Czech law, has no suspensory effect on the ruling.)

o Invalidate the expulsion order for having had no legal basis in fact, and for violating due process.

A day before the case was filed, Ms. Helmova sat down with the President, Suleiman Al-Qudah, and Secretary-General Antonio Ma. Nieva, upon request of the Secretariat, for a rump session to test the soundness of our arguments and to finalize the legal brief.

1.a BACKGROUNDER ON EXPULSION

Minister Rmel's March 8, 1995 decision was issued on a petition filed three years ago by the IOJ with then Ministry of the Interior of the former Czechoslovak Federal Republic on 23 December 1991, appealing the expulsion of its headquarters from Czechoslovakia and a ban on its activities on federal territory on Aug. 1, 1991 (Ref. No. KR-2106/91).

The Federal Ministry had rejected that first appeal on 23 December 1991 (Ref. 2 D - 392/L-91) to confirm the expulsion order, prompting the IOJ to ask for reconsideration. This, too, was turned down by the Ministry in a ruling on 7 December 1992 (Ref. 2 D - 246/L-92). A second petition has remained unacted on to this day.

That Federal Ministry action of 7 December 1992 reconfirmed the expulsion of the IOJ but rescinded the ban on the conduct of its its activities, as a result of a decision by the Constitutional Court on an appeal by the World Federation of Trade Unions, one of the three international organizations expelled by the government (the third organization is the International Students Union).

The IOJ's protest of the 7 December 1992 federal ruling formed the basis for Rmel's March 8 decision.

1.b NO LEGAL BASIS FOR RMEL RULING

We maintain that Rmel's ruling, Ref. LK-4747/93-537, has no legal basis and, in fact, violated due process and the rule of law (Czech Statute 116/1985, as amended by Statute 157/1989).

The IOJ contends that the ruling is grounded on mainly political reasons that are moreover unspecific and very general and, therefore, grossly unjust.

Minister Rmel's order merely restates the government's prerogative to remove from Czech territory any international organization that ''pursues activities that are in contradiction with the conditions laid down by law.''

He justified the expulsion of the IOJ by arguing that, in the first place, the decision to allow the Organization to establish its headquarters in Czechoslovakia was a political one by the former totalitarian regime, and that it supported the political and ideological goals of that regime.

Because the totalitarian regime had been swept away, therefore, there is no reason for the IOJ to remain in the Czech Republic.

The decision noted that ''the changes in personnel and in the internal structure of the Organization after 1989 have not changed the essen of the Organization's character today.''

Nowhere in that decision is there any mention of any paricular violation by the IOJ of Statute 116/1985, as amended by Statute 157/1989.

We have pointed out that it was not the former totalitarian regime that allowed the IOJ to set up its headquarters in Prague but the freely elected Czechoslovak government of 1946.

We are also maintaining that nowhere in its basic documents, including its statutes before or after 1989, has the IOJ advocated support for totalitarianism or the subversion of the Czech government or developed any activity in conflict with Czech law or its own statutes.

We cited CSFR Ruling No. 208 of 4 April 1991 by a government body that investigated the IOJ and exonerated it of any wrongdoing. That ruling stated there was no legal basis to end the Organization's activities in the Czech territory.

We argued that Rmel's characterization of the IOJ as an organization that undertakes activities contrary to law in no way corresponds to our orientation and actual activities, much less to the democratic transformation of the IOJ since Harare in 1991 that followed the political changes in Czechoslovakia itself.

We are reiterating that the IOJ is an international, non-governmental, democratic and professional organization of journalists, committed solely to defending the professional rights of media practitioners and the principles of freedom of information and expression as guaranteed by the Universal Declaration of Human Rights.

1.c PROSPECTS OF THE CASE

It will take the Administration Court at least two months to adjudicate the case, according to our legal advisers.

We have a fairly strong chance of winning the case since most of the accusations raised to justify the IOJ's expulsion are unsubstantiated and without legal basis.

Our arguments are sound. and we are closely monitoring the legal proceedings. Only a most biased judge will be blind to the injustice inflicted on the IOJ.

ANTONIO Ma. NIEVA
Secretary-general

Prague, May 26 1995

APPENDIX 33. IOJ HOMEPAGE 1995

International Organisation of Journalists http://www.anet.cz/iojgs/#Index

International Organisation of Journalists

Home page in Prague

You are 00079 visitor of this page.

French Spanish

PRIMER

Know your IOJ

This primer introduces the journalist to the International Organization of Journalists, describing its vital role in the advocacy of the journalists' cause.

The times as that folk song goes they are a changing. The world has grown much smaller, circumscribed in cyberspace by the Computer and Internet, the cold war is over, but the dangers confronting the journalist have not lessened. They are more pronounced.

Newsmen everywhere are still dying violently. Many are languishing in jail. Wherever they are, media professionals must confront intolerance in various forms.

For the IOJ, the work is never done. Vigilance continues.

In these new and more perilous times, the IOJ assumes more crucial responsibilities in promoting freedom of expression and safeguarding the rights of the working press.

Read on, and find out why and how.

ANTONIO Ma. NIEVA
Secretary-General
E-mail: iojgs@bohem-net.cz
Prague, August 15,1995

What's it all about?

It's about press freedom, and caring and feeling for the working newsman, promoting his welfare and protection, ensuring his professional development, and securing his right to practice his profession freely and without fear or moral reservation.

The International Organisation of Journalists (IOJ) unites 250,000 journalists in print, television and broadcast around the world. It embraces 94 affiliate unions and organisations in 94 countries.

How did it come to be?

The IOJ was organised in June 1946 in Copenhagen, Denmark in a landmark International Congress of Journalists participated in by 21 national journalists organizations encompassing 130,000 newsmen.

Among the watershed resolutions passed by that first Congress of' the IOJ was a document abduring war and calling on all journalists to lent themselves to the cause of peace.

What does it hope to accomplish?

The IOJ endeavours to
- Improve job security and working conditions of journalists through the mechanism of collective bargaining.
- Raise their professional standards and strengthen their social responsibility.
- Secure their protection on while on dangerous missions.
- Work for the democratisation of media at all levels, and the people's right to truthful and unbiased information on the basis of the Universal Declaration of Human Rights.
- Articulate the journalists' cause before the United Nations and its agencies.
- Struggle against censorship.
- Promote new technologies, and the covenants on copyright and intellectual property rights (IPR).

How fares the IOJ?

It fares vigorous and well, in an atmosphere of democracy and pluralism, committed to advance the advocacy of journalism and press freedom into the 2lst century.
The IOJ maintains its headquarters in Prague, the CzechRepublic, and regional centers in Mexico, for Latin America; Paris, for Europe; Pyongyong, People's Democratic Republic of Korea, for Asia; and Sanaa, Yemen, for the Arab world.

Is the IOJ 'political'?

It is, in the advocacy of journalism, freedom of expression, and journalists' rights.
The IOJ is independent of any government, political ideology or party. It is a pluralistic, non-profit international non-government organization holding consultative status with the the U.N. Economic and Social Commission (Ecoosoc) and UNESCO.
It works in close collaboration with the U.N. Commission for Human rights, the International Labor Organisation, and the World Intellectual Property Organisation (WIPO), the International Committee of the Red Cross, Amnesty International, as well as other international and regional medial organisations.

Who funds the IOJ?

The IOJ derives its revenues from the membership dues paid by its affiliate organisations, and mainly from the business activities of its enterprises.
These are limited-liability companies engaged in printing, car-rental, restaurant, hotel and pension house operations, and interpreting and translation services.

How does it work?

The Congress of affiliate unions is the highest policy making body of the IOJ. It convenes every four years to review the IOJ's programs, approve new member-organizations, and lay down programs of action.
In between congresses, the IOJ is governed by the Executive Committee, a 21-man body that includes the President, two Vice Presidents, The Secretary General and a Deputy, the Treasurer and a Deputy, seven Regional Vice Presidents, and seven other members representing the regions. The E.C. supervises the work of the IOJ and implements the decisions of the Congress.
The Secretariat is the executive body of the IOJ. It carries out the day-to-day work of the organization. It is headed by the Secretary-general, the chief executive officer, who is accountable to the E.C.

Who can join the IOJ?

Any journalist's union or professional organization can affiliate with the IOJ as a regular member, for as long as it meets the conditions set forth in the IOJ's statutes.
If it does not meet all the conditions but agrees with the aims of the IOJ, it can qualify as an associate member.
Associate members cannot vote nor seek representation in an elective office in the IOJ.

Who are the leaders of the IOJ?

The President is Suleiman Al-Qudah, from Jordan.

Juan Carlos Camano, of Argentina, is First Vice president, while Moses Nagamootoo of Guyana, is Second Vice President.
The Secretary-General is Antonio Ma. Nieva of the Philippines, and the Deputy, Kindness Paradza of Zimbabwe.
The Treasurer is Alexander Angelov of Bulgaria while his Deputy is Shahul H. Abdul Careem of Sri Lanka.
The Seven Regional Vice Presidents are Jean-Francois Tealdi of France, for Europe; Kevin Lynch of the United States, for North America; Tubal Paez Hernandez of Cuba, for Latin America; Earl Bousquet of Sta. Lucia for the Caribbean; Ladi Lawal of Nigeria, for Africa; R. Naem Toubase of Palestine, for the Arab Region; and Phang Quang of Vietnam, for Asia and Oceania;
The other members of the E.C. are Hilario Manuel Matusse, representing Africa; Luis Carlos de Assis Bernardes of Brazil, Latin America; Stanley Palmoen Sidoel of Surinam, Caribbean; Abdel Allateef Aouad of Morroco, Arab Region; Jose Armando Martins Morim of Portugal, Europe; and Ram K. Karmacharya of Nepal, Asia and Oceania.

APPENDIX 34. REPORT OF THE EXECUTIVE COMMITTEE IN PRAGUE 1995

R A I S E T H E I O J B A C K
T O I T S F E E T

A DRAFT ACTION PLAN FOR 1995-96

1 - RATIONALE

THIS is a draft Program of Action for 1995 designed to enable the International Organization of Journalists to fulfill its statutory mandate as well as to carry out the resolutions of the X11 Congress in Amman, Jordan.

It was evolved from a critical analysis of the IOJ's problems, external and internal, and is therefore circumscribed by the limitations of the 1995 Budget (See Financial Annex).

The budget, at the very least, ensures only the most minimal operations for the IOJ, enabling the Organization to remain alive but without the logistical reserve to exercise the full range of its functions unless a determined and sustained effort is exerted to source funds from non-traditional sources for the IOJ's political and professional work.

If so, it would require innovative networking and linkaging with IOJ and non-IOJ institutions and organizations, and sustained cost-cutting. The austerity policy would have to be kept in balance with priorities to prevent the IOJ from coming to a complete paralyzation/standstill.

The reality is the IOJ is financially at its most critical period where it must go through intensive care in order to keep itself alive. Our enterprises, the limited-liability companies, are in no position to deliver surplus revenues for the Organization, having themselves been the victims of the internal crises that plagued the leadership these last four years.

Our cash position is down and will remain so in the near future.

The IOJ has lost considerable ground around the world, the process of attrition from the collapse of the Socialist bloc eroding its influence and chipping away at its membership.

From scores of personnel, the Secretariat has been reduced to a skeleton staff without the capability of maximum performance but unable to hire new people to strengthen the work force because of our financial debilitation.

In Prague itself, the IOJ is locked in a court case with the Ministry of the Interior to retain its headquarters in the Czech Republic. Four years since 1991, when the government ruling expelling the IOJ was handed down, the Organization has remained in political isolation, under siege from the Czech government and media.

This is the general environment in which the IOJ must perform its work in 1995, the eve of its 50th founding anniversary.

II - MOBILIZATION AND CONSOLIDATION

For the IOJ to surmount its most difficult period, it has to mobilize and consolidate, a minimum requirement for organizational survival, and consciously anchor political and professional work on an economic orientation. It must go through a period of purging and rehabilitation in the process of renewal.

All forms of profligate practices must cease, while all affiliate Unions must share the burden of putting the IOJ back on its feet through payment of dues and involvement in the Organization's economic projects.

Three priorities must be addressed, not necessarily in the order of their presentation. The IOJ must

o Generate new money from non-traditional sources (funding institutions: the UNESCO, private foundations, commercial sponsorships, revenue-generating projects, i.e., publications, and annual dues from the member organizations), while realigning or expanding -- where the situation calls for it -- the business activities of our enterprises and tightening management control over them.

o In support of the above, mobilize in the widest possible way the Organization's biggest -- and heretofore largely untapped -- resource, its 121 affiliate unions and media associations in 94 countries, for economic projects.

o Systematically campaign to build up a more favorable environment in Prague for the Organization to operate in.

III - IMMEDIATE, MEDIUM-TERM OBJECTIVES

This program shall encompass two mutually inclusive objectives, namely:

a. Raise the the IOJ back to its feet, in the short term, which attainment shall

b. Into the second year of this administration, the intermediate target, stabilize the IOJ enough to restore normalcy to its functions in the long term.

IV - FOUR LEVELS OF ACTION

Strategies of work must be developed at four levels:

1. International

Involves the following concerns:

1.a The IOJ's continuing effort to work out closer linkage with the International Federation of Journalists, i.e., unification of the world journalists movement, joint action to protect journalists, rapid unilateral response to incidents of violence inflicted on media practitioners.

1.b The campaign to upgrade the IOJ's consultative status with UNESCO from Category B to Category A before the end of 1995, acquire official accreditation with the United Nations as well as the newly established World Trade Organization, and secure consulting status with existing inter-government regional blocs.

1.c Closer rapport with United Nations institutions and international non-government organizations in the promotion of human rights, trade union organizing and protection of workers' rights, the environment, peace, and other concerns; linkaging with other fraternal organizations and institutions involved in mass communication advocacy.

1.d Preparations for the IOJ's Golden Anniversary celebration in June 1996.

1.e Reactivation of All-China Journalists Association's membership in the IOJ.

(See Work Plan 1)

2. Regional

2.a More comprehensive interaction with the IOJ Regional Centers' in recruitment, mobilization and consolidation of the general membership, and expansion of their role of carrying out the Organization's political and professional work to include tasking for economic projects.

2.b Linkaging with regional non-government organizations and other media institutions, in furtherance of the ends defined in 2.a.

(Work Plan 11 Appended, Incorporates Plans of Action of the Centers)

3. National

3.a Continuous networking with member unions and other affiliates, and their reorientation toward self-reliance through sustainable economic ventures undertaken independently or jointly with the IOJ.

3.b The organization of cost-effective, self-liquidating projects, professional and economic -- trade union seminars, skills-upgrading workshops, publications, etc.

3.c Purging of the membership roster to remove ''ghost'' unions.

3.d Revival of the membership drive (The IOJ lost at least 19 unions from 1991): Reestablishing contact with the affiliate organizations in the former Soviet Union, reactivating the membership of the All-China Journalists Association, recruitment of new affiliates.

(The Secretariat, Regional Centers' operations)

4. The Czech Republic

4.a The creation of more favorable conditions in the Czech Republic, particularly in Prague, to end the IOJ's political isolation.

4.b Networking an outreach program with the Association of Czech Journalists and the diplomatic community to reestablish goodwill with the Czech government and media.

4.c More positive exposure of the Organization and its activities worldwide, particularly in the protection of journalists, in the international press -- and specifically in the Czech media.

(See Work Plan 111)

V - METHODS

o The Secretariat shall exercise the dual role of implementing body for the IOJ's mandate and catalyst for business development for the Organization, opening new journalism-related projects that could generate revenue for IOJ and networking market connections for the enterprises.

o Where it is applicable, professional work and revenue generation shall be carried out by the Secretariat directly or via the companies through the strategic projects outlined in the work plans.

o Tighter management control over the enterprises by the Supervisory Board, the process to include expansion or realignment of their lines of activities.

Non-profitable companies either to be dissolved or merged with the more liquid enterprises; non-performing and idle assets in the general inventory to be converted into cash or networked with econonic activities for revenue generation.

(Requirements: Regular weekly briefings with company managers and fortnightly meetings of the Board, and the possible conversion of Mondiapress into a holding company.

o Sustained cost-cutting in operational costs, adoption of less expensive modes of communication, i.e., E-mail in lieu of fax, special telephone discount services.

o Possible further reduction of IOJ workforce, if necessary, and elimination of non-productive cost areas, i.e., parking at Intercon, utilization of vehicles.

CONCLUSIONS OF THE SESSION

The Executive Committee (EC) of the International Organization of Journalists convened on 21-23 June 1995 in Prague, the Czech Republic.

The participants are listed in Annex 1.

During the session, the Action Plan for 1995-97 was unanimously approved on the basis of availability of funds. The EC agreed to replace former Secretary General Gerard Gatinot as general manager of Mondiapress with Secretary General Antonio Ma.Nieva. It decided to deny as well claims for indemnification of presumed urgent expenses presented both by Gatinot and former Treasurer Marian Grigore. In the case of expenses of the Paris Center and of the former IOJ legal counsel, Mojmir Moravec, it was agreed to leave it up to the SG to settle in accordance with law.

The EC approved the reports presented by the General Secretary and Treasurer Alexander Anguelov and the budget for 1995-96. In a departure from previous practice, the EC agreed to assign a salary only to the Secretary General. The President and Treasurer, along with the Vice Presidents, would be alloted only minimal funding to cover costs connected with their work. Some of the EC members expressed concern over the disproportion between the early expenditure in the budget and the activities of IOJ. It was explained that such cost was incurred during the first three months of the year and corresponds primarily to the expenses of the former leadership.

Among the most discussed subjects was the management of IOJ property. The reports of Mrs Ivana Kuberová as well as of the President of the Audit and Control Commission, Luis Castro, are enclosed in Annex II of this document. The EC resolved to authorize the Secretary General to shut down non-productive enterprises and take other steps to build up the productive ones. As regards the proposal for an external audit, the EC decided it would be commissioned only if there are funds for it and if the new management considers it indispensable.

The body decided to intensify the activities of the regional centers. In the case of Africa, it was agreed to reserve 5000 USD for a Center until the African group reaches a definite decision on how and where it shall function. .

It was further agreed to mobilize the affiliate organizations to send solidarity assistance, in cash or kind, to the Association of Journalists of Cuba. During the session, some EC members gave positive answer to this initiative while others said they would discuss it with their unions but gave assurance they would support the campaign.

As regards relations between the IOJ and the International Federation of Journalists, the EC resolved to send a positive response to the IFJ on their Congress resolution for concrete cooperation with the IOJ.

The EC resolved as well to support the proposal of journalists of Latin America to proclaim April 11 as a Day of Solidarity with journalists in the region and to support FELAP's 7th Congress in Argentine.

On the proposal of the Arab group, the EC agreed to include in the final declaration an expression of support for journalists of Iraq, Palestine, Egypt and Algeria. It was agreed as well to open an IOJ office in Jerusalem.

The EC agreed to support a meeting of journalists of the Caribbean region in Santa Lucia.

It also agreed to look into the status of the printing equipment at the Addis Ababa center and its possible transfer to Sana'a, as well as the recovery of the printing machine donated to the Indian Federation of Working Journalists. The EC agreed to delete the IFWJ from the IOJ's roster and to authorize the Secretary General to bring legal action against its president, Vikram Rao.

A resolution was approved on the promotion of closer relations with the UNESCO and support for ties with other United Nations organizations.

The EC approved a resolution expressing appreciation to Miguel Rivero for his work during the session.

The last item in the agenda, the offer of the Vietnam Journalists Association to host the next meeting of the EC, was accepted and approved subject to the availability of funds. Otherwise, the next meeting shall again be held in Prague to save on expenses.

The President said he was gratified by the results of the meeting. At its conclusion, Suleiman Al-Qudah said: "We are going in the right direction ... I would like to say that this organization can maintain its position." He asked all participants to have confidence in themselves and in each other if we want to go further." He expressed for the work of the Secretary General, and added that the accomplishments in the last three months were the result of the collective effort of the President, General Secretary, and Treasurer.

Prague, June 23, 1995.

ATTESTED

Antonio Ma. Nieva
Secretary General

NOTED

Suleiman Al-Qudah
President

PROCEEDINGS

[...]

Secretary General Nieva read his report on the current situation of the organization and presented the accounts of former Secretary General Gérard Gatinot to the Executive Committee for decision. He noted the disorder in the archivers and the lack of documentation, mainly on the transfer of printing machines to the Center at Addis Ababa and to the Indian union.

Tealdi intervened to remind about the importance of contacts with the International Federarion of Journalists as well as the results of its last congress. He said the UNESCO was ready to cooperate with the IOJ. Explaining the activities of the IFJ, he said about 75 % its funding came, from external sources, two-thirds of its budget is covered by the European Union. The FIJ, he said, owned offices in Algeria and Peru, and helps Palestinians by means of Scandinavian funds. Further more, he said, there were organizations with membership both in IOJ and FIJ. They uphold important activities on all-European scope, he said, for instance organizing in the former Yugoslavia seminars about European television supported by the European Union, a conference on copyright as well as a seminar about independent journalists. They organized meetings also in the Czech Republic.

Tealdi recalled that during the IFJ Congress in Santander, which he attended as observer, relations with the IOJ provoked a general discussion. His speech, he said, was mainly about the IOJ's wish for exchange and cooperation. Great Britain proposed a fusion of both organisations, he said, triggering a big discussion that could be summarized, thugly: The, Czech syndicate declared that IOJ remained a tool of „Soviet imperialism" and said that 60 communists of the extreme left were in the organization. The French declared that the IOJ could "poison" the IFJ. The Nepalese declared that the IOJ was cooperating with non-existent organizations and that it was financing personalities who were non-journalists. Linde, the IFJ President, said, he was ready to cooperate but not to carry things too far. He called on the delegates to wote against union with the IOJ. In spite of the IFJ President's position, the congress woted in favour of union and joint actions with the IOJ. The result of vote was: 133 for, 70 against, and 40 abstentions. There were organizations with dual membership, such as South Korea, Romania and Costa Rica which voted against or abstained, according to Tealdi.

[...]

The Secretary General proposed a resolution reciprocating the IFJ's own resolution urging unification of the World journalists movement and the creation of contact group to discuss joint projects with the IOJ. He said the IOJ should react positively on the IFJ initiative. Morim said he was for initiating moves toward unification but would like first to read the text of any formulation. The formulation must be clear, he said.

The Secretary General said the idea had already been incorporated into the Plan of Action. He said the proposal was for this session of the Executive Committee to organize a working group that would study 4 possibilities as a reciprocal gesture for the IFJ's resolution.

Bousquet said that talking of a merger of the two organizations always stirred trepidation among some IOJ members. He reminded the body that the IOJ Congress was for cooperation and solidarity actions but not an obligation of merger.

President said it was purely a response to the IFJ. This trend could be supported as discussed in Amman and by the previous day's session, as the IOJ's answer to the IFJ. It was put to a vote, and unanimously approved.

[...]

The President opened the session and gave the floor to Auditing Commission President Luis Castro.

Citing the Statutes, Castro said the Audit and Controls Commission should have met prior to a session of the Executive Committee, but was nevertheless accepting the reports of the Secretary General and President and confirmed the need to apply strict measures to save the IOJ. Because he exercised no voting right, he proposed to review the report of Ivana Kuberová and to conduct an inspection of accounts,on the bassis o which he would present a report on the financial situation of the organization. The body approved the proposal.

Mrs Kuberová explained that her report was prepared by the of Board of management of IOJ enterprises and that it discussed utilization of capital of the IOJ in the Czech Republic. The results of the period, January-April 1995, reflected considerable improvement in all economic indices, she said. Equally, Editpress and Gatus achieved positive results. The same positive trend was also reported by Technical Services, which incurred no losses. The Secretary General participate in the meetings of the supervisory Board. Previously no such thing happened. Directors of establishments asked to be informed about changes in the IOJ's top leadership as well as other statutory of changes.

Treasurer Anguelov asked Mrs. Kuberová to explain the current condition of IOJ property as there was lack of information about the legal situation of these assets.

Mrs. Kuberová said immovables owned by IOJ and its limited-liability companies in the Czech and Slovak territory as follows:
- A house in Bratislava, managed by Sprint Press, s.r.o. is part of its capital stock.
- A building in Prague, used by establishment Technickal Services, it is rented out, with the company maintaining its offices on the ground floor.
- A house in Brno, part of basic capital of Engineering Services, s.r.o.
- A building at the Harrachov, mountain resort, with 20 beds, belonging to Mondiapress.
- An apartment building with 4 flats in which the Secretary General, Mrs. Navarette, and Gamal are living. It belongs to Mondiapress.
- A building in Prague 4 where delegates are accommodated. It is a villa bringing profit to Mondiapress.

Rented flats which do not belong to the IOJ:
Donovalská-Street: It is necessary to move out.
Českolipská-Street: A cooperative flat. It is registered under the name of a former Germasn Secretary of the IOJ.
Prague 5: Owned by the administration of Services of Diplomatic Corps, now used as storage place by the former Secretary General.. There is a notice to vacate.
Rybná-Street Prague 1: Property of the municipality of Prague. Since 1991 there is a notice to vacate but an agreement with the tenants cooperative was signed. It is residential flat of Mr. Gatinot.
Jevany, including, building, and woods: It is unused.
Bílá Hora: IOJ has been using it since 1982 free of charge on a usufruct contract for 30 years. The building has been restituted to the owner, it is managed by Gatus.
A recreation center Godollo in the vicinity of Budapest.
Aflat in Mexico: A The Latin-American center uses it.
A flat in Paris: Site of the former center.

[...]

The Secretary General said the IOJ had little money left. While it owned companies, in the course of political changes it lost property which ended in the hands of private individuals. Personal conflicts within the organization contributed to the catastrophe. In the last four years, he said, the IOJ lost USD 10 million, and therefore he proposed to create new sources o. incomes -- to improve management of companies whis operated previously with little control, to found new commercial activities, and to introduce new systems. While the conditions of the companies are expected to improve, he said, their contribution to the budget is not likely to exceed 1%. He said the IOJ could not afford to give thousands of dollars to member organizastions. Even the IFJ is not that charitable to its members -- their delegates were required to pay part of their travell expenses to their Congress. The IOJ must adopt similar measures. He said he had analyzed the situation in the last two months and reviewed internal matters. He proposed to find help abroad.

[...]

APPENDIX 35. REPORT TO THE EXECUTIVE COMMITTEE IN HANOI 1996 (EXCERPTS)

The IOJ: It lives yet to fight one more year

The good news is the International Organization of Journalists, against all predictions to the contrary, is still alive, albeit not exactly vigorously kicking, to celebrate the golden anniversary of its founding in 1946.

It is a small blessing to be thankful for on this 50th year of the Organization's existence when ill-wishers, both within and without, were trumpeting in 1995 that the XIIth Congress in Amman, Jordan was the IOJ's final gasp of breath.

This means that each additional year of its existence from 1995 represents a major victory, moral and institutional, for the IOJ and the world journalists' movement.

The bad news is the IOJ has enough funds to support operations only for one more year despite the most rigorous belt-tightening. We have about US$ 400,000 left in our account, or less than 50 per cent of last year's approved budget of US$ 826,460 – effectively US$ 416,000, since US$ 410,000 had already been spent on the Amman Congress even before the new leadership took over.

But the IOJ has also learned to cope with the exigencies of survival under harsh conditions. It is adapting to the new realities.

Bracing for harder times

Belt-tightening continues in the manner prescribed by the Executive Committee in June 1995. The payroll of both Mondiapress and IOJ has been slashed by 20 employees to realize savings of

2,010,700 Czech crowns (about US$ 73,116) for 1995–96, and annually thereafter from 1997, at least 3,406,980 Kč, or $123,887.

Among those who were given their walking papers were the Administrative Manager, Chief Accountant, and Building and Maintenance Supervisor of Mondiapress.

From the 15 vehicles already sold, we generated 1,486,000 Kč ($54,036), from which proceeds the separation benefits for the 20 employees estimated at of 386,930 Kč ($11,161) are being drawn. Eight more vehicles are up for sale.

The dismantling of the Transport Service has also removed a source of petty graft among employees – and an unnecessary cost, 680,000 Kč or $24,727 representing yearly amortization of the vehicles, from the accountancy books of the IOJ.

The relocation to *Bílá Hora* of both the IOJ and Mondiapress accountancies from No. 7 *Washingtonova Street* in Prague 1 was accomplished in mid-January 1995 (the Secretariat is gradually moving to the same place) despite attempts by some conspirators within the company to sabotage the move.

The same disruptive elements, in collusion with outside parties, were thwarted in their plot – uncovered late last year – to wrest control of the Secretariat and IOJ Accountancy, obviously with the goal of eventually liquidating from within the Organization in the Czech Republic.

The Organization has since taken measures to reestablish its statutory control and authority over the companies.

Our transfer to *Bílá Hora* (about 15 km in the suburbs from downtown Prague) saves us 720,000 Kč ($26,181) in rentals annually. It also generated 900,000 Kč (US$ 32,727) for the IOJ – 700,000 Kč ($25,454) representing the balance of our original 9-million Kč (US$ 327,272) (of which 6.4 million Kč ($232,727) was forfeited through a bad rental contract that the dismissed Administrative Manager signed in 1993 with the building owner) and 200,000 Kč ($7,272) in payment for structural fixtures (boiler, etc.) left behind.

Complementing these fiscal moves, two companies are being merged with Mondiapress, s.r.o., the IOJ's flagship enterprise, a third has been sold, while a fourth is being offered for sale to interested buyers.

The objective is to reduce the number of IOJ companies from 10 to four or five for easier controls.

(For details, see Report on IOJ Enterprises.)

Payback time for previous errors

The radioactive fallout from the errors of 1991–94 continues to keep the Organization catatonic well into the 18th month of this administration, and we have paid through the nose for it, a total 855,050 Kč ($31,093) thus far, summarized as follows:

A fine of 50,000 Kč ($8,818) paid late last year to the Municipal Finance Office of Prague 1 for a serious shortcoming in the accounting system in 1992–93 that the dismissed Administrative Manager, as the IOJ's authorized tax representative, never bothered to rectify.

235,943 Kč ($8,580) paid last April to the Municipal Finance Office for unremitted value added tax collected on services by the IOJ in 1994.

A total 213,408 Kč or $7,760 (156,468 Kč of it, about $5,617, in claims for back wages, plus lawyer's fees and judicial costs) coughed up also last April to Milos Jakeš, the former Director- general for Enterprises, as per ruling of the Prague 1 District Court upholding his suit for illegal dismissal in 1990.

300,812 Kč ($10,939) paid in May to Czech Customs on import taxed incurred in 1991 that remained unpaid despite two previous collection notices in 1993 and 1994 to the former Administrative Manager.

54,887 Kč, or $1,996, in lawyer's fees paid again last April to a legal counsel, Dr. Čechová, for services rendered in successfully prosecuting a 5-million Kč. collection suit against a debtor firm, Nanka, Ltd. for the IOJ in 1993–94.

Direct/indirect losses

Since June 1995, through painstaking reconstruction of "misplaced" or "lost" documents, we have uncovered roughly 17 million Kč. ($618,182) in losses, direct or indirect, resulting from willful neglect, errors and questionable acts of omission or commission by the previous leadership and management in Prague.

This is apart from the 855,050 Kč. ($31,093) in unscheduled but obligatory payments made recently by the IOJ on old payables, fines, unpaid import taxes, etc., which may be written down as part of the losses.

There is no way of ascertaining the pecuniary damage wrought on the IOJ down to the last crown, much less any chance of recovering any money, but he inquiry continues nevertheless if only to establish ex- post facto responsibility for the tragedy.

Direct total losses include the overpayment to Mondiapress of 1,332,328 Kč/ $48,448 – 1,062,328 Kč. ($38,630) to cover the January–September 1995 salaries of IOJ personnel on its payroll and 270,000 Kč ($9,818) for the 13th month pay of the employees in June 1995, through outright misrepresentation by the former Administrative Manager.

Still another instance of direct loss for the IOJ has been the misappropriation of 1.5 million Kč ($54,545) in rentals of construction equipment owned by the inactive IOJ company, Combild, s.r.o., for the year 1995 (1994 figures are not available because of scant documentation) alone.

'Sweetheart' rental contracts

In two instances, the IOJ lost 13,627,216 Kč ($495,535) non-refundable investments on building repairs and reconstruction forfeited via "sweetheart" rental contracts signed by the dismissed Administrative manager.

In the capacity of "IOJ General Manager", a non-existent position, the former Administrative Manager of Mondiapress signed a rental contract for the Washingtonova offices under terms grossly inimical to the interest of the Organization because of its "indefinite duration" clause. This provision legally enables the landlord to evict his tenant at any time, without giving justifiable cause.

That same contract, finalized without the knowledge or consent of the former Secretary General or consultation with our legal counsels, downgraded the Organization's investment of 9 million Kč ($94,545).

Coupled with this enormous indirect loss of 6.4 million Kč ($232,727) was the discovery only this June by the Supervisory Board of a similar loss, under starkly similar circumstances, of 7,227,216 Kč ($262,808) invested by the IOJ for the reconstruction of a building housing Editpress' printing plant in Rudná, about 30 km from Prague.

[...]

Doing so much with so little

We have not been able to accomplish much on the basis of the Plan of Action for 1995–97 adopted by the Executive Committee in June 1995 – but the little that has been achieved, however modest the gains, is definitely a breakthrough against the financial debilitation that had effectively immobilized us.

It means that we are at last moving forward in spite of our prostration from the troubles of 1991–94. Where before the IOJ encountered only setbacks, we have started to score minor victories.

The Organization made its presence felt in the Arab world last January during the Regional Seminar for the Promotion of an Independent and Pluralistic Arab Media in Yemen and in Latin America during the Federation of Latin American Journalists' VIIth Congress and the Third Encounter of Ibero-American Journalists in Buenos Aires in October 1995.

Relations with the UNESCO are cordial, and prospects are rife for expanding contacts and co-operation not only with this U.N. agency but also with other international institutions involved in professional and trade union work in mass media.

The IOJ is online on the Internet with its own website – http://www.anet.cz/iojgs – installed March 16, 1995 through a hookup with the Czech server company, Cesnet, s.r.o., and electronic mailbox: iojgs@ bohem-net.cz. The homepage, which carries basic information on the IOJ, may be accessed in English, French, or Spanish with any browser program.

[...]

Slightly better political situation

The onset of the 50th anniversary of the IOJ finds the Organization enjoying a slightly improved political situation in Prague, vis-a-vis the expulsion issue, as a result of a legal opinion by the Ministry of the Interior that the Organization "may continue pursuing its operations in the Czech Republic with the existence of its office in the Republic being envisaged".

The opinion was rendered Jan. 15, 1995 in response to an order by the Supreme Court, before which the IOJ had appealed the expulsion of its headquarters from the Czech Republic, on the ground of unsubstantiated accusations.

Previously, the Ministry's position stipulated only that the IOJ could continue its operations in the country, without mention of an office. This particular clause was pounced on by certain mischievous fringe elements to stress the IOJ's dependency on them, with the self-serving interpretation that only through a local organization could it carry out any activities in Prague.

The Ministry's January 1995 stand is unquestionably an expansion of its previous ruling on the IOJ's presence, this time allowing it to set up a bureau or office in the country.

New status with Unesco

In June 1996, the Secretariat was informed that the United Nations Educational, Scientific and Cultural Organization had upgraded the IOJ from Category B to the new status of "Operational Relations", along with 47 other international non-government organizations.

"Operational Relations" is the second level of formal accreditation under the new system approved by the UNESCO General Assembly. The first level consists of "Associate Relations" and "Consultative Relations", in that order.

[...]

Fourteen Category-A NGOs and 11 networks were admitted to "Consultative Relations".

Eight Category-A NGOs were downgraded to "Operational Relations" while one was dropped to the deferred list along with 314 organizations for incomplete documentation or failure to comply with requirements.

The International Federation of Journalists, a Category-A status, was among those organizations whose reclassification was deferred until the 150th session of the UNESCO Executive Board next year.

In the meantime, working journalists have no representation on the first level ("Associate" or "Consultative") of formal relations, into which two publishers groups have been admitted – the International Newspaper Publishers Association.

[...]

New, more creative survival measures

This is how it has been for the IOJ in the 12 months since the last Executive Committee meeting in Prague.

The leadership, collectively, has done its best to steer the Organization past the most critical period of its existence, but we are not yet over the crisis.

We have adopted draconian fiscal measures to slash costs and minimize spending, but we have only succeeded in staving off the inevitable.

It will take time for the IOJ to recover, and we are in short supply of it. If the Organization is to live on, we must resort to new, creative measures of survival.

This should be the primal concern of everyone within the IOJ family.

For a long time, the Organization extended a generous helping hand to many affiliate organizations around the world, dispensing hundreds of thousands of dollars in solidarity assistance.

This time around, it is the IOJ that is need of a helping hand.

APPENDIX 36. IOJ LETTER TO THE IFJ CONGRESS IN ANGERS 2016

Message to the 29th IFJ Congress in Angers, France, on 7–10 June 2016

Dear delegates – fellow journalists!

On this occasion we are invited to recall the history of our international movement. It is indeed a long and complicated story. The movement started over 120 years ago in 1894, when the first international conference of "press people" took place in Antwerp. But it took until after World War I for the first proper association of professional journalists to be established in 1926 with the encouragement of the International Labour Organization ILO and the League of Nations. It took as its name *Fédération Internationale des Journalistes* (FIJ) and its secretariat was located in Paris. The FIJ was destroyed by the German army's occupation of France in 1940. During World War II the movement was hosted by the British Union of Journalists, which helped to set up the *International Federation of Journalists of Allied or Free Countries.* This federation in exile organized new beginning for the movement in 1946 in Copenhagen, where the *International Organization of Journalists* (IOJ) was founded among Europeans together with Russians, Americans and Australians – as the legal successor of the FIJ.

The Cold War since the late 1940s led to a split in the movement, whereby the Western member unions left the IOJ and in 1952 established a new association, the present *International Federation of Journalists* (IFJ). Meanwhile, the IOJ consolidated itself in Eastern Europe and spread to the developing world. The world of journalist associations was divided between the Prague-based IOJ and the Brussels-based IFJ, with some, like the French and the Finns, having membership of both. The two internationals followed the Cold War division between "Communist East" and "Free West" leading to a politicization of the movement and a competition for new associations in the Third World.

The two world associations began to cooperate on common professional issues only in the 1970s, when a spirit of détente entered international politics. Bridge builders were especially the Italian and Finnish associations with a strategy for maximal unity of the international movement of professional journalists. This development was supported by UNESCO, leading to consultative meetings between the IOJ, IFJ and regional associations in Africa, Asia and Latin America, with joint measures in many professional questions, including ethics and safety of journalists. By 1991 both world associations were ready to negotiate on how to achieve a unity of the movement.

However, the fall of the Berlin Wall and the collapse of the Soviet Union led in the IOJ to a deterioration of what used to be the world's largest international organization of journalists and the IOJ withered into a nominal entity. Meanwhile, the IFJ grew in size and importance as most IOJ members joined it while retaining their formal membership in the IOJ. By the end of the millennium the movement had reverted to the pre-Cold World War situation, when journalists from all continents and geopolitical areas had effectively one platform for cooperation – first the FIJ and then the IOJ.

Today it is obvious that the IFJ is the sole representative of professional journalists around the world. This does not mean that the IFJ is the direct successor of the pre-war FIJ, whose legal heritage was passed to the IOJ. On this occasion of the 29th IFJ Congress in 2016 it is important that the IFJ perceives itself correctly in history as a successor of both the pre-war FIJ and the post-war IOJ. While celebrating the 90th anniversary of the founding of the FIJ, we should not forget that a common IOJ was founded in Copenhagen exactly 70 years ago, on 3–9 June 1946 – with high hopes, until it was split by the unfortunate Cold War.

Dear colleagues,

As the President of the IOJ and its Honorary President elected in the last IOJ Congress in Amman in 1995, we note that the historical development has led to a natural demise of the IOJ as an operational organization. While closing this page in history, we are pleased to pass on to the IFJ the heritage of the pre-war FIJ. We wish you every success in taking good care of this valuable heritage.

Amman and Maputo, 3 June 2016

Suleiman Al-Qudah, IOJ President

Manuel Tomé, IOJ Honorary President

BIBLIOGRAPHY

Books and articles cited

1er Congrès International de la presse (1894 – Anvers) (1984). Renseignements, Procès-vebaux des Séances et Discours communiqués. Antwerp: J. E. Buschmann.

4th Consultative Meeting of International and Regional Journalists' Organizations, Prague June, Paris November 1983 (1984). Prague: IOJ.

Agee, Philip (1977). *Inside the Company: CIA Diary*. Harmondsworth, UK: Penguin.

Beyersdorf, Frank and Nordenstreng, Kaarle (forthcoming). From Liberty of the Press to Advocacy of Peace: How the International Organization of Journalists Was Embroiled in the Cold War. (To be completed in the proofs)

Björk, Ulf Jonas (1996). The First International Organization of Journalists Debates News Copyright. *Journalism History*, Vol. 42, No. 2, pp. 56–63.

The Black Book for the Persecution of the Progressive and Democratic Journalists (1982). Documents of the International Forum for the Protection of Progressive and Democratic Journalists, Varna, Bulgaria, 14–16 October 1981. Sofia: International Committee for Protection of Journalists (INTERPRESS in Budapest).

Budapest Berlin Sofia & other training centres. A World Directory (1982). Compiled by Dr. Hans Treffkorn. Prague: IOJ.

Bureš, Oldřich, ed. (1977). *Current Views on the World Information Order*. Prague: IOJ.

The Chilean Coup and its Cruel Aftermath (1974). Prague: IOJ.

Chocarro Macesse, Silvia (2017). The United Nations'. Role in Promoting the Safety of Journalists from 1945 to 2016. In Ulla Carlsson and Reetta Pöyhtäri, eds.: *The Assault of Journalism. Building Knowledge to Protect Freedom of Expression*. Gothenburg: Nordicom. Available at http://nordicom.gu.se/en/publikationer/assault-journalism.

Conditions of Work and Life of Journalists (1928). Studies and Reports, Series I (Professional Workers), No. 2, Geneva: International Labour Office.

Cowley, Robert, ed. (1999) *What If? The World's Most Foremost Military Historians Imagine What Might Have Been*. New York: Putnam.

Developing World and Mass Media (1975). Keynote papers from the International Scientific Conference of the IAMCR in Leipzig in September 1974. Prague: IOJ.

Furman, Wojciech (2017). Journalists' Associations in Poland Before and After 1980. *Media and Communication*, Vol. 5, No. 3, pp. 79–84. Available at https://www.cogitatiopress.com/mediaandcommunication/article/view/997.

Gerbner, George, Mowlana, Hamid and Nordenstreng, Kaarle, eds. (1993). *The Global Media Debate: Its Rise, Fall, and Renewal*. Norwood, NJ: Ablex.

Gopsill, Tim and Neale, Greg (2007). *Journalists: 100 Years of the NUJ*. London: National Union of Journalists.

Historical Background of the Mass Media Declaration (1982). Paris: Unesco. (Documents on the New Communication Order, No 9.) Available at http://unesdoc.unesco.org/images/0004/000476/047669eo.pdf.

Holoubek, Jaroslav (1976). The Predecessors of the International Organization of Journalists. *The Democratic Journalist*, No. 7–8, pp. 28–31.

Hudec, Vladimír (1979). *Journalism: Substance, Social Functions, Development*. Prague: IOJ.

IAMCR/AIERI Workshop on Journalism Education, Prague, August 1984 (1986). Prague: IOJ.

Idealism in Action. The Story of the IFJ (1966). Brussels: IFJ.

IFFJ. International Federation of Free Journalists of Central and Eastern Europe and Baltic and Balkan Countries (1952). London: MacNeill & Co Press Ltd.

The International Federation of Journalists. For a Free Press and Free Journalism 1952–1977 (1977). Istanbul: Union of Journalists of Turkey.

International Principles of Professional Ethics in Journalism (1985). With Comments by Kaarle Nordenstreng. Prague: Videopress. (Reprinted in 1988 by IOJ Printing House in Prague.)

Jisl, Vladislav (1968). A Sociological Inquiry among Journalists: Alarming Replies. *The Democratic Journalist*, No. 1, pp. 8–10.

Journalism and the Security Needs of States (1987). Proceedings of the 2nd International Journalists' CSCE Congress, 30th October – 1st November 1987, Hofburg, Vienna. Edited by Eva Prager-Zitterbart, Leena Paukku and Heikki Karkkolainen. Helsinki: Union of Journalists in Finland.

Journalistic Training Centres. A World Directory (1986). Compiled by Bernd Rayer. Prague: IOJ.

Journalists and Détente 30 Years after the End of the World War II: Colloquium Proceedings (1975). Edited by Tapio Varis. Tampere: Institute of Journalism and Mass Communication, University of Tampere. (Reports 25/1975)

Journalists and Détente: Documents of the Conference on Security and Co-operation in Europe with Finnish Comments on the 3rd Basket and a selection of Documents related to Journalism and Peace (1985). Edited by Heikki Karkkolainen. Helsinki: Union of Journalists in Finland.

Journalists and Détente: Proceedings of International Journalists' Congress, 6–9 September 1985, Finlandia-Hall, Helsinki (1986). Edited by Heikki Karkkolainen, Heli Holm, Erkki Metsälampi and Tapani Ruokanen. Photos by Kalevi Keski-Korhonen. Helsinki: Union of Journalists in Finland.

Journalists and New Technology (1988). Prepared by John Lawrence (Australian Journalists Association) on behalf of the IFJ for the International and Regional Organizations of Journalists. Prague: IOJ.

Journalists – murdered! Journalistes – assassins! !Periodistas – asesinados! (1989). Edited on behalf of the 8th Consultative Meeting of International and Regional Organizations of Journalists by R. H. L. Bakker (IFJ) and Mazen Husseini (IOJ). Prague: IOJ.

Killed for Truth. Assassines pour la verite. Asesinados a causa de la verdad (1987). Published by the 6th Consultative Meeting of the International and Regional Organizations of Journalists. Prague: IOJ.

Klimeš, Vladimír (1969). Protection of Journalists on Dangerous Missions. *The Democratic Journalist*, No. 9, pp. 199–200.

Kubka, Jiří (1977). *1200 za minutu*. Praha: Vydavatelstvi Novinár.

Kubka, Jiří and Nordenstreng, Kaarle (1986). *Useful Recollections: Excursion into the History of the International Movement of Journalists. Part I*. Prague: IOJ. Available at http://books.google.com.

Le Tribunal d'Honneur International des Journalistes (1932). Paris: FIJ.

Les Travaux du 2ème seminaire pour la formation des correspondants régionaux (1976). Organisé par l'UNAJOM en coopération avec l'OIJ. Bamako, 23 Août – 3 Septembre 1976. Budapest: INTERPRESS.

MacBride, Seán et al. (1980). *Many Voices, One World. Communication and Society, Today and Tomorrow*. Report of the International Commission for the Study of Communication Problems (MacBride Commission). Paris: Unesco. (Reprinted in 2004 by Rowman & Littlefield, USA.)

Maleček, Stanislav (1968). New Trends in the Czechoslovak Journalists Organization. *The Democratic Journalist*, No. 9, pp. 179–181.

NAM & NIICO. Documents of the Non-Aligned Movement on the New International Information and Communication Order (1986–1987) (1988). With Preface by Kaarle Nordenstreng. Compiled by W. Kleinwächter and K. Nordenstreng. Prague: IOJ. (Also in Spanish.)

Nekola, Martin (2017). International Federation of Free Journalists: Opposing Communist Propaganda During the Cold War. *Media and Communication*, Vol. 5. No. 3, pp. 103–106. Available at https://www.cogitatiopress.com/mediaandcommunication/article/view/1049.

New International Information and Communication Order: Sourcebook (1986). With Foreword by Seán MacBride. Edited by Enrique Gonzales Manet, Kaarle Nordenstreng and Wolfgang Kleinwächter. Prague: IOJ.

Nordenstreng, Kaarle (1984). *The Mass Media Declaration of UNESCO*. Norwood, NJ: Ablex.

Nordenstreng, Kaarle (2010). MacBride Report as a Culmination of NWICO. *Les Enjeux de l'information et la communication.* Available at https://lesenjeux.univ-grenoble-alpes.fr/2010-supplementA/Nordenstreng/index.html.

Nordenstreng, Kaarle (2011). The New World Information and Communication Order: Testimony of an Actor. In *Widerworte. Philosophie Politik Kommunikation. Festschrift für Jörg Becker*, edited by Frank Deppe, Wolfgang Meixner and Günter Pallaver. Innsbruck: Innsbruck University Press. Available at http://urn.fi/urn:nbn:uta-3-832.

Nordenstreng, Kaarle (2014). The International Movement of Journalists: 120 Years of Continuing Stgruggle. In Füsun Özbilgen, ed.: *Hifzi Topuz'a Armagan Kitabi. Ilet isimin Devrim Yillari* [Hizfi Topuz Festschrift. The revolutionary years of communication]. Istanbul: ILAD Hiperlink. Available at http://urn.fi/URN:NBN:fi:uta-201404291365.

Nordenstreng, Kaarle (2016). Great Media Debate. In *Towards Equity in Global Communication?*, edited by Richard C. Vincent and Kaarle Nordenstreng. New York: Hampton Press.

Nordenstreng, Kaarle; Björk, Ulf Jonas; Beyersdorf, Frank; Høyer, Svennik and Lauk, Epp (2016). *A History of the International Movement of Journalists: Professionalism Versus Politics.* Houndmills, UK: Palgrave-Macmillan.

Nordenstreng, Kaarle and Kubka, Jiři (1988). *Useful Recollections: Excursion into the History of the International Movement of Journalists. Part II.* Prague: IOJ. Available at http://books.google.com.

Nordentreng, Kaarle and Topuz, Hifzi, eds. (1989). *Journalist: Status, Rights and Responsibilities.* Prague: IOJ. Available at http://books.google.com.

Preston, William Jr.; Herman, Edward S. and Schiller, Herbert I. (1989). *Hope and Folly. The United States and UNESCO, 1945–1985.* Minneapolis, MN: University of Minnesota Press.

Professional Codes in Journalism (1979). Edited by Lars Bruun. Prague: IOJ.

Protection of Journalists (1980). Paris: Unesco. (Documents on the New Communication Order, No. 4.) Available at http://unesdoc.unesco.org/images/0004/000421/042108Eb.pdf.

Reflections Around UNESCO (1978). Presentations by the President of the International Organization of Journalists, Professor Kaarle Nordenstreng. Prague: IOJ.

Righter, Rosemary (1978). *Whose News? Politics, the Press and the Third World.* London: Burnett Books.

Roberts, Geoffrey (2014). Averting Armageddon: The Communist Peace Movement, 1948–1956. In *The Oxford Handbook on the History of Communism*, edited by Stephen S. Smith. Oxford, UK: Oxford University Press.

Ševčíková, Markéta (2015). Mezinárodní organizace novinářů (1946–1995). Unpublished PhD thesis at Charles University, Faculty of Social Sciences, Institute of Journalism Studies.

Ševčíková, Markéta and Nordenstreng, Kaarle (2017). The Story of Journalist Organizations in Czechoslovakia. *Media and Communication*, Vol. 5, No. 3, pp. 95–102. Available at https://www.cogitatiopress.com/mediaandcommunication/article/view/1042.

Towards a New World Information Order (1976). Edited by Oldřich Bureš. Prague: IOJ.

Vasilev, Radi (1970). International Comparative Research on the Social Status of Journalists. *The Democratic Journalist*, No. 6, pp. 125–127.

Vincent, Richard C. and Nordenstreng, Kaarle, eds. (2016). *Towards Equity in Global Communication?* Second Edition. New York: Hampton Press.

Reports of IOJ Congresses and other statutory meetings (in chronological order)

International Organisation of Journalists. Official Report of the First Congress, Copenhagen, June 3–9, 1946. I.O.J. Bulletin No. I. London: IOJ, July 1946. (Reproduced in *Useful Recollections, Part II*, Annex 2, pp. 101–120).
Second Congress, International Organisation of Journalists. Prague, June 3–7 1947. Prague: IOJ, 1947.
Report of the Secretary General to the Third Congress of the International Organisation of Journalists. Helsinki: IOJ, September 1950. (30 pages).
What is the International Organisation of Journalists. The I.O.J. Fifth Congress in Budapest. Prague – Budapest: IOJ, 1962.
6th Congress of the International Organization of Journalists, 10–15 October 1966 Berlin. Prague: IOJ.
The IOJ Between Two Congresses: Berlin 1966 – Havana 1971. Information about the activities of the IOJ from 1966 to 1970. 1970. Prague: IOJ.
7th Congress of the IOJ, Havana-Cuba 1971. Prague: IOJ.
Meeting of the Presidium – Ulan Bator – September 12–16th, 1974. Point 1, Report on Activities after the Executive Committee Meeting in Baghdad (September 1973), 1974.
The International Organization of Journalists Between Two Congresses: Havana – Helsinki 1971–1976. Prague: IOJ.
8th Congress of the International Organization of Journalists. Helsinki – Finland September 1976. Prague: IOJ.
Presidium de l'OIJ à Paris, les 18 et 19 novembre 1977, 1978. Prague: IOJ.
IOJ Presidium Meeting, Mexico, November 1978. Journalists' Affairs, December 1978. Prague: IOJ, 1978. (36 pages, also in French, Spanish and Russian).
Report on Activities of the Secretariat General: IOJ Presidium Meeting, Mexico City, 9–10 November 1978. Prague: IOJ, 1978. (41 pages, also in French and Spanish)
Hanoi, Ho Chi Minh City. 19th Session of the IOJ Executive Committee, November 1979. Prague: IOJ, 1980. (154 pages, also in French)
The International Organization of Journalists Between Two Congresses: Helsinki – Moscow 1976–1981. Working documentation destined for delegates of the 9th Congress, Moscow. Prague: IOJ Secretariat, 1981 (mimeographed). (180 pages)
9th Congress of the International Organization of Journalists Moscow – October 1981. Prague: IOJ, 1981. (204 pages, also in French, Spanish and Russian)
IOJ Presidium Luanda, January 27–29, 1983. Prague: IOJ, 1983. (146 pages)
IOJ Presidium Paris, November 22–23, 1983. Prague: IOJ, 1984. (160 pages)
IOJ Executive Committee New Delhi, September 1984. Prague: IOJ, 1985. (132 pages)
IOJ International Seminar New Delhi, September 1984. Prague: IOJ, 1985. (134 pages)
Presidium de la OIP Quito 1985. Prague: IOJ, 1985. (243 pages)
10th Congress of the International Organization of Journalists. Sofia October 1986. Prague: IOJ, 1987. (156 pages, also in French, Spanish and Russian)
IOJ Presidium Meeting Nicosia, October 21–23, 1987. Prague: IOJ, 1987. (77 pages)
IOJ Presidium Meeting Brasilia, April 22–25, 1988. Prague: IOJ, 1988. (63 pages)
IOJ Presidium Meeting Addis Ababa, Ethiopia, January 11–13, 1989. Prague: IOJ, 1989. (80 pages)
IOJ Presidium Meeting Lisbon-Estoril, Portugal, January 27–29, 1990. Prague: IOJ, 1990. (74 pages)
IOJ Presidium Meeting Balatonfüred, Hungary, May 6–8. 1990. Prague: IOJ, 1990. (84 pages)
IOJ Executive Committee Meeting Paris, November 17–20, 1990. Prague: IOJ, 1990. (116 pages)
12th Congress, January 28–31, 1995, Amman, Jordan. An Organization for the Third Millenium. Prague: IOJ, 1995. (40 pages)
Statutes of the International Organization of Journalists. As amended in the XIIth Congress in Amman, Jordan, January 1995. Prague: IOJ, 1995. (68 pages, including translations in French, Spanish and Arabic)

Other books by the IOJ
(in chronological order, published in Prague unless otherwise indicated)

1956–71

The International Organization of Journalists, 1956. (Also in French)

Grangeon, F. *Cours de serétariat de rédaction et de mise en page*, 1965.

La formation des journalistes à l'epoque des ordinateurs: proces-verbal. Colloque international sur les nouveaux courants dans la formation des journalistes, Prague, les 3 et 4 novembre 1967, 1967. (139 pages)

Libro Negro: La FIOPP, instrumento de la política "interamericana" de EE, 1967. (41 pages)

Die Macht des Axel Cäsar Springer, 1968. (36 pages)

The Press Acts (Sweden, Denmark, Finland, Norway), 1968. (54 pages)

Springer Power Politics, 1969. (74 pages, also in German and Spanish)

Boretsky, R. A. and Yurovsky, A. *Television Journalism*, 1970. (204 pages)

Handbook of News Agencies. Compiled by Oldřich Bureš and Jaroslav First, 1970. (74 pages)

International Centre for the Training of Journalists Budapest Hungary. Report 1971 published in the honour of the 7th IOJ Congress. Budapest: INTERPRESS, 1970. (30 pages)

Tichý, Josef. *Newspaper Production, Management and Techniques*, 1971. (93 pages)

1972

Bureš, O.; Kittelmann H. J. and Künzel, H. *Aggressionssender: Radio Free Europe, Radio Liberty, BBC, Deutschlandfunk, Deutsche Welle, Rias und andere Sender ähnlichen Charakters.* (87 pages)

Facts about the I.O.J. (68 pages)

Haškovec, Slavoj and First, J. *Introduction to News Agency Journalism.* (138 pages)

Lenin about the Press. English edition compiled by A.N. Burmistenko. Edited by M. Saifulin. (482 pages, also in French and German)

1973

Cardet, Ricardo. *Manual de Jornalismo.* (141 pages)

Chile Septiembre 1973. Edited by Oldřich Bureš. (54 pages)

Developpement des moyens de communication et nouvelles tendances dans la formation des journalistes. 1er Colloque international organisé par la Commission professionelle de l'Organisation international des journalists, en collaboration avec l'Unesco, au Centre international de l'O.I.J. pour la formation des journalistes. Hongrie, Budapest, du 18 au 22 juin 1973. Budapest: INTERPRESS. (126 pages)

Dimitrov, Georgi. *The Press is a Great Force.* (108 pages)

European Security and Cooperation: Selected Bibliography Based on Press Material on European Security and Cooperation 1966–1972. (210 pages)

Facts about the IOJ. (97 pages, also in French)

Jankovec, Miloslav. *U.S. War against Indo-China.* (76 pages)

South Africa, Apartheid, Mass Media: A Report on the Present State of Official Restrictions and Persecution. (28 pages)

1974

Banerjee, Sumanta. *India's Monopoly Press: A Mirror of Distortion.* (75 pages)

Chile: One Year Later. (34 pages, also in Spanish)

The Chilean Coup and its Cruel Aftermath. (163 pages)

Jankovec, Miloslav. *A Chronology of Events in Indo-China: January 1 – December 31, 1973.* (179 pages)

Julius Fučík and the Present. Edited by Oldřich Bureš. (35 pages, also in German)

The Media Today and Tomorrow. (130 pages)

The Present Situation of the Press in Chile: The Chilean Press before, during and after the Popular Unity Government. (19 pages, also in Czech and Spanish)

Ten Years of the International Journalist Solidarity Lottery. (21 pages)

1975
Adresses des Principales Organizations des Journalistes en Europe. (20 pages)
Bureš, Oldřich. *Egon Erwin Kisch 1885–1948: Erinnerungen zum 90. Geburtstag.* (46 pages)
Bureš, Oldřich. *Les femmes et la presse: Documents, rapports, études, bibliographie.* (44 pages)
Clash of Ideas on Modern Media: Documents: Reports: Studies: Bibliography. (98 pages)
Developing World and Mass Media. Keynote papers from the International Scientific Conference of the IAMCR in Leipzig in September 1974. (128 pages)
Directory of Press, Radio and Television in Africa. (94 pages)
The International Organization of Journalists and Africa. (79 pages, also in French)

1976
30 Years of the International Organization of Journalists in Action. (96 pages)
30 Years of the IOJ. (26 pages, also in Czech, Finnish, French, German, Russian and Spanish)
Bartoš, Jirí. *Avec la caricature contre le fascisme.* (126 pages)
Europe: Security, Understanding, Cooperation. (218 pages, also in French)
International Institute for the Training of Journalists. Report 1976 published on the occasion of the 8th IOJ Congress. Budapest: INTERPRESS. (40 pages)
Kuneitra: The Symbol of Barbarism. (27 pages, also in French)
Mass Media en Europe (quelques données statistiques). (61 pages)
Mass Media in C.M.E.A. Countries. Edited by Sepp Horlamus. (255 pages)
Mikulecká, Libuše. *Velká hospoda na Bílé Hoře.* (51 pages)
Petrusenko, Vitali. *The Monopoly Press, or, How American Journalism Found itself in the Vicious Circle of the "Crisis of Credibility".* (143 pages)
South Korea – Persecution of Journalists and Mass Media. (44 pages)
Tausk, Petr. *An Introduction to Press Photography.* (125 pages)
Towards a New World Information Order. Edited by Oldřich Bureš. (76 pages)
Les Travaux du 2ème seminaire pour la formation des correspondants régionaux. Organisé par l'UNAJOM en coopération avec l'OIJ. Bamako, 23 Août – 3 Septembre 1976. Budapest: INTERPRESS. (125 pages)
Vasilev, Radi. *La Condition sociale des journalistes: enquête comparative internationale.* (209 pages, also in Russian and Spanish)

1977
Current Views on the World Information Order. Edited by Oldřich Bureš. (115 pages)
Hermann, Jean-Maurice. *L'éthique internationale des journalistes.* (28 pages)
Kubka, Jiří. *Explosion der Informationen.* Budapest: INTERPRESS. (133 pages)
Máté, György. *Vietnam: It Happened in front of our Very Eyes.* (206 pages)
Petrusenko, Vitaly. *A Dangerous Game: CIA and the Mass Media.* (190 pages)
Saxlund, Ricardo. *El Fascismo y la Prensa Uruguaya.* (46 pages)
Todorov, Dafin. *Freedom Press: Development of the Progressive Press in Western Europe and the USA.* (97 pages)

1978
La Décolonisation de l'information et le role des mass media dans le développement et dans la creation d'un nouvel odre economique international. Les travaux du 3ème Colloque international organisé par l'O.I.J en cooperation avec UNESCO et l'Union des Journalistes d'Iraq. Bagdad, du 1er au 7 novembre 1977. Budapest: INTERPRESS. (284 pages)
Europe: Security, Understanding, Cooperation Volume Two. (126 pages, also in French)
Journalists Press Apartheid. Edited by Oldřich Bureš. (114 pages)
Kuznetsov, Vladlen. *Operation "N": The Latest Lethal Nuclear Weapon that Menaces Mankind!.* (55 pages)
La Larga mano de la "Freedom House": Los medios de comunicacion en Jamaica.
La OIP y America Latina. (83 pages)

Reflections Around UNESCO. Presentations by the President of the International Organization of Journalists, Professor Kaarle Nordenstreng. (69 pages)
South Korea: Suppression of the Press. (23 pages)
The IOJ in the Struggle Against Apartheid. Compiled by Hans Treffkorn and Štefan Rybár. (158 pages)

1979

20 Years: The International House of Journalists at Varna 1959 - 1979. (52 pages)
Exposición Interpressfoto-79, La Habana-Cuba. Edited by Aurelian Nestor. (97 pages, in Spanish, French, English and Russian)
Hudec, Vladimír. *Journalism: Substance, Social Functions, Development.* (60 pages, also in French, Spanish and Portuguese)
IOJ and Vietnam. (122 pages)
Manet, Enrique González. Descolonización de la Información. (125 pages)
Professional Codes in Journalism. Edited by Lars Bruun. (127 pages)
Repression, Torture and Death: South Africa. (44 pages)
Tsukasov, S.V. *The Organization of Work in an Editorial Office.* (88 pages, also in Spanish)

1980

Children and the Mass Media. Edited by Oldřich Bureš. (128 pages)
Goban-Klas, Tomasz. *The Mass Media – an Advocate of Peace or an Advocate of Conflict?* (48 pages)
Haškovec, Slavoj. *The News Agency in the System of Mass Media.* (65 pages, also in Spanish)
Mass Media and Disarmament. Edited by Oldřich Bureš. (41 pages)
Minkov, Mihail. *Radio Journalism.* (79 pages, also in Spanish)
Mongolia and its Mass Media. Edited by Oldřich Bureš. (63 pages)
Organisations Internationales et Régionales de Journalistes. (88 pages)
Rivero, Miguel. *Infierno y amanecer en Kampuchea: a manera de presentacion.* (259 pages)
The Action: the assault on Moncada. Budapest: INTERPRESS. (20 pages)
Villares, Ricardo. *Abel Santamaría, the most generous, beloved and couraeous of our youth.* A biographical sketch of the second in command of the assult on the Moncada Barracks. Budapest: INTERPRESS. (23 pages)

1981

35 Years in Service of Peace, Cooperation and Understanding among Nations. (68 pages, also in French, Russian and Spanish)
5th International Symposium of Journalists: Ulan-Bator, October 26–29, 1981: The Role of Journalists in the Struggle for Peace, Understanding among Nations, Humanism and Social Progress. (44 pages)
Boretsky, R.A. and Kuznetsov, Georgy. *Journalistic Work and Television.* (101 pages, also in Portuguese: O trabalho do journalista e a televisao)
Facts about the IOJ. (30 pages, also in French, Russian and Spanish)
Gargurevich, Juan. *A golpe de titular: CIA y periodismo en América Latina.* (109 pages)
Polská krajina od poloviny 19. století do roku 1939: katalog výstavy. (91 pages)
Tausk, Petr. *Textbook of Press Photography.* (188 pages)

1982

The Black Book for the Persecution of the Progressive and Democratic Journalists. Documents of the International Forum for the Protection of Progressive and Democratic Journalists, Varna, Bulgaria, 14–16 October 1981. Sofia: International Committee for Protection of Journalists. Budapest: INTERPRESS. (164 pages)
Budapest Berlin Sofia & other training centres. A World Directory. Compiled by Dr. Hans Treffkorn. Prague: IOJ. (95 pages)
First Conference of Journalists from the Caribbean Area, St. George, Grenada, April 1982. (100 pages)
Jankovec, Miloslav. *South-East Asia in International Relations.* (173 pages)

1983

4th International Scientific Conference held on the occasion of the 20th anniversary of the "Werner Lambertz" Institute in Berlin, September 1983. (110 pages)
From Camp David to Beirut: An Outline of the Fifth Israeli-Arab War – Its Roots and Results. (118 pages)
Fučík, Julius. *Reporter of Revolution. Part I, Selection of Newspaper Articles.* (137 pages, also in Spanish)
Fučík, Julius. *Reporter or Revolution. Part II, Report from the Gallows.* (105 pages, also in Spanish)
Hemánus, Pertti and Varis, Tapio. *Mass Media Yesterday and Today.* (79 pages)
Janata, Michael. *The Phony Connection: Background to the Attempted Assassination of Pope John Paul II.* (136 pages)
Kashlev, Jurij. *The Mass Media and International Relations.* (168 pages)
The Nuclear Threat. (85 pages)
Peace, Development and Cooperation and the Responsibility of the Mass Media: Berlin, September 1983. (100 pages)

1984

Benítez, José Antonio. *Técnica periodística.* (205 pages)
García, José M. Ortiz. *Angola: from the Trenches.* (235 pages)
Hoffmann, Arnold. *How to Write a Journalistic Contribution.* (58 pages)
International Organization of Journalists: IOJ Solidarity Schools. (52 pages)
IOJ Videopress Introducing. (58 pages)
Radics, Vilmos and Ritter, Aladár. *Make-Up and Typography.* (175 pages)
Women and Media: European Seminar, 2–5 October 1984, Warsaw, Poland. (29 pages)
Yermoshkin, Nikolai. *Spiritual Neo-colonialism.* (89 pages)

1985

Carew, Jan. *Grenada: The Hour Will Strike again.* (278 pages)
E.E. Kisch: Journalist and Fighter. Biography written by Danica Kozlová and Jiří Tomáš. Selections from Works by E. E. Kisch. (306 pages)
Ford, Glen. *The Big Lie: Analysis of U.S. Press Coverage of the Grenada Invasion.*
International Principles of Professional Ethics in Journalism. With Comments by Kaarle Nordenstreng. (18 pages, reprinted in 1988)
Lopez, Diana Valle and Silva, Osvaldo Zamorano. *Periodismo libre en patrias libres.* (105 pages)
Memoria de la cuarta Bienal Internacional de Humorismo 1985, San Antonio de los Baños, Cuba.
Suárez, Luis. *The Other Face of Afghanistan: Reportage from the Heart of Asia.* (129 pages)
Syruček, Milan. *Dien Bien Phu: Sur les sentiers de la victoire.* (221 pages)
Witnesses of the Great Victory: World War 2 in Reports, Epics, Memoirs. (174 pages)

1986

Cheporov, E. A. *Democracy and the Press.* (201 pages)
Faits et données – MON. (26 pages)
Finková, Dagmar. *The Militant Poster 1936–1985.* (143 pages)
Gurevich, Semyon. *Karl Marx the Publicist.* (287 pages)
Handbook of News Agencies in the World. (167 pages)
IAMCR/AIERI Workshop on Journalism Education, Prague, August 1984. (102 pages)
International Meeting of Journalists, Torgau '85, Held in Berlin the Capital of the German Democratic Republic: Session on the Responsibility of Journalists for the Safeguarding and Preservation of Peace. (95 pages, also in German)
IOJ facts and figures. (26 pages, also in French)
Jean-Maurice Hermann se souvient. (47 pages)
Journalistic Training Centres. A World Directory. Compiled by Bernd Rayer. (342 pages)

Kubka, Jiři and Nordenstreng, Kaarle. *Useful Recollections: Excursion into the History of the International Movement of Journalists. Part I.* (121 pages)

New International Information and Communication Order: Sourcebook. With Foreword by Seán MacBride. Edited by Enrique Gonzales Manet, Kaarle Nordenstreng and Wolfgang Kleinwächter. (392 pages, also in Spanish)

Solidarity School of Julius Fučík. Scientific and Technological Progress in Present-day Printing. (86 pages)

1987

Eyes See what Eyes Want to See: Western Media and the Peace Movement: What Actually Happened at the World Peace Congress in Copenhagen. Edited by Eva Bendix; Susanne Bjorkenheim; Leif Larsen and Ron Ridehour. (125 pages, also in Danish)

Killed for Truth. Assassines pour la verite. Asesinados a causa de la verdad. Published by the Sixth Consultative Meeting of International and Regional Organization of Journalists in the IOJ Publishing House. (54 pages)

Luis, Julio Garcia. *Géneros de Opinión: Apuntes y sugerencias sobre el artículo periodístico.* (149 pages)

Modern Science and Technology in Journalism and Graphic Arts. Seminar Lectures. Compiled by Břetislav Hofbauer. (212 pages)

Rácz, Juraj. *It All Began with Suez.* (69 pages)

Szentesi, György; Tolnay László and Vajda Péter. *Military Balance & Doctrines: Four Essays* by György Szentesi, László Tolnay and Péter Vajda. (154 pages)

1988

Journalists and New Technology. Prepared by John Lawrence (Australian Journalists Association) on behalf of the IFJ for the international and regional organizations of journalists. (155 pages)

Kashlev, Juri and Lebedeva, Tatiana. *Information Serving Peace and Progress: the International Program for the Development of Communication in the Context of the Struggle for a New Information Order.* (198 pages)

NAM & NIICO. Documents of the Non-Aligned Movement on the New International Information and Communication Order (1986–1987). With Preface by Kaarle Nordenstreng. Compiled by W. Kleinwächter and K. Nordenstreng. (119 pages, also in Spanish)

Nordenstreng, Kaarle and Kubka, Jiři. *Useful Recollections: Excursion into the History of the International Movement of Journalists. Part II.* (195 pages)

Novák, Miloslav. *Munich Pact 1938: Betrayal of Collective Security.* (56 pages)

Tausk, Petr. *A Short History of Press Photography.* (232 pages)

Uribe, Hernán. *La guerra secreta de las noticias.* (158 pages)

1989

Application of Modern Technology in Editorial Work: seminar lectures. Edited by Rudolf Převrátil. Compiled by Břetislav Hofbauer. (142 pages)

Journalism and the Challenge of the Year 2000: 5th International Scientific Conference and Graduates' Workshop, Berlin, September–October 1988: International Institute of Journalism Berlin, 1963–1988. (53 pages)

Journalist: Status, Rights and Responsibilities. Edited by Kaarle Nordenstreng and Hifzi Topuz on behalf of the IOJ, IFJ, FELAP, FELATRAP, UAJ, FAJ and CAJ. (317 pages)

Journalists – murdered! Journalistes – assassins! !Periodistas – asesinados! Edited on behalf of the 8th Consultative Meeting of the International and Regional Organizations of Journalists by R. H. L. Bakker (IFJ) and Mazen Husseini (IOJ). (96 pages)

Šnajder, Bohuslav et al. *The Last Days of a Restless Peace.* (140 pages)

Solidarity School of Julius Fučík in the Czechoslovak Socialist Republic. (16 pages)

1990

Faut-il casser les consoles? Nouvelles technologies. (87 pages)

Intifada: Year Two. (89 pages, also in French)
Mrázková, Daniela and Remeš, Vladimír. *The Great Pictures of World Photojournalism.* (250 pages)
Mukherjee, Sadhan. *Media Handbook for South Asia.* (167 pages)
Šnajder, Bohuslav. *Years of Hope: Reminiscences of War Reporters.* (260 pages, also in Russian)

1991
Computer Terminals: The Health Hazards. (95 pages, also in French)

1992
Media Freedom in Former Yugoslavia: A Special Report for the Citizen's Peace Conference, Ohrid, Macedonia, November 5–8, 1992. (51 pages)

1993
Delalandre, Jean-Philippe and Novak, Adam. *Reporters and Medias in Ex-Yugoslavia. Reporters et médias en ex-Yougoslavie.* (100 pages)
Mamadou, Fofana; Lebedeva, T. and Alin, A. Maiga. *Mass média en Afrique: théorie et pratique.* (100 pages)
The State of the Media in 1992: The Yearly Report of the IOJ. (46 pages)

1995
IOJ Unites the Journalists of the World. Primer. (12 pages)

Journals and magazines (in alphabetical order)
Africa Mass Media / Afrique Mass Media: Revue Professionnelle. Budapest: INTERPRESS, 1976–77.
The Democratic Journalist, 1952–91 / *Demokratische Journalist,* 1952–61 / *Le Journaliste démocratique,* 1953–91 / *El Periodista demócrata* / Demokratikus Ujságíró, 1953–91 / *Demokratičeskij žurnalist,* 1961–90.
Hungarofilm Bulletin (in English, French and German). Budapest: INTERPRESS, 1981–88.
INFO. Newsletter of the IOJ Training Commission, 1982–85.
Interpress Expo (in English, Russian and German). Budapest: INTERPRESS, 1978–86.
Interpress Magazín (in Czech and Hungarian, also in English 1976). Budapest: INTERPRESS, 1968–92.
Interpress-Foto: die Welt in Bildern = Interpress-photo = Interpresse photo, 1960–66.
Interpressgrafik: International Quarterly for Graphic Design (in English-Russian-French-German-Spanish). Budapest: INTERPRESS, 1969–85.
IOJ Bulletin, 1946–52.
IOJ News and Information (occasional supplement of *The Democratic Journalist*), 1953–73.
IOJ Newsletter (biweekly), 1980–94 – in Spanish (*Correo de la OIP* 1983–1991), in German (*IOJ Nachrichten* 1985–91, in French (*Les Nouvelles de l'OIJ* 1985–91), in Russian (*Novosti MOŽ* 1988–91) and in Arabic (1988–91).
Journalists' Affairs (biweekly), 1974–80 / *Les affaires des journalistes,* 1974–80.
Journalists International, 10 issues in 1995–97.
Le Monde des Journalistes, one issue in 1992.
United voice: Organ of the IOJ Training Center for Journalists. Budapest: INTERPRESS, 1970–75.

INDEX OF NAMES

Index covers the book except documentation and bibliography (pp. 343–541).